Communications in Computer and Information Science 1825

Rationale

The CCIS series is devoted to the publication of proceedings of computer science conferences. Its aim is to efficiently disseminate original research results in informatics in printed and electronic form. While the focus is on publication of peer-reviewed full papers presenting mature work, inclusion of reviewed short papers reporting on work in progress is welcome, too. Besides globally relevant meetings with internationally representative program committees guaranteeing a strict peer-reviewing and paper selection process, conferences run by societies or of high regional or national relevance are also considered for publication.

Topics

The topical scope of CCIS spans the entire spectrum of informatics ranging from foundational topics in the theory of computing to information and communications science and technology and a broad variety of interdisciplinary application fields.

Information for Volume Editors and Authors

Publication in CCIS is free of charge. No royalties are paid, however, we offer registered conference participants temporary free access to the online version of the conference proceedings on SpringerLink (http://link.springer.com) by means of an http referrer from the conference website and/or a number of complimentary printed copies, as specified in the official acceptance email of the event.

CCIS proceedings can be published in time for distribution at conferences or as post-proceedings, and delivered in the form of printed books and/or electronically as USBs and/or e-content licenses for accessing proceedings at SpringerLink. Furthermore, CCIS proceedings are included in the CCIS electronic book series hosted in the SpringerLink digital library at http://link.springer.com/bookseries/7899. Conferences publishing in CCIS are allowed to use Online Conference Service (OCS) for managing the whole proceedings lifecycle (from submission and reviewing to preparing for publication) free of charge.

Publication process

The language of publication is exclusively English. Authors publishing in CCIS have to sign the Springer CCIS copyright transfer form, however, they are free to use their material published in CCIS for substantially changed, more elaborate subsequent publications elsewhere. For the preparation of the camera-ready papers/files, authors have to strictly adhere to the Springer CCIS Authors' Instructions and are strongly encouraged to use the CCIS LaTeX style files or templates.

Abstracting/Indexing

CCIS is abstracted/indexed in DBLP, Google Scholar, EI-Compendex, Mathematical Reviews, SCImago, Scopus. CCIS volumes are also submitted for the inclusion in ISI Proceedings.

How to start

To start the evaluation of your proposal for inclusion in the CCIS series, please send an e-mail to ccis@springer.com.

Lorna Uden · I-Hsien Ting
Editors

Knowledge Management in Organisations

17th International Conference, KMO 2023
Bangkok, Thailand, July 24–27, 2023
Proceedings

Springer

Editors
Lorna Uden
Staffordshire University
Stoke-on-Trent, UK

I-Hsien Ting
National University of Kaohsiung
Kaohsiung, Taiwan

ISSN 1865-0929   ISSN 1865-0937 (electronic)
Communications in Computer and Information Science
ISBN 978-3-031-34044-4   ISBN 978-3-031-34045-1 (eBook)
https://doi.org/10.1007/978-3-031-34045-1

This Springer imprint is published by the registered company Springer Nature Switzerland AG
The registered company address is: Gewerbestrasse 11, 6330 Cham, Switzerland

Preface

The 17th International Conference on Knowledge Management in Organisations took place at Srinakharinwirot University, Bangkok, Thailand from 24 to 27th July 2023.

The conference was preceded by one day of free tutorials for participants who wished to learn state-of-the-art research relating to the topics of KMO and Learning Technology for Education Challenges. The tutorials were held on the 24th of July 2023. The conference itself commenced on the 25th of July 2023.

Knowledge Management benefits organisations in many ways, especially during and after the pandemic. Knowledge is an important asset and the foundation for the digital workplace. Companies are beginning to recognise how critical knowledge is for collaboration - especially for remote workers. Businesses depend on a reliable Knowledge Management system for smooth information sharing and internal operations. Effective Knowledge Management supported by technology enables organizations to become more innovative and productive. Knowledge sharing matters now, more than ever since the pandemic. Regardless of the industry, size, or knowledge needs of the organization, we need people to lead, sponsor, and support knowledge sharing.

The use of social media should be a part of the Knowledge Management system. This will enable collaboration at the click of a button and give employees a common space in which to interact. By adding these features, we will be able to provide employees with a better experience than their current ones.

AI is increasingly used in Knowledge Management. Knowledge mining is a new AI-driven idea that entails combining several intelligent services to quickly study data, uncover hidden insights, and discover linkages at scale. Knowledge workers will be able to access unstructured data more efficiently and make better business judgments because of this.

Chatbots powered by Knowledge Management can be used by employees to retrieve documents from the Knowledge Management system as personal assistants on the intranet and in messaging apps like Teams, Skype For Business, and Skype.

In a constantly digitalizing world, companies' success depends on Knowledge Management more than ever before. Digital transformation along with adoption of digital technologies offers almost endless opportunities for companies' development, value creation, and profit. In order to utilize these possibilities, organizations need to simultaneously enable innovative, quick, and dynamic ways of learning and adopt more flexible Knowledge Management strategies. Digital transformation is a process facilitated to a large extent by Knowledge Management.

KMO 2023 aimed to encourage research on various aspects of managing knowledge in the process or supporting the process of global digital transformation.

This conference series provides an interdisciplinary platform for researchers, practitioners, and educators to present and discuss their most recent work, trends, innovation, and concerns as well as to share the practical challenges encountered, and solutions adopted in the fields of Knowledge Management in Organisations.

These proceedings consist of thirty-four papers covering various aspects of Knowledge Management. All published papers have undergone a rigorous review process involving at least four reviewers. The authors of these papers come from many different locations, including Austria, China, Colombia, Ecuador, Finland, Hong Kong, India, Indonesia, Japan, Malaysia, Palestine, Poland, Portugal, Puerto Rico, Slovenia, South Africa, South Korea, Spain, Taiwan, Tunisia, and the UK.

The papers are organised into the following topics:

Knowledge Transfer & Sharing
Knowledge in Business & Organisation
Digital Transformation and Innovation
Data Analysis and Science
KM and Education
KM Process and Model
Information & Knowledge Systems
IT & New Trends in KM
Healthcare

Besides the papers, we also had invited keynote speakers and tutorials. We would like to thank our authors, reviewers, and program committee for their contributions and Srinakharinwirot University, Bangkok, Thailand for hosting the conference. Special thanks to the authors and participants at the conference. Without their efforts, there would be no conference or proceedings.

We hope that these proceedings will become a useful reference tool and that the information in this volume will be used to further advancements in both research and industry in Knowledge Management.

Lorna Uden
I-Hsien Ting

Organization

Conference Chair

Lorna Uden   Staffordshire University, UK

Program Chair

Derrick I-Hsien Ting   National University of Kaohsiung, Taiwan

Local Chairs and Organizing Team

Somchai Santiwatanaku   Srinakharinwirot University, Thailand
Prit Supasetsiri   SWU, Thailand
Adul Supanut   SWU, Thailand
Suppanunta Romprasert   SWU, Thailand
Nattaya Prapaipanich   SWU, Thailand
Peera Tangthamrak   SWU, Thailand
Danai Thanamee   SWU, Thailand
Thongthong Bowonthamrongchai SWU, Thailand

Program Committee

Reinhard C. Bernsteiner   Management Center Innsbruck, Austria
Marjan Heričko   University of Maribor, Slovenia
GAN Keng Hoon   Universiti Sains Malaysia, Malaysia
Thomas Jackson   Loughborough University, UK
George Karabatis   University of Maryland, Baltimore County, USA
Eric Kin-Wai Lau   City University of Hong Kong, China
Dario Liberona   Seinajoki University of Applied Sciences, Finland
Furen Lin   National Tsing Hua University, Taiwan
Jari Kaivo-Oja   University of Turku, Finland
Mariusz Kostrzewski   Warsaw University of Technology, Poland
Remy Magnier-Watanabe   University of Tsukuba, Japan
Magdalena Marczewska   University of Warsaw, Poland

Victor Hugo Medina Garcia	Universidad Distrital Francisco José de Caldas, Colombia
Derrick I-Hsien Ting	National University of Kaohsiung, Taiwan
Fernando Tiverio Molina Granja	National University of Chimborazo, Ecuador
Luka Pavlič	University of Maribor, Slovenia
Christian Ploder	MCI Management Center Innsbruck, Austria
Stephan Schlögl	MCI Management Center Innsbruck, Austria
Dai Senoo	Tokyo Institute of Technology, Japan
Hanlie Smuts	University of Pretoria, South Africa
Kamoun-Chouk Souad	Manouba University, ESCT, Tunisia
Lorna Uden	Staffordshire University, UK
Iraklis Varlamis	Harokopio University of Athens, Greece
Costas Vassilakis	University of the Peloponnese, Greece
William Wang	University of Waikato, New Zealand
Mingzhu Zhu	Apple Inc, USA

Contents

IT and New Trends in KM

Healthcare

Knowledge Transfer and Sharing

Startups Knowledge Sharing Through Entrepreneurial Networks and the Catalytic Role of Incubators

Roberta Dutra de Andrade[(✉)] and Paulo Gonçalves Pinheiro

Research Center for Business Sciences - NECE, University of Beira Interior, Covilhã, Portugal
{roberta.andrade,pgp}@ubi.pt

Abstract. Based on the theories of networks and structural holes, exchange and social capital and reasoned action, this article aims to understand the functioning of entrepreneurial networks for startups and the role incubators and accelerators play in acquiring and exchanging knowledge of these companies. Qualitative research was conducted through in-depth individual and focus group interviews, and data were subjected to content analysis using NVivo software. The results indicate that startups resort to networks to access scarce resources, absorb technical knowledge and use the relationship network of incubators and accelerators. These institutions play a crucial role in startups' acquisition and exchange of expertise since they make available physical spaces with shared resources, business development support services and extensive relationship networks. Furthermore, results reveal that knowledge sharing in entrepreneurial networks happens informally, based on the sense of collectivism, truth and trust between the links and to mature the recognition, image and individual and organisational reputation. The present study explored the theme of data triangulation from the perspective of several members of startups of distinct industries and maturity levels and incubation and acceleration program managers. This study innovates by analysing the management and sharing of knowledge at the individual, intra, and inter-organisational levels of startups in entrepreneurial networks originating from emerging economies considering their idiosyncrasies.

Keywords: Knowledge sharing · Knowledge management · Startups · Incubators · Networks

1 Introduction

Knowledge in organisations is seen as a critical resource to obtain a sustainable competitive advantage, and, in recent years, researchers have concentrated efforts on studying knowledge sharing [1]. Shorter time in developing and completing new product projects, team performance, innovation capacity and overall organisational performance explain the growing interest [2]. In emerging economies, startups appear as potential development promoters, creating jobs, tax revenues and exports [3]. In their early stages, startups face difficulties that can compromise their survival in the first few years and not have significant capital investments [4]. To overcome these challenges, look for incubators and

© The Author(s), under exclusive license to Springer Nature Switzerland AG 2023
L. Uden and I-H. Ting (Eds.): KMO 2023, CCIS 1825, pp. 3–16, 2023.
https://doi.org/10.1007/978-3-031-34045-1_1

accelerators to compensate for resource deficits since these institutions provide physical spaces with shared resources, business development support services and extensive relationship networks [5, 6].

Especially for startups, network interactions and knowledge exchange with the environment can be particularly useful to access information, allow exchanges and provide more excellent connectivity to businesses [7]. Knowledge sharing has been adopted as an instrument for development with an impact on the innovation and performance of organisations [8]. This study result deals with how knowledge is created flows and can be appropriated by individuals, teams, and organisations along the network links. The objective is to understand the functioning of entrepreneurship networks for startups and the role that incubators and accelerators play in acquiring and exchanging knowledge of these companies.

The theme's relevance is confirmed by the lack of qualitative studies incorporating dynamic elements in network analysis. To date, the inclusion of sociopsychological variables is missing research, joining the perspective of startups, incubators, and accelerators. It is still missing studies of emerging economies, considering their peculiarities, and emphasising the various extensions of sharing. This study also advances and adheres to the proposed theme from multiple points of view through the triangulation of data from founding partners, directors and employees of startups and managers of incubators and accelerators.

2 Literature Review

Startups are an essential source of organisational innovation generated from identifying the need to develop products in high-potential target markets [9]. Perceived as an intrinsic part of the entrepreneurial ecosystem, startups play an essential role in the progress of emerging markets. Therefore, have been awakening a growing interest in the literature and government development policies [10].

Entrepreneurs usually find themselves involved in new administrative activities and unstable economic scenarios and seek partners who can provide knowledge to help them fill institutional gaps in administrative matters [11]. Organisational networks promote the creation, development and share knowledge among their components, impacting the innovation and performance of organisations. It allows cooperation and partnerships between organisations. The creation of organisational networks is a strategy to increase the competitiveness of organisations. To contribute to the development and survival of these companies, Incubators, Accelerators and Universities are strengthening actions to help entrepreneurs achieve business development and connect them with the most diverse partners [12].

The use of newly acquired information to overcome critical factors in the development of startups must be aligned with the implementation of strategies to manage this knowledge to maintain its agility and organisational learning curve [13]. Thus, the purpose of investigating knowledge management in entrepreneurship networks is to foster innovation by creating new knowledge through adopting new collaborative and innovative technologies.

The theories of exchange and social capital reasoned action, social networks, and structural holes were used to understand better the path of information and how relationships in networks can positively or negatively influence this flow [14]. While the approach of reasoned actions seeks to understand the consequences of alternative behaviours in the face of sharing knowledge, attitudes and subjective norms, the theory of exchange and social capital seeks to understand structural, relational, and cognitive issues [15]. Finally, the approach of networks and structural holes seeks to understand how the relational ties between individuals, inside and outside organisations, influence the links in the network and how the size of the network, degree of connectivity, and perceived benefits fill or cause gaps in the network—the flow of information [16].

2.1 Theory of Structural Networks and Holes

The network is a phenomenon commonly explored to explain the interconnections between individuals and the flow of information to exchange knowledge. The analysis of relationships comprises three main dimensions: structural [17], relational [18] and cognitive [19]. Each size is itself a composite of many variables. Structural holes and solid and weak relational ties, respectively. Based on the theory of Structural Holes, considered a valuable form of social capital, several authors indicate that the size of an organisation's network can be regarded as an essential factor for innovation, through the degree of connectivity or lack thereof, between the partners generating more benefits and opportunities [20].

2.2 Social Exchange and Share Capital Theory

The social exchange theory is a predictor in understanding the conceptual paradigms of knowledge sharing through a set of behaviours developed among individuals in an organization [21]. Feelings such as gratitude, trust, personal obligation, justice, and commitment are reported in previous studies investigating the main conditions of knowledge transfer within organisations. Previous research has shown that leaders who encourage employees to have innovative thinking and who empower them to share their information management create a better organisational climate without judgments and obtain a feeling of justice, which is an antecedent of corporate trust and commitment [22].

Knowledge sharing among the team is a process that predominantly involves the dimensions of social capital, constituted by structural, relational, and cognitive issues. The structural aspect would be related to the patterns of connections and influences in information. The relational scope refers to the interactions between the organisation's stakeholders. The cognitive perspective concerns the resources contributing to the interpretations, representations and shared systems of cultural and social norms [23].

2.3 Grounded Action Theory

Grounded action theory suggests that individuals consider the consequences of alternative behaviours in the face of attitudes toward knowledge sharing. Perspectives, subjective norms, the richness of the communication channel and the ability to absorb information are predictors that shape a person's intention to share knowledge [24]. The theory of action based on the incentive to knowledge sharing advocates the combination of extrinsic rewards, the feeling of reciprocity in the relationship with leaders, the sense of self-esteem and the organisational climate [25].

3 Methodology

3.1 Research Methods

This study is classified as exploratory-descriptive research [21], with a qualitative app-roach [26] and a multiple case study was carried out [27] as a scrutiny strategy in which one or more processes, activities, or individuals over a limited period. Figure 1 shows the choice of samples.

Semi-structured in-depth interviews were conducted [27] in a focus group [28] to realise the information and feelings of individuals on specific issues. Data triangulation was performed [29] to map the institutional practices performed and perceptions about knowledge sharing. The content analysis was structured into categories defined from the literature on knowledge management, social networks, and structural holes so that the core of meanings could be investigated and subsequent recognition of agglomerations in themes [30] as shown in Fig. 2.

3.2 Research Framework

A study framework of knowledge sharing in entrepreneurship social networks was devel-oped, favouring the visualisation of their motivations, specificities, and perceived results, as shown in Fig. 3.

4 Results and Analysis

Startups were considered the centre of the network, and the interaction and knowledge flows were analysed from the links of education, knowledge and growth through insti-tutions that permeate and interconnect universities, startups, public and private develop-ment agencies and access to capital and support. They are incubators and accelerators and co-accelerator.

Regarding knowledge management in startups, all had some mechanism for collect-ing, storing, and distributing explicit knowledge. Early-stage startups used free cloud storage repositories with broad access to all members. Companies in more advanced stages have developed their warehouses with limited access levels. Still, they understand that this policy also influences the integration of new employees and reduces training time [27].

The most significant benefits perceived were access to physical spaces and shared resources, support services and consultancies for business development and, mainly, access to the networking of these extensive incubation and acceleration institutes. The most recurrent statement in all respondents was the pacified idea that connections move the world. Startups stated that much of the technical knowledge, access to capital and

INTERVIEWED	INDUSTRY	OPERATING TIME	NUMBER OF EMPLOYEES	TYPES OF INTERVIEWEES	MATURITY	INCUBATION/ ACCELERATION	INVESTMENT SUPPORT
STARTUP A	EduTech	6 years	60	founder & directors	operates in the national market	nacional	bootstrap & capital venture
STARTUP B	SoftTech	3 years	10	founder & directors	operates in the regional market	nacional	bootstrap & capital venture
STARTUP C	HardTech	2 years	5	all team	beginning to selling	regional	bootstrap
STARTUP D	HardTech	6 years	15	founder & directors	internationalized	regional, national & international	bootstrap & economic subsidy
STARTUP E	SoftTech	4 years	8	all team	operates in the national market	nacional	bootstrap & economic subsidy
STARTUP F	HardTech	2 years	6	all team	operates in the regional market	regional	bootstrap & capital venture
STARTUP G	Fintech	7 years	38	founder & directors	internationalized	international	bootstrap & capital venture
STARTUP H	Construtech	5 years	6	all team	internationalized	national & international	bootstrap & capital venture
STARTUP I	Agrotech	2 years	9	all team	beginning to selling	nacional	bootstrap & capital venture
STARTUP J	SoftTech	4 years	47	founder & directors	operates in the national market	nacional	bootstrap & economic subsidy
STARTUP K	Agrotech	1,5 years	12	all team	beginning to selling	nacional	bootstrap & economic subsidy
STARTUP L	Fintech	8 years	69	founder & directors	internationalized	national & international	joint venture
INCUBATOR 1	All	10 years	12 employees+ 120 volunters	coordinators & managers	regional	own program	private & governmental
INCUBATOR 2	All	7 years	11 employees+ 67 volunters	coordinators & managers	nacional	own program	private & governmental
INCUBATOR 3	IT	8 years	18 employees+ 43 volunters	coordinators & managers	nacional	own program	private & governmental
ACCELERATOR 1	All	3 years	22 employees+ 54 volunters	coordinators & managers	regional	own program	private & governmental
ACCELERATOR 2	IT	4 years	72 employees+ 58 volunters	coordinators & managers	nacional	own program	private & governmental
CO-ACCEL 1	IT	1 year	4 employees+ 40 volunters	coordinators & managers	nacional	colab	private only

Fig. 1. Characterisation of the sample

contact with the market to form partnerships and customer portfolios came through participation in incubation and acceleration programs [31]. The central recognised values were creating and exploiting knowledge and promoting and supporting innovation. 90% of mentors are made up of volunteers who consider their activity beneficial due to the gain of learning and knowledge exchange. A large part of the network, which grows yearly, expands through the indication of participants, who invite other people of notorious expertise in the market to help strengthen the entrepreneurial ecosystem [32].

4.1 Moderating Variables

The primary constructs of the structural holes' theory were used as moderating factors to distinguish the acquisition and sharing of knowledge between individuals, intra- and inter-organisational in startups, incubators, and accelerators. The variables considered were network density and cohesion, the intensity of ties, the position of connections and the volume of information and knowledge exchanged. The strong links highlighted by the interviewees were the incubation and acceleration programs. The weak link in the chain was considered access to capital which, despite the relevant number of public and private development institutions, credit lines and volume of investments in this type of company, is still growing at a slower pace compared to other links in the network [33].

MODERATING VARIABLES	size/density
	network cohesion
	relational ties
	position of links/actors
	volume/quality of information

NETWORK INFLUENCES	EXOGENOUS	Political development
		Cultural development
		Economic development
		Technological development
	ENDOGENOUS	Effort of the organization to reach resources
		Structuring relationships efficiently
NETWORK RELATIONSHIPS	STRUCTURAL	Pattern of connections and influences
	RELATIONAL	Interactions between stakeholders
	COGNITIVE	Interpretations of cultural and social systems and norms
TYPE OF SHARING	PROVIDE KNOWLEDGE (Know how)	managerial knowledge
		improve competitiveness
		create innovation
	GET KNOWLEDGE (Know that)	reproduce routines
		improve qualification
		e-learning

NATURE OF KNOWLEDGE	TACIT		
	EXPLICIT		
SHARING EXTENSION	BETWEEN INDIVIDUALS		
	INTRA-ORGANIZATIONAL		
	INTERORGANIZATIONAL		Financial, strategic, and marketing results
REASONS FOR SHARING	EXTERNAL	ENVIRONMENTAL FACTORS	Organizational context
			Interpersonal and team characteristics
			cultural characteristics
	INTERNAL	Individual characteristics/factors	
		Characteristics / motivational factors	
		Behavioral characteristics/factors	

Fig. 2. Content analysis categorisation tree

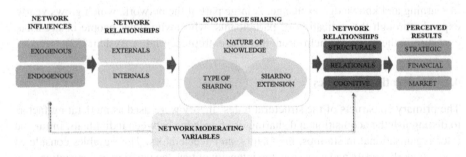

Fig. 3. Study framework of knowledge management in entrepreneurship networks

The cost-benefit perception focused on the return on knowledge and improvement in reputation. Common sense was that strengthening the ecosystem was above any individual gain since a robust ecosystem supports the entire network. And that, if one-day mature startups benefit, it is part of their social role to return new knowledge to the network and pave the way for new businesses. It is also worth emphasising the existence of groups of online practices in which startups, including competitors, exchange experiences to grow together [34].

Relational bonds were considered intense since interactions were daily and fueled by what respondents called a "feedback loop" based on reciprocity and collaboration. The position of the links was deemed adequate and accessible with considerable ease of access and robustness of the communication channels throughout the entire network. All interviewees claimed to have quick access, including with organisations and individuals still unknown through the immediate indication of partners in the online communities of practices. The investment link was cited as the weakest and most challenging to access [35]. Organisations in transition economies have knowledge transfer patterns that can differ depending on their maturity level. All startups linked their current stage of maturity to participate in incubation and acceleration programs [36]. The interviewees understood that programmes should be guided by networking, providing knowledge based on absorptive capacity. The type of industry directly influenced the sharing practices adopted by entrepreneurs [37].

4.2 Network Influences

Among the main endogenous influences of the entrepreneurial network, the efforts of startups were cited, which continue to seek continuous incubation and acceleration programs to gain access to resources they still do not have. Many have participated in programs to expand their technical capacity, access networks, and build new links. Structuring relationships efficiently was also cited. Communities of practice, investment communities, customer communities and others were reported, and a large communication group with everyone involved in the network for questions and general and random sharing. Political development was mentioned by creating new bodies in public institutions and universities to develop entrepreneurship and innovation. The culture of belonging stimulated the branching and expansion of the knowledge flow and economic development with the entry of new businesses generating jobs and income with little investment [35].

4.3 Motivations to Share

4.3.1 External Motivations

All startups actively participate in communities, providing and obtaining knowledge and having a stimulus to the culture of sharing information among employees. No feeling of rivalry or superiority was identified in sharing information among members. Respondents demonstrated a spirit of collectivism and cooperation, pointing out that an organisational climate promotes competition between individuals and creates barriers to fostering a culture of sharing [38]. Statements that the return perceived by sharing information results from the recognition and credibility acquired, in addition to a possible approximation that may arise with investors and mentors. Promoting organisational incentives and rewards is essential to motivate individuals to pass on their knowledge. Heterogeneity was a positive factor among the focus groups [35].

4.3.2   Internal Motivations

Integrating the team inside and outside the work environment influences the sharing of knowledge among employees when stating that individuals tend to prioritise sharing their information with people they relate to and trust. Startups pointed to recognition and meritocracy as pillars to promote greater knowledge integration. Intra-organizational incentive, recognition and reward campaigns were used to encourage knowledge sharing [39].

4.4   Specificities of Knowledge Sharing

4.4.1   Nature of Knowledge

It was identified that in all the interviewed companies, this tends to occur more informally than through formal communication channels, and much of this process depends on the organisational culture. The hierarchical level directly influences the type of information and the members' access level. Tacit knowledge is shared in daily face-to-face or virtual meetings, with everyone present and stimulated through coexistence between senior and junior individuals. Because they are organisations with peculiar characteristics, startups have a very lean composition and only necessarily intimate knowledge is restricted to founding partners. Explicit knowledge is elaborated and formalised mainly by team leaders, does not require approval from the highest leadership and can be proposed by everyone. The most significant benefit pointed out by the investigated startups in formalising knowledge was the reduction of the integration time of new members and the need to hire external basic training since the internal processes already mapped encourage organisational learning [16].

4.4.2   Sharing Type

Interorganizational knowledge transfer was seen from the perspective of network relationships based on connections and affinities between the knowledge giver and recipient. The decision to provide and obtain knowledge inside and outside organisations was left to the private judgment of the members about the receptor's absorption capacity, their motivation to teach and learn, and the intra-organizational transfer capacity [40]. Although all startups had a pro-knowledge-sharing culture with direct actions from management and managerial support, including some recognition practices, providing knowledge was more concentrated on members who considered themselves experts in the topics to be shared. Members' main reasons for improving skills and creating innovations were to provide knowledge among their peers and in communities of practice. They were obtaining knowledge, although a generalised approach by the individuals interviewed was actions based on rules in the sense of reproducing routines and improving their self-perception of qualification. E-learning was the most used channel for converging knowledge between managerial and operational levels [41].

4.4.3   Share Extension

Knowledge was quickly shared by members of organisations among themselves, between teams and between organisations, individually motivated by peer recognition and a sense of self-efficacy. The motivation was attributed to learning mechanisms promoted by participatory and decentralised leaderships, such as participation in skills development programs, external training, promotion of internal workshops and collective assessment of teams [15]. Individuals who have undergone training or considered themselves mature enough have voluntarily passed on their learning to their team and other groups through manuals and flowcharts that promote interdisciplinary cooperation [42]. Internal relationships, values and norms shared by the group were listed as impulses to sharing. Until then, the investigated startups claim not to have presented levels of conflicts that have interfered with the learning processes and knowledge sharing. They all listed interference from external factors such as public opinion, organisational reputation, and market variations. All startups participate in online groups and communities of practice at the individual initiative of their members. The leaders encouraged their teams by highlighting the strong bonds of emotional proximity and the social relationships that facilitate knowledge transfer and increase the quality of the information exchanged [43].

4.5 Network Relationships

Most of the startups developed within incubation and acceleration programs, and the few reported that did not follow the same path were born in universities and had an informal technical follow-up. Organisations formed business and support networks to the point where one interviewee stated that "an incubator or accelerator that does not have an excellent network of contacts is useless (...) all the clients that my organisation today came as a result of these interactions if it were not for this great effort to create connections, we would not be who we are today". Competing startups often share even access to their customers because they understand that this can generate collaborative growth for all and the development of new technologies with open innovation. One of the interviewees stated that he was not afraid of unethical attitudes in these relationships and emphasised, "here, everyone knows each other by name and surname, we often sit down at the table (...) negative effect on individual and organisational reputation would be grave" [14]. Respondents understand that their reputation outweighs any temporary gain and that a good reputation guarantees future employability and reasonable access to market opportunities, even in the event of company closure. The main improvements from network interactions were expanding innovative and entrepreneurial capacity, reflecting comparative advantages and more significant impact of solutions launched in the market. Individually, increased creativity and qualification were cited, in addition to the possibility of retaining talent. Institutions stated technical nature is of extreme relevance for the composition of teams. Priority is given to absorbing members best suited to the organisational culture who already relate to other links in the network [31].

4.6 Perceived Results

Interorganizational exchanges were seen as a dynamic 'feedback loop' structure where antecedents and consequences of transfer intertwine in environments of constant change that promote learning. Feedback relationships between peers and immediate superiors and causal links between specific organisational knowledge were listed as direct influencers of company performance [44]. All interviewees perceived strategic results in enjoying the benefits of networking in a satisfactory and balanced way. All cited bene-fits in sharing knowledge between organisations, especially concerning the relationship network. Startups stated that a large part of their customers and investors were accessed from the incubation and acceleration programs they participated in and that, without these network contacts, it wouldn't have been possible to position themselves in the market the way they are currently placed [45].

4.7 Emerging Categories

4.7.1 Information Security

The information security category emerged during the investigation due to the concern and need of startups losing talent and information related to their core business. They all saw security as a market entry and survival strategy. However, only startups with higher maturity levels presented a contingency plan and formally signed documents to prevent information leakage and loss of knowledge [46].

5 Conclusion

In methodological matters, the study innovated by qualitatively analysing startups, incu-bators and accelerators from emerging economies in different degrees of maturity and belonging to various industries. It was not limited to measuring knowledge sharing and considered relational aspects of the cooperation network from a social perspective in different links and hierarchical levels to address network management, influences and characteristics of the links. It also revealed how situational factors reflected in the development of social relationships and influenced knowledge sharing in organisations, directly affecting individual and organisational results.

As for the practical implications, the findings showed that knowledge sharing in entrepreneurial networks happens informally, based on the sense of collectivism, truth, and trust between the links and with the mature and organisational recognition, image and reputation. More specifically, the top results perceived were access to physical spaces and shared resources, support services and consultancies for business devel-opment and, mainly, access to the networking of extensive incubation and acceleration institutes. Technical knowledge, access to capital and contact with the market for forming partnerships and customer portfolio was also widely reiterated.

The strong links in the entrepreneurial network highlighted by the interviewees were the incubation and acceleration programs. The weak link in the chain was consid-ered access to capital. Despite the relevant number of public and private development institutions, credit lines and the volume of investments in this type of company is still growing slower than other links. The perceived return focused on knowledge gained and improved individual and organisational reputation. Common sense was that strength-ening the ecosystem was above personal gain since a robust ecosystem supports the entire network. And that, if one-day mature startups benefit, it is part of their social role to return new knowledge to the network and pave the way for new businesses. The "feedback loop" was based on intense relational ties, reciprocity and collaboration.

Among the main influences of the entrepreneurial network, the efforts of startups were cited, which continue to seek continuous incubation and acceleration programs to gain access to resources they still do not have. Political development with the creation of new bodies and the culture of belonging has stimulated the branching and expansion of knowledge flow. Economic growth with the entry of new businesses generated employment and income with little investment, and technological development was cited as an influencing factor.

Organisations claimed to form business and support networks based on participation in incubation and acceleration programmes. They also revealed that competing startups tend to share access to their customers because they understand that this can generate collaborative growth for all and the development of new technologies with open innovation. The absence of fear of unethical attitudes in these relationships was based on the perception that the negative cost on individual and organisational reputation would be buried.

For future research, we suggest identifying managerial behaviours and actions that support strengthening bonds and knowledge sharing. As a future administrative contribution, we recommend developing a guide of reasonable and possible scales that can measure the willingness of individuals to share different types of knowledge in various communication channels.

References

1. Slotte-Kock, S., Coviello, N.: Entrepreneurship research on network processes: a review and ways forward. Entrep. Theory Pract. **34**, 31–57 (2010). https://doi.org/10.1111/j.1540-6520. 2009.00311.x
2. Sundin, E.: People and places in the global economy article information. J. Enterp. Commun. **10**, 29 (2016)
3. Ahadi, S., Kasraie, S.: Contextual factors of entrepreneurship intention in manufacturing SMEs: the case study of Iran. J. Small Bus. Enterp. Dev. **27**, 633–657 (2020). https://doi.org/ 10.1108/JSBED-02-2019-0074
4. Roundy, P.T.: Start-up community narratives: the discursive construction of entrepreneurial ecosystems. J. Entrep. **25**, 232–248 (2016). https://doi.org/10.1177/0971355716650373
5. Soriano, D.R., Castrogiovanni, G.J.: The impact of education, experience and inner circle advisors on SME performance: insights from a study of public development centers. Small Bus. Econ. **38**, 333–349 (2012). https://doi.org/10.1007/s11187-010-9278-3
6. Gattringer, R., Wiener, M.: Key factors in the start-up phase of collaborative foresight. Technol. Forecast. Soc. Change. **153**, 119931 (2020). https://doi.org/10.1016/j.techfore.2020. 119931
7. Rahim, N.A., Mohamed, Z.B., Amrin, A.: From lab to market: challenges faced by academic entrepreneur in technology transfer pursuit. Int. J. Bus. Soc. **22**, 1256–1268 (2021). https:// doi.org/10.33736/ijbs.4300.2021
8. Tumelero, C., Sbragia, R., Borini, F.M., Franco, E.C.: The role of networks in technological capability: a technology-based companies perspective. J. Glob. Entrep. Res. **8**(1), 1–19 (2018). https://doi.org/10.1186/s40497-018-0095-5
9. Polzin, F., von Flotow, P., Klerkx, L.: Addressing barriers to eco-innovation: exploring the finance mobilisation functions of institutional innovation intermediaries. Technol. Forecast. Soc. Change. **103**, 34–46 (2016). https://doi.org/10.1016/j.techfore.2015.10.001

10. Bischoff, K.: A study on the perceived strength of sustainable entrepreneurial ecosystems on the dimensions of stakeholder theory and culture. Small Bus. Econ. **56**(3), 1121–1140 (2019). https://doi.org/10.1007/s11187-019-00257-3

11. Bergmann, H.: The formation of opportunity beliefs among university entrepreneurs: an empirical study of research- and non-research-driven venture ideas. J. Technol. Transf. **42**(1), 116–140 (2015). https://doi.org/10.1007/s10961-015-9458-z

12. Malerba, F., McKelvey, M.: Knowledge-intensive innovative entrepreneurship integrating Schumpeter, evolutionary economics, and innovation systems. Small Bus. Econ. **54**(2), 503–522 (2018). https://doi.org/10.1007/s11187-018-0060-2

13. Kashani, E.S., Roshani, S.: Evolution of innovation system literature: intellectual bases and emerging trends. Technol. Forecast. Soc. Change. **146**, 68–80 (2019). https://doi.org/10.1016/j.techfore.2019.05.010

14. Muñoz, P., Branzei, O.: Regenerative organizations: introduction to the special issue. Organ. Environ. **34**, 507–516 (2021). https://doi.org/10.1177/10860266211055740

15. Kroll, H.: How to evaluate innovation strategies with a transformative ambition? A proposal for a structured, process-based approach. Sci. Public Policy. **46**, 635–647 (2019). https://doi.org/10.1093/scipol/scz016

16. Casson, M.: Entrepreneurship: theory, institutions and history. Eli F. Heckscher Lecture, 2009. Scand. Econ. Hist. Rev. **58**, 139–170 (2010). https://doi.org/10.1080/03585522.2010.482288

17. Dey, A., Gupta, A., Singh, G.: Open innovation at different levels for higher climate risk resilience. Sci. Technol. Soc. **22**, 388–406 (2017). https://doi.org/10.1177/0971721817723242

18. Todericiu, R.: The impact of intellectual capital on the SMEs performance: a study of the Romanian central region SMEs. Stud. Bus. Econ. **16**, 198–209 (2021). https://doi.org/10.2478/sbe-2021-0016

19. Blair, C.A., Shaver, K.G.: Of horses and jockeys: perceptions by academic entrepreneurs. Entrep. Res. J. **10**, 20190011 (2020). https://doi.org/10.1515/erj-2019-0011

20. Attour, A., Lazaric, N.: From knowledge to business ecosystems: emergence of an entrepreneurial activity during knowledge replication. Small Bus. Econ. **54**(2), 575–587 (2018). https://doi.org/10.1007/s11187-018-0035-3

21. Cánovas-Saiz, L., March-Chordà, I., Yagüe-Perales, R.M.: New evidence on accelerator performance based on funding and location. Eur. J. Manag. Bus. Econ. **29**, 217–234 (2020). https://doi.org/10.1108/EJMBE-10-2017-0029

22. Shepherd, D.A., Covin, J.G., Kuratko, D.F.: Project failure from corporate entrepreneurship: managing the grief process. J. Bus. Ventur. **24**, 588–600 (2009). https://doi.org/10.1016/j.jbusvent.2008.01.009

23. Fazlagić, J., Sulczewska-Remi, A., Loopesko, W.: City policies to promote entrepreneurship: a cross-country comparison of Poland and Germany. J. Entrep. Manag. Innov. **17**, 159–185 (2021). https://doi.org/10.7341/202117226

24. Forsstrom-Tuominen, H., Jussila, I., Goel, S.: Reinforcing collectiveness in entrepreneurial interactions within start-up teams: a multiple-case study. Entrep. Reg. Dev. **31**, 683–709 (2019). https://doi.org/10.1080/08985626.2018.1554709

25. Delanoë-Gueguen, S., Fayolle, A.: Crossing the entrepreneurial rubicon: a longitudinal investigation. J. Small Bus. Manag. **57**, 1044–1065 (2019). https://doi.org/10.1111/jsbm.12419

26. Brandao, T.: Shaping Portuguese science policy for the European horizon: The discourses of technological change. Technol. Forecast. Soc. Change. **113**, 168–184 (2016). https://doi.org/10.1016/j.techfore.2015.09.014

27. Zhao, W., Wang, A., Chen, Y., Liu, W.: Investigating inclusive entrepreneurial ecosystem through the lens of bottom of the pyramid (BOP) theory: case study of Taobao village in

China. CHINESE Manag. Stud. **15**, 613–640 (2021). https://doi.org/10.1108/CMS-05-2020-0210

28. Elena García-Ruiz, M., Lena-Acebo, F.J.: FabLab movement: research design by mixed methods. Obets **14**, 373–406 (2019). https://doi.org/10.14198/OBETS2019.14.2.04

29. Pornparnomchai, M., Rajchamaha, K.: Sharing knowledge on the sustainable business model: an aquaculture start-up case in Thailand. Cogent Bus. Manag. **8**, 1924932 (2021). https://doi.org/10.1080/23311975.2021.1924932

30. Pillai, T.R., Ahamat, A.: Social-cultural capital in youth entrepreneurship ecosystem: Southeast Asia. J. Enterp. Communities **12**, 232–255 (2018). https://doi.org/10.1108/JEC-08-2017-0063

31. Mian, S., Lamine, W., Fayolle, A.: Technology business incubation: an overview of the state of knowledge. Technovation **50–51**, 1–12 (2016). https://doi.org/10.1016/j.technovation.2016.02.005

32. Lamine, W., Mian, S., Fayolle, A., Wright, M., Klofsten, M., Etzkowitz, H.: Technology business incubation mechanisms and sustainable regional development. J. Technol. Transf. **43**(5), 1121–1141 (2016). https://doi.org/10.1007/s10961-016-9537-9

33. Miles, M.P., Morrison, M.: An effectual leadership perspective for developing rural entrepreneurial ecosystems. Small Bus. Econ. **54**(4), 933–949 (2018). https://doi.org/10.1007/s11187-018-0128-z

34. Aminullah, E., Adnan, R.S.: The role of academia as an external resource of innovation for the automotive industry in Indonesia. ASIAN J. Technol. Innov. **20**, 99–110 (2012). https://doi.org/10.1080/19761597.2012.683946

35. Castañer, X., Oliveira, N.: Collaboration, coordination, and cooperation among organizations: establishing the distinctive meanings of these terms through a systematic literature review. J. Manage. **46**, 965–1001 (2020). https://doi.org/10.1177/0149206320901565

36. Rogge, K.S., Reichardt, K.: Policy mixes for sustainability transitions: an extended concept and framework for analysis. Res. Policy. **45**, 132–147 (2016). https://doi.org/10.1016/j.respol.2016.04.004

37. Lee, J., Park, C.: Research and development linkages in a national innovation system: factors affecting success and failure in Korea. Technovation **26**, 1045–1054 (2006). https://doi.org/10.1016/j.technovation.2005.09.004

38. Aleksandrova, E., Gerry, C.J., Verkhovskaya, O.: Missing entrepreneurs: the importance of attitudes and control in shaping entrepreneurial intentions in Russia. J. Entrep. Emerg. Econ. **12**, 1–33 (2020). https://doi.org/10.1108/JEEE-11-2018-0133

39. Guerrero, M., Urbano, D., Herrera, F.: Innovation practices in emerging economies: do university partnerships matter? J. Technol. Transf. **44**(2), 615–646 (2017). https://doi.org/10.1007/s10961-017-9578-8

40. Kim, J., Choi, H.: Value co-creation through social media: a case study of a start-up company. J. Bus. Econ. Manag. **20**, 1–19 (2019). https://doi.org/10.3846/jbem.2019.6262

41. Alves, A.C., Fischer, B., Schaeffer, P.R., Queiroz, S.: Determinants of student entrepreneurship: an assessment on higher education institutions in Brazil. Innov. Manag. Rev. **16**, 96–117 (2019). https://doi.org/10.1108/INMR-02-2018-0002

42. Roundy, P.T.: Rust belt or revitalization: competing narratives in entrepreneurial ecosystems. Manag. Res. Rev. **42**, 102–121 (2019). https://doi.org/10.1108/MRR-01-2018-0019

43. Zhou, J., Ge, L.G., Li, J., Chandrashekar, S.P.: Entrepreneurs' socioeconomic status and government expropriation in an emerging economy. Strateg. Entrep. J. **14**, 396–418 (2020). https://doi.org/10.1002/sej.1361

44. Radacsi, L., Filep, J.C.: Survival and growth of Hungarian start-ups. Entrep. Sustain. Issues. **8**, 262–279 (2021). https://doi.org/10.9770/jesi.2021.8.4(15)

45. Villegas-Mateos, A.: Regional entrepreneurial ecosystems in Chile: comparative lessons. J. Entrep. Emerg. Econ. **13**, 39–63 (2021). https://doi.org/10.1108/JEEE-11-2019-0168
46. Melnyk, M., Korcelli-Olejniczak, E., Chorna, N., Popadynets, N.: Development of regional IT clusters in Ukraine: institutional and investment dimensions. Econ. Ann. **173**, 19–25 (2018). https://doi.org/10.21003/ea.V173-03

Knowledge Gaps Implementing Electronic Content Management in the Third Sector

Ejovwoke Onojeharho[1], Thomas Jackson[1(✉)], Lisa Jackson[2], and Corneliu Cotet[1]

[1] School of Business and Economics, Loughborough University, Loughborough, UK
t.w.jackson@lboro.ac.uk

[2] Aeronautical and Automotive Engineering, Loughborough University, Loughborough, UK

Abstract. PURPOSE: This paper reports the challenges encountered and successfully overcome in designing and implementing a knowledge management (KM) system in a third sector organisation. In particular, it highlights the academic contribution to the implementation of Electronic Content Management (ECM) systems and exposes the gap between academic theory and practice.

DESIGN/METHODOLOGY: The research adopts a case study and mixed methods approach following an exploratory sequential design in a third sector national sports organisation.

FINDINGS: The findings highlight that a holistic academic approach is required for successful system implementation. The result is a co-created framework from both academics and practitioners that will facilitate the successful implementation of an ECM system in a third sector organisation.

RESEARCH LIMITATIONS: The research was carried out in a single case study organisation and therefore caution should be taken in generalising the conclusions across multiple different contexts.

PRACTICAL IMPLICATIONS: The outcome of the research offers a practical tool (the EKESNA system) and framework that will be of potential assistance in successful implementation of an ECM system.

ORGINALITY/VALUE: The research builds upon academic theory that is applied to the design and implementation of KM systems. It extends current academic thinking through exploration of the approach taken to develop a more holistic implementation framework for ECM; detailing the relevance of social network analysis for stakeholder analysis, combined with the use of expertise profiling to aid the development of a corporate taxonomy for information structuring.

Keywords: Social Network Analysis · Knowledge Sharing · ECM Implementation · Not-for-Profit Organisations · Stakeholder Analysis

1 Introduction

The purpose of this article is to provide insight into the challenges encountered in successfully implementing Knowledge Management (KM) systems within a not-for-profit organisation, commonly referred to as "third sector organisations". There is a significant distinction between knowledge sharing and expertise sharing; according to the authors

L. Uden and I-H. Ting (Eds.): KMO 2023, CCIS 1825, pp. 17–37, 2023.
https://doi.org/10.1007/978-3-031-34045-1_3

the former "takes a perspective in which externalization of knowledge in the form of computational or information technology artefacts or repositories play an important role" [1, p.532]. This suggests a transfer from tacit to explicit knowledge described in the externalization phase from the four modes of knowledge conversion which were identified as: tacit to tacit (S)ocialisation; tacit to explicit (E)xternalisation; explicit to explicit (C)ombination, and explicit to tacit (I)nternalisation (SECI) [2]. In contrast expertise sharing is described as the ability for one to solve problems or to engage with their work, by having discussions amongst knowledgeable actors, but necessarily with significant a priori externalization support [1]; this again suggests a transfer from tacit-to-tacit knowledge described of the socialization phase in the SECI Process [2]. The two perspectives have been a result of the developments brought about by the technological advancement of knowledge management over the years, leading to a generational classification in terms of the models in which they are represented. Two model generations were proposed in [1] and [3]; the repository (codification) model, and the sharing expertise (community) model.

1.1   The 1st Generation: The Repository Model

Codifying and documenting knowledge in large repositories is the repository model. For centuries, libraries utilized this method. However, between the late 1980s and the early 1990s, organisations exploited networked and distributed systems to discover "what they know." In this generation, organisations created massive, shared repositories of manuals, standard operating procedures, process maps, best practises, and emails that other employees could use to complete their tasks. The model focused on optimising retrieval and improving knowledge sharing through optimised tagging and filtering in modern repositories like Content Management Systems (CMS) and Customer Relationship Management (CRM) Systems [1]. By allowing many people to search and retrieve context-specific knowledge without having to contact the original developer, this approach can scale knowledge reuse [24]. Motivating users to author, organise, and update their information was the biggest issue with this approach [1]. However, the model's dissociative assumption that collective memory could be captured without individuals was its main flaw. Information is produced by specific people in specific contexts for specific purposes, according to Bannon and Kuutti. The authors explain that while this does not mean it is bound solely to the context in which it was created, it does mean that one cannot easily extract and abstract from this web of signification items of "information" that can be stored in some central resource for later use [4].

1.2   The 2nd Generation: The Sharing Expertise Model

The second generation prioritised directed interpersonal communications between topic experts over information artefact externalisation, identifying a gap in the repository model. Technology that helps find suitable experts to share knowledge or expertise filled the gap. The second generation focused on finding the right person and sharing tacit knowledge, which contained contextual knowledge needed to understand information but was not always documented with the repository model [1]. The growing popularity of Communities of Practice (CoP), which identified relevant groups of people to work together in a domain and share common practise, spurred the shift to the second generation. CoPs form the foundation of a social learning system by allowing competence and experience to converge [23]. The authors also stressed social capital, which they defined as collective abilities from social networks. Thus, systems must support the "finding-out" task of finding suitable people to play a significant role in expertise sharing. Expertise Locator became the preferred technology for answering "who knows about this" in an organisation [31]. Thus, organisations began using software like IBM's "SmallBlue" people mining system, which ranked people by search terms that should represent knowledge or skills.

Thus, this research proposes a holistic, context-specific future based on interconnected practises. The paper continues: Sect. 2 discusses the research context and the case study's KM issues. Section 3 examines models that could aid third-sector ECM implementation. Section 4 discusses research methodology. Sections 5 and 6 report data findings. Section 7 discusses findings' significance. Section 8 concludes.

2 Case Study Context

The case study organisation is a National Sport Organisation (NSO); NSOs "are not-for-profit organisations (NPO) that are responsible for the development of their particular sport in their own country" [5, p.264]. NPOs are institutions that self-govern, distribute non-profits, and employ volunteers [22]. The organisation has grown to a multi-regional operation with a diverse expertise pool, and in 2011, it conducted an internal Knowledge Management (KM) audit to assess its knowledge sharing competence. Surveys and interviews revealed communication and information awareness issues. Staff reported poor inter-departmental communication, but good intra-departmental communication. Regarding information awareness, staff felt that while they had the knowledge and skills to do their job, they did not always have the right amount of information from other sources to execute it efficiently, which led to duplication of effort at least. The KM audit recommended implementing Information and Knowledge Management (IKM) tools and strategies to reduce knowledge loss, realise information assets, and reduce work duplication.

The case organisation in [5] described how their rapid growth since the 1990s had caused communication issues and breakdowns and inefficiencies. As a result, the organisation "has worked to implement a number of solutions (that could be classified as KM) to alleviate these challenges including a network of e-communication and the adoption of a database-driven website launched in 2002, [but] success has been limited." [5, p.273]. IKM system implementation research is even rarer than third sector or voluntary sector KM research. While NPOs and for-profit organisations (FPOs) have some similarities, NPOs face unique challenges like decreasing government funding, difficulty recruiting and retaining volunteers, and the need for effective outreach programmes to connect with stakeholders [26]. NPOs are knowledge-intensive organisations. "Studies that look specifically at sport organisations [within this sector] are scarce in the literature [… as] NPOs' in general often lack the resources to embark on major supply-side initiatives (e.g., data warehousing, intranet, web boards)" [6, p.17]. [3, p.270].

Given the many failed KM implementations in literature, this type of organisation seems uninterested in expensive KM initiatives. Oxfam, a charity, treats its KM initiative as a project and has six senior staff members from different departments who are champions for knowledge management in their divisions [7]. Given the unique challenges, including limited finances, NSOs may not be able to afford sophisticated and expensive KM tools and technologies. There appears to be a gap in the literature on KM implementation in NSOs. A KM perspective on NPO technology needs fills a gap in current literature [28, p.720]. Thus, the current case study offers a unique opportunity to explore pragmatic solutions and academic theory.

3 Theoretical Background

KM implementation in FPOs may not directly apply to NPOs' KM needs due to their unique work context [27]. However, successful FPO-KM systems implementation research should be considered. [8] was the only relevant ECM implementation framework for SMEs (see Fig. 1). The framework provides a longitudinal CMS implementation study at a similar-sized organisation to this paper. No other framework had directly applied to NSOs, so this was the best comparison and starting point.

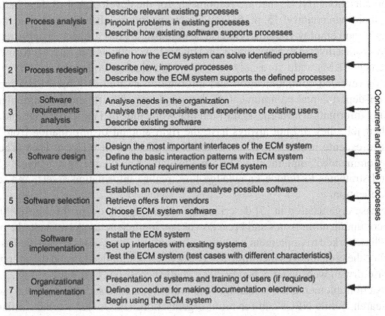

Fig. 1. A process model of the implementation of the ECM system at Altan.dk. Source: [8, p.354]

The implementation model derived by [8] shown in Fig. 1, focuses extensively on the IT system selection and acquisition; labelled as step 5 on the framework. However, when comparing the three-content management strategy plan proposed in [9], it becomes evident that the existing model overlooks elements concerning information content and governance, while implementing a CMS (see Fig. 2).

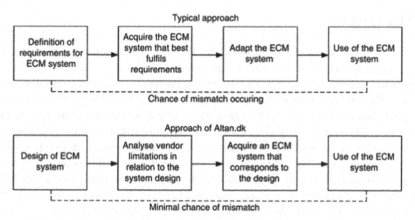

Fig. 2. The ECM approach at Altan.dk. Source: [8, p.355]

The existing model does not make any mention of the need for foundation work, in terms of proposing a systematic approach to identify and recruit the key stakeholders and drivers, who will play a major role in shaping and promoting the initiative within the organisation. The successful design of an effective KM team requires the identification of key stakeholders, both within and outside the organisation, with experience to design, build and deploy systems, whilst balancing the technical and managerial requirements [29]. Identifying the right individuals for these roles early in the project may be crucial to its success; it is therefore valuable to find central members within the organisation's structure with controlling influence [32].

In addition, part of the foundation which is seemly overlooked by the model is content structuring referred to in [9]; this involves the process of documenting guidelines for governing how information content is described and stored within the new CMS. As such taxonomies or ontologies need to be present prior to implementation of the new CMS: this is potentially a key stage in the implementation, which is overlooked by the existing model, as it is assumed that the organisation already has a corporate taxonomy or that there is no need for planning the acquisition and design of one during the CMS implementation. Finally, the existing model also fails to address life after the new CMS has been implemented within the organisation: there needs to be strategy in place to help the organisation take full ownership of the new system, solicit feedback from end users, as the system is always in transition resulting from the growing needs of users as they become accustomed to the system, but also continuous update of the taxonomy/ontology as the organisation is constantly moving into new areas of operation.

The issues identified within the case study organisation presented an opportunity to explore specific challenges of implementing a combination of practices and tools identified in both first and second-generation models and overcoming these challenges though a pragmatic new framework for conducting knowledge management projects in Non-Governmental Organisations (NGOs) and NSOs specifically. The findings, however, could be generalised and potentially applied to other third sector organisations.

4 Methodology

This research was conducted in a national third sector organisation that governs all levels of aquatic sports. The case study organisation is the National Governing Body for aquatics in England and is a vibrant modern organisation providing leadership to the industry of swimming in many ways. It supports over 1,200 affiliated swimming clubs through a National/Regional/and Sub-regional structure. At the time of the research the organisation had over 350 employees; 245 were permanent staff, and the rest were volunteering members. A decision was made for this research to focus only on permanent staff; volunteering members were not considered because they did not actively participate in functions that directly impact decision making at the organisation; additionally, operating remotely across the regions meant that reaching this group for data collection was impractical. Alongside the case study organisation, this project involved working with British Swimming, which is the National Governing Body for Swimming, Diving, Synchronized Swimming, Water Polo and Open Water in Great Britain. It is responsible internationally for the high-performance representation of the sport. British Swimming seeks to enable its athletes to achieve gold medal success at the World Championships, Paralympics, Commonwealth Games, and Olympics. To ensure this, the organisation's main focus was to capitalise upon the residual knowledge held by their employees to generate income. Through identifying what they knew, their aim was to codify the knowledge to gain commercial value. A key part of this was conducting a knowledge audit of the organisation to map out the knowledge flows between individuals and/or systems and potential value of the knowledge.

Understanding the organization's issues was essential to assessing barriers. Table 1 presents KM survey results. After identifying these issues, the organisation could determine the best ways to improve knowledge sharing or remove barriers. This paper does not discuss the survey results because they were published in [11]. That study suggested KM systems for organization-wide knowledge sharing. It also mapped the organization's IT systems to determine their suitability. Informal interviews and observation helped identify the organization's KM barriers. These showed that the organisation lacked a suitable expert-finding method and information repository. The next step was to determine if an expertise locator and content management system would improve knowledge management and sharing at the organisation.

The organisation used Social Network Analysis (SNA) to identify key information players to assess value. We then asked them to champion the proposed knowledge management tools to promote system adoption. After identifying the SNA network, we used an expertise locator system to measure organisational knowledge flows. The Email Knowledge Extraction and Social Network Analysis (EKESNA) system helped build knowledge profiles, which, when combined with the SNA, visualised the organization's knowledge flows. When reviewing social networks, node importance should be combined with contextual information about the node itself. The system identified the company's knowledge enablers and blockers. After SNA identified key information players, the Feature Analysis Matrix (FAM) was used in a seven-step sequence [12, p.124]. After FAM identifies potential solutions, end-users provide their requirements and score-rank the selected systems. The scoring matrix indicates which system may be best for the organisation. The seven steps include (1) select candidate solutions to

Table 1. Case study organisation's issues to be addressed following the results of a Knowledge Management Audit

Preliminary KM Investigation Use questionnaire, interview, and observation		
Issues to Address	Method	Method Outcomes
Employees have difficulty discovering files or media within their own organisation or storage?	Expert locator system (EKESNA) + Social Network Analysis (SNA)	Implementing a Content Management system can improve information sharing Assess the organisations knowledge network to identify key players in the organisation when it comes to knowledge sharing, as can be seen in Fig. 8, the Email Knowledge Extraction and Social Network Analysis (EKESNA) system was able to capture information relating individuals to media files and folders
Employees find it difficult knowing who to contact for information or expertise?	EKESNA + SNA	EKESNA system was trialled as a method to create an expertise repository where employees can find experts to contact regarding their queries, see Fig. 8
If the organisation electronically stores information, either structured or unstructured inside or outside of a CMS	EKESNA + SNA Focus Group	Using the SNA feature of the EKESNA system would help identify key topic experts to help build the /ontologies which may be used to improve an employee's access to the information stored The SNA coupled with data collected on individual's expertise from the EKESNA system was used to identify key players within the organisation to provide the requirements for a new CMS in a focus group, but also to champion its implementation going forward

(continued)

Table 1. (*continued*)

Preliminary KM Investigation Use questionnaire, interview, and observation

Issues to Address	Method	Method Outcomes
Employees have difficulty communicating between departments or across geographically dispersed departments?	EKESNA + SNA	EKESNA system was trialled as a method to discover the information flow network The EKESNA system collects SNA data which the organisation can use to improve connectivity between departments and teams, and improve collaboration

evaluate, (2) identify the user requirements, (3) prioritise features with respect to the user requirements by using a scoring system, (4) agree on a scoring system that can be applied to all features, (5) carry out the evaluation to score the solutions against the criteria, (6) analyse and interpret the results and (7) Present conclusions on the evaluation to decision-makers.

A focus group of four SNA-identified key players in their department was used to understand the current information sharing and storage situation, the current systems, how they were being used and whether they were fit for purpose, and the requirements for a potential new CMS. "Based on their common characteristics relative to the issue being discussed" [13, p.81], key information brokers and eigenvectors were used to select focus group members. The IT manager helped integrate the new system into the organization's infrastructure. Five people including the IT manager formed the focus group. The SNA results revealed the four most influential nodes through which a significant amount of the organization's information traffic passed [13 & 14]. The recommended manageable size is six to twelve participants. These individuals could accurately estimate the organization's system requirements. In focus groups, one or two people often dominate the discussion [15], making it hard for other members to contribute. The researcher chaired the group to ensure everyone could speak. The FAM process included a focus group assessment of current systems and requirements for the new system. The findings section lists FAM-selected systems. Next, the case study organization's ECM implementation was evaluated using an FPO-KM-derived framework [8]. (see Fig. 3). In the discussion section, the researcher adapted the framework to emphasise the importance of a holistic approach to identify the right tools and stakeholders to facilitate and promote knowledge sharing project acceptance.

4.1 SNA Approach

Surveys, ethnographic interviews, and electronic activity mapping can collect sociogram data [33]. The case study organisation collected data using questionnaires, which "method is not practical for groups larger than 150 to 200, the results within this range provide broad coverage and actionable results within groups up to this size" [33, p.336].

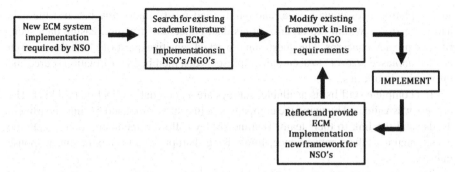

Fig. 3. Case Study Evaluation approach. Adapted from [8, p.355]

[34] proposes snowball and full network social network analysis. The snowball approach works best when there is a natural starting point [35]. It works by asking the pre-determined individuals who they contact, then asking the list obtained who they connected to. The full network approach collects population data at once. This research method was preferred because it quickly represented the organisation and was easier to administer if respondents were asked to identify a limited number of specific individuals [35].

4.2 SNA Sampling

As mentioned, the case study organization's volunteers were excluded from the SNA sample because they mostly did low-level tasks like survey data collection. Volunteers typically only stayed for a surveying exercise or other short-term projects, which also influenced the decision to exclude them. A missing node in the dataset can affect the SNA [34]. For this project, a complete network was necessary to understand current information and knowledge sharing connections and identify the organization's key players/influencers.

4.3 SNA Data Collection

Online questionnaires were the obvious data collection tool with the right reach for the case study organisation, which had a near 60/40 split of local and remote workers. This method saved time, money, and effort by collecting data simultaneously across the organization's geographically divided sections. The case study organisation had members across the UK, making data collection easier. However, this data collection method is difficult to ensure a high response rate. An incomplete data set may hinder social network analysis conclusions. However, data analysis should show basic information and knowledge sharing and organisational social network trends.

4.3.1 SNA Online Survey

Surveys show current conditions in a cross-section [36]. They usually involve questionnaires or interviews, but this study used a questionnaire. The organisation used an online survey platform for convenience, anonymity, and most importantly because the data had to be stored within the organization's data collection structure, easing data security and privacy concerns. The questionnaire asked sensitive questions, and the research needed unbiased answers to accurately represent each member's information source and informal network ties.

If a complete staff list is available, surveys are a good data collection tool [37]. The process was validated by using the company's online survey tool and having department heads send the link to their teams. Online surveys allowed members to complete the questionnaire at their convenience, minimising disruption, and maximising response rates.

The survey was extensively piloted before deployment to ensure question clarity and ease of access and completion. After approval from the project manager and human resources manager, the survey was launched. The company required their approval before collecting internal data.

As mentioned earlier, one of the drawbacks of online surveys was that participants couldn't directly contact the researcher for clarification or problems while completing the survey. However, self-completed questionnaires must be simple to use and answer [38]. Due to their scepticism of the survey's use, some participants were hesitant to participate. Clear instructions and background information about the survey helped the researcher address most of these issues. The survey noted that participants could opt out at any time. The survey was easy to complete with instructions, allowing participants to answer "N/A" for irrelevant questions. Any survey process requires extra effort to achieve 100% response rate. The authors set a one-month deadline for data collection, but as the deadline approached, participants who had not completed the questionnaire were prompted via email to either complete it online or schedule an assisted telephone interview at their convenience. These efforts increased survey response.

Table 1 listed the case study organization's issues and resolution strategy. Based on this research, it suggests where an organisation can improve knowledge sharing and the best tool and approach. If the organisation can accurately determine where to focus its efforts, following the method in this section will reduce the likelihood of failure in implementing the best solution.

5   Findings and Analysis of SNA Data

This section summarises SNA data. The authors provide an overview of the network and analyse its properties, roles, and key players.

5.1   Network Properties

Reviewing network characteristics is essential before analysing its properties. As shown in Fig. 4, the socio-gram shows that not all nodes are connected in the network. The social network is developed from each member's responses regarding their information sources channel, unlike an ego network, which focuses on a single member's communication links with the rest of the organisation. Bi-directional links between nodes are also shown in the socio-gram. These links improve idea exchange in an organisation [43]. "Networks where we study how all actors are tied to one another according to one relation, like friendship" [44, p.16] are 1-mode networks, which contain data on nodes of a similar type.

Fig. 4. Socio-gram of the case study organisation.

The previous section helps calculate network density. For this network, the overall density was 0.035, indicating that the organisation is using only 3.5% of its communication channels or that 96.5% are underutilised. This suggests that most members ask a small group of people.

5.2 Descriptive Measures Analysis

The data was imported into UCINET [48] where calculations were made on the centrality measures; these highlight the node's position in the network and their value to the network. The most important and frequently calculated centrality measures are highlighted in [45] as the degree centrality, betweenness, closeness, and the eigenvector centrality. The author explains that these centrality measures are used to indicate "prestige, importance, prominence and power" [45, p.112]. The findings from the analysis of the centrality measures are given below, showing the nodes with the highest values for each measure.

5.2.1 Degree Centrality

Since the network is directed, degree centrality includes in-degree and out-degree centralities. Thus, the two centralities refer to the node's inquests: those received and those made to other nodes in the network. In the study organisation, degree centralities indicate how well members interact. The higher the in-degree, the more important the information provider. The out-degree emphasises an individual's information seeking confidence; the higher the value, the more comfortable they are contacting organisation members for information. A network communicator with equal in-degree and out-degree may give and take equally.

Table 2. In-degree and Out-degree

Node Unique ID	In-degree	Out-degree
289	120	17
291	80	20
125	73	29
247	71	0
248	67	17
73	4	33
265	7	29
249	13	28
123	27	28
251	33	28
283	42	28

Table 2 lists the top five nodes with the highest in-degree or out-degree ratios in this network. 289, 291, 125, 247, and 248 were the highest in-degree nodes. The questionnaire allowed participants to explain their information sources, and the following statements supported the high dependence on node "289": *(a) "Knows everything, makes time for you straight away.", (b) "I would speak to "289" because "289" is very helpful:)", (c) "Friendly and approachable", (d) "In my office, and is a wiz with these things", (e) "Who Else?" and (f) "Only < department > officer within company".* The statements emphasise the person's approachability, efficiency, and helpfulness. The statements show confidence in "289's" general expertise, but more interestingly, they show that "289" is the only information source for that department. The researcher found this person to be the organization's most popular. Node "73" had the highest out-degree value, followed by 125, 265, 249, 123, 251, and 123, which had equal values. The top five nodes for both in-degree and out-degree were analysed to determine the ratio. Nodes "123" and "251" have the most balanced network communication due to their in-degree to out-degree ratios.

5.2.2 Betweenness Centrality

Table 3 lists the five highest-betweenness nodes. Betweenness is related to "path" and "closeness" because it calculates how often a node is on the geodesic between two other nodes. The path is defined in [35] as the distance travelled from one node to another without returning to any node in the network, and a geodesic distance is simply the shortest (most efficient) travel path between two nodes.

Table 3. Betweenness Measures

Node Unique ID	Betweenness
241	4236.41
338	4171.48
125	3450.19
251	3348.15
23	3341.30

Nodes "241" and "338" had the highest betweenness value, making them vital to the information network. These individuals are vital to the organisation because they are well positioned within the most efficient communication channels, allowing them to influence information flow within the network, potentially the best way to introduce new information.

5.2.3 Eigenvector Centrality

Table 4 lists the six highest-eigenvector nodes. The eigenvector centrality shows how well connected a node is and how well connected its neighbours are. Nodes "289" and "291" had the highest eigenvector values, making them the most connected. These individuals regularly communicate with organisation members, who are important information channels. Due to their network connectivity, these individuals know most people-of-interest and can make the right introductions. The authors relied on social network analysis (SNA) to find the case study organization's most influential members to drive the project.

Table 4. Eigenvector results

Node Unique ID	Eigenvector
289	0.274
291	0.202
248	0.191
125	0.186
247	0.177
241	0.173

6 Discussion of Results

The study found that SNA was a reliable and crucial method for quickly identifying key organisation members who could be enlisted early in the project to ensure success and impact. The authors were able to access existing trial groups within departments and groups of people from different departments and regions who wanted to be involved in new solutions that could be implemented in the organisation. After reviewing previous KM and staff surveys, the authors agreed with the recommendations and stated that the primary reason for conducting SNA for this research was to identify champions for KM initiatives. The results could also be analysed to discuss emerging patterns and suggest knowledge flow initiatives to support business goals.

6.1 Identifying Individuals

6.1.1 Thought Leaders

These are overlooked group supporters. The SNA identified such employees (degree centrality and eigenvector). Node "289" had the highest In-degree centrality value, indicating that this source receives a lot of traffic and is trusted. The same node had the highest eigenvector, indicating network connectivity. This person was hired early in the project to help spread awareness quickly to a wider audience within the network and recruit organisation members for the pilot and trial. This decision paid off as participants were mostly cooperative throughout the study.

6.1.2 Boundary Spanners

Those who facilitate communication and information flow between groups in the social network [45]. These nodes connect informal subgroups [40]. High betweenness scores, high degree centralities, and boundary spanners are linked to identify these nodes [46]. The researcher found 241,125,251,289,236, 291, 338, 23, 16, 77, 83, and 174 nodes with the highest degree centralities and betweenness scores. KM initiatives recruited many of these nodes.

6.1.3 Bottlenecks/Information Brokers

Information brokers and boundary spanners create bottlenecks by overusing that channel for information. Overloading the communication channel with these nodes causes network disintegration [40]. After analysing betweenness measures, the researcher found that 241, 125, 251, 289, 236 and 291 are overused nodes in the network. These nodes often serve as information sources and communicate across network subgroups, making them bottlenecks.

6.1.4 Proposed Newly Updated ECM Implementation Framework

In the theoretical background, the University of Arizona library's ECM implementation framework was reviewed [8]. It discussed its limitations and suggested a more comprehensive framework for an implementation plan. The NSO used an updated ECM implementation framework shown in Fig. 5, which other organisations could use to improve knowledge sharing by using existing information that is often a by-product of their daily processes. Figure 6's framework helps implement ECM systems and helps employees find and document relevant information for daily operations. Figure 5 updates [8]'s ECM system implementation process model. The current research case study organization's holistic approach informed the model's additions. The purple-highlighted new inserts "2, 4, and 10" describe steps taken to prepare the organisation for the ECM system implementation and ensure project continuity afterward. Following the "Process Analysis" phase, the new ECM framework is used to implement an Electronic Document and Records Management (EDRM) subsystem at the organisation.

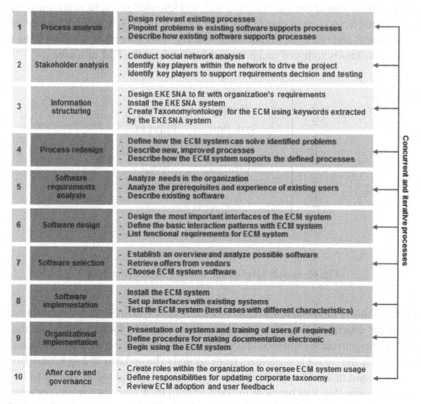

Fig. 5. An updated process model of the implementation of ECM system. Adapted from [8, p.354]

6.1.5 Stakeholder Analysis

Stakeholder analysis involves brainstorming and assessing their impact on the project [17 & 18]. Olander suggested four stakeholder evaluation categories [19]. (see Fig. 6). The method's advantage over a simple list of stakeholders is that the project manager can maintain good relationships with the right people, helping to plan and mitigate each group's impact on the project. Project managers must understand stakeholders' often-hidden power and influence. Even if the project manager met the original time, budget, and scope, a project may not be successful without considering the needs and expectations of a diverse range of stakeholders [20, p.650]. Figure 6 shows how much a stakeholder can help a project on the y-axis. Stakeholder analysis has worked well for managing construction projects and KM implementation projects, according to Olander [19 & 29]. SNA was used to identify these four groups within the organisation to ensure consistency with the research approach and simplicity in selecting and categorising stakeholders. This stakeholder analysis evaluated the updated sections of the model's new ECM implementation framework and helped the case study organisation identify strong facilitators to drive the project and test and provide feedback on the entire process. To understand the organization's social dynamics and knowledge interactions, the research used traditional SNA (survey questions). SNA data identified key individuals who could drive the project and reach the organisation quickly. SNA data also identified influential knowledge brokers who tested and provided feedback on the KM initiative.

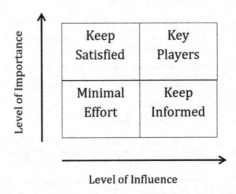

Level of Influence

Fig. 6. Stakeholder impact matrix. Adapted from [19]

Figure 7 shows this research's stakeholder analysis. The SNA-identified information brokers were crucial to the implementation of information tools, so they are the key players. The eigenvector influenced project connectivity and recruitment. At each stage of the research, the senior management team needed to be updated and approved. Boundary spanners and members with high out-degree were highlighted as groups to be kept informed because they can promote the project with their reach across the organisation and high outward communication. The Internal Communications team falls under this group because they can update the rest of the organisation using official information channels like the weekly newsletter.

6.1.6 Information Structuring

White noted that their CM strategy plan needed a governance element—a medium or documentation with a set guideline for creating metadata to describe the organization's content [9]. The updated model's Information Structuring section required the case study organisation to use keywords extracted by the Email Knowledge Extraction and Social Network Analysis (EKESNA) system after it was installed.

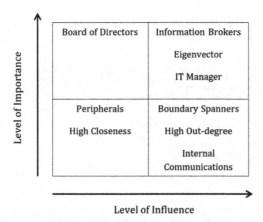

Fig. 7. Stakeholder analysis for ECM project using SNA

Over 18,600 key phrases were extracted during EKESNA testing, of which 2,300 were rated as valid expertise by participants. EKESNA did not use a taxonomy, so it had a higher recall but lower precision. However, allowing the system to collect as many terms as possible can be seen in each user's profile and when creating a taxonomy or document structure. A focus group of experts from the organisation would create the taxonomy. This required a good participant selection. The researcher used SNA results from the stakeholder analysis to choose one participant from each department to create the corporate taxonomy.

Figure 8 shows a search for "learn to swim" and a few variations of the term held within the system, such as {learn2swim and learntoswim}, which reflects how staff may document information about the term (while communicating via email or when saving files on a shared network drive). This causes a problem when another employee searches for a file called "learn2swim" within the organisation. The system will allow the researcher to quickly develop a corporate taxonomy using frameworks like the Dublin Core Metadata Initiative (DCMI) [30], which will become the CMS's standard for cataloguing the organization's information content.

6.1.7 Software Requirements Analysis and Selection

The case study organisation found SNA to identify key stakeholders for the ECM implementation project and EKE profile expertise area to evaluate them useful in implementing Sects. 4–7 of the implementation framework. M-Files DMS Professional scored highest on the Feature Analysis Metrics (FAM) and was recommended to meet the organization's current and future needs. All four FAM systems could scan and store files for the organization's immediate need, replacing an outdated InView system. M-Files and SharePoint can search scanned documents in-text with powerful optical character recognition. M-Files recognises and computes values from scanned forms. M-Files can also solve the organization's information management issues in the future by implementing an EDRM system. M-Files' customers are small and medium-sized businesses like the case study organisation, so they need better implementation support than SharePoint and

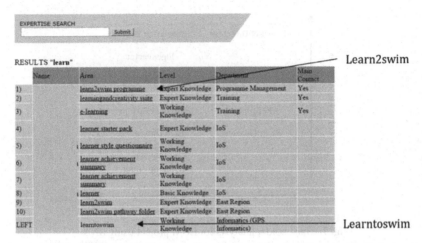

Fig. 8. EKESNA search showing multiple variations of "Learn to Swim"

Huddle. Huddle guarantees user adoption, but M-Files is easy to use and stakeholders have few problems migrating their document libraries.

In contributing to the gap in literature, the surprising findings indicate the limited use of open source-based productivity software, as opposed to commercial systems, even though NPOs are presumed to prefer these low-cost or free systems [28]. The authors note that this was not the case for respondents in their study and suggest further investigation to understand why, speculating due to organisational (finance) or human (staff) factors. For the current knowledge gap research, the FAM also compared an open-source solution (Alfresco), which scored well and was a lower-cost option, since cost was a major focus group topic. The IT manager explained that a low-cost commercial package had more technical support than open source, which swayed the decision. The case study organisation chose to outsource its complex IT needs because it lacked the IT staff to support an open-source system.

6.1.8 Implications for ECM Implementation

This research addressed ECM implementation "process dimension" issues with KM tool implementation [21]. After reviewing the literature and conceptual framework, the authors identified process and people research gaps. Current research addresses "Process" and "People" gaps. A literature review found that the current research can fill these gaps, particularly for NSOs, and discussed the framework for ECM implementation in the case study organisation. SNA was used to identify early project leaders and plan ECM implementation, according to the research. The research suggested using the EKESNA system to help implement ECM because it was able to collate and compute the organization's network faster than a survey technique over a longer period. This could replace SNA in identifying the key players needed for project success. The tool may also help the case study or other organisations without a corporate taxonomy bootstrap one for information content structuring [9, p. .36] The literature suggests a "more holistic approach to intranet and content management strategy planning, [which] is based on three core elements: information content (referring to content structuring), technical infrastructure and governance". Stakeholder analysis, knowledge structuring, and governance and aftercare were added to the model based on this research.

The study used the framework to implement a potential CMS at the case study organisation, but budget and redirected commitments prevented the CMS's full implementation, limiting the framework's validity. The CMS's feature analysis at the case organisation provides a ready-vetted solution that integrates into the existing IT infrastructure and has the features needed to efficiently manage the organization's information.

7 Conclusion

In this paper, we first review the research context, and then examine the KM issues facing the case study organisation. The paper uses a pragmatic approach to address the niche of frameworks available for the implementation of knowledge management (KM) systems in Not-for-Profit Organisations (NPO's), and further propose a holistic framework which includes social network analysis as a tool to facilitate stakeholder analysis; by identifying and enlisting influential nodes to support the KM system implementation within the organisation. While the totality of the new framework was not realised within this research as a result of shifting priorities for the organisation; the findings make significant contribution to the understanding of implementing KM tools within this type of organisation, but also signposts the value of applied social network analysis for supporting business processes.

Acknowledgements. This work was supported by the Amateur Swimming Association (ASA) by means of funding, and through access for exploration as the case study organisation.

References

1. Ackerman, M.S., Dachtera, J., Pipek, V., Wulf, V.: Sharing knowledge and expertise: the CSCW view of knowledge management. Comput. Support. Coop. Work (CSCW) **22**(4–6), 531–573 (2013). https://doi.org/10.1007/s10606-013-9192-8
2. Nonaka, I., Toyama, R., Konno, N.: SECI, Ba and Leadership: a Unified Model of Dynamic Knowledge Creation (2000). https://doi.org/10.1016/S0024-6301(99)00115-6
3. Handzic, M., Durmic, N.: Knowledge management, intellectual capital and project management: connecting the dots. **13**, 51–61 (2015)
4. Bannon, L., Kuutti, K.: Shifting perspectives on organizational memory: from storage to active remembering. In: Proceedings of the Hawaii International Conference on System Sciences (HICSS-29) (1996)
5. O'Reilly, N.J., Knight, P.: Knowledge management best practices in national sport organizations. **2**, 264–280 (2007)
6. Lettieri, E., Borga, F., Savoldelli, A.: Knowledge management in non-profit organizations. **8**, 16–30 (2004)
7. Stephen, J.: Knowledge management in Oxfam. **17**, 107–110 (2001)
8. Haug, A.: The implementation of enterprise content management systems in SMEs. **25**, 349–372 (2012). https://doi.org/10.1108/17410391211245838

9. White, M.: Selecting a content management system. **32**, 34–39 (2002). https://doi.org/10.1108/03055720210473830
10. Riege, A.: Three-dozen knowledge-sharing barriers managers must consider. **9**, 18–35 (2005)
11. Onojeharho, E., Jackson, T.W., Cooke, L.: Introducing the email knowledge extraction with social network analysis (EKESNA) tool, for discovering an organization's expertise network. In: proceedings of the BCS Quality Specialist Group's Annual International SQM (Software Quality Management) and INSPIRE (International conference for Process Improvement, Research and Education). Loughborough, United Kingdom (2015)
12. Kitchenman, B., Linkman, S., Law, D.: DESME: a methodology for evaluating software engineering methods and tools. **8**, 120–126 (1997)
13. Henczel, S.: The Information Audit: A Practical Guide. K.G. Saur, München (2001)
14. Krueger, R.A.: Focus Groups: A Practical Guide for Applied Research. Sage, London (1994)
15. Robson, C.: Real World Research: A Resource for Users of Social Research Methods in Applied Science. John Wiley and Sons, Chichester (2011)
16. Griman, A., Perez, M., Mendoza, L., Losavio, F.: Feature analysis for architectural evaluation methods. **79**, 871–888 (2006). https://doi.org/10.1016/j.jss.2005.12.015
17. Pouloudi, A., Whitley, E.: Stakeholder identification in inter-organizational systems gaining insights for drug use management systems. **6**, 1–14 (1997)
18. Pan, G.: Information systems project abandonment: a stakeholder analysis. **25**, 173–184 (2005)
19. Olander, S.: Stakeholder impact analysis in construction management. **25**, 277–287 (2007)
20. Bourne, L., Walker, D.H.T.: Visualizing and mapping stakeholder influence. **43**, 649–60 (2005)
21. Alalwan, J.A., Weistroffer, H.R.: Enterprise content management research: a comprehensive review. **25**, 441–461 (2012). https://doi.org/10.1108/17410391211265133
22. Anheier, H.: Nonprofit Organizations: Theory, Management, Policy. Routledge, New York, NY (2005)
23. Wenger, E.: Communities of Practice and Social Learning Systems (2000). https://doi.org/10.1177/135050840072002
24. Hansen, T.M., Nohria, N., Tierney, T.: What's Your Strategy for Managing Knowledge? Harvard Business Review, March-April 1999
25. Renshaw, S., Krishnaswamy, G.: Critiquing the knowledge management strategies of nonprofit organizations in Australia. In: Proceedings of the World Academy of Science, Engineering and Technology (WASET) (2009)
26. Gregory, A., Rathi, D.: Open source tools for managing knowledge in a small non-profit organisation. **7**, 285–297 (2008)
27. Ragsdell, G., Espinet, E.O., Norris, M.: Knowledge management in the voluntary sector: a focus on sharing project know-how and expertise. **12**, 351–361 (2014)
28. Rathi, D., Given, L.M.: Non-profit organizations' use of tools and technologies for knowledge management: a comparative study. **21**, 718–740 (2017). https://doi.org/10.1108/JKM-06-20-2016-0229
29. Warier, S.: Knowledge Management. Vikas Publishing House Pvt Limited, Kolkata (2003)
30. Haynes, D.: Metadata for Information Management and Retrieval. Facet Publishing, London (2004)
31. Ehrlich, K., Shami, N.S.: Searching for expertise. In: Proceedings of the SIGCHI Conference on Human Factors in Computing Systems (CHI '08). ACM, New York, NY, USA (2008)
32. Yang, Y., Xie, G.: Efficient identification of node importance in social networks. **52**, 911–922 (2016). https://doi.org/10.1016/j.ipm.2016.04.001
33. Anklam, P.: Social Network Analysis in the KM Toolkit. Elsevier Butterworth-Heinemann, London (2005)

34. Cross, R.L.C., Parker, A.: The Hidden Power of Social Networks: Understanding How Work Really Gets Done in Organizations. Harvard Business School Press, Boston (2004)
35. Hanneman, R.A., Riddle, M.: Introduction to social network methods. Riverside, CA (2005)
36. Cornford, T., Smithson, S.: Project Research in Information Systems. Palgrave Macmillan, Basingstoke (1996)
37. Evans, J.R., Mathur, A.: The value of online surveys. **15**, 195–219 (2005)
38. Bryman, A., Bell, E.: Business Research Methods. Oxford Press, New York (2007)
39. Baruch, Y.: Response rate in academic studies-a comparative analysis. **52**, 421–438 (1999)
40. Chan, K., Liebowitz, J.: The synergy of social network analysis and knowledge mapping: a case study. **7**, 19–35 (2006)
41. Van Bennekom, F.: Customer Surveying: A Guidebook for Service Managers. Customer Service Press, Boston (2002)
42. McKinlay, A.: The limits of knowledge management. **17**, 76–88 (2002)
43. Dozier, A., Lurie, S., Fogg, T.: Social network analysis as a method of assessing medical-centre culture; three case studies. **84**, 1029–1035 (2009)
44. Prell, C.: Social Network Analysis: History, Theory and Methodology. Sage Publications, London (2012)
45. Long, J.C., Cunningham, F.C., Braithwaite, J.: Bridges, brokers and boundary spanners in collaborative networks: a systematic review. **13**, 1–13 (2013)
46. Matthews, L., Richard, P.: Who is central to a social network? It depends on your centrality measure (2012). http://www.activatenetworks.net/blog/who-is-central-to-a-social-network-it-depends-on-your-centrality-measure
47. Helms, R., Ignacio, R., Brinkkemper, S., Zonneveld, A.: Limitations of network analysis for studying efficiency and effectiveness of knowledge sharing. **8**, 53–68 (2010)
48. Borgatti, S.P., Everett, M.G., Freeman, L.C.: UCINET for Windows: Software for Social Network Analysis. Analytic Technologies, Harvard, MA (2002)

Knowledge Sharing During Natural Disasters: Key Characteristics of Social Media Enablement

Naomi Naidoo and Hanlie Smuts[✉] [iD]

Department of Informatics, University of Pretoria, Pretoria, South Africa
u18337482@tuks.co.za, hanlie.smuts@up.ac.za

Abstract. Modern social media platforms have transformed how individuals engage, exchange information, collaborate and communicate as it promotes communication and knowledge sharing. There is a growing awareness of the need to lower the risk of disasters and build resilient communities that can recover from disasters by sharing information over social media. This paper investigated the role that social media plays in knowledge sharing during a natural disaster and categorised the key characteristics of social media enablement of knowledge sharing during natural disasters. The categorisation process identified 7 key themes namely, accessibility, communication, data collection, decision-making, digital philanthropy, improved knowledge base, knowledge sharing channel, learning and situational awareness. These themes were then allocated across all stage of disaster management and the type of knowledge exchange identified. Identification of various ways of using social media is important, as it helps in providing high level guidance on disaster management to federal, state, territory and local governments and it is first step towards longer term goals of delivering sustained behaviour and enduring partnership within the communities.

Keywords: knowledge sharing · information sharing · social media · natural disasters · disaster management

1 Introduction

Within half a decade, social media has evolved from a recreational pastime to a fully integrated component of every facet of people's lives [1]. More than half the population has some form of social media which translates into over 4.62 billion people [2]. Social media can be utilised and has proved to be beneficial, however, social media can also become detrimental when used excessively and relied on without verifying the source of the information [3].

Knowledge sharing during a natural disaster deals specifically with providing information about how severe a situation is and what is required. When information is shared about the situation, decisions can be made as to how to handle the disaster [4]. Disaster management has benefited from knowledge sharing on social media since it allows people to contribute by reporting incidents relating to disasters [5]. Although this is crucial when handling a natural disaster, decisions made can only be of assistance when the data that is provided is accurate [6].

L. Uden and I-H. Ting (Eds.): KMO 2023, CCIS 1825, pp. 38–48, 2023.
https://doi.org/10.1007/978-3-031-34045-1_4

There have been instances where individuals report inaccurate and untrue information in order to gain popularity and this does occur when reporting information about a natural disaster [7]. This has a negative impact on how decisions are made. Spreading fake news has become a constant when considering social media [8]. Individuals may not grasp the severity of this act, especially when spreading fake news during a natural disaster. This impacts how the disaster management plan is conducted and places the lives of multiple individuals at risk [9]. Furthermore, lack of knowledge sharing results in low visibility of decision making, low capability of disaster support teams, communities and stakeholders, and potential lack of coordination [10].

The purpose of this study is to investigate the role that social media plays in knowledge sharing during a natural disaster. Hence, the research was guided by the following main research question: *"What are the key characteristics of social media enablement of knowledge sharing during a natural disaster?"* The key characteristics were identified through a systematic literature review process and mapped to the dynamic knowledge creation model proposed by Nonaka and Takeuchi [11, 12]. By understanding the role that social media as a knowledge sharing mechanism may play during a natural disaster, government, local authorities, first responders and disaster relief organisations may optimise their engagement during these critical times.

In Sect. 2 we present the background to the study followed by the research approach in Sect. 3. Section 4 details the data analysis and findings, while Sect. 5 concludes the paper.

2 Background

One may argue that during a natural disaster, social media is not a priority and should not be taken into consideration [13]. However, during a natural disaster many people utilise social media for different purposes. These include checking on whether friends or family members are safe, ascertaining who and which areas require assistance [14] and trying to gain an overview of the scope of the natural disaster [15]. Social media provides a platform for individuals to share their first-hand experience of the natural disaster and provide real time updates [16]. However, during a disaster, especially the response phase, the exchange of information is essential [13].

In the next sections we consider information exchange during a disaster, as well as dynamic knowledge sharing.

2.1 Information Exchange During a Disaster

Throughout a natural disaster event, the rate of communication need to increase significantly [1] during a time when technical and communication facilities may be under extreme pressure and unable to operate properly [17]. However, the operation of communication facilities has improved through the enhancement of different telecommunication networks, the pervasive distribution and relatively low barrier to entry of mobile devices, and the proliferation of web technologies such as social media, and messaging services [13, 17]. This improvement of communication facility operations supports a disaster resilient community as it augments the timely and consistent transmission of valuable, relevant information throughout the disaster management life cycle [1, 13].

Typically during a natural disaster the information and knowledge that is required ranges from establishing how serious the situation is, what supplies are needed and the relevant location of the disaster [18]. Disasters are complex in nature, and social media sites often serve a breaking-news role for natural disasters [19]. Furthermore, the news announcement of natural disasters reaches a large mass of people quickly as millions of users regularly visit these sites and share headline news [20].

2.2 Knowledge Management and Natural Disasters

The success of disaster management is based on disaster preparedness, as well as the effectiveness of response and improved recovery [21]. Disaster efficacy relates to effectively anticipating and responding to, and recovering from, disasters [22]. Therefore, disaster preparedness consists of developing capability and knowledge by individuals, citizens, communities, humanitarian organisations and local and national governments [21, 22]. Knowledge management (KM) has been recognised as a vital part of disaster management as KM increases visibility, coordination, humanitarian operations and enhances the capacity to act and make decisions [22]. KM enhances the capacity to act through the creation and transfer of tacit and explicit knowledge among support teams and communities [22, 23]. Tacit knowledge refers to knowledge that is internalised and is often developed through a person's experience, this can be thought of as personal knowledge [24]. Explicit knowledge relates to knowledge that can be documented or transcribed [25].

Nonaka and Takeuchi [12] proposed that the creation and development of knowledge take place through the interaction between explicit and tacit knowledge. They defined four individual, group, organisational and inter-organisational knowledge conversion modes namely (S)ocialisation, (E)xternalisation, (C)ombination and (I)nternalisation referred to as the SECI model [12]. Socialisation (shared experiences) converts tacit knowledge to tacit knowledge, externalisation (experiences articulated as concepts) converts tacit knowledge to explicit knowledge and combination (process of combining different kinds of explicit knowledge into a knowledge system) converts explicit to explicit knowledge. Finally, internalisation (enriching and improving internal knowledge) converts explicit knowledge to tacit knowledge [12]. Therefore, in the context of natural disasters, KM can be implemented at the individual and community levels both at the disaster preparedness phase, as well as during the response phase [10].

3   Research Approach

The main aim of this paper was to investigate the role that social media plays in knowledge sharing during a natural disaster. In order to achieve this outcome, a 2-step process was followed. Cases of social media based knowledge sharing during a natural disaster were studies through a systematic literature review (SLR) process. Specifically, we executed the 3 steps as applied by Berniak-Woźny and Szelągowsk consisting of 3 steps: (1) scoping and planning based on the objectives of the study, (2) identification and selection of publications through rigorous execution of the plan and (3) synthesis, analysis and reporting of the results of the SLR [26]. A literature search was performed in Google Scholar with the keywords ("Knowledge Sharing" or "Information Dissemination") and "Natural Disaster" and "Social Media" and "Disaster Management". The search returned 143 papers that were screened based on title and abstract, after 3 duplicates were removed. Papers that did not specifically dealt with knowledge sharing using social media during a natural disaster, non-English papers, and research theses were excluded resulting in a set of 83 full-text papers that were studied in detail. Papers that did not specifically contain a statement of findings related to the role that social media plays in knowledge sharing during a natural disaster, were excluded resulting in a set of 43 papers that were analysed in detail, extracting the key characteristics of social media enablement of knowledge sharing during natural disasters. The theme identification process was executed by reading the extracted papers in detail and by conducting thematic analysis [27]. Thematic analysis refers to a qualitative data analysis method where a researcher look for patterns in the meaning of the data to find themes [27]. Once the themes were identified (refer Themes in Table 1), axial coding was applied where the categories related to the themes were assembled (refer Categories in Table 1) [28].

Organisations are given the chance to communicate emergency alerts via social media sites, which have been classified as broadcasting instruments. Self-reported location is utilised on social media as a tool to identify areas in need of relief efforts or medical aid, with map development being a frequent technique to illustrate data. Social media analysis showed promise in previous studies as a way to speed up response times and pinpoint people's whereabouts.

Social media creates a platform for many people to share information. These platforms are open to the public and easily accessible to everyone. In addition, social media supported urgent assistance, information about the natural disaster and information about supplies and donations.

Social media sites provides a platform for people to interact and share their expertise and information in a fast and easily accessible way. In instances when a natural disaster occurs the information needs to be provided in real time which is why traditional news sharing methods are not effective. During natural disasters, social media has focused on serving as a news source. With instantaneous information accessible across various devices, this is undoubtedly invaluable. Often, during a natural disaster there will be landlines and TV stations being disconnected due to power outages.

Key themes regarding knowledge sharing over social media also emerged. First responders rely on the information, that social media provides about the whereabouts of people and which areas need urgent assistance. Additionally, in the case of the flooding, there will be roads that are badly affected, which is information that can be shared via social media. This will allow people to plan properly and avoid badly damaged areas. Situational updates where communities and neighbours communicate vital information among themselves about the road closures, power outages, fires, accidents, and other associated issues save people time and allow them to make informed decisions about routes to travel. In terms of financial support, people are able to make requests on social media and this information is sent globally. With online facilities such as crowd-funding and platforms such as GoFundMe, more people are able to assist. Social media is also

Table 1. Number of themes identified

	Knowledge Sharing Categories	Themes	Reference
1	Accessibility	Knowledge availability; Knowledge accessibility; Low barrier to entry	[29, 30]
2	Communication	Information efficiency (as opposed to traditional media); Multiple channels; Disaster response communication tool; Immersive communication tool; Knowledge integration for effective communication; Communication channel; Real time information provisioning	[31–37]
3	Data collection	Information gathering; Knowledge accuracy; Data points for real-world calamities	[29, 38]
4	Decision-making	Information accuracy; Knowledge reliability; Crisis situation management; Crisis situation response; Support recovery rate improvement; First responder resource; Support decision-making; Disaster effect minimisation; Globalise disaster management; Provide actionable information; Disaster relief opportunity visibility; Government interaction	[29, 35, 39–47]
5	Digital philanthropy	Assist with family reunification; Personal experience reflection; Personal experience sharing; Promote individual communication	[44, 48, 49]
6	Improved knowledge base	Foster shared intelligence; Multiple disaster phase relevance; Global information dissemination; Foster knowledge-based development initiatives	[43, 50–52]

(continued)

Table 1. (*continued*)

	Knowledge Sharing Categories	Themes	Reference
7	Knowledge sharing channel	Information sharing triggers; Quick access to situation-sensitive information; Information distribution; Proven usefulness; Engagement mechanism; Enable fast-paced warning sharing (spreading)	[16, 50, 53–56]
8	Learning	Information exchange; Improve disaster resilience; Knowledge exchange value; Promote socialisation; Re-usability i.t.o. disaster management framework	[30, 43, 48, 49, 57]
9	Situational awareness	Foster situational awareness; Sharing valuable knowledge; Improve situational awareness	[50, 54, 56]

used to ask for assistance and volunteers. Social media facilitates the correspondence between people and thus creates greater awareness and will receive more help. Communication with family members is often used during a natural disaster for status updates and response preparation. Social media is an essential platform for sharing because it links individuals to each other and is relatively simple to use.

Social media platforms enable people to actively crowdsource localised information from community organisations and the general public, which they actively monitor and then send to the emergency responders on the ground together with geospatial data. Localised, real-time emergency warning information is immediately sent to the public via SMS alerts, messages to their social networks, and other conventional media including radio, TV, and the internet. Through a variety of channels, including webpages, mobile-friendly websites, smartphone apps, video-sharing websites, and social networking sites, they are directly accessing links to online content. They are actively boosting the warnings and forwarding messages from emergency organisations to their social networks.

Information about where to find supplies must be communicated. This is important since there will be a limited amount of products available in stores. When a store gets stock this is communicated over social media. In instances where people have medical conditions and need medication, a request can be made and assistance can be provided.

There are a few key takeaways summarised from Table 1:

- Delivers useful information to persons in a disaster area before and after the event
- Create driver awareness for those who might not be aware of the condition of the roads
- Being able to communicate with loved ones and family members

- Provide important information to first responders and rescuers about where people are located
- Information dissemination which emergency responders can provide to locals and vice versa

In order to practically apply the key characteristics, we mapped the key characteristics identified to the SECI model knowledge conversion phases and indicated the particular step of disaster management it relates to in the next section.

4 Discussion

The aim of this study was to consider the role that social media plays in knowledge sharing during a natural disaster. In order to apply the knowledge sharing categorisation, we mapped the themes identified in Table 1 to knowledge exchange based on the SECI model, as well as its application to the particular phase of disaster management. The mapping is shown in Table 2.

Table 2. Application characteristics of social media in knowledge sharing during a natural disaster

	Disaster management phases [22]	Knowledge sharing categorisation (Refer Table 1)	Knowledge exchange based on SECI [12]	Knowledge exchange type [12]
1	Preparation	Accessibility	Combination	Explicit to explicit
		Communication	Socialisation	Tacit to tacit
		Data collection	Internalisation	Explicit to tacit
		Improved knowledge base	Combination	Explicit to explicit
		Knowledge sharing channel	Externalisation	Tacit to explicit
2	Immediate response	Improved knowledge base	Combination	Explicit to explicit
		Decision-making	Combination	Explicit to explicit
		Situational awareness	Internalisation	Explicit to tacit
		Knowledge sharing channel	Externalisation	Tacit to explicit
3	Reconstruction	Improved knowledge base	Combination	Explicit to explicit
		Digital philanthropy	Socialisation	Tacit to tacit
		Knowledge sharing channel	Externalisation	Tacit to explicit
		Learning	Internalisation	Explicit to tacit

The proposed application characteristics (Table 2) apply to different stages of the disaster management process and the same characteristic may be relevant to more than one disaster management phase. However, the knowledge exchange based on the particular combination of disaster management stage and characteristics, may change.

Each of the knowledge sharing categories in Table 2 were evaluated against the definition of a knowledge exchange process (refer description in Sect. 2.2). *Knowledge sharing channel* and *improved knowledge base* are knowledge sharing categories that apply to all 3 of the disaster management stages as in each stage, citizens and responders utilise social media as knowledge sharing channel and in that way, improve the knowledge base. The context of the disaster management stage is different though.

As accessibility, improved knowledge base and decision-making relate to knowledge availability and accessibility in explicit forms, we associated it with explicit codified knowledge sources and therefore combination. Communication and digital philanthropy refer to knowledge that is shared through practice, guidance and observation, and we therefore associated it with socialisation. Data collection, situational awareness and learning are associated with internalisation as explicit knowledge sources are used and learned, the knowledge is internalised, and the knowledge then modifies citizens' and responders' existing tacit knowledge. Knowledge sharing channel includes quick access to situation-sensitive information, information distribution and proven usefulness, it is associated with externalisation, tacit to explicit, as tacit knowledge is codified into documents, manuals, etc. so that it can be shared more easily.

During the preparation phase of disaster management [22], the role that social media plays in knowledge sharing during a natural disaster, focuses on communication and using social media as a channel of communication. This knowledge sharing is combined and socialised (data collection, learning), enabling quick decision-making and enriching the body of knowledge with new knowledge and learning. During the immediate response phase [22], decisions are executed based on the knowledge and situational awareness. Learning is applied and decision-making now executed in order to take decisive action. For the reconstruction phase, knowledge sharing relates to internalising lessons learned and thus improving the knowledge base. Furthermore, digital philanthropy support further confirmation of status of families and communities and ensure that status is socialised as post-disaster activity commences.

5 Conclusion

The study set out to investigate the role that social media plays in knowledge sharing during a natural disaster. Forty-three papers were purposefully extracted and analysed and knowledge sharing characteristics during a natural disaster were categorised into 7 key themes namely, accessibility, communication, data collection, decision-making, digital philanthropy, improved knowledge base, knowledge sharing channel, learning and situational awareness. These categories were mapped across all stages of disaster management and the type of knowledge exchange identified. Identification of various ways of using social media for knowledge sharing during a natural disaster promotes knowledge sharing and communication in support of communities. Furthermore, first responders and rescue teams draw from the social media reports to fast track decision-making and improve disaster response.

In terms of future research, we acknowledge that different disaster management stakeholders would need different information sets as a natural disaster and follow-up actions unfold. It is likely that the different stakeholders would benefit from different kinds of knowledge. A deeper analysis of the knowledge sharing categories and its importance to stakeholders during different stages of a natural disaster may be investigated. In addition, further research may be conducted to compare knowledge sharing categories for man-made disasters.

References

1. Wang, B., Zhuang, J.: Crisis information distribution on Twitter: a content analysis of tweets during Hurricane Sandy. Nat. Hazards **89**(1), 161–181 (2017). https://doi.org/10.1007/s11069-017-2960-x
2. Gogulamudi, A., Prabhu, S.: Consumer decisions under the influence of social media & behavioral targeting. In: 2022 International Conference on Decision Aid Sciences and Applications (DASA). IEEE (2022)
3. Sharma, B., Lee, S.S., Johnson, B.K.: The dark at the end of the tunnel: doomscrolling on social media newsfeeds. Technol. Mind Behav. **3**(1) (2022)
4. Hariharan, A., Park, J.Y.: A flagged or spam? Social media driven public interactions for natural disaster response and recovery. In: Proceedings of the 8th ACM International Conference on Systems for Energy-Efficient Buildings, Cities, and Transportation (2021)
5. Nyame, H.B.: The role of radio in combatting misinformation about Covid-19: an assessment of potters FM in The Bono Region. Ghana Institute of Journalism (2021)
6. Phengsuwan, J., et al.: Use of social media data in disaster management: a survey. Future Internet **13**(2), 46 (2021)
7. Rajdev, M., Lee, K.: Fake and spam messages: detecting misinformation during natural disasters on social media. In: 2015 IEEE/WIC/ACM International Conference on Web Intelligence and Intelligent Agent Technology (WI-IAT). IEEE (2015)
8. Puraivan, E., et al.: Fake news detection on Twitter using a data mining framework based on explainable machine learning techniques (2021)
9. Bhavaraju, S.K.T., Beyney, C., Nicholson, C.: Quantitative analysis of social media sensitivity to natural disasters. Int. J. Disast. Risk Reduct. **39**, 101251 (2019)
10. Kusumastuti, R.D., et al.: Indicators of community preparedness for fast-onset disasters: a systematic literature review and case study. Nat. Hazards **110**(1), 787–821 (2021)
11. Nonaka, I., Toyama, R., Konno, N.: SECI, Ba and leadership: a unified model of dynamic knowledge creation. Long Range Plan. **33**, 5–34 (2000)
12. Nonaka, I., Takeuchi, H.: The Knowledge Creating, vol. 304. New York (1995)
13. Abedin, B., Babar, A., Abbasi, A.: Characterization of the use of social media in natural disasters: a systematic review. In: 2014 IEEE Fourth International Conference on Big Data and Cloud Computing. IEEE (2014)
14. Chair, S., Charrad, M., Saoud, N.B.B.: Towards a social media-based framework for disaster communication. Procedia Comput. Sci. **164**, 271–278 (2019)
15. Muniz-Rodriguez, K., et al.: Social media use in emergency response to natural disasters: a systematic review with a public health perspective. Disaster Med. Public Health Prep. **14**(1), 139–149 (2020)
16. Matar, S., et al.: Social media platforms and its applications in natural disaster and crisis events–the case of Bosnia & Herzegovina. J. Inf. Knowl. Manag. **6**(5), 50–56 (2016)
17. Eriksson, M.: Lessons for crisis communication on social media: a systematic review of what research tells the practice. Int. J. Strateg. Commun. **12**(5), 526–551 (2018)

18. Sobel, R.S., Leeson, P.T.: The use of knowledge in natural disaster relief management. In: The Political Economy of Hurricane Katrina and Community Rebound. Edward Elgar Publishing (2010)
19. Dong, R., et al.: Information diffusion on social media during natural disasters. IEEE Trans. Computat. Soc. Syst. 5(1), 265–276 (2018)
20. Feng, Y., Huang, X., Sester, M.: Extraction and analysis of natural disaster-related VGI from social media: review, opportunities and challenges. Int. J. Geogr. Inf. Sci. 36(7), 1275–1316 (2022)
21. Sardjono, W., Perdana, W.G.: Improve understanding and dissemination of disaster management and climate change by using knowledge management systems. In: IOP Conference Series: Earth and Environmental Science. IOP Publishing (2020)
22. Kusumastuti, R.D., et al.: Knowledge management and natural disaster preparedness: a systematic literature review and a case study of East Lombok, Indonesia. Int. J. Disaster Risk Reduct. 58, 102223 (2021)
23. Seneviratne, K., Baldry, D., Pathirage, C.: Disaster knowledge factors in managing disasters successfully. Int. J. Strateg. Prop. Manag. 14(4), 376–390 (2010)
24. Ksiazkiewicz, A.: Implicit political knowledge. PS Polit. Sci. Polit. 46(3), 553–555 (2013)
25. Rumanti, A.A., Samadhi, T.A., Wiratmadja, I.I.: Impact of tacit and explicit knowledge on knowledge sharing at indonesian small and medium enterprise. In: 2016 IEEE International Conference on Industrial Engineering and Engineering Management (IEEM). IEEE (2016)
26. Berniak-Woźny, J., Szelągowski, M.: Towards the assessment of business process knowledge intensity–a systematic literature review. Bus. Process. Manag. J. 28(1), 40–61 (2022)
27. Leedy, P.D., Ormrod, J.E.: Practical Research, vol. 108. Pearson, Upper Saddle River (2016)
28. Bhattacharya, K.: Fundamentals of Qualitative Research: A Practical Guide. Taylor & Francis (2017)
29. Pathirage, C., et al.: Managing disaster knowledge: identification of knowledge factors and challenges. Int. J. Disaster Resilience Built Environ. 3(3), 237–252 (2012)
30. Yates, D., Paquette, S.: Emergency knowledge management and social media technologies: a case study of the 2010 Haitian earthquake. Int. J. Inf. Manage. 31(1), 6–13 (2011)
31. Osatuyi, B.: Information sharing on social media sites. Comput. Hum. Behav. 29(6), 2622–2631 (2013)
32. Reuter, C., et al.: Social media in emergencies: a representative study on citizens' perception in Germany. Proc. ACM Hum.-Comput. Interact. 1(CSCW), 1–19 (2017)
33. Ishak, S., et al.: Examining the fit of social media as a tool to share disaster-related knowledge: from the perspective of task-technology fit theory, pp. 867–872 (2014)
34. Brambilla, M., et al.: Spatial analysis of social media response to live events: the case of the milano fashion week. In: Proceedings of the 26th International Conference on World Wide Web Companion (2017)
35. Lateef Saeed, N.A., Zakaria, N.H., Ahmad, M.N.: The use of social media in knowledge integration for improving disaster emergency management task performance: review of flood disasters. Indian J. Sci. Technol. 9(34), 1–12 (2016)
36. Jayasekara, P.K.: Role of Facebook as a disaster communication media. Int. J. Emerg. Serv. 8(2), 191–204 (2019)
37. Mohanty, S.D., et al.: A multi-modal approach towards mining social media data during natural disasters-a case study of Hurricane Irma. Int. J. Disaster Risk Reduct. 54, 102032 (2021)
38. Kompatsiaris, I.: Multimodal social media mining. In: Proceedings of the 1st International on Multimodal Sentiment Analysis in Real-life Media Challenge and Workshop (2020)
39. Popoola, A., et al.: Information verification during natural disasters. In: Proceedings of the 22nd International Conference on World Wide Web (2013)

40. Imran, M., et al.: Processing social media messages in mass emergency: survey summary. In: Companion Proceedings of the the the Web Conference 2018 (2018)
41. Lee, K.S.: Explicit disaster response features in social media: safety check and community help usage on Facebook during Typhoon Mangkhut. In: Proceedings of the 21st International Conference on Human-Computer Interaction with Mobile Devices and Services (2019)
42. Rodzi, M., et al.: Flood sensor development with ontology-based knowledge integration using design science research methodology (2017)
43. Oktari, R.S., Munadi, K., Ridha, M.: Effectiveness of dissemination and communication element of tsunami early warning system in Aceh. Procedia Econ. Financ. **18**, 136–142 (2014)
44. Chen, T.Y.: Multi-temporal deep learning-based social media analysis for disaster relief. In: Proceedings of the 20th Annual International Conference on Mobile Systems, Applications and Services (2022)
45. Nagar, S., Seth, A., Joshi, A.: Characterization of social media response to natural disasters. In: Proceedings of the 21st International Conference on World Wide Web (2012)
46. Nazer, T.H., et al. Finding requests in social media for disaster relief. In: 2016 IEEE/ACM International Conference on Advances in Social Networks Analysis and Mining (ASONAM). IEEE (2016)
47. Al-Saggaf, Y., Simmons, P.: Social media in Saudi Arabia: exploring its use during two natural disasters. Technol. Forecast. Soc. Chang. **95**, 3–15 (2015)
48. Nur, W., et al.: Knowledge sharing and lesson learned from flood disaster: a case in Kelantan. J. Inf. Syst. Res. Innov. **9**(2), 1–10 (2015)
49. Dwivedi, Y.K., et al.: Examining the effects of enterprise social media on operational and social performance during environmental disruption. Technol. Forecast. Soc. Chang. **175**, 121364 (2022)
50. Kankanamge, N., et al.: Determining disaster severity through social media analysis: testing the methodology with South East Queensland Flood tweets. Int. J. Disaster Risk Reduct. **42**, 101360 (2020)
51. Stieglitz, S., et al.: The Adoption of social media analytics for crisis management–challenges and opportunities (2018)
52. Yigitcanlar, T., et al.: Can building "artificially intelligent cities" safeguard humanity from natural disasters, pandemics, and other catastrophes? An urban scholar's perspective. Sensors **20**(10), 2988 (2020)
53. Haq, A.M.: Knowledge sharing in social media as moderating variable between social capital online and response to humanitarian crises (2021)
54. Nguyen, D.T., et al.: Damage assessment from social media imagery data during disasters. In: Proceedings of the 2017 IEEE/ACM International Conference on Advances in Social Networks Analysis and Mining (2017)
55. Haq, E.-U., et al.: Weaponising social media for information divide and warfare. In: Proceedings of the 33rd ACM Conference on Hypertext and Social Media (2022)
56. King, L.J.: Social media use during natural disasters: an analysis of social media usage during Hurricanes Harvey and Irma (2018)
57. Ahmed, Y.A., et al.: Social media for knowledge-sharing: a systematic literature review. Telemat. Inform. **37**, 72–112 (2019)

Knowledge in Business and Organisation

Telework Experience and Frequency, and Knowledge Management During COVID-19 in Japan

Remy Magnier-Watanabe[✉]

Graduate School of Business Sciences, University of Tsukuba, Tokyo, Japan
magnier-watanabe.gt@u.tsukuba.ac.jp

Abstract. In Japan, successive states of emergency due to COVID-19 have sent office workers into mandatory telework, leading to radical changes in terms of how they manage knowledge on the job. This paper investigates how mandatory telework has affected knowledge management based on telework frequency. It makes use of two large groups of full-time Japanese employees, one with prior telework experience and the other one without.

Results highlight differences based on prior telework experience, whereby experienced teleworkers displayed higher knowledge management than telework novices. Moreover, for those with prior telework experience, an increase in telework frequency from 1 to 4 days a week meant an increase in knowledge management, but full telework resulted in lower knowledge management. This inverse U-shaped relationship suggests that full telework is detrimental to knowledge management for experienced teleworkers. In other words, higher telework frequency helps experienced teleworkers manage knowledge, as long as they go to the office once a week.

These findings suggest first that training and practice of using remote work can significantly increase knowledge management efficiency when forced to telework, and second that working one day a week in the office contributes to higher knowledge management among experienced coworkers, owing to the dual explicit and tacit nature of knowledge.

Keywords: Telework · Experience · Frequency · Knowledge management · Japan

1 Introduction

As of November 2022, COVID-19 has developed into a significant epidemic with 634 million confirmed cases and excess mortality of at least 6.6 million deaths (WHO, 2022). It has led to extraordinary precautionary measures, such as the mandatory confinement of millions of employees. Similarly, Tokyo and its metropolitan area declared successive states of emergency, forcing many office workers to work from home. The central government of Japan has limited enforcement power but it can count on private businesses to comply with the state of emergency and the stay-at-home directive by instructing their

L. Uden and I-H. Ting (Eds.): KMO 2023, CCIS 1825, pp. 51–63, 2023.
https://doi.org/10.1007/978-3-031-34045-1_5

staff to transition to home-based telework. In April 2020, a significant portion of employees in Japan made the switch to 100% telework, with the service sector accounting for the largest share. Just a few weeks prior, telework was rarely permitted by company management and frequently restricted to one or two days per week, making such a shift unthinkable.

We are only at the beginning of COVID-19 and no empirical research to date has been conducted on the effect of telework experience and frequency on how employees managed knowledge when they were thrust into mandatory telework in Japan. But given the ever-growing role of knowledge work in today's digital economy (Vuori et al., 2019), these findings will be crucial for companies to regain their lost competitiveness and adjust to the "new normal" of social distancing and widespread telework.

A survey in Japan highlighted both positive and negative effects from telework specifically related to subjective well-being, knowledge management, and job performance (Japan Times, 2020). Positive consequences were reported to be reduced stress from the absence of commuting (68%), being able to work and care for family members at the same time (48%), and less time spent on unproductive overtime (42%). Negative effects included work that has to be done at the office (72%), reduced closeness with work colleagues (39%), and difficulties communicating with bosses and coworkers (36%). These undesirable consequences are directly related to the management of knowledge, which depends on location-specific knowledge and to the creation, sharing, and application of knowledge.

COVID-19 has in effect changed how people interact, communicate and work, because of the fear of infection, social distancing and telework. This drastic change in working conditions – working from home organized primarily for private activities, rather than from an office designed to achieve organizational goals – is inevitably having an effect of how employees cope with knowledge and eventually their job performance. In particular, prior telework experience and the frequency of telework need to be examined (Allen et al., 2015; Taskin and Bridoux, 2010) as they can affect knowledge management (KM), or the selective handling of knowledge to fulfill one's duties and help the firm achieve its goals (Jennex, 2009). It is therefore crucial to investigate how knowledge can still be created, shared, and applied under these new conditions, and propose countermeasures. This paper therefore investigates how mandatory telework has affected the amount of KM activities based on prior telework experience and telework frequency. The results will help Japanese and foreign practitioners update their organization's work practices in order to raise knowledge and worker productivity adapting to the new demands of COVID-19 and eventually recover faster from the economic recession brought about by COVID-19.

2   Literature Review

2.1   Telework from Home

Regular salaried employment performed at the employee's home is referred to as telework. It is also known as home-based teleworking or working from home. Leaving aside less frequent instances, it can range from 1 day to 5 days a week (Aguilera et al.,

2016). Numerous studies have been conducted on the factors influencing the acceptance of home-based telework, which are mainly concerned with the nature of work, its perceived advantages and disadvantages, and fit with the company or country cultures (Peters and Batenburg, 2015; Aguilera et al., 2016). Telework from home has been found to be better suited for highly skilled and independent workers who see it as beneficial to their professional and personal lives (De Graaff and Rietveld, 2007; Pérez et al., 2003).

Key success factors of telework are many and include "time-planning skills, possibility to work during the most productive time, reduced time for communication with co-workers, possibility to work from home in case of sickness, supervisor's trust; supervisor's support, possibility to save on travel expenses, possibility to take care of family members, suitability of the working place at home and possibility to access the organization's documents from home" (Nakrošienė et al., 2019, p. 97).

In Japan, the Ministry of Health, Labor, and Welfare has shared public recommendations for telework since 2004 and updated them in 2008 to highlight the benefits and drawbacks of such work arrangement (MHLW, 2008). Some benefits of telework for businesses include: business operations can continue in the event of a natural disaster, in accordance with a Business Continuity Plan; attracting and keeping talent by enabling flexible working styles; promoting work-life balance and corporate social responsibility; and lowering costs for office space and commuting allowances (For regular employees, the entire cost of the commute between home and work is covered by the employer in Japan) (MHLW, 2008).

Additionally, there are benefits for employees, such as being able to work while taking care of children or elderly parents, having more free time because they don't have to commute, expanding employment opportunities for the elderly and disabled who have trouble traveling, and being able to work in a more peaceful environment that promotes concentration and productivity. According to employee data, the guidelines also list the drawbacks of telework, including separating work and personal time, working long hours, evaluating one's work, accessing documents located at the office, managing one's health, communicating with superiors, improving one's skills, and earning less money (MHLW, 2008).

Telework is called mandatory when the employee's employer required it in order to abide by the COVID-19 emergency declaration orders issued by the prefectures where their offices are located. This environment allowed for home-based telework to be deployed without consideration for suitability as long as tasks could be completed remotely using a computer and a phone. The distinction between voluntary and mandatory telework has been made in the past by examining whether telework was based on the employee's personal preference or rather on the employee feeling obliged to accept (De Cuyper and De Witte, 2008; Lapierre et al., 2016). Notably, whether telework is voluntary bears consequences on teleworkers' level of training and preparedness for telework.

2.2 Knowledge Management

KM is "the process for acquiring, storing, diffusing and applying both tacit and explicit knowledge inside and outside the organization's boundaries with the purpose of achieving corporate objectives in the most efficient manner" (Magnier-Watanabe and Senoo,

2008, p. 22). This description highlights the dual nature of knowledge (Polanyi, 1966), and it follows that telework – which induces a loss in face-to-face interactions – could strain KM because of a shortfall in tacit knowledge. KM matters because it has previously been found to be an important source of individual and organizational performance, especially in knowledge-intensive industries and firms (Abubakar et al., 2019).

A dominant conceptualization of KM is the knowledge value chain, which separates the knowledge activities of the firm into a series of knowledge-related tasks during which employees participate in building an organization's competitive advantage (Wong, 2004). Several models have been developed, and although they may vary slightly in terms of stages and terminology (Chen and Chen, 2006), they generally consist of the three major categories of knowledge acquisition or creation (or capture), sharing or storage (or transfer), and application or usage (Heisig, 2009).

Knowledge acquisition, made up of knowledge identification and creation (Heisig, 2009), is the process of gaining new knowledge from either inside or outside the organization and in either tacit or explicit form (Massa and Testa, 2009). Identification presumes that knowledge already exists and is then accepted as such, while creation assumes the formation of previously non-existent knowledge into new knowledge for the firm.

Knowledge sharing consists of formal and informal movements of knowledge between organizational agents (Kianto et al., 2018) and it involves both giving and receiving knowledge. Knowledge sharing is a function of trust, motivation, job satisfaction, norms and values of an organization and leadership support (Hooff and De Ridder, 2004). Tacit knowledge, which is difficult to articulate, is inherently more difficult to share, while explicit knowledge, which is easy to codify by nature, is easier to share (Polanyi, 1966).

Last, knowledge application is the process of incorporating acquired or created knowledge into the firm's products, services and or practices to derive additional value from it (Massa and Testa, 2009). It is intricately linked to learning, which can be either exploitative or explorative (March, 1991). The former takes place along an existing trajectory that has already been followed, while the latter occurs along an entirely different trajectory that is new to the firm (Gupta et al., 2006).

2.3 Development of Hypotheses

2.3.1 Prior Telework Experience and KM

Prior telework experience is predicated on whether employees had previous training and practice of remote work before COVID-19. Because telework almost always requires technology to remotely communicate with coworkers or business partners, access documents, and more generally create, share, and apply knowledge, it presupposes high ICT literacy and mastery (Nakrošienė et al., 2019). Furthermore, the advent of the technology-mediated virtual office has made telework location-independent (Messenger and Gschwind, 2016). Consequently, employees skilled in new technologies have been found to be more willing to telework and conversely, those lacking such mastery to be reluctant to work away from the office (Dias et al., 2022).

Lee and Choi (2003) had shown early the importance of collaboration, trust, learning, skills, and information technology support, among others, for knowledge creation and other knowledge-related processes. Learning, skills and IT support can be related to prior experience with telework, which can benefit from the study and practice of specific competences. It follows that prior experience with telework will have a positive effect on KM when working remotely. Therefore, we formulate the following hypotheses:

H1: For those with prior telework experience, KM activity will be higher during COVID-19-related mandatory telework, compared to those without prior telework experience.

2.3.2   Telework Frequency and KM Activity

Telework frequency, or intensity, depends on the amount of time spent working remotely (Gajendran and Harrison, 2007; Pérez et al., 2003). Occasional or ad-hoc telework happens when someone works from home on an as-needed basis, in the event of an illness or of impromptu child care. Part-time or partial telework takes place when an employee works some of the time from home, the workplace or a client location in an intentional and prearranged manner. And full telework occurs when a worker continuously works from home or another location besides the office, only rarely visiting the company workplace (Nakrošienė et al., 2019).

Taskin and Bridoux (2010) have stressed the relationship between telework frequency and KM. They argued that the loss of face-to-face communication, such as that enabled through colocation, deprives employees of important channels such as nonverbal and paralinguistic (Thatcher and Zhu, 2006) and therefore dilutes the quality and depth of communication. This loss in media richness, previously highlighted by research on telework using media richness theory, can lead to a decline in knowledge-related activities (Magnier-Watanabe, 2022). Another deleterious consequence of telework frequency is the disconnect between teleworkers and non-teleworkers, who have limited opportunities to establish and maintain trust because of a lack of face-to-face interactions (Taskin and Bridoux, 2010). To a certain extent, higher telework frequency inhibits the transfer of knowledge.

Nakrošienė et al. (2019) have confirmed a link between telework and higher productivity, brought about by less time interacting with colleagues, a suitable working environment at home, and the possibility to care for family members when teleworking. In the context of Japanese workers, Kazekami (2020) has established that telework increased life satisfaction, which in turn improved productivity at work. Similarly, telecommuters often report higher job productivity stemming from fewer interruptions at home and being able to work while at their most productive during the day (Hartman et al., 1992).

However, at the same time, high telework frequency had also been shown to have a negative impact on organizational knowledge creation and transfer (Bridoux and Taskin, 2005). This is because these two kinds of knowledge are directly related to interpersonal relationships and organizational commitment (Szulanski, 1996; Nahapiet and Ghoshal, (1998). High telework frequency is thought to have a harmful effect on social inclusion and relationships with colleagues and supervisors, resulting in inferior creation and transfer of knowledge identification with the firm and consequently on knowledge creation and transfer. Therefore, past research seems to indicate that telework is beneficial to KM up to a certain frequency.

Based on the previous review of the literature, we argue that, for experienced teleworkers, telework frequency will be related to higher KM activity, as long as they can meet their colleagues face-to-face once a week to acquire, share, and apply tacit knowledge otherwise impossible to do remotely. Mandatory telework has a lesser influence on KM habits, since those had already been developed and practiced in that setting. We predict that, for those with prior telework experience, there is an inverse U-shaped relationship between telework frequency and KM activity, whereby KM activity increases with telework frequency until they reach a peak at 4 days a week and drop when telework is 5 days a week. Conversely, mandatory telework was a drastic change for those without prior experience in telework, regardless of frequency. Those inexperienced employees had to relearn how to work isolated for several days a week, leading to inefficiencies and lower KM activity in general and at any telework frequency. Therefore, we put forth the following hypotheses:

H2a: For those with prior telework experience, there is a U-shaped relationship between telework frequency and KM activity peaking when telework is 4 days a week.
H2b: For those without prior telework experience, there is no relationship between telework frequency and KM activity.

3 Methodology

3.1 Survey and Sample

The data was gathered in December 2021 using an Internet survey company. The sample was made up of full-time Japanese employees in the Tokyo area, some with prior telework experience, and some without, and all had been engaged in telework to some degree over the period of interest between July 12 and September 28, 2021. In this sample of 945 respondents, 575 are without and 370 with prior telework experience. There is a majority of male employees (73%), most with a university degree (72%), having subordinates (62%), working as general employees (55%) in very large companies with more than 500 employees (49%) for more than 10 years (53%), having teleworked from home during the period of study 3 days a week (24%), 3 days a week (20%), or 5 days a week (29%) (Table 1).

3.2 Measures

KM activity related to acquisition, sharing, and application were assessed using three items each from Kianto et al. (2018) on a 7-point scale; those asked for the respondents' level of agreement with the following: Acquisition: we are stimulated to acquire or develop new knowledge; we are focused on learning and exploring new ways of working; we have systems to capture new ideas and experiences; sharing: the management motivates us to share our knowledge; we spend time to share ideas and experiences with each other; we have the right systems to support knowledge sharing; application: we are encouraged to make use of the available knowledge; we apply knowledge to improve in our job; we have systems that make it easier to make use of available knowledge. And telework frequency took the following values: 3: 1 day a week; 4: 2 days a week; 5: 3 days a week; 6: 4 days a week; 7: 5 days a week. Table 2 shows telework frequencies for both groups of respondents.

Table 1. Sample demographics

Indicator	N	%	Indicator	N	%
Gender			Function		
Men	686	72.6	General employee	522	55.2
Women	259	27.4	Section chief	194	20.5
Age			Manager	105	11.1
20-24	36	3.8	Senior manager	33	3.5
25-29	178	18.8	Top management	43	4.6
30-34	69	7.3	CEO	16	1.7
35-39	87	9.2	Other	32	3.4
40-44	93	9.8	Company size		
45-49	138	14.6	<10	29	3.1
50-54	98	10.4	10-49	91	9.6
55-59	103	10.9	50-249	223	23.6
60-64	143	15.1	250-499	144	15.2
Education			500+	458	48.5
High school	64	6.8	Tenure		
Professional school	50	5.3	2-5yrs	265	28.0
Associate degree	28	3.0	5-10yrs	175	18.5
University degree	684	72.4	10yrs+	505	53.4
Master degree	93	9.8	Prior telework exp.		
PhD degree	24	2.5	None	575	60.8
Other	2	.2	1-3 times per month	86	9.1
Occupation			1 day a week	66	7.0
Top management	223	23.6	2 days a week	79	8.4
Profess. / tech. work.	230	24.3	3 days a week	59	6.2
Office worker	332	35.1	4 days a week	54	5.7
Sales staff	83	8.8	5 days a week	26	2.8
Service staff	31	3.3	Telework frequency		
Other	46	4.9	None	0	0
Subordinates			1-3 times per month	0	0
0	356	37.7	1 day a week	74	7.8
1-5	262	27.7	2 days a week	179	18.9
6-10	124	13.1	3 days a week	230	24.3
11-30	102	10.8	4 days a week	188	19.9
31+	101	10.7	5 days a week	274	29.0

For the KM constructs, Cronbach's alpha was 0.893, 0.891, and 0.873, respectively, thus denoting internal consistency. A factor analysis of those items confirmed three factors explaining 6% for acquisition, 72% for sharing, and 5% for application, for a combined total of 83%, thus confirming convergent validity. Constructs related to KM show some collinearity (above 0.8) but were kept as is to evaluate each of them separately (Table 3).

Table 2. Telework frequencies among the two groups

Telework frequency	Without prior telework experience		With prior telework experience	
	N	%	N	%
1 day a week	55	9.6	19	5.1
2 days a week	116	20.2	63	17.0
3 days a week	150	26.1	80	21.6
4 days a week	92	16.0	96	25.9
5 days a week	162	28.2	112	30.3
Total	575	100.0	370	100.0

Table 3. Means, standard deviation and correlations of study variables

	Mean	SD	1	2	3	4	5	6	7	8	9	10
1. Gender	1.274	0.446	1									
2. Age range	6.330	2.559	-.293**	1								
3. Education	3.817	1.019	0.001	-0.055	1							
4. Tenure	4.254	0.867	-.229**	.614**	-0.022	1						
5. Subordinates	2.291	1.349	-0.045	0.014	.087**	.137**	1					
6. Company size	3.964	1.176	-.106**	.152**	.129**	.223**	.148**	1				
7. Telework frequency	5.433	1.295	0.013	0.022	0.052	-0.039	-.110**	0.041	1			
8. ACQ	4.835	1.326	.074*	-.275**	.072*	-.221**	.165**	-0.006	0.043	1		
9. SHARE	4.780	1.370	0.060	-.251**	0.061	-.194**	.190**	0.010	0.056	.829**	1	
10. APPLY	5.007	1.243	.082*	-.241**	.075*	-.176**	.152**	0.034	.078*	.806**	.861**	1

Gender: 1=male; 2=female
Age range: 2=20-24; 3=25-29; 4=30-34; 5=35-39; 7=40-44; 7=45-49; 8=50-54; 9=55-59; 10=60-64
Education: 1=High school; 2=Prof. school; 3=Associate degree; 4=University; 5=Master degree; 6=PhD; 7=Other
Tenure: 3=2-5yrs; 4=5-10yrs; 5=10yrs+
Subordinates: 1=0; 2=1-5; 3=6-10; 4=11-30; 5=31+
Company size: 1=<10; 2=10-49; 3=50-249; 4=250-499; 5=500+
Telework freq.: 3=1 day a week; 4=2 days a week; 5=3 days a week; 6=4 days a week; 7=5 days a week
KM: 7-point Likert scale
*p<0.05; **p<0.001

4 Results

4.1 Differences in KM Activity Based on Prior Telework Experience

In order to test H1, a t-test was conducted between those with and without prior telework experience. All differences in KM activity between the two groups are highly significant ($p < 0.001$). Those with prior telework experience display higher levels of KM activity compared to those without prior experience, providing support for H1 (Fig. 1) (knowledge acquisition: M = 4.611 SD = 1.344 vs. M = 5.182 SD = 1.220, t(943) = –6.606, p = 0.000; knowledge sharing: M = 4.24 SD = 1.396 vs. M = 5.177 SD = 1.228, t(943) = –7.346, p = 0.000; knowledge application: M = 4.812 SD = 1.272 vs. M = 5.311 SD = 1.134, t(943) = –6.140, p = 0.000). Differences notwithstanding, all KM activity modes were above 4.5, mildly indicating positive evaluations for all, and more so for those with prior telework experience with KM activity above 5, on a 7-point scale.

4.2 Relationship Between Telework Frequency and KM Activity

In order to test H2, analyses of variance (ANOVA) were conducted to examine differences based on telework frequency per week. Figure 2 plots KM activity based on telework frequency per week. For respondents with prior telework experience (n = 370), there are statistically significant differences based on telework frequency per week for all three KM activity modes, with the highest levels of KM activity when teleworking 4 days a week, thus providing support for H2a: knowledge acquisition (F(4,365) = 10.582, p =

0.000); knowledge sharing ($F(4, 365) = 8.396$, $p = 0.000$); knowledge application ($F(4, 365) = 7.879$, $p = 0.000$). In addition, post-hoc comparisons using Tukey HSD tests show that statistically significant differences exist based on telework frequency, albeit not between every frequency (not shown); however, the trends are clear, with a peak at 4 days a week, and a drop at 5 days a week.

Furthermore, for respondents without prior telework experience ($n = 575$), there are no statistically significant differences for KM activity, providing support for H2b.

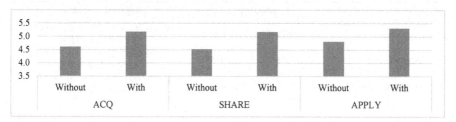

Fig. 1. Means of KM activity for those without and with prior telework experience (all differences significant at $p < 0.001$)

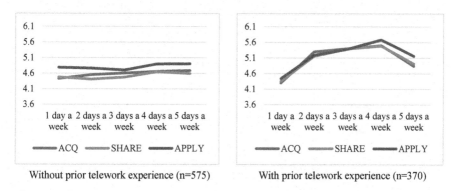

Fig. 2. KM during mandatory telework

To provide further evidence for H2, quadratic regression analyses were conducted and indeed established that nonlinear relationships exist (Salkind, 2010) between telework frequency and KM activity on the hand, and between telework frequency for those with prior telework experience (Table 4, Fig. 3).

An increase in telework frequency from 1 to 4 days a week meant an increase in KM activity, but telework frequency of 5 days a week – that is full telework – resulted in lower KM activity. This inverse U-shaped relationship suggests that telework frequency is detrimental to KM activity when teleworking every day without a single day in the office. In other words, increased telework frequency helps employees master collaboration tools and results in higher KM activity, as long as they can also meet colleagues and partners face-to-face at least once a week. Beyond 4 days a week, telework causes diminishing returns with a decline in KM activity.

Although our analyses confirm a U-shaped relationship between telework frequency and KM activity, it should be noted that R^2 is low, meaning that the model accounts for a low amount of variability, suggesting that other explanatory variables not evaluated here may be important.

Table 4. Quadratic regressions between telework frequency and KM activity for those with prior telework experience

	ANOVA	Regression equation
Knowledge acquisition	F(2,367)=14.177, p=0.000	$Y = -0.761 + 2.400*x - 0.228*x*x$; $R^2=0.072, p=0.000$
Knowledge sharing	F(2,367)=11.344, p=0.000	$Y = -0.468 + 2.233*x - 0.209*x*x$; $R^2=0.058, p=0.000$
Knowledge application	F(2,367)=11.432, p=0.000	$Y = -0.009 + 2.015* x - 0.181*x*x$; $R^2=0.059, p=0.000$

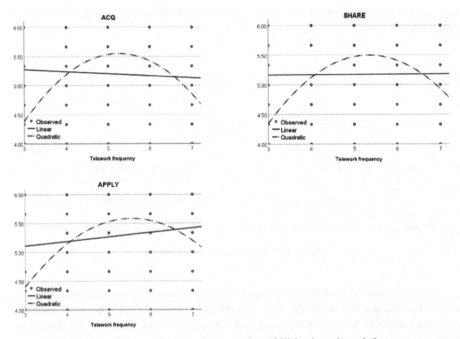

Fig. 3. Curve fitting with quadratic regression of KM using telework frequency

5 Conclusion

This research investigated how mandatory telework has affected KM activity based on prior telework experience and telework frequency. First, we found differences based on prior telework experience, whereby experienced teleworkers displayed higher KM activity compared to telework novices, during mandatory telework. This outcome suggests that training and practice of using remote work can significantly increase KM activity when forced to telework. As part of business continuity planning, now standard when trying to mitigate the adverse effects of disruptive incidents, firms should provide basic training as well as opportunities to experience telework to key knowledge workers. The need for telework education and try-out was further supported by the fact that there was no relationship between telework frequency and KM activity for those without prior telework experience; it indicates that telework novices had to relearn how to work, isolated at home, leading to persistently low KM activity.

Second, for those with prior telework experience, an increase in telework frequency from 1 to 4 days a week meant an increase in KM activity, but full telework – that is telework frequency of 5 days a week – resulted in lower KM activity. This inverse U-shaped relationship suggests that full telework is detrimental to KM activity for experienced teleworkers. In other words, higher telework frequency helps experienced teleworkers manage knowledge, as long as they go to the office once a week. Beyond four days a week, telework causes diminishing returns with a decline in KM activity. Low telework frequency is probably facing the issue of having absent colleagues at the office, resulting in lower KM activity due to a lack of colocation, even when the respondent is at the office. And those who telework fully without setting foot in the office end up engaging in less KM because the absence of face-to-face interactions deprives them of a critical channel for managing tacit knowledge. Some companies have recently come to the same conclusion and asked engineers to come to the office once a week (Japan Times, 2022).

In conclusion, this research has found that, first, prior telework experience results in higher KM activity when forced to telework, and second, that one day a week in the office contributes to higher KM activity among experienced coworkers, owing to the dual explicit and tacit nature of knowledge.

References

Abubakar, A.M., Elrehail, H., Alatailat, M.A., Elçi, A.: Knowledge management, decision-making style and organizational performance. J. Innov. Knowl. **4**(2), 104–114 (2019)

Aguilera, A., Lethiais, V., Rallet, A., Proulhac, L.: Home-based telework in France: characteristics, barriers and perspectives. Transp. Res. Part A Policy Pract. **92**, 1–11 (2016)

Allen, T.D., Golden, T.D., Shockley, K.M.: How effective is telecommuting? Assessing the status of our scientific findings. Psychol. Sci. Public Interest **16**(2), 40–68 (2015)

Bridoux, F., Taskin, L.: Telework: Despatialisation as a challenge to knowledge creation and transfer. Center for REsearch in Change, Innovation and Strategy, Working paper 03/2005 (Reprint IAG W.P. n°145–05), 1–19 (2005)

Chen, M.Y., Chen, A.P.: Knowledge management performance evaluation: a decade review from 1995 to 2004. J. Inf. Sci. **32**(1), 17–38 (2006)

De Cuyper, N., De Witte, H.: Volition and reasons for accepting temporary employment: associations with attitudes, well-being, and behavioural intentions. Eur. J. Work Organ. Psychol. **17**(3), 363–387 (2008)

De Graaff, T., Rietveld, P.: Substitution between working at home and out-of-home: the role of ICT and commuting costs. Transp. Res. Part A Policy Pract. **41**(2), 142–160 (2007)

Dias, P., Lopes, S., Peixoto, R.: Mastering new technologies: does it relate to teleworkers' (in)voluntariness and well-being? J. Knowl. Manag. **26**(10), 2618–2633 (2022)

Gajendran, R.S., Harrison, D.A.: The good, the bad, and the unknown about telecommuting: meta-analysis of psychological mediators and individual consequences. J. Appl. Psychol. **92**(6), 1524–1541 (2007)

Gupta, A.K., Smith, K.G., Shalley, C.E.: The interplay between exploration and exploitation. Acad. Manag. J. **49**(4), 693–706 (2006)

Hartman, R.I., Stoner, C.R., Arora, R.: Developing successful organizational telecommuting arrangements: worker perceptions and managerial prescriptions. S.A.M. Adv. Manag. J. **57**(3), 35–42 (1992)

Heisig, P.: Harmonisation of knowledge management – comparing 160 KM frameworks around the globe. J. Knowl. Manag. **13**(4), 4–31 (2009)

Japan Times (2020). 70% in Japan want telecommuting to continue after pandemic, survey finds, 22 June 2020. https://www.japantimes.co.jp/news/2020/06/22/business/japan-telecommuting-continue/

Japan Times (2022). Japanese firms re-imagine offices to make them hubs of communication, 24 November 2022. https://www.japantimes.co.jp/news/2022/11/24/business/office-redesign-communication-boost/

Jennex, M.E.: Knowledge Management, Organizational Memory and Transfer Behavior: Global Approaches and Advancements: Global Approaches and Advancements. Hershey, PA: IGI Global (2009)

Kazekami, S.: Mechanisms to improve labor productivity by performing telework. Telecommun. Policy **44**(2), 101868 (2020)

Kianto, A., Shujahat, M., Hussain, S., Nawaz, F., Ali, M.: The impact of knowledge management on knowledge worker productivity. Balt. J. Manag. **14**(2), 178–197 (2018)

Lapierre, L.M., van Steenbergen, E.F., Peeters, M.C.W., Kluwer, E.S.: Juggling work and family responsibilities when involuntarily working more from home: a multiwave study of financial sales professionals. J. Organ. Behav. **37**(6), 804–822 (2016)

Lee, H., Choi, B.: Knowledge management enablers, processes, and organizational performance: An integrative view and empirical examination. J. Manag. Inf. Syst. **20**(1), 179–228 (2003)

Magnier-Watanabe, R.: The effect of telework frequency on communication media and knowledge sharing in Japan. In: Uden, L., Ting, I.H., Feldmann, B. (eds.) Knowledge Management in Organisations. KMO 2022. CCIS, vol. 1593, pp. 3–15. Springer, Cham (2022). https://doi.org/10.1007/978-3-031-07920-7_1

Magnier-Watanabe, R., Senoo, D.: Organizational characteristics as prescriptive factors of knowledge management initiatives. J. Knowl. Manag. **12**(1), 21–36 (2008)

March, J.: Exploration and exploitation in organizational learning. Organ. Sci. **2**(1), 71–87 (1991)

Massa, S., Testa, S.: A knowledge management approach to organizational competitive advantage: evidence from the food sector. Eur. Manag. J. **27**(2), 129–141 (2009)

Messenger, J.C., Gschwind, L.: Three generations of telework: new ICT s and the (R) evolution from home office to virtual office. N. Technol. Work Employ. **31**(3), 195–208 (2016)

MHLW (2008). Guidelines for proper labor management in telework [Terewāku ni okeru tekisetsuna rōmu kanri no tame no gaidorain]. Ministry of Health, Labor, and Welfare. https://www.mhlw.go.jp/content/000553510.pdf

MHLW (2020). Work style called "telework from home" ['Jitaku de no terewāku' to iu hatarakikata]. Ministry of Health, Labor, and Welfare. https://www.mhlw.go.jp/bunya/roudou kijun/dl/pamphlet.pdf

Nahapiet, J., Ghoshal, S.: Social capital, intellectual capital, and the organizational advantage. Acad. Manag. Rev. **23**(2), 242–266 (1998)

Nakrošienė, A., Bučiūnienė, I., Goštautaitė, B.: Working from home: characteristics and outcomes of telework. Int. J. Manpow. **40**(1), 88–101 (2019)

Pérez, M.P., Sanchez, A.M., de Luis Carnicer, M.P.: The organizational implications of human resources managers' perception of teleworking. Pers. Rev. **32**(6), 733–755 (2003)

Peters, P., Batenburg, R.: Telework adoption and formalisation in organisations from a knowledge transfer perspective. Int. J. Work Innov. 1(3), 251 (2015)

Polanyi, M.: Tacit Dimension. Peter Smith, Gloucester, MA (1966)

Salkind, N.J.: Encyclopedia of Research Design, vol. 1. SAGE Publications Inc., Thousand Oaks, CA (2010)

Szulanski, G.: Exploring internal stickiness: Impediments to the transfer of best practice within the firm. Strateg. Manag. J. 17(S2), 27–43 (1996)

Taskin, L., Bridoux, F.: Telework: a challenge to knowledge transfer in organizations. Int. J. Hum. Resour. Manag. 21(13), 2503–2520 (2010)

Thatcher, S.M., Zhu, X.: Changing identities in a changing workplace: identification, identity enactment, self-verification, and telecommuting. Acad. Manag. Rev. 31(4), 1076–1088 (2006)

Van Den Hooff, B., De Ridder, J.A.: Knowledge sharing in context: the influence of organizational commitment, communication climate and CMC use on knowledge sharing. J. Knowl. Manag. 8(6), 117–130 (2004)

Vuori, V., Helander, N., Okkonen, J.: Digitalization in knowledge work: the dream of enhanced performance. Cogn. Technol. Work 21(2), 237–252 (2019)

WHO (2022). Weekly epidemiological update on COVID-19 - 23 November 2022. World Health Organization. https://www.who.int/publications/m/item/weekly-epidemiological-update-on-covid-19---23-november-2022

Wong, H.: Knowledge value chain: implementation of new product development system in a winery. Electron. J. Knowl. Manag. 2(1), 77–90 (2004)

The Role of Tacit Knowledge for Enhanced Quality Service Delivery in Organizations

Rexwhite Tega Enakrire[ID] and Hanlie Smuts[(✉)][ID]

Department of Informatics, School of Information Technology, University of Pretoria, Pretoria, South Africa
hanlie.smuts@up.ac.za

Abstract. The developments in cutting-edge technologies, such as mobile systems, artificial intelligence (AI), robotics, the Internet of Things (IoT), embedded computing, 3D printing, genetic engineering, and quantum computing are the role of tacit knowledge embedded in the human brain. The rationale that necessitates this study is that tacit knowledge, hidden in the human brain/mind, has become an enabler that results in quality service delivery in organizations. To establish the role of tacit knowledge for enhanced quality service delivery in organizations in the context of Africa, three research objectives were used to guide the study, namely: examine tacit knowledge in organizations, determine cutting-edge technologies, and explore the role of tacit knowledge in organizations. In this study, a multi-stage approach that comprised qualitative content analysis and a phenomenological research approach was employed. Findings reveal that tacit knowledge is applied in all aspects of the organization especially when the organization is in a critical situation, employees come together as a team using their various expertise in ensuring the organization is viable, competitive, productive, and sustained irrespective of the context. The carriers (human beings/brain/mind) know more than they thought, especially when engaging in discussion. Cutting-edge technologies of mobile systems, AI, robotics, IoT, embedded computing, 3D printing, genetic engineering, and quantum computing serve as supporting tools in the roles that tacit knowledge plays in the organization. Findings revealed that the role of tacit knowledge in organizations is to solve certain problems, decision-making, plan, and execution of tasks. The study recommends the need to value and treat the carriers of the tacit knowledge better than the technologies itself which serve as tools only.

Keywords: Information · Knowledge · Tacit · Service delivery · organization · productivity · private and corporate organization

1 Introduction

Tacit knowledge has proven to be the panacea to organizational problems [1], because of hidden expertise in the human brain/mind. The hidden know-how in the human brain/mind which is unveiled when actions/activities take place in the organizations is seen as an enabler that results in quality service delivery in the organizations. [2]

notes that tacit knowledge comprises insights, innovations, human behaviour, intelligence, and fresh ideas that are products of organizational sustainability. The insights, innovations, human behaviour, intelligence, and fresh ideas cannot work in isolation, but rather through humans effort. As employees continue to engage in one task or the other where they discuss with each other, even though certain challenges with situations abound in the organization, the employees show capability in their work performance. This is also supported by [2] who attests that most activities experienced in corporate and private organizations were the effort of tacit knowledge. The impact of tacit knowledge is shown through its sharing among colleagues' behaviour thus leading to innovative work performance of tasks exhibited.

While employees exhibit their tasks in tacit knowledge application in work productivity or performance in the organization, the study by [3] indicates that cutting-edge technologies of mobile systems, artificial intelligence (AI), robotics, the Internet of Things (IoT), embedded computing, 3D printing, genetic engineering, and quantum computing have only served as supporting tools for enhanced quality service delivery in the organizations. Consumers have continued to interact with cutting-edge technologies to support their business transactions. The behind the scene activities and success of results achieved in work performance by employees, competition, daily accomplishment, planning, and decision-making is the tacit type of knowledge in humans. The tacit type of knowledge being an enabler to the success of activities in the organization is supposed to be recognized and appreciated more than cutting-edge technologies that only gave birth to transformation and development in organizations. Therefore, the focus of this paper is to investigate the role of tacit knowledge in enhanced quality service delivery in organizations.

The paper applied the qualitative content analysis and phenomenological research approach based on the authors' lived experiences and expositions in their careers. The adopted research approach has helped to addressed the role which tacit knowledge has brought for enhanced quality service delivery in organizations. The purpose of this paper reflects on tacit knowledge (knowledge in the human brain/mind) and how it has supported and transformed the organization compared to the cutting-edge technologies of mobile systems, AI, robotics, IoT, embedded computing, 3D printing, genetic engineering, and quantum computing mostly celebrated today. The implication of the identified variables "tacit knowledge and cutting edge technologies" and roles of tacit knowledge in organization were buttressed.

In this paper, we provided an overview of the literature surrounding the capability of tacit knowledge, and cutting-edge technologies in Sect. 2, followed by the research approach for the study in Sect. 3. Section 4 entails the findings/contribution of the study, while Sect. 5 connotes the implication of the study while 6 is the conclusion of the paper.

2 Background

To survive as an organization, especially in a continuous fluctuating economy where certainty is not sure, pressures from customers are increasing and opportunities declining, it is essential to advance abilities that will support them to effortlessly adjust [4]. These abilities are time-consuming with substantial organizational effort. It would help accomplish the level at which the organization operates with reliance on employees [4]. Tacit knowledge has previously been situated as one of these abilities. Several tasks/work operations, transformation, planning, and implementation of innovations have advanced from one phase to another through the support which cutting-edge technologies of mobile systems, AI, robotics, IoT, embedded computing, 3D printing, genetic engineering, and quantum computing offered in the organizations. These were the result of tacit knowledge embedded in human beings. These cutting-edge technologies have been implemented in many sectors in Africa, where effectiveness, efficiency, and quality service delivery are ensured. Most of the effectiveness, efficiency, and quality of services delivered in private and public corporations make the organization more viable, competitive, and sustainable hence staff members continue to put in their best in what they know to do. The tasks/job performance carried out in the organizations (private and/or corporate) depends mostly on the support which the employee (humans), put into their services.

The efforts that employees exert on work operations or practices are reflected in how much tacit type of knowledge is used. For example, solving a financial account for an organization through the support of mobile systems, using AI to diagnose a patient with a certain ailment, applying robots for security detections in a company or homes, and embedded computing for the operation of systems and application software and formulating a program for any kind of tasks in the organization [5]. The feasibility of these services and tasks which became a reality through the effort of cutting-edge technologies could not have been possible if humans were not involved. The tacit type of knowledge embedded in them [6] in this context relates to the humans effort. There were other reflective quality services in organizations found in the cutting-edge technologies that include: AI, Machine learning, and algorithms serving commercial applications purposes of information, data, images, and text storage [7]. Another point of concern with AI is the study by [8] that refers to intricate matters that surround decisions making about people's job recruitment and the government distribution of services and well-being payments.

The use of systems for computerized decision-making by companies and governments, brought thoughtful influences on livelihoods [7]. Another dimension of influence in cutting-edge technologies experienced in digitalization programs of audit processes is the modernization and enhancement that surrounds the working condition of the audit profession, audit process, and auditor [9]. These events involve the application of critical thinking skills [10], hence the need for the tacit type of knowledge embedded in the human mind/brain. The reason for the tacit type of knowledge embedded in the human mind/brain is that all the ideas, innovation, and creativity resulting in cutting-edge technologies were proven to take the attention of humans in all organizations globally. The abilities that reside in human beings [6] are not the same in relation to the application of critical thinking skills [10], nurtured by humans hence the tacit type of knowledge cannot be undermined for enhanced service delivery in the organizations.

3   Research Method

To achieve the aim of this study, a multi-stage approach was employed. First, the researchers applied the qualitative content analysis of literature harvested from online database of Google Scholar. The qualitative content analysis was internalized where salient points extracted in relation to tacit knowledge, cutting-edge technologies and the role of tacit knowledge are used by employees to support their operations/work performance on daily basis in the organizations. Second, a phenomenological research approach was also considered in this study. A phenomenological approach was considered appropriate due to its usefulness to understand the lived experience and exposition of the researchers have worked in different organizations in the context of Africa. The study by [11] and [12] assert that a phenomenological approach is dedicated to the orderly investigation of personal experience based on the lifestyle lived, career track records and the impact made on people in society which could be remembered or used as the basis for reference. The authors of this study considered the qualitative content analysis and phenomenological research approach based on their expertise in knowledge management (where tacit knowledge is situated) and cutting-edge technologies of mobile systems, AI, robotics, IoT, embedded computing, 3D printing, genetic engineering, and quantum computing. The two variables have had significance in corporate organization with relation to work performance, innovation, and transformation.

In the qualitative content analysis of literature [13] and phenomenological research approach applied [14], the authors interpreted different literature based on experiences and exposition on work carried out in different organizations (private and public). The work practice attributes to the authors expertise progression, career, and published articles they have read on their own, which also supports the role of tacit knowledge and how it is used in the organization. The study by [11, 15–17] and [12] to mention a few, have also applied the use of qualitative content analysis and a phenomenological research approach in their study. The authors established that the qualitative content analysis and phenomenological research approach helps to explore better understanding of internalised literature and the lived experience of the various phenomenon of the authors. In this study, the authors made an intelligent critique of their personal lives and social world. The authors experience on how much they have learned in their careers puts transformation and impact on the use of tacit knowledge and cutting-edge technologies to support quality service delivery in the organization. While the study emphasized the authors' shared experience with cutting-edge technologies and the role of tacit knowledge for enhanced quality service delivery in the organization, a lot of differences and similarities of the components emerged as well.

The next sections addressed the findings and implication of the study based on qualitative content analysis and phenomenological approach of the lived experiences and exposition of the authors in their career progression. The main emphasis highlighted is tacit knowledge, cutting-edge technologies, and the role of tacit knowledge for enhanced quality service delivery in the organization.

4   Findings and Implication of the Study

This study investigated the role of tacit knowledge in enhanced quality service delivery in organizations. This section presents the findings and implication of the study as it relates to tacit knowledge, cutting-edge technologies, and the role surrounding tacit knowledge for enhanced quality service delivery in the organization. The findings obtained were based on qualitative content analysis of literature harvested from online database of

Google Scholar and the phenomenological approach of lived experiences and expositions of the authors in their career progression. The specific work, and research carried out in different organizations (private and public) were part of the phenomenological approach adopted in the study.

4.1 Tacit Knowledge in the Organization

Tacit knowledge is key to organizational productivity. Most of what employees carry (knowledge) is hidden until a certain responsibility/task is given. The tasks begins to unveil itself based on what the knower do. One remarkable emphasis that has lasted the test of time is the one made by [18] regarding tacit knowledge embedded in the SECI model [18]. [19] emphasized that what employees do in the organization is knowledge-generating processes where they create new knowledge through their product design and service delivery. Apart from Nonaka, several studies by [20–22] has made use of SECI model based on its usefulness in explaining tacit knowledge application in service delivery. For example, in the mobile technology industry, prior to when the Apple, iPhone, Samsung, and computer is designed, the expert uses their tacit knowledge to assemble all the raw materials or different apparatus and devices required in each stage of production of the technology. The SECI model [18] enables all the employees to socialize (sharing experiences and interact wiht employees through tacit knowledge) [23], externalize (conversion of tacit to explicit) [23], combination (explicit renewed to explicit knowledge) [24], and internalization (converting explicit to tacit knowledge) [18]. [2] alludes that tacit knowledge being innovation, ideas, and creativity of human beings led to the development of cutting-edge technologies of mobile systems.

The tacit knowledge is the innovation, ideas, and creativity emanated from the discourse of individual expertise. It can also be attributed to experiences and knowledge acquired over the years among employees on what they know best. Tacit knowledge would continue to remain an incubator of innovations and cutting-edge technologies that resulted in transformation of the organizations.

This has been the experience of the authors throughout their career progression having worked in different private and public organizations in Africa, where they converted explicit knowledge to tacit and vice versa. The reason the authors of this paper felt the qualitative content analysis of literature and phenomenological research approach is more appropriate in this study is aligned with where they showcase their thoughts and experiences on how tacit knowledge remains an enabler to organizational productivity. The extent to which employees could tell how much know-how they posses and have acquired reflects on knowledge application in the production of goods and services being enabler in this ever-changing world of uncertainty.

4.2 Cutting-Edge Technologies

Cutting-edge technologies have become the panacea through which organizations are sustained on daily basis in the present-day knowledge economy. The position or roles which cutting-edge technologies of mobile systems, AI, robotics, IoT, embedded computing, 3D printing, genetic engineering, and quantum computing has played cannot be underestimated in organizations globally, including those in the African context. The cutting-edge technologies described in this paper are considered evolving in the growth of the organization for better and quality service delivery. For example, in the health sector, the study by [25] emphasized that AI has become a cornerstone incorporated into real-life sciences that focuses on faster innovation in the form of human support.

Another point of departure according to [26] is robots which are now used worldwide for cyber security measures in companies and homes. The reason for its infusion is to avoid exposures, outbreaks/attacks into systems. The level of insecurity in organizations is becoming alarming and also increasing on daily basis, hence alternative measures of plating robots, cameras, gadgets, and other chips to combat the insecurity threat. These measures have helped to a large extent in combating and reducing attacks witnessed in many organizations. The infusion of cutting-edge technologies has helped organizations to compete among its counterparts in several ways. It is as a result of this practice that its relevance continue to add value to the organizations.

4.3 Role of Tacit Knowledge in Organizations

By"role", the authors of this paper refers to what employees do in the organization. Role are aligned with responsibility/obligation of employees. The role of employees ranges from leadership role, mentorship, managing innovation, service manager, executive officer, section officer among others in the organization. The role of tacit knowledge are hidden treasures or secrets that could safeguard an organization from getting into a difficult situation. The role of tacit knowledge in organization helps to eradicate complexity which could have been difficult to handle ordinarily [27].

The study by [27] which have a link to [19] emphasizes on conversion phase of knowledge having different dimensions as earlier mentioned by [18]. Could you have thought or imagine that knowledge are converted from tacit to explicit and verse versa [18]. It was the effort by [18], now replicated in other studies, making the practice come into existence. The act of tacit knowledge application which is seen in the role of employees is interesting because depending on the type of knowledge the seeker requires, conversion usually take place. It has enabled the exchange of currency in monetary value in the business world. The exchange of currency in monetary value implies that money is converted from one context to another to serve a specific purpose. In this study the authors understood and appreciated [18] work that knowledge can be converted depending on the purpose for which it is required in the organization.

[28] refer to the reduction of uncertainty and collective interface of organization knowledge. It is believed that the role of tacit knowledge would solve problem of uncertainty that were difficult ordinarily. The impact of organizational culture [29] is crucial because it helps to determine the extent to which the organization could grow irrespective of the context. When there are well-cultured people in the organization, it affects everything they do. The authors of this paper would like to draw a salient point from the study by [30] that dwells on the reconciliation of different thoughts of employees. It is important because people agree to disagree based on their different beliefs, exposition, and philosophy about life. The reason employee apply their beliefs, exposition, and philosophy is to ensure all have a consensus on what needs to be addressed for the

progress of the organization and the tasks assigned to them. The role of tacit knowledge is overwhelming when debated especially with quality service delivery because employees apply it in ensuring success is attained in the organization.

5 Implication of the Study

The implication of the study is that tacit knowledge is fundamental in all spheres of human endeavours. Tacit knowledge refers to the voice of the individual/employees through which his/her position is acknowledged in the organization. Without tacit knowledge, it is difficult to tell what an individual or employee is capable of, especially when it relates to showcasing talent in best practices in the organization and ever-changing world. The vitality of the corporate world today results in the know-how (tacit of human beings) of employees in the organization. A situation where employees do not have what it takes (know-how), to function, it therefore means, there is a serious problem, possibly because the individual is not capable in relation to having sufficient knowledge application in service delivery in the organization (private or public) [6].

The strength which organizations have depends largely on the carrier of the knowledge (humans) portrayed in what they do, hence the role of tacit knowledge discussed in this context cannot be overemphasized. The qualitative content analysis and phenomenological approach used in this study have assisted the authors to understand that organization cannot survive without the role of tacit knowledge which employees exhibit in their tasks. In this ever changing economy where certainty is not sure, and the information needs of customers are on the increase, application of the role (hidden treasure) of tacit knowledge becomes necessary for competition among organization/business enterprises. One of the roles (hidden treasures) of tacit knowledge identified in this study is the need to harness, tap, and shared stored knowledge embedded in employees. This is one of the best ways management of the organization would gain confidence in retaining their customers and other business partners. Among the quality of services envisaged in a public and private organization in relation to the role of tacit knowledge application is to ensure customers are served timeously and treated with respect and utmost priority. The employees should collaborate with one another thus taking deliberate steps in ensuring teamwork is continuous among employees. Most activities and tasks carried out in corporate and private organizations globally were the effort of tacit knowledge application in work productivity or performance.

6 Conclusion

The study established that the role of tacit knowledge for enhanced quality service delivery in the organization is multi-faceted. There is no organization in the present-day context that could survive without the application of tacit knowledge utilized for different service delivery. The tacit type of knowledge expressed by employees differs in job descriptions and fields of expertise. The study emphasized that organizational strength depends more on the effort of their employees based on the know-how (humans) portrayed in the tasks performed. The understanding surrounding the role of tacit knowledge as unveiled in this study indicates that as employees begin to share what they know, they filter old knowledge and gain new ones for better and quality service delivery.

The study reveals that in the infinite shifting economy where certainty is not guaranteed, and customer information needs increasing, the organization has to offer strategic ways to survive. Tapping into the role (hidden treasure) of tacit knowledge becomes necessary, especially among young and growing competitive organization and other business enterprises. It is believed that when employees share their hidden treasure (deep knowledge-tacit) identified in this study the employees and organization will be sustained. While the study emphasizes that the role of tacit knowledge for enhanced quality service delivery in an organization differs from one context to another, the need to harness, tap, and shared stored knowledge embedded in employees is crucial because no knowledge is lost. Although cutting-edge technologies of mobile systems, AI, robotics, IoT, embedded computing, 3D printing, genetic engineering, and quantum computing has and would continue to support and transform the organization.

The role of tacit knowledge has proven beyond measures because it gave birth to the cutting-edge technologies promoted today. The study concludes that since tacit knowledge (hidden know-how in the human brain/mind) is what gave birth to cutting-edge technologies, the time to promote and showcase tacit knowledge for task accomplishment is now. Although much emphasis debated among scholars, and research publication in recent times are on cutting-edge technologies in all sectors, rethinking the potential surrounding tacit knowledge becomes imperative. A constraint of this research is that only a few studies in the context of African private and public organizations have been carried out. There is a knowledge gap in existing literature, methodological approach and theoretical framework in relation to role of tacit knowledge application in organizations which this study has filled.

In terms of future research, we acknowledge the position of different stakeholder in higher education and health institutions, thereby giving consideration to the roles of stakeholder tacit knowledge in sustaining the organization.

References

1. Alzoubi, M.O., Alrowwad, A.A., Masa'deh, R.E.: Exploring the relationships among tacit knowledge sharing, communities of practice and employees' abilities: the case of KADDB in Jordan. Int. J. Organ. Anal. **30**(5), 1132–1155 (2022)
2. Malik, S.: Emotional intelligence and innovative work behaviour in knowledge-intensive organizations: how tacit knowledge sharing acts as a mediator? VINE J. Inf. Knowl. Manag. Syst. **52**(5), 650–669 (2022)
3. Ameen, N., Hosany, S., Tarhini, A.: Consumer interaction with cutting-edge technologies: implications for future research. Comput. Hum. Behav. **120**, 106761 (2021)
4. Domingo, N.P., Víctor Raúl LÓ, P.R., Leonardo, B., George Ciprian, G.: Knowledge management - the key resource in the knowledge economy. Theor. Appl. Econ. **06**(547)(06(547)), 27–36 (2010)
5. Hatziapostolou, T., Dranidis, D., Sotiriadou, A., Kefalas, P., Nikolakopoulos, I.: An authentic student research experience: fostering research skills and boosting the employability profile of students. In: Proceedings of the 23rd Annual ACM Conference on Innovation and Technology in Computer Science Education, pp. 254–259, July 2018
6. Enakrire, R.T., Smuts, H.: Efficacy of knowledge and skills in teaching and learning and research in higher education institution. In: Uden, L., Ting, I.H., Feldmann, B. (eds.) Knowledge Management in Organisations. KMO 2022. CCIS, vol. 1593, pp. 16–24. Springer, Cham (2022). https://doi.org/10.1007/978-3-031-07920-7_2

7. Bradley, F.: Representation of libraries in artificial intelligence regulations and implications for ethics and practice. J. Aust. Libr. Inf. Assoc. **71**(3), 189–200 (2022)
8. Krafft, P.M., Young, M., Katell, M., Huang, K., Bugingo, G.: Defining AI in policy versus practice. In: Proceedings of the AAAI/ACM Conference on AI, Ethics, and Society, pp. 72–78, February 2020
9. Schreuder, A., Smuts, H.: Perspective Chapter: Audit Digitalization-Key Impacts on the Audit Profession (2023)
10. Snyder, L.G., Snyder, M.J.: Teaching critical thinking and problem solving skills. J. Res. Bus. Educ. **50**(2), 90 (2008)
11. Tomkins, L.: Using interpretative phenomenological psychology in organisational research with working carers. In: Brook, J., King, N. (Ed.), Applied Qualitative Research in Psychology, pp. 86–100. Palgrave, London (2017)
12. Noon, E.J.: Interpretive phenomenological analysis: an appropriate methodology for educational research. J. Perspect. Appl. Acad. Pract. **6**(1) (2018)
13. Given, L.M.: The SAGE Encyclopedia of Qualitative Research Methods, vol. 1. SAGE Publications, Inc., Thousand Oaks, CA (2008)
14. Greening, N.: Phenomenological research methodology. Sci. Res. J. **7**(5), 88–92 (2019)
15. Smith, J.A., Flower, P., Larkin, M.: Interpretative phenomenological analysis: theory, method and research. Qual. Res. Psychol. **6**(4), 346–347 (2009). https://doi.org/10.1080/147808809 03340091
16. VanScoy, A., Evenstad, S.B.: Interpretative phenomenological analysis for LIS research. J. Doc. (2015)
17. VanScoy, A., Bright, K.: Articulating the experience of uniqueness and difference for librarians of color. Libr. Q. **89**(4), 285–297 (2019)
18. Nonaka, I.: A Dynamic Theory of Organizational Knowledge Creation, Institute of Business Research, Hitotsubashi University, Kunitachi, Tokyo, Japan, pp. 14–3 (1994)
19. Nonaka, I., Byosiere, P., Borucki, C.C., Konno, N.: Organizational knowledge creation theory: a first comprehensive test. Int. Bus. Rev. **3**(4), 337–351 (1994)
20. Andreeva, T., Ikhilchik, I.: Applicability of the SECI model of knowledge creation in Russian cultural context: theoretical analysis. Knowl. Process. Manag. **18**(1), 56–66 (2011)
21. Adesina, A.O., Ocholla, D.N.: The SECI model in knowledge management practices: past, present and future. Mousaion **37**(3) (2019)
22. Canonico, P., De Nito, E., Esposito, V., Iacono, M.P., Consiglio, S.: Knowledge creation in the automotive industry: Analysing obeya-oriented practices using the SECI model. J. Bus. Res. **112**, 450–457 (2020)
23. Farnese, M.L., Barbieri, B., Chirumbolo, A., Patriotta, G.: Managing knowledge in organizations: a nonaka's SECI model operationalization. Front. Psychol. **10**, 2730 (2019). https://doi.org/10.3389/fpsyg.2019.02730
24. Nonaka, I., Toyama, R., Konno, N.: SECI, Ba and leadership: a unified model of dynamic knowledge creation. Long Range Plan. **33**(1), 5–34 (2000)
25. Noorbakhsh-Sabet, N., Zand, R., Zhang, Y., Abedi, V.: Artificial intelligence transforms the future of health care. Am. J. Med. **132**(7), 795–801 (2019)
26. Yaacoub, J.P.A., Noura, H.N., Salman, O., Chehab, A.: Robotics cyber security: vulnerabilities, attacks, countermeasures, and recommendations. Int. J. Inf. Secur. 1–44 (2022)
27. Mitchell, V.W., Harvey, W.S., Wood, G.: Where does all the 'know how' go? The role of tacit knowledge in research impact. High. Educ. Res. Dev. **41**(5), 1664–1678 (2022)
28. Oğuz, F., Elif Şengün, A.: Mystery of the unknown: revisiting tacit knowledge in the organizational literature. J. Knowl. Manag. **15**(3), 445–461 (2011)

29. Mambo, S., Smuts, H.: The impact of organizational culture on knowledge management: the case of an international multilateral organization. EPiC Ser. Comput. **85**, 184–195 (2022)
30. Muñoz, C.A., Mosey, S., Binks, M.: The tacit mystery: reconciling different approaches to tacit knowledge. Knowl. Manag. Res. Pract. **13**, 289–298 (2015)

Cybersecurity Management in Micro, Small, and Medium Enterprises in Colombia

Flor Nancy Díaz-Piraquive[1]([✉]) [iD], Yasser de Jesús Muriel-Perea[1] [iD],
and Rubén González-Crespo[2] [iD]

[1] Fundación Universitaria Internacional de la Rioja, Bogotá, Colombia
{flornancy.diaz,yasserdejesus.muriel}@unir.edu.co
[2] Universidad Internacional de la Rioja, Madrid, Spain
ruben.gonzalez@unir.net

Summary. The aim of this research study is the analysis of the cybersecurity management in micro, small and medium enterprises (MSMEs or MIPYMES) in Colombia. To reach this objective, the quantitative approach methodology was used, with a descriptive exploratory scope, in coherence with the research approach.

To collect the information, a questionnaire was used, applied to 130 MSMEs companies from 23 states in Colombia. The results of the research study show that a considerable percentage of MSMEs in Colombia is aware of what cybersecurity is, and the main procedures that they carry out, depending on the Information Technology and Communications is about payments. The analysis leads to conclude that, while the enterprises know what cybersecurity is, they do not develop actions to mitigate risks originated from cyberattack threats. This is evident, among several other reasons, because in its great majority, they do not count with a unit in charge of managing cybersecurity, and when they make third party agreements of information services, they do not establish confidentiality agreements. These steps are essential for a safe digital transformation of MSMEs in Colombia.

Keywords: Cyberattacks · Cybersecurity · MSMEs · Risk management

1 Introduction

Throughout history, several industrial revolutions have taken place, which have brought changes that have impacted society as a whole. Each revolution has been recognized by the appearance of a pivotal milestone: first revolution: mechanization; second revolution: electricity; third revolution: the computer, and the fourth revolution: Cyber-physical systems, being understood as an integration between physic, digital, and biological processes [1]. The fourth industrial revolution has brought opportunities and challenges for people as well as for enterprises.

As far as opportunities are concerned, this revolution has allowed in a snappy way, the democratization of access to information, and the use of pillars such as data analysis, big data, artificial intelligence, internet of things, among others. These opportunities,

L. Uden and I-H. Ting (Eds.): KMO 2023, CCIS 1825, pp. 74–85, 2023.
https://doi.org/10.1007/978-3-031-34045-1_8

unlike the previous industrial revolutions, are accessible to companies, regardless of size; Micro, small and medium enterprises (MSMEs) - are among the most benefitted, since costs are more affordable than in the past.

Regarding challenges, due to every time bigger digital transformation of business processes of organizations, threats have increased against availability, integrity, and confidentiality of information. Digital security attacks in the big corporations, are more publicized, and therefore are better known. Most usual ones are user accounts compromise, ransomware, web application vulnerabilities, and denial of services. Some recent cases in Colombia: case EPM, one of the main enterprises of the power generating sector in Colombia; case Sanitas, a Health Care Services promoting company, whose access to health services was disabled by a cyberattack for several weeks, to nearly 5,5 million users, as well as services of the Superintendence of Industry and Commerce. [2]. However, (MSMEs) are the most vulnerable enterprises that face these threats. The situation becomes relevant with respect to acceleration of digital transformation caused by the Covid 19 pandemic, and keeping in mind that MSMEs represent more than 90% of the national productive sector, which generate about 35% of the GDP (Gross Domestic Product), and 80% of employment throughout Colombia [3].

This paper analyzes cybersecurity management by MSMEs in Colombia, inquiring if they know the threats that they represent for continuity of their processes, and the development of the value chain, and what steps are being taken on that respect. The document is organized as follows: The problem is displayed in the first part, as well as the justification and purpose of the research study. Then, the theoretical framework, and the methodology. Finally, the results and conclusions are presented.

The paper is structured as follows: Sects. 2 and 3 describe the concept of cybersecurity, regulations in Colombia, and typology of Micro, Small and Medium Enterprises in Colombia. Section 4 defines the research methodology, and the design of the paper. Section 5 shows the results of the research study. Section 6 includes a discussion about the research study. Section 7 defines an improving suggested route addressed to MSMEs. Finally, Sect. 8 presents the conclusions and proposed future works.

2 Cybersecurity and Regulations in Colombia

Cybersecurity refers to the guarantee of confidentiality, integrity, and availability of information in the cyberspace. This last factor refers to the environment product of people interaction, software, and internet services [4]. Cyberattacks not only happen to corporations, but also to individuals, with the intention of accessing their personal information. A cyberattack includes all actions to deviate, alter, or destroy information systems [5]. In the same sense, there are several types of threats to cybersecurity.

Cyberattack is an aggressive cyber action taken against people, corporations, networks, systems, and services, with the intention of causing loss or damage [4].

Cyberspace is an environment resulting from the interaction of people, software, and internet services, by means of technological devices and networks connected to each other, but which physically do not exist [4].

Vulnerability is the intrinsic property of something resulting sensitive to a risk source, that can lead to an event with a consequence [4].

Spoofing (Phishing) consists in sending misleading electronic mails similar to electronic mails from reliable sources. The intention is the stealing of neuralgic information from credit/debit cards, etc.

Ransomware is a type of malicious software. It is a kind of extortion with the purpose of demanding money, to unlock files or systems of the affected user. It is possible for a company to be subject to a ransomware attack and be forced to pay for the ransom to decrypt their data [4].

Malware is a type of built software to get restricted access, or to cause damage to a computer.

Social Engineering is a strategy used by delinquents to cheat and have personal information disclosed. It is used to get money, or to access confidential information for multiple purposes.

Many of the cybersecurity problems are also caused by the lack of expertise, or the neglect of people in charge of managing the information [4]. These inconvenient are caused due to the lack of understanding the risks implied in the use of cyberspace, by staff not trained properly to do their work.

A cyberattack seeks two basic aspects: On one side, to somehow tampering with or removing valuable information, and/or on the other side, make extortions or fraudulent maneuvers with such information, chasing profit.

All organizations look for the achieving of strategic objectives, rigorously planned; for that, an adequate custody and utilization of information is essential. A cyberattack can jeopardize the Core Business of a company, according to that, [6] those are the neuralgic activities of an institution, that's to say, the ones that give meaning to the company, its reason for being. That is why cyberattacks are real hazards to business continuity.

In the innovation age, counting with tools that keep up with technological advances is more than essential, to understand their duality, that is to say, their positive characteristics, but also the challenges it brings, [7] in the Oslo manual, innovation is defined as the entrance of a new or improved product (good or service), of a process, of a new strategy of commercialization, or of a new organizational method. The impact it would bring to a company, the filtration of information on a new launching of a product or service in the market, would be very important.

There are tools to get protected from cybercrime, such as for example the cyber insurance, this is an important tool to reduce risks derived from damages for cyberattacks, while big corporations contract more and more cyber insurance, MSMEs are more reluctant to do it, it could be due to lack of knowledge, or because they are not conscious of real consequences of cyber risks [8].

Regarding international legislation, the following organizations are relevant to fight the threats against cyber security: The Agreement on cybercrime of the European Council– CCC (Agreement on cybercrime of Budapest), and Resolution AG/RES 2004 (XXXIV- 0/04) General Assembly of the Organization of American States.

As far as national legislation is concerned, efforts have been made in Colombia to relieve cybercrime, that is why on 2018, a law was signed on cybercrime, adhering to guidelines of the Budapest Treaty of 2001, on that topic. Such law [9], seeks the prevention of crimes directed against the confidentiality, integrity, and availability of systems, and the assumption of sufficient powers to vigorously confront such crimes, facilitating its detection, through investigation both, at national and international level, allowing an efficient international cooperation. It is also relevant: Law 527 of 1999, electronic commerce; Law 1273, Cybercrime; Law 1581 of 2012, protection of personal data; CONPES 3854 of 2016, guidelines on Cybersecurity, and Cyber-defense.

3   Micro, Small and Medium – Sized Enterprises in Colombia

In Colombia, according to Law 905/2004, Colombian Enterprises Typology is based on two criteria: number of employees and assets [10]. (See Table 1).

Table 1. Enterprise Classification

Size	Work unit or Total assets $COP
Micro	Work <= 10 employees, or total assets, excluding house <= $368.858.500
Small	Work >= 11 and <= 50 employees, or total assets > $368.858.500 and <= $3.688.585.000
Medium	Work >= 51 and <= 200 employees, or total assets > $3.688.585.000 <= $22.131.510.000
Large	Work > 200 employees, or total assets > $22.131.510.000

Source [13]

Micro-Companies generate 50.3% of employment, while Small and Medium create 30.5% of it. MSMEs are mostly concentrated in Bogota, Antioquia, Valle del Cauca, Atlántico and Santander regions. Exports grew up to $1.437 million in 2016, experienced a contraction, by 5.7% since 2015. United States of America and Ecuador are the most relevant Colombian products importers. Indeed, industrialists represent about 90.6% of exports. Regarding legal aspects, 40% of businesses establish as companies' society and 60% operates under legal natural person. Furthermore, "Productive Colombia" Program refers to current situation for MSMEs, aiming efficiency. According to MINCIT, MSMEs require double employees to generate the average value of a large company. Because of this situation, MINCIT objectives for 2032 remain in competitiveness. Data confirm that MSMEs are key to achieve this goal [11].

3.1   MSMEs Weaknessess

Colombian MSMEs weaknessess are similar to other countries: poor use of technology (see Fig. 1), lack of experience in technology of information and communication and unawareness of real opportunities given by the State or market. As a result of this, MSMEs are operating under low efficiency and competitiveness rates [12].

3.2   MSMEs Strength

Access to credit is one of the most relevant advantages for Colombian MSMEs. According to the World Bank "Doing Business, 2017" Report, Colombia scores second at this dimension, overpassed by New Zealand [13]. In addition, MSMEs size favour flexibility and quick change.

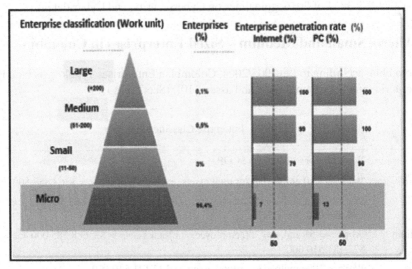

Fig. 1. Internet penetration rate for enterprises. Source [15]

4   Study

The purpose of this research study is the analysis of the cybersecurity management, in the Colombian MSMEs' (MIPYMES). To define the study universe, the total number of MSMEs was taken into account in Colombia, while for calculation of the minimum sample size, Mertens [14] was taken into account, who indicates that, according to the purpose, for descriptive analysis and large-scale surveys, the minimum size is 100 cases. The study included a sample of 130 MSMEs. The study is solid, since it was heterogeneous thanks to the fact that SMSs correspond to different regions of the country, from 23 states. This condition lends weight to the research study.

4.1   Research Methodology

There are several approaches for research, according to Johnson and Christensen [15] "a particular investigation can be completely qualitative or mixed, with qualitative emphasis, completely quantitative or mixed with quantitative emphasis, or mixed with both, qualitative and quantitative emphasis." (p. 81). In the case of this study, to achieve the purpose of the research, the quantitative approach was used.

Scope: Descriptive – Exploratory. Descriptive, to the extent that they consider the studied phenomenon, and its components, and exploratory, since a little-known problem is studied, and prepares the ground for future studies [16]. Data collection technique:

Questionnaire. Population: established MSMEs (MIPYMES) in Colombia. Sampling technique: Probabilistic.

Sample: One hundred thirty (130) MSMEs from 23 states in Colombia, with the following distribution: Valle del Cauca, 28; Antioquia, 19; Bogotá, 17; Norte de Santander, 11; Santander, 9; Tolima, 8; Cundinamarca, 6; Magdalena, 5; Atlántico 4; Putumayo, 3;Risaralda, 3; Caldas, 3; Amazonas, 2; Huila, 2; Quindío, 2; Bolívar, 1; Boyacá, 1; Cauca,1; Cesar, 1; Choco, 1; Guainía, 1; Guaviare, 1; Nariño. For the calculation of the sample, the probabilistic sampling, simple random technique was used. For this purpose and in order to make the sample representative, in the universe of the one hundred thirty companies, it was taken into account that they were heterogeneous in terms of economic sectors.

4.2 Research Design

The on-line survey integrates 14 questions. The questions of survey come from, mainly, concepts about Cyber Security and characteristic of MSMEs. It was sent to Colombian MSMEs. Each enterprise received a link in order to response the survey.

The on-line survey was structured as follows: three questions about general aspects (Size, Economic sector and job position); then, eleven questions regarding Cyber Security (see Table 2).

4.3 Research Question

The question that conducts this research is: What actions are carried out by MSMEs in Colombia in order to guarantee the preservation of confidentiality, integrity and availability of information in the Cyberspace?

5 Result of the Survey

As it can be seen (Table 3), most of the surveyed companies belong to the commercial sector, which is consistent with the conformation of the business network in Colombia. While it is true that these companies state that they know what cybersecurity is, and that the key processes of their value chain depend on the Information Technology and Communications, and on the cyberspace, it is evident that they do not take actions or measures to guarantee the availability, integrity, and confidentiality of information.

The results show that very few companies take actions to mitigate cybersecurity risks, such as: procedures, confidentiality clauses, encourage the importance of cybersecurity, and management of their users, and passwords, among others. Their main efforts are restricted to antivirus software tools, antispyware, or firewall. This research study shows that an important percentage of MSMEs (MIPYME) has suffered some type of cybersecurity incident during the last two years.

Table 2. Survey

No.	Question	Answer Options
1	Size of enterprise by number of employees	Micro (1–10) Small (11–50) Small (11–50)
2	¿What economic sector does the Enterprise belong to?	Financial activities and insurance; Public Administration and defense; social security, education; Services; Wholesale and retail trade; Transportation, logistics, storage, accommodation; Industry; Manufacture; Health, Pharmaceutical; Technology; Taxes; professional activities; scientific and technical; artistic activities, training and entertainment, and recreation; Real estate activities; Electricity, gas, vapor, water and air; Mines and quarries; Agricultural Information and communications; Construction, Other
3	Position	Manager/Coordinator/,External Consultant, Professional (Accountant - Engineer - Developer), Technician/Technologist, Helper/Assistant, other
4	¿Do you know what cybersecurity is? informatic security or information security?	Yes, No
5	¿Which of your processes are more dependent from Information Technology and Communication, and from Internet? (Please check all options that you consider)	Inbound logistics. Outbound logistics, Business operation (main processes), Administration and Management, Marketing and sales, Services, Payments or transactions, Communication with third parties (customers, suppliers, partners, etc.), None of the above
6	¿Does your company have an area to take care of cybersecurity, or information security?	Yes, it has an internal area, exclusively assigned to the topic. Yes, it does, but it is part of another area of the company. Yes, it does, but it is contracted with a third party, outside the company
7	¿Are there procedures known by employees, about security measures to be considered, to guarantee security of the company's information?	Yes No

(*continued*)

Table 2. (*continued*)

No.	Question	Answer Options
8	¿Does the company provide orientation as of how management should be done by its users, and passwords in applications and other information systems?	Yes No
9	¿Does your company use software (programs) antivirus, antispyware, or firewall?	Yes No
10	¿Are actions and mechanisms developed to generate awareness about cybersecurity or information security, to guarantee confidentiality, integrity, and availability of the company's information? customers', suppliers and employees'?	Yes No
11	¿Do contracts with the company's suppliers explicitly include confidentiality and security clauses of the information, to indicate that the information must be protected, and the computational resources of the company, in case of having access to them?	Yes No
12	¿For how long can your key business processes operate, without having access to internet?	Minutes, Hours Days Weeks Months
13	¿Which do you consider is the most important aspect to guarantee cybersecurity or information security in the company?	Technology Processes People All the above
14	¿During the last 2 years, did your company suffer from any type of incident of cybersecurity? (For example: virus, loss of information, fake e-mails, on-line payments not authorized, etc.)	Yes No

6 Discussion

This research study shows that, while it is true that most of the surveyed MSMEs companies consider that they know about the cybersecurity concept, they have not appropriated the concept, they have not internalized it in the organizations. Even though their processes depend on the cyberspace, and that the tolerance threshold with respect to failures is low, they do not assume the necessary measures to guarantee cybersecurity.

The results allow us to infer that the surveyed MSMEs do not make an adequate management of cybersecurity risk, and that they allocate real few resources to guarantee availability, integrity, and confidentiality of information. The first concept is reflected

Table 3. Answers Obtained

Question	Responses
1	Regarding the size of the company: Microenterprises: 22%; Small enterprises: 49%; Medium enterprises: 29%
2	Regarding the economic sector which the enterprises belong to, the largest participation corresponds to the commercial sector with 25%, followed by sectors of artistical activities, training and recreation, and construction with 16% and 13%, respectively
3	50% of people who answered the survey, hold management positions
4	68% of surveyed companies, stated that they know what Cybersecurity is, while 32% declared that they do not know
5	Regarding the question inquiring about which of the processes were more dependent from Information Technology and Communication, and internet, 80% of the companies stated that the most dependent one, is the process of payments and transactions; 52%, administration of human resources; 44% services, and 35%, marketing and sales
6	Regarding the question whether the company has an area to take care of cybersecurity or information security: No, it does not, 64%. Yes, it does, it has an internal area, exclusively dedicated to the topic, 11%. Yes, it does, but it is part of another company, 15%. Yes, it does, but it is contracted through a third party outside of the company, 10%
7	Regarding the existence of procedures, known by employees, about the security measures to be considered, 70% of the companies stated that they do not have them, 30% stated that they do have them
8	Regarding the question about the management orientation of their users, and passwords, 64% of the companies stated that they do not do it, 36% stated that they do it
9	As far as the use of antivirus software is concerned, antispyware o firewall, 71% stated Yes, while the rest stated that they do not use it, or that they do not know those tools
10	About awareness of the importance of cybersecurity of the company, 69% stated Yes, while 31% stated that they do not take any action in that sense
11	About the inclusion of confidentiality clauses and security of information, in third party contracts, 54% stated Yes, they do it, while 46% stated that they do not do it
12	Regarding the time during which the business key processes can operate, without having access to internet, 67% of the companies consider that they can tolerate minutes, and as a maximum hour
13	Regarding the question about the most important point to guarantee cybersecurity or information security of the company, the answer was: technology 22% of the companies, processes 7%; people 12%, and all the above, 80%

(*continued*)

Table 3. (*continued*)

Question	Responses
14	About the question whether during the last 2 years, their companies have had some type of cybersecurity incident, 70% stated that they have not had it, while 30% stated that Yes, they have had it

in that, for example, no procedures and campaigns are established for awareness of cybersecurity risks, and neither user management nor passwords, among others. The second concept is evident to the extent that they do not have an organizational structure, a unit in charge of the topic, and when they sign third party contracts, they do not set confidentiality clauses.

The research study allows to confirm that these companies consider that to guarantee cybersecurity, the most important thing is the technological dimension, and they ignore the organizational and human dimensions. In fact, these last two concepts are the ones that weight more out of causes for cybersecurity incidents. This agrees with the given answers in the sense that they do not make awareness campaigns on the cybersecurity risks, and they consider that, with antivirus software, antispyware or firewall is enough. The Discovery in the sense that 30% of the surveyed MSMEs has suffered cybersecurity incidents, is of great impact, for if we extrapolate the universe of MSMEs in Colombia, which represent more than 95% of the companies network in the country, there is no doubt that they certainly are in a situation of vulnerability and cyberattacks.

7 Adoption Roadmap

Based on the current study and theoretical framework – such as PDCA of Deming, - we propose this step-in order to incorporate strategies for to guarantee cybersecurity at MSMEs in Colombia (see Fig. 2).

The details of the step of roadmap for MSMEs are:

- Step 1: To study about Cyber Security.
- Step 2: To diagnose current situation of enterprise related to Cyber Security
- Step 3: To define the strategy including three dimensions: technological, organizational, and human.
- Step 4: To train and to make aware employees.
- Step 5: To measure the Cyber Security Strategy.
- Step 6: To do based on the measurement.

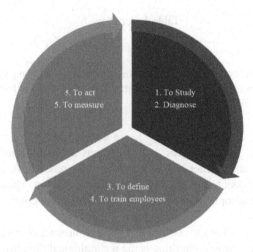

Fig. 2. Adaptation Roadmap. Source. Author

8 Conclusions and Future Works

The research carried out allows us to reach the following conclusions:

- A considerable percentage of MSMEs in Colombia, know what cyber security is, and the main process they carry out depend on Information Technology and Communications (ITC). In spite of that, they do not have a responsible area of cyber security or information security, neither they have procedures known by their employees for the information management.
- When MSMEs companies contract information services through third parties, it is evident that a high percentage of them does not include confidentiality clauses, and information security, with their suppliers, situation which makes them more vulnerable to cyber-attacks.
- MSMEs are aware that to guarantee the information security, the mixture of the three dimensions combined must be considered (people, procedures, and technology). However, they have a technological bias. It is convenient that they give the three dimensions the same importance.
- To reach an effective digital transformation, it is suggested that MSMEs implement as a priority, permanent actions, within the dimensions of technology, procedures, and people, to manage cybersecurity risks to which they are exposed. One must move from theory to practice, although awareness is considered, however, no actions are evident to mitigate cybersecurity risks.
- Future work needs to confirm and reinforce the project conclusions. In the future, it will be necessary to expand the sample. In this study there was a restriction, as it was developed only with a sample of 130 enterprises in Colombia.

References

1. Schwab, K.: The fourth industrial revolution. World Economic Forum (2017)

2. MINTIC. Obtenido de (2023). https://mintic.gov.co/portal/inicio/Sala-de-prensa/Noticias/ 273464:En-el-ultimo-mes-y-medio-MinTIC-ha-recibido-36-reportes-de-ataques-ciberneti cos-en-Colombia
3. Ministerio del Trabajo de Colombia. MIPYMES (2019). https://www.mintrabajo.gov.co/pre nsa/comunicados/2019/septiembre/mipymes-representan-mas-de-90-del-sector-productivo-nacional-y-generan-el-80-del-empleo-en-colombia-ministra-alicia-arango
4. Sutton, D.: Cyber Security: A Practitioner's Guide. BCS Publishing, London (2017)
5. Abello, R., Ramírez, W., Mejía, A.: Diálogos y casos iberoamericanos sobre derecho internacional penal, derecho internacional humanitario y justicia transicional. Editorial Universidad del Rosario (2020)
6. Michaux, S., Cadiat, A.-C.: Las cinco fuerzas de Porter: Cómo distanciarse de la competencia con éxito. 50Minutos.es (2016)
7. OCDE. Oslo Manual 2018: Guidelines for Collecting, Reporting and Using Data on Innovation, The Measurement of Scientific, Technological and Innovation Activities. OECD Publishing (2018)
8. Del Saz, J., De Ávila, R.: Los seguros de la empresa y el empresario: Todo lo que siempre quiso saber para proteger su negocio. Libros de Cabecera (2020)
9. Consejo de Europa (2018). http://es.presidencia.gov.co. Obtenido de. http://es.presidencia. gov.co/normativa/normativa/LEY%201928%20DEL%2024%20DE%20JULIO%20DE% 202018.pdf
10. Congreso de la República de Colombia. Ley 905 de 2004. Capítulo 1
11. Productive transformation program. Recovered from the page. https://www.ptp.com.co/cat egoria/Colombia_Productiva.aspx. Accessed 1 Dec 2017
12. DANE. Departamento Administrativo Nacional de Estadísticas. Informe estadístico 2015
13. World Bank. Doing Business 2017: Equal Opportunity for All. Washington, DC: World Bank. DOI: https://doi.org/10.1596/978-1-4648-0948-4. License: Creative Commons Attribution CC BY 3.0 IGO (2017)
14. Mertens, D.M.: Transformative mixed methods research. **16**(6), 469–474 (2010)
15. Johnson, B., Christensen, L.: Educational research: Quantitative and qualitative approaches. Allyn & Bacon (2014)
16. Hernández-Sampieri, R., Mendoza, C.: Metodología de la investigación: las rutas cuantitativa, cualitativa y mixta. Mcgraw-Hill, Boston (2020)

Study on the Impact of the Telework on the Employee's Productivity Improvement and Its Business Performance -Based on a Case Analysis of a Major Japanese IT Company-

Akira Kamoshida[1]([✉]), Toru Fujii[2], and Yu Yating[2]

[1] HOSEI University, Chiyoda, Japan
akira.kamoshida.34@hosei.ac.jp
[2] KITAMI Institute of Technology, Kitami, Japan
toru-fujii@live.jp, yuyating@mail.kitami-it.ac.jp

Abstract. The purpose of this paper is to focus on major Japanese IT companies whose usage rate of telework has increased rapidly due to the COVID-19 disaster, and to consider issues and measures for improving productivity and performance by using telework.

In this survey, we conducted a questionnaire survey of employees at major IT companies based on Herzberg's theory of motivation, and we analyzed the correlation between the work environment and productivity awareness before and after the COVID-19 pandemic.

As a result, we confirmed that major Japanese IT companies have not been able to actively utilize telework and adapt to the working environment, work environment, and corporate culture [18] that contribute to productivity improvement.

In addition, because of the correlation analysis, "The working environment for telework in companies has not changed explicitly before and after the corona crisis. There are large individual differences." The situation was confirmed. However, the absolute number of samples in this questionnaire survey is small, and it is necessary to increase the number of samples and conduct a detailed examination in the future.

Under these circumstances, major Japanese IT companies introduced telework relatively quickly compared to many other companies in other countries and Japan, demonstrating the resilience of their operations.

However, to continuously improve the productivity and performance of employees using telework in the future, it will be necessary to reshape the working environment surrounding telework.

Keywords: telework · productivity improvement · IT company · business performance · work environment

L. Uden and I-H. Ting (Eds.): KMO 2023, CCIS 1825, pp. 86–97, 2023.
https://doi.org/10.1007/978-3-031-34045-1_9

1 Introduction

The global COVID-19 pandemic, which began at the end of 2019, has wrought havoc on societies, industries, and people's lives around the world. Many companies took advantage of this opportunity to quickly introduce telework, and as a result, the usage rate of telework, which had been stagnant until now, increased sharply. In the case of Japan, according to [1], the number of companies that had introduced telework increased from 7.6% at the end of 2006 to 19.0% at the end of 2009, and decreased to 12% in January 2011, the rate of increase was declining. However, because of the COVID-19 pandemic, the telework usage rate has increased rapidly to about 60% since April 2020, and in 2021 it is almost the same level as in 2020 [2]

Looking at the changes in telework usage before and after the COVID-19 pandemic across OECD countries compared to Japan, [3] almost 40% of Eurozone workers used telework in April 2020, and this figure will increase to about 45% by summer 2020. However, it was also found that across OECD member countries, the telework usage rate increased significantly from about 16% before the COVID-19 pandemic to about 37% in the first wave (April 2020). Also, in the United States, the proportion of employees working from home has increased from about 15% before the pandemic to about 50% (Brynjolfsson et al., 2020). [4] documented that around 34% of the European Union workforce worked exclusively from home during the COVID-19 pandemic.

From here, the use of telework has risen sharply in all countries triggered by the corona crisis.

Faced with the need to curb the spread of the virus, governments around the world have introduced strict lockdown measures and mandated social distancing. For many companies, implementing telecommuting (telecommuting, remote work, or work from home) has been the only way to keep business running and avoid employee furloughs or layoffs [3].

Telecommuting has enabled businesses and workers to rely on what his Eberly, Haskel, and Mizen (2021) called "latent capital," represented by housing and workers' internet connectivity, thus reducing the economic impact of the pandemic and increased resilience.

On the other hand, in Japan, the percentage of telecommuting users was high at companies with the top 20% of salaries even before the COVID-19 pandemic, but in 2020 with the pandemic, the difference became more pronounced. There is a clear trend that the ratio of telecommuting users is high [5].

The purpose of this paper is to conduct a questionnaire analysis of the employees of major Japanese IT companies, and to consider the issues and measures for improving productivity and performance using telework.

2 Literature Review

2.1 Definition of Telework

According to Japan's Ministry of Internal Affairs and Communications and Ministry of Health, Labor, and Welfare, telework is defined a flexible work style that makes effective use of time and place using information and communication technology (ICT). It is a coined word that combines Tele (remote) and Work (work). In short, it is to work using ICT in a place away from the home office. (Omitted) Telework can be categorized from the perspective of "working place" into "telecommuting" working at home, "satellite office work" working at a facility other than the home base, and "mobile work" working while traveling or on the go [6, 7].

2.2 Issues Faced by Japanese Companies When Introducing Telework

With the outbreak of the COVID-19 pandemic, many companies moved to introduce telework all at once, but the introduction and implementation did not all proceed smoothly.

The first problem is a labor management.

According to [8], the Japanese-style personnel system based on lifetime employment and seniority, which has emphasized face-to-face human relationships, is not suitable for employment forms such as telework that do not necessarily involve face-to-face management. Said to have a negative impact on the adoption of In addition, [9] cites "unclear job scope" and "evaluation of human resources by emotional evaluation" as factors that hinder the introduction of telework.

These are also characteristics of Japanese-style management, and it can be said that membership-based employment, which has been the source of the strength of Japanese companies, has become a major obstacle in terms of labor management when telework is introduced.

The second is the security problem [10]. Leakage of information and confidential information, unauthorized access to servers, and infection by computer viruses are major obstacles to promoting telework.

When working remotely from home, the security system at home is generally weaker than the security level in the office. There is a problem that it must rely heavily on the knowledge and actions of individual employees regarding security.

The third problem is whether employees can carry out their duties autonomously and efficiently. This problem is a theme that is directly related to the awareness of the problem in this paper.

The problems of business execution by individual employees using telework are (1) the IT environment for telework at home, (2) the level of security knowledge and IT literacy of employees, and (3) the efficiency and effectiveness of telework and (4) incentives for employees to use telework.

(1) Regarding the telework environment at home, it has been pointed out that the space at Japanese home is small, there is no dedicated space, and the Internet environment is inadequate [11], so corporate support is important.
(2) If the level of security awareness and IT literacy among employees is insufficient, it is necessary to raise the level through in-house training, etc. In addition, each employee must be aware of the benefits of using telework. Is important [12].
(3) In order to promote work efficiently and effectively using telework, it is necessary to develop an appropriate working environment. In addition to the hardware development of the telework environment for employees mentioned in (1) and the use of technology tools to facilitate telecommuting, it is important to manage working

hours during telework and develop business processes [2]. Employees are also very interested in how telework will affect their performance evaluation [11], and in the case of Japanese companies, membership-type employment with ambiguous job scopes is also a hindrance.

(4) The extent to which employees are willing to use telework largely depends on the relative comparison of advantages and disadvantages compared to office work. According to [12], it is to what extent telework is more advantageous in terms of work and life. For example, the characteristics of the employee's work (whether there is a lot of work that involves teamwork, whether there is a lot of work that aims to develop new business and increase added value, whether there is a lot of creative work that requires originality and ingenuity, and whether there is a lot of work that is done in cooperation with people outside the company (e.g., is there a large number of employees in the workplace), the introduction of new technologies, the effectiveness of workplace communication, clarification of duties and responsibilities, work engagement, and a self-transforming workplace atmosphere [13].

2.3   Introduction of Telework and Herzberg's Theory of Motivation

Several studies have been conducted on the relationship between labor productivity and the introduction rate of telework. In general, it has been reported that the introduction of telework improves labor productivity.

According to [3], telework enables companies and workers to rely on what his Eberly, Haskel, and Mizen (2021) called "latent capital," represented by housing and workers' internet connectivity. Made the economy more resilient to the pandemic. This mobilization of "potential capital" could have contributed up to 10% of GDP across Japan, the UK, Germany, Spain, France, Italy, and the US (Eberly, Haskel and Mizen, 2021).

In addition, a study conducted in 2015 targeting Japanese companies [14] confirmed that the introduction of telework improved productivity and job satisfaction.

Frederick Herzberg has proposed a theory of what causes job satisfaction and job dissatisfaction [15]. According to this, human job satisfaction does not increase when a certain factor is satisfied and decreases when it is not satisfied and the factor (hygiene factor) related to "dissatisfaction" are different things.

In this paper, based on Herzberg's theory of motivation mentioned above, we investigate incentives for employees of major IT companies to use telework.

3   Purpose and Method of Questionnaire Survey

In this study, we conducted two questionnaires. (Conducted from December 15, 2022, to January 15, 2023 for employees of major Japanese IT companies (Hitachi, Toshiba, IBM, and Ricoh affiliates)).

In the first survey, we conducted a questionnaire survey of employees working at major IT companies and analyzed the correlation between the work environment and productivity awareness before and after the COVID-19 pandemic. At this time, we created a questionnaire based on Herzberg's theory of motivation to improve the work environment (labor management, work environment → motivational factors, organizational culture → hygiene factors) and productivity questionnaires.

Herzberg's two-factor theory is a theory that analyzes the factors that cause job satisfaction and dissatisfaction.

In the two-factor theory, a person's motivation factor is.

• Motivational factors (motivators)
• Hygiene Factor

It is said that it should be divided into two [15].

Motivators are "factors that cause job satisfaction," and specifically include the following.

• Sympathy of ambition
• Awareness of connection with friends
• A sense of accomplishment
• Approval from others
• Challenging job
• Self-growth
• A sense of mission for the role
• Approval from society and family

Hygiene Factors Refers to factors related to dissatisfaction at work.

• Easy-to-understand personnel system
• Fair wage system
• Working conditions, social insurance
• Working hours, number of days off
• Stable salary level
• Clear rules of employment
• Comfortable work environment
• Welfare system, etc.

In the questionnaire survey, based on the above, correlation analysis was performed using Excel for each questionnaire item, using the question item "Do you feel that telework has increased productivity compared to face-to-face work?" 77 survey respondents (60 valid responses). Respondents with less than three years of service were excluded to compare face-to-face before COVID-19 with telework that began during the COVID-19 period. There were 60 respondents who answered 3 years or more. There were 25 questions about problems that arise in telework, which is a free description.

In the second survey, a total of 26 questions were asked based on the three major items of "labor management," "work environment," and "organizational culture," extracted from previous research [16, 17] in papers and reports. We created it and conducted a questionnaire survey.

4   Questionnaire Results and Discussion

In this survey, the subjects of the questionnaire survey were employees of major Japanese IT companies (Fig. 1).

In addition, although labor management is also at a high level, there were more results-based responses than seniority-based systems, and it was confirmed that fewer employees were considering changing jobs. This may be because employees are generally satisfied with the status quo, or they do not actively change the status quo (Table 1).

Regarding the organizational culture, support systems for childcare, etc. and measures against harassment are being handled, but even major IT companies still have opportunities to use meetings and seals that feel useless. This indicates that they have not been able to fully adapt to the working environment, work environment, and corporate culture [18] that contribute to productivity improvement (Table 2).

Table 1. Survey Attribute information

Working years	Less than 3 years	17
	3–10 years	6
	10–20 years	20
	20–30 years	17
	30 +	17
	Total	77
Age	20–30	5
	30–40	13
	40–50	20
	Over 50	21
	Total	59
Occupation	Manufacturing/SE	29
	Sales/Marketing	8
	Management	18
	Others	2
	Total	57
Director	Position in charge	24
	Manager	11
	Head of Department/General Manager	11
	Manager/Executive	2
	Others	2
	Total	50
Employment format	Regular	60
	Non-regular	0
	Total	60

Table 2. 1st Questionnaire items related to attributes (18 items) and response results

Answer item	Answer item	Answer result
1. How much ratio did you use telework out of your total work hours (2021)?	100% to 75%	14
	75% to 50%	5
	50% to 25%	9
	25% to 0%	32
	Total	60
2. How much ratio did you use telework out of your total work hours (2020)?	100% to 75%	34
	75% to 50%	10
	50% to 25%	9
	25% to 0%	6
	Total	53
3. How much ratio did you use telework out of your total work hours (2019)?	100% to 75%	32
	75% to 50%	11
	50% to 25%	8
	25% to 0%	8
	Total	59
4. Were there more internal meetings than you thought were appropriate before COVID-19?	Many	5
	Somewhat high	36
	Slightly less	11
	Less	1
	Not implemented	2
	Total	55
5. How much has the time of internal meetings changed in a week before and after the introduction of telework?	Reduced by 2 h or more	0
	1 ~ 2 h decrease	5
	1 ~ 2-h increase	6
	Increased by 2 h or more	12
	No change	33
	Total	56
6. Has the amount of internal work increased due to the introduction of telework?	1.26 times more	4
	1.01–1.25 times more	10
	0.76–0.99 times less	7
	0.75 or less	1
	No change	33
	Total	55
7. How much has your internal work time changed in a week before and after the introduction of telework?	Reduced by 2 h or more	4

(*continued*)

Table 2. (*continued*)

Answer item	Answer item	Answer result
	1 ~ 2 h decrease	20
	1 ~ 2-h increase	14
	Increased by 2 h or more	5
	Not implemented	14
	Total	57
8. Is communication within the company sufficient compared to before Corona?	Is enough	4
	Sufficient to some extent	19
	Somewhat inadequate	27
	Poor	10
	Total	60
9. What is the evaluation of work in telework?	Emphasis on working hours	0
	Somewhat focused on working hours	2
	More focused on results	31
	Emphasis on results	24
	Not rated	2
	Total	59
10. Is fairness maintained in job evaluation between office work and telework?	Kept	40
	Maintained to some extent	12
	Somewhat unretained	2
	Not kept	2
	Not rated	3
	Total	59
11. Do you agree with the evaluation of your work compared to before Corona?	Convinced	29
	Somewhat satisfied	26
	Somewhat unconvinced	2
	Not convinced	0
	Total	57
12. Do you think the company's telework system, goals, and effects are clear?	Clear	28
	Somewhat clear	28
	Somewhat abstract	2
	Abstract	0
	Total	58
13. When you telework, do you clearly separate your work time and your own time?	Divided	34
	Divided to some extent	18

(*continued*)

Table 2. (*continued*)

Answer item	Answer item	Answer result
	Somewhat undivided	3
	Not divided	4
	Total	59
14. How do you manage your time when teleworking?	Determined by the company	5
	Decide for yourself	37
	Decided by myself and the company	16
	I work without deciding	0
	Total	58
15. Do you feel more tired from telework than face-to-face work?	Increased	5
	Increased to some extent	15
	Slightly decreased	26
	Decreased	12
	Total	58
16. Has the amount of unproductive work (Irrelevant meetings, too much confirmation work, etc.) changed before and after the introduction of telework?	Increased	5
	Increased to some extent	25
	Slightly decreased	23
	Decreased	3
	Total	56
17. Do you think that the production volume per person has increased in the new business after Corona?	Increased	6
	Increased to some extent	32
	Slightly decreased	16
	Decreased	1
	Total	55
18. Do you feel more productive working remotely than working face-to-face?	Up	6
	Up to some extent	32
	Slightly down	14
	Down	3
	Total	55

As a result of the correlation analysis, no clear correlation could be confirmed. Among them, Figs. 2, 3 and 4 showed a slight correlation.

However, from the question items set in this questionnaire survey, it can be said that there is no clear correlation between the work environment before and after the corona crisis and the awareness of productivity due to telework.

What are the possible reasons for this?

H1: The work environment for telework at companies has not changed explicitly before and after the COVID-19 pandemic.

H2: Even within the same company, due to differences in generations and IT literacy,

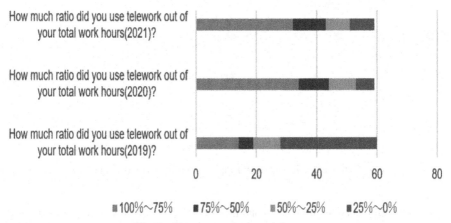

Fig. 1. Usage rate of telework by year

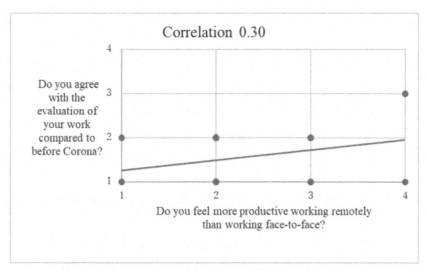

Fig. 2. Impact of Telework on Employee Productivity (Finding #1)

There are large individual differences in attitudes and results regarding the use of telework.

This indicates that "employees who feel that their productivity has increased through the use of telework are more satisfied with their work evaluations" "Employees who felt that their productivity increased due to the use of telework had less fatigue due to the use of telework.", "Employees who felt that their productivity increased through the use of telework had smoother communication within the company".

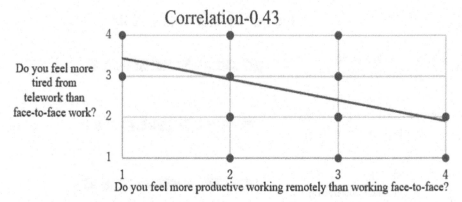

Fig. 3. Impact of Telework on Employee Productivity (Finding #2)

However, the absolute number of samples in this questionnaire survey is small, and it is necessary to increase the number of samples and conduct a detailed examination in the future.

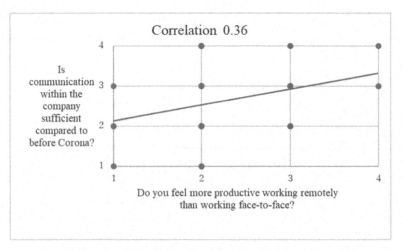

Fig. 4. Impact of Telework on Employee Productivity (Finding #3)

5   Conclusion

The global COVID-19 pandemic, which began at the end of 2019, has wrought havoc on societies, industries, and people's lives around the world. Many companies took advantage of this opportunity to quickly introduce telework, and as a result, the usage rate of telework, which had been stagnant until now, increased sharply.

Under these circumstances, major Japanese IT companies introduced telework relatively quickly compared to many other companies in other countries and Japan, demonstrating the resilience of their operations.

However, even in major IT companies, there are still many opportunities to use unnecessary meetings and stamps, and the transformation to an environment where employees can actively use telework is still halfway through.

To improve the productivity and performance of employees by using telework in the future, it will be necessary to reshape the working environment surrounding telework.

In future research, we would like to greatly expand the number of samples from this perspective and further explore medium- to long-term changes in the work environment that are suitable for telework.

References

1. Ministry of Internal Affairs and Communications, p.18 (2010a). Ministry of Internal Affairs and Communications, p.37 (2011)
2. Nikkei Smart Work Management Study Group. Report on Smart Work Management, 7 (2022). 5 July 2022
3. Criscuolo, C., et al.: OECD productivity working papers. The Role of Telework for Productivity During and Post Covid-19: Results From an Oecd Survey Among Managers and Workers, vol. 31, p. 14 (2021)
4. Eurofound. Living, Working and COVID-19, COVID-19 series, Publication Office of the European Union, Luxembourg (2020).https://doi.org/10.2806/467608
5. Nikkei Smart Work Management Study Group. Report on Smart Work Management 7 (2022). 31 July 2022
6. Ministry of Internal Affairs and Communications. The White Paper on Information and Communications in Japan 2021 (2021)
7. The Telework Comprehensive Portal. https://telework.mhlw.go.jp/telework/about/
8. Shimozaki, C.: Conformity and contradiction between telework and Japanese personnel system reform. Kokumin Keizai Zasshi **184**(1), 1–17 (2001)
9. Sato, A.: Telework and workplace transformation, the Japan Institute of Labor **627,** 58–66 (2012)
10. Furukawa, Y.: Telework and the productivity of white-collar workers. J. Policy Studies **39** (2011)
11. Nikkei Smart Work Management Study Group.Report on Smart Work Management 7 (2022). 7 July 2022
12. Sahori, D.: A Study on Implementation of an Organizational Telework. Japan Telework Soc. **1**(1), 79–96 (2002)
13. Nikkei Smart Work Management Study Group. Report on Smart Work Management, vol. 7, pp. 10 (2022)
14. Sato, S., Nakamura, H.: A study on the introduction of telework-exploring the relationship between work style and productivity improvement. Keio Business School. Japan (2015)
15. Herzberg, F.: Motivation to Work (English Edition), Routledge (2017)
16. Doshisha University. Study on the Improvement Effect of Productivity and Treatment of Japanese Software Engineers: Achievements Report on the Use of a Framework for International Comparative Analysis with Asian and Western Countries (2016)
17. Okamuro, H.: The effect of inter-firm business collaboration: a comparative analysis of small and large companies using individual data. J. Bus. Res. **10**, 35-54 (2007)
18. Saloner, G., Shepard, A., Podolny, J.: Strategic management, John Wiley & Sons, Inc., 89 (2005)

Digital Transformation and Innovation

National Innovation Systems, Knowledge Resources and International Competitiveness

Magdalena Marczewska[1]([envelope]) and Marzenna Anna Weresa[2]

[1] University of Warsaw, Warsaw, Poland
mmarczewska@wz.uw.edu.pl
[2] Warsaw School of Economics, Warsaw, Poland
mweres@sgh.waw.pl

Abstract. In the contemporary world economy, understood as a set of mutual connections and interdependencies, innovations are crucial for economic growth and competitiveness. Internationalization and globalization processes in the world economy also concern the innovativeness of economies, and are visible in international use of technologies developed within national innovation systems,globalization of the creation and implementation of innovations, international (global) cooperation in research and development and innovation activities, international (global) protection of intellectual property. The interdependencies between countries in terms of their innovative activity are gradually deepening. This overlaps with the links and interdependencies that exist between the national innovation system of a given country and regional, metropolitan and industry systems.

The purpose of this study is to analyze the existing links and interdependencies between the national innovation systems of various countries and to determine their impact on international competitiveness. The research focuses on national innovation systems and their international linkages, knowledge resources and international competitiveness. It proposes a conceptual approach to characterize and study the interdependencies indicated above. With reference to theoretical approaches, it shapes a framework that could be the basis for further empirical analyses.

Keywords: National innovation systems · Knowledge resources · Competitiveness · Innovation

1 Introduction

In the contemporary world economy, understood as a set of mutual connections and interdependencies, innovations are crucial for economic growth and competitiveness. This then has already been widely emphasized by both theoretical and empirical works (e.g. [1–10]). Internationalization and globalization processes in the world economy also concern the innovativeness of economies, and are visible in:

- international use of technologies developed within national innovation systems,
- globalization of the creation and implementation of innovations,

© The Author(s), under exclusive license to Springer Nature Switzerland AG 2023
L. Uden and I-H. Ting (Eds.): KMO 2023, CCIS 1825, pp. 101–114, 2023.
https://doi.org/10.1007/978-3-031-34045-1_10

- international (global) cooperation in research and development and innovation activities,
- international/global protection of intellectual property [8].

This means that the interdependencies between countries in terms of their innovative activity are gradually deepening. This overlaps with the links and interdependencies that exist between the national innovation system of a given country and regional, metropolitan and industry systems. These two types of compounds, i.e.: (1) between different types of innovation systems functioning within the national innovation system of a given country, (2) between different countries, and more precisely between their national innovation systems, may affect changes in the international competitiveness of economies.

The purpose of this study is to analyze one of the types of interdependence mentioned above, i.e. the existing links between the national innovation systems of various countries and to determine their impact on the international competitiveness of countries. The research focuses on national innovation systems and their international linkages, knowledge resources and international competitiveness. It proposes a conceptual approach to characterize and study the interdependencies indicated above. With reference to theoretical approaches, it shapes a framework that could be the basis for further empirical analyses.

2 Methodology

This exploratory, conceptual paper is based on desk research methods. First, it uses a semi-systematic literature review following Snyder's approach [11] with the goal to describe national innovation systems and their international linkages, knowledge resources and international competitiveness. Then, the narrative synthesis approach is applied to analyze most relevant papers selected for this semi-systematic literature review. This analysis was aimed at indicating the interdependence between innovative activity carried out in different countries and the competitiveness of economies. An extensive literature review allowed to conceptualize these relationships. Last, the conceptual approach has been complemented by an analysis of the results of previous empirical research conducted by various authors using different methodological approaches.

3 Knowledge Resources in the Internationalization of National Innovation Systems

There are many dimensions describing the relationship between the innovativeness of countries and their international competitiveness. These interdependencies can be included in the analytical framework referring to the national innovation system (NSI). This concept integrates the achievements of evolutionary economics relating to innovation with concepts based on the analysis of interactive learning processes, complementing them with institutional threads. The national innovation system can be defined as a system of connections and mutual interactions between entities using the knowledge resources accumulated in the economy, operating within a specific institutional order applicable in a given country and participating in the creation and commercialization of new knowledge [8]. Such an approach to innovation processes from the perspective of the entire economy allows them to be related to the concept of competitiveness of economies.

When looking for interdependence in the innovative activity of countries, one should take into account the growing internationalization of national innovation systems, which is conditioned by the openness of these systems to cooperation with foreign countries. Comparisons of the degree of interdependence existing between innovation systems from different countries can be made at the level of countries, regions and industries [12]. Focusing on the national (macroeconomic) dimension of innovation systems, the focus is on interactions between NSIs from different countries. Internationalization processes cover all components of the innovation system, i.e. domestic enterprises, universities and other scientific units, administration that shapes regulations in the sphere of science and technology (including innovation policy). The openness of national innovation systems is determined by the intensity of links between their individual elements and foreign countries [13]. Referring to the indicators of internationalization and globalization of innovative activity presented above, at least three main dimensions of interdependence between national innovation systems can be indicated. These include:

- Diffusion of innovations on an international scale,
- International cooperation in research and innovation activities,
- International protection of intellectual property.

The degree of interdependence between the national innovation system and the international environment is conditioned, among others, by country's level of development, its innovative potential, and technological specialization. Small countries tend to be more dependent on international flows of technical knowledge. They also apply different mechanisms of shaping cooperation with foreign countries, including interdependence in the field of patent activity, developing publications, and the movement of scientific personnel [14, 15].

Table 1 summarizes the national and international (global) elements of innovation systems, which are closely related.

Comparative research on the national innovation systems of various countries and their degree of dependence on the international environment indicate a significant diversification of the internationalization of individual NSI areas. NSI's openness to international cooperation in scientific research is relatively high, while cooperation with foreign countries in innovative activities or the application of new technologies in practice is undertaken with greater caution, as these are areas of direct competition of enterprises on the global market. In addition, empirical research on the interdependence between national innovation systems shows that public sector research units and non-profit organizations relatively more often undertake scientific and research cooperation with foreign entities than private sector entities. This is to some extent due to the support for the internationalization of the R&D sphere by means of innovation policy tools [14, 16]. There are two basic models of internationalization of NSI, which are related to science and innovation policy of a given country. These are:

1. A model of controlled opening of the innovation system,

2. Liberal model.

In the model of the controlled opening of the NSI, the innovation policy is aimed at stimulating the absorption of technologies from abroad, but at the same time actions are taken to significantly protect the country's own scientific and technological thought. The liberal model, on the other hand, lacks state interference in shaping cooperation with foreign countries in science, technology and innovation. The connections of national innovation systems and their individual elements with the international environment are formed spontaneously and are the effect of market forces.

An example of a country that applies the model of controlled opening of the innovation system is Japan. This was especially evident in the Japanese science and technology policy in the last two decades of the 20th century. The aim of this policy was to absorb foreign technical thought, while at the same time striving to limit the influence of foreign entities on the technological development of this country was visible [17]. A similar model is used by other Asian countries, e.g. South Korea or China [18].

The interdependencies between national innovation systems in Europe are shaped differently, based on the model of internationalization similar to the liberal one. For example, the priorities of the European Research Area (ERA) include the free movement of qualified scientific staff, effective transfer of knowledge, as well as the opening of innovation systems between ERA countries and the rest of the world [19].

Table 1. National and international elements of innovation systems - synthesis. Source: adapted from [8].

National	Transnational/Global
General structure of the innovation system	
Differences between countries in the historical development of innovation corresponding to different institutional factors in individual countries	Worldwide trajectories of technological development
System entities	
National enterprises, educational and research organizations, local administration units shaping innovation policy	Transnational corporations, international organizations (e.g. World Intellectual Property Organization - WIPO, World Trade Organization - WTO, international research consortia)
System institutions	
National and local regulations - legal standards, formal and informal rules (customs) regarding development of technologies, markets and industries; national and local regulations on education system and conducting R&D works	International and supranational regulations regarding markets (e.g. competition rules, regulations on intellectual property rights), as well as technologies and industries (e.g. technical standards, security standards); coordination of innovation policy

(continued)

Table 1. (*continued*)

National	Transnational/Global
Knowledge resources	
Scientific papers published in local languages and journals; national patents and trademarks; local know-how etc	Scientific publications in international journals; internationally granted patents (PCT); foreign patents obtained locally, etc
Interactions and connections of entities and institutions in the process of creating, sharing and using new knowledge	
Intra-national transfer and diffusion of technology; cooperation of national units in R&D and innovative activity, internal flow of R&D personnel	International transfer and diffusion of technology; international cooperation in research and innovation activities; joint patents of domestic and foreign entities, foreign licenses, international mobility of R&D personnel - international scientific networks

Summing up the analysis of the interdependence of national innovation systems in the global economy, it can be noted that the tightening of links between them results from the globalization of research and innovation activities. Globalization processes concern not only companies operating on international markets, but also universities, research centers as well as inventors and innovators. Competing on foreign markets involves not only products, but also resources (including knowledge resources). In addition, the development of information and communication technologies (ICT) accelerates the international knowledge flow and facilitates access to its resources accumulated in other countries. Similar processes can also be observed in relation to universities - international research cooperation is developing dynamically.

In this context, the question arises how to measure these growing interdependencies between national innovation systems? Attempts to quantify them were undertaken by [13, 16]. Traditionally used measures are the volume of international turnover in licenses and patents, the balance of technological turnover with foreign countries, the volume of exports of high-tech goods, the international mobility of scientists and doctoral students [13, 16]. Other measures of interdependence between innovation systems from different countries include, for example, cooperation with foreign countries in the field of scientific publications, the intensity of cooperation with foreign countries in the preparation of scientific publications, joint patents of domestic and foreign inventors, the extent of international cooperation in innovative activity [8, 20–22]. Table 2 presents a list of various measures allowing to determine the degree of interdependence between innovation systems.

The measures of interdependence between the national innovation systems of various countries presented in Table 2 do not provide an exhaustive list of all possible ways of measuring this phenomenon. These basic measures can help to create indexes, and their changes over time can be supplemented. The construction of indicators in empirical analyzes depends on the selection of the analyzed sample of countries, and their practical application depends on the availability of statistical data.

Table 2. Measures of interdependence between national innovation systems of different countries. Source: own elaboration based on the author's earlier works (cf. [8]).

Main dimensions of interdependence between national innovation systems	Selected measures
Diffusion of innovations on an international scale	- Exports of high-tech products as a percentage of exports of a given country/region/industry - The share of patents of a given country in the total number of patents in the world - The share of scientific publications of a given country in the total number of publications in the world - Relation of expenditure on R&D from foreign sources to domestic expenditure - R&D expenditures of transnational corporations - Foreign personnel employed in the R&D sector in relation to all R&D employees - Foreign doctoral students as a percentage of all doctoral students - Liabilities and receivables from international trade in patents as a percentage of national expenditure on R&D or in relation to GDP - The degree of coverage of a given country's expenses for international license purchases to the proceeds from this title
International cooperation in research and innovation activities	- The number of innovative companies that have started cooperation with foreign countries in the area of innovation as a percentage of all innovative companies in a given country/region/industry - Share of patent applications prepared in international cooperation in the total number of applications (%) - Number of research projects carried out by domestic entities in cooperation with foreign countries - Number of scientific publications prepared in cooperation with foreign partners per capita - Number of foreign scientists and doctoral students in a given country in relation to the number of domestic scientists and doctoral students working abroad (in total and by industry/technology) - Number of cooperation agreements regarding the exchange of technical information, know-how, equipment (in total and by industry/technology)

(*continued*)

Table 2. (*continued*)

Main dimensions of interdependence between national innovation systems	Selected measures
International/ global intellectual property protection	- Number of patent applications in the international procedure (PCT) in relation to GDP (total and/or by industries/technologies) or per capita - Patent applications in the international procedure (PCT) in the fields of high technology per 1 million inhabitants - Dynamics of patent applications filed by residents of a given country under the international PCT procedure (total and/ or by industry/technology) - Share of international PCT patent applications from a given country/region by field (industry) in the total number of world patents in a given field (industry) - The number of patent applications in the Triad countries (*triadic patent families*) in relation to the number of inhabitants

4   Innovation Systems and International Competitiveness

The interdependencies between the national innovation systems of various countries, which have been synthetically presented above, mirror the competitiveness of economies understood as "the ability to improve the standard of living of the society, strengthen the position on foreign markets and increase the attractiveness of a given territory for foreign investments" [23]. Comparing the definition of the national innovation and competitiveness system, it can be seen that some elements of innovation systems, e.g. technology, innovation, human capital, institutions are factors of competitiveness of economies, while entities that are of key importance for the functioning of innovation systems, such as: enterprises, research units, administration bodies, directly and indirectly affect competitiveness. Therefore, the concepts of the innovation system and the competitiveness of countries have a number of common elements, which implies their mutual two-way interactions. The direction of these influences can be traced based on the concept of the innovative capacity of countries, which combines the micro- and macroeconomic elements of innovation research, integrating the achievements of economics and management sciences [24]. This concept refers to three trends in innovation research [24]:

- so-called the "new" theory of economic growth, in which knowledge and innovation are endogenous factors [1],
- the concept of a national innovation system [25],
- the cluster - based concept of the competitive advantage of nations [3].

National innovative capacity means the ability of a given country to create and commercialize new, previously unknown solutions (innovations) in the long term [24]. The key aspects included in the definition of innovative capacity are the originality of innovations on a global scale, their creation in a given economy in a continuous manner over a long period of time and the use of novelties in business practice (commercialization of innovations).

In this approach, the national innovative capacity includes the location conditions of innovative activity that determine the resources possessed, as well as the activities of the countries' innovation policy for the creation and improvement of these resources [24]. The national innovation capacity is affected by many different mutually influencing factors, such as the country's tangible and intangible resources, the stream of investments that allows not only the use of existing resources, but also the improvement of their quality and the creation of new resources. An important element of the national innovative capacity is the state policy on science, technology and innovation. It determines the scope of public support for research and development as well as innovative activities of enterprises, creates a regulatory framework for the protection of intellectual property, and indicates which areas (or industries) are considered priority in a given country.

Figure 1 illustrates the conceptual framework of national innovation capacity in the context of countries' competitiveness.

The determinants of the national innovative capacity of countries can be divided into three broad categories [24]:

- innovation infrastructure common to the entire economy (resources, institutions),
- specific environment for innovation created within clusters,
- quality of links (interactions) between innovative infrastructure and clusters.

One issue imprecisely explained in the model, is its connection with the competitive advantages of nations described by the Porter's Diamond Theory of National Advantage [3]. On the one hand, the existence of a bilateral interdependence between the national innovative capacity and competitiveness can be discerned (cf. Figure 1), but on the other hand, the existing feedback between the two phenomena cannot be precisely defined. Nevertheless, the model helps to understand national innovation system and is widely applied in empirical research [26].

The concept of the national innovative capacity shows the relationships between the above-mentioned determinants of the country's innovativeness in the form of a function based on the function of knowledge production [24]:

$$A^{\cdot}j,t = \delta j,t(X^{INF}j,t \, , \, Y^{CLUS}j,t \, , Z^{LINK}j,t \,) \, H^{A\lambda}j,t \, A^{\phi}j,t \tag{1}$$

where:

A˙j, t - streams of globally new technologies from country j in year t,

$H^{A\lambda}$j,t - human capital and material resources in the research sector of a given economy,

A^{ϕ}j,t- accumulated knowledge in country j,

X^{INF}j,t - resources allocated for the implementation of the innovation policy,

Y^{CLUS}j,t - a specific environment for innovation created within industrial clusters,

Z^{LINK}j,t - links between innovative infrastructure and industrial clusters.

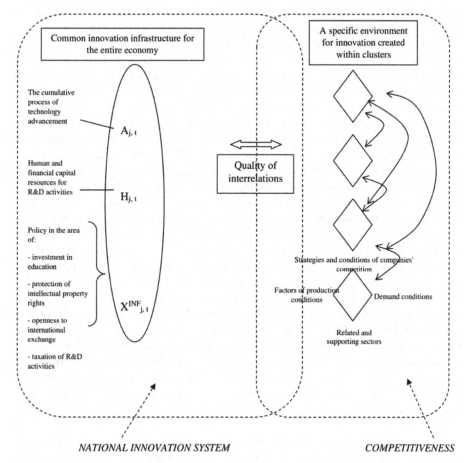

Fig. 1. National innovation capacity: linking the concept of innovation systems with competitiveness (Source: elaboration based on [24]; dashed lines and elements written in italics are elements added by the author's)

All variables (except qualitative variables or percentage variables) are expressed in logarithmic form. Empirical verification of the model was carried out for 17 OECD countries and covered the period 1973–1996. Due to the fact that the description of function variables is quite general, their operationalization required the adoption of specific measures for which statistical data are available. The stream of world-new technologies developed in a given country was described by means of international patent activity, assuming a 3-year lag between the factors determining the national innovative capacity and patent indicators. Independent variables describing the determinants of innovative capacity are a combination of indicators characterizing the development of science and technology and the state of human capital resources, as well as managers' ratings collected in an anonymous survey. Indicators based on statistical data include expenditure on R&D, employment in the science and technology sector, expenditure on education related to GDP. Qualitative variables based on managers' assessments (on a scale of 1 to 10) are: the level of openness of the economy, the degree of protection of intellectual property, the scope of antitrust policy, the availability of venture capital [24].

This approach is an attempt to quantify qualitative and quantitative factors in order to determine their impact on the innovativeness of the country. It allows to analyze whether differences in innovation intensity and R&D productivity can be explained by sources of national innovation capacity. However, this model has some limitations. Such a limitation is the assumption that only innovations that are unique on a global scale are taken into account, which is a narrowing down of the definition of innovation adopted in the Oslo Manual, according to which an innovation is a new or significantly improved solution being a novelty on a market or company scale [27]. Therefore, the model does not take into account the transfer of technology from abroad and innovations introduced as imitation/adaptation of foreign solutions. Moreover, considering the number of patents as the dependent variable excludes from the model innovations that have not been patented (e.g. organizational innovations are not patentable), but includes patents that may never be commercialized. The model could also be supplemented with a variable describing the creativity of societies - e.g. the measure could be expenditure on education in a given country as a percentage of national income. Creativity and the ability to commercialize ideas are recognized in the literature as key features of innovative companies [28]. Moreover, the model lacks internal determinants of creativity of innovator, such as intuition, psychological and personality traits, knowledge and training [29] were also not included in the model. Creativity is essential in the process of economic development, which, according to Florida's concept of the creative class, follows the 3T model, i.e. a combination of technology, talent and tolerance [30]. The growing importance of competition in terms of attracting talent from abroad cannot be overlooked. A creative economy that can base competitiveness on innovation, uses the achievements of science, technology and design, and fosters the development of creativity in every area of activity [31].

Despite its limitations, the model proposed by [24], and especially its conceptual basis, is an approach often used for empirical research on the links between innovation and competitiveness. However, when conducting empirical research and interpreting their results, adjustments should be made to the innovation indicators used. Those that were used in earlier periods of development of the global economy may turn out to be useless and inadequate today [32].

The determinants of the national innovative capacity defined by the groups of factors indicated above are closely related to the concept of competitiveness. Furman and Hayes

[33] using a modified version of this model conducted empirical research for 29 developed countries[1] in the period 1978–1999, assuming as a dependent variable the number of patents obtained by inventors from the analyzed countries in the United States Patent Office. The estimation of the model allowed to distinguish four groups of countries: leaders, moderate innovators (*middle tier*), innovation-weaker countries (*third tier*) and emerging stars of innovation (*emerging innovators*). The research proves that innovative leadership relies mainly on investments in R&D and innovative activities, as well as the quality of innovation policy. Interestingly, the research results prove that countries with high openness to international trade and various international interdependencies in country's innovation system has negative impact on the number of patents obtained abroad (in this case in the United States) [33]. This comes as no surprise, as global cooperation allows easier access to obtaining foreign solutions through licensing or direct purchase.

Another example of the research based on the model described above with relevant modification is a study in which five countries from East Asia were analyzed. Here additional variables were included in the model, such as technological specialization in selected key areas [34]. The results regarding factors determining the national innovative capacity and competitiveness of these countries are in principle similar to those obtained by [33] for highly developed countries, with the increase of public sector expenditure on R&D playing a much greater role in Asian countries. The difference also concerns the importance of interdependence between innovation systems measured by openness to international trade. In the case of the analyzed five Asian countries, a positive, albeit very slight, impact of increasing openness on the innovativeness of the country was shown [34]. Further analyzes conducted for China, however, showed that the role of public expenditure on R&D was not crucial in this case, and the impact of the level of openness on international patent activity turned out to be positive, but it could only be demonstrated when adding to the model a variable describing protection of intellectual property (which turned out to have a negative impact) [35]. Comparing China with other Asian tigers allows to formulate a conclusion that as a higher level of innovation is achieved, there will be a gradual change in the importance of individual factors determining the national innovation capacity [35]. Further analysis of China's economy, its innovative capacity and competitiveness conducted for a later period (1999–2012) proved that the opening of the Chinese economy and the increase in international interdependence of the Chinese innovation system, especially in relation to certain industries, allowed the improvement of the country's national innovation capacity and its international competitiveness [36].

Another approach to analyze the relationship between innovation and competitiveness enriching the concept of Furman, Porter and Stern [24] is the use of the *European Innovation Scoreboard* (more on this methodology in [37]). It has been recently used to analyze the impact of welfare state systems on innovation performance and competitiveness [38]. Another alternative is to combine the concept of the national innovation capacity with the competitiveness research methodology proposed by the World Economic Forum (WEF) and used in the *Global Competitiveness Report* [39]. Use of the WEF methodology allowed for the development of the innovation capacity index, but it does not include the interdependence between national innovation systems in a direct

---

[1] Ultimately, due to lack of data, the sample amounted to 23 countries (cf. [30]).

way, but rather serves to analyze the position of individual countries in the international innovation ranking (cf. e.g. [40]).

5   Conclusion

The results of this semi-systematic literature review aimed at indicating the interdependence between innovative activity carried out in different countries and the competitiveness of economies can be summarized by juxtaposing the indicators of the competitiveness of the economy, including the ability to innovate [41] with the factors determining national capacity to innovate according to the model by Furman, Porter and Stern [24]. The summary of various indicators of international competitiveness of the economy and determinants of innovation capacity are presented in Fig. 2.

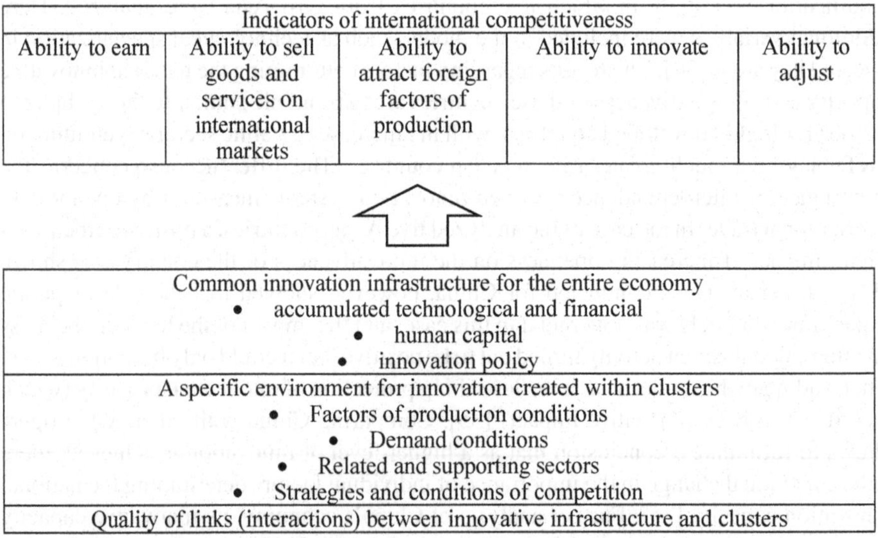

Indicators of international competitiveness				
Ability to earn	Ability to sell goods and services on international markets	Ability to attract foreign factors of production	Ability to innovate	Ability to adjust

Common innovation infrastructure for the entire economy • accumulated technological and financial • human capital • innovation policy
A specific environment for innovation created within clusters • Factors of production conditions • Demand conditions • Related and supporting sectors • Strategies and conditions of competition
Quality of links (interactions) between innovative infrastructure and clusters

Fig. 2. Various indicators of the international competitiveness of the economy and determinants of the ability to innovate (Source: own elaboration based on [23, 40])

To sum up, based on the review of theoretical literature and previous empirical research, it can be concluded that there is a two-way relationship between the links existing between various innovation systems and the international competitiveness of economies. By synthesizing the contents of Tables 1 and 2 with the dependencies presented in Fig. 1–2, it can be concluded that the interdependencies between national innovation systems of different countries are directly reflected in such symptoms of competitiveness as the ability to sell goods and services on international markets (ability to sell) and the ability to attract foreign factors of production (ability to attract). Indirectly, however, the determinants of national innovative capacity also affect other indicators of international competitiveness, i.e. the ability to adjust and the ability to earn. This conclusion is confirmed both by theoretical concepts and the results of the empirical analyzes cited above, conducted for different countries in different periods.

Future research could provide more empirical evidence from various economies presenting this two-way relationship between the links existing between various innovation systems and the international competitiveness of economies. Such evidence from different economies would allow to better illustrate this phenomenon and provide a bigger picture of these processes. Moreover, additional empirical evidence could further support the frameworks proposed in this paper based on semi-systematic literature review.

References

1. Romer, P.: Endogenous technological change. J. Polit. Econ. **98**, 71–102 (1990)
2. Aghion, P., Howitt, P.: The Economics of Growth. MIT Press, Cambridge MA, London (2009)
3. Porter, M.: The Competitive Advantage of Nations. The Free Press, New York (1990)
4. Porter, M.: On Competition. Harvard Business School Press, Boston MA (2008)
5. Clark, J., Guy, K.: Innovation and competitiveness: a review. Technol. Anal. Strateg. Manag. **10**(3), 363–395 (1998)
6. Gomułka, S.: Theory of innovation and economic growth. Center for Social and Economic Research CASE, Warsaw (1998)
7. Kubielas, S.: Innovations and the Technological Gap in the Knowledge-Based Global Economy. University of Warsaw Publishing House, Warsaw (2009)
8. Weresa, M.A.: Innovative systems in the contemporary global economy. Wydawnictwo Naukowe PWN, Warszawa (2012)
9. Bresson, G., Etienne, J.M., Mohnen, P.: Inclusive growth and innovation: a dynamic simultaneous equations model on a panel of countries. STI Pol. Rev. **6**(1), 1–23 (2015)
10. Sener, S., Delican, D.: The causal relationship between innovation, competitiveness and foreign trade in developed and developing countries. Procedia Comput. Sci. **158**, 533–540 (2019). https://doi.org/10.1016/j.procs.2019.09.085
11. Snyder, H.: Literature review as a research methodology: an overview and guidelines. J. Bus. Res. **104**, 333–339 (2019)
12. Orlov, E.V., Machabeli, M.S., Mingaliev, K.N., Ivanova, O.E., Ivanov, M.G.: Mechanisms for increasing industry competitiveness in the context national innovation systems. In: Bogoviz, A.V., Ragulina, J.V. (eds.) Industry Competitiveness: Digitalization, Management, and Integration. ISCI 2019. LNNS, vol. 280, pp. 112–117. Springer, Cham (2021). https://doi.org/10.1007/978-3-030-80485-5_16
13. Niosi, J., Bellon, B.: The global interdependence of national innovation systems - evidence, limits, and implications. Technol. Soc. **16**(2), 173–197 (1994)
14. Carlsson, B.: Internationalization of innovation systems: a survey of the literature. Res. Policy **35**, 56–67 (2006)
15. Marčeta, M., Bojnec, Š: Innovation and competitiveness in the European Union countries. Int. J. Sustain. Econ. **13**(1), 1 (2021). https://doi.org/10.1504/ijse.2021.113316
16. Niosi, J., Bellon, B.: The globalization of national innovation systems. In: De la Mothe, J., Paquet, G. (eds.) Evolutionary Economics and the New International Political Economy 1996. Pinter, New York (1996)
17. Fransman, M.: Visions of Innovation: The Firm and Japan. OUP Catalogue, Oxford University Press (1999)
18. Weresa, M.A.: Innovation Policy. Wydawnictwo Naukowe PWN, Warszawa (2014)
19. ICF International (2015) Assessment of progress in achieving ERA in Member States and Associated Countries. ICF Consulting Services Limited, London. http://ec.europa.eu/research/era/pdf/era-communication/era_final_report_2015.pdf

20. Frietsch, R., Schuller, M. (Eds.): Competing for global innovation leadership: innovation systems and policies in the USA, Europe and Asia. Fraunhofer Institute for Systems and Innovation Research ISI, Fraunhofer Verlag, Stuttgart (2010)
21. Greenhalgh, C., Rogers, M.: Innovation, Intellectual Property and Economic Growth. Princeton University Press, Princeton, Oxford (2010)
22. Autretsch, D.B., Heblich, S., Lederer, A.: The Handbook of Research on Innovation and Entrepreneurship. E. Elgar, Cheltenham (2011)
23. Weresa, M.A.: Foreword. In: Weresa, M.A. (ed.) Poland: Competitiveness Report 2016. Importance of economic policy and institutional factors. Oficyna Wydawnicza, Warsaw School of Economics, Warsaw (2016)
24. Furman, J.L., Porter, M.E., Stern, S.: The determinants of national capacity. Res. Policy **31**, 899–933 (2002)
25. Nelson, R. (ed.): National Innovation Systems: A Comparative study. Oxford University Press, New York (1993)
26. Afzal, M., Lawrey, R., Gope, J.: Understanding national innovation system (NIS) using porter's diamond model (PDM) of competitiveness in ASEAN-05. Compet. Rev. **29**(4), 336–355 (2019). https://doi.org/10.1108/cr-12-2017-0088
27. OECD/Eurostat (2018) Oslo Manual 2018: Guidelines for Collecting, Reporting and Using Data on Innovation, 4th Edition, The Measurement of Scientific, Technological and Innovation Activities. OECD Publishing, Paris/Eurostat, Luxembourg. https://doi.org/10.1787/978926 4304604-en
28. Govindarajan, V.: The Three-Box Solution: A Strategy for Leading Innovation. Harv. Bus. Rev. (2016)
29. Poskrobko, B.: Creativity of employees as a tool for shaping the sustainable development of the company. Scientific Papers of the Wrocław University of Economics 376, Wrocław University of Economics Publishing House, Wrocław (2015)
30. Florida, R.: The Rise of the Creative Class: Revisited. Basic Books, New York (2012)
31. Florida, R.: The flight of the creative class: the new global competition for talent. Lib. Educ. **92**(3), 22–29 (2006)
32. Freeman, C., Soete, L.: Developing science, technology and innovation indicators: what we can learn from the past. Res. Policy **38**(4), 583–589 (2009)
33. Furman, J.L., Hayes, R.: Catching up or standing still? National innovation productivity among followers countries. Res. Policy **33**(9), 1329–1354 (2004)
34. Hu, M.C., Mathews, J.A.: Innovative capacity in East Asia. Res. Policy **34**, 1322–1349 (2005)
35. Hu, M.C., Mathews, J.A.: China's national innovative capacity. Res. Policy **37**, 1465–1479 (2008)
36. Usman, K., Liu, Z., Anjum, M.N., Bi, S.: The evaluation of innovation capacity of China and its influencing factors. Asian Soc. Sci. **11**(13), 180–189 (2015)
37. EIS (2016) European Innovation Scoreboard 2016. European Union, Belgium. http://ec.eur opa.eu/growth/industry/innovation/facts-figures/scoreboards/index_en.htm
38. Hajighasemi, A., Oghazi, P., Aliyari, S., Pashkevich, N.: The impact of welfare state systems on innovation performance and competitiveness: European country clusters. J. Innov. Knowl. **7**(4), 100236 (2022). https://doi.org/10.1016/j.jik.2022.100236
39. WEF (2015) Global Competitiveness Report 2015-16. World Economic Forum, Geneva
40. Mouhallab, S., Jianguo, W.: Standing points of innovation capacity. J. Econ. Bus. Manag. **4**(1), 53–57 (2016)
41. Misala, J.: Theoretical grounds of the development of long-term competitive advantages in international trade. In: Weresa, M. (eds.) Innovation, Human Capital and Trade Competitiveness. Innovation, Technology, and Knowledge Management, pp. 3–51. Springer, Cham (2014). https://doi.org/10.1007/978-3-319-02072-3_1

Exploring the Context with Factors of Cloud Computing to Digital Transformation and Innovation

Ju-Chuan Wu[1]([✉]), Shu-Mei Lee[1], and Chih-Jou Chen[2]

[1] Department of Business Administration, Feng Chia University, Taichung 40724, Taiwan
katejcwu@mail.fcu.edu.tw

[2] Department of Marketing and Logistic Management, National Penghu University of Science and Technology, Magong, Taiwan

Abstract. As Cloud computing has been considered as key pillar of the digital transformation technology ecosystem recently, this study aims to explore the factor of cloud computing to digital innovation as well as the relationships among them. A hybrid approach combining with content analysis and formal conceptual analysis was used to explore the relevant factors and context of 174 use cases which including cloud natives and startups, the research design supports the researchers on how to come across the research findings. The results indicate that relative advantages, financial costs, ease of use, security and privacy, and supplier computing support are significant in cloud computing on digital innovation, especially in startups. The context of cloud computing with our proposed research model and approach provides objective findings with evidence to demonstrate the critical position of cloud computing to digital transformation and provide managerial implications for both of academical and practical.

Keywords: Cloud computing services · Activity theory · Organizational Agility · Content Analysis · Formal Concept Analysis (FCA)

1 Introduction

Over the last decade, the evolution of Internet has enabled the information and communication technologies (ICTs) rapid growth and broaden application. Both industrial and academia has increasingly focused on enterprise transformational developments brought by ICTs. Cloud computing, one of the ICTs appeared based on the Internet and information technology (IT) industry revolution, has been seen as the critical strategy technology and the digital transformation enabler in next few years. It is indeed a technology and business composite issue. It serves as the foundation for other disruptive trends including the Internet of Things, artificial intelligence, and digital business.

Forrester report states that "Cloud computing has moved past its self-centered teenage years to become a turbocharged engine powering digital transformation around the world" [1]. Cloud computing has been established as a prominent research topic with the rise of a ubiquitous provision of computing resources over the past years. However,

© The Author(s), under exclusive license to Springer Nature Switzerland AG 2023
L. Uden and I-H. Ting (Eds.): KMO 2023, CCIS 1825, pp. 115–136, 2023.
https://doi.org/10.1007/978-3-031-34045-1_11

many researchers focus exclusively on the technical aspects of cloud computing, thereby neglecting the business opportunities and potentials cloud computing and services can offer [2, 3]. And some of scholars also mentioned that the attention to the cloud computing and services related articles have now moved from technical issues to business issues [4]. Using web crawler with Python, this study searched the key word "cloud computing" and "cloud services" through Google scholar engine on Jan 4th, 2019 and found out that only 11% was discussing on the business perspective. Apparently, there are still an obvious research gap from technology to business application.

Cloud computing have revolutionized traditional IT delivery [5] with its essential characteristics including on-demand self-service, broad network access, resource pooling, rapid elasticity, measured service [6]. With these characteristics, organizations need only low cost to achieve the effectiveness of the original information system infrastructure [3, 7]. On the other hand, the reduction in in-house ICT sunk costs and the lower risks associated with developing new ICT-related or supported projects [8] has become the chances for entrepreneurs; therefore, facilitate the famous tech unicorn [9] such as Dropbox, Airbnb, Spotify, Uber and so on. Since most of the startups nowadays are increasingly built on emerging Internet-based technologies [8, 10] Those startups become enablers of change and influence the traditional firms to start transformation [11]. Wu and Lee [12] have discussed the activities and elements which should be involved in the adoption of cloud computing and services scenarios and proposed a conceptual framework with activity theory. Therefore, this study mainly focusses on the relevance between adoption factors in startup cases in this study.

2 Literature Review

2.1 Cloud Computing and Service

National Institute of Standards and Technology (NIST) release the cloud computing definition document in 2011 and define "Cloud computing is a model for enabling ubiquitous, convenient, on-demand network access to a shared pool of configurable computing resources (e.g., networks, servers, storage, applications, and services) that can be rapidly provisioned and released with minimal management effort or service provider interaction. This cloud model is composed of five essential characteristics (on-demand self-service, broad network access, resource pooling, rapid elasticity, measured service), three service models (software as a service, platform as a service, infrastructure as a service), and four deployment models (private cloud, community cloud, public cloud, hybrid cloud) [6]." The NIST definition has been broaden adopted by scholars and become the reference for this research.

In cloud computing and services industry structure, there are several providers including application service provider (SaaS), cloud service provider (PaaS), cloud provider (IaaS), hardware provider, fundamental software provider [13]. SaaS providers offer productivity applications and programs including customer relationship management (CRM), enterprise resource planning (ERP), electronic commerce (EC), supply chain management (SCM), business intelligence (BI), office automation (OA) etc. Google

Docs and Salesforce are some well-known SaaS solutions. PaaS providers offer application developers to develop and run their software solutions on a cloud platform, typically including operating systems, a programming language execution environment, databases, and web servers. Amazon Web Services, Google's App engine, Microsoft's Azure and are early market leaders. IaaS providers offer infrastructure resources including virtual computers, servers, storage devices and data center space to support enterprise operations. Modern firms may have very large data computing and storage requirements which can be met by cloud service providers. Examples include Amazon's Elastic Compute Cloud (EC2), Simple Storage Service (S3), VMware [14–16].

The future research direction has turn from technology development to business and application such as the critical adoption factors, privacy and security, and the relevance between cloud computing and services adoption and enterprise performance [4, 17]. This study concentrates on the situation and performance after adoption and focus on the enterprises that have adopted cloud computing and services for their information systems.

In addition, cloud computing and services adoption empirical research start to use the Technology, Organization and Environment (TOE) theory of technological innovation adoption [18, 19] as its main theoretical foundation, which includes more types of adoption factors. In Senyo et al. (2018) review, TOE is also the most used research framework [4]. TOE factors are di-vided into three main types: technological factors (perceived technological characteristics of cloud computing and services), organizational factors (firm internal characteristics) and environmental factors (characteristics of firm's external environment). To examine the technological factors, previous studies adopt Diffusion of Innovation (DOI) theory [20] to define with five critical characteristics of innovation which are the degree of relative advantage, compatibility, complexity, trialability and observability.

Summarizing, the main empirical studies that investigate the factors determining cloud computing and services adoption at firm level, particularly a series of firm characteristics, are shown in Table 1, and the factors are classified in the next section through the activity theory framework.

2.2 Activity Theory

Activity Theory describes the analysis of the activity from the element performance and communication process, and the activity involves the object, the activity goal, the applied tools and language-related projects are set in the framework [27], and the dynamic knowledge view of activity theory echoes the knowledge view based on practice [28]. It has three main intermediary paths: (1) The subject and object will be affected by the intermediary of the tool unit. (2) The community and the subject will also be subject to rules. (3) The community unit and the object unit will be affected by the division of labor. In addition, other additional lines may have secondary mediating relationships (Georg et al., 2015). It is also the basis for the development and transformation of the activity system. Activity analysis helps in multiple fields to understanding of complex work and social activities [29], that used to explore the complex process relationships in activities, has now become the founding theory of understanding the changes and development of work and social activities [30], activities theory-related framework and analysis unit.

Table 1. Previous empirical studies examining the effects of firm characteristics on cloud computing/services adoption

Related Research	Factor			Country Industry
	Technological	Organizational	Environmental	
Gutierrez, Boukrami [21]	Relative advantage, Complexity (−), Compatibility	Top management support, Firm size, Technological readiness (+)	Competitive pressure (+), Trading partners pressure (+)	UK firms
Gangwar, Date [22]	Relative advantage (+), Compatibility (+), Complexity (−)	Organizational readiness (+), Top management commitment (+), Training/education (+)	Competitive pressure (+), Cloud Computing services providers' support (+)	Indian information technology firms
Hsu and Lin [23]	Relative advantage (+), Ease of use, Compatibility, Trialability, Observability (+), Security (+)	Firm size, Global scope, financial costs (+), Satisfaction with existing IS (−)	Competition intensity (+), Regulatory environment	Taiwanese firms
Loukis, Arvanitis [24]	Degree of sophistication of firm's ICT infrastructure (+)	Adoption of ICT investment reduction strategy (+), Adoption of an innovation oriented strategy, Employment of specialized ICT personnel (+), Sufficiency of ICT skills of firm's employees, Previous experience of ICT outsourcing (+),Size	Price competition, Quality competition	European countries (Germany, Spain, France, Italy, UK, Poland) manufacturing firms
Kandil, Ragheb [25]	Relative Advantage (+), Complexity (+), Compatibility (+), Security and Trust (+)	Top Management Support (+), Technology Readiness and Manpower (+), Technology Readiness and Manpower (+)	Telecommunication Infrastructure (+), Trading Partner support (+), Trading Partner Pressure (+)	Egypt firms

(continued)

Table 1. (*continued*)

Related Research	Factor			Country Industry
	Technological	Organizational	Environmental	
Skafi, Yunis [26]	Relative Advantage	Cost, Security and Privacy (+), Compatibility, Complexity (+), Trialability, Size, Top Management Support (+), Innovativeness, Prior Technological Experience (+)	Competitive Pressure, Supplier Computing Support	Lebanon small and medium-sized enterprises (SMEs)

To describe the elements which are included in the adoption of cloud computing/services, this study uses the framework of activity theory proposed by Engeström (1999) and refers to the eight-step model proposed by Mwanza (2001), which is clarified by eight open-ended questions (See Table 2). The six elements involved should be summarized and explored to establish the relevant factors that should be involved in the adoption of cloud computing and services to more clearly describe the issues discussed in this study.

2.3 Organizational Agility

In the "21st Century Manufacturing Development Strategy" proposed by the Iacocca Institute (1991), it is pointed out that the 21st century market competition environment is unpredictable, technology is developing faster, products are customized, life cycle is short, etc., if enterprises cannot adapt in time Such changes and seizures will be eliminated [31]. Therefore, articles discussing agility have emerged, and many scholars have proposed relevant definitions for the term agility. Youssef (1992) pointed out that Agile manufacturing is related to both quick response and time-to-market. Quick response means that the product is presented at the right time and place [32]. Time to market is the time it takes to define a product and publish a product. Sharifi and Zhang (1999) argue that agility contains two important concepts, one is to respond to expected or unexpected changes in an appropriate manner and time, and the other is to use changes and turn them into opportunities, which need to be perceived. And the basic ability to predict changes in the organization's business environment [33]. Nagel and Bhargava (1994) argue that agility is a rapid response to market movements through continuous improvement to gain the ability to grow in a changing competitive market and drive products and services based on customer value [34, 35]. Goldman, Nagel, and Preiss (1995) point out that agility is a comprehensive system that involves all processes within the enterprise and the suppliers and customers of the enterprise [35]. The Global Logistics Research Team believes that agility depends on the company's ability to restructure and position these components. Agility is there-fore an opportunity to integrate the necessary assets,

Table 2. Eight-step-model open-ended questions describe the activities components of adopting cloud computing and services

Analysis process and units	Open-ended question	Components
Activity of interest	What sort of activity does this study interest in?	Enterprise adopting cloud computing/services situation
Objective of activity	Why is this activity taking place?	The cloud computing/services have been broaden applied to enterprises, the purpose is to explore the situation of adoption
Subjects in this activity	Who is involved in carrying out this activity?	The enterprises which have adopt cloud computing/services
Tools mediating the activity	By what means are the subjects carrying out this activity?	Cloud computing/services: SaaS, PaaS, IaaS Relative advantage, Compatibility, Complexity, Trialability, Observability, Ease of use, Perceived benefits, Security and privacy, Uncertainty, Geo-restriction
Rules and regulations	Are there any cultural norms, rules or regulations governing the performance of this activity?	Market scope Industry regulations Government policy Sophistication of firm's ICT infrastructure
Division of labor	Who is responsible for what, when carrying out this activity and how are the roles organized?	Top management support/commitment Innovativeness ICT investment strategy Specialized ICT personnel and non-ICT employees' IT capability, readiness, and prior IT experience Human resource training/education
Community	What is the environment in which this activity is carried out?	Competitor pressure, Trading partner pressure, Supplier computing support, Government support
Outcome	What is the desired outcome from carrying this activity?	Digitalization Organizational agility

knowledge, and relationships within and outside the organization to perceive innovation and market competition at an unexpected rate.

Agility includes exploration and exploitation of market arbitrage opportunities [36]. Exploring is the organization's experimental approach to finding new alternatives to pursue currently unknown competitive opportunities. Exploitation is the organization's use and development of known things, through the improvement and expansion of existing capabilities, technology, and knowledge. Agility could be divided into three areas, including capabilities related to interactions with customers, orchestration of internal operations, and utilization of its ecosystem of external business partners [36]. Customer agility is the ability of an organization to obtain market intelligence and identify competitive opportunities through its customers [37]. In customer agility, the role of information technology is to maintain a virtual customer community as the basis for product design, feedback, and testing [36]. Partnering agility is the ability to explore and develop innovation through alliances, partnerships, or joint ventures that combine the capabilities of suppliers, manufacturers, and logistics providers with technology, assets, and knowledge. Information technology accelerates collaboration among internal partners in partner agility [36]. Operational agility reflects the ability of an organization's business processes to achieve speed, accuracy, and economic cost in developing innovation and competitive opportunities. Operational agility ensures that companies can quickly redesign existing processes and create new processes for dynamics. In the market situation, the role of information technology in operational agility is to help build modular and integrated business processes [36]. These three dimensions together reflect agility, and organizations that have developed these three dimensions of agility should achieve better competitive positions by combining customers, partners, and operational agility [36]. This study adopts organizational agility as a represent of organization performance after adopting cloud computing and services.

2.4 Content Analysis

Content Analysis is a set of procedures for researching and analyzing the content of communication through quantitative and qualitative methods and making effective inferences [38]. The most valuable part of the research is to analyze the information, calculate it in a systematic, objective, and quantitative way, calculate the frequency of occurrence, and assign the frequency to the value, according to the statistics of the category, from the most mentioned times Reflects the most concerned vocabulary [39]. It is a technology that can confuse a large amount of data and change it systematically [40], and this analysis technology enables us to discover and understand in depth about individuals, groups, institutions. Or the focus of attention in society [38].

Content analysis can be used to study the analysis of the changing trends of things [39]. The analytical data used in content analysis is also quite diverse, such as: website content [41], paper, TV commercial, news media coverage, etc. [42–44]. This study conducts open data from cloud computing provider official website content including text type and video type description of startup case studies. The text type data is used directly into analysis, and the video type data has been converted into subtitle for analysis. The theme is the analysis unit, and the language is to express the startup cases on a certain topic. It is also regarded as the most useful unit of analysis in content analysis, exploring the factors that enterprises adopt cloud computing and services.

2.5 Formal Concept Analysis

Formal Concept Analysis (FCA) is a data analysis theory that discovers conceptual structures from data sets [45]. Based on a matrix theory (Lattice Theory) proposed by German scholar Wille in 1982, FCA was constructed on the algebraic principle of Galois Connection and used in mathematical methods of data analysis [46], structuring data into human thought. An abstract object in the form of a concept that turns the material into a meaningful and understandable interpretation that is used to derive an implicit relationship between a set of attributes and those attributes in another description object. FCA is mainly based on matrix theory, a quantitative method for data analysis, the data analysis theory of conceptual structure is found from the data set, and the attributes of objects based on common characteristics [47]. As a grouping action, FCA provides a conceptual architecture to construct (Structure), analyze (Analyze) and visualize (Visualize) data, making these materials easier to understand and through the concept matrix (Concept Lattice) defines the binary relationship between objects and attributes to find clusters of objects with similar properties [48].

Regarding the use of FCA, FCA has been rapidly developed and applied to many fields such as: sociology, medicine, psychology, anthropology, musicology, linguistics, database, library science, information science, software engineering, ecology, and in the other fields, conceptual analysis is also widely used in social sciences, especially in social sciences, which often cannot adequately capture quantitative analysis. This study used FCA to further understand the relationship between factors after encoding from the content analysis, and then develop the hypotheses via FCA results.

3 Methodology

3.1 Research Design

The research subjects are the enterprises with cloud computing and services adoption. The research process includes three stages (Fig. 1). First, systematically review the cloud computing and services articles and found out the critical adoption factors for the conceptual framework through activity theory [49]. Second, collect the secondary data from cloud providers' website and use content analysis to examine the conceptual framework. Third, convert the content analysis result into the essential data for formal concept analysis for further analysis and discussion.

This study used web crawler for systematically review on the research articles related to cloud computing and services, a systematic review of cloud computing/services literature on the adoption factors. And then the study collects the case studies on AWS case studies official website for content analysis. The type of data from text of case studies for content analysis. After collecting case studies from website, these contents are encoding by two or more coders. This study uses the ConExp (Concept Explorer) software to explore the formal concept analysis. The regular matrix is composed of objects and attributes, and the content analysis method is carried out through the collected data of case studies, including extraction categories, coding, and reliability analysis. The analysis unit and category obtained from the content analysis method are input to objects and attributes to establish formalize content.

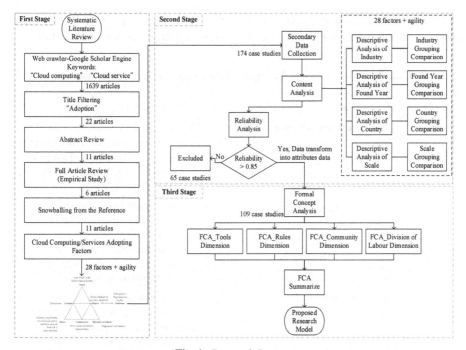

Fig. 1. Research Process

In first stage, using Python web crawler to search "cloud computing" and "cloud service" through Google Scholar Engine in July 2021. The result included the first hundred pages with total 1,825 articles, and then excluded the same articles from two key words, the number of initial articles was reduced to 1,639. In second stage, the articles were excluded based on titles, and reserve the article title which included "adoption". After article title limitation, the number of relevant articles was reduced to 22. The third stage put all the remaining articles under abstract examination. Based on key information of the papers, the excluding articles in this stage are the study which cloud computing/services are not adopted by enterprise or focus on the technical issues. There were 11 articles remained in this stage. The fourth stage review full texts with all remaining articles. There are 5 empirical studies used the qualitative methodology which did not identify the significant factors in the result; therefore, excluded in this stage and remained 6 articles. In the fifth stage, reference lists of the remaining articles were searched to find key articles which were not recovered during the earlier stages in the literature selection process. Snowballing increased the number of relevant articles to 11, which was the final number of the included studies.

The Secondary data in second stage is collected from the AWS official website. The customer case study information includes the company name, industry, found year, country, firm size (employees' number), company website, the used of cloud computing/services, and the reason of using cloud computing/services and choosing this provider. The third stage data is converted from the content analysis results, including two coders encoding data of 28 adopting factors which are collected from the first stage articles and "agility" factor as outcome. Table 3 present the definition of 29 factors.

Table 3. Adopting factors for content Analysis and formal concept analysis

AT	Factors	Code	Definition
Tools	Relative advantage	TL01	Relative advantage is defined as the degree to which innovation is perceived by potential adopters as providing greater benefits than the current practices
	Compatibility	TL02	Compatibility is defined as the degree to which innovation is perceived to be consistent with existing values, current needs, and previous experience of potential adopters
	Complexity	TL03	Complexity is defined as the extent to which an innovation is perceived as difficult to understand and use
	Trialability	TL04	Trialability is the degree to which an innovation may be experimented with on a limited basis
	Observability	TL05	Observability is the degree to which the results of an innovation are visible to others
	Ease of use	TL06	Ease of use is defined as the degree to which an individual believes that using a cloud service would be free of effort
	Perceived benefits	TL07	Perceived benefits are referred to the operational and strategic benefits a firm can expected to receive from cloud computing
	Security and privacy	TL08	Security and privacy in organizations concerns are about having their own control than any other serious issue
	Uncertainty	TL09	Uncertainty is the short lifetime of an innovation may often lead to some degree of uncertainty

(*continued*)

Table 3. (*continued*)

AT	Factors	Code	Definition
	Geo-restriction	TL10	Geo-restriction is identified as the enterprises concern about the geolocation which their data is stored
Rules	Industry regulations	RU01	The implementation of national system from government may lead to the intensity in industry competition. These competitive pressures will force firms to adopt new IS quickly to provide better services and increase strategic advantages typically in hospitalize and financial industry
	Government support	RU02	Government support may give from several ways such as issuing regulations for protecting data security and confidentiality, issuing policies to lowering bandwidth cost and hardware/software procurement tax, and improving national IT infrastructure providing incentives and financial support as well as by adopting cloud computing and services within government institutions
	Degree of sophistication of firm's ICT infrastructure	RU03	Cloud computing and services are valuable to firms with highly sophisticated ICT infrastructures, since it enables them to reduce their high ICT operations, support, and maintenance costs
Community	Market scope	CM01	Market scope is identified as the horizontal extent of a company's operations
	Competitor pressure	CM02	Competitor pressure refers to the intensity and pressure levels from the competitors in the same industry

(*continued*)

Table 3. (*continued*)

AT	Factors	Code	Definition
	Trading partner pressure	CM03	Trading partner is which firms rely on for their IT design and implementation tasks
	Supplier computing support	CM04	Supplier activities can significantly influence adoption decisions and identify the importance of activities such as targeting and communication to reduce the perceived risk from the potential customer
Division of Labour	Firm size	DV01	Firm size is the scale of employee numbers and firm capacity
	Financial costs	DV02	Cloud computing and services pay-as-you-go basis lead to the lower financial costs including set-up, operations, management, maintenance, and training
	IT capability	DV03	IT capability consists of IT resources and IT employees. IT resources refer to the firm's annual budget for its IT department to install, maintain, and upgrade the company's information systems. The number of IT employees is an indicator to determine whether a firm has sufficient IT employees to support daily operations; perform installation, maintenance, and upgrades; and handle emergencies

(*continued*)

Table 3. (*continued*)

AT	Factors	Code	Definition
	Organizational readiness	DV04	Organizational readiness has been described into three dimensions including managers perception and evaluation of the degree to their organization aware-ness, resources, commitment, and governance to adopt IT; financial readiness (financial resources for cloud computing implementation and for ongoing expenses during usage); technological readiness (infrastructure and human resources for cloud computing usage and management)
	Satisfaction of existing IS	DV05	The satisfaction level with existing systems
	Prior IT experience (outsourcing)	DV06	Firm's personnel have previous experience and skills concerning any type of ICT outsourcing can be useful
	Specialized ICT personnel	DV07	Specialized ICT personnel has been identified as the critical importance human capital for ICT-related innovation who's technical and business knowledge and skills can be quite useful for the adoption and adaption to the cloud computing and services

(*continued*)

Table 3. (*continued*)

AT	Factors	Code	Definition
	ICT investment reduction strategy	DV08	ICT investment reduction strategy is the firm adopts a greater or lesser degree strategy of investment reduction due to unfavorable economic conditions (e.g., overall recession or sectoral economic problems). Cloud computing and services costs can transform the ICT capital investments to operating expenses to cope with this problem
	Top management support	DV09	Top management plays an important role on integration of resources and reengineering of processes during cloud computing and services implementation
	Innovativeness	DV10	Innovativeness means the openness to new technologies, and often links to the human characteristics of the decision maker such as CEO, CIO
	Training Education	DV11	An organization needs to train and educate its employees before the implementation to reduce employees' anxiety and stress about the use and to provide motivation and better understanding about cloud computing and services benefits for their tasks

After the encoding process of content analysis, descriptive analysis is used to describe the secondary data and the demographic variables. Then the reliability analysis of content analysis is adopted to ensure the stability, reproducibility, and accuracy before the data transformed to attributes data for formal concept analysis. Formal concept analysis is processed by ConExp (Concept Explorer) software with four dimensions of the conceptual framework and then proposed the association rules result as the research model. The minimum support was set to 9 and the minimum confidence was set to 85% [50]. In this study, the minimum support was set to 10 and the minimum confidence was set to 85%.

3.2 Data Collection and Analysis

The subjects of this study are the startups with AWS cloud computing and services adoption. The data is collected from AWS case studies official website (https://aws.amazon.com/tw/solutions/case-studies/) on August. 25, 2021. The total number of case studies is 174, including 145 text type cases and 29 video type cases.

The profile of our use cases including industry, found year, country, and scale of employee number. The classification of industry is referred from North America Industry Classification System (NAICS). 69% of cases are from professional, scientific, and technical services industry such as cloud consultant company and digital marketing company. 9% of cases are from finance and insurance industry, many of them are doing FinTech business. The found year of cases is distinguished into three groups which is before 2006 (11%), between 2006–2009 (25%), and after 2010 (64%). The reason of grouping is due to the cloud vendor appearance. 2006 is the year that Amazon Web Services launch their first two cloud services EC2 and S3. After 2010, Microsoft Azure and Google Cloud Platform (GCP) join in the cloud vendor align and now share the market together with AWS. The proportions of the cases are also similar with the startup raising rate in USA which dramatically increased between 2008–2013 and then drop from 2014. USA (43%), UK (9%), and Taiwan (6%) cases are in the lead, and Australia (4%) and Sweden (4%) are followed by. This study further compared the USA cases and Taiwan cases. The employee numbers of these cases are mostly under 200. For further grouping, this study divided the scale into three groups which are 2–50 employees (37%), 51–200 employees (37%), and over 200 employees (26%).

3.3 Findings from Content Analysis

The content analysis results indicate that the top five mentioned factors are TL01_Relative Advantage (3.47), DV02_Financial Costs (2.07), TL06_Ease of Use (0.94), TL08_Security and Privacy (0.93), CM04_Supplier Computing Support (0.90). Those five factors are the most mentioned factors that influence the decision of adopting cloud computing and services and play important roles in the adoption context. For further descriptive analysis, this study groups these cases by industry, found year, country, and scale. The grouping criteria have been mentioned in the case studies profile section and only the average of the factor has exceeded/below 0.3 of the total average of the factor would be further discussed.

In industry comparison, this study only presents four types of industry which are professional, scientific, and technical services (120 cases), Finance and Insurance (15 cases), Health Care (8 cases), and Arts, Entertainment, and Recreation (11 cases). Professional, Scientific, and Technical Services industry is the majority in the secondary data set, and without doubt, the average of each factor doesn't show the big difference with the total average. TL04_Trialability was found higher in finance and insurance industry. Since the industry has higher flexibility need to react to immediately changes, while firm developing and integrating the FinTech solutions, cloud computing and services characteristic could fulfil their need on rapid respond. Therefore, trialability was found to be important in this industry. On the other hand, the health care industry and the finance and insurance industry have higher-level data transfer regulations than the other industries. Both show higher results on RU01_Industry regulations, this makes sense because of worldwide standard regulations such as Payment Card Industry Data Security Standard (PCI DSS) or The Health Insurance Portability and Accountability Act (HIPAA). Once the firms adopted cloud computing and services from vendors, the vendor has responsibility for meeting the requirements from those regulations, so the firm should not need to concern about meeting the standard. In addition, both industries also result in lower TL06_Ease of use, this may occur to the differences on the end-user. The cloud computing and services tools may not use by every employee, and instead, the ease of use on cloud computing and services may only influence the IT staff. For the end-user in these industries, their concerns are the ease of information system user interface not directly to the cloud computing and services itself. In arts, entertainment, and recreation industry, TL06_Ease of use result is much higher than average. Those creators or developers are the direct user to the cloud computing and services, the simplicity of integration and migration is the necessary concern on adoption. In the cases studies, most of the gaming firms need global deployment to maintain their applications for global users. Usually, they have a strong development team and need less support from vendors, and the scalability of cloud computing and services help them afford the unpredictable traffic; however, accompanied by unpredictable financial costs.

3.4 Analysis Results from Formal Concept Analysis

Formal concept analysis is sourced from the content analysis results. The variables data in content analysis are transformed to attributes data. Only if two coders both agreed with the case has the attribute, the case will be determined with that attribute. The transform data are recorded in the formal concept matrix for building diagrams and counting association rules. In this study, the concept structure can be discovered from the data set through FCA, and the concept matrix can be graphically generated using ConExp software, which clearly depicts the correlation between concepts. The data was input to the formal concept analysis form and result in formal concept matrix. Due to the complexity and the numerous related factors, this study divided the 28 adoption factors of cloud computing and services into four dimensions (tools, rules, community, and division of labour) which are sourced from activity theory and discussed one by one below.

According to the research purpose, this study aims to explore the context of cloud computing and services adoption and to understand the relevance between adoption factors based on the activity theory framework. This study uses a different methodology from traditional hypotheses development and attempts to discuss a complete adoption scenario in a more comprehensive framework. Summarizing the content analysis and formal concept analysis results, the proposed model is shown in Fig. 2.

In view of the systematic literature review and the factors defined process in this study, only the factors that have been evaluated with influence in previous articles would be included in the analysis process. Although some of the factors have less mentioned in the case studies, the formal concept analysis results still showed their relevance in cloud computing and services adoption. Besides, TL01_Relative Advantages, the often-mentioned factor in content analysis, also found lots of association rules with other factors in formal concept analysis. In addition, the proposed research model only includes the

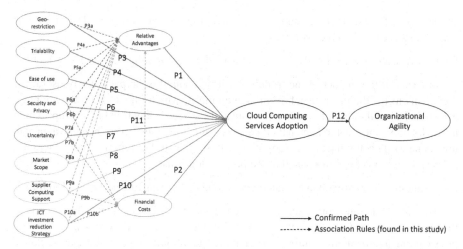

Fig. 2. Proposed Research Model

factors that has association rules with other factors and each association rules finding is discussed as below. 86% of cases indicate at least one characteristic (scalability, availability, flexibility, etc.) of cloud are the advantages that could assist them with better operations and IT expenditure rather than traditional IT options. This finding is also consistent with similar studies reported in the literature [22, 23, 51, 52]. Therefore, it is reasonable to infer the proposition as:

P1: Relative advantages are positively associated with cloud computing and services adoption.

Cloud computing and services are perceived as dramatically decreasing IS costs including costs for set-up, management, and maintenance and training, thus driving the adoption of cloud services. "By using cloud computing and services, we reduced our IT startup costs by 90%. These savings enable us to successfully launch our application" quoted in the case studies. The benefit of cloud services lies in the significant time and cost savings they offer firms. This finding is also consistent with similar studies reported in the literature [23, 53]. Therefore, it is reasonable to infer the proposition as:

P2: Financial costs are positively associated with cloud computing and services adoption.

Instead of the concern on not knowing the geolocation which firm's data is stored, the case studies result in another interesting situation. Some cases mentioned that the different regions and availability zones help them lower the latency for global users, some others even said that using cloud computing and services let engineers no longer need to worry about environment consistency; issues generated from environmental differences almost entirely stopped. The relevance is existed but may be different from the previous study which stated that geo-restriction has negative effect on adoption [51] and therefore become one of the relative advantages of cloud computing and services. Therefore, it is reasonable to infer the proposition as:

P3: Geo-restriction is positively associated with cloud computing and services adoption.

In terms of the impact of the trialability, it was found to be particularly useful for the clients to try the product before implementing it, which impacted on the adoption decision. The trialability of cloud computing and services is identified by startups which need a lot of try and error to launch their business; thus, becomes a prominent advantage in this scenario. This finding is also consistent with similar studies reported in the literature [51]. Hence, it is a fair inference that the proposition is as:

P4: Trialability is positively associated with cloud computing and services adoption.

The ease of use and convenience achieved by startups while using the cloud is one of the primary reasons for driving them to use and adopt cloud. The comparison between physical management environment and cloud has identified the ease of use as a relative advantage. This finding is also consistent with similar studies reported in the literature [53]. Hence, this study proposed the proposition as:

P5: Ease of use is positively associated with cloud computing and services adoption.

The higher and better the security and privacy regulations of the cloud, the higher are the usage and adoption of the cloud. The Clarifying Lawful Overseas Use of Data Act (CLOUD Act) law in USA is legislated in May 2018, this kind of newly established standards and federal regulations help establish organizational trust and control over data when adopting cloud computing and services. The relevance of H6b was not supported in previous study on SMEs, and had negative path coefficient [53]. The authors indicated that SMEs are fine to adopt cloud, even if it does not provide the best-in-class level of security and privacy, compensated by higher cost savings. This statement is quite similar with the content analysis result of the group which found year is between 2006 to 2009. Since the cloud security related law is not established at that time. Startups also share the characteristic of scarce resources with SMEs, the security concern may not be related to the costs at that time. However, the newly standards and laws have increased the security concerns for the startups which found later. The relevance should be further examined at this time. Hence, this study proposed the proposition as:

P6: Security and privacy is positively associated with cloud computing and services adoption.

Since the startup cases are all adopted cloud computing and services already, uncertainty is instead by reliability which has been mentioned in the cases. Their main reliability consideration is choosing cloud vendors. H7b has been supported from previous study [53], because improvements in reliability of cloud would increase the confidence to adopt cloud resulting in obvious cost savings. Hence, this study proposed the proposition as:

P7: Uncertainty is negatively associated with cloud computing and services adoption.

Due to the advantages of cloud, most of the startups could expand their market scope in the very early stage depend on their development strategy. It is responded to previous study that "Regarding the market scope, it is apparent from the results that when firms operate in a wide market area, they adopt cloud services to improve their efficiency [51]." The scenario is a bit different, because of the thought of entrepreneurship. Once the geo-restriction isn't the matter, the market expansion for startups becomes the prior concern which is mainly focused on latency and regions. Hence, this study proposed the proposition as:

P8: Market scope is positively associated with cloud computing and services adoption.

Previous research has demonstrated the availability of external support to be positively related to adoption [54]. The importance of supplier efforts and external computing support in the decision-making process [51]. However, besides from the basic support that cloud vendors could provide when adopt cloud solutions, the other support plan are chargeable; therefore, the H9b relevance is predictable. Hence, this study proposed the proposition as:

P9: Supplier computing support is positively associated with cloud computing and services adoption.

Cloud computing and services can be very useful for coping with the problem of not allow to make the required investments for upgrading and enhancing their ICT infrastructures because of the scarcity on resources in the early stage, as it enables firms to transform the ICT capital investments required for meeting the above needs into operating expenses [3, 55]. "Pay as you go", one of the characteristics of cloud computing made the operational expenses count based on the real use only. Therefore, in startups context, they all have great motivation to adopt cloud computing and services. Hence, this study proposed the proposition as:

P10: ICT reduction investment strategy is positively associated with cloud computing and services adoption.

Cost savings is confirmed as the important driver to explain the relative advantage of cloud computing and services [7, 53, 56]. However, this study discovered the bilateral relations between relative advantages and financial costs. The possible reason may occur to the better the advantages, the higher the price should pay. This phenomenon could be observed from the pricing strategy of cloud vendors. If the customer wants to get the best advantages of using cloud solutions, it will come with the relatively costs. Hence, it is reasonable to infer the proposition as:

P11: Relative advantages are associated with financial costs.
P12: Cloud Computing and Services area associated with organizational agility.

4   Conclusion

The conclusions in this study are referred to as the three stages of methodology which are systematic literature review, content analysis, and formal concept analysis. In the systematic literature review, 11 out of 1,639 articles were selected to discuss and resulted in 28 significant factors defining in previous research. Due to the case studies encoding process, this study has found relative advantages, financial costs, ease of use, security and privacy, and supplier computing support as prominent factors. The grouping comparisons have many informative and interesting results such as the financial cost consideration will decline while the scale enlarges, the security and privacy concern of finance and healthcare industry is significantly higher than other industries, and Taiwanese startups have more financial costs concern than the other countries. The formal concept analysis results divided into four dimensions to discuss and then reformed into one research framework to understand the relevance of the comprehensive context.

For academic implications, this study response with Sharma, Gupta [57] study, the findings would be useful for researchers who are currently working on cloud computing adoption research and opening up new directions of cloud computing adoption and business value research. In managerial implications, the findings indicate what customers concern about adoption and continuous adoption which would be useful for cloud computing and services providers and their partner network companies. It also provides guidance for cloud computing and services users or potential users to make advanced and multi-dimensional exploitation of cloud computing and services.

References

1. Edwards, J.: Cloud Computing 2019: The Cloud Comes of Age (2018)
2. Leimeister, S., et al.: The business perspective of cloud computing: actors, roles and value networks (2010)
3. Marston, S., et al.: Cloud computing—the business perspective. Decis. Support Syst. **51**(1), 176–189 (2011)
4. Senyo, P.K., Addae, E., Boateng, R.: Cloud computing research: a review of research themes, frameworks, methods and future research directions. Int. J. Inf. Manag. **38**(1), 128–139 (2018)
5. Hsu, P.-F., Ray, S., Li-Hsieh, Y.-Y.: Examining cloud computing adoption intention, pricing mechanism, and deployment model. Int. J. Inf. Manag. **34**(4), 474–488 (2014)
6. Mell, P., Grance, T.: The NIST definition of cloud computing (2011)
7. Dixit, S., Sharma, A.: Effect of cloud computing on enterprises: a review. Int. J. Comput. Appl. **109**(5) (2015)
8. Ross, P.K., Blumenstein, M.: Cloud computing as a facilitator of SME entrepreneurship. Technol. Anal. Strateg. Manag. **27**(1), 87–101 (2015)
9. Carey, S.: What is a tech unicorn? Here's how the tech startup landscape is changing and why you should care (2016)
10. Gagliardi, D.: Next generation entrepreneur: innovation strategy through Web 2.0 technologies in SMEs. Technol. Anal. Strateg. Manag. **25**(8), 891–904 (2013)
11. Westerman, G., Bonnet, D.: Revamping your business through digital transformation. MIT Sloan Manag. Rev. **56**(3), 10 (2015)
12. Wu, J.-C., Lee, S.-M.: Cloud Computing Services to Digital Innovation (2021)
13. Yin, C.: Cloud Computing Strategies. Common Wealth (2010)
14. Behrend, T.S., et al.: Cloud computing adoption and usage in community colleges. Behav. Inf. Technol. **30**(2), 231–240 (2011)
15. Fahmideh, M., Beydoun, G.: Reusing empirical knowledge during cloud computing adoption. J. Syst. Softw. **138**, 124–157 (2018)
16. ----------
17. Yang, H., Tate, M.: A descriptive literature review and classification of cloud computing research. CAIS **31**, 2 (2012)

18. Baker, J.: The technology–organization–environment framework. In: Dwivedi, Y.K., Wade, M.R., Schneberger, S.L. (eds.) Information Systems Theory: Explaining and Predicting Our Digital Society, pp. 231–245. Springer, New York (2012). https://doi.org/10.1007/978-1-4419-6108-2_12

19. ----------

20. Rogers, E.M.: Diffusion of Innovations. Simon and Schuster (2010)

21. Gutierrez, A., Boukrami, E., Lumsden, R.: Technological, organisational and environmental factors influencing managers' decision to adopt cloud computing in the UK. J. Enterp. Inf. Manag. **28**(6), 788–807 (2015)

22. Gangwar, H., Date, H., Ramaswamy, R.: Understanding determinants of cloud computing adoption using an integrated TAM-TOE model. J. Enterp. Inf. Manag. **28**(1), 107–130 (2015)

23. Hsu, C.-L., Lin, J.-C.: Factors affecting the adoption of cloud services in enterprises. IseB **14**(4), 791–822 (2015). https://doi.org/10.1007/s10257-015-0300-9

24. Loukis, E., Arvanitis, S., Kyriakou, N.: An empirical investigation of the effects of firm characteristics on the propensity to adopt cloud computing. IseB **15**(4), 963–988 (2017). https://doi.org/10.1007/s10257-017-0338-y

25. Kandil, A.M.N.A., et al.: Examining the effect of TOE model on cloud computing adoption in Egypt. Bus. Manag. Rev. **9**(4), 113–123 (2018)

26. Skafi, M., Yunis, M.M., Zekri, A.J.I.A.: Factors influencing SMEs' adoption of cloud computing services in Lebanon: an empirical analysis using toe and contextual theory. IEEE Access **8**, 79169–79181 (2020)

27. White, L., Burger, K., Yearworth, M.: Understanding behaviour in problem structuring methods interventions with activity theory. Eur. J. Oper. Res. **249**(3), 983–1004 (2016)

28. Simeonova, B.: Transactive memory systems and Web 2.0 in knowledge sharing: a conceptual model based on activity theory and critical realism. Inf. Syst. J. **28**(4), 592–611 (2018). https://doi.org/10.1111/isj.12147

29. Karanasios, S., Allen, D.: ICT for development in the context of the closure of Chernobyl nuclear power plant: an activity theory perspective. Inf. Syst. J. **23**(4), 287–306 (2013)

30. Karanasios, S., Allen, D.K., Finnegan, P.: Activity theory in information systems research. Inf. Syst. J. **28**(3), 439–441 (2018)

31. ----------

32. Youseff, L., Butrico, M., Da Silva, D.: Toward a unified ontology of cloud computing. In: Grid Computing Environments Workshop, GCE 2008. IEEE (2008)

33. Sharifi, H., Zhang, Z.: A methodology for achieving agility in manufacturing organisations: an introduction. Int. J. Prod. Econ. **62**(1–2), 7–22 (1999)

34. ----------

35. ----------

36. Sambamurthy, V., Bharadwaj, A., Grover, V.: Shaping agility through digital options: reconceptualizing the role of information technology in contemporary firms. MIS Q. 237–263 (2003)

37. Kohli, A.K., Jaworski, B.J.: Market orientation: the construct, research propositions, and managerial implications. J. Mark. **54**(2), 1–18 (1990)

38. ----------

39. Stemler, S.: An Introduction to Content Analysis. ERIC Digest (2001)

40. Crowley, B.P., Delfico, J.F.: Content analysis: a methodology for structuring and analyzing written material. United States General Accounting Office (GAO), Program Evaluation and Methodology Division (1996)

41. Sullivan, S.J., et al.: 'What's happening?' A content analysis of concussion-related traffic on Twitter. Br. J. Sports Med. **46**(4), 258–263 (2012)

42. Griffin, T.: Research note: a content analysis of articles on visiting friends and relatives tourism, 1990–2010. J. Hosp. Market. Manag. **22**(7), 781–802 (2013)

43. Roseman, M.G., Poor, M., Stephenson, T.J.: A content analysis of food references in television programming specifically targeting viewing audiences aged 11 to 14 years. J. Nutr. Educ. Behav. **46**(1), 20–25 (2014)
44. Carroll, B., Freeman, B.: Content analysis of comments posted on Australian online news sites reporting a celebrity admitting smoking while pregnant. Public Health Res. Pract. **26**(5) (2016)
45. Ganter, B., Wille, R.: Formal Concept Analysis: Mathematical Foundations. Springer, Heidelberg (2012)
46. Wolff, K.E.: A first course in formal concept analysis. SoftStat **93**, 429–438 (1993)
47. ----------
48. Formica, A.: Ontology-based concept similarity in formal concept analysis. Inf. Sci. **176**(18), 2624–2641 (2006)
49. Wu, J.C., Lee, S.M., Chen, L.H.: The context of cloud computing/services adoption in business: a systematic review with activity theory perspective. In: Pacific Asia Conference on Information Systems, Xi'an, China (2019)
50. ----------
51. Alshamaila, Y., Papagiannidis, S., Li, F.: Cloud computing adoption by SMEs in the north east of England: a multi-perspective framework. J. Enterp. Inf. Manag. **26**(3), 250–275 (2013)
52. Oliveira, T., Thomas, M., Espadanal, M.: Assessing the determinants of cloud computing adoption: an analysis of the manufacturing and services sectors. Inf. Manag. **51**(5), 497–510 (2014)
53. Gupta, P., Seetharaman, A., Raj, J.R.: The usage and adoption of cloud computing by small and medium businesses. Int. J. Inf. Manag. **33**(5), 861–874 (2013)
54. ----------
55. Venders, W., Whitley, E.: A critical review of cloud computing: researching desires and reality. J. Inf. Technol. **27**, 179–197 (2012)
56. ----------
57. Sharma, M., Gupta, R., Acharya, P.: Analysing the adoption of cloud computing service: a systematic literature review. Glob. Knowl. Mem. Commun. **70**, 114–153 (2020)

The Success of Business Transformation and Knowledge Management

Eric K. W. Lau[⊠]

Lee Shau Kee School of Business and Administration, Hong Kong Metropolitan University,
Hong Kong, China
ekwlau@hkmu.edu.hk

Abstract. This study is designed to identify key success factors of business transformation across different industries, create and validate scale, and formulate the success development models, all using the business transformation readiness index (BTRI). It begins with a meta-analysis of the literature covering the key success factors of business transformation and organisational changes. Using the findings of the meta-analysis, a conceptual model of the success of business transformation is developed. It involves the revision of those existing theories in organisational change, as well as knowledge management and business transformation with updated environmental variables.

Keywords: Business Transformation · Knowledge Management · Organization Capabilities · Knowledge Sharing · Functional Flexibility · Innovative Work

1 Introduction

COVID-19 has disrupted business operations on a global scale. Organisations have either been negatively affected in the business environment or have transformed in the crisis situation. This study aims to explore and analyse the success factors of business transformation readiness. The objectives of this study include the review of previous studies exploring the success of business transformations and the development of the business transformation readiness index (BTRI) with knowledge management capabilities.

The study, therefore, begins with a meta-analysis of key success factors of business transformation, knowledge management and organization changes in previous studies. Using the findings of the meta-analysis, a conceptual model of the success business transformation can be developed, validated and tested. It involves the revision of those existing theories in knowledge management, organizational change and business transformation with updated environmental variables. Building on the findings of the first phase, the theoretical model can be formulated as the key success factors within the context of organization's capabilities, and its economic and institutional environment. To investigate the applicability of the proposed model as a measurement of business transformation, an empirical study will be conducted. Hopefully, the study's subject matter will be of interest to a wide variety of potential audiences, including researchers and management consultants in the business transformation, business leaders and managers involved in the business transformation processes.

© The Author(s), under exclusive license to Springer Nature Switzerland AG 2023
L. Uden and I-H. Ting (Eds.): KMO 2023, CCIS 1825, pp. 137–146, 2023.
https://doi.org/10.1007/978-3-031-34045-1_12

2 Literature Review

2.1 Business Transformation

"Business transformation moves an organization from an existing condition to a future state that represents a targeted strategic ideal" [1]. Traditionally, the concept of change management has been used to describe organisations implementing changes in response to market pressures, new technologies, new business processes, or new business environments. "Business transformation is one such driver that provides the necessary fillip to an organization or the competitive advantage in the market place" [2].

As suggested by Cheyunski and Millard [3], earlier approaches to business transformation included business process redesign, the adoption of information technology (IT), and organisation development. They aimed to achieve breakthrough performances and gain competitive advantage by supplying cheaper or better products.

Organisations operate in a complex system; indeed, to sustain operations in such a fragile environment, organisations are increasingly resorting to changes and business transformations. The COVID-19 pandemic, in particular, brought disruptive change to all countries; with no organisations remaining unsinkable, they were forced to either confront the issue or to disappear from the environment. Organisation leaders, government policy makers, and researchers are thus identifying critical success factors for their sustainability.

In the context of digital business transformation, business transformations are always linked to information technologies. Agrawal and Haleem [4] ascertained that cultural and environmental pressures are the driving forces for IT-enabled business transformation.

Linder, Cole, and Jacobson [5] suggested the importance of business transformation outsourcing, arguing that effective outsourcing can help companies achieve sustainable business performance in terms of share price, market position, and return on capital. However, it is believed that organisations need to have sufficient capabilities for business transformation [6, 7]. Bititci [8] formulated business transformations with efficient and effective business processes and the transformational capacity for continuous learning, change, and reinvention. Alberto Pérez and Laura [9] emphasised the importance of an integrated approach to business transformation, suggesting that strategy, people, and processes are the three main pillars of change. Dutta, Choudhury, and Swarnabha [10] proposed a three-step transformation methodology (see Fig. 1), revealing that it is necessary to conduct a gap analysis to determine the key focus areas/pain points for the transformation.

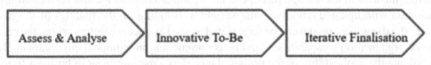

Fig. 1. Transformation Methodology Proposed by Dutta, Choudhury and Swarnabha [10]

2.2 Success Factors of Business Transformation

Change is difficult. It is necessary to determine the success factors of organisational change and business transformation [11]. Alberto Pérez and Laura [9] emphasised the importance of finding the key capabilities of business transformation. However, there is a lack of previous empirical studies on the success factors thereof.

In an earlier study, Chrusciel and Field [12] outlined the importance of organisational change in today's businesses. Using the extant literature, several factors were identified as critical success factors (CSFs) for business transformation: management involvement and fairness/justice in the planning and analysis process; evaluation of effectiveness; comprehensive communication within the organisation; and staff perception of organisational readiness to deal with change. The authors added flexibility in the organisational change curriculum and personal gain from the organisational change as additional CSFs of business transformation and organisational change.

Reinstein [13] listed the following success factors for business transformation in the case of a telecommunications company case (Avaya): building the right team with the right people, sufficient job design and training, and a relevant performance management system.

Bertoncelj, Kovac, and Bertoncel [14] reviewed the success factors and competencies in organisational evolutions, noting the importance of creativity, innovativeness, and intuition for organisational learning capacity in an innovative economy.

Based on previous studies investigating business transformation and organisational change, De Waal, Maritz, Scheepers, McLoughlin, and Hempel [15] consolidated a conceptual framework that included various paradigms and concepts related to the factors of change implementation: communicating leadership commitment; overcoming actual barriers; conducting training; performance measurement; conflict management; organisational innovation; and stakeholder communication. Similarly, Arora, Mawa, Diwvedi, Kathuria, and Sharma [16] reviewed a business case in India and proposed four key principles for its organisational realignment: innovation; agility; eco-system management; and global talent.

De Waal [17], on the other hand, listed eleven theoretical and eight practical success factors from previous case studies. With an extensive review of 290 texts in a ten-year period and a structured survey of 1,300 organisations all over the world, DeWaal went on to highlight five factors that had a positive correlation with competitive performance: continuous improvement and renewal; openness and action orientation; management quality; employee quality; and long-term orientation.

2.3 Knowledge Management, Another Perspective for the Success of Business Transformation

Due to the complexity of organisational transformation and the radical changes therein, it is necessary to build knowledge-related capabilities, including knowledge sharing and training [18–20]. As suggested by Maqsood, Walker & Finegan [21], effective knowledge management in an organisation creates innovation. Therefore, knowledge management contributes to the success of business transformation. With a sample of 202

SMEs in Malaysia, Taghizadeh, Karini, Nadarajah & Nikbin [20] found that knowledge management capability has a positive effect on SMEs' innovation strategy.

In addition, Muhammad, Yousaf, Khan & Usman [22] suggested that human capital is critical to the success of the organisational innovation process. With a sample of 894 manufacturing businesses in Pakistan, they tested their model of knowledge management infrastructure capabilities (KMICs), concluding that knowledge sharing (KS) and functional flexibility (FF) play significant mediating roles on innovative work behaviour in knowledge management.

Similarly, Ye and Tan [23] hypothesized that employees' innovation passion links with their knowledge sharing. With 318 respondents in information technology industry in China, they found that a positive and significant relationship between respondents' knowledge sharing and their innovation passion. Therefore, knowledge sharing in organization facilitate the innovation and business performance.

2.4 Impacts of Business Transformation

It is vital to identify the business outcomes from organisational changes and business transformation. Linder et al. [5] contended that it is difficult to establish objective performance indicators and metrics for business transformation in many cases due to the complex nature of the business. It is commonly believed that sustainability can result in business transformation [24–30]. In an earlier study, the sustainability maturity cube was proposed by Müller and Pfleger [31], arguing that business sustainability can be accelerated by the power of transformation.

As mentioned, IT/ICT-enabled organisational changes always take place in the process of business sustainability [15, 32]. In an earlier case study, Akemi and Bjorn-Andersen [33] concluded that, in the case of Japan Airlines, the business process change from IT applications can help the company to improve customer service, value chain logistics, competitiveness, and sales. Hanelt et al. [32] added that business eco-efficiency and new functionalities, processes and business models can be a consequence of IT-enabled business transformation.

3 Research Methods

3.1 Research Design

Business transformation is inevitable, not tomorrow but today. The study (Fig. 2) is to investigate the success factors, both key and critical, of business transformation and the development of the readiness index of business transformation (i.e., the BTRI).

The BTRI will comprise different interrelated pillars of organisational changes. This project includes a meta-analysis of the business transformation, knowledge management capabilities and organisational change literature, the identification of the key success factors of business transformation, overseeing conceptual models of business transformation in different organisation settings, and both scale development and the development of the BTRI.

Fig. 2. Research Framework of the Study

For the procedure of meta-analysis, as mentioned earlier, we produced a clear definition of the research interests identified, i.e., finding the key success factors of business transformation/organisational changes. Keywords such as "success factors", "business transformation", "organisational changes", "change capabilities", and "knowledge management" will be used for the literature search in library databases. Collecting relevant literature will be the next step. All theoretical frameworks, study designs, study samples, methodologies, variables identified, and main findings will be recorded, tabulated, and analysed.

Table 1 summarises the aforementioned studies. As we have seen, many factors have been identified, and most are from qualitative studies. Building on the findings of the first phase, the theoretical model can be formulated as the key success factors within the context of an organisation's knowledge management capabilities, in addition to its economic and institutional environment (see Fig. 3). To investigate the applicability of the proposed model as a measurement of business transformation, an empirical study will be conducted.

Table 1. Brief Summary of Past Studies on the Success Factors for Business Transformation

Year of Publication	Researchers	Methodology/Approach	Critical/Key Success Factors Reviewed and Identified
2006	Chrusciel, D., & Field, D. W.	Case study approach	Planning and analysis, assessment (i.e., evaluation of the effectiveness and feedback), "comprehensive communication", "perception of organizational readiness to deal with change", "top management support", "user training of application", "perceived utility", "staff critical mass", "flexible curriculum", "personal gain from the transformation" (i.e., fairness)
2007	Reinstein, D.	Case study approach	Building the right team (i.e., ability and willingness to work with change and the resulting ambiguity), sufficient job design and training, relevant performance management

(continued)

Table 1. (*continued*)

Year of Publication	Researchers	Methodology/Approach	Critical/Key Success Factors Reviewed and Identified
2009	Bertoncelj, A., Kovac, D., & Bertoncel, R.	Literature review	Cognitive component of competencies, affective component of competencies, and conative component of competencies
2014	De Waal, G.A., Maritz, A., Scheepers, H., McLoughlin, S., & Hempel, B.	Literature review	Communicate leadership commitment, overcome actual barriers, conduct training, performance measurement, conflict management, organisational innovation, and stakeholder communication
2017	Arora, P., Mawa, R., Diwvedi, V., Kathuria, K., & Sharma, N.	Case study approach	Organisational realignment: innovation, agility, eco-system management, and global talent
2018	De Waal, A.	Literature review and Case study approach	"continuous improvement and renewal", "openness and action orientation", "management quality", "employee quality", and "long-term orientation"
2021	Taghizadeh, Karini, Nadarajah & Nikbin 2021	Literature review and Quantitative approach	Knowledge management capability, innovation culture, innovation strategy

3.2 Research Objectives

The study investigates critical success factors of business transformation and development of business transformation readiness index. The research objectives are:

- To investigate of basic elements of business transformation, knowledge management capabilities, and organization changes;
- To conduct a meta-analysis of previous business transformation, knowledge sharing, and organizational changes studies, and identify key success factors of business transformation;
- To develop business transformation readiness index (BTRI);
- To measure the capabilities of governments, the private sectors and non-profit making organizations to face with rapid changes in their environments;
- To develop theoretical and managerial insights of business transformation with knowledge management capabilities;

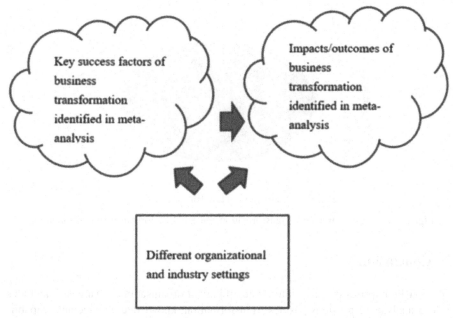

Fig. 3. Conceptual Framework Developed from the Meta-analysis

4 Implications

The BTRI framework emphasises that there is no single success path/factor toward the transformation. Empirical findings from the proposed project will provide organisations with some practical knowledge and capabilities to respond to the changes. Data and insights provided by the proposed project will allow public, private, and government policy makers to build sustainable capabilities that empower transformation processes (Fig. 4).

As a result, this affects all business models across sectors and industries. How did organisations prepare for and respond to the pandemic? A wide range of organisations including private sectors, non-profit organisations, and government agencies can adopt the models developed in this proposed project, gain insights from the BTRI so as to prepare for rapid changes in business environments, and cultivate the opportunities arising from such situations.

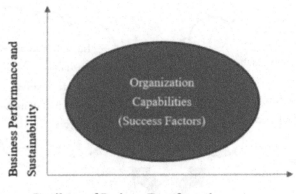

Readiness of Business Transformation

Fig. 4. Readiness of Business Transformation, Business Performance and Sustainability

5 Conclusion

The BTRI comprises different interrelated pillars of organisational changes. It includes a meta-analysis of previous business transformation, knowledge management capabilities and organisational change research, whilst also identifying key success factors of business transformation and overseeing conceptual models of business transformation in different organisational settings. Building on the findings of the first phase, the theoretical model can be formulated as the key success factors within the context of organization's knowledge management capabilities, and its economic and institutional environment. To investigate the applicability of the proposed model as a measurement of business transformation, an empirical study will be conducted. It emphasises that there is no single success path/factor toward business transformations and organizational changes.

References

1. Hoyte, D.S., Greenwood, R.A.: Journey to the north face: a guide to business transformation. Acad. Strateg. Manag. **5**(2), 7–14 (2006)
2. Sohag, S.: The art of business transformation. Telecom Bus. Rev. **6**(1), 67–77 (2013)
3. Cheyunski, F., Millard, J.: Accelerated business transformation and the role of the organizational architect. J. Appl. Behav. Sci. **34**(3), 268–285 (1998)
4. Agrawal, V.K., Haleem, A.: A cross-impact analysis of the external situation and culture on factors of IT-enabled business transformation. Glob. J. Flex. Syst. Manag. **6**(1), 21–34 (2005)
5. Linder, J.C., Cole, M.I., Jacobson, A.L.: Business transformation through outsourcing. Strategy Leadersh. **30**(4), 23–28 (2002)
6. Ashurst, C., Hodges, J.: Exploring business transformation: the challenges of developing a benefits realization capability. J. Chang. Manag. **10**(2), 217 (2010)
7. Bhatt, G.D.: A resource-based perspective of developing organizational capabilities for business transformation. Knowl. Process. Manag. **7**(2), 119–129 (2000)
8. Bititci, U.S.: An executives guide to business transformation. Bus. Strategy Ser. **8**(3), 203–213 (2007)

9. Alberto Pérez, L.R., Laura, C.H.: Integral business transformation: a global case study. Ind. Commer. Train. **43**(2), 75–78 (2011)
10. Dutta, N., Choudhury, S., Swarnabha, S.R.: Business transformation: consulting perspective. Telecom Bus. Rev. **10**(1), 8–22 (2017)
11. Savic, N., Ograjensek, I., Buhovac, A.R.: The drivers of success in business model transformation. Econ. Bus. Rev. Central South-East. Eur. **18**(1), 103–124 (2016)
12. Chrusciel, D., Field, D.W.: Success factors in dealing with significant change in an organization. Bus. Process. Manag. J. **12**(4), 503 (2006)
13. Reinstein, D.: Results matter: unlocking value through Avaya's business transformation. Organ. Dev. J. **25**(4), 55–62 (2007)
14. Bertoncelj, A., Kovac, D., Bertoncel, R.: Success factors and competencies in organisational evolution. Kybernetes **38**(9), 1508–1517 (2009)
15. de Waal, G.A., Maritz, A., Scheepers, H., McLoughlin, S., Hempel, B.: A conceptual framework for guiding business transformation and organizational change in innovative ICT projects. Int. J. Organ. Innov. (Online) **7**(2), 6–17 (2014)
16. Arora, P., Mawa, R., Diwvedi, V., Kathuria, K., Sharma, N.: IoT strategy for Telcos: critical success factors to win in the changing business landscape. Telecom Bus. Rev. **10**(1), 31–40 (2017)
17. de Waal, A.A.: Success factors of high performance organization transformations. Meas. Bus. Excell. **22**(4), 375–390 (2018)
18. Bo, B.N.: Strategic knowledge management research: tracing the co-evolution of strategic management and knowledge management perspectives. Compet. Rev. **15**(1), 1–13 (2005)
19. Cha, J., Newman, M., Winch, G.: Revisiting the project management knowledge framework: rebalancing the framework to include transformation projects [Project management knowledge framework]. Int. J. Manag. Proj. Bus. **11**(4), 1026–1043 (2018)
20. Taghizadeh, S.K., Karini, A., Nadarajah, G., Nikbin, D.: Knowledge management capability, environmental dynamism and innovation strategy in Malaysian firms [Knowledge management capability in Malaysian firms]. Manag. Decis. **59**(6), 1386–1405 (2021)
21. Maqsood, T., Walker, D.H.T., Finegan, A.D.: Facilitating knowledge pull to deliver innovation through knowledge management: a case study. Eng. Constr. Archit. Manag. **14**(1), 94–109 (2007)
22. Muhammad, K.A., Yousaf, Z., Khan, A., Usman, M.: Towards innovative work behavior through knowledge management infrastructure capabilities: Mediating role of functional flexibility and knowledge sharing [Innovative work behavior through KMIC]. Eur. J. Innov. Manag. **24**(2), 461–480 (2021)
23. Ye, P., Liu, L., Tan, J.: Influence of knowledge sharing, innovation passion and absorptive capacity on innovation behaviour in china. [Influence of knowledge sharing] J. Organ. Change Manag. **34**(5), 894–916 (2021)
24. Ahmed, M.D., Sundaram, D.: Sustainability modelling and reporting: from roadmap to implementation. Decis. Support Syst. **53**(3), 611 (2012)
25. Hussain, S., Jahanzaib, M.: Sustainable manufacturing: an overview and a conceptual framework for continuous transformation and competitiveness. Adv. Prod. Eng. Manag. **13**(3), 237–253 (2018)
26. Parida, V., Wincent, J.: Why and how to compete through sustainability: a review and outline of trends influencing firm and network-level transformation. Int. Entrep. Manag. J. **15**(1), 1–19 (2019)
27. Rajnoha, R., Lesnikova, P., Stefko, R., Schmidtova, J., Formanek, I.: Transformations in strategic business planning in the context of sustainability and business goals setting. Transform. Bus. Econ. **18**(2), 44 (2019)
28. Schroeder, H.: Post-merger integration the art and science way. Strateg. HR Rev. **11**(5), 272–277 (2012)

29. Stefan, S., Lüdeke-Freund, F., Hansen, E.G.: Business models for sustainability. Organ. Environ. **29**(3), 264–289 (2016)
30. Wadin, J.L., Ahlgren, K., Bengtsson, L.: Joint business model innovation for sustainable transformation of industries: a large multinational utility in alliance with a small solar energy company. J. Clean. Prod. **160**, 139–150 (2017)
31. Müller, A., Pfleger, R.: Business transformation towards sustainability. Bus. Res. **7**(2), 313–350 (2014)
32. Hanelt, A., Busse, S., Kolbe, L.M.: Driving business transformation toward sustainability: exploring the impact of supporting IS on the performance contribution of eco-innovations. Inf. Syst. J. **27**(4), 463–502 (2017)
33. Akemi, T.C., Bjorn-Andersen, N.: The impact of IOS-enabled business process change on business outcomes: transformation of the value chain of Japan Airlines. J. Manag. Inf. Syst. **14**(1), 13–40 (1997)

Data Analysis and Science

Dealing with Dark Data – Shining a Light

Graham Gordon Chant[✉]

Stewart Barr & Associates, Adelaide, Australia
graham.chant14@gmail.com

Abstract. Organizations today are gathering and storing more and more data in
the belief that it is necessary for compliance, legal reasons or that it may be necessary in the future. Most of this data is considered dark as it is unstructured,
uncatalogued, unmanaged, and unanalyzed. Big data consists of structured data
(business critical and redundant obsolete and trivial (ROT) data) and unstructured
data being dark data. This dark data can be in data silos isolated to specific departments or sectors in an organization unable to be accessed and analyzed by other
departments in the organization. Organizations waste time and operating budgets
searching for this data and storing the data. Data management practices, policies
and procedures need to be reviewed by organizations. The creation of a position
solely to be responsible for the storage, curation, and general good health of data
should be considered. Dark data can have inherent security risks for organizations
that can damage reputations, harm revenue, and leave the organization vulnerable to cybersecurity threats and risks such as personal data breaches or stolen
data. Data governance principles need to be established and implemented in all
organizations. The three main components of data governance are people (roles,
responsibilities, working groups and committees), processes, and tools and technology. This paper presents a brief review of the various aspects of dark data and
their implications for organisations.

Keywords: Dark Data · Big Data · Business Critical Data · ROT Data · FAIR ·
data security · data governance

1 Introduction

Data are observed or recorded facts. Data are usually discrete, objective, and unorganized
[1]. They have no independent meaning or value. Information is accumulated, assembled,
or processed data through processes such as referential, type, purpose, relevance, and
interpretation [2]. Information can be derived from putting data together or making
simple conclusions from experience. A workable definition of knowledge is that is data
and/or information that have been "organized and processed to convey understanding,
experience, accumulated learning, and expertise as they apply to a current problem or
activity" [3].

The aim of this paper is to discuss dark data, its importance, risks involved, the need
and techniques to structure the unstructured dark data. What are the challenges, what
are the security issues and what is the role of data governance?

L. Uden and I-H. Ting (Eds.): KMO 2023, CCIS 1825, pp. 149–160, 2023.
https://doi.org/10.1007/978-3-031-34045-1_13

A semi-systematic literature review was conducted the purpose being to identify and categorize the literature that explicitly mentions dark data. A semi-systematic literature review was the methodology chosen to provide an overview of prior research and track development over time [4]. Papers had to mention, in some capacity, dark data. A full systematic review of every single article that could be relevant to this topic is simply not possible so highly technical papers were excluded. Thematic analysis was used to read the papers in depth to identify, analyse and report repeated patterns or themes [5]. At this point I was able to define and refine the themes of this paper to be defining dark data and the challenges related to dark data (security issues and the role of data governance).

The prevailing practice of organizations today is the accumulation of vast amounts of data in the belief that this is what is necessary to generate a comparative market advantage for themselves. Data is sourced from server logs, website tracking software, customer call records, social media, video surveillance systems, audio files and networks of connected devices and sensors [6]. However, "according to research by the operational intelligence platform Splunk, much of this information is dark data, which lurks in the shadows of enterprise systems and never ends up being used" [6, 7].

Goetz [8] stated that research that doesn't yield a dramatic outcome or, the opposite of what researchers had hoped, invariably ends up stuffed in some lab drawer, unpublished. Such data counts as dark because it is a source of knowledge that does not reach the scientific and engineering community [8].

"Early accounts of dark data in scientific literature describe it as information generated by failed experiments and not published or distributed", making it "nearly invisible" to the broader scientific community [9]. Descriptions of dark data within the digital world characterize it as data that is "hidden or undigested" or "uncategorized, unmanaged, and unanalysed" [9]. While dark data is commonly unstructured, often text-based, but not "analytics ready", any data, in any form, can become dark [9]. Dark data is constantly being produced by organizations, the internet, personal mobile devices, and innumerable other sources [9].

2   What is Dark Data

Various attempts have been made over the decades to define dark data. Martin [10] described dark data as information, collected as a function of an organization's normal operations, that is rarely or never analyzed or used to make intelligent business decisions. Instead, it gets buried within a vast and unorganized collection of other data assets.

Heidorn [11] defined dark data as data that is not carefully indexed and stored so it becomes nearly invisible to scientists and other potential users and therefore is more likely to remain underutilized and eventually lost. He described dark data occurring in the long tail of science where many small research projects have neither time nor funding to accomplish the task of proper data management [11]. This led him to say that dark data is the type of data that exists only in the bottom left-hand desk drawer of scientists on some media that is quickly aging and soon will be unreadable by commonly available devices [11]. Heidorn considers dark data to be related to portable storage lost in the drawers of some researcher where the physical deterioration could easily be the cause of data becoming inaccessible [11]. He also described dark data as data that is more difficult to find and less frequently reused or preserved [11].

In a later paper Heidorn et al. [12] discusses dark data by showing how small research projects in astronomy produce dark data due to insufficient funding for research data management tasks.

A common position between Heidorn and Goetz, is that data is "dark" because it becomes invisible somehow (i.e., not carefully indexed, as Heidorn claims, and not publishable, as Goetz believes) [13].

Whilst a definition of dark data has not been established, several dark data definitions have been developed, each expressing a unique interpretation of the dark data analogy [14]. Some definitions are overlapping, or each is a consequence of the other.

Gartner defined dark data "as the information assets organizations collect, process and store during regular business activities, but generally fail to use for other purposes (for example, analytics, business relationships and direct monetizing)" [15].

Schembera & Durán [13] stated that under ideal conditions of scientific practice, standard data management workflows in high-performance computing facilities indicate that, to keep clean records of the data produced, such data must be "labelled" correctly. Metadata about the data is tagged onto the data with the purpose of identification and categorization [13]. Examples of metadata include the date and time stamps of when the data was created and modified, a string containing the full directory and ownership, and descriptive information on the content of the data [13]. Metadata, then, plays the fundamental role of structuring, informing, and identifying data by means of relevant information about them [13]. When such conditions of management workflow are not followed then data becomes dark, invisible, and undetectable by the researchers [13]. If researchers do not standardize their data and metadata or acquire updated knowledge on the standards used by a given repository, there is a subsequent loss of professional collaboration and research efforts [13]. This will also occur if they are not given incentives to share, format, and standardize their data and metadata for further use [13].

In situations where researchers leave an organization, unless the researcher leaves successors to their work, data becomes orphaned, with no responsible individual to take responsibility for such data [13]. Orphan data whose most likely future is to be forgotten on storage servers, therefore, produces more dark data [13].

3 Volume of Dark Data

The massive amounts of data that some organizations acquire are stored in data silos, isolated reserves of data that pertain to and are controlled by specific departments or sectors within a business [16, 17]. This data isolated to specific business domains throughout an enterprise can hinder an organization's ability to analyse and make meaningful data driven decisions [16]. This dark data does not yet have any monetary value, practical use, or coherent structure [16].

Veritas described databergs as being caused by adding enormous dark data volumes to poorly understood corporate data [18]. A databerg comprises of three elements. Business critical data, ROT data, and dark data. A databerg can be thought of as being like an iceberg. Business critical data is data identified as being actively used and visible to the organizations and vital to the ongoing operational success of an organization [14, 19]. This is the visible part of the iceberg above the surface of the ocean. Business critical data needs to be protected and proactively managed by organizations [19]. ROT data and dark data are like the hidden major part of an iceberg unseen below the surface of the ocean. ROT data is data identified as redundant, or duplicate data, obsolete, no longer having business value, and trivial data with little or no business value [19]. ROT data needs to be proactively minimized by securely deleting it on a regular basis [19]. Dark data is data whose value has not yet been identified [19]. It may include vital business critical data as well as useless ROT data. Either way, it consumes resources [19]. Dark data must be investigated as either ROT data or business critical data, as soon as practical [19]. Ajis [14] says the ROT data and dark data possibly provides a great opportunity for the organizations and users. Although they are hidden and unexposed, they might be keeping the data for reasons such as backup, heritage, and just-in-case situation where the data may be needed in the future [14].

A 2020 estimate suggests that at least 2.5 quintillion bytes of data are produced every day by organizations, and rather worryingly, 55% of these data are deemed dark data [20]. Organizations are failing to identify and exploit knowledge already stored within the organization [20]. This can lead to the duplication of knowledge and information assets already existing within the organization [20]. An increase in dark data can occur when employees from different divisions of the organization do not socialize the new knowledge. As time passes, this can lead to no record that the data ever existed, resulting in huge volumes of data being stored and forgotten [20]. Staff turnover, system upgrades and poor knowledge capture can lead to knowledge being forgotten and lost over time leading to data being recreated and hence an increase in dark data [20].

The sheer volume of dark data impacts the costs for searching and producing appropriate information and imposes a wasted storage cost in operating budgets [14]. To help keep storage costs down, measures should be taken to search out duplicate, stale, and other redundant data through use of deduplication technology, retention security policies and tools that give the organization insights into data usage patterns [6].

Big Data is defined [21] as huge data sets that are orders of magnitude larger (volume); more diverse, including structured, semi-structured and unstructured data (variety) and arriving faster (velocity) than any organization has had to deal with before. Zikopoulos et al. [22] defines big data as data that cannot be processed using traditional data processing tools and processes, while Mc Kinsey [23] defines big data as large pools of data that can be captured, communicated, aggregated, stored, and analyzed. Schniederjans et al. [24] suggests that big data is a collection of data sets that are so large and complex that software systems are hardly able to process them.

Big data stored by organizations is structured and unstructured [25]. Structured data can be used for business analytics as it is, but unstructured data, termed dark data, requires a good deal of pre-processing prior to utilization [25]. Studies across a range of industries indicated that less than half of an organization's structured data is actively used in making decisions, and less than 1% of its unstructured data is analyzed or used at all [25]. The subsets of big data are shown in Fig. 1.

Structured data stored in relational databases or spreadsheets can be accessed and analysed using data mining tools and can be categorized as business-critical data or ROT data [25]. Business critical data is considered the most important data to an organization whereas ROT data has little or no value to an organization [25].

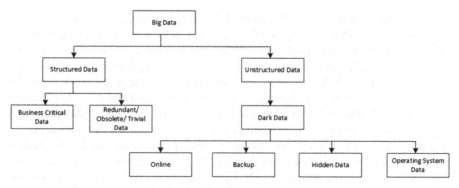

Fig. 1. Big Data Classification [25].

Unstructured data is not organized in relational databases and is uncatalogued [25]. Unstructured data has the characteristics of unstructured information or meaning which is derived not from its structure but from its values and context [14]. Analysis of unstructured data is difficult because of the content and data value that is buried inside unstructured data which requires human interpretation [14]. The inability to access data puts the accuracy of data analysis at risk, which may lead to poor decision making based on incorrect data [14]. Images, movies, and audio in their context provide significant information that can't be accessed by computer keyword analysis of unstructured data [14]. This unstructured dark data can be of many forms but is generally online data, backup data, hidden data or operating system's data [25].

Splunk [7] found that often, organizations ignore potentially valuable data because they don't have the time or resources to prepare it for use. They also found that organizations lacked the necessary skill sets [7]. Indeed, they found that 81% of respondents agreed that "every office worker will need to have a basic level of data analysis skills in the near future" [7].

4 Making Dark Data Discoverable

A study by Gimpel [26] analyzed hundreds of industry reports, news briefs and scholarly articles, and conducted interviews with 22 leading executives and subject matter experts. Findings indicated that executives who want to benefit from dark data must do two things, build dark data awareness within their organizations, and motivate their firms to allocate the resources needed to exploit these data [26].

To build dark data awareness Gimpel [26] suggested informing all levels of employees, from line-level workers to senior management, about the types of places where they can find dark data. A vast amount of data stays trapped within data silos where it remains unknown to those who could use it to improve the business [26]. To break down information silos and shine light on data, managers need to conduct a data audit [26]. Organizations can be aware that data exists, but they are stuck in a data collection rather than a data analysis mode [26]. To improve awareness, Information Technology (IT) people and data scientists must educate business executives about what can be achieved with dark data [26].

Gimpel [26] found that the allocation of the resources needed to exploit dark data requires business leaders to overcome the status quo, move beyond competing priorities and overcome the difficulty predicting returns on technology investments.

Commvault [27] identified five approaches that can reveal dark data. This entails managing storage growth by keeping only data that has value to the business, whilst ensuring that data produced within the organization is collected and stored [27]. Giving users access to be able to search within the organization for data to support their duties will aid their productivity [27]. Another approach is to define a clear lifecycle for the data from the time it is created to when it is deleted and assure compliance and discovery to reduce costs and risks with enterprise-wide search [27]. Finally, ensure that the discovered information is simple and defensible [27]. To truly illuminate dark data in organizations, there is a need for an archive with intelligence [27]. It's that intelligence that will manage storage growth, capture data comprehensively and provide users with simple self-service access, all the while managing it throughout its lifecycle for lower compliance and litigation risk and cost [27].

Ryan [28] singled out four stages of illuminating dark data in an organization. The Identification phase tries to find out what data the organization has and where it is stored (either within or outside the organization) [28]. Classification organizes the data into groups to reflect the structural organizational needs or processes within the organization [28]. The control stage manages the data that has been organized to ensure its security and integrity [28]. It is during this stage that data analysis is conducted [28]. The fourth stage, continuous monitoring, is to ensure that proper mechanisms are put in place to safeguard that the data is continually maintained to serve the needs of the organization and identify areas for improvement [28]. Ryan [28] posits that taking this approach enables analytics to be used on the data within organizations. This is because data is usually unstructured and can only be made usable if the firm is able to mine it and extract useful patterns and relationships which would allow the firm to make the best business decisions [28].

5 Managing Dark Data

There are three basic aspects to handling dark data problems: preventing the problem from arising in the first place, detecting the presence (or perhaps "absence") of dark data, and correcting or at least making allowance for it when it arises [29].

A second study by Ajis et al. [30] was conducted to investigate current dark data management practices by Malaysian SMEs for business operations. Findings of the study indicated that all businesses were employing Dark Data Lifecycle Management (DDLM), which entails appointing a data expert or caretaker and undertaking data caretaking or data stewarding duties [30]. DDLM was identified as a strategy that would contribute to the suppression of dark data while also allowing for the mitigation of the risk and effect of dark data [30]. Not only did business owners utilize DDLM to manage the data in the repository, but also to avoid the emergence of dark data [30].

5.1 Security Issues with Dark Data

Imdad et al. [25] identified dark data as having inherent security risks for organizations. Reputations would be damaged, and revenue would be harmed if their data security was compromised, leaving the organization vulnerable to cybersecurity threats and risks such as personal data breaches and stolen data [14]. Being unstructured in nature makes dark data very difficult to categorize as it is diverse in character or content [25]. As these data streams cannot be categorized it can be difficult to define proper access control mechanisms for data [25]. Some if not all of the data is confidential in nature and unauthorized access to that data can cause a data breach [25]. The implementation of authentication and proper control lists for accessing data, and the concept of having more than one person required to complete a task (Separation of Duty) can help mitigate overly permissive access that leads to malicious insider breaches [31]. Researchers found that restricting access to data, constantly monitoring data protection to uncover security gaps, and treating data catastrophe planning as a critical contingency plan all contributed to the safety of dark data [30]. Identifying the users and groups with access to data, matching them to who should or shouldn't have access and recognizing anomalies reduces security risks and increases organizational effectiveness [32].

Should data be required for legal or financial matters, it may not be located immediately due to its random nature [25]. This may lead to a legal and financial liability to an organization [25]. When the Hypertext Transfer Protocol (HTTP) was introduced, there was no concept for caching sensitive data [25]. Now the recent web servers have a way to cache data on the basis of permissions in the server header [25]. In a web cache attack the content delivering websites are targeted and create latency to access this content getting into this cache [25]. It is difficult to audit data creation trails and the flow of data because of its storage [25]. There are no proper guidelines about access so data flow, replication and usage cannot be identified [25]. When someone internal to the organization gets access to data and exploits it, the organization has no audit trails to track the responsible entity [25].

Information that is not managed properly can also expose an enterprise to considerable vulnerabilities. Distributed and duplicated content, without explicit oversights, weakens security [10]. Hackers can have more potential entry points and leaked, lost, stolen, or breached dark data can result in damaged reputations as well as loss of competitive strength [10].

To better harness dark data, the first step is to secure and encrypt all data to prevent it from being exploited. Second, prevent it from piling up and getting out of control, which requires analyzing it regularly [10]. Classify legacy data to give it meaning going forward and assign owners to data, so they can review and decide if there is value [10]. Retention policies can be set up to automate how data is handled going forward and delete dark data that's considered redundant, obsolete, and trivial. [10].

Dark data is huge and unstructured, but machine learning offers tools and techniques to study this information and recognize patterns in it [10]. The data can be processed using smart algorithms because it cannot be analyzed manually [10]. Frameworks like Hadoop provide a platform to break this data into chunks that can be managed and studied [10]. Additionally, metadata can be employed to identify, link, curate, and cross-reference information in a way that unlocks its relevance and usefulness [10]. A file analysis (FA) tool may further help to sift through dark data [10].

Schniederjans et al. [24] described the business analytics process as a three-stage process mining the information out of the data to unlock the valuable or problem-solving information locked in the sources of the data. Descriptive analytics analysis sorts out the data as the size of some data sources can be unimaginable, complex, and confusing [24]. This makes some sense out of its informational value indicating patterns or business behavior that can be identified representing targets of business opportunities and possible future trend behavior [24]. Predictive analytic analysis uses multiple regression analysis, or other forecasting methods such as exponential smoothing and smoothing averages to develop forecasts of business trends [24]. Prescriptive analytic analysis applies various operations research methodologies to optimally allocate a firm's limited resources to take best advantage of the opportunities it found in the predicted future trends [24]. Using business analytics solutions, organizations can identify the factors that impact their performance, create more accurate forward-looking strategies, enhance efficiency, increase profitability, and improve customer satisfaction and loyalty [33].

5.2 Role of Data Governance

Dark data should be seen as a business opportunity however there are challenges that it presents [6]. Data governance, data compliance, and cost-efficient storage are three such challenges. To address these challenges an organization must have clear visibility into their data [6].

There are various definitions of data governance. Researchers differ in defining data governance. The Data Governance Institute (DGI) defines it as "data governance is a system of decision rights and accountabilities for information-related processes, executed according to agreed-upon models which describe who can take what actions with what information, and when, under what circumstances, using what methods" [34]. Newman and Logan [35] define data governance as "the collection of decision rights, processes, standards, policies and technologies required to manage, maintain and exploit information as an enterprise resource".

Almeida [36] says that data governance is a set of policies and practices that an organization can establish to support their data management. Policies and procedures that govern data management will help eliminate inconsistencies from dark data and improve data quality, thus helping to reduce data management costs [6]. Henderson [37] defines data governance as the exercise of authority and control (planning, monitoring, and enforcement) over the management of data assets.

Data governance plays an essential role in fulfilling the organization's strategy and growth by providing visibility to what data is available and how it can be used [36]. Engineering aspects such as the data architecture, access controls and tooling are important in data governance [36]. One of the most crucial tasks for data governance to accomplish is to continuously discover new data sources and maintain a living catalog of data within the organization [36].

Schembera [13] stated that any attempt to diminish or even try to eliminate dark data from facilities cannot be tackled exclusively with technical efforts, but a profound change in the administrative structure of how institutions manage and control their users and their data is also needed. His proposal was to create a Scientific Data Officer (SDO) responsible for the storage, curation, and general good health of data in the computing facilities following the FAIR principles of scientific data management [13]. Wilkinson et al. [38] developed a measurable set of principles to act as a guideline for those wishing to enhance the reusability of their data holdings. All research objects should be Findable, Accessible, Interoperable and Reusable (FAIR) both for machines and for people [38]. Henderson [37] suggested that a person appointed as a data steward would have accountability and day-to-day responsibility for data and processes to ensure effective control and use of data assets.

Data governance principles make compliance standards easier to audit and help an organization find ways to comply with privacy regulations in multiple jurisdictions [36]. Data governance requires an entire shift in an organization's culture and its practices associated with data [36]. Henderson [37] says effective and long-lasting data governance programs require a cultural shift in organizational thinking and behavior about data, as well as an ongoing program of change management to support the new thinking, behaviors, policies, and processes to achieve the desired future state of behavior around data.

Panian [39] said that the goals of data governance are to ensure data meets the needs of the business, protect, manage, and develop data as a valued enterprise asset and lower the costs of managing data. The successful implementation of a data governance program addresses and enhances all six of the key data attributes of accessibility, availability, quality, consistency, auditability and security [39].

Koltay [40] said that adopting data governance is advantageous, because it is a service based on standardised, repeatable processes and is designed to enable the transparency of data-related processes and cost reduction. It is also useful, because it refers to rules, policies, standards; decision rights; accountabilities and methods of enforcement [40].

[41] The belief that increased use of governance practices is good for firm performance may not seem unusual, particularly if these practices are intended to enable innovative uses of information or to suppress risky activities that might lead to an erosion of value from using information [41]. Over-governance could limit information-led innovation, motivating users to work around policies and to take unnecessary risks with their information [41].

6 Discussion

This paper examined the management of dark data which led to a discussion of the challenges related to dark data (security issues and the role of data governance).

Donnelley Financial Solutions [42], along with Morning Consult, surveyed 300 professionals at large U.S. and U.K. public and private companies to understand their cybersecurity experiences and expectations. The most revealing finding was that seven of 10 enterprise leaders surveyed said that storing detailed information presents more risk than value [42]. The report also revealed that nearly half of the respondents don't have the technical tools required to adequately do the job of safeguarding dark data [42]. More research is needed to discover and evaluate the tools necessary to provide security for an organization's dark data.

Al-Ruithe et al. [43] suggest that since data governance is still under researched, there is need to advance research in data governance to deepen practice. The three main components of data governance people (roles, responsibilities, working groups and committees), processes, and tools and technology need to be researched. Every organization is composed of stakeholders with different values, views, beliefs, and ideals that they bring to the organization. The data governance roles and responsibilities of each of these stakeholders needs to be researched.

Data governance tools and technology is one of the critical success factors in the successful implementation of data governance [44]. Research into data governance tools and technologies can form an important part of an overall data governance strategy and implementation as they can automate repetitive activities and processes, enhance productivity, and reduce operational costs. This investigation will cover the organization's readiness for purchasing data governance tools as well as aspects that need to be considered when assessing the data governance tools and technology in the marketplace.

Data governance focuses on how decisions are made about data and how people and processes are expected to behave in relation to data [37]. A Data Governance program will develop policies and procedures, cultivate data stewardship practices at multiple levels within the organization, and engage in organizational change management efforts that actively communicate to the organization the benefits of improved data governance and the behaviors necessary to successfully manage data as an asset [37]. For most organizations, adopting formal Data Governance requires the support of organizational change management, as well as sponsorship from Senior Management.

7   Conclusion and Future Work

Dark data is not going to go away anytime soon. As data storage costs decrease organizations will see this as an opportunity to store more and more data. The appointment of an SDO or similar position can provide a point of focus and direction for an organization. This person would be responsible for the storage, curation, and general good health of data in the computing facilities following the FAIR principles of scientific data management.

However, this does not excuse the researcher or business user for not practicing good data governance and ensuring that their data is structured and catalogued as it is being stored. In the future research should be expended in investigating how organizations manage the three main components of data governance, the roles and responsibilities of all stakeholders and the data governance tools and technologies that organizations use.

Data security and cybersecurity are central to ensuring that an organization's data is not breached or stolen. Corruption of data or loss of data can have catastrophic effects to an organization. It can lead to loss of valuable research data gathered over many years or cause major financial problems for a business, even leading to bankruptcy. We are hearing almost daily of such issues, so it is becoming more important to conduct research to discover and evaluate the tools necessary to provide security for an organization's dark data.

Tallon et al. [41] said that a relevant but under-researched area comprises the effectiveness of data governance. Current research only provides brief evidence of the intermediate performance effects and the ways how to measure those effects [41]. If organizations use too bureaucratic, complex, and use restrictive data governance mechanisms, this 'over-governance' could lead to a performance decrease by limiting data led innovations and motivating users to bypass policies and take unnecessary risks with their data [41]. Future research should conduct a more in-depth analysis of this relationship between restrictive data governance mechanisms and performance decrease, which determines the optimal data governance design.

References

1. Ackoff, R.L.: From data to wisdom. J. Appl. Syst. Anal. **16**, 3–9 (1989)
2. Allen, G.D.: Hierarchy of knowledge – from data to wisdom. Int. J. Curr. Res. Multidisc. (IJCRM) **2**(1), 15–23 (2017)
3. Turban, E., Rainer, R.K., Potter, R.E.: Introduction to Information Technology, 3rd edn. Wiley, New York (2005)
4. Snyder, H.: Literature review as a research methodology - An overview and guidelines (2019)
5. Braun, V., Clarke, V.: Using thematic analysis in psychology (2006)
6. Ashbel, A.: Dark data: a challenge enterprise data management can't ignore. https://bluexp. netapp.com/blog/cds-blg-dark-data-a-challenge-enterprise-data-management-cant-ignore. Accessed 11 Nov 2022
7. Splunk: The state of dark data (2019). Accessed 11 Nov 2022
8. Goetz, T.: Freeing the dark data of failed scientific experiment. Wired Mag. **15**(10), 7–12 (2007). http://www.wired.com/science/discoveries/magazine/15-10/st_essay. Accessed 11 Nov 2022
9. Grimm, D.J.: The dark data quandary. Am. Univ. Law Rev. **68**(3), 768 (2019)
10. Martin, E.J.: Dark Data: Analyzing Unused and Ignored Information (2016)
11. Heidorn, P.B.: Shedding light on the dark data in the long tail of science. Libr. Trends **57**(2), 280–299 (2008)
12. Heidorn, P.B., Stahlman, G.R., Steffen, J.: The astrolabe project: identifying and curating astronomical 'dark data' through development of cyberinfrastructure resources. Astrophys. J. Suppl. Ser. **236**(1), 3 (2018). https://doi.org/10.1051/epjconf/201818603003,lastaccessed 2022/11/11
13. Schembera, B., Durán, J.M.: Dark data as the new challenge for big data science and the introduction of the scientific data officer (2019)
14. Ajis, A.F.M., Zakaria, S., Ahmad, A.R.: Demystifying dark data characteristics in small and medium enterprises: a Malaysian experience (2022)
15. Gartner Inc.: Innovation Insight: File Analysis Innovation Delivers an Understanding of Unstructured Dark Data, Alan Dayley, March (2013)
16. Cadariu, S.: Dark Data at the Enterprise Level: What is it and What Risks Does it Pose? https://www.aitimejournal.com/dark-data-at-the-enterprise-level-what-is-is-and-what-risks-does-it-pose. Accessed 11 Nov 2022
17. Cadariu, S.: Data Fabric and Cloud Computing as Enterprise Technologies, https://www.ait imejournal.com/data-fabric-and-cloud-computing-as-enterprise-technologies, last accessed 2022/11/11
18. Veritas: The databerg report - see what others don't (2015)
19. Dimitrov, W., Siarova, S., Petkova, L.: Types of dark data and hidden cybersecurity risks (2018)

20. Jackson, T.W., Hodgkinson, I.R.: Keeping a lower profile: how firms can reduce their digital carbon footprints (2022)
21. Intel: A vision for big data
22. Zikopoulos, P., Eaton, C., Dirk, D., Deutsch, T., Lapis, G.: Understanding Big Data: Analytics for Enterprise Class Hadoop and Streaming Data, 1st edn. Mcgraw-Hill, New York (2012)
23. McKinsey: Big Data: The Next Frontier For Innovation, Competition and Creativity (2011)
24. Schniederjans, M.J., Schniederjans, D.G., Starkey, C.M.: Business Analytics Principles, Concepts and Applications, 1st edn. Gill Editorial Services, Pearson Education, Inc., Upper Saddle River (2014)
25. Imdad, M., et al.: Dark Data: Opportunities and Challenges (2020)
26. Gimpel, G.: Dark data: the invisible resource that can drive performance now (2021)
27. CommVault: 5 ways to illuminate your dark data (2014)
28. Ryan, S.: Illuminating Dark Data (2014)
29. Hand, D.J.: Dark data: why what you don't know matters (2020)
30. Ajis, A.F.M., Ishak, I., Harun, Q.N.: Modelling dark data management framework - a grounded theory (2022)
31. Bertino, E.: Data protection from insider threats. Synthesis Lect. Data Manage. 4(4), 1–91 (2012). https://doi.org/10.2200/S00431ED1V01Y201207DTM028
32. CommVault.: Turning dark data into smart data (2014)
33. Kevin, N.M., Wanyaga, F.M., Kibaara, D., Dinda, W.A., Ngatia, J.K.: Dark data: business analytical tools and facilities for illuminating dark data (2016)
34. The Data Governance Institute: Definitions of Data Governance (2015). https://datagovernance.com/defining-data-governance/. Accessed 08 Dec 2022
35. Newman, D., Logan, D.: Governance is an essential building block for enterprise information system. Gartner Research (2006). https://www.gartner.com/en/documents/492444. Accessed 08 Dec 2022
36. Almeida, B.: Data governance challenges just got easier to solve (2021). https://bluexp.net app.com/blog/clc-blg-data-governance-just-got-easier-to-solve. Accessed 11 Nov 2022
37. Henderson, D.: DAMA-DMBOK-Data-Management-Body-of-Knowledge, 2nd edn. (2017)
38. Wilkinson, M.D., et al.: The FAIR guiding principles for scientific data management and stewardship. Sci. Data 3 (2016). https://www.nature.com/articles/sdata201618. Accessed 11 Nov 2022
39. Panian, Z.: Some practical experiences in data governance (2010)
40. Koltay, T.: Data governance, data literacy and the management of data quality. IFLA J. 42(4), 303–312 (2016)
41. Tallon, P.P., Ramirez, R.V., Short, J.E.: The information artifact in it governance: toward a theory of information governance. J. Manage. Inf. Syst. 30(3), 141–177 (2014)
42. Donnelley Financial Solutions: Understanding Risk: The Dark Side of Data (2022). https://www.dfinsolutions.com/sites/default/files/documents/2022-10/DealMaker_Meter_Security_Report. Accessed 08 Dec 2022
43. Al-Ruithe, M., Benkhelifa, E., Hameed, K.: Systematic literature review of data governance & cloud data governance (2019)
44. Mahanti, R.: Data governance components and framework. In: Mahanti, R. (ed.) Data Governance Success, pp. 127–166. Springer, Singapore (2021). https://doi.org/10.1007/978-981-16-5086-4_5, https://doi.org/10.1007/978-981-16-3583-0_4. Accessed 08 Dec 2022

Social Network Analysis to Accelerate for R&D of New Material Development

Hideki Hayashida[1]([✉]) and Hiroki Funashima[2]

[1] Department of Industrial Technology and Innovation, Tokyo University of Agriculture and Technology, Fuchu, Japan
hideki-hayashida@go.tuat.ac.jp
[2] Department of Comprehensive Engineering, Kindai University Technical College, Higashiosaka, Japan

Abstract. A feasibility study on the technology and market trends of organoids was conducted by analyzing information using published patent information and network analysis. It was found that the organoid market exhibits a scale-free network structure among complex networks, and that Japanese research is isolated and domestic-only. On the other hand, the largest research clusters were found to have research institutions with structural holes, indicating that collaboration with foreign research institutions with such holes is desirable to accelerate Japanese research. This suggests the effectiveness of an analytical method that combines patent analysis and network analysis for practitioners.

Keywords: Organoid · Network analysis · R&D management · Data analysis

1 Introduction

The essence of innovation is the creation of new knowledge. It is essential to build a "place (Ba)" where teams and organoids can create new "knowledge", where people can gather in a flexible manner, and where mutual support can be provided, in other words, how to build a network. As an example of how to construct and manage knowledge that leads to innovation, we attempted to analyze a network related to cancer organoid research.

Since cancer organoids can reproduce the properties of a patient's cancer tissue, they are expected to be applied to cell modeling in drug discovery, development of new therapies, and evaluation of drug efficacy. They are also being studied as disease models suitable for elucidating the mechanisms of cancer development, recurrence, and metastasis. Given these factors, organoids are expected to be a next-generation medical tool contributing new drug development, cancer treatment, and personalized medicine. Its market is expected to expand in the future.

Although many research institutes in Japan are currently conducting R&D for practical applications using organoids, obtaining a complete picture of research activities on a global scale is difficult. In addition, it has been pointed out that one of the challenges of global Japanese R&D is the lack of joint research with foreign countries. On the other

L. Uden and I-H. Ting (Eds.): KMO 2023, CCIS 1825, pp. 161–168, 2023.
https://doi.org/10.1007/978-3-031-34045-1_14

hand, it can be assumed that even those who wish to exchange information and conduct joint research with overseas researchers may not be able to take concrete action because they do not have an overall picture of the situation. Under such an R&D environment, "If Japan's R&D position in the global R&D network can be clarified, it will be possible to efficiently build networks with overseas countries. We thought that this was a good idea. Therefore, this study aimed to clarify Japan's R&D position in the global R&D network analyzing the network centrality using applicant data of patent information.

2 Literature Review

2.1 Organoid Innovation (OI)

Cancer metastasizes from tumor tissue to the whole body and causes organ dysfunction, leading to the patient's death. Effective therapies have been developed and investigated for many years to inhibit cancer metastasis and improve the survival rate of cancer patients. In developing novel therapeutics, pathological models such as 2D-cultured cancer cell lines and patient-derived xenograft animal models (PDX) in preclinical studies have been used to elucidate the pathogenic mechanisms of cancer and screen for therapeutic agents. However, these disease models have difficulty reflecting the in vivo microenvironment, and it has been reported that 90% of development candidates have no confirmed therapeutic effect in humans [1]. Organoids have, therefore, recently attracted attention as a new culture model [2]. Organoids are 3D disease models with features similar to in vivo tissues and are formed by the three-dimensional culture of stem cells in a medium containing multiple growth factors required for stem cell self-renewal and a laminin-rich basement membrane matrix called Matrigel [3]. The ability to reproduce the unique cancer characteristics of individual patients has led to the selection of personalized therapies, which are expected to have applications in novel drug screening and personalized medicine [4]. Indeed, the reproducibility of the derived patient's drug response in cancer patient-derived organoids has been reported, indicating that organoids can be applied to the evaluation of anti-cancer drugs [5].

On the other hand, cancer cells are known to have intracellular heterogeneity at the single-cell level [6], and it has been reported that cancer treatment resistance increases with the increasing frequency of subclonal mutations that cause heterogeneity development [7, 8].

Since heterogeneity in size, proliferative capacity, shape, and gene expression is also known to exist in organoids, which reflect tumor tissue characteristics [9, 10], organoids are a suitable model for analyzing heterogeneity within cancer tissue model for analyzing heterogeneity within cancer tissues. On the other hand, since the process and causes of heterogeneity within tumors that cause treatment resistance are not yet understood, temporal observation and analysis of the process of heterogeneity development would be helpful for elucidating the mechanism of cancer treatment resistance acquisition. However, the method of embedding stem cells in a dome-shaped solidified Matrigel, which is commonly used in organoid culture, poses challenges in that stem cells are randomly arranged in the Matrigel, resulting in overlap of cells in the same xy-axis and binding of adjacent organoids, causing differences in size and growth rate during culture [11], challenges [11, 12]. Therefore, in evaluating anti-cancer drugs using organoid models, the effects of drugs may not be accurately assessed depending on the organoid culture environment. Based on the above, it is expected to control the arrangement of organoids in Matrigel, array single cancer stem cells, and monitor the process of organoid formation from single cancer stem cells to analyze heterogeneity in anti-cancer drug response using cancer organoids.

We have developed a microcavity array (MCA), a cell trapping device for the highly efficient accumulation of hematopoietic cells, etc. The MCA consists of a nickel substrate with several microns of microscopic holes at equal intervals, and a cell suspension is sucked from the back of the device. It has been confirmed that MCAs can be used to hold and single culture cells at regular intervals [13]. In a previous study, diatom and yeast cells were arrayed on micropores using MCA and embedded in agarose gels followed by time-lapse imaging, demonstrating that MCA is effective for observing single cells over time and analyzing heterogeneity among single cells and cell behavior in culture [14]. Such cell capture devices make it possible to monitor cellular changes over time on a single cell-by-cell basis.

2.2 Network Analysis (NI)

Granovetter has researched social networks on the "strength of weak ties" where novel and valuable information is more likely to come from people with weak social ties, such as acquaintances of acquaintances or people who know each other briefly (weak It is more likely to come from people with weak social ties (weak ties), such as acquaintances of acquaintances, or people with little acquaintances (weak ties), than from people with strong social ties (strong ties), such as one's own family, close friends, or workmates [15]. In particular, Nieminen proposed order centrality, a concept in social network analysis, showing that order centrality is a valuable method for measuring graph centrality [16]. Boissevain conducted a network analysis of how humans interact, share information, and conduct economic transactions in a village on the island of Malta [17]. Freeman defined proximity centrality as measuring proximity centrality by calculating the sum of the distances between a node and all other nodes and taking its reciprocal [18]. This definition is still used today as one of the central indicators of social network analysis, such as mediate centrality proposed by Freeman[19]. Mediocentricity is a measure of the extent to which a node plays a mediating role when it needs to take the shortest path between other nodes in the network. In other words, it indicates whether the node has is essential in transmitting information and diffusion of influence in the network. Coleman argued in the 1980s and 1990s that linkages among member in closed networks where information and resources are shared are desirable [20]. Watts and Strogatz, on the other hand, proposed the Small World Theory [21] in 1998, pointing out the importance of short-distance connections in social networks. Burt [22], in his work on the network structure of innovation creation, found that networks with structural holes are more likely to have information redundancy than networks with sparse connections. Since the 2000s, Fleming has analyzed collaborative networks among inventors in patents and found that the structure of inventor networks is also an important factor in facilitating the propagation of new ideas and knowledge. Fleming also found that a dense inventor network may facilitate information and knowledge sharing [23]. He also points out that when there is a central inventor, it is easier for information and knowledge to spread through that inventor. He also demonstrated the relationship between network structure and performance. Takashi has conducted empirical research on network structure and its impact on R&D and innovation performance [24].

In recent years, social network analysis has been applied to business and economic fields, such as online networking and recent coronary infections due to the spread of social networking services. Against this background, However, there has not yet been enough empirical research on how to construct a forum for the creation of "knowledge" that is useful in practical terms.

3   Research Methods

3.1   Research Framework

This study used the Patent Information Platform (J-PlatPat) to analyze technical trends related to organoids. Of the patent information using the word "organoid" in the full text of the patents, 920 patents that were made known after 2009, when the organoid culture system was established, were included in the analysis.

In this work, we derived three different concepts of centrality to estimate network properties. The first one is eigenvector centrality. The simplest form of centrality is the degree at a node. However, the degree is an extremely crude measure of centrality. In effect, it gives one "centrality point" for each neighborhood a node has. However, not all neighbors are necessarily equal. Often a node's importance in a network is increased by having connections to other nodes that are themselves important. We can the eigenvector centrality using node's several points proportional to the centrality score of its neighbors rather than one point for each neighbor in the network it has. The graded equation is given as.

$$u(t + 1) = Au(t)$$

where A and $u(t) \equiv (u_1, u_2, \ldots, u_n)^T$ are the neighbor matrix and the vector aligned centrality u_i of the node v_i respectively.

Interpreting the above equation as the influence u_i of a node is the sum of u_j over adjacent points, we can regard variable t as the index of updates for the iteration. Since the above equation is an incremental equation with t as the index, we consider repeating it to find the centrality at each vertex. In general, however, it is not possible to find the number of updates for $u_1, u_2, \ldots, u_N$ diverges. Therefore, we impose a bound condition each time such that the sum of $u_1, u_2, \ldots, u_N$ is equal to 1, and iterate. The linear algebra show us that these iterations are shown to be maximal eigenvectors of A if there is at least one closed odd angle in the network. Therefore, if the largest eigenvalue of A is λ_N, eigenvector centrality is given as.

$$Au = \lambda_N u .$$

With eigenvector centrality defined in this way, a node can achieve high centrality by having many neighbors with modest centrality or a few neighbors with high centrality (or both). This situation is natural. The node can influence by knowing many nodes or the node can influence by knowing a few nodes.

Second, we evaluated the closeness centrality. The closeness centrality is defined that how close on average, the node are from itself to others. Mathematically, the closeness centrality is defined as

$$\frac{N-1}{\prod_{j=1,\, j\neq i}^{N} d(v_i,\, v_j)} = \frac{1}{L_i}$$

where $d(v_i,\, v_j)$ is the distance between nodes v_i and v_j. L_i is the average distance from node v_i to other nodes.

The betweenness centrality is the degree to bridge and control the flow of information in a network for the nodes. Mathematically, betweenness centrality is defined as

$$b_i = \frac{\sum_{i_s=1,\, i_s\neq i}^{N} \sum_{i_t=1,\, i_t\neq i}^{i_s-1} \frac{g_i^{(i_s,\, i_t)}}{N_{i_s,\, i_t}}}{(N-1)(N-2)/2}$$

where $g_i^{(i_s,\, i_t)}$ is the number of vertices in the shortest path going from the start point v_{i_s} to the endpoint v_{i_t}. $N_{i_s,\, i_t}$ is the number of shortest paths from the start point to the endpoint.

4   Results and Discussion

4.1   Network Analysis

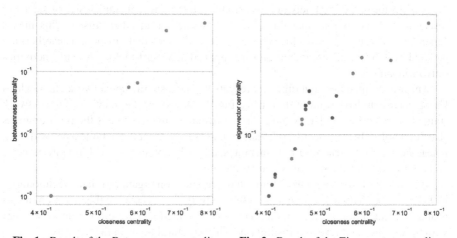

Fig. 1. Result of the Betweenness centrality   **Fig. 2.** Result of the Eigenvector centrality

Where $g_i^{(i_s,\, i_t)}$ is the number of vertices in the shortest path going from the start point v_{i_s} to the endpoint v_{i_t}. $N_{i_s,\, i_t}$ is the number of shortest paths from the start point to the end point. Figure 1 and Fig. 2 are not clear due to the small number of data, however, both logarithmic graphs show a straight line with both graphs rising steadily. This assumed to resemble a typical scale-free network structure [26].

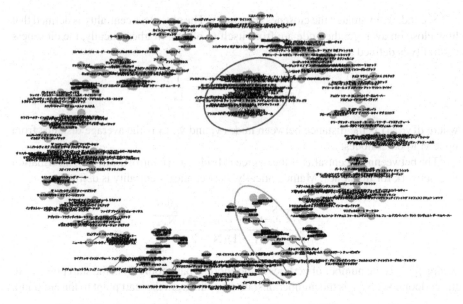

Fig. 3. Result of Total network of organoid technology (Color figure online)

Figure 1 and Fig. 2 are not clear due to the small number of data, however, both logarithmic graphs show a straight line with both graphs rising steadily. This assumed to resemble a typical scale-free network structure [26]. Within the Fig. 3, red circle is the biggest cluster in the total network and orange circle represents the cluster of Japanese researchers. It is obvious that this cluster is isolated from other cluster. This means Japanese researchers make a closed network. It can be seen that Japanese researchers are isolated from overseas researchers and are engaged in inward-looking research activities only in Japan.

The area framed in red in Fig. 3 represents the most significant network class, which European research institutions dominated Fig. 4. Shows an enlarged view of the network framed in red in Fig. 3. The two red circle institute or university has the positioning as structural hole." In other words, if isolated Japanese researchers can build a network with researchers at these structural-hole institutes, they will obtain much helpful information, and their research can be expected to accelerate.

As a result, it was found that although the research on organoid-related technologies is the scale-free network of complex systems. To further accelerate this research, it was found that much helpful information could be obtained if it were possible to network with universities and research institutions with structural holes in the network.

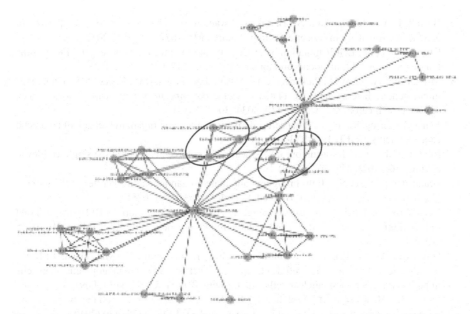

Fig. 4. Focused on the biggest network from total network of organoid technology (Color figure online)

5 Conclusion

The outcome of this study is that Japanese researchers are isolated from large overseas R&D networks. Our analysis regarding the network centrality of the largest overseas network cluster revealed that two research institutions are positioned to have a structural hole. It was suggested that information exchange and joint research with research institutions with such a structural hole would promote research in Japan.

By combining such patent data analysis and network analysis, we found a practical and effective way to determine what kind of research institutions and companies to establish an information network with to promote research.

References

1. Hutchinson, L., Kirk, R.: High drug attrition rates-where are we going wrong? Nat. Rev. Clin. Oncol. **8**(4), 189–190 (2011)
2. Sato, T., et al.: Single Lgr5 stem cells build crypt-villus structures in vitro without a mesenchymal niche. Nature **459**(7244), 262-U147 (2009)
3. Sato, T., et al.: Long-term expansion of epithelial organoids from human colon, adenoma, adenocarcinoma, and Barrett's epithelium. Gastroenterology **141**(5), 1762–1772 (2011)
4. Dekkers, J.F., et al.: Characterizing responses to CFTR-modulating drugs using rectal organoids derived from subjects with cystic fibrosis. Sci. Transl. Med. **8**(344), 344–384 (2016)
5. Vlachogiannis, G., et al.: Patient-derived organoids model treatment response of metastatic gastrointestinal cancers. Science **359**(6378), 920–931 (2018)

6. Burrell, R.A., McGranahan, N., Bartek, J., Swanton, C.: The causes and consequences of genetic heterogeneity in cancer evolution. Nature **501**(7467), 338–345 (2013)

7. Chen, Z.Y., et al.: EGFR mutation heterogeneity and the mixed response to EGFR tyrosine kinase inhibitors of lung adenocarcinomas. Oncologist. **17**, 978–985 (2012)

8. Mroz, E.A., Tward, A.D., Pickering, C.R., Myers, J.N., Ferris, R.L., Rocco, J.W.: High intra-tumor genetic heterogeneity is related to worse outcome in patients with head and neck squamous cell carcinoma. Cancer **119**, 3034–3042 (2013)

9. Van de Wetering, M., et al.: Prospective derivation of a living organoid biobank of colorectal cancer patients. Cell **161**(4), 933–945 (2015)

10. Roerink, S.F., et al.: Intra-tumour diversification in colorectal cancer at the single-cell level. Nature **556**(7702), 457–463 (2018)

11. Brandenberg, N., et al.: High-throughput automated organoid culture via stem-cell aggregation in microcavity arrays. Nat. Biomed. Eng. **4**(9), 863–876 (2020)

12. Decembrini, S., Hoehnel, S., Brandenberg, N., Arsenijevic, Y., Lutolf, M.P.: Hydrogel-based milliwell arrays for standardized and scalable retinal organoid cultures. Sci. Rep. **10**, 10275 (2020)

13. Hosokawa, M., Arakaki, A., Takahashi, M., Mori, T., Takeyama, H., Matsunaga, T.: High-density microcavity array for cell detection: single-cell analysis of hematopoietic stem cells in peripheral blood mononuclear cells. Anal. Chem. **81**(13), 5308–5313 (2009)

14. Osada, K., Hosokawa, M., Yoshino, T., Tanaka, T.: Monitoring of cellular behaviors by microcavity array-based single-cell patterning. Analyst. **139**(2), 425–430 (2014)

15. Granovetter, M.S.: The strength of weak ties. Am. J. Sociol. **78**(6), 1360–1380 (1973)

16. Nieman, U.J.: On the centrality in a directed graph. Soc. Sci. Res. **2**(4), 371–378 (1973)

17. Boissevain, J.: Towards a sociology of social anthropology. Theory Soc. **1**, 211–230 (1974)

18. Freeman, L.C.: A set of measures od centrality based on betweeness. Sociometry **40**(1), 35–41 (1977)

19. Freeman, L.C.: Centrality in social networks conceptual clarification. Soc. Netw. **1**, 215–239 (1978)

20. Coleman, J.S.: Social capital in the creation of human capital. Am. J. Sociol. **94**, S95–S120 (1988)

21. Watts, D.J., Strogatz, S.H.: Collective dynamics of 'Small-world' networks. Nature **393**, 440–442 (1998)

22. Burt, R.S.: Structural Holes: The Social Structure of Competition. Harvard University Press, Cambridge, Mass (1992)

23. Fleming, L., Mingo, S., Chen, D.: Collaborative brokerage, generative creativity, and creative success. Adm. Sci. Q. **52**, 443–475 (2007)

24. Kishi, N.: Network characteristics and product development performance, p 218. MMRC Discussion paper (2008)

25. Konno, N.: Complex network Tokyo Japan Kindai Kagakusya (2010)

26. Biagini, F., Kauermann, G., Meyer-Brandis, T. (eds.): Network Science. Springer, Cham (2019). https://doi.org/10.1007/978-3-030-26814-5

Global Megatrends and Global GDP in 2004–2021: An Empirical Big Data Look at John Naisbitt's 12 Key Global Megatrend Variables and Global GDP PPP

Jari Kaivo-oja[1,2(✉)] and Teemu Santonen[3]

[1] Finland Futures Research Centre, Turku School of Economics, University of Turku, FFRC Unit of Tampere, Åkerlundinkatu 2 A, 33100 Tampere, Finland
jari.kaivo-oja@utu.fi

[2] Kazimieras Simonavicius University, Dariaus ir Gireno st. 21, 02189 Vilnius, Lithuania

[3] Laurea University of Applied Sciences, Ratatie 22, 01300 Vantaa, Finland
teemu.santonen@laurea.fi

Abstract. This study presents a big data-driven estimate of John Naisbitt's 12 megatrends and global economic growth. Empirical assessments and statistical monitoring analyses are presented for the years 2004–2021. The study assesses the intensity of megatrends and the direction of megatrend development based on big data from Google Trends. The study also presents a correlation analysis of the relationship between the 12 megatrend variables and global economic growth (GDP PPP). Half of the trends (N = 6) are on an upward trend, one-third of them (N = 4) are declining, and the remaining two trends follow an irregular path. The analysis of megatrends also reveals significant popularity differences between the trends. Importantly, megatrends are not stable entities, and unexpected events such as a pandemic or economic crisis appear to have a significant impact on them. Megatrends also have strong positive or negative interlinkages with each other.

Keywords: Global megatrends · Global GDP · Megatrend analysis · John Naisbitt · Google Trend · Indicator Analysis

1 Introduction

In this article, we will examine global megatrends and their related changes using Google Trend data. In 1982, a "social forecaster" named John Naisbitt wrote a global bestseller titled "Megatrends: Ten New Directions Transforming Our Lives." He later published many other popular books on megatrends. John Naisbitt [1–3] opened the eyes of many people to future megatrends. His message was quite simple: By paying attention to the underlying megatrends, you can make better decisions about what to study, where to live and invest, and what career path to pursue. The analysis of global megatrends was identified as a key issue for analyzing the decision-making environment and making strategic and visionary decisions. The analysis of megatrends was linked to global landscape and

L. Uden and I-H. Ting (Eds.): KMO 2023, CCIS 1825, pp. 169–181, 2023.
https://doi.org/10.1007/978-3-031-34045-1_15

national country analyses. A megatrend is a long-term shift in behavior or attitude with a global impact across multiple industries and societies. Megatrend analysis is defined as a technique that enables businesses to better anticipate future changes in the market by analyzing current trends and predicting future developments that will have a significant impact on businesses. Megatrends are, of course, a hot topic, but very few understand how to make sense of and apply them to growth and business strategies.

The research idea for this empirical study is to examine the same key trend variables that John Naisbitt identified in his studies, using Google Trend indicators, and to highlight the importance of twelve key megatrend indicators to global economic growth (GDP PPP US Dollars). In selecting the twelve megatrend variables, we relied on Richard Slaughter's synthesis article on the real "megatrends." In this empirical study, we have limited the number of megatrends to twelve key indicators and global GDP PPP [4, 5]. We will not analyze all the megatrend variables that John Naisbitt identified since there were many concepts and variables in his various books, and it is not possible to analyze all these listed megatrend variables in detail in this conference paper. However, we aim to cover the most important ones that are relevant for today's discussions and decision-making processes in the world.

2   Theoretical Background and Research Questions

2.1   Theoretical Background

In general terms, megatrend research refers to the study of long-term, global trends that are likely to shape the future of society, economy, technology, political systems, and cultures. Megatrend research is relevant to knowledge management activities in organizations, both in the private and public sectors, because trends can have significant implications for organizations, industries, and individuals [6, 7]. These implications are typically linked to future scenarios [8, 9]. Knowledge management has no single accepted definition, but it is widely accepted that it involves the strategies, processes, and technologies that organizations use to capture, store, share, and utilize knowledge. Thus, there is a strong link between knowledge management research and megatrend research, as knowledge management can help organizations navigate and adapt to the changes brought about by trends in their decision environment.

Many case studies of knowledge management indicate that trend and megatrend analyses are closely linked to the relevance of knowledge management practices in organizations [7, 10]. Additionally, knowledge management can assist organizations in identifying and responding to emerging trends by facilitating the creation of knowledge networks that bring together experts, practitioners, and thought leaders to share insights and best practices. Basic scenarios and strategies involve either following trends or acting against them [11, 12]. Therefore, knowledge management research is closely linked to trend research because it provides a valuable framework for understanding and responding to long-term global trends that shape the future of society and organizations.

2.2 Research Questions

As a professional futurist, John Naisbitt utilised a unique method of tracking the trends and megatrends called content analysis [1, 2, 12]. The methodology was developed during World War II, when US Army intelligence officers would obtain newspapers from behind enemy lines. They'd carefully examine them for clues such as food shortages, troop movements, political statements, strategy plans, etc. to try and discern the enemy's possible next moves. The methodology of seeking signals of change is still relevant for knowledge management research because most decision-makers want to look forward to the future. Typically signals of change are linked to megatrends, trends, scenarios, weak signals, and potential wild card events. In this study we focus on the following 12 John Naisbitt megatrend: (1) High technology, (2) Globalisation, (3) Global Economy, (4) Participatory Democracy, (5) Individualism, (6) Woman Leadership, (7) Bioage, (8) Bio Economy, (9) Art, (10) Network, (11) Pacific Rim and (12) Free Market Socialism. Research question for each megatrens is following: RQ1: What kind of trends (upward, downward, or horizontal) characterize John Naisbitt's 12 megatrends in the global context today? In addition, the following research question is defined to evaluate megatrends relationship to global GDP (PPP) development. RQ2: Is there a significant correlation between 12 megatrends variables and the global GDP PPP variable?

3 Methodology

3.1 Definition of Google Trend Data Sources and Variables

The methodology of this empirical study is including conventional statistical and index analysis of global trend variables. Megatrend variables are based on the Google Trends data. Google Trends provides access to a largely unfiltered sample of actual search requests made to Google [13–15] It's anonymized data (no one is personally identified), categorized data (determining the topic for a search query), and aggregated (grouped together). This allows us to display interest in a particular topic from around the globe or down to city-level geography. In this study we have collected data sets around the globe. The big data observations cover years 2004-2021, thus our trend analysis results bounded to this time span.

Google Trends analysis normalizes search data to make comparisons between terms easier. Search results are normalized to the time and location of a query by the following process: (1) Each data point is divided by the total searches of the geography and time range it represents to compare relative popularity. Otherwise, places with the most search volume would always be ranked highest; (2) The resulting numbers are then scaled on a range of 0 to 100 based on a topic's proportion to all searches on all topics, and (3) different regions that show the same search interest for a term don't always have the same total search volumes [13–15]. However, only five terms at the same time can be compared, which makes popularity comparison between 12 trends difficult. Therefore, trends popularity is compared in subsets of five. To make trend visualizations more readable, monthly data is averaged to annual data points. We have also considered other relevant trend and megatrend studies [16–24].

3.2   Definition of Global GDP PPP Data Sources and Variables

Google Trends analysis normalizes search data to facilitate comparisons between terms. The search results are normalized to the time and location of a query through the following process: (1) each data point is divided by the total number of searches in the relevant geography and time range to compare their relative popularity. Otherwise, regions with the highest search volume would always be ranked highest; (2) the resulting numbers are then scaled to a range of 0 to 100 based on the proportion of searches on all topics, and (3) different regions that exhibit the same search interest for a term don't always have the same total search volumes [13–15]. However, comparing the popularity of 12 trends at the same time is challenging because only five terms can be compared. Therefore, trends' popularity is compared in subsets of five. To make the trend visualizations more readable, we have averaged monthly data to annual data points. We also considered other relevant trend and megatrend studies [16–24] (Fig. 1).

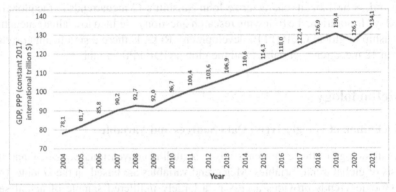

Fig. 1. World GDP PPP trend in 2004–2021. Source: International Comparison Program, World Bank I World Development Indicators database, World Bank 2023.

4   Results and Analysis

4.1   Descriptive Statistics and Correlation Analysis Results

In Table 1, we have reported descriptive statistics and the correlation analysis results for all John Naisbitt's twelve Key Global Megatrend Variables between 2004–2021.

Table 1. Descriptive statistics and the correlation analysis results.

Trend name	Mean	Range	Min	Max	Std. Dev	Year	World GDP PPP
Network	55.2	67.5	25.9	93.4	21.9	−0.974**	−0.961**
Art	51.2	53.1	37.0	90.1	15.0	−0.984**	−0.944**
Global Economy	45.9	32.2	32.8	65.0	10.8	−0.464**	−0.503**
Individualism	44.7	28.9	34.9	63.8	7.1	−0.629**	−0.656**
Women in leadership	44.3	19.1	34.9	54.0	6.0	0.359*	0.399*
Globalisation	30.7	53.9	19.6	73.5	15.2	−0.908**	−0.869**
Bioage	24.3	75.4	1.4	76.8	24.3	0.869**	0.830**
Participatory democracy	23.8	24.6	14.4	39.0	7.1	0.150	0.137
Bioeconomy	7.9	11.6	2.3	13.8	4.2	0.669**	0.708**
Hight Technology	5.2	19.8	1.5	21.3	5.1	−0.804**	−0.765**
Pacific Rim	4.2	22.0	1.0	23.0	5.4	0.294	0.308
Free Market Socialism	1.3	2.1	0.5	2.6	0.6	0.409*	0.396*

Correlation is significant ** at the 0.01 level (2-tailed) and * at the 0.05 level (2-tailed).

Table 1 includes average, minimum, maximum, range, and standard deviation values for each trends, which indicates substantial variation between the trends. Table also presents Kendall's tau b correlation values between trends, year, and world GPT PPP.

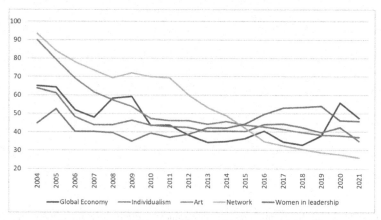

Fig. 2. Google Trend Index analyses of megatrends: Global economy, Individualism, Art, Network and Women in leadership. Source: Google Trends data 2004–2021.

This analysis method was selected, since trend data is not normally distributed data and Kendall's Rank Correlation Coefficient analysis as being a non-parametric test, it does not require normally distributed data. Based on correlation analysis results, trends can be classified into the following three categories: 1) increasing, 2) decreasing, and 3) unclear/horizontal. Upward trends include Bioage, Bioeconomy, Free Market Socialism, and Women in leadership. Downward trends are comprised of Global Economy, Individualism, High Technology, Globalisation, Network, and Art. Only two megatrend variables, "Pacific Rim" and "participatory democracy," were not statistically significantly correlating with the year or world GPT and therefore named as unclear or static. Trend correlation results with the year and GDP are somewhat similar. To gain a better understanding of each trend evolution, trends visualizations between years 2004 to 2021 are presented in Figs. 2, 3, and 4.

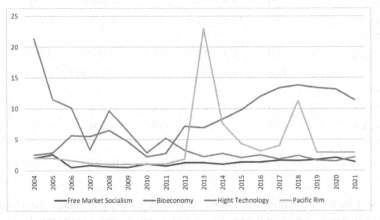

Fig. 3. Google Trend Index analyses of megatrends: Free Market Socialism, Bioeconomy, High Technology and Pacific Rim. Source: Google Trends data 2004–2021.

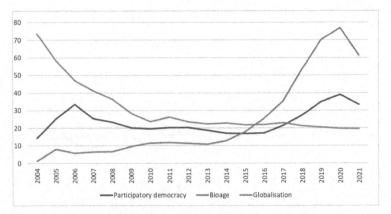

Fig. 4. Google Trend Index analyses of megatrends: Participatory democracy, Bioage and Globalisation. Source: Google Trends data 2004–2021.

4.2 Popularity Analysis

Popularity analysis revealed three subsets: highly popular, moderately popular, and low popular trends, each with substantial differences in popularity. Art is the most popular trend, followed by network as the second most popular trend. Figure 5 compares the evolution of art and network trends with the highest peaking moderate trend, globalization, to visualize the popularity differences between high and moderate groups.

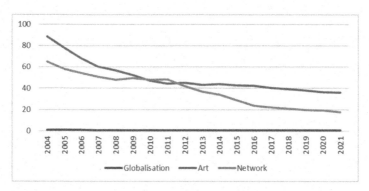

Fig. 5. Highly popular megatrends: Source: Google Trends data 2004–2021.

Figure 6 presents moderately popular megatrends, including globalization, high technology, global economy, and individualism, as well as Pacific Rim, which is the highest peaking low popular trend. Within this group, globalization is the strongest trend, followed by high technology, global economy, and individualism. Pacific Rim trend has a completely different profile than any other trend. In Fig. 7, Pacific Rim and women in leadership trends are compared. Women in leadership trend was selected for comparison

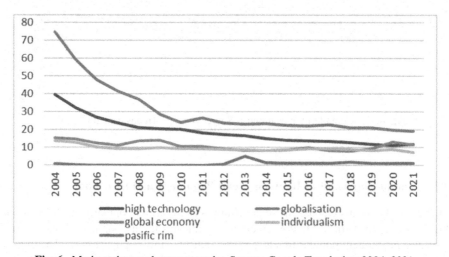

Fig. 6. Moderately popular megatrends: Source: Google Trends data 2004–2021.

since it is the most popular low trend, excluding the two high peaks in Pacific Rim trend. However, due to the annual mean value-based data points, the second peak does not exceed women in leadership popularity. These peaks can be explained by two Pacific Rim movies, whose release dates match with the peaks. Finally, Figure 8 presents low popularity megatrends, including women in leadership, bioage, participatory democracy, bioeconomy, and free market socialism.

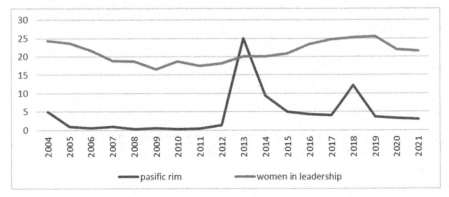

Fig. 7. Pacific rim vs. women in leadership comparison: Source: Google Trends data 2004–2021.

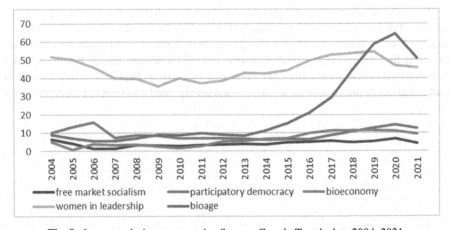

Fig. 8. Low popularity megatrends: Source: Google Trends data 2004–2021.

4.3 Relationship Analysis Between Trend Popularity and Direction

In order to better understand the relationship between trend popularity and direction, Fig. 9 was created. In the figure, green color indicates highly popular trends, yellow indicates moderately popular trends, and red indicates low popular trends. The Y-axis represents the Kendall Rank Correlation Coefficient value and the X-axis represents the trend value range. The bubble size indicates the trend mean value. Since Pacific Rim and Participatory Democracy did not have a significant correlation with the year, they are located outside of the XY-coordination.

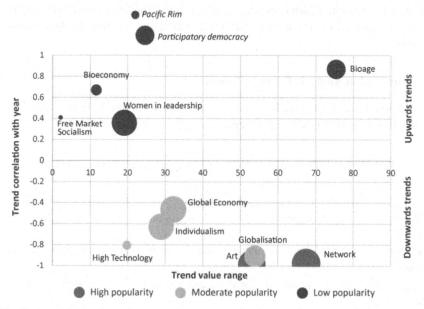

Fig. 9. Low-high popularity vs. decreasing-increasing trend quadrant. (Color figure online)

The high range increasing quadrant includes only the low popular Bioage trend. Until the year 2013, the trend's popularity remained relatively modest. However, after 2013, a steep climb can be observed, although there was a substantial drop between 2020 and 2021.

The high range decreasing quadrant includes both highly popular trend art and network trends, as well as the moderately popular globalization trend. All three trends show a strong linear decrease. Nevertheless, they still remain relevant in the year 2021 and are the top 3 trends.

The low range increasing quadrant comprises Bioeconomy, Women in leadership, and Free market socialism. Out of these three, Women in leadership is much more popular than the other two. Free market socialism is clearly the weakest trend. The Bioeconomy trend has remained relatively stable and modest over the years. The Women in leadership trend has a more modest correlation compared to the others, which can be explained by small "bumps" occurring in the years 2005 and later on between 2016 and 2019. As mentioned earlier, the Pacific Rim trend is an anomaly. Participatory democracy also follows a two "bump" profile. There was a steep increase between the years 2004 and 2006, which was followed by a steady decrease until 2016, when another steep increase occurred until the year 2020.

The low range decreasing quadrant contains three moderately popular trends: high technology, global economy, and individualism, which currently share similar popularity.

The global economy trend contains two "bumps," one between 2008–2010 and the other one from 2019 to 2021. However, both of the bumps can be linked to major economic crises. In the literature, the era between 2007–2008 has been referred to as the Global Financial Crisis (GFC). At that time, the GFC was the most serious financial crisis since the Great Depression, which occurred in the year 1929.The latter global economy trend bump can be linked to the Covid-19 pandemic, which was affecting the whole world at the time.

4.4   Correlation Analysis Between Trends

Table 2 presents Kendall's tau b correlation values between trends. In the Table 2, only significant correlation values are presented.

Table 2.   Kendall's tau b correlation value for trends, year and world GPT PPP.

	3	4	5	6	7	8	9	10
1. Women in leadership	.647**	−.399*		−.386*	−.367*		.386*	.551**
2. Global Economy		.503**	.477**	.464**	.472**	.444*	−.359*	−.433*
3. Free Market Socialism		−.462**	−.383*	−.409*	−.417*		.422*	.364*
4. Hight Technology			.791**	.778**	.813**	.589**	−.752**	−.603**
5. Globalisation				.882**	.918**	.695**	−.778**	−.577**
6. Network					.957**	.629**	−.843**	−.695**
7. Art						.638**	−.866**	−.651**
8. Individualism							−.497**	−.385*
9. Bioage								.616**
10. Bioeconomy								
11. Pacific Rim								

** Correlation is significant at the 0.01 level (2-tailed), *. Correlation is significant at the 0.05 level (2-tailed)

Very high positive correlation (0.9 or over) can be detected between Art and Globalisation (0.918**), Art and Network (0.957**). High positive correlation (0.7 or over but less than 0.9) occurs also between Network and Globalisation (0.882**) and Network and High technology (0.778**) and Art and High technology (0.813**). There are multiple moderate (0.5 or over but less than 0.7) and low (0.3 or over but less than 0.5) positive correlation between the trends. Global economy correlates positively with High technology (0.503**), Globalisation (0.477**), Network (0.464**), Art (0.472**) and Individualism (0.444*). Also Women in leadership is correlating with multiple trends including Free market socialism (0.647**), Bioage (0.386*), Bioeconomy (0.551**) and Pacific Rim (0.482**). In addition, Free market socialism correlates with Bioage (0.422*) and Bioeconomy (0.364*). The final positive correlations can be detected between Bioeconomy and Pacific Rim (0.477**) as well as between High technology and Individualism (0. 589**).

There are four high negative correlations (−0.7 or over but less than −0.9). Bioage has high negative correlation with High technology (−0.752**), Globalisation (−0.778**), Network (−0.843**) and Art (−0.866**). Multiple moderate negative correlation is occurring with Bioeconomy including High technology (-0.603**), Globalisation (−0.577**), Network (−0.695**) and Art (−0.651**). There is also moderate negative between Global economy and Pacific Rim (−0.535**). Remaining negative correlations are low (−0.3 or over but less than −0.5).

5 Discussion and Conclusions

This empirical study presents big data-driven estimates of John Naisbitt's 12 megatrends and global economic growth. Empirical assessments and statistical monitoring analyses are presented for the years 2004–2021. In a way, we have presented a restudy of John Naisbitt's original and important megatrends. The study makes a new contribution to traditional megatrend research, now based on big data. The Google Trends study assesses the intensity of megatrends and the historical direction of megatrend development. The megatrend study also presents a correlation analysis of the relationship between 12 megatrend variables and global economic growth (GDP PPP).

The big data study on megatrends reveals that art and networking have become genuine megatrends, despite their previous downward trend. Based on the analysis, it is claimed that Free market socialism has not secured its place among the megatrends as strongly as the others. Interestingly, in the era of climate change, public interest in the bioeconomy has so far remained low. However, it is the second highest upward trend after bioage, which follows a similar trend and is still waiting to break into the same league as art and networking. Of the remaining low-popularity trends, Women in leadership is still showing an upward trend, while the prognosis for Pacific Rim and participatory democracy is unclear. Interest in all moderately popular trends was declining, and therefore, they have not gained the same success as art and networking.

We also conclude that Naisbitt's megatrends are not stable entities, and unexpected events such as an economic crisis, pandemic, or the release of a major movie can significantly impact the type of information humans seek from the internet. It is also evident that some trends appear to be associated with each other either positively or negatively. Further analysis is needed to better understand how these trends are intertwined and what kind of phenomena impact their popularity. For example, it is interesting that in the era of networks and digital connectivity, participatory democracy has remained among the low-performing trends. As a result, we can conclude that John Naisbitt's original megatrend variables are still relevant in global economic analyses, although half of them appear to be in a declining trend.

Acknowledgments. Research Director Jari Kaivo-oja is a researcher at the Strategic Research Council of the Academy of Finland, in the Manufacturing 4.0 project. The project Manufacturing 4.0 has received funding from the Finnish Strategic Research Council [Grant number 313395].

References

1. Naisbitt, J., Aburdene, P.: Megatrends 2000: Ten New Directions for the 1990's. Morrow, New York (1990)
2. Naisbitt, J.: Megatrends: Ten New Directions Transforming Our Lives. Warner Books, New York (1982)
3. Naisbitt, D., Naisbitt, J.: Mastering Megatrends: Understanding and Leveraging the Evolving New World. Kindle Edition (2019)
4. Slaughter, R.: Looking for the real megatrends. Futures **25**(8), 827–849 (1993)
5. World Bank (2023). GDP PPP. World Bank Data. World Bank. Web. https://data.worldbank.org/indicator/NY.GDP.MKTP.PP.CD
6. Covel, M.W., Ritholz, B.: Trend Following: How to Make a Fortune in Bull, Bear and Black Swan Markets, 5th ed. Wiley Trading, Hoboken, New Jersey (2017)
7. Merlo, T.R.: Understanding, Implementing, and Evaluating Knowledge Management in Business Settings. IGI Global Hersey, PA. U.S.A. (2022)
8. Polak, F.L., Boulding, E.: The Image of the Future. Elsevier Scientific Publishing Company, The Netherlands (1973)
9. Morgan, D.: Images of the future: a historical perspective. Futures **34**(9–10), 883–893 (2002)
10. Liebowitz, J. (Ed.): Knowledge Management Handbook. Collaboration and Social Networking. Second edn. CRC Press, Taylor & Francis Group, Boca Raton, London and New York (2012)
11. Kaivo-oja, J.: Tulevaisuuden tekeminen strategisen ajattelun valossa. [The shaping of futures in the light of futures studies]. Teoksessa Kamppinen, Matti & Kuusi, Osmo & Söderlund, Sari (toim.) (2002) Tulevaisuudentutkimus. Perusteet ja sovellutukset. [Futures Research. Basics and Applications]. Suomalaisen Kirjallisuuden Seuran toimituksia 896. Helsinki, pp. 224–248 (2002)
12. van Asselt, M., van't Klooster, S. (Ed.): Foresight in Action Developing Policy-Oriented Scenarios, First ed. Routledge, London (2010)
13. Google (2023). Google Trends searches "Globalisation", "Global Economy" "Participatory Democracy", "Individualism", "Woman Leadership", "Bioage", "Bio Economy", "Art", "Network", "Pacific Rim" and "Free Market Socialism". 15.1.2023. Google. Web. https://trends.google.com/trends/?geo=US
14. Google Support (2021). FAQ about Google Trends Data—How Is Google Trends Data Normalized? https://support.google.com/trends/answer/4365533?hl=en. Accessed 17 Apr 2021
15. Jun, S.-P., Yoo, H.S., Choi, S.: Ten years of research change using google trends: from the perspective of big data utilizations and applications. Technol. Forecast. Soc. Chang. **130**, 69–87 (2018)
16. Springer, S., Menzel, L.M., Zieger, M.: Google trends provides a tool to monitor population concerns and information needs during COVID-19 pandemic. Brain Behav. Immun. **87**, 109–110 (2020). https://doi.org/10.1016/j.bbi.2020.04.073

17. Jun, S.-P., Sung, T.E., Park, H.-W.: Forecasting by analogy using the web search traffic. Technol. Forecast. Soc. Chang. **115**(2017), 37–51 (2017)
18. Choi, H., Varian, H.: Predicting the present with google trends. Econ. Rec. **88**(2012), 2–9 (2012)
19. Ballantyne, R., Packer, J., Axelsen, M.: Trends in tourism research. Ann. Tour. Res. **36**(1), 149–152 (2009)
20. Borup, M., Brown, N., Konrad, K., Van Lente, H.: The sociology of expectations in science and technology. Tech. Anal. Strat. Manag. **18**(2006), 285–298 (2006)
21. Goel, S., Hofman, J.M., Lahaie, S., Pennock, D.M., Watts, D.J.: Predicting consumer behaviour with web search. Proc. Natl. Acad. Sci. **107**(2010), 17486–17490 (2010)
22. Mercer, D.: A general hypothesis of aggregated expectations. Technol. Forecast. Soc. Chang. **55**(1997), 145–154 (1997)
23. van Lente, H., Spitters, C., Peine, A.: Comparing technological hype cycles: towards a theory. Technol. Forecast. Soc. Chang. **80**(2013), 1615–1628 (2013)
24. Boumphrey, S., Brehmer, Z.: Megatrend Analysis Putting the Consumer at the Heart of Business. Euromonitor International. Web (2017). https://bluesyemre.files.wordpress.com/2019/04/wpmegatrendanalysis.pdf

Corruption Control in the BRICS and in the G7 Countries: A Benchmarking Study with World Bank Data Files from Years 1996–2021

Jari Kaivo-oja[1,2]([X]) and Teemu Santonen[3]

[1] Finland Futures Research Centre, Turku School of Economics, University of Turku, FFRC Unit of Tampere, Åkerlundinkatu 2 A, 33100 Tampere, Finland
jari.kaivo-oja@utu.fi
[2] Kazimieras Simonavicius University, Dariaus ir Girėno st. 21, 02189 Vilnius, Lithuania
[3] Laurea University of Applied Sciences, Ratatie 22, 01300 Vantaa, Finland
teemu.santonen@laurea.fi

Abstract. The aim of this study is to compare the levels of corruption control in the BRICS countries and in the G7 countries using data from 1996 to 2021 published by the World Bank. The corruption control data aims to present estimates on how corruption is controlled in the world. The BRICS countries include Brazil, Russian Federation, India, China, and South Africa, while the G7 group comprises the United States, United Kingdom, Canada, France, Germany, Italy, and Japan. This empirical benchmarking study presents both country and country-group-level analyses and results, which enable monitoring progress in corruption control in the global country groups and leading global economies. A key finding of the benchmarking study is that corruption control is higher in the G7 countries than in the BRICS countries. The average corruption control level in the G7 countries during the period 1996–2021 was 88, whereas in the BRICS countries, it was 43. The median and average corruption control difference was 40, which is a significant difference. The study reveals other relevant findings in the field of global corruption control and governance. In general, decision-makers in the G7 countries pay more attention to corruption control than those in the BRICS countries.

Keywords: Corruption control · BRICS countries · G7 countries · Benchmarking · Global governance · World Bank corruption control data · Index theory

1 Introduction

Corruption is not a new social and economic phenomenon. Historically, we have been living with it since the birth of government institutions. Corruption has two typical dimensions: public-sector corruption and private-sector corruption. As a phenomenon, corruption is a key challenge in both the political and economic spheres [1–3]. Typically seen as a form of dishonesty or criminal offense, corruption is undertaken by a person or an organization that is entrusted with a position of authority to acquire illicit

© The Author(s), under exclusive license to Springer Nature Switzerland AG 2023
L. Uden and I-H. Ting (Eds.): KMO 2023, CCIS 1825, pp. 182–196, 2023.
https://doi.org/10.1007/978-3-031-34045-1_16

benefits or abuse power for personal gain. Corruption can involve anyone who is doing business or public transactions, including politicians, government officials, public servants, businesspeople, or members of the public [4]. Corruptive practices make it more difficult to achieve fairness in economic and political decision-making. It is no wonder that more and more attention has been paid to this issue in both research and political decision-making.

Benchmarking is a process of comparing the performance of a system or process to a set standard, other systems/processes in the same domain, or the best or toughest competitors in order to improve one's own performance [4]. The benchmarking analysis method is one of the basic methods in information and knowledge management, which focuses on how organizations capture, store, share, and utilize knowledge. David Snowden and other key scholars of knowledge management research argue that benchmarking is a very appropriate data-driven method for evaluating and comparing social systems [5–7]. In knowledge management, benchmarking methods can help organizations to 1) identify best practices and areas for improvement, 2) identify strengths and weaknesses in general or specific areas, 3) set performance goals, and 4) measure progress of development [8]. Thus, benchmarking studies in the context of knowledge management research can provide clear value.

2 Theoretical Backgrounds

Key studies of corruption have primarily been a matter of political science and sociology [9–13]. However, the scientific scenario of corruption research has changed since the 1970s. Professor Rose-Ackerman's article "The Economics of Corruption," published in the Journal of Public Economics in 1975 [14], marked a turning point. Since then, more than 4,000 articles have been written with 'corruption' in the title, at least 500 of which directly focus on different aspects related to corruption using an economic framework. Some books have also been published on the subject [3, 9, 10, 13, 15, 19]. In the field of scientific investigation, the economics of corruption deals with the misuse of public power for private benefit and its economic impact on society. The key hypothesis is that economies afflicted by high levels of corruption are not capable of prospering as fully as those with low levels of corruption. It has been proven that countries with relatively low levels of GDP per capita tend to have higher levels of corruption. From this economic perspective, active and broad corrupt practices can lead countries and companies to a low level of prosperity. The impact of corruption on income inequality was investigated in the empirical study of Gupta et al. (2002). They found a significant positive impact of corruption on inequality while considering exogenous variables. Corruption has an impact on income inequality through numerous channels, such as economic growth, biased tax systems, asset ownership, etc. [17–19]. Corruption is also a question of social justice. In this study, the theoretical background is linked to the current understanding of economic thinking, especially to the World Bank's statistical analyses of corruption control. The World Bank produces an annual "Control of Corruption" index (CCI) that uses similar sources to the International Country Risk Guide and Corruption Perception Index [20–23].

3 Methodology

Kaufmann, Kraay, and Mastruzzi [22] developed a complementary measure called "Control of Corruption," which draws from a large set of data sources. Their definition of corruption is broader and includes most cross-country indices that report rankings on some aspect of corruption. They also use a different strategy than Transparency International to aggregate corruption indicators, and their index is applied in this study. However, definitions and aggregation choices seem to matter only marginally. The simple correlation between Control of Corruption (from 2002) and the Corruption Perceptions Index (from 2003) is 0.97, and the correlation between Control of Corruption or the Corruption Perceptions and corruption scores from the International Country Risk Guide (from 2001) is 0.75. The main difference between the three indicators is the countries and years they cover [21].

This study is based on the benchmarking methodology [25–30]. Benchmarking has become a central instrument for improving the performance of the public sector and companies, reflecting that comparison can be a powerful driver of better performance. Benchmarking is based on key ideas such as assessing performance objectively, identifying areas for improvement and underlying problems in organizations/countries or country groups, identifying best practices, focusing on the links between processes and results, and testing the success of improvement. All these principles are relevant in the context of anti-corruption activities. In this benchmarking study, we focus on comparing performance and evaluating programs, rather than re-engineering or total quality management [26].

It would be good if different countries around the world were to compete to see who can root out corruption the most, thus reducing the negative impact of corruption on their citizens' productivity. Benchmarking typically helps decision-makers (1) identify strengths and areas for improvement, (2) facilitate the formulation of institutional development plans to build upon strengths and address identified gaps, (3) prioritize corruption interventions, and (4) monitor progress and achievements in anti-corruption policies [24–29]. By using benchmarking in this new way, businesses can gain strategic advantages over competitors and improve industry averages. The dimensions typically measured in benchmarking studies are quality, time, and cost. In this international benchmarking study, the dimensions are limited to corruption control measures in time. We perform country and country group benchmarking analyses in this study using World Bank's corruption control data covering years 1996–2021 [31].

4 Data and Measures

4.1 Statistical Analyses of County Groups

In Fig. 1 we report corruption control estimates of the BRICS countries for the years 1996–2021.

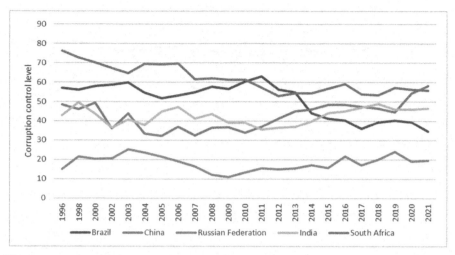

Fig. 1. Corruption control level estimates of the BRICS countries for the years 1996–2021. Source: World Bank 2023.

The Kendall Rank Correlation Coefficient analysis is a non-parametric test and therefore does not require normally distributed data. Therefore, it was selected as an analysis method. We can observe a high decrease in the corruption control level in South Africa (−0.700**) and a moderate decrease in Brazil (−0.520**). South Africa has been in a somewhat steady downshifting trend since 1996, whereas Brazil has taken a steeper decrease since 2011. A very weak and steady corruption control level can be observed in the Russian Federation throughout the years between 1996 and 2021. India is also following a steady path but has a higher corruption control level than the Russian Federation.

China is the only country showing weak positive progress in corruption control (0.356*). In 2021, China gained the top position among the BRICS countries but is still performing weaker than South Africa did in the late 90s and early 2000s.

In Fig. 2, we report corruption control estimates of the G7 countries for the years 1996–2021.

We can observe corruption control level trends in G7 countries. Italy has the lowest corruption control level among G7 countries and is showing a weak declining trend (−0.375*) due to a long downfall trend from the year 2000 until 2014 when an upwards trend was introduced. Italy is clearly the weakest among the G7 countries, whereas all other G7 countries have had quite strong corruption control levels. In fact, Japan (0.509**) and Germany (0.479**) have improved their corruption control during these years, whereas the USA is showing the strongest declining trend (−0.557**). France, the United Kingdom, and Canada are following steady paths. As a group, both BRICS (−0.415*) and G7 (−0.396**) have been in a downward trend. There is a weak negative correlation between the groups (−0.396**).

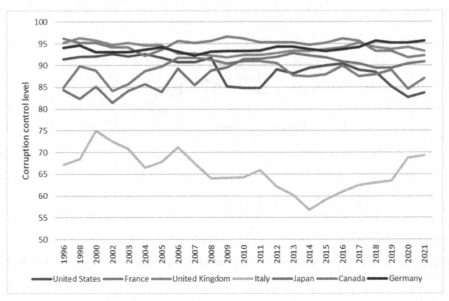

Fig. 2. Corruption control level estimates of the G7 countries for the years 1996–2021. Source: World Bank 2023.

4.2 Statistical Analyses of BRICS Countries

In Fig. 3, we report on the corruption control level of Brazil, along with the average corruption control level estimate for the BRICS countries. Since 2011, Brazil has weakened its own corruption control measures and it is currently below the average corruption control level of the BRICS countries.

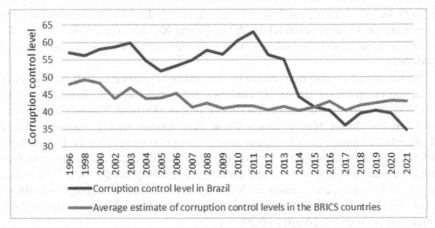

Fig. 3. Corruption control level in Brazil and average estimate of corruption control levels in the BRICS countries for the years 1996–2021. Source: World Bank 2023.

In Fig. 4 we report on the corruption control level of China, along with the average corruption control level estimate for the BRICS countries. We can clearly see from Fig. 5 that China has strengthened its corruption control since 2010. China has now surpassed the BRICS countries average corruption control level.

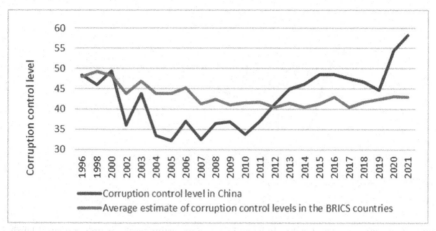

Fig. 4. Corruption control level in China and average estimate of corruption control levels in the BRICS countries for the years 1996–2021. Source: World Bank 2023.

In Fig. 5, we report on the level of corruption control in the Russian Federation, along with the average corruption control level estimate for the BRICS countries. The graph clearly shows that Russia is by far the weakest country in terms of controlling corruption among the BRICS countries. The difference from the average corruption control index for the BRICS country group is about 25 units.

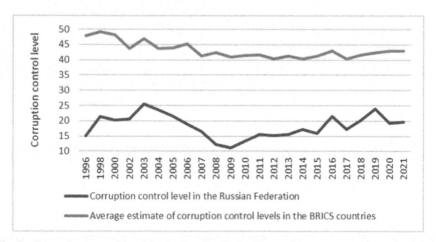

Fig. 5. Corruption control level in the Russian Federation and average estimate of corruption control levels in the BRICS countries for the years 1996–2021. Source: World Bank 2023.

In Fig. 6 we report on the level of corruption control in the India, along with the average corruption control level estimate for the BRICS countries. India's level of control over corruption is pretty close to the BRICS country group average.

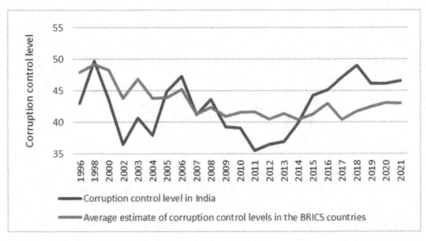

Fig. 6. Corruption control level in India and an average estimate of corruption control levels in the BRICS countries for the years 1996–2021. Source: World Bank 2023.

In Fig. 7, we present the corruption control level of South Africa, along with the average estimate of corruption control levels for the BRICS countries. The long-term review shows that South Africa has had stronger corruption control compared to the average for the BRICS country group. However, the fight against corruption in South Africa has not been very successful in recent years, as corruption control has slowly

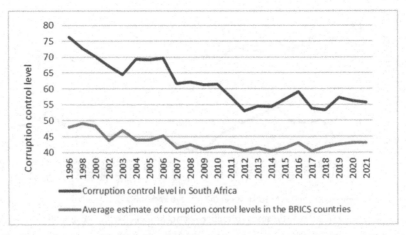

Fig. 7. Corruption control level in South Africa and an average estimate of corruption control levels in the BRICS countries for the years 1996–2021. Source: World Bank 2023.

deteriorated over time. In 1996, the corruption control level was almost 80, but now it is less than 60.

By identifying areas (for example, corruption control) you wish to improve on in your business and benchmarking your existing performance against competitors, your business can strive to enhance your execution tenfold. Using benchmarking in this kind of new way, we can allow businesses to gain strategic advantages over competitors and grow industry averages. Dimensions, typically measured in benchmarking studies, are quality, time, and cost. In this international benchmarking study, dimensions are limited to corruption control measures in time. In this study, we perform country and country group benchmarking analyses with World Bank´s corruption control data covering years 1996–2021 [31].

4.3   Statistical Analyses of G7 Countries

In Fig. 8, we present the corruption control level of the United States, along with the average estimate of corruption control levels for the G7 countries. In the United States, the control of corruption has weakened since the late 1990s and early 2000s. The strong decline began after 2008. While there was a period of strengthening in the CC index after 2012, corruption control continued to weaken after 2016. Historically, the weakest value of the CC index was achieved in 2020.

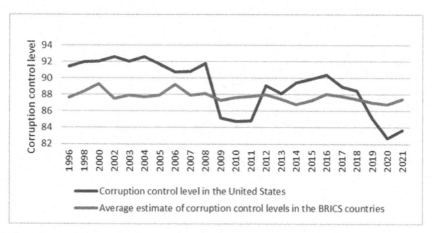

Fig. 8. Corruption control level in the United States and an average estimate of corruption control levels in the G7 countries for the years 1996–2021. Source: World Bank 2023.

In Fig. 9 we report the corruption control level of France with an average estimate of corruption control levels of the G7 countries. In France, the level of control over corruption has been slightly higher than the average for the G7 group.

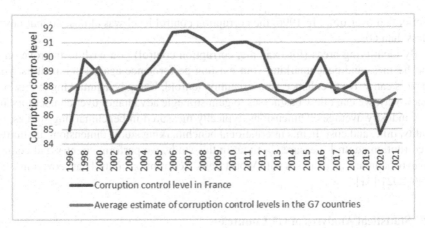

Fig. 9. Corruption control level in France and an average estimate of corruption control levels in the G7 countries for the years 1996–2021. Source: World Bank 2023.

In Fig. 10 we report the corruption control level of the UK with an average estimate of corruption control levels of the G7 countries. In the UK, the level of control over corruption has been clearly higher than the average for the G7 group.

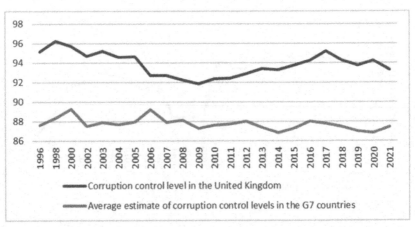

Fig. 10. Corruption control level in the United Kingdom and an average estimate of corruption control levels in the G7 countries for the years 1996–2021. Source: World Bank 2023.

In Fig. 11 we report the corruption control level of Italy with an average estimate of corruption control levels of the G7 countries. In Italy, the level of control over corruption has been clearly lower than the average for the G7 group. The difference has been about 20 CC index units. It is worth noting that since 2014, the control of corruption in Italy has been strengthened due to numerous political scandals in Italy.

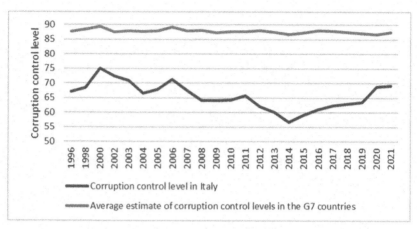

Fig. 11. Corruption control level in Italy and an average estimate of corruption control levels in the G7 countries for the years 1996–2021. Source: World Bank 2023.

In Fig. 12 we report the corruption control level of Japan with an average estimate of corruption control levels of the G7 countries. In Japan, the control of corruption has clearly intensified over a long period of time, reaching an average level above the 90 CC index. At the end of the 1990s, the level was at the level of the 85 CC index. In Japan, the level of control over corruption is currently at a higher level than the G7 average level of corruption control.

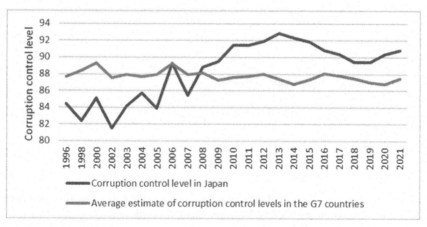

Fig. 12. Corruption control level in Japan and an average estimate of corruption control levels in the G7 countries for the years 1996–2021. Source: World Bank 2023.

In Fig. 13 we report the corruption control level of Canada with an average estimate of corruption control levels of the G7 countries. Canada has had very high and stable level of corruption control among the G7 countries throughout the history of CC index monitoring.

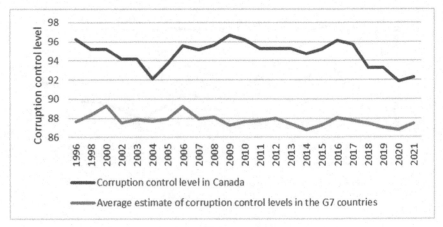

Fig. 13. Corruption control level in Canada and an average estimate of corruption control levels in the G7 countries for the years 1996–2021. Source: World Bank 2023.

In Fig. 14 we report the corruption control level of Germany with an average estimate of corruption control levels of the G7 countries. Germany like Canada has had very high and stable level of corruption control among the G7 countries throughout the history of CC index monitoring.

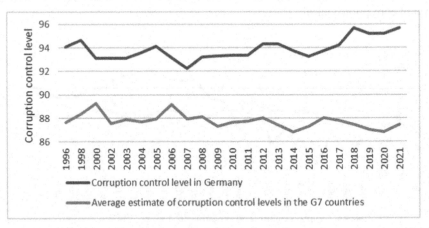

Fig. 14. Corruption control level in Germany and an average estimate of corruption control levels in the G7 countries for the years 1996–2021. Source: World Bank 2023.

5   Results and Analysis

In this section, we report the main benchmarking results of the BRICS and G7 countries. First, we present the statistical benchmarking results of the BRICS countries in Table 1. To interpret the results, the strongest corruption control in the period 2016–2021 was in

South Africa, and the weakest corruption control was in the Russian Federation. Brazil was ranked second in the corruption control (CC) index comparison, while China and India were ranked third and fourth, respectively.

Table 1. Benchmarking results of the BRICS country group. Source: World Bank 2023.

	Median	Average	Max	Min	Range
Brazil	54,9	50,8	63,0	34,6	28,4
China	44,7	42,8	58,2	32,2	26,0
Russian Federation	19,0	18,3	25,4	11,0	14,4
India	43,6	42,6	49,7	35,5	14,2
South Africa	61,2	61,6	76,3	53,1	23,3
Average BRICSA	42,5	43,2	49,2	40,4	8,8

First, we present the statistical benchmarking results of the G7 countries in Table 2. To interpret the results, the strongest corruption control in the period 2016–2021 was in Canada, while the weakest corruption control was in Italy. Germany and the UK were ranked second or third best in the corruption control (CC) index comparison, and Japan was ranked fourth. The USA was ranked fifth, and France was ranked sixth in the CC index comparison.

Table 2. Benchmarking results of the BRICS country group. Source: World Bank 2023.

	Median	Average	Max	Min	Range
United States	89,9	89,1	92,6	82,7	9,9
France	88,8	88,6	91,7	84,1	7,6
United Kingdom	93,8	93,9	96,3	91,9	4,4
Italy	65,9	65,7	75,0	56,7	18,3
Japan	89,4	88,4	92,9	81,5	11,4
Canada	95,2	94,7	96,7	91,8	4,8
Germany	93,8	93,9	95,7	92,2	3,4
Average G7 countries	87,7	87,8	89,3	86,8	2,5

Table 3 presents the statistical benchmarking results of the BRICS and G7 countries. The average corruption control (CC) index of BRICS countries is 45, while the average CC index of G7 countries is 88. The average difference in CC index is 43, which is a significant difference.

Table 3. Benchmarking results of the BRICS and G7 country groups. Source: World Bank 2023.

	Median	Average	Max	Min	Range
Average BRICS	43	43	49	40	9
Average G7 countries	88	88	89	87	2
Difference	45	45	40	46	−6

In Fig. 15 we visualize the key statistical results of BRICS and G7 country groups benchmarking.

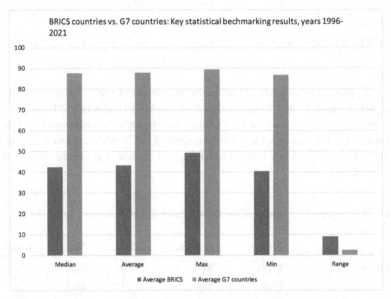

Fig. 15. BRICS countries vs. G7 countries: Key statistical benchmarking results, years 1996–2021. Source: World Bank 2023 [31].

6   Discussion and Conclusions

In this empirical benchmarking study, we present new results on the development of corruption control levels in the BRICS and G7 country groups. The benchmarking results reveal that the differences in the control of corruption between the G7 and BRICS country groups are still large and significant. If the negative social and economic effects of corruption are to be reduced, the fight against corruption should be strengthened, especially in countries where corruption control is low according to the results. Such countries are the Russian Federation in the BRICS country group and Italy in the G7 country group. The champion in the BRICS group is South Africa, and in the G7 group, it is Canada. The benchmarking results are relevant for knowledge-based decision-making in these leading countries in the world.

A key finding of the benchmarking study is that corruption control is higher in the G7 countries compared to the BRICS countries. The average corruption control level in the G7 countries from 1996–2021 was 88, while in the BRICS countries, it was 43. The median and average corruption control difference is considerable at 40. The study reveals many other relevant findings in the field of global corruption control and governance. A general conclusion of this benchmarking study is that decision-makers in the G7 countries pay more attention to corruption control than decision-makers in the BRICS countries.

Acknowledgments. Research Director Jari Kaivo-oja is a researcher at the Strategic Research Council of the Academy of Finland, in the Manufacturing 4.0 project. The project Manufacturing 4.0 has received funding from the Finnish Strategic Research Council [Grant number 313395].

References

1. Buchan, B.: Changing contours of corruption in Western political thought, c. 1200–1700. In: Barcham, E. (ed.) Corruption: Expanding the Focus, pp. 73–96. ANU Press (2012). https://doi.org/10.22459/cef.09.2012.05
2. Dearden, S.J.H.: The challenge to corruption and the international business environment. In: Kidd, J.B., Richter, F.-J. (eds.), Corruption and Governance in Asia, pp. 27–42. Palgrave, Houndmills (2003)
3. Fisman, R., Golden, M.: Corruption: What Everyone Needs to Know. Oxford University Press, New York (2017)
4. Camp, R.C.: Benchmarking: the search for industry best practices that lead to superior performance. Asq Press (1989)
5. Kurtz, C., Snowden, D.: The new dynamics of strategy: sense-making in a complex and complicated world. IBM Syst. J. **42**(3), 462–483 (2003)
6. Snowden, D.J., Boone, M.E.: A leader's framework for decision making. Harv. Bus. Rev. **85**(11), 68–76 (2007)
7. Snowden, D., Rancati, A.: Managing Complexity (and Chaos) in Times of Crisis. A Field Guide for Decision Makers Inspired by the Cynefin Framework. Publications Office of the European Union, Luxembourg (2021)
8. Stapenhurst, T.: The Benchmarking Book. A How-to-Guide to Best Practice for Quality Managers and Practitioners. Routledge. Taylor and Francis, London and New York (2009)
9. Fontana, B.: Sallust and the politics of Machiavelli. Hist. Polit. Thought **24**(1), 86–108 (2003)
10. Ekpo, M.U., Vine, V.L. (eds.): Bureaucratic Corruption in Sub-Saharan Africa, Toward a Search for Causes and Consequences. University Press of America, Washington (1979)
11. Klitgaard, R.: Controlling Corruption. University of California Press, Berkeley, CA (1988)
12. Mauro, P.: The Effects of Corruption on Growth, Investment, and Government Expenditure. Economic Growth, IMF Working Paper No. 96/98. International Monetary Fund. Washington D.C. (1996)
13. Nicholls, C., Daniel, T., Polaine, M., Hatchard, J. (eds.): Corruption and Misuse of Public Office. Oxford University Press, Oxford (2006)
14. Rose-Ackerman, S.: Corruption - A Study in Political Economy. Academic Press, New York (1978)

15. Hough, D.: Corruption, Anti-corruption and Governance. Political Corruption and Governance Series. Palgrave Macmillan, Basingstoke (2013)
16. Kijang, S., Onn, J.D.: Enhancing Government Effectiveness and Transparency. The Fight Against Corruption. Global Report. International Bank for Reconstruction and Development. The World Bank. Kuala Lumpur, Malaysia (2020)
17. Khan, M.M.: Economic research of corruption: its consequences. Res. Humanit. Soc. Sci. **8**, 12–16 (2018)
18. Svensson, J.: Eight questions about corruption. J. Econ. Perspect. **19**(3), 19–42 (2005)
19. Euben, J.P.: Corruption. In: Ball, T., Farr, J., Hanson, R.L. (eds.) Political innovation and Conceptual Change, pp. 220–46. Cambridge University Press, Cambridge(1989)
20. World Bank (1999). Fostering Institutions to Contain Corruption. PREM Notes No. 24, World Bank, Washington, DC
21. Howell, L.D.: The Handbook of Country and Political Risk Analysis. Political Risk Services. IBC USA Publications Inc., East Syracuse, N.Y.: PRS Group. (2001)
22. Kaufmann, D., Kraay, A., Mastruzzi, M.: Governance Matters III: Governance Indicators for 1996–2002. World Bank Policy Research Working Paper No. 3106, Washington, D.C. (2003)
23. Transparency International (2022). Corruption Perceptions Index 2022. Berlin, Germany. Web. https://images.transparencycdn.org/images/CPI2021_Report_EN-web.pdf
24. United Nations Development Programme (UNDP) (2005). Institutional Agreements to Combat Corruption: A Comparative Study, UNDP Regional Center, Bangkok
25. Boxwell, R.J., Jr.: Benchmarking for Competitive Advantage. McGraw-Hill, New York (1994)
26. Helgason, S.: International Benchmarking Experiences from OECD Countries. Paper Presented at a Conference organised by the Danish Ministry of Finance on: International Benchmarking Copenhagen, 20–21 February 1997. Copenhagen, Denmark (1997)
27. Quah, J.S.T.: Benchmarking for excellence: a comparative analysis of seven Asian anti-corruption agencies. Asia Pac. J. Public Adm. **31**(2), 171–195 (2009). https://doi.org/10.1080/23276665.2009.10779362
28. Gemperle, S.M.: Comparing anti-corruption agencies: a new cross-national index. Int. Rev. Public Adm. **23**(3), 156–175 (2018). https://doi.org/10.1080/12294659.2018.1518002
29. Quah, J.S.T.: Evaluating the effectiveness of anti-corruption agencies in five Asian countries: a comparative analysis. Asian Educ. Dev. Stud. **4**(1), 143–159 (2015)
30. Recanatini, F.: Anti-corruption authorities: an effective tool to curb corruption? In: Rose-Akerman, S., Soreide, T. (eds.) International Handbook on the Economics of Corruption, Chapter 19, pp. 528–564. Edward Elgar Publishing (2011)
31. World Bank (2023). Corruption Control. Worldwide Governance Indicators. World Bank. Voice and Accountability; Political Stability and Absence of Violence/Terrorism; Government Effectiveness; Regulatory Quality; Rule of Law; Control of Corruption. Web. https://databank.worldbank.org/source/worldwide-governance-indicators

KM and Education

Doctoral Program in Computer Science: A Study of Demand and Employability in Ecuador

Fernando Molina-Granja(✉), Lida Barba-Maggi, and Lorena Molina-Valdiviezo

Faculty of Engineering, National University of Chimborazo, Riobamba, Ecuador
{fmolina,lbarba,lmolina}@unach.edu.ec

Abstract. Information systems in companies and public and private organizations until the previous decade were frequently characterized by a lack of assimilation of new technologies, the underuse of computer equipment, the widespread discontent of users due to the obsolescence of computer applications, the lack of planning of information systems and the partial solutions proposed, that was not integrated, produced mechanization islands and manual processes difficult to control and expensive to maintain. This article aims to determine the demand and employability of the doctoral-level study program in the area of computer science to be applied at the National University of Chimborazo, the required competencies, and the relevance of the study program. With a descriptive and cross-sectional study, through a virtual survey of professionals and companies in Ecuador, 336 and 133 responses are obtained respectively and allow to respond positively to the objective of the study, concluding that there is great interest in the study program and it is considered relevant to society, therefore its implementation is recommended.

Keywords: Doctoral program · Computer science · demand, and employability · doctoral relevance

1 Introduction

Academic training and specialization of knowledge are undoubtedly the paths to the sustained development of a society and a country, so professionals seek the means to improve the processes by which to strengthen knowledge, transmit it and apply it for the benefit of society.

The doctorate is a degree derived from a training program known as a postgraduate, whose object is the academic preparation of the participant in techniques and methodology of research applied to a specific area of knowledge.

"Knowledge is the most important asset that we can transmit to future generations" this phrase is intended to demonstrate the need to invest in science, technology, and innovation for the development of society and with-it higher education institutions have the responsibility to generate and promote an optimal scenario for training processes. So, for professionals to be trained and acquire the necessary skills to generate that asset called knowledge, they must obtain the academic title of the highest educational degree in our country: the doctorate [1].

© The Author(s), under exclusive license to Springer Nature Switzerland AG 2023
L. Uden and I-H. Ting (Eds.): KMO 2023, CCIS 1825, pp. 199–209, 2023.
https://doi.org/10.1007/978-3-031-34045-1_17

The most appropriate and used mechanism to promote research processes is doctoral training. Through the doctoral programs of the universities, dynamic foci are concentrated on the generation of new knowledge and technological development. A professional who graduated from a doctoral program is expected to make a novel contribution that transcends the frontier of knowledge, with contributions of original solutions to disciplinary or interdisciplinary problems.

With the advancement of communications, the ICT sector has developed rapidly in recent years, governmental and non-governmental organizations require qualified personnel with knowledge of computer techniques and tools for the management of new computer technologies, information processing, control, and computer security, professionals who can incorporate computer management to organizations and facilitate decision making at the Executive and managerial. According to the study, this situation has caused a growing demand for professionals in the area of computing and informatics who have the necessary skills and abilities and based on the analysis of existing information and computer infrastructure, can advise and potentiate the different strategic areas raising competitiveness and productivity [2].

In addition to the above in a globalized society, ICTs are a tool that transcends devices and their operation, so it should be considered as an "opportunity" the fact that small and medium-sized companies or organizations, both public and private, at the national level are moving their business models to the internet, as it allows them to have a complete portfolio of products and services, improving and facilitating e- commerce transactions between suppliers and buyers, as well as access to their services [3–6].

In Ecuador, according to the CES, 23 doctoral programs are listed in various areas, of these in the area of industries and construction there are 4 offers in Electrical Engineering, and 3 programs in the broad field of ICT Information and Communication Technologies, specifically with the Computer Science program, one in the province of Guayas and two in the province of Azuay (Fig. 1) [7].

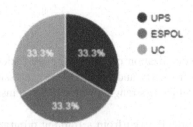

Fig. 1. Offer of current doctoral programs in ICT in Ecuador. Source: [7]

The Doctor of Computer Science will be able to:

- Systematically understand the field of information technologies and mastery of related research skills and methods; conceive, design or create, implement and adopt a substantial IT research process through original research, with critical analysis and evaluation and synthesis of new and complex ideas.
- Communicate and disseminate adequately to the academic, and scientific community and with society about its scientific achievements and advances.

- Analyze and act in contexts in which specific information is deficient, through the definition of specific questions that allow solving a complex problem, with a critique and intellectual defense of solutions.

In the specific field, the doctor in Computer Science will be able to:

- Acquire advanced knowledge at the frontier of knowledge, with a mastery of the theoretical and practical aspects, as well as scientific methodology in the fields of Information and Communication Technologies.
- Propose effective solutions, aligned with the government and societal needs within the field of Information and Communication Technologies.
- Contribute with original and significant research that is recognized by the international scientific community.
- Propose innovative research projects and scientific collaborations, national or international within the field of Information Technologies in multidisciplinary contexts and, as the case may be, with a transfer of knowledge.

For the above, it is necessary to find a way to articulate higher education with the world of work, offering new educational programs of scientific training that allow covering the demand for qualified professionals in the use and generation of knowledge in the field of IT, with skills for decision making, problem-solving, ease of communication with their work environment and with a commitment to their organization, Competences that will guarantee their permanence and the employability of future professionals in the area [8, 9].

Higher education institutions and in particular those in the central area of the country, for several years, have been training third and fourth-level professionals in the career of Systems and Computer Engineering, Computer Engineering, Information Technology Engineering, and related, which today face new challenges in technological trends, Hence the University's commitment to society and the strengthening of the productive matrix [4].

2 Methodology

The demand and employability study were based on the descriptive research method and a cross-sectional study. In this way, it was possible to know in more detail the characteristics of the study population, the work they do, and to what extent they contribute to the performance and development of organizations in the area of ICT.

For the analysis, a survey was considered for possible doctoral candidates, aimed at professionals in the area of computer science, and a survey of potential employers, which would be companies and public and private institutions mainly in zone 3 of Ecuador. This calculates the sample and proposes online strategies to share and apply the information collection instrument.

2.1 Information Collection Techniques

The instrument used for data collection was a survey generated online, with the Google Forms tool, which allowed obtaining information on the need and interest of studying a doctoral program, competitive advantage, and job growth. In general, allowing to know the valuation criteria between the professional profile versus the academic offer of the doctoral program.

2.2 Population and Sample

The survey was sent to the professionals of the computer area of zone 3, as well as to the professional guilds of the sector, to know the perception of the subject matter treated and the demand for the proposal. With a defined population of 365 participants, with a 95% confidence level and a 5% margin of error, a sample of 188 participants is obtained, however, 336 responses have been obtained from potential candidates; and 133 responses have been obtained from potentially employing companies, which are part of the UNACH (National University of Chimborazo) database with agreements, informants, among others, obtaining the following responses.

2.3 Procedure

1. Design of the instrument to collect significant and relevant information for the doctoral program.
2. Validation of instruments by the Delphi method, by experts, and anonymously.
3. Survey application using virtual resources.
4. Descriptive statistics are used for the analysis of information.

3 Results and Discussion

Information and Communication Technologies (ICT) have demonstrated in a reliable way that they are a transversal axis in the transformation and development of the planet and its vision for the future.

Likewise, the advance of digital technology entails changes in the environment and ways of using it, since it is originating a new reality full of challenges and opportunities, which in turn lead to great changes in social, productive, and commercial interactions. Innovation makes it possible to adapt this technology in many aspects, which has managed to improve the quality of life of human beings.

In general terms, despite the great technological advances, the current situation of ICTs in Companies and Organizations is frequently characterized by a failure of assimilation of new technologies, an underutilization of computer equipment, a generalized discontent of users, by an obsolescence of current computer applications, by a lack of planning of information technologies, and by partially proposed solutions that, because they are not integrated, produce mechanization islands and manual processes that are difficult to control and expensive to maintain. In short, due to a lack of standards and methodologies, and a lack of training and widespread culture, especially in IT aspects [10].

At the level of Latin America, doctoral programs have become a mainstay in the development of research both locally and regionally and internationally, and the focus and research nature of the training programs allows to determine social, natural, scientific phenomena, among others. Thus, the creation of doctoral programs has been present in the universities of the Latin American region, either independently or in cooperation between universities and institutions, in the region.

In a study carried out in Latin America, it is evident that doctoral programs represent a substantial role in the social impact of academic results, with scientific and research production increasing by 72% in the last decade. In the same study, 15% of respondents said that they had been rejected in their labor insertion in business sectors because doctoral degrees are obtained to perform purely academic tasks, which also shows a social ignorance of the objectives of the degree.

The results of doctoral programs through their professionals and scientific production is analyzed in an increase of science and technology products in a social system, a tendency to favor the areas of economy, society, culture, public policies, health services, the environment, quality of life and its regional or international local environment, in the generation of health, economic and cultural benefits produced by research or projects from complex mechanisms that reflect various ways in which knowledge is produced and used, in an advance of knowledge and application of experiences for informed decision-making in the different disciplines and, with economic benefits in a broad sense—patents, companies, jobs, productivity, exports [11].

The study has obtained 336 responses from potential candidates, which are part of the database of the UNACH and other IES in the central area and surroundings, of its graduates and graduates, and has been applied to computer personnel of companies in the sector and the guilds of professionals in the area.

Obtaining the following information:

59.6% of the participants in the meeting are between 30 and 40 years old, 29.8% are over 40 years old, and 10.5% are between 20 and 30 years old; 72.8% of respondents are male (Fig. 2).

56% of respondents reside in the province of Chimborazo, 13% in Pichincha, coincide in 6% both in the province of Cotopaxi, Bolivar, Santo Domingo, and Guayas, the rest are distributed in the other provinces of the Ecuadorian continental territory.

61.4% work in the public sector, 23.7% work in the private sector, 8.8% in mixed enterprises, and 6.1 percent do not work at the time of the survey; As for the type of institution in which they work, 47.4% work in Higher Education Institutions-IES, 20% work in companies with commercial purposes of goods or services and/or production, 11.4% work in government agencies, 9.6% work in educational institutions in general (except IES), 2.6% work in academic-social-scientific-commercial research institutions, 0.9% work in a non-profit, non-governmental organization.

26.3% have a Master's degree with an academic career in the field of IT, 21.1% have a Master's degree with a research trajectory in the field of IT, 14.9% have a Master's degree with a research trajectory in other fields of knowledge and 9.6% a Master's degree with an academic trajectory in other fields of knowledge. 28.1% do not have a master's degree.

81.6% indicate that they are not pursuing a Master's degree, and 11.4% are studying a master's program either with a research or academic trajectory in the field of IT. The remaining 7% are pursuing master's degrees in other areas.

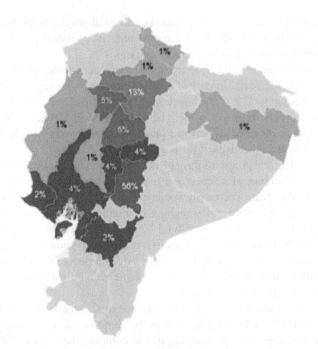

Fig. 2. Province of residence

95.6% of respondents consider it pertinent to carry out a Doctoral Program in Computer Science.

43% of respondents consider it extremely necessary for their profession to have specialized knowledge in research in the field of IT, and 55.3% consider between very necessary and moderately necessary for their profession to have specialized knowledge in research in the field of IT. 1.2% consider it not necessary or not at all necessary for their profession to have specialized knowledge in research in the field of IT.

28.1% are extremely interested in studying a Doctoral Program in Computer Science, 36% are Very interested, and 28.9% are moderately interested in studying a Doctoral Program in Computer Science. 7% are little or not at all interested.

Specifically, if you want to study at the National University of Chimborazo, 92.9% are between Extremely interested, very interested, and Moderately.

52.6% indicate that their main reason for choosing to study a Doctoral Program is the generation of knowledge, 37.7% mention that it is scientific production, and 57% mention that their main reason for opting for a doctoral program is the possibility of improving workspace. 46.5% want a professional update and 9.6% have a particular interest.

To study a Doctoral Program, 67.5% consider the important Degree offered, 61.4% the faculty, 43% the infrastructure of the higher education institution, 81% consider the Cost of the Program important and 59.6% consider the Duration important.

As for the financing modality for choosing to study the doctoral program, 31.6% prefer semester payments, 22.8% prefer educational credit, 21.9% prefer to use a credit card, and 14% prefer annual payments.

On the other hand, the potential employers or occupational fields for this study are obtained:

The place of residence of the potential employers that applied to the survey is 69% in Chimborazo, 10% in Pichincha, 7% in Napo, and between 2 and 3% distributed in the other provinces.

54.54% of the companies surveyed are from the public sector, 33.33% from the private sector, and 12.13% are mixed.

27.3% of the institutions surveyed are higher education institutions, 24.2% are without educational institutions, non-HEI, 18.2% are government agencies, 9.1% are non-profit non-governmental organizations, and 21.2% are for-profit companies.

97% of respondents consider it pertinent to carry out a Doctoral Program in Computer Science.

93.3% of the institutions surveyed would be interested in supporting their computer staff to study a Doctoral Program in Computer Science.

77.4% mention that they could provide support with flexibility in work schedules so that staff can pursue a doctoral program, 6.5% would support with scholarship or with financial support, while the rest would support with various ways.

57.6% indicate that the main reason to support their computer staff to study a Doctoral Program in Computer Science is the generation of knowledge, 51.5% is the possibility of improving labor skills, 48.5% indicate that it is the Search for efficient solutions, 30.3% mention that it is due to the invention of products and/or processes, and 36.4% indicate that their main reason would be the probable Innovation of products and processes.

Additionally, it is indicated that there is a probable need for doctoral programs in the area of education 45.5%, 27% in the area of administration, 24.2% in the area of engineering, industry, or construction, and 21% in the area of services.

As for generic and specific competences, the following are determined as priorities:

1. Demonstrate a high level of theoretical and methodological knowledge of Computational Sciences in the resolution of problems in the professional, scientific or academic field.
2. Carry out high-level scientific and applied research, with support in Computer Science to provide relevant solutions to problems of various kinds in the field of their professional practice
3. Communicate the results of their research clearly and effectively in professional and non- professional environments
4. Work with scientific rigor, participatory leadership, social responsibility, ethics, and humanism, in multidisciplinary teams, problem-solving in situations of chaos or uncertainty

It is obtained between 85% and 88%, coinciding with the generic competences that the doctoral student must develop.

It is determined that 67% consider that the specific competence that the doctoral student must develop is Cybersecurity and IT Infrastructure and Data Science and Intelligent Systems.

61% consider that the specific competence that the doctoral student must develop is IT Service Management.

58% consider that the specific competence that the doctoral student must develop is Fraud and Electronic Crimes Legislation, and good practices of ethical leadership in all the actions carried out by the Computer Science professional.

57% consider that the specific competence to be developed by the doctoral student is Machine Learning Models and Data Science and Applied Mathematics.

54% consider that the specific competence that the doctoral student must develop is Industry 4.0.

All other competences are also considered important, in percentages less than 50% for the institutions consulted.

Currently, companies and organizations manage a globalized trend in the business or services they provide, being necessary that the internal control systems they use are as efficient and effective as possible without neglecting other broader concepts such as information risk, continuity of operations, management of the information center, etc. Hence the importance of updating and continuous improvement through research on the work performance of professionals and teachers who opt for the doctoral program.

The evolution of computer science has forced professionals to a higher degree of training, becoming experts in specific areas within companies or organizations fulfilling independent functions within a computer environment, and the analysis of information, this program aims to provide that opportunity.

Computer systems are increasingly present in the activities we carry out and surround us, hence the need to promote research, training, and training to generate knowledge and tools that allow establishing adequate mechanisms for the control and treatment of information by applying technologies to establish adequate and specific mechanisms in IT processes that allow cost savings and maximize productivity.

On the other hand, reviewing information published on the website of the Ministry of Education, Higher Science, Technology [7], we obtained data that reflect the demand and employability of fourth- level professionals during the last 5 years, with a cut to 2018. Results that we consider pertinent to mention and analyze to support the doctoral project.

3.1 Demand

The following table shows the number of fourth-level degrees registered per year, in the period from 2013 to 2018, also the total number of titles with a cut-off to the year 2018, and whether they were obtained in the country or abroad (Table 1).

Analyzing between the last three years, that is, 2016, 2107, and 2018 where there is a decrease of 6,133 and 5,872 records of titles for each year respectively and therefore a decrease of professionals between 2017 and 2018, meanwhile there is an increase of 2,643 and 669 titles and professionals respectively per year who decided to study abroad for some reason.

Now let's analyze the total number of fourth-level degrees that were obtained in the area of Information and Communication Technologies, between the years 2013–2018 (Fig. 3).

Table 1. Total fourth-level degrees in Ecuador, by year of registration 2013–2018.

Title type	2013	2014	2015	2016	2017	2018	Titles Total
National	13.307	12.745	19.206	21.675	15.542	9.670	**92.145**
Foreign	5.090	7.681	9.795	6.239	8.882	8.213	**45.900**
Total	**18.397**	**20.426**	**29.001**	**27.914**	**24.424**	**17.883**	**138.045**

Source: Ministry of Education, Higher Science, Technology and Innovation [12] - National Information System of Higher Education of Ecuador [13]

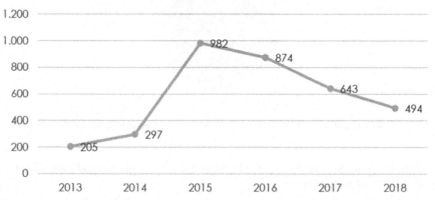

Fig. 3. Fourth-level degrees in the broad field of information and communication technologies registered Senescyt 2013–2018. **Source: Ministry of Education,** Higher Science, Technology and Innovation - National Information System of Higher Education of Ecuador [12, 13].

As can be seen in the frequency polygon, since 2015 there has been a clear decrease in records of degrees and professionals in the area, so it is of utmost urgency to diversify the academic offer, in tune with social needs, since the curriculum must go hand in hand with the progress of science and technology.

3.2 Employability

Similarly, reviewing the official website of the National Institute of Statistics and Census [14] it was possible to find information on the total number of companies with investment in ICT, in the detailed field, information with the cut to the year 2015 that we use as a reference.

From a micro social analysis, the changes produced in productive and service organizations are recognized, as we can see in the table small, medium and large companies make investments of 66%.73%, up to 85% in Information and Communication Technologies. Therefore, it is necessary to have educational programs focused on the improvement and specialization of workers who have been developing in the area, guaranteeing their job permanence and in the same way it is the opportunity to hire new qualified personnel in the management of computer technologies and information processing and generation of new knowledge in the area that allows being more effective, efficient and competitive [15].

Similarly, and based on the records of INEC 2015, the data on investment in ICT according to the economic activity they carry out are shown in the following graph and can be considered as a reference for the study of demand and employability (Fig. 4).

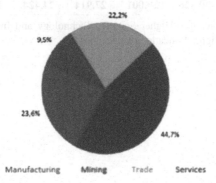

Fig. 4. Amount of investment in ICT (281 MM*) of each economic sector. Source: [14]

It is important to note that it is the latest information published and available on the official INEC website [14].

4   Conclusions

The realization of postgraduate programs through interdisciplinary and transdisciplinary studies allows for the establishment of adequate and specific mechanisms to promote research, education, and training. The doctoral program in Computer Science contributes to the development of the territory not only in zone 3 but also, at the national level since a large part of medium and large companies are modernizing their computer operations and therefore innovative, relevant, and competitive solutions are required.

The doctorates, since they are the highest level in vocational training, are called to be protagonists of first hand in the productive context of the country, it cannot be expected that those who achieve this academic level stay or are their only claims to remain linked to the academy exclusively, but they are the ones who must potentiate the productive development of the country, To be the promoters of ideas and developments that allow closing the gaps that the country is currently experiencing in technological matters.

In this sense, the study program that is presented, in addition to defining professional profiles, demand and employability, has as an independent function to train research professionals in the area of Information Technologies capable of generating solutions to the real problems of our context.

This program contributes to the general mission of the National University of Chimborazo, to the Creating Opportunities Plan in its short and long-term vision, in addition to training professionals according to trends and scientific-technological development, through processes that involve teaching with research, management, and linkage with society, capable of proposing integral solutions based on local problems, national and international. In addition, it is justified by the projection made concerning the demand for professionals and the need to have a fourth-level program that helped to acquire scientific and technological knowledge, with social responsibility, as a result of the dynamic articulation of the academic and the demand of Ecuadorian society.

References

1. Navas, A.: Vale la pena hacer un doctorado. Innov. Ciencia **XXIV**(2) (2017)
2. Varquillas, C., Velasco, D., Cejas, M., Moreno, P.: Evaluación sobre la pertinencia del modelo educativo pedagógico y didáctico vigente de la unach. UNACH, Riobamba (2021)
3. MINTEL: Agenda de transformación digital del Ecuador 2022–2025. Ministerio de Telecomunicaciones y de la Sociedad de la Información, Quito, (2022)
4. Bnamericas: Panorama de inversión y financiamiento de TIC: Lavca, Ativy. Aerialoop (2022)
5. Chui, M., Roberts, R., Yee, L.: McKinsey technology trends outlook 2022. McKinsey Digital (2022)
6. FIBK: Las grandes tendencias tecnológicas que vienen esta década. Fundación Innovación Bankinter (2022)
7. CES: Comisión Permanente de Doctorados, 4 November 2022. http://appcmi.ces.gob.ec/ofe rta_vigente/especializaciones/especializacion.php
8. AuraQuantic: Top 10 tendencias tecnológicas 2023. Aura quantic, Miami (2022)
9. IEBS: Tendencias tecnológicas para la próxima década (2022–2030) (2022)
10. Leon, D., Martinez, J.; Tendencias Tecnológicas de Mayor Impacto en el Ecuador para el Año 2022: Evolucionando digitalmente los negocios. itAhora (2022)
11. Higher Education Funding Council: Annual report and accounts 2013–14. England (2015)
12. SENESCYT: Secretaría de Educación Superior, Ciencia, Tecnología e Innovación, 22 January 2023. https://www.educacionsuperior.gob.ec/
13. SNIESE: Sistema Nacional de Información de Educación Superior del Ecuador - SNIESE | Quito, Ecuador, 13 January 2023. https://public.tableau.com/app/profile/sniese
14. INEC: Empresas y TIC. INEC, Quito (2015)
15. Coba, G.: Nueve de cada 10 pymes en Ecuador invierte en tecnología. Primicias, Quito (2022)
16. OMS: Objetivos de Desarollo Sostenible. OMS (2015)

Developing an Effective ICT Strategic Framework for Higher Education Institutions: A Case of Mataram University

Surya Sumarni Hussein[1]([⊠]), Muhamad Wisnu Alfiansyah[1], Rohaizan Daud[2], Suraya Ya'acob[3], and Anitawati Mohd Lokman[1]

[1] College of Computing, Informatics, and Media, Universiti Teknologi MARA, Shah Alam, Malaysia
`{suryasumarni,anitawati}@uitm.edu.my`
[2] Institut Tadbiran Awam Negara (INTAN), Jabatan Perkhidmatan Awam Malaysia, Kuala Lumpur, Malaysia
`rohaizan@intanbk.intan.my`
[3] Advanced Informatics Department, Faculty of Technology and Informatics, Universiti Teknologi Malaysia, Kuala Lumpur, Malaysia
`suraya.yaacob@utm.my`

Abstract. This study proposes an Information and Communication Technology (ICT) Strategic Plan (ISP) framework aimed at providing organizations with a practical guide to implementing successful ICT strategies. The proposed framework is based on the identified as-is situation and gap analysis using Enterprise Architecture (EA) and Knowledge Management (KM) approaches. The most significant limitation of most developed ISP frameworks is the inadequate requirement gathering and analysis, leading to a lack of a comprehensive understanding of the organization's true goals. To address this, the proposed framework integrates EA and KM practices, enabling organizations to develop models and diagrams to visualize organizational objects and capture, transfer, and create new ICT strategies. The study's contribution lies in providing organizations with a valuable resource for developing dynamic and meaningful ICT strategies, culminating in the translation of the resulting ISP into an Enterprise Architecture diagram, called a Landscape Map Viewpoint (LMV), as a communication medium for decision-making purposes.

Keywords: Enterprise Architecture · Knowledge Management · ICT Strategic Plan · Case Study

1 Introduction

The success of an organization's implementation of an Information and Communication Technology (ICT) strategic plan has become increasingly critical in recent times, and the ability to make strategic decisions is closely linked to the organization's chances of success. To achieve this goal, the ICT strategic plan must be easily understood and

L. Uden and I-H. Ting (Eds.): KMO 2023, CCIS 1825, pp. 210–221, 2023.
https://doi.org/10.1007/978-3-031-34045-1_18

adaptable to the current environment. According to Abu Bakar et al. [1] and Guerra et al. [2], two elements must complement each other for successful implementation of ICT strategic plan initiatives: clear visualization of the goals and comprehensive information. Visual aids such as diagrams and matrices can provide the necessary clarity, while the ICT strategic plan should include details on processes, data, and technology, among other important information.

The current framework for the ICT strategic plan has fallen short of its purpose to provide clear visualization of initiatives for organizations to successfully implement ICT projects. As a result, there is a pressing need for information to be visible and readily available to create useful and dynamic ICT strategies [3, 4]. Saiya and Arman [5] echo this sentiment, stating that a robust framework is built on complete and thorough information. Furthermore, as outlined by Abu Bakar et al. [1], Enterprise Architecture (EA) is a detailed structure that comprises various components such as context, service, business, application and data processing, data space, technologies, and physical infrastructures, along with stakeholder perspectives. Thus, incorporating EA and Knowledge Management (KM) in the ICT strategic plan framework allows for the capturing and visualization of information that is crucial in formulating effective and dynamic ICT strategies.

This paper intends to develop meaningful and dynamic ICT strategies. At the end of this study, ICT strategic plan will be translated into an EA diagram known as a Landscape Map Viewpoint (LMV) and represent a communication medium for decision-making purposes.

2 Material and Method

2.1 The Concept of ICT Strategic Plan

ICT strategic plan is an organisation's long-term plan related to its information system or information technology. This plan is influenced by several factors such as grants and funds management, financial management, budgeting and planning, and human capital management (HCM) according to Luić et al. [6]. Kamariotou and Kitsios [7] suggest that a good ICT strategic plan should incorporate success constructs, alignment, analysis, cooperation, and capabilities. It is important to note that the ICT strategic plan cannot be developed in isolation from the company's strategic plan, which includes business processes, information systems, and information technology [8]. The ICT strategic plan should provide detailed information about how information systems and technologies are influenced, specifically in areas such as IT governance, IS application, IT infrastructure, and IT human resources, according to Gandhi et al. [9].

The success of ICT strategic plan implementation is dependent on various interrelated factors, including the rapidly changing technology landscape, individual IT expertise, budgetary constraints, and the presence of meaningful strategic plans [10]. Moreover, the alignment between information and business strategy plays a crucial role in ensuring the success of the ICT strategic plan [10]. Therefore, the use of EA as an approach in developing the ICT strategic plan is appropriate, given that it focuses on aligning the information and business strategy [12, 13].

2.2 EA Framework

The literature reviews discover EA frameworks prominently used to develop a strategic plan in an organization [12, 13]. The first framework is known as the Zachman Framework, which is a logical and straightforward framework developed for overall EA, and it can be used to manage the infrastructure information of an enterprise [14, 15]. The second framework is called the TOGAF Framework, which offers a comprehensive approach to designing, planning, implementing, and controlling an enterprise information architecture. The TOGAF framework follows a holistic approach to design and is typically modelled at four levels: business, application, data, and technology [15–19]. Figure 1 illustrates the TOGAF framework, which is suitable for this research due to the detailed process it provides [12, 13, 20].

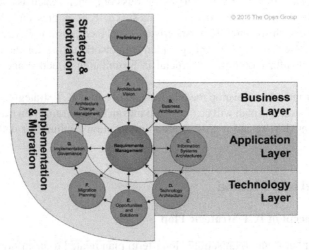

Fig. 1. TOGAF Framework [19]

2.3 KM Framework

A KM framework can greatly improve an organization's knowledge gathering, sharing, application, and retention, making it a vital tool for the effective implementation of an ICT strategic plan [22, 23]. The objective of knowledge management is to boost organizational performance by delivering the right information to the right people at the right time. Although the concept of KM has been around for decades, it has not been widely adopted in ICT project development, particularly in ICT strategic plans [24, 25]. By using a structured approach to manage knowledge, timely and informed decision-making can be enabled, quality and productivity can be enhanced, and new products can be delivered to stakeholders. The four critical components of KM are people, process, content/IT, and strategy. Regardless of the industry, size, or knowledge needs of an organization, people are essential to lead, sponsor, and support knowledge sharing [24]. Techniques to manage and evaluate the flow of knowledge must be defined, and knowledge material and IT systems that connect the right individuals with the right content at the right time must be provided. Finally, a well-defined and documented strategy is required to use KM to meet the organization's most critical and urgent needs. All of these processes are interdependent on one another and influenced by various factors. This is why KM frameworks can differ in many ways and can be implemented in various ways.

Different models of knowledge management may vary in their presentation, with some models being sequential, while others show processes overlapping. However, as knowledge management is dependent on other aspects of an organization such as project management, information management, and strategy, and involves multiple systems and processes, some models can become complex. The KM framework by CEN [22], which is illustrated in Fig. 2, takes a clear process-oriented approach that aims to describe core business and knowledge-related processes. This framework extends those processes by enablers: knowledge capabilities on both organizational (such as vision and strategy) and individual levels (such as skills, competencies, methods, and tools). The CEN framework has provided a common terminology, structure, and guidelines around these processes. However, it does not cover the main aspects of globally distributed knowledge management but provides options for extension, such as adding enablers and additional components or extending processes. It also does not incorporate research perspectives, such as aspects studied, or models validated.

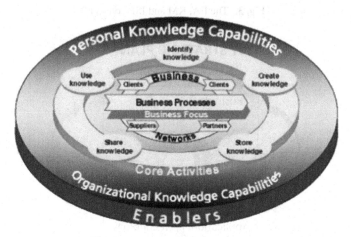

Fig. 2. KM framework by CEN [22]

2.4 Research Model Formulation

The development of the ICT strategic plan framework is rooted in both the KM and EA frameworks. To create the framework, the first step involves reviewing published literature by conducting searches using the keywords 'knowledge management', 'enterprise architecture', and 'ICT strategic plan' on three e-libraries: ACM Digital Library, Springer Link, and SCOPUS. These searches yielded articles from various fields, such as Computer Science, Decision Science, Social Science, Education, Finance, Nursing, Business Management, and Psychology. To avoid duplications, any articles with the same title or DOI were removed, followed by a cleaning process of the title and abstract. In addition, manual exploration using Google Scholar and the "snowball" concept by Dusek et al. [26] was used to ensure that all relevant works were included. After that, a thorough analysis was conducted to eliminate any articles that lacked a description of the organization or statement from the authors. Finally, appropriate journal titles were selected, and the EA, KM, and ICT strategic concepts were formulated.

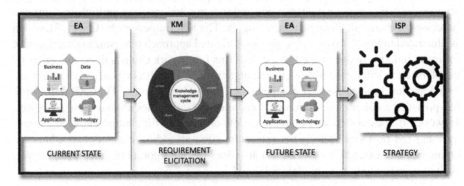

Fig. 3. The EA, KM and ISP concept

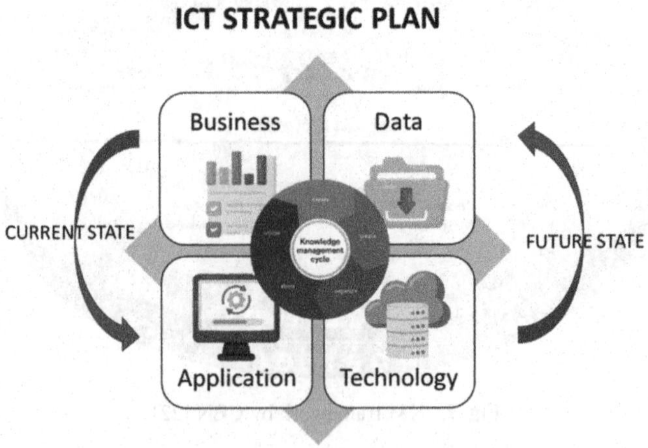

ICT STRATEGIC PLAN

Fig. 4. The ICT Strategic Plan Framework

The conceptual framework proposed in Fig. 3 integrates both the EA and KM frameworks with a process that includes creating, curating, organizing, sharing, and utilizing knowledge. The KM components have been modified to collect up-to-date information in four domains: business, data, application, and technology, to develop the ICT strategic plan. Figure 4 illustrates the ICT strategic plan framework, which was utilized as a benchmark during stakeholder interviews.

2.5 Methodology

This study utilized two primary data sources for each case: a literature review and in-depth case study interviews to ensure high reliability and validity. The theoretical framework for the ICT strategic plan was identified through a thorough literature review. Meanwhile, in-depth case study interviews were conducted with three participants from Mataram University who were involved in ICT initiatives, namely the Vice Chancellor for Field 4, the Head of IT Department, and the CTO IT Department. These participants, referred to as P1, P2, and P3, all met the inclusion criteria, having worked for more than 10 years with at least five years of IT-related expertise. Questions for the case study interviews were based on the four domains defined in the EA framework selected, TOGAF. The purpose of these interviews was to evaluate the proposed framework.

On November 29, 2022, the P1 interview was conducted in the Vice Chancellor field 4 room, while the interviews with P2 and P3 were held on November 24, 2022, in the Mataram University IT department building. These interviews followed a semi-structured format and were analysed using the thematic analytic method. This method helps to identify patterns in the data, which are then used to address the research or raise concerns over any issues that may arise. The researcher chose thematic analysis because it is a process of identifying themes or patterns within qualitative data collected during the previous phase. The development process adhered to the existing TOGAF framework, which involves four domains: business, data, application, and technology.

3   Results and Discussion

The results of the interviews were analysed using a thematic analysis to identify the key elements related to each domain. These elements will serve as inputs for the development of an ICT strategic plan for the IT department at Mataram University, using the proposed ICT Strategic framework. The TOGAF framework has four architectural domains which include business, data, application, and technology. Section 3.1 of the report outlines the findings of the thematic analysis conducted on the interview data.

3.1 Business Domain

The Business domain is crucial to all activities at Mataram University, including organizational units, actors, roles, processes, functions, and business services. The thematic analysis of the interview excerpts revealed that the COVID-19 pandemic has caused a surge in online learning and research activities, resulting in a high demand for systems and infrastructure procurement. To meet the growing demands, it is essential that the developed systems are easily accessible and user-friendly. The University has primarily focused on web-based development and has yet to implement an application base. Mataram University is also expanding its cooperation with external parties, providing numerous opportunities for collaboration in the ICT field. The top management is also supportive of ICT development and has been increasing funding in this sector. However, due to the vast capital needed, development needs to be done in stages. Effective communication and cooperation among all internal parties at the University are critical to the success of various plans, particularly in developing the ICT sector. Currently, the IT Department handles development without the use of external vendors due to past failures and vendors not taking responsibility. Although the Department's employees are experienced, their numbers are relatively low, so increasing the workforce in the coming years is necessary. The excerpts that support these findings are:

> *"Several systems have been created to support the decision-making process, such as the executive portal and IKU.... The system is more in the form of graphs or charts, which can later be considered for management. Meanwhile, no system recommends decision-making. Although Mataram University already has a system, they still use direct correspondence (not ready to go paperless)." (P1)*

> *"To support collaboration in any department by providing various systems or websites needed. In addition, the data integration process continues to this day. Strengthening was also done on the infrastructure side regarding data servers, bandwidth, and Wi-Fi. Regarding the MBKM government program, the integration process is carried out even faster." (P2)*

> *"In the future, information technology will become fundamental. The hope is that it can become an institution that can meet all IT-related needs at Mataram University." (P2)*

Thus, Mataram University's collaboration with various parties, including the government, other universities, and industry, is needed. Furthermore, Mataram University needs to improve both its infrastructure and systems in the ICT field.

3.2 Data Domain

Transparency of data is becoming increasingly important, with many parties demanding access to it. As a result, it is crucial to standardize the collection, storage, conversion, and use of data and information within businesses. At present, Mataram University has systems in place that provide access to a significant amount of information. However, these systems are still under construction and only partially functional. Data has been stored centrally, and some of it has been integrated to facilitate user access. Mataram University aims to reduce data redundancy and integrate data from various sources. Despite this, the process of inputting data remains relatively slow, making it difficult to keep up to date. The excerpts that support these findings are:

> *"For transparency, we create a system where everyone can see directly. But it may not have included the budget, such as absorption and spending today..."* P1.

> *"Because Mataram University is under the government, the data or information must be open"* P2.

> *"Some data has been integrated, such as data on students, staff/lecturers, UKT payments, courses, and data for organizational needs."* P2.

3.3 Application Domain

The application domain is integral to all processes related to planning, development, and maintenance at Mataram University. Several systems have already been built and integrated, with each system tailored to meet the specific needs of the university. However, the development of these systems depends on the skill set of the staff responsible for creating them, resulting in the use of different programming languages such as Laravel, Code Igniter, Javascript, among others. This lack of standardization in the IT Department's system development process has resulted in inconsistencies. Recently, the department has developed "MyUnram", an application that simplifies system access for users. The excerpts that support these findings are:

> "Several integrated information systems are already available at Mataram University."(P3).

> "ICT development can be maximized for profit/income at the University of Mataram." (P1).

> "Increasing demands for the continuity of updating information systems within Mataram University". (P2).

As stated in the excerpt, a number of systems have been integrated. In addition, academic, management, and monitoring systems have been established and utilised. Nonetheless, certain systems remain undeveloped due to inadequate infrastructure. Addressing this issue is crucial for their inclusion in the future state.

3.4 Technology Domain

The use of technology at Mataram University encompasses various service platforms and technology components. Although the existing infrastructure may not be optimal, it is still capable of meeting the institution's needs. The helpdesk services provided are comprehensive and accessible through multiple channels, including the web, Telegram, and email. The recent procurement of data centres is a significant milestone, as it has enhanced the control system and database storage process. However, the maintenance of the data centre is still carried out manually, as there is currently no automation system in place.

The current technology policy is accompanied by a Service Level Agreement (SLA) policy, which has been implemented at the highest management level, i.e., Vice Chancellor 4. However, there is a need to develop a corresponding SLA policy at the IT Department level. Furthermore, there is a lack of appropriate documentation for risk management across all owned systems, making it necessary to establish policies and frameworks to manage risks effectively in the future. The excerpts that support these findings are:

> The number of ICT facilities is not proportional to the number of human resources. (P3).

> Internet bandwidth is still inadequate, so internet access is still slow. (P2).

> The availability of technology that supports smart campuses (education 4.0) is insufficient. (P3).

> The rapid development of ICT so that the University of Mataram must continue to renew/revitalize facilities/infrastructure and software to avoid technology lags and delays in ICT services. (P2).

The excerpt highlights the significant role of technology in education and how Mataram University's technological records contain crucial information in this regard. While deploying the necessary infrastructure facilities can undoubtedly improve the quality of education for students, professors, and staff, the current implementation is considered suboptimal. To address this, the ICT strategic plan for Mataram University has been illustrated in an LMV diagram, which provides enough flexibility to integrate a wide range of categories and concepts derived from earlier findings. During the interview process, it was revealed that the application domain requires improvement.

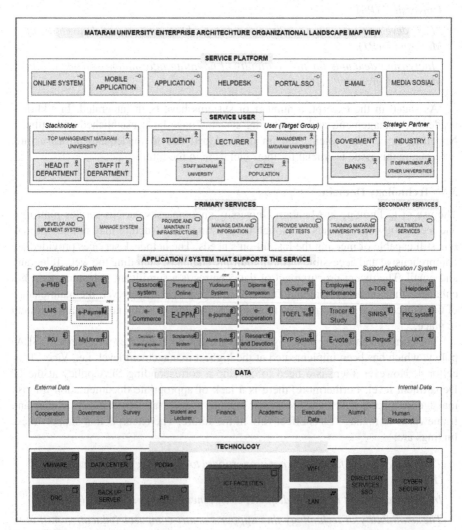

Fig. 5. Future states of Mataram University Enterprise Architecture Organizational Landscape Map Viewpoint

As a result, the LMV diagram visualises the ICT strategic plan for Mataram University, as shown in Fig. 5, with the dotted line indicating the proposed applications in the future state of the plan.

4 Conclusion

This research presents a framework for an ICT strategic plan and uses a Landscape Map Viewpoint (LMV) to visualise the plan based on the findings. KM is not a new concept, but its application in the ICT domain is still limited. EA provides a common approach to transferring and visualising knowledge across organisational and geographic boundaries in a manner that is easily understood and shared, leading to consistent execution quality, increased efficiency, and ongoing improvement in ICT implementation. Developing a culture of seeking and sharing knowledge, as well as aligning business and technology, including people and ICT, are critical to successfully integrating KM and EA into ICT strategic planning development and implementation. Formulating an ICT strategic framework is the starting point for developing an ICT strategic plan, and further interview sessions were conducted to evaluate the framework. Ultimately, the ICT strategic plan is visualised using the LMV approach, illustrating the landscape map of ICT initiatives in Mataram University. This research can serve as a valuable resource for organisations seeking to develop meaningful and dynamic ICT strategies.

Acknowledgement. The authors gratefully acknowledge the financial grant 600-RMC 5/3/GPM (040/2022) provided by Research Management Centre, and the College of Computing, Informatics and MediaUniversiti Teknologi MARA, Malaysia, as well as Mataram University, Indonesia for all support and resources.

References

1. Abu Bakar, N.A., Yaacob, S., Hussein, S.S., Nordin, A., Sallehuddin, H.: Dynamic metamodel approach for government enterprise architecture model management. Procedia Comput. Sci. **161**, 894–902 (2019). https://doi.org/10.1016/j.procs.2019.11.197
2. Guerra, E., de Lara, J., Malizia, A., Díaz, P.: Supporting user-oriented analysis for multi-view domain-specific visual languages. Inf. Softw. Technol. **51**(4), 769–784 (2009). https://doi.org/10.1016/j.infsof.2008.09.005
3. Gonçalves, D., Ferreira, L., Campos, N.: Enterprise architecture for high flexible and agile company in automotive industry. Procedia Comput. Sci. **181**, 1077–1082 (2021). https://doi.org/10.1016/j.procs.2021.01.303
4. Yuliana, R., Rahardjo, B.: Designing an agile enterprise architecture for mining company by using TOGAF framework. In: Proceedings of 2016 4th International Conference on Cyber and IT Service Management (CITSM 2016) (2016). https://doi.org/10.1109/CITSM.2016.7577466
5. Saiya, A.A., Arman, A.A.: Indonesian enterprise architecture framework: a platform for integrated and connected government. In: Proceeding - 2018 International Conference on ICT for Smart Society: Innovation Toward Smart Society and Society 5.0 (ICISS 2018) (2018). https://doi.org/10.1109/ICTSS.2018.8549990

6. Luić, L., Kalpić, D., Bojović, M., Milasinović, B., Radivojević, Z.: Principal risk in implementation of a sophisticated ERP system at a higher education institutions. In: Proceedings of Papers from the 10th International Conference on Telecommunications in Modern Satellite, Cable and Broadcasting Services (TELSIKS 2011), pp. 357–360 (2011). https://doi.org/10.1109/TELSKS.2011.6112069

7. Kamariotou, M., Kitsios, F.: How managers use information systems for strategy implementation in agritourism SMEs. Information (Switzerland) 11(6), 331 (2020). https://doi.org/10.3390/info11060331

8. Szabo, Z., Ori, D.: Information strategy challenges in the digital era how enterprise architecture management can support strategic IS planning. In: Proceedings of the International Conference on Software, Knowledge Information, Industrial Management and Applications (SKIMA), vol. 2017-Decem, no. March 2018 (2018). https://doi.org/10.1109/SKIMA.2017.8294114

9. Gandhi, A., Ruldeviyani, Y., Sucahyo, Y.G.: Strategic information systems planning for bureaucratic reform. In: Proceedings of the International Conference on Research and Innovation in Information Systems (ICRIIS), no. Dc (2017). https://doi.org/10.1109/ICRIIS.2017.8002474

10. Sudirman, S., Mohammad Yusof, Z.: Public sector ICT strategic planning: framework of monitoring and evaluating process. Asia Pac. J. Inf. Technol. Multimedia 06(01), 85–99 (2017). https://doi.org/10.17576/apjitm-2017-0601-07

11. Kurniawan, N.B.: Enterprise architecture design for ensuring strategic business IT alignment (integrating SAMM with TOGAF 9.1). In: Proceedings of the Joint International Conference on Rural Information and Communication Technology and Electric-Vehicle Technology, rICT and ICEV-T 2013 (2013). https://doi.org/10.1109/rICT-ICeVT.2013.6741505

12. Hussein, S.S., Abu Bakar, N.A., Yaacob, S., Nordin, A., Sallehuddin, H., Ahmad, S.: Development and validation of enterprise architecture (EA) readiness assessment model meta-model for enterprise architecture (EA) data management: case study of Malaysian public sector (MPS). Int. J. Adv. Sci. Eng. Inf. Technol. 10(1), 1–12 (2020). https://doi.org/10.18517/ijaseit.10.1.9007

13. Batmetan, J.R.: Model enterprise architecture for information technology services in universities. Int. J. Inf. Technol. Educ. 1(4), 18–34 (2022). http://ijite.jredu.id/index.php/ijite/article/view/73

14. Lapalme, J., Gerber, A., Van Der Merwe, A., Zachman, J., De Vries, M., Hinkelmann, K.: Exploring the future of enterprise architecture: a Zachman perspective. Comput. Ind. 79, 103–113 (2016). https://doi.org/10.1016/j.compind.2015.06.010

15. Abunadi, I.: Enterprise architecture best practices in large corporations. Information 10(10), 5–7 (2019). https://doi.org/10.3390/info10100293

16. Saiya, A.A., Arman, A.A.: Indonesian enterprise architecture framework: a platform for integrated and connected government. In: Proceedings - 2018 International Conference on ICT for Smart Society: Innovation Toward Smart Society and Society 5.0, ICISS 2018, 0-5 (2018). https://doi.org/10.1109/ICTSS.2018.8549990

17. Soares, S.: University in Timor Leste to support the strategic plan of integrated information system. In: Aung, M.W., Adeli, H. (eds.) Proceedings of the 2014 International Conference on Information Science and Applications (ICISA 2014), pp. 4–9. Springer (2014). https://doi.org/10.1007/978-3-319-06758-3_2

18. De Fatima Gusmao, U., Setyohadi, D.B.: Strategic planning for the information development of IPDC (Instituto Profissional de Canossa) library using TOGAF method. In: Proceedings of the 2017 5th International Conference on Cyber and IT Service Management (CITSM 2017), pp. 1–6. IEEE (2017). https://doi.org/10.1109/CITSM.2017.8089289

19. Jnr, A., Regulation, D.P.: Digital transformation with enterprise architecture for smarter cities: a qualitative research approach. Digit. Policy Regul. Gov. **23**(2), 121–146 (2021). https://doi.org/10.1108/DPRG-08-2020-0045

20. Hussein, S.S., Ismail, Z., Mat Taib, M.Z.: Towards sustainability of EA practices: a systematic review. In: First International Conference on ICT for Transformation (2016)

21. Desfray, P., Raymond, G.: Togaf®: in modeling enterprise architecture with TOGAF, pp. 1–24 (2014). https://doi.org/10.1016/B978-0-12-419984-2.00001-X

22. Pawlowski, J.M., Bick, M.: The global knowledge management framework: towards a theory for knowledge management in globally distributed settings. Electron. J. Knowl. Manag. (2012)

23. Bhat, M., Shumaiev, K., Biesdorf, A., Hohenstein, U., Hassel, M., Matthes, F.: Meta-modelbased framework for architectural knowledge management (2016).https://doi.org/10.1145/2993412.3004848

24. Karagoz, Y., Whiteside, N., Korthaus, A.: Context matters: enablers and barriers to knowledge sharing in Australian public sector ICT projects. J. Knowl. Manag. **24**(8), 1921–1941 (2020). https://doi.org/10.1108/JKM-12-2019-0691/FULL/XML

25. Ragsdell, G.: Knowledge management in the not-for-profit sector. J. Knowl. Manag. **20**(1) (2016). https://doi.org/10.1108/JKM-11-2015-0483/FULL/HTML

26. Dusek, G.A., Yurova, Y.V., Ruppel, C.P.: Using social media and targeted snowball sampling to survey a hard-to-reach population: a case study. Int. J. Dr. Stud. **10**, 279–299 (2015). https://doi.org/10.28945/2296

Peer Online Training (POT) as Learning Activity in Computer Security Audit and Risks Management Teaching Module

Rabiah Ahmad[1]([⊠]), Aslinda Hassan[2], Lee Hwee Hsiung[2],
and Mohd Fadzrin Othman[3]

[1] Faculty of Engineering Technology, University Tun Hussein Onn, Parit Raja, Malaysia
rabiah@uthm.edu.my
[2] Faculty of Information and Communication Technology, UTeM CyberSecurity Competence Center, Universiti Teknikal Malaysia Melaka, Durian Tunggal, Malaysia
[3] CyberSecurity Malaysia, Cyberjaya, Selangor Darul Ehsan, Malaysia

Abstract. Teaching and Lecturing Computer Security Audit & Risks Management module is challenging. With the increase demand of high skilled talent in computer security by industries, all subjects at Bachelor Degree Program are required to be up to date and complete with practical skill training. Many technical universities in Malaysia promote Practical Application Oriented Approach (PAO) as mode of delivery in teaching and learning. As we know, an online learning received serious attention due to pandemic Covid 19. Inspired from Professional Training in Cybersecurity, we implemented method call Peer Online Training (POT) as learning activity in teaching Computer Security Audit and Risks Management module. There are ten (10) students were given a task to conduct mini project related to ISMS, risks analysis and Incident Management. The project required students to conduct information searching, practical exercises and industry communications. Students need to utilize their skill in Microsoft Power point, Infographics, and Multimedia applications for developing a Training Contents. Each training video uploaded to Youtube Channel and the link shared among themselves. We also share the Youtube link to five panels from industry for content validations. The panels are from Cybersecurity Malaysia, Finance Officer at Higher Institution, and Inland Revenue ICT Director. All students were asked to participate for physical training and technique called "Ireland Hopping" were applied to improve training contents. The training also required students to conduct self and peer assessment. We observed students' performance by (1) distributing feedback survey form and (2) personal interview. The results show that 95% students enjoyed Peer Online Training. Their feedback shows that POT increased understanding and improve their skill to explore audit activity. They recommended for more on online practical exercise in future. We concluded that POT able to act as value added tool in learning activity. It creates new insight for students to have better understanding in learning Computer Security Audit & Risk Management.

Keywords: Computer Security Audit · Online Training · Risk Management · Practical Application Oriented (PAO)

© The Author(s), under exclusive license to Springer Nature Switzerland AG 2023
L. Uden and I-H. Ting (Eds.): KMO 2023, CCIS 1825, pp. 222–229, 2023.
https://doi.org/10.1007/978-3-031-34045-1_19

1   Introduction

Computer Security has become important area in formal education. Many countries around the world put a lot of effort to create academic program in Computer Security either at Diploma, Degree or Postgraduate. There are various type of name referring to Bachelor program in Computer or Information Security at global market. Universities and College offers various type of courses related to Cybersecurity recently. According to Cybersecurity Malaysia, Malaysia needs 20,000 talent in Cybersecurity by 2025 [8]. The demand in Cybersecurity talent is due to dramatic growth of cyber attacks and crimes [1]. We need experts that able to design countermeasures for future attack on computer and cyber world. It is highlighted by industry report that, competent people are needed to secure internal system against cyber attack. Report by [2] addressed that highly skilled people in cybersecurity able to reduce cases involve cyber attack and data breaches. Academic program at university is designed to meet criteria of talent in cybersecurity.

It is important to note here that in cybersecurity there are four important parameters must meet industry criteria. Those parameters are content, competency, method of delivery and assessment. Computer and Cybersecurity were set to be professional job skill. There are a lot of professional certifications available in the market. However, certifications that get highly attention from industry are CISSP, COMPTIA, ISACA and GlobalACE [7]. It is important to note here that some certifications are product-based cert and limited number of certifications program are designed to meet generic industry requirement cross country.

Collaborations industry, community, university and government agency termed as quadruple helix innovated solutions and talent for global challenge. Malaysia started implemented Quadruple Helix approach to all public universities. Technical universities in Malaysia were designed to bring more high skilled talent and solutions provider. Applying practical application oriented approach (PAO), most technical university in Malaysia implemented quadruple helix approach for high demand academic program like information security. Industry feed university with information like shortage of highly skilled talent in cybersecurity. On top of that Cybersecurity industry keep sharing what type of skill sets require for industry-ready graduate.

As lecturer at technical university we are committed to execute PAO for industry-driven academic module. We offer Bachelor Degree in Network Security at the faculty of Information Communication System, University Technical Malaysia. One of the module is Computer Security Audit and Risks Management. The program designed aligned with content of Global Ace Scheme offered at Cybersecurity Malaysia. We also apply online learning and in this program we introduce Peer Online Training as part of learning activity.

This article presents our innovation in teaching Computer Security and Risks Management. The learning activities for this module consists of group discussion, "Ireland hopping" and Peer Online Training (POT). This article is structured into five sections which include introduction, previous work, method, result and conclusion. The detail of the program will be presented as follow.

2 Previous Work

Online learning has gained popularity since year 2000 when the world was introduced to the concept of Open University. It becomes more popular when we are facing with pandemic Covid 19. The post pandemic gave pressures to learning community and it enforces people to be familiar with online learning. As we can see, online teaching and learning has gained popularity to learned community particularly those who are in the area of computer science and ICT.

Industry 4.0 demands transformation in learning ecosystem. Students not just seat in the lecture room to study, yet word learning is most appropriate. Students must be able to learn, unlearn and re-learn as mechanism to equip themselves with appropriate knowledge and information. From industry perspective, high skilled talent produced through effective training. Professional certifications offer as value add to students at diploma and bachelor degree level. Realizing the needs of professional certification in cybersecurity, Ministry of Higher Education Malaysia funded a group of expert at one of the technical university to establish competency center in cybersecurity. Industry approach for training integrated with online learning implemented to a group of students who are taking Computer Security Audit and Risks Management.

Online learning is turn to the new term called online-training. As we can see from websites, there are various type of online training available in the market. Cybersecurity training is available on YouTube Channel organized by either companies, NGO or training institution [2–5]. Udacity, Coursera and Google offer online training for cybersecurity awareness with the minimal cost [7]. Meanwhile, some Professional Cybersecurity Training Provider creates a thriller as promotion of their training materials. Several education institutions offer training via their learning management system platform but to our knowledge none of them offer cybersecurity online training.

3 Methods

Our study employed hybrid methods in conducting lecture for 10 students who enrolled Computer Security Audit and Risks Management module. The lecture executed for 14 weeks as stated in academic calendar. University learning management system was used as online learning platform. Physical lectures schedule every Monday from 2.00 pm to 4.00 pm Malaysia time. The module consists of 14 topics related to ISMS, Risks Management, Incident Analysis and Contingency Planning. Assessment for students categorized in two main categories which are summative and formative. Summative assignments included Mini Project, Short Quizzes, Workshops and Peer Training. Formative assessment executed after week 14.

Practical online training (POT) is part of learning activity in class. Week 6 students received Task for mini project. Before proceed with POT student were as to complete mini project. The objective of mini project is to expose student with real experiences in simulation mode. The detail on POT described below.

Development of POT comprises ten (10) activities as described below.

Activity 1
Setting Mini Project
The Course coordinator delivered Tasks to students. The instruction sets to students as in Table 1. Students were given 14 days to complete the project.

Table 1. Instruction Sets for Mini Project

	Task 1	Task 2	Task 3	Task 4
Group 1	Identify Group Member	Simulate Cases	Conduct Risks Analysis	Report
Group 2	Identify Group Member	Plan Audit	Conduct Audit	Report
Group 3	Identify Group Member	Simulate Cases	Conduct Incident Management	Report

Activity 2
Develop Report

Progress report presented at Week 9 and peers feedback is required to value add the content. Each group will then improve the content for final report.

Activity 3
Established Focus Group Discussion.

Inspired from leadership training model, "Ireland Hopping" concept was introduced. Each group presented their works. During the presentation, everyone must participate in commenting all aspects as mechanism to improve contents of final project report and also the lesson learns. Students exchanged tasks after completed progress presentation which mean those who were given Task 1 will exchange to group who was responsible for task two and so on. All inputs taken from different group members will be analysed for better outcome.

Activity 4
Content Development for training

Once the final report ready, each member of the group identified what are the main skill that they wanted to train others. In this case group one decided to conduct training in risks analysis, group two for ISMS and group three agree for Incident management. They were given two weeks for content development. They explored and improved in power point, info-graphics, web setting and prepare YouTube Links.

Activity 5
Content Evaluation by Industry Panel

Before sharing the link to class members, the course coordinator forwarded the link to industry expert to get initial feedback. The experts background are Cybersecurity Malaysia, Inland Revenue, and Auditors from Technical University.

To speed the process, the experts were given the YouTube link and they spend around one hour to watch the video. They need to provide feedback via WhatsApp Application. Comments by industry experts were taken by students and action for improvement begun.

Activity 6
Launching the Practical Online Training. The student started to create actual link for the improved training materials.

Activity 7
Sharing Content to Peer

On week 10 the students shared the link to their peers and everyone was asked to spend three hours take part in the training by watching to the video and extract information as much as they can. They also need to answer questions distributed via WhatsApp Application developed by course coordinator.

Activity 8
Physical Training Discussion

Week 11, 27 December 2022 the students conducted Physical Training Outside University. This session was designed to expose students how does real training environment executed. Venue was set as real training set up. Training manager appointed among them and Fig. 1 presents some picture on activity.

Fig. 1. Training

Activity 9
Peer Review

We let the students to discuss among themselves professionally. They need to rank and provide positive comments so that all participants able to learn and improve.

Activity 10
Giving Feedback

Finally the students we asked to complete survey form. Survey is designed to get student opinion on POT. The survey questions as in Table 2 was developed as for POT instruments.

Table 2. Survey Form for Students

Feedback Peer Online Training	
Please complete the questions below and submit to *rabiah@utem.edu.my* before Friday 6/1/2023	
(1)	What are your key learning objectives for this course?
(1)	Better Understanding
(2)	For Fun
(3)	Fulfil Assignment
(2)	How confident are you that the course will deliver on the learning objectives?
(1)	High
(2)	Moderate
(3)	Low
(3)	At the end of the course, what do you hope to have achieved?
(1)	Get A for Module
(2)	Explain the subject to others
(3)	Be able to practise
(4)	What types of learning do you like best?
(1)	Online Learning
(2)	Online Training with and By Peers
(3)	Physical Lecture and Discussion
(5)	What areas of this topic do you struggle with the most?
(1)	Risk Analysis
(2)	BCP
(3)	ISMS
(4)	Incident Management
(6)	What are the biggest barriers to you achieving your learning goals?
(1)	Understanding
(2)	Practising
(3)	Writing
(7)	Have you completed any other training in this field before taking this course?
(8)	How do you hope this course will improve on previous education experiences?
(9)	Nominate which group provide effective training and easy to follow

Table 3. Content Validation by Industry Expert

	Expert 1: Cyber Security Malaysia	Expert 2: Finance Officer Risks Finance - UTeM	Expert 3: Auditor UTeM	Expert 3: IT Management LHDN	Expert 4: Cybersecurity Senior Officer
Group 1	*Able to get general idea on risks analysis. Content can be more interesting*	*Understood whats the video try to explain*	*Interesting*	*Presentations not attractive but content wise okay*	*Creative !*
Group 2			*Able to understand ISMS*		*Creative !*
Group 3			*Interesting*		Creative !

All video shared and experts were asked for content understanding

4 Results

We presented two results; first content validation by expert in Table 3.

The second results were taken by students when they were asked to evaluate their peers.

We disturbed survey questions to 10 students end of the physical training. The survey measured students perceptions and their opinion for future improvement. Results shows students feedback from practical value and the other feedback all of them enjoyed the learning activity.

Practical Value proposed

(i) One of the student highlighted group X should provide practical skill for vulnerability assessment module.
(ii) Student recommended that in some situation earlier data audit is required to early detection of data breache

Overall Feedback

a. All students (100%) enjoyed both online training and the best part is the Physical Training at outside campus.

5 Conclusion

Peer Online Training (POT) provide excitement in learning. It boosting students interest in self explore Computer Security Audit and Risks Management. Self-Explore for developing content material able to develop understanding and initiate practical skill to students. The skill to run risks analysis, conduct computer audit and incident handling. The students also develop their communication skill and industry linkages. As a summary we concluded that our approached technique known as Practical Online Training

(POT) is a consider success trial. However it needs to be tested in the bigger volume. Future work will take part in leveraging POT for modules with more practical work and bigger sizes.

Acknowledgements. High appreciation to Information Security, Digital Forensic and Computer Networking (INSFORNET) Research Group; Center for Advanced Computing Technology (C-ACT); and Faculty of Information and Communication Technology (FTMK), Universiti Teknikal Malaysia Melaka (UTeM) for their continuous financial support and the use of the existing facilities for our non-funded Research in Exploring Learning Methods for Teaching Computer and Cyber Security. Special Thank to University Tun Hussein Onn.

References

1. Harkins, M.: Managing Risks and Information Security Protect to Enable, Apress Open Publication, New York (2013)
2. Martin, F., Sun, T., Westine, C.D.: A systematic review of research on online teaching and learning from 2009 to 2018. Comput. Educ. **14**. Elsevier (2020)
3. Katsantonis, M.N., Mavridis, I., Gritzalis, D.: Design and evaluation of COFELET-base approaches for cyber security learning and training. Comput. Secur. **12**. Elsevier (2021)
4. Karjalainen, M., Kokkonen, T., Puuska, S.: Pedagogical aspects of cyber security exercises. In: 2019 IEEE European Symposium on Security and Privacy Workship (EuroS & PW) (2019)
5. Bishop, M.: Computer security education: training, scholarship, and research. Secur. Priv. IEEE (2002)
6. Hatzivasilis, G., et al.: Modern aspects of cyber-security training and continuous adaptation of programmes to trainees. Appl. Sci. 10, 5702 (2020). MDPI
7. Selamat, S.R., Hsiung, L.H., Yusoff, R.: Development of examination framework for cyber security professional competency certification. OIC-CERT J. Cybersec. **3**(1), 57–67 (2021)

Knowledge Management Process and Model

Development and Validation
of a Knowledge Audit Framework
for SMEs

Arno Rottensteiner[1]([✉]), Christian Ploder[1], Thomas Fritz[2],
and Reinhard Bernsteiner[1]

[1] MCI - The Entrepreneurial School, Universitaetsstrasse 15, 6020 Innsbruck, Austria
arno.rottensteiner@mci.edu
[2] Tiroler Rohre GmbH, Innsbrucker Straße 51, 6060 Hall in Tirol, Austria
thomas.fritz@trm.at

Abstract. With knowledge becoming a central component of an organization's internal resource structure, managing this valuable asset gained on importance and developed to one of the most critical activities over the last few years. Successfully managing intellectual expertise and securing a comprehensive and gap-less knowledge base will contribute and enhance centralized and distributed decision making and furthermore help to sustainably maintain and increase competitive advantages. Especially regarding ISO 9001 certified Small and Medium-sized Enterprises (SMEs) and complying to its general principle of continuous improvement, auditing and reassessment of the current state of Knowledge Management is crucial. Therefore, this paper will propose a three step incremental Knowledge Audit Framework that helps SMEs to identify, assess and manage knowledge gaps in knowledge intense business processes. Building up on the underlying research method of a Case Study, the framework was designed using relevant literature and results of previous research endeavors. In order to identify and asses the potential knowledge gaps the framework will triangulate the following three data collection methods: (1) participating observation, (2) direct observation, and (3) structured questionnaire. After a detailed description of the proposed Knowledge Management Audit Framework, this paper will focus on the results and limitations by implementing the framework in a SME operating in the production of ductile iron pipe systems. After applying the framework in the aforementioned SME a general knowledge gap, mainly in the field of procedural knowledge, was identified. In order to close the identified knowledge gaps and build up a sustainable and effective Knowledge Management System this paper will be concluded by highlighting and suggesting several recommended actions.

Keywords: Knowledge Management · Knowledge Assessment · Knowledge Audit

© The Author(s), under exclusive license to Springer Nature Switzerland AG 2023
L. Uden and I-H. Ting (Eds.): KMO 2023, CCIS 1825, pp. 233–244, 2023.
https://doi.org/10.1007/978-3-031-34045-1_20

1   Introduction

Whereas the concept of Knowledge Management was initially introduced for bigger organizations [15], the implementation of practices and processes connected to the concept of Knowledge Management made inroads in Small and Medium-sized Enterprises over the last few years [6]. Although the need for managing intellectual expertise and its connected benefits for SMEs are evident for most organizations, the entailed challenging factors are sometimes hindering Knowledge Management implementations in Small and Medium-sized Enterprises [5]. Bridge and O'Neill [5] mainly associated a non-implementation of Knowledge Management measures in SMEs to two main factors: (1) a general constraint of resources and (2) a concentration of power and decision making in SMEs. By mitigating and not counteracting to these limiting factors, an implementation of a comprehensive Knowledge Management Strategy can be at risk, leading to simply relying on centralized knowledge stored in employees' minds [28]. In order to contribute to a successful implementation of a sustainable and comprehensive Knowledge Management Strategy in SMEs, this paper will suggest a framework [23] to audit the current state of knowledge and Knowledge Management, identify potential knowledge gaps and assess and quantify these gaps. Especially the initial audit of the current state of knowledge and Knowledge Management can be seen as a crucial activity to flatten the knowledge landscape and close potential gaps [20]. Underestimating this initial assessment will not only have an impact on the Knowledge Management Strategy formulation process and the outcome but could, according to Probst [20, p. 21], furthermore lead "to inefficiencies, uninformed decisions, and redundant activities" in SMEs. Therefore this paper should serve as a blueprint for analyzing knowledge, formulating a Knowledge Management Strategy and by this answering the posed research question:

How to identify and overcome organizational knowledge gaps between documented and non-documented knowledge by implementing Knowledge Management measures?

After a short literature review in the upcoming chapter, Sect. 3 will focus on the methodology used for the data collection in this research endeavour. After applying the developed Knowledge Audit Framework, the results are represented and furthermore discussed in Sect. 4 and 5. The paper will be concluded by listing some of the encountered limitations and giving an outlook on further research opportunities.

2   Literature Review

After introducing the term of knowledge itself, this section will focus on the definition of Knowledge Management, and the concept of using the principle of knowledge audits in Small and Medium-sized Enterprises.

2.1 Definitions of Knowledge

To fully understand and formulate a comprehensive Knowledge Management strategy, it is crucial to understand the term knowledge, its peculiarities and the different types of appearance. The most used definition of the term knowledge derives from the so-called "DIKW" (Data, Information, Knowledge, Wisdom) framework [7]. This model represents a hierarchical structure by describing each of the layers and furthermore highlighting the relation and interconnection between each of the components. Whereas the DIKW-framework was first limited only to three layers [1] added the Wisdom layer by referring to it as applying the knowledge and "the ability to increase effectiveness". While data can be seen as raw, unprocessed facts and figures, information can be described as data that has been organized and brought into context in order to add a meaning to this data and therefore make it more useful. To generate knowledge this information has to be understood and applied in order to solve problems and make well-founded decisions [1]. The highest level of the pyramid, wisdom, can be reached when knowledge is coupled with experience in order to take decisions and judgements that are both effective and ethical [7]. Especially when implementing Knowledge Management measures the DIKW model could help SMEs to understand the importance of not only collecting, but furthermore developing raw data into valuable knowledge to further improve informed decision marking and expand the sustainable competitive advantage [27]. Whereas the DIKW model can be used for generally defining knowledge, Probst et al. [21, p. 23] defines knowledge in an organizational and business context using the following definition: "Knowledge refers to the totality of knowledge and skills that individuals use to solve problems. This includes theoretical knowledge as well as practical everyday rules and instructions for action. Knowledge is based on data and information and, in contrast to these, is always linked to individuals". As this definition also represents the general approach of a hierarchical knowledge structure based on data used as a foundational layer, Probst's definition furthermore underlines the link between knowledge and individuals.

When it comes to the classification of knowledge based on its characteristics a general distinction between tacit and explicit knowledge can be made [17]. Tacit knowledge can generally be refereed to as knowledge that is difficult to formalize and is often held by individuals within an organization. It can include things like expertise, skills, and insights that are gained through experience. Based on these characteristics it is not easily transferable unless it is brought to a formal and general level of abstraction [11]. Howells [8] furthermore simplifies this definition by referring to tacit knowledge as "know-how". As tacit knowledge is mainly generated by the process of individual learning [8] it can be described as "highly individual and subjective" [25, p. 18]. Although because of its information richness tacit knowledge can be seen as a valuable intangible knowledge asset within an organization, its characteristics mentioned above make it hard to articulate and transfer to other individuals [24]. Explicit knowledge on the other hand can be seen as the counterpart to tacit knowledge. Whereas tacit knowledge is highly individual and hard to document, explicit knowledge can be defined as knowledge that is easier to formalize and can be easily shared within an organization. It can include knowledge like policies, procedures, and manuals that are documented using letters, numbers and graphics [10]. Smith [24, p. 314] refers to explicit knowledge as "academic knowledge" and "know-what". Due to the fact that explicit knowledge can be documented using common documentation methods, this type of knowledge can be brought to a common level of abstraction and understanding and facilitate searching of stored knowledge using keywords [16]. From an organizational viewpoint Lam [9] defined four different knowledge dimensions based on the relation between explicit and tacit knowledge and individual and organizational knowledge. By matching each of the dimensions, Lam developed the following four different organizational knowledge dimensions: (1) Encoded knowledge, (2) Embedded knowledge, (3) Embodied knowledge, and (4) Embrained knowledge [9].

2.2   Knowledge Management in SMEs

The idea of managing intellectual expertise has since centuries always been in the nature of human beings. Whereas at the beginning this task involved storing information and documentations for upcoming generations, Knowledge Management evolved to a much more complex task over the last decades, involving a numerous amount of sub-processes [26]. Whereas the first approaches to Knowledge Management were paper-based, major developments in information technology allowed for digitally storing knowledge and facilitating knowledge sharing within and beyond organizational borders [2]. As Knowledge Management usually spreads over several different units of organizational structures it is important to observe it from the following three perspectives according to Lindner [13]: people, organization, and technology. Whereas the technological aspect describes the foundation digitally supporting the different processes involved in Knowledge Management, the organizational perspective looks at Knowledge Management, taking into account different aspects like organizational structures, cultures and climates. The last perspective focuses on the social aspects of people interacting with a Knowledge Management system. Rosenbichler [22] furthermore highlights the importance of finding a good balance between all perspectives and not underestimating the importance of a good interconnection between them. Nonaka & Takeuchi [18, p. 3] were some of the first ones coming up with a definition of Knowledge Management by referring to it as "the capability of an organization to create new knowledge, disseminate it throughout the organization and embody it in products, services and systems". Whereas Nonaka & Takeuchi were mainly focusing on the three processes of creating knowledge, distributing it within an organization and lastly implementing it into products, services and systems, Probst [20] enhanced this definition by adding a strategic layer including knowledge goals and measurements. On an operational level Probst focused on the three different processes of identifying knowledge, acquiring knowledge and preserving knowledge within an organization [20].

As at first mostly bigger corporations tried to successfully implement Knowledge Management measures, in the last couple of years also SMEs recognized the importance of Knowledge Management and included it as a key process into their organizational process landscape [6]. While Knowledge Management can be beneficial for SMEs, it can be challenging to implement and sustain due to the limited resources, infrastructure, and support that these organizations may have. Some of the critical success factor that are specific to SMEs include limited resources to devote Knowledge Management initiatives, limited organizational support due to a high concentration of power, and a more entrenched culture often leading to a general resistance to change [5].

2.3 Knowledge Audit

In general a knowledge audit can be seen as a systematic review of an organization's knowledge assets, including its knowledge processes, systems, and culture [4]. The aim of a knowledge audit is to identify the organization's strengths and weaknesses in terms of its Knowledge Management, as well as to identify opportunities for improvement. There are several approaches to conducting a knowledge audit, including structured interviews, focus groups, surveys, and document analysis [3]. The choice of approach will highly depend on the specific objectives and context of the knowledge audit. A knowledge audit can furthermore provide valuable insights into an organization's Knowledge Management practices, and can help to identify areas for improvement and the resources required to address them [3]. A knowledge audit could not only be used in order to improve Knowledge Management measures in place but additionally contribute to an increase of effectiveness of the use of knowledge and with that contribute to better decision making [20].

3   Methodology

In order to methodologically support this research endeavour and respond to the posed research question, a case study analysis following Yin's approach [29] was deemed as an appropriate method of investigation. According to Yin [30, p. 45] a case study can be described as an "empirical method that investigates a contemporary phenomenon in depth and within its real-world context". Due to these characteristics the researcher takes a more observant role in the process and has no or only little influence on the outcome of the study [29]. For this publication a single case study was selected, focusing on one single unit of inquiry. This could furthermore provide the opportunity for a longitudinal study in order to evaluate the progress made by the "case" after implementing some first measures in the field of Knowledge Management.

The data collection of the case study evidence took place in the department for application technology at Tiroler Rohre GmbH (TRM). TRM is on of the major players in the production of ductile iron pipe systems on the international market. The company was founded in 1947 in order to respond to the urgent demand for pipes to rebuild key infrastructure destroyed during world war two. After the production site run into a risk of closure in 2013, together with a local bank Max Kloger stepped in and performed one of the largest management buy outs in Austria and brought the business back to life. In the upcoming years TRM innovatively expanded their product portfolio, entered new markets and became one of the major ductile iron pipe producers in Europe. During these more than 70 years in business, a lot of important knowledge was generated in different technical and administrative areas. With an increase of long-term employees retiring, TRM became aware of the potential knowledge loss and tried to focus on implementing Knowledge Management measures to prevent such events. In order to audit the current state of knowledge and Knowledge Management at TRM, a Knowledge Audit Framework was developed and at first applied on the department for application technology which is responsible for the technical customer support and to answer all technical inquiries regarding products available at TRM.

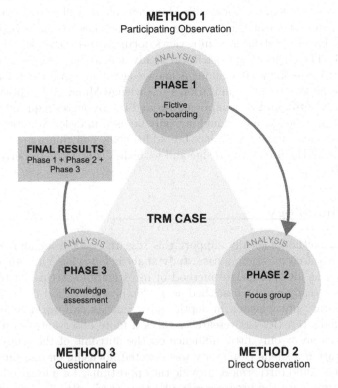

Fig. 1. Knowledge Audit Framework

As displayed in Fig. 1, the Knowledge Audit Framework is based on a methodological triangulation based on three different methods. What is also pretty unique to this framework is the analysis sphere surrounding each of the phases. This means that all the collected data is being immediately analyzed after each phase and handed over to the upcoming phase. This provides the possibility for an iterative contribution of each phase to the final result. To maximize the quality of the information outcome it is necessary to base the framework on different sources of evidence, always containing a chain of evidence, and especially taking care when using and relying on external resources within the framework.

3.1 Knowledge Audit Framework

To gather the necessary data for analyzing the framework depicted in (Fig. 1) was designed. The main purpose of this framework is to acquire a comprehensive overview of the knowledge landscape in place, and to identify potential gaps between documented and non-documented knowledge.

In order to delineate the process and collect all necessary documented knowledge to perform the task of technical customer support, phase 1 consisted out of a participating observation in form of a fictive on-boarding. Based on the impressions collected in the fictive on-boarding a current state of the process can be documented using a Business Process Modelling Notation BPMN [19]. All identified process flaws were documented, further described and improved in a re-modelled version of the process of technical customer support. This modeled to-be process was handed over to phase 2 where the process was discussed in a focus group based on the methodological approach of a direct observation. During this focus group each of the process tasks and it's connected necessary knowledge was collected and documented using a whiteboard and sticky notes. Clustering the collected knowledge bits revealed a list of knowledge modules that are necessary in order to perform the to-be process. By comparing these knowledge modules with the documented knowledge, collected in phase 1, first knowledge gaps between documented and non-documented knowledge can be identified. Phase 3 serves as a knowledge assessment to the identified knowledge gaps using a standardized questionnaire. This will not only help to quantify the knowledge gaps but furthermore to prioritize the closure of the gaps. To do so, the authors decided to use a framework proposed by Magnier-Watanabe [14]. Using this framework knowledge can be classified by the two dimensions breadth and depth. Whereas breadth describes if knowledge is only focused to one discipline (narrow = 1) or even spans over several different disciplines (broad = 4), knowledge depth describes if the knowledge falls under the classification of know-what (shallow = 1) or can be seen as know-how (deep = 4). By multiplying both of the dimensions, a knowledge score can be calculated. A high knowledge score indicates high importance and value to the organization [14]. The knowledge module with a high knowledge score should therefor be prioritized when closing the knowledge gaps.

4 Results

The following Table 1 will display the average knowledge scores of each knowledge module and identified gaps by listing the current status of the knowledge. Additionally to the quantitative data displayed in the table several qualitative data was collected during phase 1 and 2 of the Knowledge Audit Framework. Whereas employee 2 highlighted the lack of standardization in answering service requests by mentioning that "every employee has his or her unique approach to it", employee 1 shares the same opinion but rather associates this lack to the "unique character of each support request". Employee 4 furthermore supports this statements but underlines, beside the lack of documentation in the field of support requests, the Knowledge Management and documentation of technical knowledge and instructions already in place.

Table 1. Ranking of the identified knowledge modules based in their importance

	Knowledge Module	Avg. breadth	Avg. depth	Avg. score	Status
1	Basic Technical Knowledge	3.6	3.4	**12.24**	+
2	Technical Instructions	3.4	3.4	**11.56**	+
3	Already answered support requests	3.2	3.4	**10.88**	~
4	List of request levels and keywords	3.8	2.8	**10.64**	−
5	Skills Matrix	3.2	3.0	**9.60**	−
6	Customer Knowledge	2.2	3.8	**8.36**	−
7	Technical Certifications	2.6	2.8	**7.28**	+
8	Technical Norms	2.0	3.6	**7.20**	+
9	Product Information	2.6	2.6	**6.76**	+
10	Process Handbook	2.2	2.4	**5.28**	−
11	Software Manual	2.0	2.0	**4.00**	−

As displayed in Table 1, technical knowledge, consisting of basic technical knowledge and technical instruction, was identified as the most important knowledge with the company TRM. Furthermore, the importance of already answered customer support requests was highlighted by ranking it third with an overall score of 10.88. When observing the average breadth values, the knowledge module of "list of request levels and keywords" displays the highest value with 3.8. Looking at the average depth values, the knowledge module of "customer knowledge" indicates the highest value with 3.8. The two lowest values can be found in the knowledge module "software manual" which reflects the characteristics of narrow and shallow knowledge with an average breadth and depth of 2.0. The identified knowledge gaps can be observed looking at the column "Status" in Table 1. Whereas a "+" indicates a fully documented knowledge module (no knowledge gap) a "−" displays a high discrepancy between documented and non-documented but necessary knowledge (knowledge gap). A "~" indicated a partially documented knowledge module. In the case of the "already answered support questions" this means that they are already documenting some of the support requests but without following common guidelines and no consistency. Although the two most important knowledge modules do not show any knowledge gap, six out of eleven knowledge module exhibit a partial or complete knowledge gap.

5   Discussion

As all of the knowledge modules are already available within TRM in some form, closing the knowledge gap means to transform tacit knowledge into explicit knowledge and document the intellectual expertise. This concept can also be referred to as externalisation [18]. Especially in the context of technical customer support, externalisation plays a fundamental role. When processing a customer support request, the responsible employee of the department of application technology will build up experience originating from the interaction with the client and the elaboration of the answer to the request. As participants of phase 3 assigned a high importance to the knowledge modules "already answered support requests" and the "customer knowledge" closing the knowledge gaps concerning these modules should be prioritized in order to furthermore support better decision making in customer support requests. Another highly relevant aspect when closing the identified knowledge gap is the combination of individual explicit knowledge and creating new organizational knowledge. As experienced during the fictive on-boarding, some of the employees already used simple Knowledge Management approaches in order to document their individual knowledge. As this knowledge is only stored on the employees' individual end devices, no organizational knowledge sharing was initiated. Combining it with the concept of socialization [18], which describes the exchange of experience (tacit knowledge) between different people in a company, could initiate and establish a culture of knowledge sharing within TRM. To facilitate this process and incentivize knowledge sharing the process could be supported and furthermore propelled using different concepts of gamification [31]. Knowledge Management should furthermore not be used as a static tool but needs a more agile approach to it. Lin et al. [12] suggest using the concept of Six Sigma's Define-Measure-Analyze-Improve-Control cycle in order to update and improve the implemented Knowledge Management System. This agile improvement cycle will allow for direct response to changing environmental factors and early detection of possibly arising knowledge gaps. In order to do so, the following list derives from best practice examples and literature, and can be seen as a road-map of recommended actions to succeed in the field of Knowledge Management.

1. Further expand the knowledge analysis using the Knowledge Audit Framework to other departments
2. Close all identified knowledge gaps by documenting the knowledge, before implementing a Knowledge Management strategy
3. Analyse the different stakeholder requirements and include them into the strategy formulation process
4. Coordinate and align the Knowledge Management goals with the overall company goals
5. Implement concepts of gamification in order to increase motivation in Knowledge Management
6. Use supporting technological systems with the main focus on usability and functionality

7. Constantly reassess and improve the strategy in order to prevent new arising knowledge gaps

These recommended actions will not only allow for a quick reaction when it comes to closing knowledge gaps, but furthermore assure a consistent and stable Knowledge Management at TRM.

6   Limitations and Potential Further Research

In conclusion this paper proposed a Knowledge Audit Framework combined with recommended action items that will contribute to identify and overcome current flaws, increase effectiveness, and optimize the knowledge process in SMEs. In terms of limitations even though the author has dealt intensively with TRM, an external view on the company was still obtained throughout the study. During the course of this study, the company tried to already implement different measures in the Knowledge Management field. This led to a distortion of the initially captured status quo. Nevertheless, the author decided to stick to the initially collected data and use them as a basis for further evaluations. Another limitation that can be mentioned is the language barrier, as all the empirical research of this study was performed in the mother tongue of the participants (German), but had to be translated to English. Last but not least a holistic view and validation of the framework would require an application and implementation of the framework in other industries. Whereas future research endeavours could not only include a cross industry application, expanding the research geographically is also a research opportunity that it's aimed at.

Acknowledgements. The authors would like to express their sincere gratitude to TRM - Tiroler Rohre GmbH for commissioning and supporting this research project. This work would not have been possible without the support, resources and knowledge provided by the company. The authors would furthermore like to extend their thanks to the employees of the department for application technology who provided valuable assistance and insights throughout the research process. Finally, we would also like to express our appreciation to Max Kloger, the CEO of TRM, for his vision and leadership in supporting this research. His support has been crucial in driving this project forward and we are deeply grateful for his commitment to advancing research in the field of Knowledge Management.

References

1. Ackoff, R.: From data to wisdom. J. Appl. Syst. Anal. **15**, 3–9 (1989)
2. Akscyn, R.M., McCracken, D.L., Yoder, E.A.: KMS: a distributed hypermedia system for managing knowledge in organizations. Commun. ACM **31**(7), 820–835 (1988). https://doi.org/10.1145/48511.48513. https://dl.acm.org/doi/10.1145/48511.48513
3. Alavi, M., Leidner, D.E.: Review: knowledge management and knowledge management systems: conceptual foundations and research issues. MIS Q. **25**(1), 107 (2001). https://doi.org/10.2307/3250961. https://www.jstor.org/stable/3250961?origin=crossref

4. Ayinde, L., Orekoya, I.O., Adepeju, Q.A., Shomoye, A.M.: Knowledge audit as an important tool in organizational management: a review of literature. Bus. Inf. Rev. **38**(2), 89–102 (2021). https://doi.org/10.1177/0266382120986034. http://journals. sagepub.com/doi/10.1177/0266382120986034
5. Bridge, S., O'Neill, K.: Understanding Enterprise: Entrepreneurs & Small Business, 5th edn. Palgrave, London, (2018)
6. Durst, S., Runar Edvardsson, I.: Knowledge management in SMEs: a literature review. J. Knowl. Manag. **16**(6), 879–903 (2012). https://doi.org/ 10.1108/13673271211276173. https://www.emerald.com/insight/content/doi/10. 1108/13673271211276173/full/html
7. Henry, N.L.: Knowledge management: a new concern for public administration. Public Adm. Rev. **34**(3), 189 (1974). https://doi.org/10.2307/974902. https:// www.jstor.org/stable/974902?origin=crossref
8. Howells, J.: Tacit knowledge. Technol. Anal. Strateg. Manag. **8**(2), 91–106 (1996). https://doi.org/10.1080/09537329608524237. http://www.tandfonline. com/doi/abs/10.1080/09537329608524237
9. Lam, A.: Tacit knowledge, organizational learning and societal institutions: an integrated framework. Organ. Stud. **21**(3), 487–513 (2000). https://doi.org/10.1177/ 0170840600213001. http://journals.sagepub.com/doi/10.1177/0170840600213001
10. Lee, C.K., Foo, S., Goh, D.: On the concept and types of knowledge. J. Inf. Knowl. Manag. **05**(02), 151–163 (2006). https://doi.org/10.1142/S0219649206001402. https://www.worldscientific.com/doi/abs/10.1142/S0219649206001402
11. Liebowitz, J., Beckman, T.: Knowledge Organizations: What Every Manager Should Know. St. Lucie Press, Boca Raton (1998)
12. Lin, C., Frank Chen, F., Wan, H., Min Chen, Y., Kuriger, G.: Continuous improvement of knowledge management systems using Six Sigma methodology. Robot. Comput.-Integr. Manuf. **29**(3), 95–103 (2013). https://doi.org/10.1016/j.rcim. 2012.04.018. https://linkinghub.elsevier.com/retrieve/pii/S0736584512000646
13. Lindner, F.: Projektwissensmanagement: Status quo, Gestaltungsfaktoren und Erfolgsdeterminanten des Wissensmanagements in der Projektabwicklung. No. Bd. 8 in Controlling und Management, Lit, Berlin Münster (2010)
14. Magnier-Watanabe, R.: Recognizing knowledge as economic factor: a typology. In: 2015 Portland International Conference on Management of Engineering and Technology (PICMET), Portland, OR, USA, pp. 1279–1286. IEEE (2015). https://doi.org/10.1109/PICMET.2015.7273065. http://ieeexplore. ieee.org/document/7273065/
15. McAdam, R., Reid, R.: SME and large organisation perceptions of knowledge management: comparisons and contrasts. J. Knowl. Manag. **5**(3), 231–241 (2001). https://doi.org/10.1108/13673270110400870. https://www.emerald.com/ insight/content/doi/10.1108/13673270110400870/full/html
16. Mescheder, B., Sallach, C.: Wettbewerbsvorteile durch Wissen. Springer, Heidelberg (2012). https://doi.org/10.1007/978-3-642-27896-9
17. Nonaka, I., Peltokorpi, V.: Objectivity and subjectivity in knowledge management: a review of 20 top articles. Knowl. Process Manag. **13**(2), 73–82 (2006). https:// doi.org/10.1002/kpm.251. https://onlinelibrary.wiley.com/doi/10.1002/kpm.251
18. Nonaka, I., Takeuchi, H.: The Knowledge-Creating Company: How Japanese Companies Create the Dynamics of Innovation. Oxford University Press, New York (1995)
19. (OMG) Object Management Group: Business Process and Notation (BPMN) (2013). https://www.omg.org/spec/BPMN/2.0/PDF

20. Probst, G.: Practical Knowledge Management: A Model That Works, p. 14 (1998)
21. Probst, G., Raub, S., Romhardt, K.: Wissen managen: wie Unternehmen ihre wertvollste Ressource optimal nutzen. Gabler Verlag, Wiesbaden, 7. aufl. 2012, korr. nachdruck 2013 edn. (2010)
22. Rosenbichler, U., Grünwald, A., Kallinger, M., Nikolov-Bruckner, E., Wenzel, C.: Wissensmanagement - Leitfaden und Toolbox zur Wissenssicherung bei Personaländerungen. Technical report, Bundeskanzler Amt, Wien (2017)
23. Rottensteiner, A., Ploder, C.: Identifying and assessing knowledge gaps in ISO 9001 certified SMEs using a knowledge audit framework. In: Proceedings of the 14th International Joint Conference on Knowledge Discovery, Knowledge Engineering and Knowledge Management, Valletta, Malta, pp. 158–162. SCITEPRESS - Science and Technology Publications (2022). https://doi.org/10.5220/0011539600003335. https://www.scitepress.org/DigitalLibrary/Link.aspx?doi=10.5220/0011539600003335
24. Smith, E.A.: The role of tacit and explicit knowledge in the workplace. J. Knowl. Manag. 5(4), 311–321 (2001). https://doi.org/10.1108/13673270110411733. https://www.emerald.com/insight/content/doi/10.1108/13673270110411733/full/html
25. Sternberg, R.J.: Successful Intelligence: How Practical and Creative Intelligence Determine Success in Life. Plume, New York (1997)
26. Sveiby, K.E.: The New Organizational Wealth: Managing & Measuring Knowledge-Based Assets, 1st edn. Berrett-Koehler Publishers, San Francisco (1997)
27. Teece, D., Pisano, G.: The dynamic capabilities of firms: an introduction. Ind. Corporate Change 3(3), 537–556 (1994). https://doi.org/10.1093/icc/3.3.537-a. https://academic.oup.com/icc/article-lookup/doi/10.1093/icc/3.3.537-a
28. Yew Wong, K., Aspinwall, E.: Characterizing knowledge management in the small business environment. J. Knowl. Manag. 8(3), 44–61 (2004). https://doi.org/10.1108/13673270410541033. https://www.emerald.com/insight/content/doi/10.1108/13673270410541033/full/html
29. Yin, R.K.: Case Study Research: Design and Methods. Applied Social Research Methods, vol. 5, 4th edn. Sage Publications, Los Angeles (2009)
30. Yin, R.K.: Case Study Research and Applications: Design and Methods, 6th edn. SAGE, Los Angeles (2018)
31. Duriník, M.: Gamification in knowledge management systems. Central Eur. J. Manag. 1(2) (2015). https://doi.org/10.5817/CEJM2014-2-3. https://journals.muni.cz/cejm/article/view/2445

Development of a Knowledge Transfer Model for Family-Owned SMEs

Alina Nagl, Christian Ploder[(✉)], Thomas Dilger, and Stephan Schlögl

MCI - The Entrepreneurial School, Universitaetsstrasse 15, 6020 Innsbruck, Austria
christian.ploder@mci.edu

Abstract. Ninety percent of family-owned small and medium-sized enterprises (SMEs) cannot survive the 3rd handover in their company history. So one idea to improve this ratio could be to think about a much-improved knowledge transfer from the predecessor to the successor. Various models for knowledge transfer have been developed in the past decades, but none were specially designed or applied in family-owned SMEs. Especially this non existing match with the special needs of family-owned businesses is the trigger for the created framework adapted to the unique needs of family-owned businesses. The framework was developed based on a preliminary study held in the summer of 2022 and will be implemented in some consulting projects in 2023.

Keywords: Knowledge Management · Knowledge Transfer · Family Businesses

1 Introduction

Companies around the world are exposed to increasing competition as a result of advancing globalization. In this context, resource knowledge is a critical factor that must be taken into account to achieve an advantage in the market and to be able to hold one's own against the competition [2] based on the additional deep improvement of the intellectual capital [22]. The knowledge transfer process is critical regarding succession since it affects the business's survival [4]. This is particularly important in the case of generational shifts within family businesses. Around 70% of all family businesses fail when the founding generation hands over to its successor, and only 10% of companies survive the transition to the third generation [16]. Due to the desire of family businesses to ensure the company's continuity for a long time [19,31], the intergenerational management of knowledge is, therefore, essential for family-owned businesses [6]. Especially to be able to innovate the business ether incrementally or in huge steps radical, the use of the intellectual capital of the organization has to be taken into account [11]. Yet, knowledge transfer in family firms is not planned, or rather, it does not work as expected [4]. In the literature, several models already depict knowledge transfer mechanisms; however, there is a gap in research related to knowledge transfer in family-owned SMEs. Since the Austrian economy consists

L. Uden and I-H. Ting (Eds.): KMO 2023, CCIS 1825, pp. 245–254, 2023.
https://doi.org/10.1007/978-3-031-34045-1_21

of 99,6% of SMEs and 50% of all companies are family-run, there is a great need for a model that meets these criteria (www.kmuforschung.ac.at). A very similar picture of the SME situation can be seen in our neighborhood country Germany [8]. Therefore, this paper aims to define a process model of knowledge transfer that specifically meets the requirements of SMEs and, subsequently, family businesses. So the research question for this paper was: How can family-driven SMEs implement Knowledge Transfer in their handover process? The given research question is answered through a literature review (Sect. 2), which forms the basis for the framework, and in a second step, the modeled framework is discussed with four experts in a focus group setting, who are both academics and owners of a family-owned business. Thus, the framework presented in this paper is already validated in the first iteration. After this introduction, the theoretical background is laid out in Sect. 1, followed by the methodology used in Sect. 3. Section 4 shows the results and the discussion. The paper summarizes the limitations and ideas about future research in Sect. 5.

2 Literature Review

The selection of literature is primarily based on the "Global ranking of knowledge management and intellectual capital academic journals: 2017 update". The authors suggest a total of 27 journals after preliminary analysis of a survey with 482 active knowledge management scientists and reference to journal citation indices [28]. The heyday of knowledge management was several years ago, which explains why most of the literature was published between 2000 and 2010. This section will examine the concept of knowledge before concentrating on knowledge management and transfer.

2.1 Concepts of Knowledge

In their publication "the knowledge-creating company", Nonaka and Takeuchi (1995) make an essential contribution to the differentiation of the two concepts of tacit and explicit knowledge [20]; their considerations go back to Polanyi (1966) [23]. Explicit knowledge can be recognized because it is tangible for others and can be documented effortlessly. Accordingly, explicit knowledge can also be easily stored and communicated [17,20]. In direct comparison to tacit knowledge, explicit knowledge is characterized as formalized knowledge [13], which exists in verbal form and is transferable with the support of information and communication technologies [21]. Implicit knowledge, on the other hand, is context-specific and personal and, therefore, difficult to verbalize and share with others. Because of these characteristics, it is almost impossible to formalize [20]. Researchers disagree about which type of knowledge is more significant [1]. This conflict can be countered by the fact that tacit knowledge always reflects the background and structure essential for the construction and interpretation of explicit knowledge [23]. Moreover, the separation of tacit and explicit knowledge should not be considered since both presuppose each other [20].

2.2 SECI-Model of Knowledge Transfer

For a company's success, it is crucial to consider both tacit and explicit knowledge [21]. Knowledge is created through the interaction between tacit and explicit knowledge. Four different modes of knowledge transformation can be derived from this, which are illustrated in the SECI model [20]. The four parts and their connection to family-owned businesses will be explained in the next paragraphs.

The SECI model is developed by Ikujiro Nonaka and Hirotaka Takeuchi in the 1990s. It emphasizes the creation and sharing of knowledge within an organization through a continuous cycle of four stages: Socialization, Externalization, Combination, and Internalization.

Family-owned businesses are unique in that they often have a strong sense of family values and culture, which can be difficult to translate into clear business strategy and standardised operations. In the authors perspective the SECI model is particularly useful for family-owned businesses because it emphasizes the importance of socialization and externalization, which can help to capture and transfer tacit knowledge (i.e., knowledge that is difficult to codify or transfer explicitly).

Socialization involves the sharing of tacit knowledge. This stage is particularly relevant for family-owned businesses, where family members often have a deep understanding of the company's values and culture that may not be easily communicated to non-family members.

Externalization involves the articulation of tacit knowledge into explicit knowledge, such as through documentation or storytelling. This stage is important for family-owned businesses because it can help to preserve and codify the family's values and culture for future generations. But especially this externalization often lacks in the family-owned business handover.

Combination involves the integration of explicit knowledge from different sources, such as through knowledge management systems or databases, wehich are not of high interest to this type of business because their system landscape is most often simple.

Internalization involves the application of explicit knowledge to tacit knowledge, such as through training or apprenticeships. This stage is important for family-owned businesses because it can help to ensure that the family's values and culture are maintained and passed down to future generations.

An alternative model used would be the DIKW (Data-Information-Knowledge-Wisdom) model [27]. This model suggests that knowledge is a hierarchical process that begins with data and progresses to wisdom. While this model may be useful for some businesses, it may not be well-suited for family-owned businesses that place a high value on tacit knowledge and the sharing of experiences and stories. In family-owned businesses, knowledge is often passed down through personal relationships and direct experience, rather than through formal data and information systems.

Socialization. This first step is about exchanging experiences, from which knowledge such as technical skills or thought models can emerge. It is possible to acquire tacit knowledge without having to use language. Furthermore, it is advantageous to acquire tacit knowledge if the transferor of the knowledge has everyday experiences with the transferee. If these experiences are missing, it is almost impossible to put oneself into the thinking process of another person [20].

Externalization. Externalization is the transformation of tacit knowledge into its explicit form. This process is the core component of knowledge creation, as tacit knowledge is transformed into explicit knowledge and takes the form of, for example, models, metaphors, comparisons, or assumptions [20].

Combination. Once knowledge has been externalized, the next step is the combination of knowledge. New knowledge is created through the exchange and combination of knowledge, which also includes the sorting or categorization of knowledge. This can also be the case in meetings or telephone conversations [20].

Internalization. Internalization is converting explicit knowledge into tacit knowledge, closely related to learning by doing. When experiences through the previous phases of the SECI model (socialization, externalization, and combination) are incorporated into the tacit knowledge base, they become valuable resources. For the creation of organizational knowledge, the tacit knowledge accumulated by the individual must be shared with other members of the organization. For this purpose, the SECI spiral is rewound. For transforming explicit knowledge into tacit knowledge, using manuals or storytelling is beneficial as it enables the reliving of experiences [20].

Overall, the SECI model is useful for family-owned businesses because it emphasizes the importance of capturing and sharing tacit knowledge, which is often a critical component of the family's values and culture. By using the SECI model, family-owned businesses can ensure that their unique knowledge assets are preserved and leveraged to drive business success for generations to come.

3 Methodology

As part of a preliminary study, model interrogation was conducted based on the literature review (Sect. 2) to get a first draft of the model derived from the literature based on the author's work. To ensure some objectivity and validity of the built model, the draft version was discussed in a focus group [18] with four experts. The focus group had mainly two goals in mind, which influenced the expert selection: (1) proof of the framework from a theoretical viewpoint and (2) practicability for implementation in family-owned businesses. Therefore the focus group members existed of one academic expert in Knowledge Management and three owners of family-businesses which were different companies. One of the owners was a transferor, and two of them were successors. Two of the focus group experts were male, and two were female and their age was between 35 and 65 years. The focus group discussion was based on introducing the topic and presenting the theoretically derived model following a semi-structured procedure to get family business participants. The focus group session was additionally recorded to avoid missing any argument, which helped improve the final framework. The workshop was held for two and a half hours with a coffee break in between in August 2022.

Within the focus group setting, the model was elaborated and evaluated. This model then provided the basis for a further study dedicated to developing practical recommendations for action to improve knowledge transfer within family businesses.

4 Results and Discussion

In research, several models can be found that depict knowledge transfer. However, none of these models describes knowledge transfer within family-owned SMEs. This section introduces a process model for facilitating knowledge transfer within family-owned SMEs (Fig. 1). In doing so, The theory referred to in Sect. 2 will be discussed.

4.1 Process Model for Knowledge Transfer in Family-Owned SMEs

A variety of frameworks are used to represent the mechanisms of knowledge transfer [17]. All of these theories share the same basic idea of communication and cooperation between sender and receiver [17], which was first expressed in the mathematical approach to communication and information in Shannon and Weaver's (1948) sender-receiver model [5,29]. This model was the basis for developing Deutsch's communication theory [7]. In the corporate context, knowledge transfer includes not only oral communication but also takes into account other methods, such as intermediary or technological interventions [17]. Liyanage, Elhag, Ballal, and Li (2009) developed a process model to illustrate knowledge transfer based on Deutsch's (1952) communication theory and Holden and Kortzfleisch's (2004) theory of translation [7,12,17]. The authors mention four prerequisites for successful knowledge transfer: the identification of the required and most appropriate knowledge, the willingness to share the knowledge, the willingness to learn, and finally, the receptivity of the recipient [17]. The process model is divided into five phases and refers to the elements network and barriers [17], which can be seen as framework conditions in the following figure. Probst (2000) also illustrates the core processes of knowledge management on six different levels, which were revised by Fink and Ploder (2009) to meet the specific requirements of small and medium-sized enterprises [9,24].

Based on these two approaches, a third model can now be derived that encompasses the essential aspects of both concepts and thus forms a comprehensive solution (Fig. 1). This scheme reflects the necessary process parts of Liyanage et al. (2009) and supplements them with those building blocks that play a role, especially in SMEs [9,17]. In addition, information was added that plays a role, particularly in knowledge transfer in family businesses based on the outcomes of the focus group workshop. For this reason, the additional frame condition "Relationships" was added to the figure. A process model was designed to ensure knowledge transfer in family-owned businesses (Fig. 2).

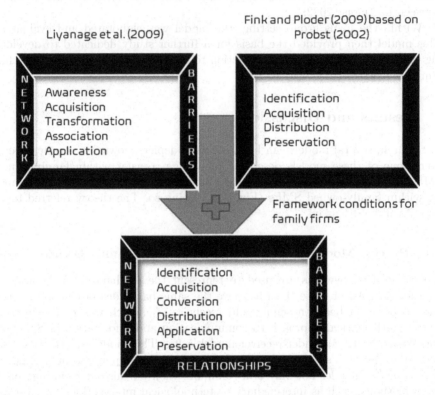

Fig. 1. Process Model for Knowledge Transfer in family-owned SMEs

Knowledge Identification. Knowledge identification measures deal with analyzing a company's knowledge environment [24] and thus aim to identify valuable knowledge [17]. A challenge for family businesses is that the transferor is not directly aware of their knowledge [3]. Consequently, the person has to reflect on their previous actions to derive the knowledge hidden in them [14]. The same applies to the successor [10] to avoid knowledge deficits. This process of "unlearning" increases the flexibility of the business [25], can also be achieved in other ways by involving the successor in the business at an early stage [15].

Knowledge Acquisition. Knowledge acquisition refers to the forms of knowledge that the organization should acquire from the outside world through relationships with stakeholders [17]. It can also be characterized by the ability to obtain crucial information for the organization that originates in the outside world of the company [30]. Considered essential for this step is the ability and also the will of both sender and receiver to hand over the knowledge [17].

Knowledge Conversion. The result of knowledge conversion is to make the knowledge usable, thus improving old knowledge or subsequently (see knowledge application) being able to generate new knowledge. This area can be divided into two parts. One is knowledge transformation, which can be achieved by adding or deleting information, and the other is knowledge association. The latter refers to relating the knowledge transformed in the previous step to the internal needs of the organization [17].

Knowledge Distribution. Knowledge distribution is the process of spreading knowledge, and the basic principle here is "as little as possible and as much as necessary". This means that knowledge should be distributed to the extent that it is useful [24].

Knowledge Application. Measured against the rationale that value creation occurs only when knowledge is successfully moved from its origin to its destination and applied purposefully, the "knowledge application" item is arguably the essential [1]. All the preceding activities in this model neither improve performance nor effectively lead to value creation [17].

Knowledge Preservation. The last part of the process deals with the actualization of knowledge. It thus also includes the disposal of redundant and obsolete knowledge [9].

Framework Conditions. In addition to the parts of the process just described, it is also possible to identify framework conditions that lead to successful knowledge transfer. A dense network is advantageous for effective knowledge transfer because, this way, a strong interaction of all persons involved in the organization can be achieved. As a result, knowledge is distributed efficiently [17]. Furthermore, barriers, i.e., factors negatively influencing knowledge transfer, must be considered. In addition, the analysis should also include forces that promote success. The last framework condition is the relationship between the predecessor and the successor. Positive feelings between those involved in the succession process contribute to a smooth transition between generations. If this is not the case, there is a risk that the successor will reject the knowledge of the predecessor [4].

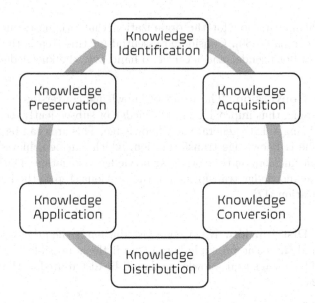

Fig. 2. Circular Model of Knowledge Transfer for family-owned SMEs

Finally, the framework presented in Fig. 2 is an assumption of the frameworks presented in Fig. 1 combined with the outcomes of the focus group interviews. The circular relationship ensures the continuity of the knowledge transfer and the need for permanent communication in a family-based company to stabilize the transferred knowledge for the next generation. This framework shows how family-driven SMEs can implement Knowledge Transfer in their handover process and answers the given research question.

5   Summary, Limitations and Potential Further Research

The elaborated framework will help mainly family-owned businesses to improve their knowledge management to ensure the long-term existence based on competetive advantages [26] of the company. The SECI model fits best to the special situation of family businesses, and the process models derived from the literature built the base for the new framework. The framework was additionally validated by a focus group of experts and will, in the next step, be tested in the field with current consulting topics for family-owned businesses. One limitation is the small number of workshop participants in the pre-study. It could be assumed that most of the same kinds of businesses have to deal with the same issues, but this should be investigated in an expanded focus group setting. Additionally, there was no implementation or testing of the developed process model for knowledge transfer in companies. Maybe the first implementations will show some flaws in the model, which can later the fixed by the adoption of the model. Therefore future research needs to expand the pool of experts and their localization and try to implement the model for a concrete handover in practical project situations in 2023.

References

1. Alavi, M., Leidner, D.E.: Review: knowledge management and knowledge management systems: conceptual foundations and research issues. MIS Q. **25**(1), 107 (2001). https://doi.org/10.2307/3250961
2. Bender, S., Fish, A.: The transfer of knowledge and the retention of expertise: the continuing need for global assignments. J. Knowl. Manage. **4**(2), 125–137 (2000). https://doi.org/10.1108/13673270010372251
3. Brown, J.S., Duguid, P.: Organizing knowledge. Calif. Manage. Rev. **40**(3), 90–111 (1998). https://doi.org/10.2307/41165945
4. Cabrera-Suárez, K., de Saá-Pérez, P., García-Almeida, D.: The succession process from a resource- and knowledge-based view of the family firm. Fam. Bus. Rev. **14**(1), 37–46 (2001). https://doi.org/10.1111/j.1741-6248.2001.00037.x
5. Carlile, P.R.: Transferring, translating, and transforming: an integrative framework for managing knowledge across boundaries. Organ. Sci. **15**(5), 555–568 (2004). https://doi.org/10.1287/orsc.1040.0094
6. Chaudhary, S., Batra, S.: Absorptive capacity and small family firm performance: exploring the mediation processes. J. Knowl. Manage. **22**(6), 1201–1216 (2018). https://doi.org/10.1108/JKM-01-2017-0047, http://www.sxf.uevora.pt/wp-content/uploads/2013/03/Glaser_1967.pdf
7. Deutsch, K.W.: On communication models in the social sciences. Public Opin. Q. **16**(3), 356 (1952). https://doi.org/10.1086/266399
8. Döring, H., Witt, P.: Knowledge management in family businesses-empirical evidence from Germany. Knowl. Manage. Res. Pract. **18**(2), 175–187 (2020)
9. Fink, K., Ploder, C.: Knowledge management toolkit for SMEs. Int. J. Knowl. Manage. **5**(1), 46–60 (2009). https://doi.org/10.4018/jkm.2009010104
10. Hatak, I.R., Roessl, D.: Relational competence-based knowledge transfer within intrafamily succession: an experimental study. Fam. Bus. Rev. **28**(1), 10–25 (2015). https://doi.org/10.1177/0894486513480386
11. Hayaeian, S., Hesarzadeh, R., Abbaszadeh, M.R.: The impact of knowledge management strategies on the relationship between intellectual capital and innovation: evidence from SMEs. J. Intellect. Cap. **23**(4), 765–798 (2022)
12. Holden, N.J., von Kortzfleisch, H.F.O.: Why cross-cultural knowledge transfer is a form of translation in more ways than you think. Knowl. Process. Manage. **11**(2), 127–136 (2004). https://doi.org/10.1002/kpm.198
13. Koulopoulos, T.M., Frappaolo, C.: Smart Things to Know About Knowledge Management, 1st edn. Capstone US, Dover, NH (2000)
14. Kransdorff, A., Williams, R.: Managing organizational memory (OM): the new competitive imperative. Organ. Dev. J. **18**(1), 107–117 (2000)
15. Le Breton-Miller, I., Miller, D., Steier, L.P.: Toward an integrative model of effective fob succession. Entrep. Theory Pract. **28**(4), 305–328 (2004). https://doi.org/10.1111/j.1540-6520.2004.00047.x
16. LeMar, B.: Generations- und Führungswechsel im Familienunternehmen: Mit Gefühl und Kalkül den Wandel gestalten, 2nd edn. Springer, Heidelberg (2014)
17. Liyanage, C., Elhag, T., Ballal, T., Li, Q.: Knowledge communication and translation - a knowledge transfer model. J. Knowl. Manage. **13**(3), 118–131 (2009). https://doi.org/10.1108/13673270910962914
18. Mikkonen, K., Elo, S., Kuivila, H.M., Tuomikoski, A.M., Kääriäinen, M.: Culturally and linguistically diverse healthcare students' experiences of learning in a clinical environment: a systematic review of qualitative studies. Int. J. Nurs. Stud. **54**, 173–187 (2016)

19. Moss, T.W., Payne, G.T., Moore, C.B.: Strategic consistency of exploration and exploitation in family businesses. Fam. Bus. Rev. **27**(1), 51–71 (2014). https://doi.org/10.1177/0894486513504434
20. Nonaka, I., Takeuchi, H.: The Knowledge-Creating Company: How Japanese Companies Create the Dynamics of Innovation. Oxford University Press, Oxford (1995)
21. North, K.: Wissensorientierte Unternehmensfuhrung: Wissensmanagement Gestalten. Springer Gabler, Wiesbaden, Cham. 6 edn. (2016). https://doi.org/10.1007/978-3-658-11643-9
22. Oliveira, M., Curado, C., Balle, A.R., Kianto, A.: Knowledge sharing, intellectual capital and organizational results in SMEs: are they related? J. Intellect. Cap. **21**(6), 893–911 (2020)
23. Polanyi, M.: Personal Knowledge, 1st edn. University of Chicago Press, Chicago (1958)
24. Probst, G., Raub, S., Romhardt, K.: Managing Knowledge: Building Blocks for Success, 1st edn. Wiley, Chichester (2000)
25. Rebernik, M., Širec, K.: Fostering innovation by unlearning tacit knowledge. Kybernetes **36**(3/4), 406–419 (2007). https://doi.org/10.1108/03684920710747039
26. Rehman, S.U., Bresciani, S., Ashfaq, K., Alam, G.M.: Intellectual capital, knowledge management and competitive advantage: a resource orchestration perspective. J. Knowl. Manage. **26**(7), 1705–1731 (2022)
27. Rowley, J.: The wisdom hierarchy: representations of the DIKW hierarchy. J. Inf. Sci. **33**(2), 163–180 (2007). https://doi.org/10.1177/0165551506070706
28. Serenko, A., Bontis, N.: Global ranking of knowledge management and intellectual capital academic journals: 2017 update. J. Knowl. Manage. **21**(3), 675–692 (2017). https://doi.org/10.1108/JKM-11-2016-0490
29. Shannon, C.E.: Weaver, Warren: a mathematical theory of communication. Bell Syst. Tech. J. **27**(3), 379–423 (1948). https://doi.org/10.1002/j.1538-7305.1948.tb01338.x
30. Zahra, S.A., George, G.: Absorptive capacity: a review, reconceptualization, and extension. Acad. Manage. Rev. **27**(2), 185 (2002). https://doi.org/10.2307/4134351
31. Zellweger, T., Astrachan, J.: On the emotional value of owning a firm. Fam. Bus. Rev. **21**(4), 347–363 (2008). https://doi.org/10.1111/j.1741-6248.2008.00129.x

Theoretical Model of New Ways of Knowledge Creation and Their Impact on Exploratory and Exploitative Innovation

Thomas Jackson[1]([⊠]), Lisa Jackson[2], and Matthew Day[1]

[1] Loughborough Business School, Loughborough University, Loughborough, UK
`t.w.jackson@lboro.ac.uk`
[2] Aeronautical and Automotive Engineering, Loughborough University, Loughborough, UK

Abstract. The main purpose of this paper is to model the new ways of knowledge creation and their relationship with both exploratory and exploitative innovation. Based on Dubin's quantitative method of theory building, a conceptualization of a model concerning transformations in the creation of knowledge in an organization embedded in technology is presented. The authors construct and analyze a novel model called Persistent Leveraging of Artificial Intelligence (AI) Systems Tapers Innovation Capability 'PLASTIC', which models on-going transitions in knowledge management practices. The theoretical model aids in the understanding of the specific knowledge processes within an organization and the main prospective challenges, obstacles and difficulties for knowledge management over the next decade. It discusses the role of a changeable environment and the interactions between technology-driven transformations and human-oriented practices, and it enables the evaluation of the future adaptation in knowledge management processes. This research is the first to challenge the impact of AI aided searching on the workforce and provides the catalyst for discussion of long-term innovation implications.

Keywords: Knowledge Management · Impact of AI Searching · Information Retrieval · Innovation stagnation · Exploratory Innovation · Exploitative Innovation

1 Introduction

Ensuring the creation of new knowledge is an important concern for organizations. The creation of new knowledge leads to innovation [1] and provides a competitive advantage [2], while also enabling effective adaptation against changes in the environment [3]. Digital technology plays an important role in supporting the process of creating and refining organizational knowledge [4]. To account for the different ways of knowledge creation in an organization, scholars tend to rely on existing models: the SECI model [5] and the knowledge-creating spiral to illustrate knowledge creation processes [6–9]. As a result of ubiquitous technology and the rapid development of digitalization in the last decade [10], the attributes within these models have transformed and require both re-examination and critical analysis.

© The Author(s), under exclusive license to Springer Nature Switzerland AG 2023
L. Uden and I-H. Ting (Eds.): KMO 2023, CCIS 1825, pp. 255–272, 2023.
https://doi.org/10.1007/978-3-031-34045-1_22

Changes in knowledge creation pertain to both processes associated with refining existing resources and creating new organizational knowledge [11]. The main purpose of this paper is to identify and model the factors of how new ways of knowledge creation can affect organizational ambidexterity, the capacity to achieve both exploratory and exploitative innovation. Exploitative innovation refers to the refinement of existing resources [12–14], while exploratory innovation concerns the creation of novel solutions based on the generation of new knowledge [15].

A number of studies argue that emerging technologies provide new opportunities by facilitating knowledge processes in organizations [16–18]. However, there is still a lack of comprehension about the long-term consequences and shortcomings of the technological consequences for knowledge creation. Although research has examined the relationship between modern technology and knowledge management processes in organizations [19–25], the consequences of using modern technological solutions in knowledge creation for organizational creativity are not fully established. Ribiere *et al.* [26] calls for a deep understanding of how to best align knowledge management in organizations with the digital transformation. Furthermore, Di Vaio *et al.* [27] points to the need to implement new ways of knowledge creation in organizations to enable the modeling and refinement of business strategies for knowledge creation. Lanzolla *et al.* [26] emphasized that further reflection is needed on the optimal balance between the use of digital methods and cognitive skills in the context of organizational knowledge. They noted that, despite widespread hype, more digital solutions do not always mean better knowledge. Therefore, it is important to examine the interrelationships between the changes in interaction and knowledge acquisition in organizations, triggered by increasing adoption of technology and technological breakthroughs, and the exploratory and exploitative innovation that is affecting organizational ambidexterity.

Altered information acquisition strategies may lead to an increase in knowledge reuse [29], which can have significant implications for the creation of new knowledge. Previous research indicates that exploratory innovation, in particular, enhances organizational competitiveness [30]. Therefore, examining the relationship of technological transformation affecting the modification of organizational knowledge creation patterns is an important contribution to management practice. The theoretical contribution of this study focuses on the creation of a model using Dubin's model building theory. The primary purpose of this paper is to model the ongoing changes resulting from ubiquitous technology that is altering patterns of organizational knowledge creation and to diagnose these changes in organizational creation processes for exploratory and exploitative innovation. In creating the model, it builds upon the foundations from intensely researched and well understood areas, such as the SECI model and organisation learning. It is only by using these as a foundation that we can start to model potential relationships behind leveraging artificial intelligence technology for knowledge reuse and further explore the relationships with innovation.

This paper begins by providing the research design that was used to create the model (Sect. 2). Section 3 reviews the literature and identifies and defines factors (units) that contribute to or hinder exploratory and exploitative innovation. Section 4 determines how these factors interrelate, which, enables the theory boundaries to be set as discussed in section five. The paper concludes by providing the Plastic model and discusses the contribution of this research and its limitations.

2 Research Design

Dubin's model-building method [31, 32] was chosen for this study, and concepts from this method with the positivism paradigm were used to develop the conceptual model of factors and examine the interrelationships between the changes in interaction and knowledge acquisition in organizations, triggered by technological breakthroughs, and the exploratory and exploitative innovation. Dubin's model addresses the 'paradox of embracing prior research while at the same time not being bound by it' [33]. Dubin's eight-step theory building methodology consists of two parts, conceptual development and research operation. This research focused on developing the conceptual model and providing a starting place for further research and debate. To do this, an interdisciplinary approach was used to compile a comprehensive list of factors. As a result, data was collected from articles from various fields of study, such as knowledge management, psychology, computer science, information system management, marketing, organisational studies and information science. The two steps followed in this study are part one of Dubin's method: (1) Identification and definition of the units of the theory (Sect. 3 of this paper); (2) Determination of interaction that state the relationships between the units of the theory (Sect. 4 of this paper); and (3) Definition of the boundaries of theory to help focus attention on forces that might impact the interplay of the units (Sect. 5 of this paper).

3 Identification and Definition of the Units of the Model

3.1 Research Framework

Before any conceptual model can be built it is important to understand **knowledge creation in organizations**, and **knowledge reuse and innovation**, to identify the basic building blocks in those areas. Through a theoretical literature review approach, it was possible to focus on a pool of theory that has accumulated from seminal knowledge management building blocks, like socialization, externalization, combination and internalization [5]. In this section, through analyzing the theories, we identify the units that make up the building blocks in relation to **knowledge creation in organizations**, and **knowledge reuse and innovation**, such as altered creative potential, information location, reuse reasoning and time constraints. This approach provides an insight into the factors that need to be considered when developing the PLASTIC model.

3.2 Factors of Knowledge Creation in Organizations

One of the basic classifications of knowledge is the distinction between explicit and tacit knowledge [34]. Explicit knowledge, that is to say, knowledge that is codifiable, in the form of language, included in documentation or reports [5]. In turn, hidden knowledge is contextual, subjective and difficult to formalize and communicate [35]. It is situated in the mind of the individual, which makes it challenging not only to articulate, but also to transmit.

Tacit knowledge in itself is a complex process of thinking. It can be described as a triangle, comprising focal content, subsidiary awareness and a knower, who links these two components [35]. Tacit knowledge includes the complex and dynamic relationship between these three components. Furthermore, this integration between these components can be mostly acquired by personal experience and cannot be imprinted mechanically. So, knowledge (especially tacit) is personal, and derived from an individual, subjective perspective. Tacit knowledge is regarded as an essential component of knowledge creation in organizations [5, 36]. However, its nature makes it really challenging to share [37]. Since tacit knowledge is embedded in individual experience and highly elusive, the successful sharing can occur on the basis of collective experience rather than language. Therefore, four areas that may influence knowledge creation in organizations, and knowledge reuse and innovation, have been applied from the knowledge creation model (SECI) developed by Nonaka and Takeuchi [5]. These four main stages impact knowledge conversions and are: *socialisation* (tacit to tacit); *externalisation* (tacit to explicit); *combination* (explicit to explicit); and *internalisation* (explicit to tacit). However, the research to date analyzing the application of the SECI model in organizations is not complete; and among other things, it has not been explained how changes in employees' interactions caused by the use of information technology and new ways of knowledge acquisition affect the creation of organizational knowledge and, consequently, its innovativeness.

The SECI model provides a lens for considering the ongoing changes in relation to knowledge creation in organizations. The conceptualisation of the relationship of the SECI model to organisational innovation has been confirmed in previous research [38]. However, this theory anchors the complex dual processes concerning the formation of organisational ambidexterity in the SECI model in the context of technological immersion. Since the pursuit of exploratory and exploitative innovation requires different processes and abilities, these two types of actions may respond differently to the widespread adoption of technology in knowledge creation processes. This is why it seems so relevant to consider two divergent types of innovation, which significantly extends the cognitive scope of the model.

Referring to this theory, some of the core implications of the technologization of interaction and the use of technology-enabled new channels for knowledge acquisition are indicated. Elements of the model will be used to create the PLASTIC model units that aid the exploration of the interrelationships of knowledge acquisition in organizations, and the exploratory and exploitative innovation [6].

3.3 Factors of Knowledge Reuse and Innovation

Understanding the ongoing changes in available knowledge utilization could help to identify ways to facilitate knowledge reuse in organizations and subsequently innovation. Innovation is a critical factor for an organization to sustain in business [39]. The source of innovation is viewed as a differentiating factor of innovation models, and one type of innovation refers to the novel solution generated in an organization [40]. Such innovation is driven from within and comes from the organization's members. In this closed-innovation model, organizations focus on internal research, development and implementation [41]. Another type of innovation is represented by a different approach: organizations are sourcing new ideas from the outside environment [42]. Open innovation enables organizations to gain ideas from outside and develop effective concepts. Regardless of its source, innovation capability depends on knowledge [43]. New knowledge creation is critical for developing innovation [7]. However, it is often difficult to execute due to the high cost of resources needed to create new knowledge. Therefore, employees rely on knowledge reuse as a strategy to deal with challenges and develop novel solutions [44]. Exploitation of available knowledge is likely to enhance innovation [45, 46], but availability of knowledge does not necessarily mean that it will be reused in organizations [47]. In summary, *knowledge reuse* is a crucial factor that enables organizations to effectively reinforce knowledge. In an organizational context, knowledge reuse refers to identifying and exploiting available knowledge in organizations [45, 46]. It comprises of four low-level steps, namely the *formulation* of a search question; formation of the *search* question for given knowledge; *identifying* the required knowledge; and finally, *applying* this knowledge [47]. These identified units provide a means of explaining the processes of knowledge management in an organization and will enable identification of the most important stages of knowledge creation, which are affected by the technological analyzed organizational changes.

3.4 Factors of Organization Learning

The organizational learning, as a collective process [48], is inevitably linked to joint participation in knowledge creation [49]. Thus, the SECI model is an integral aspect of organizational learning. Organizational learning is perceived as a process of processing information which results in changed behaviours [50] in a specific context [48]. As such, it encompasses a range of social processes based on interactions. Taking the seminal work of Huber [50], we will use the four stages of organization learning in our proposed model and these are: The *knowledge acquisition* which is based on a mechanism for obtaining information, and the primary driver is attention. Attention influences what is being highlighted in organizations, what aspects or problems are the most important challenges on which organizational activities are focused; In contrast, *information distribution* refers to the sharing and exchange of knowledge within an organization; The *interpretation of information* includes giving meaning to knowledge held; and finally *organizational memory* which refers to the use of new knowledge and is a key factor in the process of organizational learning. These four areas, knowledge acquisition, information distribution, interpretation of information, and organizational memory will be included in the proposed model as units that influence knowledge creation in organizations, knowledge reuse and innovation.

3.5 Factors of Technologically Enhanced Knowledge Seeking

Individual learning is an important part of creating organizational knowledge [9]. Individuals are analyzing, evaluating and applying knowledge to create a novel idea. Technology can enhance the search for required information and it can provide a diverse perspective and potentially induce Eustress. However, even though technology enables employees to access a greater amount of data, for some employees it does not necessary increase their innovative potential. Due to "technostress", employees can become less productive and innovative [51]. Innovation potential may be hindered by factors related to new, just-in-time, technologically enhanced knowledge. Within this perspective, factors that could hamper innovation are; overload, invasion, uncertainty, insecurity, complexity, lack of time, poor engagement, and a diminished ability to think critically [1]. Amabile et al. [52] conducted empirical research on employees engaged in creative and innovative projects. The results suggested that higher creativity is related to greater time spent on a given task, whereas fragmented focus hinders an individual's creative potential. This longitudinal study indicates the negative effect time-pressure has on developing new ideas.

Other studies suggest that information overload and interrupted focus due to technology hampers innovation [53]. The consequences of technological advancement become a part of a complex process that affects innovation capability. Some aspects of this process (such as information overload, interrupted focus and lack of time) can lead to a decrease in the individual's innovation potential. Deeper reflection, in-depth understanding, prolonged focus and data mindfulness can prevent the development of these innovation constraints [51]. The addition of technostress as a unit will model both its negative and positive influence on knowledge creation in organizations, and knowledge reuse and innovation.

4 Interacting Units of the Model

4.1 Basic Blocks of PLASTIC Model

As mentioned in section three, the basic building blocks of the PLASTIC model are *socialisation*, *externalization*, *internalisation*, and *combination*. The focus of the PLASTIC model is based around knowledge creation in organizations, knowledge reuse and innovation, organization learning, and technologically enhanced knowledge seeking. The theories of the building blocks and areas of focus are mainly built upon characteristics, such as, knowledge acquisition, technostress, available time, interpretation of information. These characteristics have provided units for the PLASTIC model and Dubin [32] referred to these types of units as 'enumerative'. In this research, all factors associated with knowledge creation in organizations, and knowledge reuse and innovation, were considered as enumerative units by which the knowledge phenomena could be illustrated. The specific units, which will be derived from the factors in section three, that form the PLASTIC model are discussed in the following sections using the seminal building blocks as high-level categories, with the addition of two more, technostress and available time.

4.2 Socialisation (Tacit to Tacit)

The dynamic of social disconnection in the workplace, which may affect knowledge creation processes at the organizational level by hindering socialization and externalization. The extant studies link IT tools with the *socialization* and *externalisation* of tacit knowledge, yet there is a lack of convincing empirical evidence confirming IT as a capable tool facilitating tacit knowledge sharing [54]. It can be the packaging of the new knowledge, through socialization, which can cause us to reflect on what we have learnt and what we would do differently next time (denoted by path C in Fig. 1). A potential interesting link between socialization, externalization and technostress is the dynamic of social in-person disconnection in the workplace. This may affect knowledge creation processes at the organizational level by hindering socialization and externalization; and *altered creative potential* at the individual level, in the context of modification of individuals' behaviors and cognitive patterns, focusing on instant solutions and just-in-time knowledge given the working constraints to get the task done. The following units have been identified:

- Unit 1 - *Altered creative potential*: In the model (Fig. 1) we view the knowledge source subsystem as the AI enhanced information brokers. We have defined AI enhanced information brokers as everyday search engines like Google and Bing, through to the more sophisticated systems like, IBM Watson. For example, an end-user requires information to complete a task and requests information through an information broker to retrieve relevant information for the required task. Available time is always a factor (Unit 12), but the speed of technology can help, but also maybe hinder as employees may rely on quickly retrieved knowledge without proper validation of the provenance of sources which could instigate the risk of processing incorrect information [55]. Consideration has to be given to the potential over-reliance on technology, on information brokers and their personalized filters. An interesting dynamic is around knowledge reuse, which can be defined as an activity aimed at managing disposable knowledge in an organization that involves formulation, search, identification and application. With the advent of easily accessible internet knowledge, accessing organisational knowledge can become the harder route and offer increased resistance due to the lack of Google like search systems for internal knowledge stores, remote working and access to employees. Altered creative potential can be defined at the individual level, in the context of modification of individuals' behaviors and cognitive patterns, focusing on instant solutions and just-in-time knowledge given the working constraints to get the task done.

- Unit 2 - *Formation of the search question for given knowledge*: With the emergence of sophisticated AI questioning and answering systems like IBM's Watson [56], the end-user is required to do less of the assimilation of the data and information to formulate answers to the task in hand. While this may save time in the short-term, long-term these are skills that we may forget, and we could question whether we need them again. In addition, moving to a black-box neuromorphic system like Watson makes it impossible to determine how the answer was calculated, providing another level of obscurity to the knowledge economy. This is especially the case with regard to the issue of explainability and causality of AI [83]. Currently, the leveraging of knowledge supports the successful application of knowledge and creation of a new innovation. Information brokers can provide a cognitive shortcut, which allows us to quickly rely on technology (especially AI-assisted technology), yet it could result in innovative stagnation.

4.3   Externalisation (Tacit to Explicit)

Expressing tacit knowledge entails using explicit, understandable concepts such as metaphors, analogies or models. Externalization involves dialog, creative discussion or collective thinking which facilitate a common understanding of concepts. These two phases take place in a social context and require interaction [5]. Therefore, knowledge creation in an organizational context is inherent in social relations. As such, it is based on collective exchange of expertise and knowledge. It is also important that the employee has enough time (unit 12) to develop wisdom, which can be derived from the process of distributing and *externalization* of new knowledge.

- Unit 3 - *Information distribution* refers to the sharing and exchange of knowledge within an organization. Knowledge sharing and reciprocal relationships are an important element in strengthening an organisation's innovative capacity [36]. These processes are also being transformed by the implementation of remote working solutions and more frequent mediation of interpersonal communication by ICT tools [58].
- Unit 4 – *New Organizational memory* refers to the use of new knowledge and is a key factor in the process of organizational learning [50]. This concerns the storage and retention of knowledge in organisations based on knowledge management systems and established procedures.
- Unit 5 - *Reuse Reasoning* is often based on wrong answers and flawed reasoning [59]. Its success relies on sources which can be biased. Hence, application of such knowledge may result in a lack of success.
- Unit 6 – *Knowledge Loss* occurs when knowledge is not codified into an organization's resources and is forgotten [60], and therefore such knowledge cannot be reused.

4.4   Combination (Explicit to Explicit)

Within organisations employees trying to complete a knowledge task start by *combining* existing information and could call upon existing human knowledge within the organisation (path B in Fig. 1), or by using an information broker to search and retrieve, data, information and knowledge (path A in Fig. 1). The power of the information brokers to provide just-it-time knowledge is immense and understanding those dynamics will enable organisations to determine the 'right' organisational balance.

- Unit 7 - *Anchoring* of a search question, which is different to unit 2 because this is the step before knowing what new knowledge currently exists. This unit is embedded in the problem to be solved and the anchoring effect is a cognitive bias which is influenced by a particular reference point or 'anchor' in an individual's decision-making process [61].
- Unit 8 – *Information Location*: Previous studies imply that around 50 per cent of knowledge reuse attempts fail in engineering firms [62], due to difficulty in finding the

source of information. For instance, empirical data indicates that information workers in Western Europe waste around 4.9 h weekly on fruitless searches for existing information [63]. Information overload can also contribute to the difficulty in locating the required information [64, 65].

- Unit 9 - **Knowledge acquisition** is based on a mechanism for obtaining information, the primary driver of which is attention. Attention influences what is being highlighted in organizations, what aspects or problems are the most important challenges on which organizational activities are focused. In the quest for knowledge acquisition, technological immersion may influence knowledge management practices among current employees. Surface learning, just-in-time knowledge, quick information availability, and information overload are emerging issues related to the ongoing shift in the contemporary workforce. The technological innovation shapes cognitive patterns of employees and affects their behaviors. An example of AI aiding information retrieval is Google Personalized Search. If an individual searches the internet using Google, the search engine will use their browser cookie record to provide more relevant information to the user. Search results presented are based on the relevance of each web page in relation to the search term and which websites the user (or someone else using the same browser) visited through previous search results Google (2009). This approach provides a personalized search, that increases the relevance of search results, and which many of us use today without knowing about the technology behind it. However, such filtering has side effects, such as creating a filter bubble [66]. A filter bubble is where a search engine user encounters only information and opinions that conform to and reinforce their own beliefs. In summary, personalized searching can save the end-user time and reduce the risk of information overload, but could lead to less serendipity and innovative thinking.

4.5   Internalisation (Explicit to Tacit)

On retrieving the information, the user then **internalises** and **socialises** the information to get an understanding of what might answer the clients' issues. However, due to time restrictions and not being able to find colleagues (due to their time pressures or increased remote home working due to the pandemic) to socialise the ideas, socialising doesn't take place. This could lead to the creation of a peculiar information broker bubble. The bubble occurs when existing knowledge stops being challenged or changed. Additionally, it could catalyze competency traps [67], when once useful knowledge turns into outdated information as a result of never being revised or challenged. The critical evaluation of existing knowledge is essential for the successful application of knowledge. It needs to be constantly re-adjusted to an ever-changing environment. However, it is at the internalization process (path E) that we may see the biggest challenges to knowledge growth and innovation in the digital business. With technology providing just in-time knowledge at the click of a search button, the need to follow path C becomes less clear for the employee, due to time pressures and more importantly the bigger picture of not understanding the need to feedback into the organisation and the technology data, information and knowledge sources, so others can benefit from their wisdom in the future.

The pinch point for organisational learning lies with Path E, where employees might follow the surface-learning route and do not retain the newly gained knowledge as they can easily locate that information in the future through the use of technology (just-in-time knowledge); or process and store the new knowledge for later use. The decision-making process around path E would certainly benefit from future research in discovering the true impact of surface-learning on the employee, and on the development of organizational knowledge. Again, an important issue is to verify the long-term impact of the aforementioned changes in knowledge creation processes for the innovative potential of the organizations.

- Unit 10 - The *interpretation of information* includes giving meaning to knowledge held. However, it also implies that one day technology (AI) will take over some knowledge assessment processes. Yet nowadays, the technology depends solely on human input, for instance, deep-learning mechanisms are based on the dataset placed by a programmer. Without this human-driven contribution, technology might lack out-of-the box thinking. The learning process requires exploitation, exploration, evaluation and integration. So far, only humans are capable of such a complex learning process (such as evaluative judgment) [68, 69]. Therefore, this approach to sourcing knowledge could trigger a possible decrease in creativity. The repetitive re-used knowledge might bring about innovative stagnation.
- Unit 11 – *Technostress*: Involves a combination of factors and may vary from very little or no technostress to becoming overwhelmed due to factors such as information overload; interrupted focus; lack of time leading to diminished ability to think critically; and poor engagement. Furthermore, an intensive use of AI/ML may reduce the time an individual spends interacting with other people for the use of systems [70]. As a consequence of reduced social interaction at work collective reflection or joint dialogue and discussion may be constrained (unit 1 and unit 2). As a result, the valuable contribution of employees to knowledge creation in the organization may be diminished. AI/ML solutions can be used to help to compensate for potential losses in collective knowledge creation. However, such partial replacement of interaction-based knowledge by algorithms may also lead to a change in the way new knowledge is created in organizations. As a result, the knowledge creation process undergoes significant changes.
- Unit 12 - *Available Time* - This factor was reinforced by Schick et al. [71] in their definition as 'capacity of time available' and was considered as a common facilitator of knowledge reuse [57]. Consequently, time restrictions are a barrier to knowledge utilization and allowing more time for task performance can improve knowledge reuse.

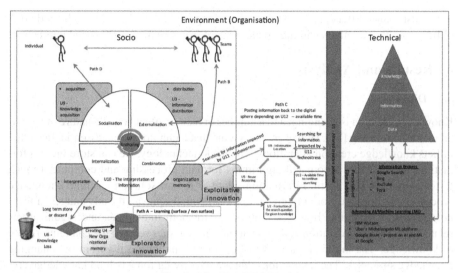

Fig. 1. The PLASTIC Model

5 Theory Boundaries

In this research, three system boundaries were specified for the PLASTIC model taken from the socio-technical perspective, socio, technical, and the environment. The term socio-technical was first suggested by Emery and Trist [72] to describe a method of analyzing the social and technological subsystems of the organization and the relation of the organization as a whole to the environment in which it operates. According to Pasmore, et al. [73], "the sociotechnical system view contends that organizations are made up of people that produce products or services using some technology," and that each "affects the operation and appropriateness of the technology as well as the actions of the people who operate it" (p. 1182). The boundaries provided by the socio-technical perspective emphasize the interconnecting social and technical factors in the way people work in searching for information and knowledge. Using the theory as a lens enables researchers and practitioners to understand the complex interrelations between various elements of systems in organizations.

The key assumption of this approach is that interaction between social and technical aspects of an organization contributes to its success. Within the **technical boundary** it comprises of the devices, tools and techniques needed to transform inputs into knowledge outputs in a way which enhances the economic performance of the organization. Within the **social boundary** it comprises of the employees (at all levels and generations) and the knowledge, skills, attitudes, values and needs they bring to the work **environment** as well as the reward system. We note that there could be very different social systems within an organization given the varying specifics of employees. In terms of the environment boundary in our PLASTIC model, both the technical and social boundaries reside within the **environment boundary** and are viewed as sociotechnical microcosms that help form the overall environment, but extend their knowledge independence through the varying depth of knowledge of AI searching technologies. The reward in the sociotechnical microcosms also differs greatly with some seeking adrenaline fixes due to the addiction of being on-line; to others gaining greater reward from the traditional social interaction.

6   Results and Analysis

6.1   Discussion

Knowledge creation is changing, and a number of factors affect how the nature of knowledge is transforming [74]. However, we assume that technology is an essential facet that inflicts knowledge creation alterations. Thanks to technology, we can store more information; we can build automated algorithms for data processing and compute it much faster to quickly find useful information. State-of-the-art solution leverage knowledge processes can improve work organizations. However, despite all the advantages of technological growth, it also brings several issues for both individuals and organizations related to knowledge creation and innovation. These issues refer to the changing nature of knowledge. The individual aspect of this transformation results from the changing knowledge strategies. The interactions that are the driving force behind knowledge creation in an organization are being altered by the use of technology [75]. Their nature is changing and, as a result, knowledge creation immanently related to the social aspect of collaboration is also being reshaped. Moreover, the way knowledge is acquired and used is transformed by technology. Hence, this contributes to a change in knowledge creation in the organization and can lead to both increased innovation potential and decreased organizational knowledge generation. Consequently, these transformations can contribute to changes in organizational ambidexterity, affecting the potential for exploratory and exploitative innovation.

Technological development and social change are accelerating digital advancement of organizations [76]. The ways in which information is obtained and used are altered, hence the creation of knowledge in organizations also undergoes modifications. On the one hand, the use of AI/ML potential enables modern solutions and indicates the optimal use of data (e.g. adjusting the strategy to the algorithmic prediction). On the other hand, however, there is also fast, shallow and unreflective knowledge, therefore ready-made knowledge, which is only a superficial processing of easily accessible and superficially studied information.

This reusable knowledge is based on instantly-obtainable, just-in-time information and fast feedback. It is quickly forgotten and might lack in-depth reflection and critical analysis. PLASTIC knowledge is a major step forward as it enables us to operate quickly and provide prompt answers. However, it can lead to information overload and burnout [77], technology addiction [78, 79], and knowledge deficiency resulting from surface-learning and over-reliance on technology. Where further research is required on it is in determining the impact of it lowering the organization's innovation potential.

There are a number of organizational challenges concerning knowledge processes and information deficiency:

- Over-reliance on technology as a knowledge storage can cause difficulties in case of equipment malfunction or a changed business model (for instance the introduction of fees for access to information resources or information brokers). The potential data loss might negatively affect the organization's PLASTIC knowledge capability.

- Employees' creative capability may be limited. What we could see in the near future is technological omnipotence might limit human creativity [80].

These challenges need to be researched in order to maintain sustainable business. Managers need to determine ways of using the strength of technological advancement without compromising the creativeness of employees. Technology is a robust tool to support decision-making processes and information processing in organizations. It significantly accelerates data analysis and enables access to large data sets of facts. However, it can also, in some cases, contribute to the smoothing of knowledge creation processes by limiting reflection and in-depth dialogue, providing just-in-time plastic knowledge. For many years organisations have been positioning themselves for rapid information and knowledge reuse, and it appears that we are nearly there. However, there are potential unforeseen consequences of the use of plastic knowledge that need to be considered and require further research. PLASTIC knowledge imposes the mechanism of non-reflective re-usage of information. It promotes the throw-away approach to information; you obtain it, use it and dispose of it quickly. It is within this approach that we are likely to see a lack of knowledge refinement and improvement that could hinder organisational knowledge development due to the reduced analysis, evaluation and reflection. As we move further into the PLASTIC knowledge mindset, it will mean that we heavily rely upon available information resources and exploit them, yet greatly reduce our contribution to the development of new knowledge, and as a result, organizations may face innovative stagnation. Successful knowledge management oriented towards innovation assumes that we should consciously manage knowledge as a valuable resource [81, 82]. The responsible knowledge management will not only focus on effective re-usage of existing knowledge resources, but will contribute to the knowledge-pool by developing refined knowledge. Leverage knowledge brings about long-term benefits as a renewable source of innovation, whereas plastic knowledge decreases innovative potential by narrowing our focus onto the re-usage of existing information resources. Hence, sustainable knowledge management enables innovation and facilitates creativity. By encouraging reflection, analytical thinking and in-depth information analysis, it enhances the long-term competitive advantage arising from creative potential. Moreover, sustainable knowledge management emphasizes the importance of mental development. It boosts knowledge generation as the main source of knowledge supply. To incorporate sustainable knowledge management, organizations should design a business process to support knowledge growth and refinement. The result will be an organization in a better position to maintain sustainable knowledge processes and thus achieve innovation. In summary, the PLASTIC model provides insight into the mechanisms of the changing knowledge practices caused by interactions between humans and AI. The model raises new research questions for knowledge management and information science researchers and is likely to inflict further transition in knowledge management practices.

6.2 Future Work

Since this paper is theoretical and indicates the directions of the observed changes, further research may refer to the empirical verification of the presented concept. The analysis of relations between advanced information brokers and the consequences for particular phases of the SECI model seems to be particularly important. Another limitation of the presented concept is the lack of data related to the described processes. Future research should focus on the dynamics of changes and modification of information acquisition in organizations. Similarly, observation of knowledge creation processes will constitute an important complementary element of the presented discussion.

7 Conclusion

The PLASTIC knowledge model presented contributes to the knowledge management literature in at least three ways. First, a conceptualization based on a critical analysis of knowledge creation and organizational learning theories provides needed clarification to this burgeoning research area. Second, this model indicates what underlying mechanisms are associated with the implications for knowledge creation embedded in technological change. More specifically, the PLASTIC model highlights how changes in the social interactions and the knowledge acquisition methods affect transformations in the organizational knowledge creation. In addition, it outlines the implications of these alterations for exploratory and exploitative innovation. Therefore, this model is a call for a more thorough and in-depth theoretical and empirical investigation of this topic. The synthesis of empirical research, carried out in line with Dubin's method, outlines perspectives for further research and practical applications related to knowledge creation in a technological environment. The outcome of PLASTIC model is to support both scholars and practitioners in critically reflecting on the implications of changes resulting from the embeddedness of organizational knowledge creation processes in technology.

Knowledge management is critical for an organization's success. Knowledge processes such as creation, utilization and refinement are the cornerstone of innovation [67]. The developed model aids in the understanding of the specific knowledge processes within an organization through using a socio-technical theoretical lens. It emphasizes the role of a changeable environment and the interactions between technology-driven transformations and human-oriented practices. It allows for evaluation of the future adaptation in knowledge management processes. Additionally, it implies the main prospective challenges, obstacles and difficulties for knowledge management over the next decade. The model illustrates how technology-inflicted alteration may shape human cognitive strategies and the impact it will have corporate innovation. Moreover, it provides an insight into knowledge management mechanisms embedded into the AI technological evolution. Taken together, this model points to a comprehensive picture where technological immersion in organisational knowledge searching can relate in different ways to exploratory and exploitative innovation. By identifying the key points that determine the effective use of knowledge and the achievement of innovation, we assume that a deliberate and purposeful focus will be directed at critical risk areas that may hinder organizational innovation.

References

1. Love, P.E.D., Matthews, J., Zhou, J.: Is it just too good to be true? Unearthing the benefits of disruptive technology. Int. J. Inf. Manage. **52**, 102096 (2020)

2. Pinheiro, J., Silva, G.M., Dias, Á.L., Lages, L.F., Preto, M.T.: Fostering knowledge creation to improve performance: the mediation role of manufacturing flexibility. Bus. Process. Manag. J. **26**(7), 1871–1892 (2020)
3. Rindova, V., Courtney, H.: To shape or adapt: knowledge problems, epistemologies, and strategic postures under Knightian uncertainty. Acad. Manag. Rev. **45**(4), 787–807 (2020)
4. Cai, W., McKenna, B., Wassler, P., Williams, N.: Rethinking knowledge creation in information technology and tourism. J. Travel Res. 004728752094610 (2020)
5. Nonaka, I., Takeuchi, H.: The Knowledge-Creating Company: How Japanese Companies Create the Dynamics of Innovation. Oxford University Press, New York (1995)
6. Flores Torres, C.L., Olvera-Vargas, L.A., Sánchez Gómez, J., Contreras-Medina, D.I.: Discovering innovation opportunities based on SECI model: reconfiguring knowledge dynamics of the agricultural artisan production of agave-mezcal, using emerging technologies. J. Knowl. Manag. **25**(2), 336–359 (2020)
7. Li, M., Liu, H., Zhou, J.: G-SECI model-based knowledge creation for CoPS innovation: the role of grey knowledge. J. Knowl. Manag. **22**(4), 887–911 (2018)
8. Chatterjee, A., Pereira, A., Sarkar, B.: Learning transfer system inventory (LTSI) and knowledge creation in organizations. Learn. Organ. **25**(5), 305–319 (2018)
9. Baldé, M., Ferreira, A.I., Maynard, T.: SECI driven creativity: the role of team trust and intrinsic motivation. J. Knowl. Manag. **22**(8), 1688–1711 (2018)
10. Arias-Pérez, J., Velez-Ocampo, J., Cepeda-Cardona, J.: Strategic orientation toward digitalization to improve innovation capability: why knowledge acquisition and exploitation through external embeddedness matter. J. Knowl. Manage. (2021)
11. Mardani, A., Nikoosokhan, S., Moradi, M., Doustar, M.: The relationship between knowledge management and innovation performance. J. High Technol. Managem. Res. **29**(1), 12–26 (2018)
12. Hung, K.-P., Chou, C.: The impact of open innovation on firm performance: the moderating effects of internal RandD and environmental turbulence. Technovation **33**(10–11), 368–380 (2013)
13. Lai, H.-C., Weng, C.S.: Exploratory innovation and exploitative innovation in the phase of technological discontinuity: the perspective on patent data for two IC foundries. Asian J. Technol. Innov. **24**(1), 41–54 (2016)
14. Zang, J.: Structural holes, exploratory innovation and exploitative innovation. Manag. Decis. **56**(8), 1682–1695 (2018)
15. Koryak, O., Lockett, A., Hayton, J., Nicolaou, N., Mole, K.: Disentangling the antecedents of ambidexterity: exploration and exploitation. Res. Policy **47**(2), 413–427 (2018)
16. Papa, A., Santoro, G., Tirabeni, L., Monge, F.: Social media as tool for facilitating knowledge creation and innovation in small and medium enterprises. Balt. J. Manag. **13**(3), 329–344 (2018). https://doi.org/10.1108/BJM-04-2017-0125
17. Stachová, K., Stacho, Z., Cagáňová, D., Stareček, A.: Use of digital technologies for intensifying knowledge sharing. Appl. Sci. **10**(12), 4281 (2020). https://doi.org/10.3390/app101 24281
18. Dwivedi, Y.K., et al.: Artificial intelligence (AI): multidisciplinary perspectives on emerging challenges, opportunities, and agenda for research, practice and policy. Int. J. Inf. Manage. **57**, 101994 (2021)
19. Wild, R., Griggs, K.: A model of information technology opportunities for facilitating the practice of knowledge management. VINE J. Inf. Knowl. Manage. Syst. **38**, 490–506 (2008)
20. Skok, W., Kalmanovitch, C.: Evaluating the role and effectiveness of an intranet in facilitating knowledge management: a case study at surrey county council. Inf. Manage. **42**(5), 731–744 (2005)
21. Sher, P., Lee, V.: 'Information technology as a facilitator for enhancing dynamic capabilities through knowledge management'. Inf. Manage. **41**(8), 933–945 (2004)

22. Benitez, J., Castillo, A., Llorens, J., Braojos, J.: IT-enabled knowledge ambidexterity and innovation performance in small U.S. firms: the moderator role of social media capability. Inf. Manage. **55**(1), 131–143 (2018). doi:https://doi.org/10.1016/j.im.2017.09.004

23. Almeida, F., Miranda, E., Falcão, J.: Challenges and facilitators practices for knowledge management in large-scale scrum teams. J. Inf. Technol. Case Appl. Res. **21**(2), 90–102 (2019)

24. O'Connor, C., Kelly, S.: Facilitating knowledge management through filtered big data: SME competitiveness in an agri-food sector. J. Knowl. Manag. **21**(1), 156–179 (2017)

25. Archer-Brown, C., Kietzmann, J.: Strategic knowledge management and enterprise social media. J. Knowl. Manag. **22**(6), 1288–1309 (2018)

26. Ribiere, V., Gong, C., Yang, K.: Knowledge management from a technology perspective. In: Liebowitz, J. (ed.) A Research Agenda for Knowledge Management and Analytics, pp. 43–66. Edward Elgar Publishing (2021)

27. Di Vaio, A., Palladino, R., Pezzi, A., Kalisz, D.E.: The role of digital innovation in knowledge management systems: a systematic literature review. J. Bus. Res. **123**, 220–231 (2021)

28. Lanzolla, G., Markides, C.: A business model view of strategy. J. Manage. Stud. **58**(2), 540–553 (2021). https://doi.org/10.1111/joms.12580

29. Chhim, P.P., Somers, T.M., Chinnam, R.B.: Knowledge reuse through electronic knowledge repositories: A multi theoretical study. J. Knowl. Manag. **21**(4), 741–764 (2017)

30. Tang, M., Xu, P., Llerena, P., Afshar Jahanshahi, A.: The impact of the openness of firms' external search strategies on exploratory innovation and exploitative innovation. Sustainability **11**(18), 4858 (2019)

31. Dubin, R.: Theory building in applied areas. In: Dunnette, M.D. (ed.) Handbook of Industrial and Organizational Psychology, pp. 17–39. Rand McNally, Chicago (1976)

32. Dubin, R.: Theory Building, Rev. edn. Free Press (1978)

33. Holton, E.F., Lowe, J.S.: Toward a general research process for using Dubin's theory building model. Hum. Resour. Dev. Rev. **6**(3), 297–320 (2007)

34. Massingham, P.: Knowledge sharing: what works and what doesn't work: a critical systems thinking perspective. Syst. Pract. Action Res. **28**(3), 197–228 (2014). https://doi.org/10.1007/s11213-014-9330-3

35. Polanyi, M.: The Tacit Dimension. Routledge and Kegan Paul, London (1967)

36. Ganguly, A., Talukdar, A., Chatterjee, D.: Evaluating the role of social capital, tacit knowledge sharing, knowledge quality and reciprocity in determining innovation capability of an organization. J. Knowl. Manag. **23**(6), 1105–1135 (2019)

37. Hislop, D.: Linking human resource management and knowledge management via commitment: a review and research agenda. Empl. Relat. **25**(2), 182–202 (2003). https://doi.org/10.1108/01425450310456479

38. Sian Lee, C., Kelkar, R.S.: ICT and knowledge management: Perspectives from the SECI model. Electron. Libr. **31**(2), 226–243 (2013). https://doi.org/10.1108/02640471311312401

39. Walcher, F., Wöhrl, U.: Measuring innovation performance. In: Friedl, G., Kayser, H. (eds.) Valuing Corporate Innovation. Management for Professionals, pp. 71–110. Springer, Cham (2018). https://doi.org/10.1007/978-3-319-64864-4_4. ISBN 978-3-319-64863-7

40. Phillips, J.: Defining your innovation model: 10 facets of innovation. Int. J. Innov. Sci. **1**(1), 1–12 (2009)

41. Huang, H., Lai, M., Lin, L., Chen, C.: Overcoming organizational inertia to strengthen business model innovation: an open innovation perspective. J. Organ. Chang. Manag. **26**(6), 977–1002 (2013)

42. Chesbrough, H.: Open Innovation: The New Imperative for Creating and Profiting from Technology. Harvard Business School Press, Boston (2003)

43. Martín-de-Castro, G., Delgado-Verde, M., López-Sáez, P., Navas-López, J.E.: Towards 'an intellectual capital-based view of the firm': origins and nature. J. Bus. Ethics **98**(4), 649–662 (2011)
44. Paraponaris, C., Sigal, M.: From knowledge to knowing, from boundaries to boundary construction. J. Knowl. Manag. **19**(5), 881–899 (2015)
45. Majchrzak, A., Cooper, L.P., Neece, O.E.: Knowledge reuse for innovation. Manage. Sci. **50**(2), 174–188 (2004)
46. Cheuk, K.P., Baškarada, S., Koronios, A.: Contextual factors in knowledge reuse. VINE J. Inf. Knowl. Manage. Syst. **47**(2), 194–210 (2017)
47. Markus, M.L.: Toward a theory of knowledge reuse: types of knowledge reuse situations and factors in reuse success. J. Manage. Inf. Syst. **18**(1), 57–93 (2001)
48. Lau, K.W., Lee, P.Y., Chung, Y.Y.: A collective organizational learning model for organizational development. Leadersh. Org. Dev. J. **40**(1), 107–123 (2019)
49. Belle, S.: Organizational learning? Look again. Learn. Organ. **23**(5), 332–341 (2016). https://doi.org/10.1108/TLO-01-2016-0007
50. Huber, G.P.: Organizational learning: the contributing processes and the literatures. Organ. Sci. **2**(1), 88–115 (1991)
51. Tarafdar, M., D'Arcy, J., Turel, O., Gupta, A.: The dark side of information technology: is overuse of information technology sapping your employees' productivity, innovation, and well-being? MIT Sloan Manage. Rev. **2015** (2015)
52. Amabile, T.M., Mueller, J.S., Simpson, W.B., Hadley, C.N., Kramer, S.J., Fleming, L.: Time pressure and creativity in organizations: a longitudinal field study. In: Harvard Business School Working Paper, No. 02-073 (2002)
53. Akorfu, G.K.S.: Costs of information overload to organisations – an information technology perspective. Afr. J. Comput. ICT **6**(2), 11–30 (2013)
54. Panahi, S., Watson, J., Partridge, H.: Towards tacit knowledge sharing over social web tools. J. Knowl. Manag. **17**(3), 379–397 (2013)
55. Hershatter, A., Epstein, M.: Millennials and the world of work: an organization and management perspective. J. Bus. Psychol. **25**(2), 211–223 (2010)
56. IBM: Put AI to work (2019). https://www.ibm.com/thought-leadership/smart/uk-en/watson/. Accessed 27 June 2019
57. Paulin, D., Winroth, M.: Facilitators, inhibitors and obstacles - a redefined categorization regarding barriers for knowledge sharing, transfer and flow. In: Washington DC, ACAD Conferences LTD, pp. 320–328 (2013)
58. Leonardi, P.M.: COVID-19 and the new technologies of organizing: digital exhaust, digital footprints, and artificial intelligence in the wake of remote work. J. Manage. Stud. (2020). https://doi.org/10.1111/joms.12648
59. Liebowitz, J., Beckman, T.J.: Knowledge Organizations: What Every Manager Should Know. CRC Press, Boston (1998)
60. Levallet, N., Chan, Y.: Organizational knowledge retention and knowledge loss. J. Knowl. Manag. **23**(1), 176–199 (2019)
61. Ni, F., Arnott, D., Gao, S.: The anchoring effect in business intelligence supported decision-making. J. Decis. Syst. **28**(2), 67–81 (2019). https://doi.org/10.1080/12460125.2019.162 0573.ISSN1246-0125
62. Irnazarow, A., Heisig, P.: Designed to fail? Challenges in sharing engineering knowledge across a global company. In: Proceedings of the European Conference on Knowledge Management, ECKM (2015)
63. IDC. The Information Worker Productivity Gap in Western Europe: New Challenges and Opportunities for IT (2012). https://denalilabs.com/static/ProductivityWhitepaper.pdf. Accessed April 2021

64. So, J.C.F., Bolloju, N.: Explaining the intentions to share and reuse knowledge in the context of IT service operations. J. Knowl. Manag. **9**(6), 30–41 (2005)
65. Jackson, T.W., Farzaneh, P.: Theory-based model of factors affecting information overload. Int. J. Inf. Manage. **32**(6), 523–532 (2012)
66. Pariser, E.: The Filter Bubble: What the Internet is Hiding from You. Viking/Penguin Press, London (2011)
67. Hislop, D., Bosua, R., Helms, R.: Knowledge Management in Organizations: A Critical Introduction, 4th edn. Oxford University Press, Oxford (2018)
68. Bearman, M., Luckin, R.: Preparing university assessment for a world with AI: Tasks for Human intelligence. In: Bearman, M., Dawson, P., Ajjawi, R., Tai, J., Boud, D. (eds.) Re-imagining University Assessment in a Digital World. TEPA, vol. 7, pp. 49–63. Springer, Cham (2020). https://doi.org/10.1007/978-3-030-41956-1_5
69. Kao, Y.F., Venkatachalam, R.: Human and machine learning. Comput. Econ. 1–21 (2018). https://doi.org/10.1007/s10614-018-9803-z. Accessed 20 June 2019
70. Brougham, D., Haar, J.: Smart technology, artificial intelligence, robotics, and algorithms (STARA): employees' perceptions of our future workplace. J. Manag. Organ. **24**(2), 239–257 (2018). https://doi.org/10.1017/jmo.2016.55
71. Schick, A.G., Gordon, L.A., Haka, S.: Information overload: a temporal approach. Acc. Organ. Soc. **15**(3), 199–220 (1990)
72. Emery, F.E., Trist, E.L.: The causal texture of organizational environments. Hum. Relat. **18**, 21–32 (1965)
73. Pasmore, W., Francis, C., Shani, A.: Social technical systems: a North American reflection on empirical studies of the seventies. Hum. Relat. **35**(12), 1179–1204 (1982)
74. Choi, H.-J., Ahn, J.-C., Jung, S.-H., Kim, J.-H.: Communities of practice and knowledge management systems: effects on knowledge management activities and innovation performance. Knowl. Manag. Res. Pract. **18**(1), 53–68 (2020)
75. Laitinen, K., Valo, M.: Meanings of communication technology in virtual team meetings: framing technology-related interaction. Int. J. Hum. Comput. Stud. **111**, 12–22 (2018)
76. Priyono, A., Moin, A., Putri, V.: Identifying digital transformation paths in the business model of SMEs during the COVID-19 pandemic. J. Open Innov.: Technol. Mark. Complex. **6**(4), 104 (2020)
77. Kouvonen, A., Toppinen-Tanner, S., Kivisto, M., Huuhtanen, P., Kalimo, R.: Job characteristics and burnout among aging professionals in information and communications technology. Psychol. Rep. **97**(2), 505–514 (2005)
78. Widyanto, L., Griffiths, M.: 'Internet addiction': a critical review. Int. J. Ment. Heal. Addict. **4**(1), 31–51 (2006). https://doi.org/10.1007/s11469-006-9009-9
79. Emmens, B., Thomson, P.: Organizational culture, and the impact of the digital overload. In: Thomson, P., Johnson, M., Devlin, J. (eds.) Conquering Digital Overload. Palgrave Macmillan, Cham (2018)
80. Runco, M.: The real creativity crisis. Creat. Hum. Dev. 1–10 (2015)
81. North, K., Kumta, G.: Knowledge in organisations. In: North, K., Kumta, G. (eds.) Knowledge Management. STBE, pp. 31–61. Springer, Cham (2018). https://doi.org/10.1007/978-3-319-59978-6_2
82. Venkitachalam, K., Willmott, H.: Strategic knowledge management—insights and pitfalls. Int. J. Inf. Manage. **37**(4), 313–316 (2017)
83. Shin, D.: The effects of explainability and causability on perception, trust, and acceptance: Implications for explainable AI. Int. J. Hum Comput Stud. **146**, 102551 (2021)

Applying a Combination Model of Knowledge Management and Visitor Relationship Management in the Study of the Visitors of Historical Museum

Mei-Yun Hsu[1] and I-Hsien Ting[2(✉)]

[1] National Museum of Taiwan History, Tainan City, Taiwan
`myhsu@nmth.gov.tw`
[2] Department of Information Management, National University of Kaohsiung,
Kaohsiung City, Taiwan
`iting@nuk.edu.tw`

Abstract. Museum is a place that not only provides service but also content, no matter public or private. In recent years, customer relationship management is increasingly important for museums that want to attract visitors or promote the museum's core concept and value. In this paper, we will propose a new model combining knowledge management and customer (visitor) relationship management as a process. In the new model, data analysis is the main focus and plays the core role of the model. This paper will use the National Museum of Taiwan History as a case study to raise some research questions. According to the questions, data are collected and analyzed by various data analysis techniques to form knowledge that can be used for taking action to provide better services and content for museum visitors. In conclusion, we will also provide future research suggestions in knowledge and visitor relationship management for museum study.

Keywords: Historical Museum · Data Analysis · Knowledge Management · Customer Relationship Management · Visitor Relationship Management · Seasonal Analysis

1 Introduction

Knowledge management has been considered a fundamental model to better use knowledge in organizations, such as industries, enterprises, governments, schools, etc. In recent years, the concept of knowledge management has also been adopted to be applied in libraries and museums to improve the organization process. In addition to knowledge management, customer relationship management has also been combined with the concept of knowledge management. This concept has also been adopted in many organizations where customers are their primary focus, not only in selling physical products but also in providing services [14].

L. Uden and I-H. Ting (Eds.): KMO 2023, CCIS 1825, pp. 273–286, 2023.
https://doi.org/10.1007/978-3-031-34045-1_23

In order to apply knowledge management and customer relationship management, data is the essential factor for the process. The data needs to be processed into information to manage better and use the information to achieve the concept of knowledge. We then can use the knowledge for customer relationship management to keep old customers and attract new ones. Therefore, data play the most critical success factor in knowledge management and customer relationship management in organizations [7].

In previous research, museums, and libraries are places that provide not only service but also content, no matter public or private museums and libraries. In recent years, customer relationship management is increasingly important for museums that want to attract visitors or promote the core concept of the museum. The term visitor relationship management is therefore proposed. In order to achieve the idea of visitor relationship management, they need to understand their visitors first. Moreover, the museum is also concerned about the gap between what they want to deliver and what visitors receive in the exhibitions [8]. Data analysis is the best way to understand the visitors among all other ways. Thus, some researchers are focusing on knowledge management and customer relationship management. However, gaps still exist when combining knowledge and customer relationship management, especially when including data analysis in the two models and processes. A new model for this kind of organization is, therefore, essential [6].

Therefore, in this paper, we will propose a new model in which knowledge and customer relationship management are combined as a process. In the new model, data analysis will be the main focus as the core of the model. Then, we will use the National Museum of Taiwan History as a case study to raise some research questions. According to the questions, data are collected and analyzed to form knowledge that can be used for taking action to provide better services and content for museum visitors.

The rest of the paper is organized as follows. In Sect. 2, related literature, research, and backgrounds will be reviewed, including historical museums and visitors, knowledge management for museum research and customer relationship management, and data analysis techniques. A new research model of knowledge management and customer relationship management will be proposed, and six research questions will be raised in Sect. 3. In Sect. 4, we will introduce the data that was used in this research, and appropriate data analysis techniques will be used to analyze the data. The analysis results will also be presented in this section. The paper will finally be concluded, and future research directions and suggestions will be provided in Sect. 5.

2   Literature Review

2.1   Museum and Visitors

Since ancient times, museums have been treated as the highest and the best palace to present cultural achievement [6], and it intends to affect the visitors with an implicit cultural power. However, the ideological role of museums has been questioned in recent years. Museums are increasingly moving towards a democratic trend. Whether in terms of interpreting high-level cultural terms or curating themes, they are increasingly trying to embrace the public.

The museum has four basic functions of research, collection, display, and education, among which the research and collection department is the basic foundation through the exhibition to achieve the goal of education. Visitors can practice knowledge, social, and dream functions in the museum. These functions show that the resources that the museum expects to provide the audience are not only knowledge but include social and other feelings formed by history, culture, and memory [1].

However, did the visitors learn? How to learn? What do the visitors want to learn? What have the visitors learned? What does the museum want to interpret? What to communicate? Who is the target? How to communicate? These are the must-haves for museum curators when interpreting collections, planning exhibitions, and educational activities.

The types of museum visitors can be roughly divided into three categories: adult audience, family audience, and primary school audience. Student audiences' learning behavior is expected to be changed during museum visits. Whether guided tours by museum guides or self-exploration by children, the delivery of out-of-school instruction can produce significant changes in children's learning and behavior [2,10,11]. The peer influence of co-visiting is also significant, which may hinder learning or improve learning efficiency; family audiences will regard visiting museums as a social activity, and they hope museums provide learning functions and relaxing activities. Environment for socializing among family members without an excessive study load. General adult audiences are characterized by valuing learning, seeking the challenge of discovering new things, and enjoying doing meaningful things in leisure time [3,4].

An audience survey is an essential bridge for museum interpretation and audience communication. Currently, there is a tendency to pay more and more attention to educational functions because more and more social pressure requires museums to prove the reasonable use of their existence. Most of these pressures are reflected in the market research reports made by museums. The investigators usually make appeals, asking museums to confirm where their audiences are. At the same time, we should plan popular exhibitions and educational activities to attract different customers. Museum practitioners have gradually become aware of the possible role of museums in education and have begun to re-evaluate the relationship between museums and audiences [5]. Therefore, the needs and feelings of museum audiences, such as expectations, satisfaction, preferences, learning, and social interaction, have become essential issues between museums and audiences, and audience research has received much attention.

This paper uses The National Taiwan Museum of History as a case study. The National Taiwan Museum of History with the purpose and mission of promoting Taiwan's history. It is also an essential base for contemporary cultural tourism and for international tourists to understand Taiwan and its history and culture. Thus, through continuous audience surveys to understand the needs and expectations of the audience, we can develop exhibitions that connect and resonate with the public's emotions during exhibition planning and become a museum that meets the needs of the public and meets the trends.

The issue discussed here is actually a research topic in knowledge management and customer relationship management. So, a model for knowledge and customer relationship management for museums can be proposed. The model can be used for future research in museum studies. Moreover, we do hope some novel data analysis techniques can be used in the data that is collected by using traditional survey methods from museums, which may provide more interesting results and findings for museums to take action and provide better exhibition contents and services.

2.2   KM for Museum Research and CRM

Knowledge management is a process for an enterprise to gather, organize, manage, share, and use knowledge. In order to acquire knowledge, many information techniques need to be used for data analysis and by this to get valuable knowledge, such as data mining and machine learning. Information systems are also crucial for managing knowledge well and sharing knowledge via information systems [12], virtual communities or social networks [13].

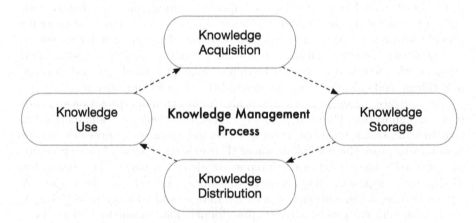

Fig. 1. The common knowledge management process [9].

Figure 1 shows the process of knowledge management, and it is very commonly used in different areas. In the process, there are four main steps of knowledge management: knowledge acquisition, knowledge storage, knowledge distribution, and knowledge use. In some research, externalization, combination, internalization, and socialization are used instead of the four steps in Fig. 1 that focus on the knowledge transformation process [9].

In the field of museum study, some researchers are starting to apply the concept of knowledge management. Most of the literature focuses on information systems for museums, such as knowledge management systems, content management systems, visitor management systems, etc. [7]. However, only some of these researches are about the process of knowledge management and the model. Therefore, there are still gaps between the knowledge management process and the lack of a total solution model to complete the process [14].

Fig. 2. Traditional customer relationship management model.

In addition to knowledge management, customer relationship management is another concept that focuses on attracting new customers and keeping old customers through a process. Data analysis is also essential for achieving the idea in customer relationship management. Traditional customer relationship management has three focuses: marketing, service, and sales. Figure 2 shows the traditional customer relationship management model.

However, museums treat their customers as visitors, focusing on something other than sales but more on the exhibition's content. Therefore, we propose a visitor relationship management model modified from traditional customer relationship management as shown in Fig. 3, which is the visitor relationship management model. The three visitor focuses are marketing, service, and content. Like traditional customer relationship management, data analysis also plays an essential role in the model.

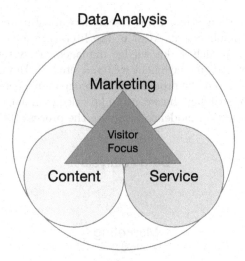

Fig. 3. Modified customer relationship management model for museum (Visitor relationship management).

3   Research Model and Questions

Based on the literature reviewed in the previous section, we proposed a model combining the knowledge management process and visitor relationship model. The model is shown in Fig. 4. The model is helpful for museums to manage their knowledge for visitor relationship management. The process is from knowledge acquisition to gathering knowledge for visitor relationship management. The second step is knowledge storage, about how to store the gathered knowledge in a knowledge base. The third step is knowledge distribution, which spreads and shares stored knowledge. The last step is about how to use the knowledge to take into practice for museums to manage the relationship of visitors well.

In the following sessions, we will use a real case to demonstrate how Fig. 4 works from research questions to acquire data and from data to knowledge by data analysis. The questions are raised according to the three dimensions, marketing, service, and content. Then analyze the results to provide suggestions for using the knowledge.

Most of the audience's learning in the museum is informal, but they can enjoy a more pleasant learning experience. In the museum learning research literature, it is generally agreed that the three indicators of "attraction," "sustainability," and "participation" can be used as the basis for examining audience learning behavior. In addition, relevant research has also proved that the five visiting behaviors of "asking questions, answering questions, commenting or explaining the content of the display, silently reading the display instructions or reading the display instructions aloud" can infer that learning is ongoing [2,10,11].

In addition, factors that affect audience behavior include display design factors, audience factors, and architectural factors. Display design factors include

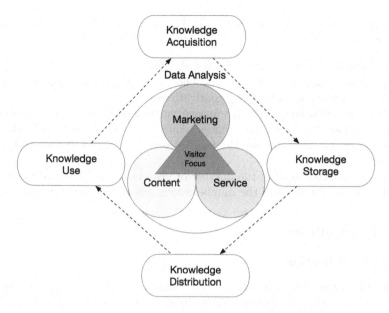

Fig. 4. A combined model with knowledge management and visitor relationship management.

the size of cultural relics displayed, the difficulty of displaying descriptions, aesthetics, novelty or rarity, feeling, interaction, and other factors related to display design, etc.; audience factors include audience participation and interaction, satisfaction with the displayed cultural relics, whether they are tired, Special interests, cultural background factors, personal living environment, and other psychological factors; architectural factors include the brightness of the visiting space, the degree of proximity to the exhibits, the degree of authenticity of the exhibition area, the degree of sensory (attraction given by the sense of space design) and other factors related to the Related space factors, etc. [3].

In other words, the factors that affect audience learning are the interaction among personal context, social context, and physical context. Personal context refers to demographic and socio-economic information such as visitor motivation, information source, cultural background, educational background, age, income, occupation, gender, and place of residence; social context refers to the composition and characteristics of the audience; environmental context refers to the cultural relics in the museum. Collection theme, type, material, degree of difficulty, display method, architecture, display field space, graphic description, guide commentary and whether to charge or not, etc. [4].

According to this paper's background and literature review, six research questions are raised to understand the historical museum's visitors better. According to the proposed visitor relationship management model, the six questions are based on the focus: marketing, service, and content. In this paper, these questions will be answered by applying novel data analysis techniques. The research questions are:

(1) Do visitors who like historical relics also like digital media?
(2) The demographics of the visitors who like historical relics including age, gender, education and visiting motivations.
(3) Does the exhibition positively improve the understanding of Taiwan Culture Associations? and their age, gender, education and visiting motivations.
(4) Does the exhibition inspire the motivations to understand Taiwan Culture Associations?
(5) The seasonal analysis of the number of visitors of the historical museum.
(6) The climatic analysis of the number of visitors of the historical museum.

4   Data Analysis

4.1   Data Collection

In order to answer the six questions, two datasets have been collected. The first data is the statistics of museum visitors from January 2022 to September 2022. Thus, the data can be used for the seasonal analysis of museum visitors. The data are daily visitor statistics based on different visitor categories: ordinary visitors, ordinary group visitors, and student group visitors. The weather condition for each day is also collected in the dataset for climatic analysis. The data can be accessed via https://ppt.cc/fT1Yfx.

The second data set is collected by a questionnaire, which can be accessed via https://ppt.cc/f1sPtx. The main idea of the data is about the feedback of an exhibition from visitors. The impression of the Taiwan culture association when visitors visit the exhibition is also included in the questionnaire. In the dataset, the demographic data of visitors are also collected which can be used to answer the questions in the previous section.

4.2   Results of Data Analysis

In the following subsections, the collected data will be analyzed by using appropriate data analysis techniques. We will provide some insights for each analysis to explain the data analysis results and answer the questions.

Do Visitors Who Like Historical Relics Also Like Digital Media? From the data analysis results. 92% of the visitors agree that they like historical relics and 8% of visitors disagree. Among the visitors who like historical relics, 95% of the visitors also like digital media and only 5% dislike digital media. Table 1 shows the results of the visitors who like historical relics, and Table 2 shows the results of the visitors who like historical relics and digital media.

Historical relics are the soul of historical museums. Therefore, the visitors usually hope they can see actual historical relics, not only photos and text or digital media. This exhibition presented historical relics and digital media, including

Table 1. The percentage of visitors who like historical relics

Total samples	Agree	Disagree
572	531	41
100%	92%	8%

Table 2. The percentage of visitors who like historical relics also love digital media

Total samples	Agree	Disagree
531	505	26
100%	95%	5%

photos, diagrams, graphs, videos, illustrators, audio, interactive digital media, etc. From the result, we can learn that an exhibition with a combination style (historical relics and digital media) is an ideal one that is acceptable for most visitors and expected more visitors can be attracted.

The Demographics of the Visitors Who Like Historical Relics Including Age, Gender, Education and Visiting Motivations. Table 3 shows the

Table 3. The demographics analysis of museum visitors

Gender	Male	160	30%
	Female	363	68%
	Unspecific	8	2%
Age	Under 12	63	12%
	12–18	51	10%
	18–35	205	38%
	35–55	181	34%
	Above 55	31	6%
Education	Primary School	61	11%
	Junior High School	25	5%
	Senior High School	48	9%
	Bachelor	241	45%
	Master	135	25%
	Ph.D	21	5%
Motivation	Pass By	151	28%
	Interested in Taiwan History	262	49%
	Recommended By Friends/Family	113	21%
	Other	5	2%

demographics analysis of the data. Demographics analysis is easy data analysis. However, the result is always of interest in the questionnaire. From the result, the ratio of females and males is about 7:3, where the ratio of males to fill the form is lower than the normal museum visitors ratio (6:4). About age and education, due to the content of the exhibition is a little bit difficult to understand, 84% of the visitors' education is higher than senior high school, and 79% of the visitors' age is between 18–55. It shows the significant visitors of this exhibition, and the knowledge can be used for future exhibition marketing and promotion.

Does the Exhibition Positively Improve the Understanding of Taiwan Culture Association? The analysis result of the question is shown in Table 4. From the result, 94% (536 visitors) of the visitors agree that the exhibition improves the understanding of the Taiwan Culture Association. It means the main idea of the exhibition is achieved. Only about 6% (36 visitors) of the visitors disagree that the exhibition is helpful for the understanding of the Taiwan Culture Association. This knowledge can also be used in the future to curate related exhibitions.

Table 4. The percentage of visitors who understand more of Taiwan Culture Association after visiting the museum

Total samples	Agree	Disagree
572	536	36
100%	94%	6%

Does the Exhibition Inspire the Motivation to Understand Taiwan Culture Association? The analysis result is shown in Table 5. In Table 5, 90% (513 visitors) of the visitors agree that they have been inspired to understand more about Taiwan Culture Associating after visiting the exhibition. Only 10% (59 visitors) of the visitors disagree about this. From the feedback comments from visitors, they are interested to understand more about not only the association but also Taiwan history. Some visitors even think the exhibition can be treated as the supplement material in addition to the textbook.

Table 5. The percentage of visitors who has been inspired to understand Taiwan Culture Association after visiting the museum

Total samples	Agree	Disagree
572	513	59
100%	90%	10%

The Seasonal Analysis of Number of Visitors of the Historical Museum. The seasonal analysis is an interesting data analysis technique. In order to perform seasonal analysis, a long period of data must be collected. Usually, the period should be longer than three months. Seasonal analysis can help us discover interesting knowledge with an extended data monitoring period. In this paper, we collected data from about nine months and used the data for seasonal analysis about the number of visitors in other months.

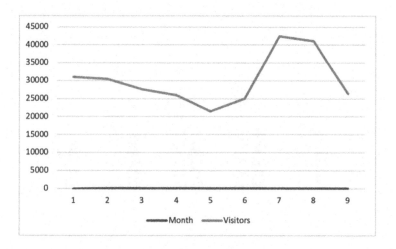

Fig. 5. Seasonal analysis of number of museum visitors.

The analysis result presented in Fig. 6 shows that the number of visitors is high during the summer vacation period and drops down very fast right after summer vacation. January and February are the months of winter vacation and the Lunar new year period, which is lower than the summer vacation period but higher than other months. This finding benefits the curator and the museum in curating and scheduling the exhibitions. For example, some popular exhibitions may consider arranging in lower seasons to attract more visitors. During peak season, the museum may need more volunteer workers and better traffic control strategies. After practicing the knowledge, the museum can consider collecting data continuously for the next round of data analysis.

The Climatic Analysis of Number of Visitors of the Historical Museum. The climatic analysis is not a usual data analysis technique. In order to perform climatic analysis, the climatic data must be collected first each day. Another way to do this is to adopt open weather data. The climatic analysis is another critical analysis for museums to predict the number of visitors. The climatic analysis result is shown in Fig. 5.

From the result, whether it is a weekday or a holiday, a sunny day is a day that most visitors visit the museum. Then, the second is partly cloudy on weekdays, but the second one on holidays is rainy. On a sunny day, most visitors visit the museum because the museum is an air-conditioned place where visitors prefer to stay indoors to enjoy the cold air. For holidays, rainy days have the second highest number of visitors because indoor activity is better than an outdoor activity. Climatic analysis is essential knowledge for museums. The museum can expect the number of visitors and provide appropriate service and strategy accordingly.

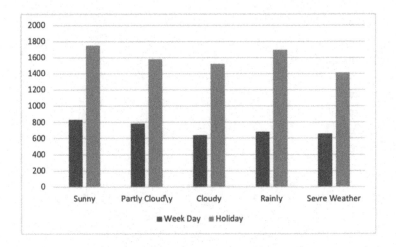

Fig. 6. The climatic analysis result.

Fig. 7. Text cloud analysis graph of museum visitors' comments (In traditional Chinese characters).

In addition to answering the six questions, we also do a so-called text-cloud analysis to analyze the comments from visitors' comments. The text-cloud analysis is a fashion and visualization way for text analysis. However, it is a challenging data analysis technique. First, all the comments need to be pre-processed by word segmentation, a natural language processing technique. After word segmentation, the frequency of each word will be counted. Finally, visualization techniques will be used to visualize words according to the frequency, such as the words' location, the words' size, and the color of the words in the text cloud.

Figure 7 is the text cloud analysis graph of museum visitors' comments, which is presented in traditional Chinese characters. The most central and biggest word is "Exhibition" and then "History," "Like," Great," "Culture Association," "diligently," and "Design". From the visualized graph, it is easy and quick to know the most important words used in the visitors' comments. The comments are very optimistic that the visitors like the exhibition a lot and the museum can also understand the important focuses of visitors.

5   Conclusion and Future Research Suggestions

In this paper, we propose a combination model of knowledge management and visitor relationship management for historical museums. The proposed visitor relationship management is a modified model based on traditional customer relationship management. In the new model, we introduce a new focus, "content," in visitor relationship management and keep data analysis as the most crucial role of the model.

In order to demonstrate the proposed new model, six questions have been raised that cover the process of knowledge management and visitor relationship management. Two data sets are collected for answering the questions, and appropriate data analysis techniques were used to analyze the data for answering the six questions. The data analysis results have been presented in the paper and explained. Suggestions about how to put the discovered knowledge into practice for museums to attract more visitors are also provided in the paper.

Future research is suggested to focus on each element in the model and the process to discuss how to apply the model in museum-related studies. In this paper, we only proposed the model and demonstrated an example. However, many studies and researchers are of interest in the area of museum study. There are also many possible future research directions about data analysis techniques in the area of knowledge and visitor relationship management in museum study. For example, there are few types of research on social network analysis for museums and social media marketing. Some machine learning and AI-related data analysis techniques are also worth trying for museum data analysis.

References

1. Annis, A.: The Museum as a staging ground for symbolic action. Mus. Int. **38**(3), 151–168, 168–171 (1986)

2. Bitgood, S., Shettel, H.: An overview of visitor studies. J. Mus. Educ. **21**(3), 6–10 (1996)
3. Falk: A framework for diversifying museum audience. Mus. News **77**(5), 36–39, 61 (1998)
4. Falk, J.H., Dierking, L.D.: Lessons Without Limit: How Free-Choice Learning is Transforming Education, p. 189. Altamira Press, Walnut Creek (2002)
5. Hein, G.: Learning in the Museum, p. 3. Routledge, London (1998)
6. Hooper-Greenhill, E.: Museums and Their Visitors, 1st edn. Routledge (1994). https://doi.org/10.4324/9780203415160
7. Marty, P.F., Soren, B.J., Armstrong, J.: Building community among museum information professionals: a case study of the Museum Computer Network. Mus. Manag. Curatorship **28**(4), 394–412 (2013)
8. Moore, K.: Museum and Popular Culture, p. vii. Leicester University Press (2000)
9. Sanchez, R.: Strategic Learning and Knowledge Management. Wiley, Chichester (1996)
10. Sheng, C.W., Chen, M.C.: A study of experience expectations of museum visitors. Tour. Manag. **33**(1), 53–60 (2012). https://doi.org/10.1016/j.tourman.2011.01.023
11. Siu, N.Y.M., Zhang, T.J.F., Dong, P., Kwan, H.Y.: New service bonds and customer value in customer relationship management: the case of museum visitors. Tour. Manag. **36**(2013), 293–303 (2013). https://doi.org/10.1016/j.tourman.2012.12.001
12. Ting, I.-H.: Applications and management aspects of social networks research. Rev. Socionetwork Strat. **16**, 571–572 (2022). https://doi.org/10.1007/s12626-022-00130-y
13. Ting, I.-H.: Developing analytic talent: becoming a data scientist. Online Inf. Rev. **39**(2), 273 (2015). https://doi.org/10.1108/OIR-01-2015-0012
14. Wielinga, B., Sandberg, J., Schreiber, G.: Methods and techniques for knowledge management: what has knowledge engineering to offer? Expert Syst. Appl. **13**(1), 73–84 (1997)

Information and Knowledge Systems

The Use of No-Code Platforms in Startups

Sebastian Brühl, Reinhard Bernsteiner(✉) ⓘ, Christian Ploder ⓘ, Thomas Dilger ⓘ, and Teresa Spiess ⓘ

Department Management, Communication & IT, Management Center Innsbruck, Innsbruck, Austria
reinhard.bernsteiner@mci.edu

Abstract. One of the most critical challenges for startups is to find a market need for their product or service. The business idea has to provide a genuine solution to an existing problem to be successful. Limited resources, time pressure, and often fierce competition are typical conditions for startups. In software development, no-code platforms have emerged in the last few years. These kinds of tools have the potential to speed up software development and thus reduce time to market.

Due to its novelty, existing literature does not extensively discuss the use of no-code tools and platforms used by startups. The central aim of this paper is to give a broad overview and first insights into the usage and attitudes of startups using no-code tools. Empirical research was conducted by applying a quantitative approach to achieve this aim. A total of 120 data sets were collected and analyzed.

The results show that no-code tools are commonly used in startups. The most crucial advantage of no-code tools is the reduction of the development time of apps compared to traditional software development tools and approaches. Limited functionalities and limited possibilities to customize the developed app to the Startup's needs was the most critical disadvantage.

Keywords: No-code Platform · Software Development · Lean Startup · Startup Learning Stage · Empirical Research

1 Introduction

Software development platforms are around for several years and require profound programming knowledge to create new software. In contrast, no-code development platforms lower these requirements for the user to abstract and logical thinking [1], offering the ability to develop software for various people without the need to write a single line of code. This new way of developing software promises several advantages to its users, including the ability to create applications at a much faster pace and reduced cost without needing skilled programmers [2, 3].

As newly established organizations, startups seek a sustainable and scalable business model [4, 5]. The main challenges for these young ventures are uncertainty, the lack of resources, and time pressure [6]. Not being bound by legacy systems or the constraints of previous working experiences, startups can utilize the newest development tools and

L. Uden and I-H. Ting (Eds.): KMO 2023, CCIS 1825, pp. 289–301, 2023.
https://doi.org/10.1007/978-3-031-34045-1_24

technologies to quickly take advantage of new business and market opportunities [7, 8]. Further, no-code tools and platforms could support startups' efforts to use lean and agile methods to quickly validate their product in the market [7].

No-code platforms can help to develop minimal viable products and get customer feedback quickly. The generated feedback is then evaluated to conclude the organization's further course of action [4, 9]. To assess this assumption, this paper explores startups' usage and attitudes regarding no-code platforms.

The second section of the paper presents the theoretical background, which is the basis for the empirical part. The following section provides the problem statement along with the research design. In section four, the results are presented. Section five summarizes the research project and discusses the results. The paper ends with limitations and ideas for further research.

The contribution of this paper is threefold. First, the practical contribution of this work is based on the collection, analysis, and presentation of primary data. A quantitative approach was applied to get insights into the usage and attitude of startups towards no-code tools on a broader basis. All valid responses come from startups using those tools in their companies. They are not providers or consultants of no-code platforms. Second, the paper contributes to a theoretical understanding of application development with no-code platforms since literature forms the basis for this empirical research. Some results, in turn, may provide new research streams, which are not yet comprehensively covered. Third, the methodology used for this research project is suitable for reaching the project's aim. Getting answers from people who apply no-code platforms allows for valid responses from the field.

2   Theoretical Background

The following section lays out the theoretical background of no-code platforms and startups.

2.1   No-Code Platforms

Historically, programmers have always sought a higher level of abstraction to make the software development process faster [10]. No-code bypasses the classical step of programming and thus enables visual software development [11].

No-code is visual software development using so-called no-code tools and platforms [12]. As the name suggests, problems are solved visually - without writing code [3, 11]. No-code tools and platforms allow the software to be created via a graphical user interface with intuitive usability and design [10, 11, 13]. The user selects from existing software components and develops their application per drag & drop. These components are either reusable building blocks or complete applications [12]. No-code does not mean that no code is applied. However, it is not visible to the user and is only executed via the user interface [14]. Therefore, no-code enables people with little or no programming experience to design, create and launch their custom applications [15].

Literature reports about benefits (less development time, lower development costs, easy to understand or handle, ability to use citizen developers, quicker change management) as well as disadvantages (limited functionality, limited customization, security issues, vendor lock-in, GDPR compliance, scalability, and performance) [3, 12, 16–18]. The two lists present the most often mentioned aspects in literature.

2.2 Startups

The term "startup" has been defined in various scientific studies, yet there is no clear, universally accepted definition of what constitutes a startup. A startup is a founded company that seeks a repeatable and scalable business model in uncertain market conditions. A new business formation alone does not define a company as a startup [7]. Instead, startups strive to solve a problem through a new product or service that is not yet known or developed. In a market characterized by uncertainty, the goal is to achieve rapid growth. As newly founded companies, startups typically operate with limited resources and try to validate their business model [19].

Many startups fail due to the significant challenges of finding a sustainable and prosperous business model [20]. Business Planning describes the classical approach of existing or future companies, in which all key stakeholders come together to work out the company's vision, objectives, and goals.

Business planning is assumed to positively affect a company's success [21, 22]. According to [21], this effect of planning is also positive but noticeably more significant for existing companies than for newly founded startups. Another critical point in traditional business planning is the lack of customer feedback during compartmentalized product or service development. This can lead to the fact that nobody wants or needs the developed product after long, expensive development of sometimes several months or years [4].

Due to the specific needs of a startup, the concept of Lean Startup has been developed. Lean Startup describes an iterative and customer-centric approach for startups and enterprises. The main goal of a Lean Startup is to reduce the waste of time and money and to find a repeatable and scalable business model. This can be achieved when a product or service is developed that the customer genuinely needs and creates value [23]. Gather customer feedback and make this data measurable to draw the correct conclusions for further action. Minimal viable products are built and tested in the Lean Startup approach [9]. A minimal viable product represents a product's earliest and most straightforward version [24]. A minimal viable product consists of only the most minimal but most core features and still has value and utility to customers. Minimal viable products are a way to learn from customers [9] and can be used to evaluate central business model assumptions to reduce the risk for failure in further stages of product development and can therefore reduce the waste of time and resources [25].

Learning from customer feedback can be divided into the phases of problem definition, problem validation, solution definition, and solution validation [26]. Besides this customer-centric view, the product goes through different maturity phases: concept, in development, working prototype, functional product with limited users, functional prototype with high growth, and finally, mature product [26].

2.3 Business Planning and Lean Startups

Business Planning describes the classical approach of existing or future companies, in which all key stakeholders come together to work out the company's vision, objectives, and goals. Strategies and tactics are formulated, which should be pursued to achieve the established aims. All potential relevant influencing parameters are considered, and forecasts for the future are prepared [27, 28]. It is assumed that business planning positively affects a company's success [21, 22]. According to [21], this effect of planning is also positive but noticeably more significant for existing companies than newly founded startups. There are three reasons for this impact. Existing companies have reference values and information on to base further planning. This is not the case for startups with no history of operating in the market. These newly founded companies also lack structures and procedures that support planning. Likewise, the high degree of uncertainty makes it challenging to plan far-reaching strategic measures in the early stages of companies [21].

Another critical point in traditional business planning is the lack of customer feedback during compartmentalized product or service development. This can lead to the fact that after long, expensive development of sometimes several months or years, nobody wants or needs the developed product [4]. Lean Startup describes an iterative and customer-centric approach for startups and enterprises. The main goal of Lean Startup is to reduce the waste of time and money and to find a repeatable and scalable business model. This can be achieved when a product or service is developed that the customer genuinely needs and creates value [4, 23].

According to the Lean Startup approach, startups start with a set of untested hypotheses and go through a continuous feedback loop where ideas are materialized, and feedback and data are collected and evaluated. From these validated learnings, conclusions are drawn for further product development and strategy of the company. This is to prevent activities that do not add value and to promote those that do and, therefore, reduce the waste of resources [23]. As mentioned before, no-code platforms offer benefits that promote the fast development of working prototypes.

3   Problem Definition and Research Design

This research aims to get a broad overview of the usage and attitudes of no-code platforms in startups. A quantitative research method was applied to achieve the central aim of this research. The questionnaire questions were derived deductively from the literature presented in the theoretical background of this paper. The questionnaire was distributed online. All in all, 120 valid responses were collected.

The first section of the questionnaire consists of an introduction that briefly offers an overview of the survey and a filter question to ensure that only startups participate. In the second section, general questions about the company are asked. The founding year as well as the number of employees are gathered. The third section contains questions about the usage of no-code tools and platforms. The organizations are asked about the perceived advantages and disadvantages of using those tools and platforms. Further, questions about their current and future usage are posed.

4 Results

In this section, the startups that took part in this survey are described followed by an analysis about the usage and attitudes of no-code platforms.

4.1 Description of the Participants

The questionnaire was first distributed to friends and acquaintances, who have founded themselves or work in a startup. Additionally, over 500 emails with the link to the questionnaire were sent to startups. All contacted startups were listed on Startbasee.de. Startbase.de is a database on which over 7000 German startups are featured.

Of the 120 startups surveyed, 42 organizations were founded in 2021. This represents the largest group (Table 1). The oldest Startup was founded in 2012, while five organizations were founded in 2022, which is the most recent time of the founding.

Table 1. Foundation Year

Year Founded	%
2012	0.83%
2016	1.67%
2017	4.17%
2018	13.33%
2019	15.83%
2020	25.00%
2021	35.00%
2022	4.17%

On average, the 120 surveyed organizations have 8.68 employees. The minimum number of employees within the organization is one, while the maximum is 80. Noticeably, most startups have between 1 and 5 employees. This accounts for a total of 61,7% of the startups surveyed. Most startups have three employees. This makes up 15% of the sample size N = 120.

Most startups are indicated to be in the highest possible learning phase, called Solution Validation (Table 2). The second largest group finds itself in the second highest learning phase, Solution Definition. Both groups represent in total 92.5% of the 120 startups surveyed.

52.5% of the 120 startups have a functional product with limited users (Table 3). This represents the largest group regarding the development stages of the main product. A cumulative 17.5% of startups are in an earlier development stage from concept to functioning prototype. 30% of startups either generate a high growth rate with their functional product or already have a mature product.

Table 2. Learning Stages – Number of Companies

Learning Stage	N	%
Problem definition	3	2.5%
Problem validation	6	5.0%
Solution definition	36	30.0%
Solution validation	75	62.5%

Table 3. Software Development Stages – Number of Companies

Development Stage	N	%
Concept	3	2.5%
In development	8	6.7%
Working prototype	10	8.3%
Functional product with limited users	63	52.5%
Functional product with high growth	26	21.6%
Mature product	10	8.3%

108 startups provided feedback on how often they make structural changes to their website/app (Table 4). 34.26% of the startups change their website/app monthly. Followed by this, 25.9% implement changes quarterly.

Table 4. Website or App Changes

Frequency	N	%
Daily	51	4.6%
Weekly	19	24.1%
Monthly	3	34.3%
Quarterly	3	25.9%
Project-wise	19	9.3%
Never	2	1.9%

4.2 Usage of No-Code Platforms in Startups

In the third part of the questionnaire, data on the use of no-code tools and platforms in startups was gathered. 89 out of the 120 startups, representing 74.2% of the organizations surveyed, used no-code tools and platforms before. In contrast, 24 of the organizations, which is 20.0% of the respondents, did not use any of these tools and platforms. 70% of the 120 startups indicated they would use these tools and platforms in the future. 10.8% of the organizations would not use them in the future, while 19.2% would consider using these tools and platforms in the future.

Next, the usage frequency of no-code in startups was queried (Table 5). The evaluation of this question shows that 42.5%, representing the largest group, use the tools and platforms daily. Other results show that 15.8% use the tools and platforms weekly or project-wise, while 20% never use them. In total, 96 startups, or 80%, use these tools actively within their organization.

Table 5. Usage Frequency of No-Code Tools and Platforms

Frequency	N	%
Daily	51	42.5%
Weekly	19	15.8%
Monthly	3	2.5%
Quarterly	3	2.5%
Yearly	1	0.8%
Project-wise	19	15.8%
Never	24	20.0%

Furthermore, startups were asked about the benefits they associate with no-code tools and platforms (Table 6). Several predefined answers were possible to this question. 73,3% of the startups surveyed stated that less development time was seen as an advantage of using no-code tools and platforms. This associated benefit thus represents the largest group. The associated lower development costs follow the time advantage through the use of no-code tools and platforms, with 57.5% of organizations surveyed. 54,2% of the 120 startups state ease of use as an advantage of these tools and platforms. Increased flexibility (45%), shorter release cycles (40.8%), and improved collaboration (30%) follow. Finally, 25% of startups said they see easier change management using no-code tools and platforms. In comparison, 20% see the facilitation of in-house development, and 12.5% see the possible use of citizen developers as an advantage of these tools and platforms. It should also be emphasized that 11.7% stated that they do not see any benefits in using no-code, while 5.8% perceive other unlisted advantages.

In addition to the advantages, startups were also asked about the disadvantages they associate with no-code tools and platforms (Table 7). Multiple answers were possible for this query. 57.5% of the startups surveyed stated that limited customization using no-code tools and platforms is seen as a disadvantage. This associated downside thus represents the largest group. This drawback is followed by the associated limited functionality using such tools and platforms with 55% of the organizations surveyed. Another associated disadvantage is vendor lock-in, listed by 46.7%. 44.2% cited limited flexibility as a downside to using no-code tools and platforms.

Table 6. Benefits of No-Code Tools and Platforms

Benefit	N	%	% of cases
Easier change management	30	6.7%	25.0%
Citizen developers	15	3.3%	12.5%
Do not see benefits	14	3.1%	11.7%
Easy to handle	65	14.4%	54.2%
Improved collaboration	36	8.0%	30.0%
Increased flexibility	54	12.0%	45.0%
In-house development	24	5.3%	20.0%
Less development time	88	19.5%	73.3%
Lower development costs	69	15.3%	57.5%
Other	7	1.6%	5.8%
Shorter release cycles	49	10.9%	40.8%

Furthermore, GDPR compliance (33.3%), not being the owner of the source code (27.5%) as well as security issues (23.3%) were stated as drawbacks. It should also be emphasized that 9.2% stated they do not see any disadvantages in using no-code. Eight startups see other unlisted weaknesses, and four organizations each see increased development costs and development time as negatives.

Table 7. Disadvantages of No-Code Tools and Platforms

Disadvantage	N	%	% of cases
Do not see downsides	11	3.0%	9.2%
GDPR compliance	40	10.8%	33.3%
Increased development costs	4	1.1%	3.3%
Increased development time	4	1.1%	3.3%
Limited customization	69	18.5%	57.5%
Limited flexibility	53	14.2%	44.2%
Limited functionality	66	17.7%	55.0%
Other	8	2.2%	6.7%
Security issues	28	7.5%	23.3%
Not owner of source code	33	8.9%	27.5%
Vendor lock-in	56	15.1%	46.7%

The last question regarding no-code use in startups identified the tools and platforms most often used by organizations (Table 8). Typeform was used most frequently by 43 startups, representing 35.8% of the 120 organizations. This was followed by Notion (33.3%), Zapier (29.2%), Shopify (27.5%), Webflow (24.2%), Linktree (20%), and Airtable (15%). 38 startups, representing 31.7%, used tools and platforms not listed in the survey. In addition, 28 organizations, thus 23.3%, did not use a no-code tool or platform before.

Table 8. Used Tools and Platforms

Tool and Platform	N	%	% of cases
Adalo	2	0,6%	1,7%
Airtable	18	5,5%	15,0%
Bravo Studio	3	0,9%	2,5%
Bubble	10	3,0%	8,3%
Coda	2	0,6%	1,7%
Glide	1	0,3%	0,8%
Landbot	1	0,3%	0,8%
Linktree	24	7,3%	20,0%
Make	7	2,1%	5,8%
Makerpad	2	0,6%	1,7%
Memberstack	6	1,8%	5,0%
Notion	40	12,1%	33,3%
Not used any no-code tool	28	8,5%	23,3%
Other	38	11,5%	31,7%
Outseta	3	0,9%	2,5%
Shopify	33	10,0%	27,5%
Stacker	1	0,3%	0,8%
Thunkable	2	0,6%	1,7%
Typeform	43	13,0%	35,8%
Voice flow	2	0,6%	1,7%
Webflow	29	8,8%	24,2%
Zapier	35	10,6%	29,2%

5 Summary and Discussion

The study results show that no-code tools and platforms are highly relevant for startups. 80% of the 120 organizations surveyed actively use no-code tools and platforms. 58.3% of the surveyed ventures use no-code daily or weekly. Further, it was necessary to clarify which advantages and disadvantages startups associate with using no-code tools and platforms. Two dominant advantages could be identified.

Most often, the shortened development time of applications was stated by 73.3% of the organizations surveyed. No-code users create applications visually via drag & drop using pre-existing, reusable software components [12, 16, 17]. This shortens development time compared to traditional software development and thus leads to shorter release cycles. As a result, ideas can be validated more quickly [3, 11, 17].

Startups can use no-code tools and platforms to reduce the two main limiting factors, time and money, in the application development process compared to traditional software development. The tools and platforms promote agile development and lead to a faster validation of ideas. The short release cycles allow minimal viable products to be created, tested, and adapted faster at a lower cost. The use of no-code tools and platforms combined with the Lean Startup approach can lead to faster and more cost-effective validation of a sustainable and scalable business model. The fact that 80% of the startups surveyed actively use these tools and platforms demonstrates no-code relevance for startups.

Disadvantages also contrast the advantages of using no-code tools and platforms. As identified by startups, four significant weaknesses in the use of no-code can be derived from the survey results.

57.5% of the 120 organizations surveyed stated limited customization as the main disadvantage. Due to the predefined building blocks and limiting templates, the individuality and customization of the applications suffer. This leads to limited flexibility of what can be built [13, 17, 29].

55% of startups cited limited functionality as the second biggest downside of using these tools and platforms. The level of customization, features, and complexity of what can be built depends on the no-code tool or platform selected. While no-code use promotes agile development without a clearly defined end product, the requirements should still be defined and considered before choosing a tool or platform. Only if a tool or platform meets these requirements, the tool or platform should be used. This prevents potential problems and costs later on if functionality is required that is not available with the selected tool or platform [3, 12].

33.3% of the 120 organizations surveyed indicated that GDPR compliance is one of the main disadvantages of no-code. The ECJ's ruling and the associated expiration of the EU-US Privacy Shield agreement in July 2020 have implications for personal data processing in the EU. Most no-code providers host their applications in the US, and as soon as personal data is processed, used in the EU is thus prohibited [30].

Before starting the development of applications, the advantages and disadvantages, and requirements for the respective platforms, should be evaluated. It must be clarified whether the use of no-code tools and platforms adds value in the corresponding use case. Subsequently, which tool or platform is best suited for the use case must be clarified. This reduces the risk of a potential waste of resources during development.

6   Limitations and Future Research Opportunities

The research followed a quantitative approach. Expert interviews could have provided a basis for the lack of scientific research that is still scarce in the field of no-code. With future research, the focus should lie more on general findings over no-code as an approach to software development since the topic was hardly addressed from a scientific point of view so far. A limitation of the work is, therefore, the lack of scientific literature. One limitation represents the differences in the sample sizes concerning the frequency of use of no-code tools and platforms.

For further research, a comparison between startups that use no-code and those that do not would be an exciting research field. Furthermore, research on the different learning stages of startups would be interesting. It needs to be clarified for which groups and learning stage no-code tools and platforms are particularly relevant. It would be intriguing to see if there are differences in the usage behavior of these groups and if a higher learning stage and validation of the Startup's business model results in a system change away from no-code to coded custom software.

For further research, it would also be interesting to see how no-code as a way of creating software affects companies already existing for a longer time (non-startups). It would be intriguing to compare the usage behavior and the associated advantages and disadvantages between these organizations and startups. An additional research field is the comparison of no-code usage behavior of startups from different industries. Financial aspects, e.g. cost savings by using no-code platforms compared to traditional tools need to be investigated as well.

References

1. Moskal, M.: No-code application development on the example of Logotec App Studio platform. Informatyka, Automatyka, Pomiary w Gospodarce i Ochronie Środowiska (2021). https://doi.org/10.35784/iapgos.2429
2. Sanchis, R., García-Perales, Ó., Fraile, F., Poler, R.: Low-code as enabler of digital transformation in manufacturing industry. Appl. Sci. (2020).https://doi.org/10.3390/app10010012
3. England, S.: What is no code? The pros and cons of no code for software development. https://codebots.com/low-code/what-is-no-code-the-pros-and-cons-of-no-code-for-sof tware-development (2020). Accessed 10 Jan 2023
4. Blank, S.: Why the lean start-up changes everything. https://hbr.org/2013/05/why-the-lean-start-up-changes-everything (2013). Accessed 21 July 2022
5. Nguyen-Duc, A., Kemell, K.-K., Abrahamsson, P.: The entrepreneurial logic of startup software development: a study of 40 software startups. Empir. Softw. Eng. 26(5), 1–55 (2021). https://doi.org/10.1007/s10664-021-09987-z
6. Unterkalmsteiner, M., et al.: Software startups - a research agenda. E-Inform. Softw. Eng. J. (2016).https://doi.org/10.5277/e-Inf160105
7. Giardino, C., Unterkalmsteiner, M., Paternoster, N., Gorschek, T., Abrahamsson, P.: What do we know about software development in startups? IEEE Softw. (2014).https://doi.org/10.1109/MS.2014.129
8. Klotins, E., Unterkalmsteiner, M., Gorschek, T.: Software engineering in start-up companies: an analysis of 88 experience reports. Empir. Softw. Eng. 24(1), 68–102 (2018). https://doi.org/10.1007/s10664-018-9620-y
9. Ries, E.: The lean startup: how today's entrepreneurs use continuous innovation to create radically successful business. Currency (2011)
10. Lugovsky, V.: A guide to low-code/no-code development platforms in 2021 (2021). https://www.forbes.com/sites/forbesbusinesscouncil/2021/07/30/a-guide-to-low-codeno-code-development-platforms-in-2021/?sh=79097d5e1093. Accessed 21 July 2022

11. Adkin, D.: The future is no-code (2020). https://www.adalo.com/the-future-is-no-code/con clusions. Accessed 21 July 2022
12. Yarchevsky, M.: Is a no-code platform right for your website or app project? (2021). https://www.forbes.com/sites/forbestechcouncil/2021/08/16/is-a-no-code-platform-right-for-your-website-or-app-project/?sh=6f8a8a2a29a6. Accessed 21 July 2022
13. Tariq, H.: Low-Code Versus No-Code And The Future Of Application Development. https://www.forbes.com/sites/forbescommunicationscouncil/2021/05/07/low-code-versus-no-code-and-the-future-of-application-development/?sh=376a5f9c3568 (2021). Accessed 21 July 2022
14. Aiyer, V.: Are no-code platforms making developers redundant? (2022). https://www.forbes.com/sites/forbestechcouncil/2022/03/14/are-no-code-platforms-making-developers-redund ant/?sh=4fa74bb2f4c9. Accessed 21 July 2022
15. Nead, N.: Will no-code development put software engineers out of work? (2022). https://www.forbes.com/sites/forbesbusinesscouncil/2022/01/05/will-no-code-development-put-software-engineers-out-of-work/?sh=3338816e4597. Accessed 21 July 2022
16. Ashok, A.: Low-code and no-code in 2021: are they as useful as they seem? (2021). https://www.forbes.com/sites/forbestechcouncil/2021/05/13/low-code-and-no-code-in-2021-are-they-as-useful-as-they-seem/?sh=4ec375b1160f. Accessed 21 July 2022
17. Krajewski, R.: The rise of no-code and low-code solutions: will your CTO become obsolete? (2021). https://www.forbes.com/sites/forbestechcouncil/2021/10/14/the-rise-of-no-code-and-low-code-solutions-will-your-cto-become-obsolete/. Accessed 21 July 2022
18. Bernsteiner, R., Schlögl, S., Ploder, C., Dilger, T., Brecher, F.: Citizen vs. professional develop-ers: differences and similarities of skills and training requirements for low code development platforms. In: Gómez Chova, L., López Martínez, A., Candel Torres, I. (eds.) ICERI2022 Proceedings. 15th annual International Conference of Education, Research and Innovation, Seville, Spain, 07.11.2022–08.11.2022, pp. 4257–4264. IATED (2022). https://doi.org/10.21125/iceri.2022.1036
19. Eisenmann, T., Ries, E., Dillard, S.: Hypothesis-Driven Entrepreneurship: The Lean Startup (2012)
20. Sharp, H., Hall, T. (eds.): XP 2016. LNBIP, vol. 251. Springer, Cham (2016). https://doi.org/10.1007/978-3-319-33515-5
21. Brinckmann, J., Grichnik, D., Kapsa, D.: Should entrepreneurs plan or just storm the castle? A meta-analysis on contextual factors impacting the business planning-performance relationship in small firms. J. Bus. Ventur. (2010).https://doi.org/10.1016/j.jbusvent.2008.10.007
22. Gruber, M.: Uncovering the value of planning in new venture creation: a process and contin-gency perspective. J. Bus. Ventur. (2007).https://doi.org/10.1016/j.jbusvent.2006.07.001
23. Frederiksen, D.L., Brem, A.: How do entrepreneurs think they create value? A scientific reflection of Eric Ries' Lean Startup approach. Int. Entrepreneurship Manag. J. 13(1), 169–189 (2016). https://doi.org/10.1007/s11365-016-0411-x
24. Contigiani, A., Levinthal, D.A.: Situating the construct of lean start-up: adjacent conversations and possible future directions (2019).https://doi.org/10.1093/icc/dtz013
25. Thompson, N.T.: Building a minimum viable product? You're probably doing it wrong. Harvard Business Review (2013). https://hbr.org/2013/09/building-a-minimum-viable-prod. Accessed 19 July 2022
26. Blank, S.: The four steps to the epiphany: successful strategies for products that win (2005)
27. Ward, S.: What is business planning? (2020). https://www.thebalancesmb.com/business-pla nning-definition-2947994. Accessed 21 July 2022
28. Friend, G., Zehle, S.: Guide to business planning. Economist books. Economist in association with Profile Books, London (2004)

29. Kiguolis, L.: 7 drawbacks of using no code for your product (2021). https://codeornocode. com/no-code/no-code-is-not-a-good-idea/. Accessed 21 July 2022
30. Neiazy, V.: Invalidation of the EU–US Privacy Shield: impact on data protection and data security regarding the transfer of personal data to the United States. Int. Cybersecur. Law Rev. 2(1), 27–35 (2021). https://doi.org/10.1365/s43439-021-00018-7

Software Sustainability Requirements for Knowledge Management Systems in the Cultural Heritage Domain

Tjaša Heričko$^{(\boxtimes)}$, Marjan Heričko , and Saša Brdnik

Faculty of Electrical Engineering and Computer Science, University of Maribor,
Koroška cesta 46, 2000 Maribor, Slovenia
{tjasa.hericko,marjan.hericko,sasa.brdnik}@um.si

Abstract. As technology continues to advance and become more integrated into our society, especially in the era of digital transformations, it is imperative that software engineering practices and products are sustainable. However, in the Cultural Heritage domain, sustainability is often overlooked, even though knowledge management solutions are essential for the long-term capture, preservation, and dissemination of cultural heritage in a digital form. This paper aims to address this gap by identifying the key sustainability requirements to consider when designing and developing sustainability-aware knowledge management software solutions for the Cultural Heritage sector. A survey was conducted among professionals with experience in digitizing and managing cultural heritage materials, including cultural heritage experts and software engineers. Despite some differences in the perceived importance of sustainability requirements between the two groups of professionals, the most important sustainability features were mainly agreed upon. The acknowledged requirements encompass features from both the social and technical dimensions of sustainability, such as Usefulness, Effectiveness, and Trust for the former and Maintainability, Functional Suitability, and Efficiency for the latter. The research results provide valuable insights into how domain experts and software engineers view software sustainability in the studied domain. The findings can aid the decision-making process for prioritizing requirements related to sustainability and can serve as recommendations for developing knowledge management information systems in the Cultural Heritage domain with sustainability in mind.

Keywords: Digitized Cultural Heritage · Knowledge Management · Cultural Heritage Information System · Requirements Engineering · Sustainable Software Engineering · Sustainability Requirements

1 Introduction

Digital transformation, driven by advancements in technology, has become a prerequisite for organizations in all sectors to adapt to the digital era and take

L. Uden and I-H. Ting (Eds.): KMO 2023, CCIS 1825, pp. 302–313, 2023.
https://doi.org/10.1007/978-3-031-34045-1_25

advantage of new opportunities in the digital landscape. The Cultural Heritage domain is not exempt from this transformation, having embraced the adoption of digital technologies increasingly in recent decades [17]. Cultural heritage is the legacy of society's objects, both tangible and intangible, representing a major part of society's history, customs, identity, and cultural beliefs [1,6]. Through digitization, cultural heritage objects, e.g., historical artifacts, monuments, and audio-visual materials, are captured, preserved, and disseminated in digital form, which provides the opportunity to transfer the analog information of the cultural heritage objects in question into the digital environment [6]. This analog-to-digital conversion has the potential to benefit many cultural heritage stakeholders. For instance, it helps in conserving cultural heritage for future generations, providing online access to cultural heritage materials for both domain experts and the general public, accelerating active participation in knowledge acquisition, and promoting and commercializing cultural heritage [1,6,17].

As Information Technology plays a critical role in capturing, managing, safeguarding, and disseminating cultural heritage content, software researchers have devoted considerable effort to the digitization of cultural heritage and knowledge management of digitized cultural heritage. Many research endeavors have focused on overcoming the technical, ethical, and social challenges associated with designing and developing cultural heritage knowledge management systems. In this work, we define such a system as any information system that can gather, store, process, and distribute knowledge related to cultural heritage, to support the management of knowledge within a cultural heritage community or on a societal level. Typically, such a system supports knowledge management for a particular cultural heritage organization, while knowledge contained within the system is accessible to the general public. Europeana [9,16], Modmapng [11], and Verbo-Visuale Virtuale [8] are some examples of such systems with common functionalities that include the support for knowledge creation, storage, organization, search, and collaboration. Some specifics of knowledge management systems for the Cultural Heritage domain make such systems particularly relevant to research, namely, data heterogeneity (e.g., text, audio, video, three-dimensional models) [10], limited funding not sufficient for continuing software maintenance [1,5,17], and long-term accessibility of the knowledge contained within the systems to preserve cultural heritage for future generations [1].

In light of the impacts software systems can have on the environment, economy, society, and individuals, it is essential to take into account software sustainability when designing and developing such software. This, however, is rarely addressed in the literature. This paper attempts to fill this research gap and identify the key sustainability requirements for knowledge management solutions for digital content related to Cultural Heritage. To achieve this goal, a survey was conducted among professionals involved in digitizing cultural heritage. The most important technical and social features of software sustainability were defined based on the results. The acknowledged sustainability requirements can serve as guidelines for future knowledge management projects in the field. Given the challenges the domain faces, software development that adheres to the recognized sustainability requirements can result in more sustainable systems, which can reduce costs, extend the software's lifespan, improve long-term cultural heritage preservation, and promote sustainability-aware solutions. Thus, this research makes a new contribution by presenting a set of sustainability requirements specific to the Cultural Heritage domain that should be considered when designing and developing software to support knowledge management of cultural heritage.

The rest of the paper is divided into five sections. Section 2 provides an overview of the existing efforts to digitize cultural heritage and manage knowledge from the digitized cultural heritage. Section 3 introduces the notion of sustainability in software engineering. Section 4 presents the research design, followed by the results and discussion, reported in Sect. 5. Section 6 summarizes the findings and outlines future research directions.

2   Related Work

Technical Aspects. Information technologies have become a major driving force for the preservation and exploitation of cultural heritage. Haus [10] outlined the evolution of the role of information technologies with respect to cultural heritage. An overview of advances in cultural heritage digital processing and preservation described multiple dedicated software products for knowledge management in museums [5]. The digitization of cultural heritage is adapting well to new technologies; three-dimensional visualization and Virtual and Augmented Reality are often utilized. A specialized content management system dedicated to the Cultural Heritage domain with advanced functionalities, e.g., distributed storage capability and semantic query, has also been proposed [20]. Dragoni et al. [8] introduced a component-based architecture for knowledge management of cultural heritage to support ongoing curation activities and offer continuous access to virtual users. Huber et al. [11] presented experiences in the rapid development of an art history web portal. Best practices for web-based cultural heritage information management to facilitate the procedures for digital content management and aggregation were presented by Giannakoulopoulos et al. [9].

Social Aspects. Researchers use digitization for the long-term preservation of digital heritage. Museums expand their goals beyond preservation and generally make the collections accessible to larger audiences [5]. Government projects, such as Europeana, a digitized cultural heritage collection of more than 3,000 European institutions, share the same goal, to make cultural heritage accessible to everyone, all while addressing issues connected to information access inequality. The impact of Europeana on the digitization of cultural heritage for sustainable development in view of European Union goals has been analyzed in [16]. This work has been one of the first to address the relationship between the digitization of cultural heritage and sustainability. The cultural, economic, and social sustainability of digitization are analyzed in this domain. In a similar context, Bañuelos et al. [3] analyzed information management for sustainable conservation, and concluded that the availability of information and tools to support them is growing; however, additional progress is needed to support the interoperability, outreach, and reuse of different solutions. A historical lack of standardization and awareness about processes in the domain was also observed as a challenge.

Ethical Aspects. Cultural heritage is seen typically as being in the public domain; however, there are intellectual property-related issues that need to be considered with regard to its use. Research, documentation, and digitization projects on cultural values, as well as the production of academic and scientific works based on these projects, raise intellectual property difficulties. Borissova [6] analyzed the challenges and proposed a guide for intellectual property management along the process of digitization. Manžuch [17] focused on ethical issues in digitization, identifying multiple challenges also relevant in the Cultural Heritage Knowledge Management domain. Examples of the identified challenges include ease of sharing and manipulation of digital content, and privacy issues arising from the abundance of personal information in digitized cultural heritage documents.

3   Sustainable Software Engineering

Sustainable software engineering aims to produce long-lasting software products that meet the users' needs, while minimizing the direct and indirect negative impacts that the software may have on the economy, society, humans, and the environment during the development process or use of the software [2,7,19]. A sustainable software product can be produced only if the positive and negative impacts are considered adequately. This makes sustainability concerns manageable, and enables the professionals involved in the design and development of a software product to optimize their software product accordingly [19]. However, sustainability is a complex composite quality attribute. To promote the identification and analysis of sustainability requirements, Moreira et al. [18] proposed a configurable and reusable sustainability catalog of requirements. The catalog was created based on data acquired through a systematic mapping study, aligned further with the ISO/IEC quality model. It incorporates sustainability requirements worth considering for software products from both the technical and societal standpoints. The former refers to the longevity of software and its ability to adapt to changes in the environment in which a system operates, whilst the latter relates to society and the factors that undermine trust in communities [4]. In our research, the requirements of the proposed catalog served as the basis for identifying the requirements relevant to the domain under study. Table 1 presents and describes the social sustainability features taken under consideration in the study, and Table 2 presents and describes the technical sustainability features.

Table 1. Sustainability features of the social dimension, adopted from [18].

Feature	Definition
S1. Effectiveness	"Accuracy and completeness with which users achieve specified goals" [13]
S2. Accountability (Security)	"Degree to which the actions of an entity can be traced uniquely to the entity" [13]
S3. Authencity (Security)	"Degree to which the identity of a subject or resource can be proved to be the one claimed" [13]
S4. Confidentiality (Security)	"Degree to which data has attributes that ensure that it is only accessible and interpretable by authorized users in a specific context of use" [12]
S5. Integrity (Security)	"Degree to which a system, product or component prevents unauthorized access to, or modification of, computer programs or data" [13]
S6. Non-Repudiation (Security)	"Degree to which actions or events can be proven to have taken place, so that the events or actions cannot be repudiated later" [13]
S7. Trust (Satisfaction)	"Degree to which a user or other stakeholder has confidence that a product or system will behave as intended" [13]
S8. Usefulness (Satisfaction)	"Degree to which a user is satisfied with their perceived achievement of pragmatic goals, including the results of use and the consequences of use" [13]
S9. Pleasure (Satisfaction)	"Degree to which a user obtains pleasure from fulfilling their personal needs" [13]
S10. Comfort (Satisfaction)	"Degree to which the user is satisfied with physical comfort" [13]
S11. Efficiency	"Resources expended in relation to the accuracy and completeness with which users achieve goals" [13]
S12. Appropriateness Recognizability (Usability)	"Degree to which a product or system can be used by specified users to achieve specified goals with effectiveness, efficiency and satisfaction in a specified context of use" [13]
S13. Accessibility (Usability)	"Degree to which data can be accessed in a specific context of use, particularly by people who need supporting technology or special configuration because of some disability" [12]
S14. Environmental Risk Mitigation (Freedom From Risk)	"Degree to which a product or system mitigates the potential risk to property or the environment in the intended contexts of use" [13]
S15. Health and Safety Risk Mitigation (Freedom From Risk)	"Degree to which a product or system mitigates the potential risk to people in the intended contexts of use" [13]
S16. Legislation (Freedom From Risk)	Compliance with the laws and regulations [18]
S17. Interoperability (Compatibility)	"Degree to which two or more systems, products or components can exchange information and use the information that has been exchanged" [13]
S18. Co-existence (Compatibility)	"Degree to which a product can perform its required functions efficiently while sharing a common environment and resources with other products, without detrimental impact on any other product" [13]
S19. Fairness	Software quality of treating people equally or in a way that is reasonable, as well as being based on honesty [18]

Table 2. Sustainability features of the technical dimension, adopted from [18].

Feature	Definition
T1. Compatibility	"Degree to which a product, system or component can exchange information with other products, systems or components, and/or perform its required functions while sharing the same hardware or software environment" [13]
T2. Functional Suitability	"Degree to which a product or system provides functions that meet stated and implied needs when used under specified conditions" [13]
T3. Maintainability	"Degree of effectiveness and efficiency with which a product or system can be modified to improve it, correct it or adapt it to changes in environment, and in requirements" [13]
T4. Reliability	"Degree to which a system, product or component performs specified functions under specified conditions for a specified period of time" [13]
T5. Portability	"Degree of effectiveness and efficiency with which a system, product or component can be transferred from one hardware, software or other operational or usage environment to another" [13]
T6. Performance Efficiency	"This characteristic represents the performance relative to the amount of resources used under stated conditions" [13]
T7. Context Coverage	"Degree to which a product or system can be used with effectiveness, efficiency, freedom from risk and satisfaction in both specified contexts of use and in contexts beyond those initially explicitly identified" [13]
T8. Satisfaction	"Perception of the degree to which the customer's expectations have been fulfilled" [14]
T9. Effectiveness	"Accuracy and completeness with which users achieve specified goals" [15]
T10. Efficiency	"Resources expended in relation to the accuracy and completeness with which users achieve goals" [15]

4 Research Method

4.1 Research Objectives and Questions

The overall research goal of the study was to investigate the sustainability requirements and their relevance for knowledge management software in the domain of Cultural Heritage from the perspective of professionals working in this field. The research sought to find an answer to the following research question: *What social and technical sustainability requirements should be considered when developing knowledge management systems in the Cultural Heritage domain?*

4.2 Survey Design

A survey design was employed to address the research question. Data were gathered using a self-administered questionnaire. The sample of respondents consisted of 20 individuals; 13 participants were Cultural Heritage domain experts (referred to further as DE), with varying levels of experience in digitization and knowledge management of cultural heritage, and 7 participants were software engineers (referred to further as SE), who had been involved in the design and development of at least one knowledge management system in the Cultural Heritage domain. The questionnaire included demographic questions and questions related to social and technical sustainability requirements. The sustainability-related questions were designed to evaluate participants' opinions on the significance of social and technical sustainability features for knowledge management software in the domain under study. To measure the participants' perceptions, the participants were asked to rank the importance of each sustainability feature using a five-point Likert scale (Very Unimportant (1), Unimportant (2), Neither Important or Unimportant (3), Important (4), Very Important (5)).

4.3   Survey Response Analysis

Data gathered through the survey were analyzed using Python (v3.11.1). First, the survey results were analyzed based on the frequency distribution of responses, separately for DE and SE. Following that, the average rating for each feature was computed with respect to the responses provided by the DE and SE. In addition, a balanced average rating for each feature was computed, considering the DE and SE ratings equally, despite the different sample sizes. Finally, based on the average values, the highest-ranked features for each dimension were identified for each of the three groups. The Sørensen-Dice similarity coefficient was utilized to determine how much the resulting top-ranked features from the three groups overlapped. It was calculated as

$$Sim(A, B) = \frac{2 \times |A \cap B|}{|A| + |B|} \tag{1}$$

where $|A|$ represents the number of features in set A, $|B|$ represents the number of features in set B, and $|A \cap B|$ represents the number of features common to both sets. The coefficient value can range from 0 to 1. A coefficient value of 0 means that the two sets share no features, whereas a coefficient value of 1 means that the two sets contain exactly the same features.

5   Results and Discussion

The survey results, divided by the category of respondents, are presented in Fig. 1. Generally, there is a positive attitude towards most of the sustainability features from the view of both DE and SE. From the perspective of the former, Trust (69%) and Usefulness (69%) have the largest percentage of the highest importance in the social dimension, and Reliability (91%) and Functional Suitability (73%) in the technical dimension. In contrast, from the perspective of the latter, Effectiveness (86%) and Usefulness (86%) have the largest percentage of the highest importance in the social dimension, and Maintainability (86%) and Functional Suitability (71%) in the technical dimension. As Moreira et al. [18] have already stated, ideally, we desire a fully sustainable system. However, in most cases, selecting all sustainability features is not feasible, due to limited software project resources (e.g., time, budget, people), tight project schedules, and the lack of knowledge of the team and individuals. The most we can do is to maximize a subset of features to achieve partial sustainability. Hence, despite the expressed importance of the survey respondents towards all sustainability features, there is a need to identify a smaller set of the most important sustainability qualities in the domain based on the needs of the problem domain and stakeholders' preferences.

In Fig. 2, the average ratings for each sustainability feature are presented for social and technical sustainability. Some differences can be noticed between the perceived importance of sustainability features between the two groups of respondents. The biggest absolute difference in the average rating of social sustainability features between the two groups can be seen with Environmental Risk Mitigation ($Diff = 1.00$), Health and Safety Risk Mitigation ($Diff = 1.00$), Fairness ($Diff = 0.86$), and Confidentiality ($Diff = 0.75$). In all cases, the respondent belonging to DE assigned, on average, a higher importance to the observed feature than the respondent belonging to SE. The biggest absolute difference in the average rating of technical sustainability features between the two groups was observed for Performance Efficiency ($Diff = 1.49$), Compatibility ($Diff = 0.97$), and Context Coverage ($Diff = 0.84$). In all three cases, the respondent belonging to DE assigned, on average, a higher importance to the observed feature compared to the respondent belonging to SE. Observing the social features, the two groups had the most unified view on the importance of Appropriateness Recognizability, Trust, and Integrity ($Diff = 0.00$, $Diff = 0.04$, and $Diff = 0.10$, respectively). Observing technical features, the groups assigned the most unified importance to Functional Suitability, Effectiveness, and Maintainability ($Diff = 0.08$, $Diff = 0.08$, and $Diff = 0.13$, respectively). When ordering the nineteen social features based on average ratings, we identified major differences between the two groups in the perceived importance of Confidentiality (the 4th most important feature for DE, 14th for SE) and Accountability (11th for DE, 3rd for SE). Observing the perceived importance order of ten technical features, we identified the largest differences between the groups in the perceived importance of Efficiency (10th for DE, 3rd for SE) and Performance Efficiency (3rd for DE, 10th for SE). These differences might be due to the different perspectives of the professionals. Also, the differences might occur due to a poor understanding of sustainability requirements. More research is required to confirm or reject these assumptions.

The five highest-rated features for the social dimension, as recognized by DE, were Usefulness, Trust, Authenticity, Accessibility, and Confidentiality, while SE viewed Usefulness, Effectiveness, Trust, Accountability, and Efficiency as the most important for social sustainability in the domain. Based on a balanced average, the overall highest-rated features for social dimensions were Usefulness, Effectiveness, Trust, Authenticity, and Accountability. An overlap of three out of five features can be observed between the overall selection and the selection of the DE ($Sim = 0.6$), while an overlap of four out of five features can be observed between the overall selection and the selection of the SE ($Sim = 0.8$). The five most important technical sustainability features, as recognized by the DE, were Reliability, Maintainability, Functional Suitability, Performance Efficiency, and Compatibility, and, as recognized by the SE, Maintainability, Functional Suitability, Efficiency, Reliability, and Satisfaction. Based on a balanced average,

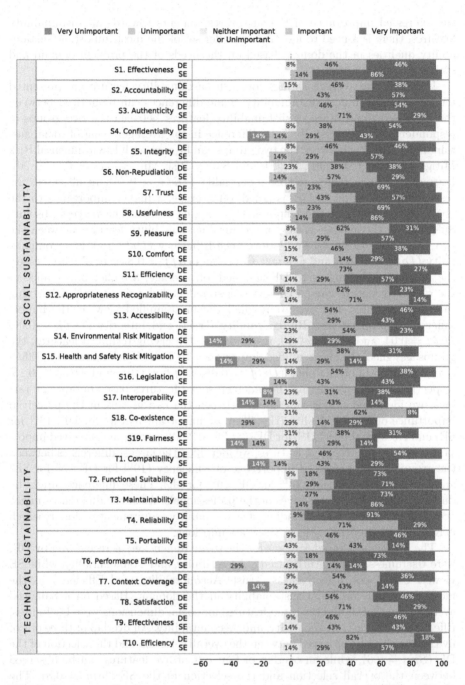

Fig. 1. Frequency distribution of survey responses of domain experts (DE) and software engineers (SE) on the perceived importance of social and technical sustainability features using a five-point Likert scale.

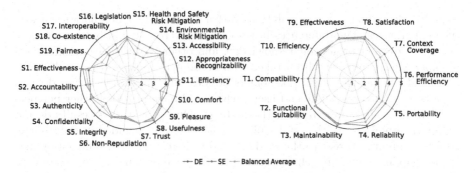

Fig. 2. The average rating for each social and technical sustainability feature, presented separately for domain experts (DE) and software engineers (SE), along with a balanced average of both categories of respondents.

the overall highest-rated features for technical dimensions were Maintainability, Functional Suitability, Efficiency, Reliability, and Satisfaction. Again, an overlap of three out of five features can be observed between the overall selection and the selection of the DE ($Sim = 0.6$), while a complete overlap of features can be observed between the overall selection and the selection of the SE ($Sim = 1.0$). Therefore, we argue that the selection of the sustainability requirements based on a balanced average of ratings from participants belonging to both groups is suitable enough to help in the choice of identifying relevant sustainability-related qualities based on the knowledge of professionals in the domain.

5.1   Implications for Researchers and Practitioners

The study offers valuable insights into how software engineers and domain experts view software sustainability in the Cultural Heritage domain. Researchers can utilize the study as a starting point for future research in the field. Following the identification of key sustainability requirements, additional research efforts are required to address them adequately. Practitioners can use the study's findings to make well-informed decisions, and prioritize sustainability requirements based on the perceptions of those in the field. The recognized requirements can serve as recommendations for designing and developing knowledge management systems in the Cultural Heritage domain, addressing the challenges posed by sustainability, and intending to impact sustainable development positively.

5.2   Validity Threats and Limitations

Several threats to the validity and limitations should be considered when interpreting and using the results and findings. The sample size used for the survey was relatively small, which hinders generalization. Despite this limitation, the small sample size was chosen to ensure that the results were representative of a focus group of professionals from the domain who have experience with knowledge management solutions rather than a larger population without such experiences. The differences in respondents were taken into consideration, i.e., their areas of professional knowledge, and other characteristics, e.g., years of experience, could have been taken into account to improve the results. The study did not include other stakeholders besides software engineers and domain experts, e.g., general public end-users, who could have provided other perspectives to the study and expanded the findings. Thus, the study's results do not reflect the opinions of other stakeholders who were not included in the sample. Another potential threat to the study's validity is related to misunderstandings by participants on what each sustainability feature represents. To mitigate this, clear definitions were provided for each sustainability feature, to ensure that participants understood them clearly. Despite this, there is still a risk of misunderstandings, particularly among domain experts who may not be familiar with the concepts. Furthermore, the study results are limited to software sustainability's social and technical dimensions, and rely on the sustainability requirement catalog used as a baseline.

6   Conclusion

With the growing importance of Information Technology in our society, the sustainability of software engineering practices and software products has become of major concern to support environmental, economic, and societal responsibility. However, despite the crucial role that knowledge management solutions play in the long-term capture, safeguarding, continuance, archiving, and promotion of cultural heritage in digital form, sustainability is considered rarely. This paper proposes a set of sustainability requirements for designing and developing sustainability-aware software in the Cultural Heritage domain. From the social dimension of sustainability, these features include Usefulness, Effectiveness, Trust, Authenticity, and Accountability. From the technical dimension of sustainability, these features include Maintainability, Functional Suitability, Efficiency, Reliability, and Satisfaction. These requirements were identified through a survey carried out among professionals with domain experience from two areas of expertise, i.e., domain experts and software engineers. The research findings can guide the development of knowledge management solutions for the Cultural Heritage domain from a sustainability perspective, especially since it has been noted that a lack of sufficient funding, long-term planning, awareness, and knowledge are the major obstacles to digitization in the domain. Future research efforts can be directed toward extending the sustainability requirements to include economic, environmental, and individual dimensions. Additionally, the viewpoints of other stakeholders in such knowledge management software solutions would provide additional insights. Furthermore, best practices and lessons learned from applying the requirements in real-world cases would be beneficial to the community.

Acknowledgements. The authors acknowledge the financial support from the Slovenian Research Agency (Research Core Funding No. P2-0057).

References

1. Adane, A., Chekole, A., Gedamu, G.: Cultural heritage digitization: challenges and opportunities. Int. J. Comput. Appl. **178**(33), 1–5 (2019)
2. Amsel, N., Ibrahim, Z., Malik, A., Tomlinson, B.: Toward sustainable software engineering (NIER Track). In: Proceedings of the 33rd International Conference on Software Engineering, pp. 976–979. Association for Computing Machinery (2011)
3. Bañuelos, K., et al.: The role of information management for the sustainable conservation of cultural heritage. Sustainability **13**(8) (2021)
4. Becker, C., et al.: Sustainability design and software: the Karlskrona manifesto. In: 2015 IEEE/ACM 37th IEEE International Conference on Software Engineering, vol. 2, pp. 467–476 (2015)
5. Belhi, A., Bouras, A., Foufou, S.: Digitization and preservation of cultural heritage: the CEPROQHA approach. In: 2017 11th International Conference on Software, Knowledge, Information Management and Applications, pp. 1–7 (2017)
6. Borissova, V.: Cultural heritage digitization and related intellectual property issues. J. Cult. Herit. **34**, 145–150 (2018)
7. Dick, M., Naumann, S., Kuhn, N.: A model and selected instances of green and sustainable software. In: Berleur, J., Hercheui, M.D., Hilty, L.M. (eds.) CIP/HCC -2010. IAICT, vol. 328, pp. 248–259. Springer, Heidelberg (2010). https://doi.org/10.1007/978-3-642-15479-9_24
8. Dragoni, M., Tonelli, S., Moretti, G.: A knowledge management architecture for digital cultural heritage. J. Comput. Cult. Heritage **10**(3) (2017)
9. Giannakoulopoulos, A., et al.: Good practices for web-based cultural heritage information management for Europeana. Information **12**(5) (2021)
10. Haus, G.: Cultural heritage and ICT: state of the art and perspectives. DigitCult - Sci. J. Digit. Cult. **1**(1), 9–20 (2016)
11. Huber, J., Gradišnik, M., Heričko, M., Seražin, H.: Rapid development of an art history web portal using the WordPress platform. In: Central European Conference on Information and Intelligent Systems, pp. 289–296 (2019)
12. ISO/IEC 25012. Standard, International Organization for Standardization (2008)
13. ISO/IEC 25010. Standard, International Organization for Standardization (2011)
14. ISO 10001. Standard, International Organization for Standardization (2018)
15. ISO 9241-11. Standard, International Organization for Standardization (2018)
16. Macrì, E., Cristofaro, C.L.: The digitalisation of cultural heritage for sustainable development: the impact of Europeana. In: Demartini, P., Marchegiani, L., Marchiori, M., Schiuma, G. (eds.) Cultural Initiatives for Sustainable Development. CMS, pp. 373–400. Springer, Cham (2021). https://doi.org/10.1007/978-3-030-65687-4_17
17. Manžuch, Z.: Ethical issues in digitization of cultural heritage. J. Contemp. Arch. Stud. **4**(2), 4 (2017)
18. Moreira, A., et al.: A social and technical sustainability requirements catalogue. Data Knowl. Eng. **143**, 102107 (2023)
19. Naumann, S., Dick, M., Kern, E., Johann, T.: The greensoft model: a reference model for green and sustainable software and its engineering. Sustain. Comput.: Inform. Syst. **1**(4), 294–304 (2011)
20. Pan, X., et al.: An enhanced distributed repository for working with 3D assets in cultural heritage. In: Ioannides, M., Fritsch, D., Leissner, J., Davies, R., Remondino, F., Caffo, R. (eds.) EuroMed 2012. LNCS, vol. 7616, pp. 349–358. Springer, Heidelberg (2012). https://doi.org/10.1007/978-3-642-34234-9_35

The Assessment of Online Games' Cyber Security Awareness Level Based on Knowledge, Attitudes, and Behaviour Model

Juliana Zolkiffli[1], Nur Azaliah Abu Bakar[1]([✉]), Suraya Ya'acob[1], Hasimi Salehuddin[2], and Surya Sumarni Hussien[3]

[1] Razak Faculty of Technology and Informatics, Universiti Teknologi Malaysia, Kuala Lumpur, Malaysia
azaliah@utm.my

[2] Faculty of Information Science and Technology, Universiti Kebangsaan Malaysia, Bangi, Malaysia

[3] Computing and Mathematical Sciences Centre of Studies, Universiti Teknologi MARA, Shah Alam, Malaysia

Abstract. Casual gamers, especially those without knowledge and unskilled with security, cause most online game cybersecurity issues. Cybercriminals exploit this thinking by breaching security. Online gamers of all ages and backgrounds have increased due to the COVID-19 suspension, exposing them to cyberattacks. These attacks exploit online players' cybersecurity ignorance to enhance cybersecurity breaches in online games. In light of these problems, this study examined Malaysian online gamer knowledge, attitude, and behaviour. This study examines passwords, email, Internet, device, and social engineering to assess online gamers' cyber security awareness. The study of 162 online gamers from Facebook, Discord, Twitter, and Twitch discovered that 55% of respondents carelessly keep their gaming account password and more than 56% of respondents' gaming PCs are not antivirus-protected. Given the in-game function that links credit and debit cards to gaming accounts, gamers' cybersecurity expertise is concerning. This shows how cybersecurity awareness may protect gamers from hackers.

Keywords: Awareness · Cybersecurity · Knowledge-Attitudes-Behaviour · Online Games

1 Introduction

In the last decade, online games have become one of the most popular entertainment information systems classes [1]. With the growth of the cyber world, an immense amount and diversity of online games are now present on various devices, including smartphones, computers, laptops, tablets, and gaming consoles. They excite citizens of all ages from all over the world. Online games differ in terms of what and where they are played. Online games are available in practically every genre of interest, including action, strategy, leap and run, shooting, simulation, role games, and sports [2]. Youngsters and adults can

L. Uden and I-H. Ting (Eds.): KMO 2023, CCIS 1825, pp. 314–328, 2023.
https://doi.org/10.1007/978-3-031-34045-1_26

play live with other community groups in online games, discuss ideas, and collaborate on campaigns or initiatives.

Browser games are also online games that can be accessed via a standard web browser. This type of game does not require the installation of any software. The browser is a point of contact between the game environment and the players. Browser games are typically basic games with low entry barriers that take only a short time to learn. PlayerUnknown's Battlegrounds (PUBG), Fortnite Battle Royale, Call of Duty, League of Legends (LOL), and Apex Legends are the most played online games around the world by the year 2021 [3]. The most popular genre of online games that attracts gamers is Massively Multiplayer Online Games (MMOGs). MMOGs are where gamers pick a virtual game character or avatar and continuously use their gaming experience to develop their skills. They work together in a clan or guild of playmates to complete quests or win the game [2]. Their popularity among gamers comes from their opportunity to interact, compete, and connect with others worldwide who share their interests [4].

When many individuals are involved in a game and try to outdo each other, suspicious behaviours to win the game using illegal methods are always possible. Cheating issues and threats are always present in real-life competitions, and multiplayer online games are no exception. As a result, most cybersecurity threats to online games are associated with cheating gamers who can either breach the system or launch distributed denial of service (DDoS) assaults against the server [5].

Cybercrimes have become serious issues for online gamers and the gaming industry. Lack of cybersecurity awareness among online gamers is the main reason why they became cybercriminals' victims of cybercriminals in the first place. Most victims are unaware that cybercriminals are targeting them. Even experienced gamers may face threats while playing or searching the web for game-related content. With the rise in online gamers due to the Covid-19 pandemic, the number of cyberattacks in the gaming industry has also skyrocketed. Cybersecurity of online gaming is highly susceptible to latency and service failure, making them ideal targets for large-scale DDoS attacks [6]. Therefore, this study investigates the relationship between cyber security knowledge, cyber security awareness, attitude, and behavioural choice protection among online gamers in Malaysia.

2   Literature Review

2.1 Online Games

According to [7], the online video game business produced $54.7 billion in sales in 2001, which is expected to increase by 2020, reaching $188.9 billion. According to a survey, 72% of teenagers play games, with 75% playing online. Of all those who played online, 54% only played with friends. On the contrary, 52% played mainly with strangers, and online games are played by 65% of adults play online games alone in the United States [8]. To date, there are 3,243.3 million gamers worldwide and most gamers are from Asia, with 1,478.9 million gamers total [9].

Significant financial incentives can encourage irresponsible players to seek an unfair advantage over other players, resulting in an underground market for game cheats. These competitions also attract clandestine groups seeking to profit from online gaming for political, financial or ideological purposes [9]. Most gaming accounts and the in-game commodities linked with them have an actual money worth that other gamers are ready to pay for in online multiplayer games. The amount of money spent on PUBG has only been increasing since April 2018, when it went from $1.5 million to $270 million in August 2021 [1]. Thus, the increasing number of gamers willing to spend their money on online games has created an interest for cybercriminals to shift their target to the online game industry.

2.2 Cyber Security Knowledge

People are increasingly relying on internet technology for their daily tasks. Because it is so easy to use, more and more people are engaging in cyber-related activities. However, awareness of the tools available to protect against cyber threats lags behind. Even basic cyber security awareness may not translate into sufficient knowledge to protect against cyber risks and threats. These would focus on operational, usage and procedural elements to increase user awareness and transform it into effective cyber security mitigation behaviour [10]. In addition, knowledge and skills are required components of competence. It is to be able to apply the associated knowledge, skills, and abilities required to successfully perform critical job functions [11]. Consequently, all technology users must be literate in cybersecurity to protect their devices from threats, highlighting the importance of cybersecurity knowledge and skills when using digital technologies [12].

2.3 Cybersecurity Awareness

The Internet has changed the way people live their lives by connecting them with new people via social networks and opening up new economic frontiers for individuals and organisations to conduct transactions via mobile devices, including recreational activities such as online gaming. Despite this, many people continue to face threats to information security from a number of sources. As a result, understanding cyber security is critical [10]. Cybersecurity awareness is a type of training designed to inspire, excite, establish, and rebuild the cyber security abilities and expected security behaviours of a specific audience. It is vital to urge and promote Internet users to take precautions and educate them on online security measures. It also teaches these users all aspects of cyber security, ensuring that not only the national network infrastructures, but also the users, are resistant to cyber attacks and dangers [11]. Training to users in order to increase their understanding of cyber security. Education, promotion, and other methods are used to promote awareness of cyber security. However, these modes must successfully make an impression on users.

2.4 Knowledge, Attitude and Behaviour Model for Information Security

A study by [10] aims to measure the level of security awareness among Palestinian students who use the Internet. Variables such as passwords, social media usage, email usage, mobile device security, and social engineering are all included in the study. According to the study, people with a higher security awareness responded more professionally against cybercrime. The study focuses on Palestinian educational institutions based on the educational environment being fully stacked with network connectivity and technologies as shown in Fig. 1.

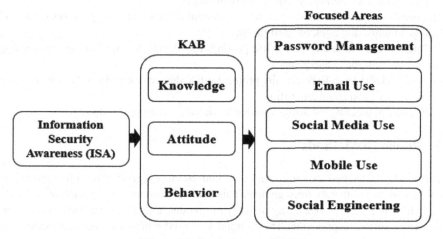

Fig. 1. ISA Study Framework [10]

The study looked at the characteristics of knowledge, attitude, and behaviour. According to this study, the best way to evaluate ISA is to measure three things:

1) Knowledge (K): What does any individual know?
2) Attitude (A): What are their thoughts on the concept?
3) Behaviour (B): How do they act?

Given the high cost of cyber risks, research has increasingly focused on the precautions and behaviours that Internet users adopt to protect their devices [11]. It has been shown that having a choice, rather than being told what to do or having only one option, has a positive impact. People are more internally motivated and perform better on the tasks they have chosen to do, and they are also more satisfied with their choices and feel in control. People tend to choose only the parts of an area that interest them. One reason for this is that decision makers and politicians, like everyone else, will react differently depending on objectively equivalent descriptions of the same problem. Communicating about cybersecurity issues and the urgent need for action is a difficult task that requires clear and convincing communication. Often, cybersecurity risk is mentioned to foresee threats to the state and create a security fantasy, a fiction that could fuel fear [12].

Based on the above discussion, this research is focused on the human factor due to the fact that individuals with a better security knowledge and awareness reacted more professionally to cyberattacks than those who did not understand [12]. This study employs the KAB model, combined with four focus areas from the Human Aspects of Information Security Questionnaire (HAIS-Q) to investigate the awareness level of knowledge, attitude, and behaviour of online gamers which covers these five (5) elements:

1) Password Management: Using the same password for many accounts, using a strong password, and sharing the password with others.
2) Email Use: Email is used to share confidential details with strangers, open harmful attachments, and click on harmful links.
3) Internet Use: Internet use for life posting, monitoring privacy settings, and taking into account the consequences.
4) Social Media Use: To physically protect mobile devices, confidential material is sent over Wi-Fi and shoulder surfing.
5) Social Engineering: Sharing confidential details and dumpster diving.

3 Research Methods

This study researched existing articles to understand cybersecurity vulnerabilities in online games and threats from gamers. This study also conducted a quantitative analysis, which is based on measuring quantity or amount, a method that outlines the characteristics of the respondents. This method was used when data were collected from respondents at a single time point.

The study population is individuals in Malaysia between the ages of 18 and sixty years old, with 250 respondents. This study will use random sampling, where the population will be chosen randomly among gaming spenders and non-gaming spenders. In this study, the questionnaire survey method was used using Google Form online. The questionnaire survey is the best method to answer the questions on their own time. The respondents are randomly selected from social media such as Facebook, Discord, Twitter, and Twitch.

One of the essential strategies in a case study is data collection, which is an effective method to collect data and discover all relevant elements. Many researchers need data collection techniques or procedures to complete their studies. The complexity, perception, structure, and management of data collection techniques can differ for each study. This study will use questionnaires as a way of collecting data. A questionnaire is a collection of questions sent to a group of respondents of which data will be collected. As discussed in the previous subchapters, the questionnaires were used to collect Information from Malaysian online gamers, then used in the study's analysis. This will help to create a complete picture of the amount of cyber security knowledge in the collection of revenues from online games.

Data will be gathered from the questionnaire survey, processed, and analysed for discussion. Data will be analysed using the appropriate computer software. Quantitative data will be evaluated via Microsoft Excel and the Statistical Package for the Social Sciences (SPSS) software to measure the level of cyber security awareness among Malaysian online gamers. Similarly, the final result will reveal the genuine picture of Malaysian online gamers' cyber security awareness level in revenue collection using tables and figures. To ensure instrument validity, the reliability of measures will be tested via Exploratory Factor Analysis (EFA) using SPSS software employing varimax rotation and principal components analysis [13]. The measure of sampling adequacy and appropriateness for element analysis will be explored via the Kaiser–Meyer–Olkin (KMO) and Bartlett sphericity tests.

In the study, the research instrument is an essential source of information for collecting data on the personal self-administered questionnaire. The questionnaire is written in straightforward English to avoid respondents' misunderstanding. This is also to ensure that the questionnaire is understandable. To avoid confusion, concise and well-defined queries will be employed. With this direct instrument, the efficiency and quality of the information collected will undoubtedly improve.

A variable is a concept that can have a variety of quantitative values. The primary goal is to examine the functional relationships between the variables. A variable is a quantity that varies from one person to the next and that varies from individual to individual. This study measures the level of security awareness of online gamers in Malaysia. This study will focus on five variables to gather data on this measurement.

4 Proposed Framework

The purpose of awareness presentations is simply to focus attention on security. Awareness presentations allow individuals to recognise IT security concerns and respond accordingly." [11]. Cybersecurity awareness is individuals' awareness of the significance of cyber security and their roles and actions in practising appropriate measures of cyber security control to secure the data and networks. According to [14], cyber security awareness programmes should educate individuals about the risks and consequences of potential security attacks to understand the security needs and their responsibility to protect information assets.

The most current focus area is Cybersecurity Awareness (CSA). The human factor has gained the attention of all stakeholders, as it has steadily become an unmanageable weak link in the security system. Cybercriminals are well aware of this mindset and are working to take advantage of it in any manner they can, such as by breaching the security chain. People of all ages and backgrounds are increasingly spending their time and money on online games, which puts them at risk of cyber threats and cyberattacks. The most common and obvious reason for these cyberattacks is a lack of awareness and understanding of cybersecurity practises, leading to a significant increase in security failures [15].

The essential purpose of CSA is to ensure that everyone follows policies and procedures and uses best practises. Although many people pay extra attention to CSA, some never believe in its effectiveness. CSA levels can be divided into low, medium, and high. For example, ignoring security recommendations and regulations is considered a low CSA level, while adopting security measures and responding appropriately to avert risks is regarded a high CSA level [11].

This study focused on five (5) areas, Password Management, Email Use, Internet Use, Device Use, and social engineering. Based on these focus areas, several questions are designed by measuring the level of awareness through a questionnaire survey. This study analysed the CSA level using the standard independent variables and Dependent Variable Relation. Finally, five (5) independent variables were proposed to measure the dependent variable as shown in Fig. 2.

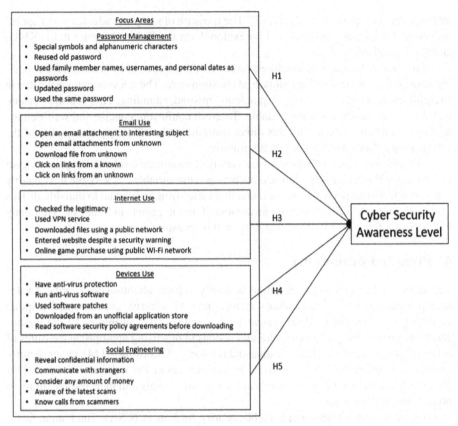

Fig. 2. Online Games' Cyber Security Awareness Framework

Password management is the characteristic of measuring cyber security awareness among Malaysian online gamers. Many have argued that how an individual manages their account's password would determine the safety of their account. Firstly, there is a positive relationship between the correct way of password management in maintaining the security levels of privileged access to certain accounts. When the password used is strong, the overall risk of a security breach is lowered. Therefore, password management would be the determinant of cyber security awareness level among Malaysian online gamers. Therefore, based on the above reasoning, this study proposes the following hypotheses.

H1: There is a significant relationship between password management and cyber security awareness level among Malaysian online gamers.

One commonly used variable to measure cyber security awareness among Malaysian online gamers is how they manage **Internet usage**. Online gamers use the Internet not only to play online games but also to purchase items in online games and download game application files onto their devices, thus causing their devices vulnerable to cyberattacks.

However, this could be avoided if online gamers protected their internet connection by turning on encryption, using multiple firewalls, and using a Virtual Private Network (VPN). Relationship between Internet usage and cyber security awareness level among Malaysian online gamers due to factors such as lack of skills or experience and unfamiliarity with internet connection protection. As such, the study proposes the following hypothesis:

H2: There is a significant relationship between Internet use with cyber security awareness level among Malaysian online gamers.

One of the traits to test the levels of cyber security awareness among Malaysian online gamers is by looking at how they use their **email.** Email usage is expressed by the way online gamers react to the different types of email from various either unknown and known senders; every online gamer could embrace different experiences, habits, or goals that could influence email usage. While certain online gamers are known to have vast experience in differentiating an email that could be a threat to them, some online gamers, on the other hand, could quickly become cybercriminals' victims. Therefore, based on the above reasoning, this study proposes the following hypothesis.

H3: There is a significant relationship between email use and cyber-security awareness levels among Malaysian online gamers.

The **device usage** variable could be associated with a cyber security vulnerability. Secure devices such as personal computers, smartphones, and gaming consoles will strive to prevent cyberattacks. Therefore, there is a positive relationship between device use and cyber security awareness among Malaysian online gamers. Good security practises such as updating the mobile operating system with security patches, keeping software up-to-date, and installing antivirus or anti-malware improve devices' protection and defence. On the other hand, an unprotected device has a negative relationship with securing devices from cyberattacks. Therefore, the hypothesis is proposed as follows.

H4: There is a significant relationship between device use and cyber-security awareness levels among Malaysian online gamers.

Cyber security awareness among Malaysian online gamers could be measured by knowing the level of knowledge of individuals about **social engineering**. Consequently, this could be described by how online gamers deal with social engineering techniques such as baiting, phishing, pretexting, and quid pro quo. As such, knowing social engineering could help reduce the chances of receiving scams and cyberattacks. Ultimately, these social engineering techniques could cause financial and even emotional damage. Thus, the hypothesis of this study is proposed as follows:

H5: There is a significant relationship between social engineering and cyber security awareness level among Malaysian online gamers.

5 Analysis and Findings

The questionnaire was sent to Malaysian online gamers. These individuals represented a proportion of the study population that was expected to be familiar with online games. Invitations to respondents were sent via Facebook, Instagram, Discord, Twitter, and Twitch, with a link to the questionnaire sent through Google Form on April 24, 2022. A total of 162 people had responded by May 14, 2022, and the information collected was utilised to perform demographic, reliability, descriptive, and correlation analyses. Table 1 shows a list of questions in the sections on password management, email use, Internet use, device use, and social engineering.

Table 1. Questionnaire's Questions

Item	Section	Question
Q1	Password Management	I created passwords that contained over eight characters of text with special symbols (e.g., @# $% &), such as numeric characters (e.g., 0â€ "9) and alphanumeric characters (e.g., AF54hhr63, jjHFay6747, @qw%$99O#)
Q2		I reused the old password that I used earlier
Q3		I used the names, usernames, and personal dates of family members as passwords
Q4		I never updated my current password to my gaming account
Q5		I never used the same password on multiple gaming accounts
Q6	Email Usage	An interesting subject line about games makes me open an email attachment
Q7		I will never open email attachments from an unknown gaming website
Q8		I will never download a file sent to me by email from an unknown gaming website
Q9		It is always safe to click on links in emails from gaming websites that I know
Q10		Nothing wrong can happen if I click on a link in an email from an unknown gaming website
Q11	Internet Usage	Before accessing it, I checked the legitimacy of a gaming website
Q12		When using the Internet to play games, I used a VPN service (a protected network connection when using public networks)
Q13		I downloaded files from a gaming website while using a public network
Q14		Despite a security warning, I entered a gaming website that said this site was dangerous
Q15		I bought an online game while connected to a public Wi-Fi network

(continued)

Table 1. (*continued*)

Item	Section	Question
Q16	Devices Usage	I do not have antivirus protection on my devices
Q17		I run antivirus software on my devices every 3 or 6 months
Q18		I use software patches on my devices
Q19		I downloaded game applications from an unofficial application store on my device
Q20		I read the game software security policy agreements before downloading them to my devices
Q21	Social Engineering	I will disclose any confidential information under any circumstances to other gamers
Q22		I will not communicate with strangers in games
Q23		I will consider any amount of money offered by an online gaming site
Q24		I am aware of the latest online gaming scams
Q25		I know the difference between original calls from official gaming websites and any calls from scammers

5.1 Demographic Analysis

Table 2 shows that male respondents (70.4%) outnumber female respondents (29.6%). Most of the respondents (49.4%) were between the ages of 18 and 30, followed by those between the ages of 31 and 40 (44.4%). Many respondents in this age group show that online games are popular among this population, and most of this population works in the private sector (32.7%) and government and public administration (30.9%). Based on Table 2, Action Role Playing (79.6%) is the genre of game that most respondents play, and most respondents spend less than RM50 (38.3%) on online game purchases in one year.

Table 2. Distribution of the demographic data of the respondents (n = 162)

Variable	Category	Number	Percentage (%)
Gender	Female	48	29.6
	Male	103	70.4
Age	18 to 30 years old	80	49.4
	31 to 40 years old	72	44.4
	41 to 50 years old	9	5.6

(*continued*)

Table 2. (*continued*)

Variable	Category	Number	Percentage (%)
	51 to 60 years old	1	0.6
Occupation	Contractor	1	0.6
	Government and Public Administration	50	30.9
	Housewife	1	0.6
	Not-for-profit sector	2	1.2
	Private Sector	53	32.7
	Self Employed	23	14.2
	Site technician	1	0.6
	Streamer	1	0.6
	Student	29	17.9
	Youtuber	1	0.6
Game Preference	Action Role Playing	129	79.6
	Real-Time Strategy	86	53.1
	Fighting and Martial Arts	78	48.1
	Puzzle	55	34
	Racing	58	35.8
	Sports	43	26.5
	Don't Know	3	1.9
	Other (Simulation, Shooter, MMORPG, Battle Royal	7	4.2
Money spends/month	None	33	20.4
	Below RM 50	62	38.3
	RM 51 to RM 100	31	19.1
	RM 101 to RM 500	19	11.7
	More than RM 500	17	10.5

5.2 Reliability Analysis

Reliability analysis is a common and widely used practice, and the SPSS performing it is user-friendly and intuitive. The reliability analysis method calculates various frequently used scale reliability metrics and figures on the correlations between certain scale items. Inter-rater reliability values can be calculated via inter-class Cronbach alpha. The reliability analysis used in this study is Cronbach's alpha coefficient as shown in Table 3.

Table 3. Total Mean Value for All Items

No	Item	Mean Value
	Q1: I created passwords that contained over eight characters of text with special symbols (e.g., @# $% &), such as numeric characters (e.g., 0â€ "9) and alphanumeric characters (e.g., AF54hhr63, jjHFay6747, @qw%$99O#)	4.22
	Q2: I reused the old password that I used earlier	3.11
	Q3: I used the names, usernames, and personal dates of family members as passwords	2.35
	Q4: I never updated my current password to my gaming account	2.94
	Q5: I never used the same password on multiple gaming accounts	2.90
	Q6: An engaging subject line about games makes me open an email attachment	2.70
	Q7: I will never open email attachments from an unknown gaming website	3.85
	Q8: I will never download a file sent to me by email from an unknown gaming website	3.93
	Q9: It is always safe to click on links in emails from gaming websites that I know	2.60
	Q10: Nothing wrong can happen if I click on a link in an email from an unknown gaming website	2.00
	Q11: Before accessing it, I checked the legitimacy of a gaming website	3.78
	Q12: When using the Internet to play games, I used a VPN service (a protected network connection when using public networks)	3.00
	Q13: I downloaded files from a gaming website using a public network	2.52
	Q14: I entered a gaming website despite a security warning saying that this site is dangerous	2.28
	Q15: I purchased an online game while connected to a public Wi-Fi network	2.17
	Q16: I do not have antivirus protection on my devices	2.17
	Q17: I run antivirus software on my devices every 3 or 6 months	2.53
	Q18: I use software patches on my devices	3.02
	Q19: I downloaded game applications from an unofficial application store on my device	2.92
		2.38
	Q20: I read the game software security policy agreements before downloading them to my devices	3.20
	Q21: I will disclose any confidential information under any circumstances to other gamers	2.22
	Q22: I will not communicate with strangers in games	3.20
	Q23: I will consider any amount of money offered by an online gaming site	2.52
	Q24: I am aware of the latest online gaming scams	3.66
	Q25: I know the difference between original calls from official gaming websites and any calls from scammers	3.66

Cronbach's alpha value greater than 0.7 is acceptable, whereas those greater than 0.8 are preferred. The overall reliability of the set used in this study is acceptable, as it generated a value of 0.730. Table 3 shows the ranking of the results of the item-total correlation analysis. Item Q13 has the most significant reliability value with 0.403, while item Q16 has the weakest reliability value with only 0.023. The higher the standard deviation, the greater the variety or spread. Most of the information is packed around the mean if the standard deviations are low. Table 4 shows the mean statistic ranking with the top five in the strongest agreement. Item Q1 has the strongest agreement with a mean value of 4.2160.

Table 4. Top Five Mean Statistic Rankings

No	Item	Mean Statistic
1	Q1: I created passwords that contained over eight characters of text with special symbols (e.g., @# $% &), such as numeric characters (e.g., 0â€ "9) and alphanumeric characters (e.g., AF54hhr63, jjHFay6747, @qw%$99O#)	4.2160
2	Q8: I will never download a file sent to me by email from an unknown gaming website	3.9321
3	Q7: I will never open email attachments from an unknown gaming website	3.8519
4	Q11: Before accessing it, I checked the legitimacy of a gaming website	3.7778
5	Q25: I know the difference between original calls from official gaming websites and any calls from scammers	3.6667

Table 5 shows the five with the strongest disagreement among the respondents. Item Q10, with a mean value of 2.0062, has the strongest disagreement among the respondents.

Table 5. Bottom Five Mean Statistic Ranking

No	Item	Mean Statistic
1	Q10: Nothing wrong can happen if I click on a link in an email from an unknown gaming website	2.0062
2	Q15: I bought an online game while connected to a public Wi-Fi network	2.1728
3	Q21: I will disclose any confidential information under any circumstances to other gamers	2.2222
4	Q14: I entered a gaming website despite a security warning saying that this site is dangerous	2.2778
5	Q3: I used the names, usernames, and personal dates of family members as passwords	2.3519

6 Conclusions

The main effect of cybercrime in online games is financial. Cybercrime can involve various types of profit-driven criminal activity, such as email and internet scams, identity fraud, and aims to steal the gamers' financial accounts and credit or debit card information. Cybercriminals may prey on the gamer's private information for theft and gaming accounts for resale. As many people resolve into remote work systems due to the Covid-19 pandemic, cybercriminals will increase in frequency by 2021, making it extremely important to protect yourself from cybercriminals. A lack of awareness of cybersecurity triggers the majority of successful attacks. There is no single human on the planet who has never made a mistake. Making mistakes is a key point in human experience. It is how humans gain knowledge and grow. Human errors are far too repeatedly ignored in cyber security. The most common reason for cyber security breaches is human error.

One of the limitations faced during the study was the lack of cybersecurity education. Participants may ask questions without understanding them. According to data analysis, some of the cybersecurity awareness topics are incorrectly answered by the respondents. The result would be different if they had a better understanding of cybersecurity. In the future, the measurement of cybersecurity awareness among online gamers should be focused on younger populations, since 49.9% of participants are between 18 and 30 years old, according to the analysis result.

The lack of sample size and the readiness of the respondents to answer the questionnaire were also faced during the data collection. Most people were unwilling to answer the questionnaire as they initially believed they were not suitable respondents, and additional explanation was needed on what cybersecurity is. This was difficult as the questionnaire was carried out online. Thus, in-person guidance was hard to perform. To exceed the study's robustness, it is appropriate to have a bigger group size, which is not deemed an appropriate sample and covers diverse controls.

Another criticism that can be gained from the assessment of the elements is the lack of expert participation and validation method in constructing the questionnaire. Only three experts willingly responded to the validation invitation when six experts were approached, and the study only managed to use the face validation method in the design of the questionnaire. The questionnaire should be validated by more experts and use more than one validation method to strengthen the reliability and validity of the questionnaire.

The significant contribution is to explore the cybersecurity awareness level among Malaysian online gamers. Cyber-attacks in online games not only lead to a data breach but also have a financial loss. Thus, to protect against such attacks, players have the leading role, which is essential to strengthening cyber-security awareness. This study evaluated and analysed the cybersecurity understanding and skills of Malaysian online gamers with respect to cybersecurity security and cybercrime. Differences in age, gender, and occupation can show different results from the data gathered from the survey. This study also proposed a framework that could serve as a guide in a future study on this topic. The research will analyse the relationship between the focus areas to answer all research questions based on the proposed framework.

Acknowledgements. This work was supported by Universiti Teknologi Malaysia under UTM Quick Win Research Grant (R.K130000.7756.4J574).

References

1. Dahabiyeh, L., Najjar, M.S., Agrawal, D.: When ignorance is bliss: the role of curiosity in online games adoption. Entertain. Comput. **37**, 100398 (2021)
2. Ahmet, E.F.E., Emre, Ö.N.A.L.: ONLINE game security: a case study of an MMO strategy game. Gazi Univ. J. Sci. A Eng. Innov. **7**(2), 43–57 (2020)

3. Grandhi, S.R., Galimotu, N.C.: Understanding social engineering threats in massively multi-player online role-playing games: an issue review. GAP Indian J. Forensics Behav. Sci. **1**(1), 66–71 (2020)

4. Taylor, D.P.J., et al.: Forensic investigation of cross platform massively multiplayer online games: Minecraft as a case study. Sci. Justice **59**(3), 337–348 (2019)

5. Munir, S., Baig, M.S.I.: Challenges and Security Aspects of Blockchain Based Online Multiplayer Games (2019)

6. Qusa, H., Tarazi, J.: Cyber-hero: a gamification framework for cyber security awareness for high schools students. In: 2021 IEEE 11th Annual Computing and Communication Workshop and Conference (CCWC). IEEE (2021)

7. Hokroh, M., Green, G.: Online video games adoption: toward an online game adoption model. Int. J. Res. Bus. Soc. Sci. **8**(4), 163–171 (2019)

8. Alturki, A., Alshwihi, N., Algarni, A.: Factors influencing players' susceptibility to social engineering in social gaming networks. IEEE Access **8**, 97383–97391 (2020)

9. Fuentes, M.R., Mercês, F.: Cheats, hacks, and cyberattacks. Trend Micro Res. 8 (2019)

10. Salem, Y., Moreb, M., Rabayah, K.S.: Evaluation of information security awareness among Palestinian learners. In: 2021 International Conference on Information Technology (ICIT), pp. 21–26. IEEE (2021)

11. Zwilling, M., et al.: Cyber security awareness, knowledge and behavior: a comparative study. J. Comput. Inf. Syst. **62**(1), 82–97 (2022)

12. Mohammad, T., Hussin, N.A.M., Husin, M.H.: Online safety awareness and human factors: an application of the theory of human ecology. Technol. Soc. **68**, 101823 (2022)

13. Amron, M.T., et al.: The validity and reliability evaluation of instruments for cloud computing acceptance study. In: 2020 6th International Conference on Information Management (ICIM). IEEE (2020)

14. Wang, Y., et al.: Framework of raising cyber security awareness. In: 2018 IEEE 18th International Conference on Communication Technology (ICCT). IEEE (2018)

15. Khader, M., Karam, M., Fares, H.: Cybersecurity awareness framework for academia. Information **12**(10), 417 (2021)

Innovations in Future Crime Decision Making Through the Codification of Temporal Expert Knowledge

Elliott MacCallum[1], Lisa Jackson[1(✉)], John Coxhead[2], and Tom Jackson[3]

[1] Aeronatuical and Automotive Engineering Department, Loughborough University, Loughborough, UK
l.m.jackson@lboro.ac.uk

[2] Policing Innovation, Enterprise and Learning Centre, University of East London, London, UK

[3] School of Business and Economics, Loughborough University, Loughborough, UK

Abstract. This paper presents a case study on the codification of temporal expert knowledge to enhance Dijkstra's route planning algorithm to reduce the time to recover stolen vehicles in the UK. The power of the predictive algorithm lies in the route costings where integration of expert knowledge on offender criminal behaviours overcomes the lack of this captured data by technology alone. According to Home Office statistics vehicle theft rates in the UK have been increasing year on year since 2014 [1]. Part of this rise can be attributed to keyless vehicle entry and ignition becoming more popular however, this does not explain the full story. Although vehicle telematics hardware is improving rapidly this has not been supported by an equal increase in use of data for vehicle tracking. This project has explored the feasibility of future innovations in policing with the focus on assisting police officers in their decision making and increasing the probability of success in apprehending offenders of stolen vehicles through codifying their knowledge. Through exploiting the growth in Internet of Things (IoT) technologies, this paper presents a novel approach to vehicle tracking with an integrated path predictive algorithm. Using Dijkstra's route planning algorithm, with real time geospatial data augmented with information from historical route data and expert knowledge, modified route costings are generated. The algorithm calculates the highest probability escape route that a thief would take and identifies an area ahead of the thief's current position where the police can position a roadblock to apprehend the criminal.

Keywords: Expert knowledge · Route Prediction · Crime prevention · IoT technology · Policing innovation

1 Introduction

Vehicle theft rates in the UK have been increasing year on year since 2014 with the main cause of increase being technology savvy criminals who can access vehicles and disable alarm and tracking systems. More significantly, recent studies demonstrate that only 45.3% of stolen vehicles are ever recovered and returned to their rightful owner [2]. This is one example where technological advances can bring advancements for society (new vehicle systems to the benefit of the user) and to the criminal (improved capability to commit crime), with the associated potential disruptors to traditional crime types and prevention and detection of criminal activity. This changing ecosystem is an ever-increasing problem with levels of technology innovation identified as a future challenge for Policing [3]. Harnessing the benefits of innovations in technology, to aid in advances in preventing and investigating crime, with a move towards evidenced-based policing [4], needs to be explored to meet the service provision capabilities of future policing. This research has focused on understanding the implications of future policing solutions with the use of a hybrid approach of emerging technology innovations and utilising police officer knowledge to harness the technology capability for a viable practical solution. These implications are explored through the investigation of novel vehicle tracking systems and utilization of the police knowledge in generating a system to aid decision making for vehicle apprehension.

With Internet of Things (IoT) based smart cities beginning to be implemented, the inter- communicating features between vehicles and other devices brings new opportunities for vehicle automation and tracking. RFID is a cost effective method to support IoT as it does not require line of sight for communication and can be retrospectively affixed to non-smart items. The potential to utilise the Radio frequency identification (RFID) coverage of smart cities, where RFID will be used in everything from street signs to ecosystem monitoring [5], for the purposes of vehicle tracking is enormous. Despite almost all new cars incorporating Global Positioning System (GPS) navigation packages as standard, the GPS devices are passive, one-way systems and therefore vehicles cannot be tracked using this system if a vehicle is stolen. In fact, even if the GPS navigation could be used to trace a vehicles location the signal from a GPS device can easily be blocked with commercially available jammers. Though not completely infallible to jamming, with passive RFID tags embedded within vehicles makes them harder to locate and block. Location in vehicles can be complicated due to their positioning next to or near to metal, however research has shown that robust communication is possible with appropriate RFID antenna designs, tested with and without metal interfaces and with materials of varying relative permittivity and thicknesses [6]. Successful use of RFID for tracking has been shown in warehouse management by large retailers as well as by the Department of Defence and the Department of Homeland Security [7, 8]. Passive RFID tags embedded within crates are interrogated as the crate progresses through a warehouse, assembly line or state border, recording information regarding the processes that the contents of the crate have undergone. A connectionless stochastic reference beacon architecture based on an RFID sensor network has also been proposed and demonstrated as a tracking solution for Humanitarian Logistics centre resource management [9]. Though currently RFID does not play a role in Car2X communication, studies are exploring its usage in the supply chain with novel tracking architectures and service provision for improved asset safety and security [10] and for autonomous vehicles as part of a multi-model positioning system [11].

This tracking of goods and vehicles, using an embedded tag, forms the basis for demonstration of the positioning prediction technology innovation in this policing application where an RFID tag embedded within a vehicle could be interrogated as it passes through junctions allowing the location of the vehicle and the route it has taken to be traced. Utilising the data from this embedded intelligence capability, the algorithms used for path prediction in autonomous vehicles can be adapted to predict the potential route a thief may take after stealing a vehicle. Observations realized that the numerical data acquired through such technology interventions does provide additional information currently not realized, yet lacks the level of granularity to make predictions that reflect the practical world – mirror the human (in this case criminal) behaviours. To this end, investigating the inclusion of expert knowledge into the mathematical prediction process is needed to give policing the superiority for detection, allowing the police to be transformative in its process – to be proactive rather than reactive – and initiate such actions as placing roadblocks ahead of the route that a thief may take, potentially increasing the number of stolen vehicles that are recovered and criminal apprehended.

The contributions of this paper are: i) investigation of the implications of innovations in technologies to enhance policing capability; ii) understanding the role of codifying changing expert knowledge plays in the transition for enabling technologies for policing interventions; and iii) highlighting some of the limitations of technology with the need for a hybridized (human and technology) solution. It is hoped that this research will provide the policing sector with a reference basis for developing future innovations and with considerations that off-the-shelf technology alone may not be the answer.

2   Literature Review

2.1   Knowledge Management in Policing

Police officers, in their role to maintain law and order, engage in a variety of activities. Often reactive (arresting an offender, increased police presence in problem areas) but sometimes proactive (directed patrols), each case involves a large amount of information. This amount of information means that police officers have to be proficient in handling and analysing this knowledge. In this era of information overload [12], effective evidence-based and intelligence-led policing operations rely on sufficient knowledge and information management, the challenge still remains however to fully leverage knowledge management surface the information and knowledge and use it for problems faced by police officers in a timely and effective manner [7, 8]. With the foreseeable transformations in future policing, due to changes in criminal activity, requiring innovations in science and technology solutions, what must not be forgotten in this innovation phase is the central role that knowledge, the implicit knowledge stored in the minds of those involved (officers, sergeants, inspectors etc.) may have in these solutions. Such knowledge, typically gained through years of experiences, can be crucial in providing an effective means to analysing and solving problems related to a variety of policing functions. How to embed this knowledge into technological solutions, may follow a codification strategy, focusing on a people to document approach, where the aim of knowledge management is to capture, codify, store, disseminate and reuse explicit knowledge in a form that is useful to achieve the end goal, to aid in the apprehension of a criminal. Examples of embedding this knowledge into mathematical models, joining qualitative and quantitative methods, includes developing If-Then rules for fuzzy inference systems in the maintenance domain [13], with coverage of RFID and semantic knowledge [14]. For consideration in Policing is the balance or changing role that codification and its integration must provide an effective solution especially in a volatile and rapidly changing industry such as for the Police. Studies have investigated how the environment and its changes may affect knowledge management, where codification and personalisation may have a varying mix over time [15]. Exploration of this mix and in particular the temporal codification strategy changes will be investigated.

2.2 RFID and Traceability Technologies

Radio Frequency Identification (RFID) is a wireless communication technology that transfers information between tagged objects and readers without line of sight. Passive RFID UHF tags require no battery, they are powered by the incoming RF wave, and they operate in the 860-960 MHz frequency range, controlled by ISO 18000–6. In addition to not requiring line of sight to function, the tags can be embedded within objects making them significantly harder to remove or tamper with than devices which require a constant power source. It has been demonstrated that passive UHF RFID tags can be read at ranges upwards of 25 m even when mounted to metal surfaces [16]. UHF RFID, in accordance to ISO 18000–6, is currently used in India, North America and Vietnam for the purpose of automated licence plate recognition for toll roads [17]. L. Mo et al. investigated the reliability of such an application of RFID by assessing the relationship between the velocity at which a vehicle passes the gantry reader and the read success rate of the RFID tag [18]. By optimising the reader refresh rate to 150 Hz, equivalent to a refresh time of 6.7 ms, the RFID tag embedded within the number plate of a passing vehicle could be interrogated up to a theoretical maximum velocity of 469 km/h, though there was a limitation of the reader being only 4 m away. Other research concluded that at a 5.5 m range, the minimum velocity a vehicle must travel at to avoid a single read is 575 km/h [19]. This is significantly above the top speed of even the fastest road legal cars and therefore it can be concluded that the speed of a vehicle passing an RFID reader will have no impact on the tag being detected by the reader.

2.3 RFID Experimentation

Experimentation with RFID technologies falls into two key categories. Firstly, positional tracking, using RFID to detect the location or direction of an object and secondly, tag and reader positioning, determining the optimal tag and reader position to ensure the most accurate measurements over the greatest range.

2.3.1 RFID Positional Tracking

A theoretical model for an RFID based vehicle tracking for a smart traffic management system using active RFID tags attached to the vehicle body and the Received Signal Strength Indicator (RSSI) used to determine the position and velocity of the vehicle when passing RFID readers along a prescribed route has been developed [20]. The use of RSSI to determine direction and position of an object with a passive UHF RFID tag mounted to its surface was carried out using 2 fixed antennae, where the time difference in peaks in RSSI could be used to form a vector dictating the direction in which the tag was moving [21]. A similar experiment was conducted where a reader with a single antenna was used to determine the location of a train along a railway track using multiple passive UHF RFID tags [22]. In this experiment the difference in time peaks of the RSSI for two different tag ID's is used, allowing the use of off-the-shelf RFID readers.

2.3.2 RFID Tag and Reader Positioning

To use RFID tags, they must be detectable when embedded within a vehicle body. This means the tags must either be detectable when mounted to metal or have antennae which can be routed to a location where they are detectable. Björninen et al. established that specially designed passive UHF RFID tags, operating at 915 MHz, can be detected from a distance of 25 m when mounted to 20x20cm cooper plates [15]. Embedding tags within a metal surface and using the surface of sheet metal as antenna to boost the range of passive UHF RFID tags operating in the 902–928 MHz frequency range has also been investigated [23]. Results showed the RFID tag was increased from 11.42m to 16.13m in comparison to when the same tags were mounted to a plastic sheet. The potential read range of 16.13 m is also significant as this is larger than the width of a 4-lane motorway in the UK (15 m with government regulation 3.75 m wide lanes). This could allow for the use of embedded tags in an automotive application as the antenna can be connected to steel sheets such as the roof, bonnet or boot of the vehicle in order to increase the read range while ensuring the tag itself is difficult to access.

2.4 Path Prediction and Probability

The most developed method for generating road networks and autonomously identifying junctions for the use of a path prediction system uses Artificial Intelligence to identify road networks and form the connection between roads. This is done through autonomous image processing from satellite imagery or digital map imagery. This has been investigated in detail using path classifiers and mixed integer programming to identify road networks [24]. Similar investigations have been conducted by using satellite and radar imagery to extract road networks from satellite data [25]. However, to reduce the significant computational power other research has used colour band separation of google maps city imagery to identify different types of road and decompose these into fixed nodes along each road [26]. On limitation is significant blind spots as the image processing is not perfect and any imperfections in the source image, such as clouds in a satellite image, can lead to highly incomplete road structures. Often used for route planning, Dijkstra's algorithm has been used with probabilistic road mapping (PRM) to navigate vehicles, including mobile robots [27]. The application of a PRM network with route costings could be used to identify the shortest potential path to an escape route.

3   Methodology

3.1   Research Overview

There are two areas of focus for this research, the technology architecture to enable a tracking capability, through RFID placement and tracking viability, and route prediction and probability. The main elements are summarized in Fig. 1.

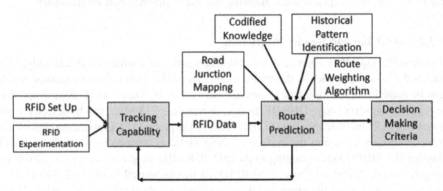

Fig. 1. Technology Innovation Components

The viability of using RFID has been determined through experiments and simulation findings, where vehicle identification, speed and direction are evidence as determinable. A vehicle has the potential to be tracked along a route based on unique tag identifiers, within the potential future IoT based smart city, providing a robust vehicle tracking method. A path predictive algorithm has been developed, using Dijkstra's algorithm as the base, in order to identify the highest probability escape route a thief would take. Codified knowledge has been used to inform the route likelihoods.

3.2   Innovation Concept - RFID Experimentation

Two experiments have been combined, (one for confirmation of vehicle identification, the second to assess direction) to validate the concept of RFID for vehicle tracking. In the real-world application of RFID tracking RFID readers would be placed at intersections with passive RFID tags embedded within vehicles.

3.2.1   Experiment 1 – Recreating Route from Tag Identifier

The initial experiment that has been developed uses a simple handheld RFID reader and passive UHF RFID tags to record the order in which tags are scanned. The scanner used throughout the experimentation in this project is a Technology Solutions Ltd 1128 Bluetooth RFID reader. This handheld reader pairs via Bluetooth to an application on a mobile phone and has a customisable Application Programming Interface (API) that allows the user to alter the reader settings as well as what tag properties the reader interrogates. The purpose of this experiment is to assess if RFID tags can be read successfully as a vehicle moves past them, and if the order in which these tags are detected can be used to retrace the route a vehicle takes around a predetermined grid. Twelve tags were laid out in a 6 by 2 grid with spacing of 10m between each tag, as is shown in Fig. 2.

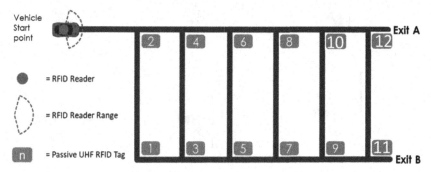

Fig. 2. Set-up for the first experiment.

A vehicle was then driven on a randomised route, determined by a MATLAB algorithm to ensure no bias, and the reader was set to scan continuously as the vehicle progressed throughout the grid. The RFID reader has a field of view of 150 degrees and therefore the reader was placed forward facing with the centre of the reader field aligned with the centre line of the vehicle. The raw data from the scanner is a continuous alphanumeric string containing the tag identifier, number of unique scans, date of scan, time of scan and time zone in which the scan occurred. In order to post-process the data, a MATLAB script was created which separates each individual category of data into its own column. This data will be used to determine the order which tags were scanned based off of the time, date and time zone. Fifty iterations of the experiment were carried out, catering for random errors though failure to scan was not expected due to speeds well below maximum [19].

3.2.2 Experiment 2 – Determining Direction from RSSI

RSSI is the most commonly used feature for RFID positioning systems where a more negative raw RSSI value in dBm is equivalent to a weaker backscattered signal strength and thus the further a tag is located away from a reader the lower the percentage of the maximum signal registered. Consideration must be given to materials directly surrounding the tags and reader, which can modify, alter or disrupt the signal. Though busy traffic scenarios may make RSSI values noisier or result in gaps, for the most part, on open roads very few interfering objects which could get between the readers and the tag antennae. For the physical experimentation proposed in this research, a 4-way junction will be used with the RFID reader placed at the intersection between two of the junctions with the 150 degree field of view of the reader facing directly into the junction centre. From this, six possible vehicle routes can be taken depending on if the vehicle approached from the front or rear of the junction, as shown in Fig. 3a–f.

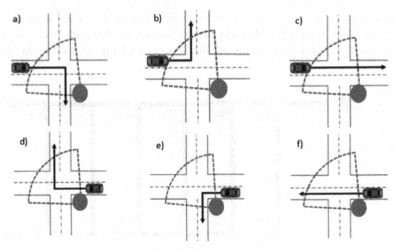

Fig. 3. Route options

3.3 Innovation Implementation - Path Prediction

3.3.1 Path Prediction Algorithm

To utilize the data provided from such an RFID tracking system, a route prediction algorithm is needed, with the key steps shown in Fig. 4. To map the road network a vehicle could take Open Street Maps (OSM) is used where junction longitudes and latitudes aid the formation of a connectivity matrix creating a virtual road map of a chosen location. From this virtual map a route costing algorithm is applied, based off a modified Dijkstra's algorithm, to evaluate costs to travel to each connected node. This cost was initially based on the proximity of each node to the next node, namely the distance between nodes. Adjustments were introduced to take into account geospatial factors and human behaviour insights that may influence an offenders chosen route. Simulation of erratic and non-logical driving that may be conducted by a thief in an escape situation, such as driving the wrong way down a one way road, was added to the modelling capability to add realism.

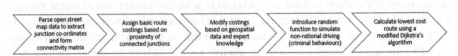

Fig. 4. Prediction pathway

3.3.2 Geospatial Factors and Codified Knowledge

In most instances when stealing a vehicle, the objective for the offender is to get to their end destination as quickly as possible. In an open space, where there are no obstructions, there is a strong correlation between distance and time taken to cover that distance.

However, in modern day road networks a number of factors can limit the time of passage including but not limited to: traffic lights, road humps, speed limits, junctions, roadworks etc. Though some of these factors are less of a hinderance to those not following the rules of the road i.e., staying within the defined safe speed limit, these factors need to be considered in determining the preferred route that may be taken. Hence, though distance can be used to as an indicator for a route preference, this route cost has been modified based on the proximity of a certain node to either an attractive or repulsive obstacle. Attractive obstacles in this research are defined as points of potential interest to an offender, such as areas of blind spots for CCTV cameras, access roads to motorways, or large parking structures, as all of these areas make it harder for the police to catch or track a vehicle. Repulsive obstacles are defined as areas a thief is likely to avoid, such as police stations, areas with road works, or narrow one-way roads, which may result in the thief raising suspicions or becoming trapped and unable to escape. Using a traditional mathematical approach, identification of these obstacles could be sought through historical crime records and analysis of the routes taken, potentially with machine learning methods to identify the patterns of behaviour. However, difficulties arise in terms of data access, sparsity of data, and inability to reflect emerging behaviours. Given the domain, huge amounts of information exist in those that work in the environment, hence the list of repulsive and attractive obstacles has been generated through knowledge capturing, using person-to-person workshops involving existing and former police officers. An insight illustration is given through the example of knowledge gained on route choices and their associated presented risks, such as those carrying more ANPR; in a form of rational choice theory application. This may equate, in practice to the use of side roads, rather than motorways, being exploited as criminal routes and rural outlying areas rather than surveillance heavy city centres. Similarly, in practice tools such as ANPR, which are essentially simply an identification and alert system, rely upon an available police mobile within distance and time to intercept any target vehicle. Such likelihood of policing mobiles, which is a calculated criminal risk, would tend to be higher closer to police stations and conurbations than outlying areas. Such considerations concerning ANPR, though, would only be a factor if the original number plates had been left on display. Each obstacle was then given a rating from 1 to 5, where 1 indicates no influence, 3 moderate influence, and 5 very strong influence. This practitioner insight and expert knowledge provides the power to the mathematical prediction.

4   Results

4.1   Tag Identification and Vehicle tracking

A MATLAB algorithm has been developed to analyse RSSI data streams, from the front and rear tags, for the six driving scenarios (shown in Fig. 5a–f). The algorithm that has been developed for this research compares the trends of data and time difference in peaks of RSSI to determine the direction the vehicle has taken through a junction. If the initial RSSI value is above 50% then the vehicle must have approached from the rear and only Fig. 5d, Fig. 5e and Fig. 5f could apply. Conversely, if the average initial RSSI is below 50% then the vehicle must have approached from the front and Fig. 5a, Fig. 5b, and

Fig. 5c could apply. The trend in the RSSI data can then be compared to expected results to identify which of the three remaining possible routes the vehicle took at the junction.

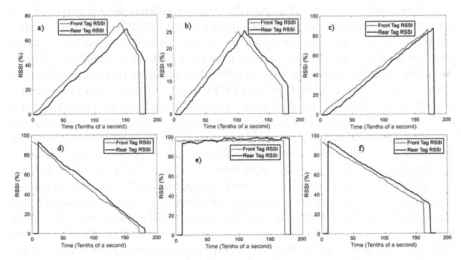

Fig. 5. RSSI Values generated

The position of the peak RSSI value relative to the initial and final values is calculated as well as the difference between the peak RSSI value and the final, non-zero, RSSI value. This allows Fig. 5a, Fig. 5b and Fig. 5c to be uniquely identified for the frontal approach scenarios. However at this point, for the rear approach scenarios, only Fig. 5e can be uniquely identified as Fig. 5d and Fig. 5f appear to have very similar RSSI traces. In order to distinguish between these scenarios the total time over which the RSSI is greater than zero can be used to determine the length of the route taken by the vehicle. The scenario presented in Fig. 5d represents a longer route, for the same velocity, than in Fig. 5f. As such the time over which RSSI values are recorded is shorter and the total time over which RSSI values are detected can be used to differentiate between the two scenarios. The algorithm developed for this experiment proves that the RSSI can be used to determine the vehicle heading and direction at a junction when the vehicle speed is known. Calculation of the vehicle speed at each time step should therefore ensure that this algorithm can correctly identify the direction any vehicle turns at a junction regardless of the vehicle velocity or if the vehicle speeds up or slows down while manoeuvring through the junction.

4.2 Path Prediction

The path prediction algorithm runs through one thousand iterations to identify the highest overall probability escape route. To illustrate the impact of geospatial factors and the process of modifying the costing can be seen in a simplified form in Fig. 6a and b, where geospatial data, such as the police station and the presence of road works, increases the cost of traveling down the road on which those obstacles are placed.

Examples of the escape routes calculated from the OSM data after applying the path prediction algorithm can be seen in Fig. 7a-c. The figures show the location of geospatial points of interest by longitude and latitude, as well as the start location at which the theoretical vehicle was stolen and the exit point(s) which are identified as a possible escape point for criminals. In this research the escape points are identified as parking structures, as shown as green points labelled 'exits' (in Fig. 7a, 7b), or access points to main roads as shown in Fig. 7c. The choice of these two types of location as exit points is based off current knowledge of typical car theft behaviour. If an offender can access main roads then they can travel at significantly higher speeds and could potentially cross county borders, making it significantly harder for the police to track down the vehicle.

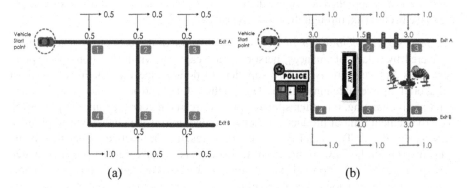

Fig. 6. (a) Basic costing (b) Modified costings

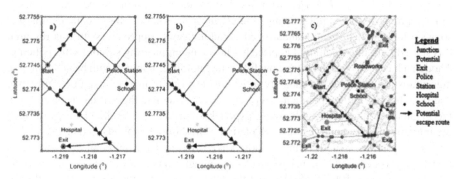

Fig. 7. (a)–(c) Map with geospatial points of interest and escape routes

Thieves have also been known to implement what is known as soaking after stealing a car. To soak a car, a stolen car is taken to a large public car park and left there for up to a week in order to assess if the vehicle is being tracked based on whether the police come to recover the vehicle. Although soaking would not be effective with RFID tracking as the vehicle would be logged entering the car park, thieves may not be aware of this and therefore, for at least a short while once the technology is first introduced, car parks may still be likely places for stolen vehicles to end up. If the RFID traceability technology and path planning algorithms were implemented in the real-world, these exit points would be defined more rigorously through further consultation with the police to highlight typical theft routes, ports where vehicles can be shipped abroad, or known garages where vehicle are taken to be stripped down and sold as parts.

5 Discussion

Although the methodology and experimentation developed in this project provide an excellent framework for the feasibility of such a system namely, implementation of an RFID based vehicle tracking system, and its subsequent use with a predictive methodology for use in apprehension of car theft offenders, there are several discussion points that have been raised through the research process.

Challenges of Technology and the Domain: Exploration of the technology space is often hampered by a lack of finances, personnel and capacity within the Force to explore new ideas and innovations, limited suppliers of domain specific solutions or lack of collaborations to enable innovations. Though the cultural and acceptance of technology solutions is changing, it is often siloed – this research being one typical example. Given the procurement time of products, if they are found, means the challenge and problem may have evolved. The majority of policing is reactive in practice, rather than being proactive. Often the view to the use of technology is to make current practices better, perhaps more efficient or provide the situational awareness or evidence for more reliable apprehension. The vision to get ahead of the criminal mind, to think out of the box, and to consider innovations for future policing rather than current policing is needed.

Integration of Human Knowledge: Typical approaches to problems becomes a discipline approach – the engineer brings the engineering solution, the social scientist the social solution, each using standardized domain specific approaches. In this research this started with this traditional approach – how can engineering solutions aid policing. Though it has been demonstrated how future technology combined with basic predictive algorithms (which have the capacity to be enhanced) can provide insight for effective decision making in the apprehension of criminals in vehicle theft, it has been realized the greater potential with embodying expert knowledge, in a codified form, through the interdisciplinary approach and adaptation of traditional methods. This research has begun the journey to understanding how knowledge management can be explored in traceability systems and the necessity of such integration and evolution to increase the effectiveness of such technologies and their acceptance. Furthering this capability to capture human knowledge with quantitative IoT based traceability to yield a knowledge system that is great than the sum of its discipline specific parts.

Data & its Agility: Firstly, a lack of access to police data and crime statistics meant that the geospatial points of interest, such as the obstacles such as police stations and hospitals, which were used to initially modify the route cost, were estimates based on the data which is publicly available including crime hotspot locations and car thief behaviour [1, 2]. The path predictive algorithm is only as accurate as the data that is entered into the system and, as a result of the publicly available data not being completely up to date and lack of accessibility of real-life data improvements are possible. The behavioural aspect, how the mind of a criminal may make decisions in a high-stress situation, is particularly difficult to gain from traditional data sources. This has been investigated through the exploration of expert knowledge, though this requires a method to codify such knowledge into a mathematical framework. How to weight human actions in a digital system is not straightforward, and this codification itself can also be improved and enhanced for increased accuracy to model and predict human behaviours.

Codification of Temporal Knowledge: Given the dynamic environment of criminal activity, where the ability to be agile in the criminal world appears to be greater than in for those trying to apprehend the criminals (partly due to the reactive rather than proactive nature), it is expected that patterns of behaviour would change. Although AI systems are being explored for continual learning from numeric datasets, the research problem is how can agile temporal knowledge be captured, codified and ingested within a continual learning AI system within a reasonable time period. The human-cyber knowledge relationship needs further research to ensure the system is capable of agile thinking in the pursuit of capturing criminals.

Creativity in Technology – does it Exist?: Many technological solutions are based on a logical approach to solution, following rational steps towards its end point. Criminal activity is typically creative, spur of the moment, non-conformist and hence the question remains as to whether technology itself can be creativity. Creativity may be viewed as an evolvement from just logic – the paradigm of poker versus chess. It may be said that poker goes beyond predictive rules, it's something the computer will struggle with even though it can handle the Cartesian mechanics of chess. The final thought is what is the art of the possible – how can technology and knowledge management be effective in creative situations?

6 Conclusion

With the emergence of new science and technology brings the potential to harness their attributes as enablers for improved products and service provision. In the field of policing services, these advances can serve two purposes – to aid those committing crimes and to facilitate capture for those trying to prevent or solve crime. Though this research had the initial perspective to consider innovative engineering solutions to advance policing capability it has realized the interconnectedness that exists between users of technology and the technology itself. The research has shown that though technology can give additional information to help inform decisions it needs to be coupled with human knowledge to give the level of sophisticated needed to work in practice, catering for the nuances that data alone does not reveal. In this application domain where the problems to be solved, namely the crimes being committed, are evolving in a dynamic environment, driven by human-centric uncertain behaviours with no clearly defined rules, innovations involving science and technology need to be coupled with expert knowledge to remain agile and fit for purpose. Clearly the study has limitations, scope of experimentation and depth of knowledge acquisition to name two, yet it is felt that it opens the door for further discussion and deepening research to advance knowledge management practices with the development of new technological solutions, in policing and beyond.

References

1. Office for National Statistics (UK). Number of motor vehicle theft offences recorded in England and Wales from 03/2002 to 22/2021. Chart. 21 July 2022. Statista. https://www.statista.com/statistics/303551/motor-vehicle-theft-in-england-and-wales/. Accessed 03 Feb 2023
2. Elkin, M.: Nature of crime: vehicle-related theft. Off. Natl. Stat. (2019). https://www.ons.gov.uk/peoplepopulationandcommunity/crimeandjustice/datasets/natureofcrimevehiclerelatedtheft
3. College of Policing. Future Operating Environment 2040 (2020). https://assets.college.police.uk/s3fs-public/2020-08/Future-Operating-Environment-2040-Part1-Trends.pdf
4. National Police Chief Council. Policing Vision 2025 (2017). https://www.npcc.police.uk/documents/Policing%20Vision.pdf
5. Luvisi, A., Lorenzini, G.: RFID-plants in the smart city: applications and outlook for urban green management. Urban For. Urban Green. **13**, 630–637 (2014)
6. Tribe, J., Hayward, S., van Lopik, K., Whittow, W., West, A.: Robust RFID tag design for reliable communication within the Internet of Things. Int. J. Adv. Manuf. Technol. **121**(3–4), 1–15 (2022)
7. Gottschalk, P.: Stages of knowledge management systems in police investigations, Knowl.-Based Syst. **19**(6), 381–387 (2006). ISSN 0950–7051
8. Poe, L., Protrka, N., Roycroft, M., Koivuniemi, T.: Knowledge management (KM) and intelligence-led policing (ILP). In: Roycroft, M., Brine, L. (eds.) Modern Police Leadership, pp. 327–343. Springer, Cham (2021). https://doi.org/10.1007/978-3-030-63930-3_25
9. Yang, H., Yang, S.: Mobile tracking architecture in ZigBee RFID sensor networks. In: EPSRC Workshop on Human Adaptive Mechatronics, May (2010)
10. Hayward, S.: A novel tracking architecture and service for improved asset safety and security through the supply chain. PHD thesis, Loughborough University Thesis (2022)
11. Wang, Z.: Vehicle positioning utilising radio frequency identification devices with geo-located roadside furniture upon urban-roads. Loughborough University Thesis (2022)
12. Jackson, T.W., Farzaneh, P.: Theory-based model of factors affecting information overload. Int. J. Inf. Manage. **32**(6), 523–532 (2012)
13. Iheukwumere-Esotu, L., Yunusa-Kaltungo, A.: Knowledge criticality assessment and codification framework for major maintenance activities: a case study of cement rotary kiln plant. Sustainability **13**, 4619 (2021)
14. Tsalapati, E., Tribe, J., Goodall, P., Young, R., Jackson, T., West, A.: Enhancing RFID system configuration through semantic modelling. Knowl. Eng. Rev. **36**, e11 (2021)
15. Bolisani, E., Padova, A., Scarso, E.: The continuous recombination of codification and personalisation KM strategies: a retrospective study. EJKM, **18**(2), 185–195 (2020)
16. Björninen, T., Espejo Delzo, K., Ukkonen, L., Elsherbeni, A., Sydänheimo, L.: Long range metal mountable tag antenna for passive UHF RFID systems. In: IEEE International Conference RFID-Technologies Applications. RFID-TA 2011, pp. 202–206 (2011)
17. Loan, D.: Vietnam starts the deployment of electronic toll collection, VNExpress International (2016). https://e.vnexpress.net/news/news/vietnam-starts-the-deployment-of-electronic-toll-collection-3429402.html
18. Mo, L., Qin, C., Tang, X.: Velocity analysis for UHF RFID vehicle license plate. In: Proceedings of the 2010 International Conference on Optoelectronics. Image Processing. ICOIP 2010, vol. 2, pp. 722–725 (2010)
19. Unterhuber, A., Iliev, S., Biebl, E.: Influence of the vehicle velocity on the number of reads in UHF RFID scenarios. In: 2019 IEEE International Conference on RFID Technology and Applications RFID-TA 2019. pp. 421–426 (2019)

20. Nafar, F., Shamsi, H.: On the design of a user interface for an RFID-based vehicle tracking system. Int. J. Wirel. Inf. Netw. **24**(1), 56–61 (2017). https://doi.org/10.1007/s10776-016-0329-9
21. Oikawa, Y.: Tag movement direction estimation methods in an RFID gate system. In: Proceedings of the 2009 6th International Symposium Wireless Communication Systems. ISWCS 2009, pp. 41–45 (2009)
22. Buffi, A., Nepa, P.: An RFID-based technique for train localization with passive tags. In: 2017 IEEE International Conference on RFID. RFID 2017, pp. 155–160 (2017)
23. Ferro, V., Luz, A., Lucrecio, A.: Small long range UHF tag for metal applications. In: 2013 IEEE International Conference on RFID- Technologies Applications. RFID-TA 2013, pp. 1–6 (2013)
24. Turetken, E., Benmansour, F., Fua, P.: Automated reconstruction of tree structures using path classifiers and Mixed Integer Programming. In: Proceedings of the IEEE Computer Society Conference on Computer Vision Pattern Recognition, pp. 566–573 (2012)
25. Chen, J., Liu, X., Liu, C., Yang, Y., Yang, S., Zhang, Z.: A modified convolutional neural network with transfer learning for road extraction from remote sensing imagery. In: Proceedings of the 2018 Chinese Automation Congress. CAC 2018, pp. 4263–4267 (2019)
26. Zhang, L., He, N., Xu, C.: Road network extraction and recognition using color clustering from color map images (2013)
27. Velagić, J., Delimustafić, D., Osmanković, D.: Mobile robot navigation system based on Probabilistic Road Map (PRM) with Halton sampling of configuration space. In: IEEE International Symposium Industrial Electronics, pp. 1227–1232 (2014)

IT and New Trends in KM

Optimal Controller Selection Scheme Using Artificial Bee Colony and Apriori Algorithms in SDN

Kyung Tae Kim[✉]

College of Computing and Informatics, Sungkyunkwan University, 2066, Seobu-ro, Jangan-gu, Suwon, Korea
kyungtaekim76@gmail.com

Abstract. Software Defined Networking (SDN) is one of the most recent Internet technology that manages the large scale network. SDN decouples the control plane from data plane, which simplifies the logic of network devices and reduces the cost of the network infrastructure. The control plane is the key component of a network which ensures smooth management and operation of the entire network. Distributed SDN controllers have been proposed to solve the scalability and a single point of failure problem. It is a critical issue for the switch to find the optimal controller among the distributed controllers. In this paper we propose a novel scheme for controller selection in distributed SDN environments. The proposed scheme decides optimal controller from distributed controllers by applying the Artificial Bee Colony (ABC) algorithm for meta-heuristic search and Apriori algorithm for effective association rule mining between switch and controller. Computer simulation reveals that the proposed scheme consistently outperforms the scheme employing only ABC and Apriori algorithms separately in terms of response time, arrival rate, number of messages, and accuracy.

Keywords: Software Defined Network · Distributed controllers · Artificial Bee Colony algorithm · Apriori algorithm · Selection of controller · Edge computing

1 Introduction

The explosive growth of the Internet of Things (IoT) and mobile devices leads to an explosion of new applications and services, increasing the burden of what today's Internet could carry [1]. Especially, since the data collected from a lot of devices can generate excessive traffic, several researchers have tried to solve this issue using Edge Computing [2, 3]. To cope with the numerous and diverse IoT devices, the edge computing infrastructure has to support a lot of connected devices and the processing of the massive data collected and complex applications. However, the edge server in edge computing has limited computational and processing resources compared to high-end servers in the cloud server [4]. Therefore, to support high scalability, ultra- low latency, high throughput, and reliable transmission of data, the SDN paradigm is regarded as one of the suitable solutions [5–7].

© The Author(s), under exclusive license to Springer Nature Switzerland AG 2023
L. Uden and I-H. Ting (Eds.): KMO 2023, CCIS 1825, pp. 347–359, 2023.
https://doi.org/10.1007/978-3-031-34045-1_28

SDN is an innovative technology in the field of computer network that separates data transmission function and control function from each other, allowing the users the flexibility of using the functions of the network in their own devices [8, 9]. SDN has numerous advantages including direct programming, centralized management, fast delivery, and flexibility. In SDN a single controller may be used as a centralized controller. If excessive packets need to be processed, however, its performance is significantly degraded because of limited processing capacity and distance to the switching devices [2]. Meanwhile, the failure of a single controller may lead to the collapse or congestion of entire network. In order to effectively resolve these issues, the distributed controller architecture was proposed [10–12]. Distributed controller architectures with more than one controller could be used to address some of the challenges of a single SDN controller such as availability [13]. Furthermore, distributed controllers can reduce the latency or increase the scalability and fault tolerance of the SDN deployment. However, this architecture increases the lookup overhead of communication between switches and distributed controllers. Moreover, this approach is difficult to maintain the consistent state in the overall distributed system [14, 15].

In this paper we propose a novel scheme which allows a switch to select an optimal controller from distributed controllers in SDN for edge computing environments. The proposed scheme decides optimal controller based on the data and weight of the controllers using the improved ABC algorithm based on Apriori algorithm for effective association rule mining between switch and controller. It can achieve controller optimization while keeping the excellent performance of the improved ABC algorithm. In the proposed scheme, the priority of each controller was determined by considering the computing and communication capacity of the controllers using an improved ABC algorithm, which includes Apriori algorithm and FCFS (First-Come-First-Served) policy. The proposed scheme significantly reduces the communication latency between the switch to the controller by selecting an optimal controller compared to the existing schemes. Also, the proposed scheme can solve the consistency problem by employing the meta-heuristic association rule mining algorithm. Furthermore, through the uniformly distributed controller, the proposed scheme increase scalability, connectivity, and flexibility of the network, which increases the communication efficiency and reduces the propagation delay of the link. Computer simulation reveals that the proposed scheme consistently outperforms the scheme employing only ABC and Apriori algorithm separately in terms of response time, arrival rate, number of messages, and accuracy.

The rest of the paper is organized as follows. Section 2 introduces the related work for proposed scheme. Section 3 describes the proposed scheme in a detailed manner. The experimental results of the proposed scheme are explained in Sect. 4. Finally, Sect. 5 concludes the paper and describes future research directions.

2 Related Work

2.1 Software Defined Networking

SDN is an effective networking paradigm which makes it easier for the network manager to control the network [16, 18]. SDN is a conceptual architecture that decouples the control plane and data plane of the network and enables network partitioning [5]. SDN architecture is divided into three categories as shown in Fig. 1: the physical infrastructure layer, the controllable control layer, and the application layer. This lets SDN not only create complex paths that cannot be configured in existing networks but also effectively cope with changing traffic patterns and quickly configure the virtual networks required in cloud environments. The control plane in SDN is decoupled from the data plane by drawing the networking functions from the forwarding devices as shown in Fig. 1. The separation of the control plane and the data plane of the network has the advantage of being able to respond more quickly to a malfunction caused by a problem and increase the flexibility and availability of the network. The control functions are deployed to logically centralized controllers so that they can be implemented on a centralized software platform [17]. Using a single, centralized controller might be efficient since the overloaded switch can migrate to a new controller from the previously connected one.

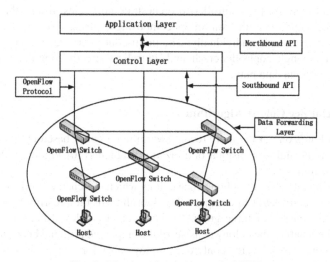

Fig. 1. The three-layer structure of SDN

2.2 OpenDaylight

OpenDaylight (ODL) is a modular open SDN platform for the networks of any size and scale [19, 20]. By sharing YANG data structure in the common data store and messaging infrastructure, ODL allows for fine-grained services to be created and combined together to solve more complex problems. In the ODL Model Driven Service Abstraction Layer (MD-SAL), any app or function can be bundled into a service that is loaded into the controller. The model-driven approach is being increasingly used in the networking domain to describe the functionality of network devices [21], services [22], policies [23, 24], and network APIs [25]. The protocols of choice are NETCONF and RESTCONF; the modeling language of choice is YANG. NETCONF [26] is an IETF network management protocol that defines configuration and operational conceptual data stores and a set of Create, Retrieve, Update, Delete (CRUD) operations that can be used to access these data stores. RESTCONF is a model that describes the mapping of YANG data to a REST-ful API [27, 28]. It is a REST-based protocol that runs over HTTP and is used to access YANG defined data, using Network Configuration Protocol (NETCONF) defined data stores. The YANG data modeling language is used to define the data sent over NETCONF [29]. It can model both the configuration data as well as the manipulated state data.

OpenDaylight SDN controller has several layers. The top layer consists of business and network logic applications. The middle layer is the framework layer, and the bottom layer consists of physical and virtual devices. The middle layer is the framework in which the SDN abstractions can manifest. This layer hosts north-bound and south-bound APIs. The controller exposes open north-bound APIs which are used by applications. OpenDaylight supports the OSGi framework and bidirectional REST for the northbound API. The business logic resides in the applications above the middle layer. The applications use the controller to gather network intelligence, run algorithms to perform the analytics, and then use the controller to orchestrate new rules, if any, throughout the network. ODL supports multi-controllers composing a cluster. If there is only a single ODL controller, it works individually. The multi-controller structure could avoid the consequence of single controller crash, and controllers directly communicate with each other rather than via data plane.

2.3   Artificial Bee Colony Algorithm

ABC algorithm is one of the more recent swarm intelligence based optimization algorithms for solving multidimensional optimization problems [30]. Figure 2 is the flowchart of ABC algorithm.

The intelligent behavior of honey bee colony which search new food sources around their hive was considered to compose the algorithm. In the algorithm, the colony of artificial bees consists of three groups of bees called employed bees, onlookers and scouts. While a half of the colony consists of the employed artificial bees, the other half includes the onlookers. There is only one employed bee for every food source. That is, the number of employed bees is equal to the number of food sources around the hive. The main steps of the algorithm are given below.

First, source initialization is the initial source to a random value.

$$X_{ij} = X_{minj} + rand(0, 1)(X_{maxj} - X_{minj}) \tag{1}$$

Second, the employed bee searches the neighbor source and estimates the amount of nectar of the source, and informs the onlooker bee of the source of higher fitness.

$$V_{ik} = X_{ik} + rand(-1, 1)(X_{ik} - X_{jk}) \tag{2}$$

Third, here a source is selected probabilistically by onlooker bee based on the source discovered by employed bee and the estimated amount of nectar. Onlooker bee selects the source by

$$P_i = \frac{f(X_i)}{\sum f(X_n)} \tag{3}$$

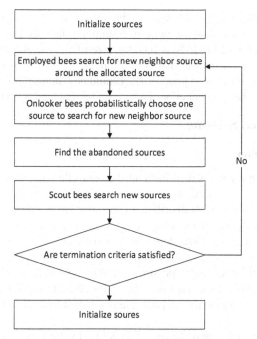

Fig. 2. The Flowchart of ABC Algorithm

2.4 Apriori Algorithm

Data Mining is a way of obtaining undetected patterns or facts from massive amount of data in a database. Association rule mining is a major technique in the area of data mining. Association rule mining finds frequent itemsets from a set of transactional databases. Apriori algorithm is one of the earliest algorithms of association rule mining [31, 32]. Apriori employs an iterative approach known as level-wise search. In Apriori, (k + 1) itemsets are generated from k-itemsets. First, scan the database for count of each candidate and compare candidate support count with minimum support count to generate set of frequent 1-itemsets. The set is denoted as $L1$. Then, $L1$ is used to find $L2$, set of frequent 2-itemsets, which is further used to find $L3$ and so on, until no more frequent k-itemsets can be found [33]. After finding set of frequent k-itemsets, it is easy to generate strong association rules. The process of finding each L_k requires the database to be scanned completely once. To improve the efficiency of the level-wise generation of frequent itemsets, an important property called the Apriori property, presented is used to reduce the search space. In Apriori property, all nonempty subsets of a frequent itemset must also be frequent. A two-step process is used to find the frequent itemsets: join and prune actions.

1) The join step: To find L_k a set of candidate k-itemsets is generated by joining L_k−1 with itself. This set of candidates is denoted C_k.
2) The prune step: The members of C_k may or may not be frequent, but all of the frequent k -itemsets are included in C_k. A scan of the database to determine the count

of each candidate in C_k would result in the determination of L_k (i.e., all candidates having a count no less than the minimum support count are frequent by definition, and therefore belong to L_k). To reduce the size of C_k, the Apriori property is used as follows. Any $(k-1)$-itemset that is not frequent cannot be a subset of a frequent k-itemset. Hence, if any $(k-1)$-subset of a candidate k-itemset is not in L_k-1, then the candidate cannot be frequent either and so can be removed from C_k.

3   The Proposed Scheme

3.1   Basic Operation

The proposed scheme gathers data from all the controllers to measure how often each controller is used, and then finds the association rules based on the items run frequently by the controllers. In the SDN distributed controller environment, the controllers are selected by Apriori algorithm according to the frequency of use. For this, the data of all the controllers are initialized to random values, and then the neighbor controllers of each controller are searched regarding the amount of nectar. Using the transaction support of Apriori algorithm, the controller's goodness of fit is estimated. In order to minimize the time for searching the association rules, the FCFS (First-Come-First-Served) policy is applied. If there exists a priority rule, the rule is selected first. Then the remaining rules are found.

In searching the source only the one of the highest value is selected, while the others are discarded. This is for minimizing the communication cost. Figure 3 is the flowchart of the proposed scheme for selecting an optimal controller based on the data and weight of the controllers.

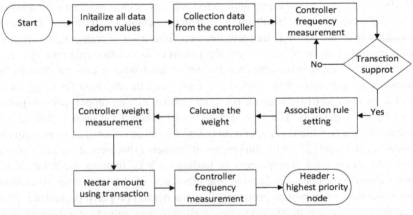

Fig. 3. The Flowchart of the proposed scheme

3.2   Priority and Weight of Controller

The priority of the controllers is decided using the ABC algorithm as follows. First, the data of the controllers are initialized to random value, and then the distance between a controller and its neighbor one is measured. The fitness of the controllers is then calculated using the transaction support of the Apriori algorithm and weight of them. The weight of each controller is defined to represent the throughput. The performance of a controller is affected by various factors such as distance to communicating controller, bandwidth, transmission delay, load, and packet loss probability, etc. Only the most frequently used controller identified by the proposed approach is selected, while the remaining controllers are excluded. By selecting the most frequently used controller, collision between the controllers and communication load can be reduced. Also, the detailed selection algorithm of controller is shown in Algorithm 1.

The following is to calculate the weight of controller_v, $w(v)$.

$$w(v) = \omega_1 P(v) + \omega_2 S(v) \tag{4}$$

where ω_1 and ω_2 are weight coefficients. $P(v)$ is the operational performance and $S(v)$ is amount nectar of controller_v, respectively.

$$W(v, s) = \alpha \cdot dis(v, s) + \beta \cdot ban(v, s)$$
$$+ \gamma \cdot del(v, s) + \delta \cdot load(v, s) \tag{5}$$

In Eq. (5) $0 \leq \alpha, \beta, \gamma, \lambda \leq 1$, $\alpha + \beta + \gamma + \lambda = 1$. The parameter of distance, bandwidth, delay, and load should be normalized:

$$dis(w_v, w_s) = \frac{dis(w_v, w_s)}{\sum_{i,j \in l(v,s) \& i \neq j} dis(w_i, w_j)}$$

$$ban(w_v, w_s) = \frac{ban(w_v, w_s)}{\sum_{i,j \in l(v,s) \& i \neq j} ban(w_i, w_j)}$$

$$del(w_v, w_s) = \frac{del(w_v, w_s)}{\sum_{i,j \in l(v,s) \& i \neq j} del(w_i, w_j)}$$

$$load(w_v, w_s) = \frac{load(w_v, w_s)}{\sum_{i,j \in l(v,s) \& i \neq j} load(w_i, w_j)}$$

Then the weight of w_v to all other $(n - 1)$ controllers in the network is:

$$All - Weight(w_v) = \sum_{s=1 \& s \neq v}^{n} weight(w_v, w_s) \tag{6}$$

The weight of w_v is calculated by

$$W(w_v) = \mu \cdot weight(w_v) + \sigma \cdot All - Weight(w_v) \tag{7}$$

ALGORITHM 1 Selection of Controller

---

1. Assume that the path of P_1 is (x_1, y_1, z_1) and that of P_2 is (x_2, y_2, z_2). The controller synchronization occurs with y_1 and y_2, and one of the new paths obtained is P_3: (x_1, y_2, y_1, z_1).
2. Deleting the duplicated switch, the new path P_3 is decided.
3. By the same way, another new path P_4 is obtained.
4. Applying the fitness function to P_1, P_2, P_3, P_4, an optimal path is selected.

3.3 Transaction

The neighbor source of an assigned source is checked, and the source of more amount of nectar is notified to the onlooker bee. They are also weighted, and the one of low nectar amount is discarded. Next, based on the source searched by employed bee and the estimated nectar amount, the onlooker bee selects the source to search. In this way, the onlooker bee selects the source of the largest amount of nectar among the ones the employed bee found.

Let S and C denote a switch and controller, respectively. Each food source, X_C^S, in the population is represented as

$$X_C^S = \left\{ X_C^S, X_C^S, \ldots, X_C^S \right\}, \forall s \in N \forall c \in P_s \qquad (8)$$

where P_s the set of controllers and N is the number of switches. It estimates the amount of nectar a switch can have from the controllers of identical schedule number. Equation (9) is used for deciding the fitness of a switch connected to a controller, F_{cs}:

$$F_{cs} = C_{cs} + \theta_{cs}, \forall cs \in P_s \qquad (9)$$

where C_{cs} indicates the sum of coverages for all schedule numbers with complete coverage, θ_{cs} shows the maximum incomplete coverage and F_{cs} represents the fitness value for the cs in the controller.

Next, each new cs in the controller for each switch is generated by only updating.

$$V_c^s = \begin{cases} s, & pri > 0.5 \ \forall c \in P_s, \forall c \in N_{nc} \\ X_c^s, & otherwise \qquad s \in \varphi \end{cases} \qquad (10)$$

Each switch will select a certain number s in the incomplete schedule vector φ as a priority.

3.4 Selection Manager

The controller of a higher weight is needed to have more networking operation. In the proposed scheme, the controller appropriate for leading the update process is elected according to the weight. The network manager has the privilege of commanding the entire network since it keeps the network view. The network manager has the privilege of commanding the entire network since it keeps the network view. The priority of controller_i, P_i, is defined as

$$P_i = \begin{cases} \lfloor S * W(c_i) \rfloor & without \ manager \\ \infty & with \ manager \end{cases}$$

where S is the scale of the network. The controllers broadcast their priority and receive the priority of other controller in a present time. They regard the controller with the highest priority as their header.

The header selection is done following three steps.

Step 1. P_i ($i = 1,2,3,\ldots,n$) are calculated.

Step 2. P_i is broadcast during T_b which is broadcast period. It also receives the priority of other controller.

Step 3. The controller saves the address and priority of the controller which priority is bigger than itself. And it considers the controller with the highest priority as its header. Once a controller receives the priority which is same with itself, its priority will be subtracted one to avoid the same priority.

4   Performance Evaluation

In this section, the performance of the proposed scheme is evaluated via computer simulation. The simulation is performed on a PC consisting of Intel i5-7500 CPU, Window OS, and 8GB memory, and the scheme was implemented with Python and MATLAB. Also, the performance of the proposed scheme is compared with two other schemes to verify its relative effectiveness, the ABC and Apriori algorithm. The test data set is from Stanford Network Analysis Project (SNAP), which is a general purpose network analysis and graph mining library. The controller appropriate to lead the update process is elected to handle massive network of hundreds of millions of nodes and billions of edges. It is efficient for manipulating large graphs, calculates structural properties, generates regular and random graphs, and supports the attributes of nodes and edges.

To investigate the effectiveness of the proposed scheme, we first evaluate the response time with various sizes of data. The comparison results with ABC, Apriori algorithm, and the proposed scheme is shown in Fig. 4. Figure 4 shows that the proposed scheme displays the smallest response time among the three schemes, while the ABC algorithm is the largest. As a result, the proposed scheme effectively reduces the communication overhead in searching the controllers than existing schemes.

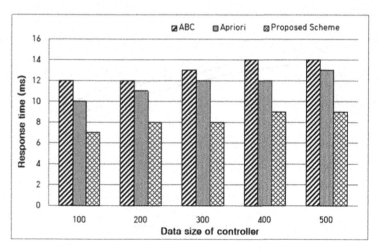

Fig. 4. The comparison of response time between proposed scheme and existing schemes

Arrival rates of the proposed scheme and existing schemes are compared in Fig. 5, which demonstrates that the proposed scheme consistently shows the lowest arrival rate with different sizes of controller data.

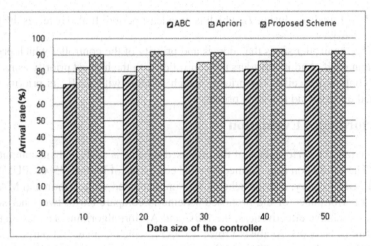

Fig. 5. The comparison of arrival rate between proposed scheme and existing schemes

Figure 6 shows the total amount of messages in ABC, Apriori algorithm, and the proposed scheme. Observe from the Fig. 6 that the proposed scheme always requires the smallest number of messages than ABC and Apriori algorithm. When the size of controller data is between 10 and 30, the ABC algorithm generates more messages than Apriori algorithm. However, Apriori algorithm needs slightly more messages than ABC algorithm after 40. This indicates that Apriori algorithm becomes overloaded when the data size grows beyond a certain level.

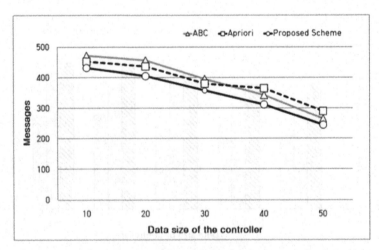

Fig. 6. The total amount of messages between proposed scheme and existing schemes

Figure 7 shows the comparison results of the accuracy in ABC algorithm, Apriori algorithm, and the proposed scheme. In Fig. 7, it demonstrates that the accuracy of the proposed scheme is about 90%, and it is the highest accuracy compared with the accuracies of the existing schemes. The accuracy of the ABC algorithm is the lowest, however, it continues getting higher accuracy as the controller data gets bigger, and it has the same accuracy as the Apriori scheme while the update data is 50 eventually.

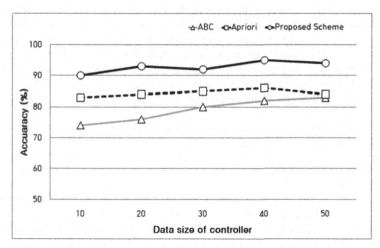

Fig. 7. The comparison of accuracy with the proposed scheme and existing schemes

5   Conclusion

The SDN paradigm shifts control to a centralized omniscient controller. The controller, however, creates a bottleneck due to the enormous amount of message exchanges between the switches and the controller in SDN for edge computing. As a result, inappropriate switch assignment to the controller reduces performance. In this paper, we have proposed a novel scheme which allows a switch to select an optimal controller from distributed controllers in order to reduce communication and propagation latency and improve throughput and reliability in SDN. The optimal controller is selected using the ABC and Apriori algorithms. Also, the priority of each controller in the proposed scheme was determined by considering the computing and communication capacity of the controllers. Moreover, the proposed scheme can solve the consistency problem by employing the meta-heuristic association rule mining algorithm. Computer simulation reveals that the proposed scheme consistently outperforms the ABC and Apriori algorithms in terms of response time, arrival rate, and number of messages exchanged. In the future, we will expand the proposed controller selection scheme by employing more sophisticated scheme such as Gaussian mixture model and artificial intelligence technique. Also, the proposed scheme will also be tested and expanded considering various environments and applications where the requirements on the energy and communication latency are diverse.

Acknowledgments. This research was supported by Basic Science Research Program through the National Research Foundation of Korea (NRF) funded by the Ministry of Education (NRF-2022R1I1A1A01053800).

References

1. Wang, A., Zha, Z., Guo, Y., Chen, S.: Software defined networking (SDN) enhanced edge computing: a network centric survey. Proc. IEEE **107**(8), 1500–1519 (2019)
2. European Telecommunication Standards Institute, Mobile Edge Computing (MEC), Technical Requirements (ETSI GS MEC 002 V.1.1.1) (2016). https://www.etsi.org/deliver/etsi_gs/MEC/001_099/002/01.01.01_60/gs_MEC002v010101p.pdf. Accessed 10 Jan 2023
3. Mao, Y., You, C., Zhang, J., Huang, K., Letaief, K.B.: A survey on mobile edge computing: the communication perspective. IEEE Commun. Surv. Tutor. **19**(4), 2322–2358 (2017)
4. Lee, C.H., Park, J.S.: An SDN-based packet scheduling scheme for transmitting emergency data in mobile edge computing environments. Hum.-Cent. Comput. Inf. Sci. **11**(28), 2–15 (2021)
5. Open Networking Foundation, Software-Defined Networking (SDN) definition (2021). https://www.opennetworking.org/sdn-definition/. Accessed 10 Jan 2023
6. Shamsan, A.H., Faridi, A.R.: SDN-assisted IoT architecture: a review. In: Proceeding of the 4th International Conference on Computing Communication and Automation (ICCCA), pp. 1–7 (2018)
7. Lv, Z., Xiu, W.: Interaction of edge-cloud computing based on SDN and NFV for next generation IoT. IEEE Internet Things J. **7**(7), 5706–5712 (2019)
8. Kirkpatrick, K.: Software-defined networking. Commun. ACM **56**(9), 16–19 (2013)
9. Khan, S., et al.: Software-defined network forensics: motivation, potential locations, requirements, and challenges. IEEE Netw. **30**(6), 6–13 (2016)
10. Balakiruthiga, B., Deepalakshmi, P.A.: Distributed energy aware controller placement model for software-defined data centre network. Iran. J. Sci. Technol. Trans. Electr. Eng. **45**, 1083–1101 (2021)
11. Radam, N.S., Faraj, S.T., Jasim, K.S.: Multi-controllers placement optimization in SDN by the hybrid HSA-PSO algorithm. Computers **11**(7), 1–26 (2022)
12. Blial, O., Mamoun, M.B., Benaini, R.: An overview on SDN architectures with multiple controllers. J. Comput. Netw. Commun. **2016**(2), 1–8 (2016)
13. Hakiri, A., Gokhale, A., Berthou, P., Schmidt, D.C., Gayraud, T.: Software-defined networking: challenges and research opportunities for future internet. Comput. Netw. **75**(24), 453–471 (2014)
14. Xiao, L., Zhu, H., Xiang, S., Vinh, P.C.: Modeling and verifying SDN under Multi-controller architectures using CSP. Concurr. Comput. Pract. Exp. 1–17 (2019)
15. Sahoo, K.S., et al.: ESMLB: efficient switch migration-based load balancing for multicontroller SDN in IoT. IEEE Internet Things J. **7**(7), 5852–5860 (2020)
16. Xue, H., Kim, K.T., Youn, H.: Dynamic load balancing of software-defined networking based on genetic-ant colony optimization. Sensors **19**(2), 1–17 (2019)
17. Ahmad, S., Mir, A.H.: SDN Interfaces: protocols, taxonomy and challenges. Int. J. Wirel. Microwave Technol. **2**, 11–32 (2022)
18. Farhady, H., Lee, H., Nakao, A.: Software-defined networking: a survey. Comput. Netw. **81**, 79–95 (2015)
19. OpenDaylight Association, Opendaylight. https://www.opendaylight.org/. Accessed 12 Jan 2023
20. Eftimie, A., Borcoci, E.: SDN controller implementation using OpenDaylight: experiments. In: Proceedings of the 13th International Conference on communications, Bucharest, pp. 1–5 (2020)
21. Clemm, A.: Navigating device management and control interfaces in the age of SDN (2014). http://blogs.cisco.com/getyourbuildon/navigating-device-managementand-control-interfaces-in-the-age-of-sdn. Accessed 13 Jan 2023

22. Wallin, S., Wikstrom, C.: Automating network and service configuration using NETCONF and YANG. In: Proceedings of the 25th Large Installation System Administration (LISA), pp. 1–13 (2011)
23. Application centric infrastructure object-oriented data model: gain advanced network control and programmability. http://docplayer.net/15876333-Application-centric-infrastru cture-object-oriented-data-model-gain-advanced-network-control-and-programmability. html. Accessed 13 Jan 2023
24. Cisco Systems, The Cisco Application Policy Infrastructure Controller. https://www.cisco. com/c/en/us/products/collateral/cloud-systems-management/aci-fabric-controller/at-a-gla nce-c45-730001.html. Accessed 12 Jan 2023
25. Alghamdi, A., Paul, D., Sadgrove, E.: Designing a RESTful northbound interface for incompatible software defined network controllers. SN Comput. Sci. **3**, 1–7 (2022)
26. Enns, R., Bjorklund, M., Schoenwaelder, J., Bierman, A.: Network configuration protocol (NETCONF) (2011). https://www.rfc-editor.org/rfc/rfc6241. Accessed 12 Jan 2023
27. Bierman, A., Bjorklund, M., Watsen, K., Fernando, R.: RESTCONF protocol, draft-bierman-netconf-restconf-04 (2014). https://datatracker.ietf.org/doc/draft-bierman-netconf-restconf/. Accessed 12 Jan 2023
28. Jethanandani, M.: YANG, NETCONF, RESTCONF: what is this all about and how is it used for multi-layer networks. In: Proceedings of the 2017 Optical Fiber Communications Conference and Exhibition (OFC), Los Angeles, CA, USA, pp. 1–65 (2017)
29. Bjorklund, M.: YANG - a data modeling language for the network configuration protocol (NETCONF), RFC 6020. https://www.rfc-editor.org/rfc/rfc6020. Accessed 12 Jan 2023
30. Karaboga, D.: Artificial bee colony algorithm. Scholarpedia (2010)
31. Agrawal, R., Srikant, R.: Fast algorithms for mining association rules in large databases. In: Proceedings of the 20th International Conference on Very Large Data Bases, pp. 487–499 (1994)
32. Zareian, M.M., Mesbahb, M., Moradic, S., Ghateec, M.I.: A combined Apriori algorithm and fuzzy controller for simultaneous ramp metering and variable speed limit determination in a freeway. AUT J. Math. Comput. **3**(2), 237–251 (2022)
33. Hu, X.G., Wang, D.X., Liu, X.P., Guo, J., Wang, H.: The analysis on model of association rules mining based on concept lattice and Apriori algorithm. In: Proceedings of 2004 International Conference on Machine Learning and Cybernetics, Shanghai, China, pp. 1620–1624 (2004)

Add-BiGAN: An Add-Based Bidirectional Generative Adversarial Networks for Intrusion Detection

Qilun Sun[1], Ran Tao[1(✉)], Youqun Shi[1], and Xia Shang[2]

[1] School of Computer Science and Technology, Donghua University, Shanghai, China
{taoran,yqshi}@dhu.edu.cn
[2] Moule Network Technology Co., Ltd., Shanghai, China
shawn@bugbank.cn

Abstract. Intrusion detection involves collecting and analyzing information about key nodes in a network to actively detect intrusions or attempts to break into the system. However, intrusion detection still faces challenges such as high false alarm and alarm rates, as well as unbalanced and unlabeled data. To address these challenges, this paper proposes an add-based bidirectional generative adversarial network (Add-BiGAN) for intrusion detection. Add-BiGAN uses an add operation for feature fusion, extracting and superimposing semantic information to achieve higher accuracy. The proposed network was tested through a binary classification anomaly detection experiment on the KDDCUP99 dataset, and the results showed that the F1 score of the proposed network was 96.11%, making it the most effective classification method. By utilizing the proposed network, a better intrusion detection system (IDS) can be built to detect intrusions in the system or network, which would reduce the alarm rate and false alarm rate.

Keywords: Intrusion Detection · Bidirectional Generative Adversarial Networks · Add-BiGAN

1 Introduction

As the use of information technology has become an integral part of our daily lives, computer security has become of paramount importance. Intrusion detection refers to the collection and analysis of information about key nodes in the network to detect signs of security breaches or attacks [29]. The Intrusion Detection System (IDS) is an active network security technology that protects against attacks. It monitors network traffic and prevents malicious requests [1], providing protection against insider attacks by monitoring the network without affecting its performance. It also offers real-time defense against external attacks and misoperations. With the increasing security threats to internet users today, malicious attacks have become more complex. The intrusion detection system, however, is not efficient in identifying unknown malicious attacks and traffic [8], which results in high alarm rates and false alarm rates. Therefore, there is an urgent need for more accurate intrusion detection models to address these challenges.

© The Author(s), under exclusive license to Springer Nature Switzerland AG 2023
L. Uden and I-H. Ting (Eds.): KMO 2023, CCIS 1825, pp. 360–374, 2023.
https://doi.org/10.1007/978-3-031-34045-1_29

Traditional machine learning methods, such as decision trees (DT) (Safavian and Landgrebe, 1991) [13], random forests (RF) (Zhang et al. 2008) [14], and support vector machines (SVM) (Hsu et al. 2003) [12], have been widely used for intrusion detection. However, with the advancement of deep learning, convolutional neural networks (CNNs) (Vinayakumar et al. 2017) [20], recurrent neural networks (RNNs) (Yin et al. 2017) [19], and long short-term memory (LSTM) networks (Roy et al. 2017) [21] have gained popularity in this field. Traditional machine learning and supervised deep learning methods require balanced datasets with labeled samples. However, obtaining attack samples can be challenging, and supervised learning may not detect previously unknown attacks. Hence, unsupervised intrusion detection methods have been proposed. These methods are generally trained using a set of normal samples and classify any samples that deviate from the normal set as abnormal to detect unknown attacks. This approach can achieve better results in unbalanced sample scenarios.

The two main commonly used unsupervised intrusion detection methods are autoencoder (AE) and generative adversarial networks (GANs) [9]. The intrusion detection based on autoencoder (AE) usually employs a reconstruction approach where the reconstruction error is calculated and used as a threshold to detect anomalies. The approach has been continuously improved by researchers from 2016 to 2021, including the people in papers [3, 5, 11, 17], and its effectiveness is confirmed in paper [4]. Aygun et al. proposed a denoising autoencoder (DAE) approach based on AE for intrusion detection in paper [15]. Torabi et al. (2023) [26] proposed a practical autoencoder intrusion detection model based on vector reconstruction error, which achieved better results compared to autoencoder. In contrast, generative adversarial networks are more effective. The first model based on GAN anomaly detection, AnoGAN, was proposed by Schlegl et al. in 2016 [16], who further proposed the f-AnoGAN (2019) [10]. The performance was further improved in the GANomaly (2018) [18] by adding two encoders. Ren et al. (2022) [27] oversampled the original dataset based on GAN networks to improve the correct classification rate.

The ability to efficiently map data to the latent space further improves the capacity to detect anomalies in bidirectional generative adversarial networks (BiGAN). For the first time, Zenati et al. (2018) [28] introduced the BiGAN architecture in the field of anomaly detection. Chen et al. (2019) proposed a bidirectional generative adversarial network that utilized Wasserstein distance in the form of L1 loss [7]. Two different training architectures were proposed by Kaplan et al. (2020), and both methods made progress in the performance of BiGAN [6]. Xu et al. (2022) proposed an improved one-class BiGAN that is more suitable for detecting network intrusion attacks [2].

At this stage, intrusion detection still faces challenges such as high alarm rates and high false alarm rates, as well as unbalanced and unlabeled data. Although unsupervised intrusion detection based on BiGAN has been relatively well-developed, the feature fusion method of the improved BiGAN mentioned above is relatively consistent. This paper proposes an add-based bidirectional generative adversarial network (Add-BiGAN) for intrusion detection, which addresses the aforementioned problems and challenges by optimizing BiGAN. First, Add-BiGAN is an unsupervised deep learning model that can address the challenges of unbalanced and unlabeled data. Second, Add-BiGAN uses the add operation for feature fusion, which increases the amount of information and improves classification accuracy while reducing alarm rates in intrusion detection. The contribution of the method proposed in this paper is demonstrated through a detailed comparison of data using the KDDCUP99 dataset in Sect. 4. The contribution of the method proposed in this paper is as follows:

1) This paper proposes an Add-BiGAN, which is an unsupervised deep learning model that can solve the problem of unbalanced and unlabeled data.
2) The proposed Add-BiGAN is different from the current BiGAN that uses a consistent feature fusion method. The Add-BiGAN uses an add operation feature fusion to increase the amount of information, which can classify more accurately, and can reduce the alarm rate when applied to intrusion detection.
3) The proposed Add-BiGAN is compared with other network on the KDDCUP99 dataset. The proposed Add-BiGAN has achieved the best results so far, and its F1 score can reach 96.11%, surpassing the results of other models.

The rest of the paper is organised as follows. Section 2 provides a review pf recent related work and relevant models for applying unsupervised deep learning to intrusion detection. Section 3 presents the methodological process and models employed in this study. Section 4 describes the experiments conducted and the analysis of the results to lay the foundation for the feasibility of our approach. Section 5 gives conclusions and makes some suggestions for future research work.

2   Literature Review

The two deep learning models, GAN and AE, are increasingly being utilized for intrusion detection. This section primarily summarizes and reviews related works on these two models, as well as BiGAN, on existing datasets.

Intrusion detection using autoencoders (AE) involves calculating reconstruction errors using reconstruction methods, which are then used to detect anomalies [3, 5, 11, 17]. In this approach, the AE can be trained with only one class of samples to learn the distribution in its latent representation. The AE uses this distribution to reconstruct the input, calculate the reconstruction loss between the output and input, and identify anomalies based on the calculated loss. A paper [4] confirmed the effectiveness of this AE-based method, which has higher accuracy in network intrusion detection compared to existing machine learning techniques. Consequently, researchers have attempted to improve AEs, resulting in several AE variants. An et al. (2015) [12] proposed a variational autoencoder (VAE) method that uses the Gaussian distribution of input samples and identifies anomalies as part of the reconstruction loss. Aygun et al. (2017) [15] used denoising autoencoders (DAEs). Torabi [26] (2023) et al. proposed a practical AE intrusion detection model based on vector reconstruction error.

The GAN-based anomaly detection task model is later than the autoencoder. In 2017, Schlegl et al. proposed AnoGAN [16], which was the first model based on GAN for anomaly detection. They also proposed f-AnoGAN [10], which allows for a direct mapping from data to potential space by adding an encoder before the generator. This model avoids expensive additional backpropagation, which improves computational efficiency. GANomaly (2018) [18] uses an encoder-decoder-encoder design to determine whether a sample is abnormal by comparing the difference between the latent variables obtained by encoding and the latent variables obtained by reconstructing the encoding. Ren et al. (2022) [27] oversampled the original dataset using a GAN network and then fed it into a classifier for training. They used GAN to augment the dataset to improve the correlation accuracy.

Bidirectional generative adversarial networks (BiGANs) improve their ability to detect anomalies by mapping data more efficiently into latent space. Compared to GANs, BiGANs have a better effect in intrusion detection. Zenati et al. (2018) [28] introduced the BiGAN architecture into anomaly detection. Chen et al. (2019) [7] proposed a BiGAN using Wasserstein distance in the form of L1 loss. This model consumes fewer computing resources, which is conducive to evaluating the anomaly scores of the target sample, significantly reducing the time cost of the training and testing process. In order to reduce the influence of this dependency of BiGAN, the learning process of the generator and the learning process of the dependency discriminator are improved. Kaplan et al. (2020) proposed two different training architectures, and both approaches have advanced in the performance of BiGAN[6]. Xu et al. (2022) proposed an improved BiGAN that is more suitable for detecting network intrusion attacks, with less training overhead and a simpler class of classifiers. This improved model achieves good results on the NSL-KDD dataset and the CIC-DDoS2019 dataset [2].

To sum up, using the optimization of BiGAN to solve the challenges of high false alarm rate and high alarm rate of intrusion detection, the Add-BiGAN is proposed. The third section is to introduce this work in detail.

3 The Proposed Add-BiGAN Model

3.1 Model Composition and Training Process

The proposed Add-BiGAN model in this paper is based the BiGAN, which consists of an encoder, a generator, and a discriminator. The model's architecture is illustrated in Fig. 1.

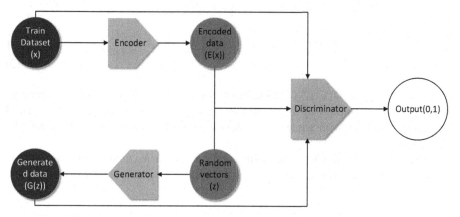

Fig. 1. The model of Add-BiGAN: modify BiGAN from paper [23]

The role of the encoder in Add-BiGAN is to map the training data to encoded data, while the generator maps random vectors to generated data. The goal is for the encoder and generator to map each other, as described in paper [22].

The main role of the discriminator of the Add-BiGAN in the training phase is to distinguish whether the input data is from the encoder or forged by the generator. In the test phase, the usage differs from that explained in the specific process of Fig. 2 below. In the Add-BiGAN proposed in this paper, the input of the discriminator is modified, which is different from the discriminator input of BiGAN. In BiGAN, the input is concatenated, which links data x (or G(z)) with its latent space E(x) (or z). Then the two concatenated data are fed into the discriminator [22, 23]. On the other hand, Add-BiGAN directly inputs the two related inputs to the discriminator simultaneously, enabling richer feature fusion. This paper proposes to use the Add operation for fusion to increase the amount of information and improve classification accuracy.

The training process for Add-BiGAN is divided into two steps. The first step trains the discriminator (D) to maximize the objective function described in Eq. (2), but does not update the generator and encoder. The second step is to train the generator and encoder to minimize the objective function related to the discriminator. It is to fix the discriminator and fix the generator and encoder separately for training at all levels, so as to achieve the encoder and generator convergence. When the training optimization is complete, G and E are inverse maps of each other and can be displayed as x = G(E(x)) and z = E(G(z)). The discriminator can distinguish between the generated data and the real data. Using the encoder and discriminator in this model to achieve binary classification, the specific training and testing process will be detailed in Fig. 2.

The encoder induces a distribution $p_E(z|x) = \delta(z - E(x))$ mapping data points x into the latent feature space of the generative model. The discriminator is also modified to take input from the latent space, predicting $P_D(Y|x, z)$, where Y = 1 if x is real (sampled from the real data distribution p_X), and Y = 0 if x is generated (the output of G(z), $z \sim p_Z$) [23].

BiGAN training objectives are defined as very large and very small objectives:

$$\min_{G,E} \max_D V(D, E, G) \tag{1}$$

where

$$V(D, E, G) := E_{X \sim p_X}\left[E_{z \sim p_E(\cdot|X)}\left[\log D(x, z)\right]\right] + E_{Z \sim p_Z}\left[E_{x \sim p_G(\cdot|Z)}\left[\log(1 - D(x, z))\right]\right] \tag{2}$$

where $E_{z \sim p_E(\cdot|X)}\left[\log D(x, z)\right]$ is equivalent to $\log D(x, E(x))$, with z being the encoding result of the real sample x by the encoder. $E_{x \sim p_G(\cdot|Z)}\left[\log(1 - D(x, z))\right]$ can be replaced by $\log(1 - D(x, z))$, with x being the generated result of the input random vector z by the generator.

Next, we will explain how the model can be trained using an unbalanced dataset to achieve good results. The specific training and testing process is shown in Fig. 2.

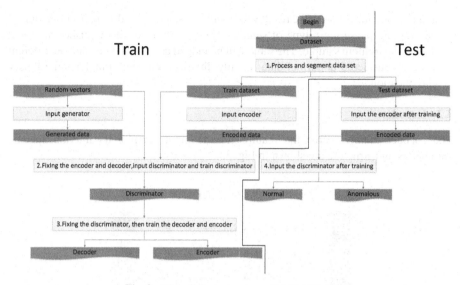

Fig. 2. Overall flow structure of Add-BiGAN

The overall process is roughly divided into a training process and a testing process, specifically divided into four steps:

1) Dataset segmentation and preprocessing. Prior to training, the dataset is divided into a random 9:1 split. A portion of the data is used as the training set, while the remaining portion is used as the test set.

2) Discriminator training. The encoder and generator are fixed, with real data used as input for the encoder and random noise used as input for the generator to obtain the encoding and decoding results. The real samples and their corresponding encoding results are simultaneously input into the discriminator and labeled as real with a score of 1. The output of the generator and its corresponding random noise input are input into the discriminator together and labeled as fake with a score of 0. The learning objective of the discriminator is to assign a high score when the input is from the encoder and a low score when the input is from the generator.

3) Training of encoder and generator. The training process of the generator involves feeding a random noise vector into the generator, which generates an output. The generated output and the noise vector are then fed into the discriminator, and a score is obtained. At this stage, the discriminator's parameters are fixed, and the generator needs to adjust its parameters to minimize the score obtained from the discriminator. In contrast, the training process of the encoder involves feeding a real vector into the encoder, which generates an output. The real vector and its corresponding output are then fed into the discriminator, and a score is obtained. At this stage, the discriminator's parameters are fixed, and the generator needs to adjust its parameters to maximize the score obtained from the discriminator.

4) Test the process. After training the discriminator, generator, and encoder, the test of the dataset uses the encoder and discriminator. The test sample is first encoded using the encoder. Then input the test sample and the encoded output into the discriminator

at the same time. Finally, the result was obtained. Since the real samples input during the training phase are a type of sample. The discriminator distinguishes the same data as the training sample. The same will be judged as normal data, and the different will be considered abnormal data. Finally, the discriminator completes the binary classification.

3.2 Encoder

The encoder mainly learns the features of the input sample. Its internal specific parameters and structure are shown in Fig. 3.

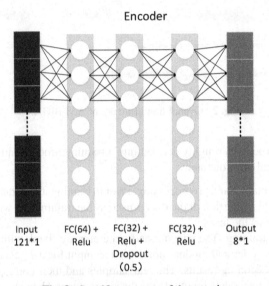

Fig. 3. Specific structure of the encoder

The encoder has a specific structure that involves using a three-layer fully connected network to transform a 121-dimensional tensor into an 8-dimensional tensor. All fully connected layers in the encoder use ReLU as the activation function. To prevent over-fitting, a Dropout layer is used after the second layer of the fully connected network, with a parameter of 0.5, causing half of the neurons to be inactivated during training. The initial input of the encoder is the tensor that results from Onehot encoding the data, which is represented as "Input" in the flowchart. The final output of the encoder is an 8-dimensional tensor.

3.3 Generator

The generator's main function is to generate fake samples using random noise or tensors. In this case, it uses 8-dimensional random noise tensors to generate 121-dimensional tensors to deceive the discriminator. The aim is to train the discriminator's ability to distinguish between real and fake data, without being able to distinguish between input from the encoder or the generator. The specific internal parameters and structure of the generator are depicted in Fig. 4.

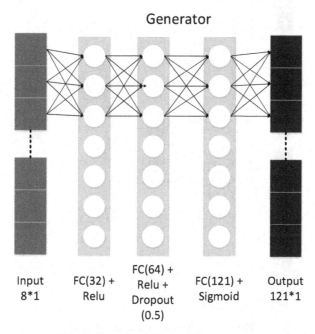

Fig. 4. Specific structure of the generator

The generator has a specific structure, which includes three fully connected layers. The first two layers use the ReLU activation function, and a dropout layer is added after the second layer to prevent overfitting. The third layer uses the Sigmoid activation function to limit the output tensor data within the range of [0, 1]. This structure is inspired by the encoder provided in the paper [2].

3.4 Discriminator

During the training phase, the discriminator's main objective is to differentiate between inputs from the encoder and generator. In the testing phase, its objective shifts to determining whether the input from the encoder for real samples is similar to previously encountered data. The specific structure of the discriminator is depicted in Fig. 5.

We propose an Add-based discriminator. The discriminator takes input from the generator and encoder and passes them through fully connected layers, activating tensors of the same dimension. It then uses additive fusion to obtain the characteristics of a 32-dimensional tensor. After passing through a dropout layer and the LeakyReLU activation function (with an alpha value of 0.3), the tensor goes through another fully connected layer to obtain a fraction, which is then transformed to a decimal value between 0 and 1 using the Sigmoid function. This decimal value represents the probability of the traffic being normal or abnormal.

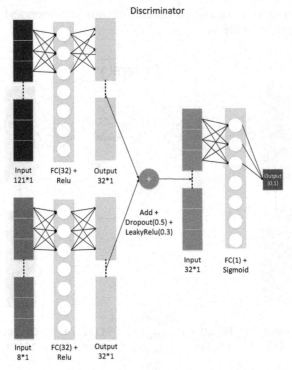

Fig. 5. Specific structure of discriminator

3.5 Loss Function

Because it is different from ordinary image generation, BiGAN is used for binary classification. The output of the discriminator is output by the activation function of Sigmoid as fixed 0 and 1, so binary cross-entropy is chosen as the loss function. Binary cross-entropy is a loss function commonly used in binary classification problems:

$$Loss = -\frac{1}{N} \sum_{i=1}^{N} y_i \cdot \log(p(\widehat{y_i})) + (1 - y_i) \cdot \log(1 - p(\widehat{y_i})) \tag{3}$$

where y_i is the label 0 or 1 of the sample.

where $p(\widehat{y_i})$ is the score after the generator and encoder input discriminator, which is a decimal between 0–1. Multiple data and label losses can be calculated, and when the prediction is completely accurate, the loss is 0.

4 Experimentation and Discussion

4.1 Experimental Setup

4.1.1 Data Set

Our experiments are based on the KDDCUP99 dataset, the 1999 Thrid International Knowlegde Discovery and Data Mining Tools Competition whose goal is to build a robust intrusion detection system. The KDDCUP99 dataset, while not a perfect representation of existing real-world networks and with some redundant data, has been widely used as a valid benchmark for comparing different intrusion detection methods due to the lack of a public dataset that can be used to build new models of network intrusion detection. Compared to some other new datasets, KDDCUP99 is the most widely used dataset. Because most of the articles use BiGAN for intrusion detection on the KDDCUP99 10 percent dataset and the data in it is fixed, it is finally determined to use this data. The KDDCUP99 dataset is the Feature Extract version of the DARPA dataset (DARPA is the original dataset). KDDCUP99 extracted 41 features for each connection and labeled the data using the Bro-IDS tool. The KDDCUP99 10 percent dataset is an official benchmark dataset with a fixed set of data records, containing a total of 494,021 records, including 396,743 anomalous records and 97,278 normal records (Table 1).

Table 1. 42 features of the KDD-99 dataset

No	Features	Type	No	Features	Type
1	duration	int64	22	is_guest_login	int64
2	protocol_type	object	23	count	int64
3	service	object	24	srv_count	int64
4	flag	object	25	serror_rate	float64
5	src_bytes	int64	26	srv_serror_rate	float64
6	dst_bytes	int64	27	rerror_rate	float64
7	land	int64	28	srv_rerror_rate	float64
8	wrong_fragment	int64	29	same_srv_rate	float64
9	urgent	int64	30	diff_srv_rate	float64
10	hot	int64	31	srv_diff_host_rate	float64
11	num_failed_logins	int64	32	dst_host_count	int64
12	logged_in	int64	33	dst_host_srv_count	int64
13	num_compromised	int64	34	dst_host_same_srv_rate	float64
14	root_shell	int64	35	dst_host_diff_srv_rate	float64
15	su_attempted	int64	36	dst_host_same_src_port_rate	float64
16	num_root	int64	37	dst_host_srv_diff_host_rate	float64
17	num_file_creations	int64	38	dst_host_serror_rate	float64
18	num_shells	int64	39	dst_host_srv_serror_rate	float64
19	num_access_files	int64	40	dst_host_rerror_rate	float64
20	num_outbound_cmds	int64	41	dst_host_srv_rerror_rate	float64
21	is_host_login	int64	42	label	object

4.1.2 Data Processing

The fields protocol_type, service, flag, land, logged_in, is_host_login and is_guest_login in the previous 41 features are one-hot encoded and the original data for these fields is removed. The Label field is encoded as 0 for normal and 1 for abnormal data. Next, 90% of the data is randomly selected as the training set, while the remaining 10% is selected as the test set. In this experiment, since abnormal data is predominant, Add-BiGAN's encoder, generator and discriminator are trained on the abnormal data. However, in real-world scenarios, normal data can also be selected for training.

4.1.3 Experimental Setup

In this study, the TensorFlow deep learning framework was used to conduct experiments on a system with an 8-core i7-7700HQ CPU, 16G of RAM, Windows 10, and a GTX-1050 graphics card. The training parameters were set to 1000 epochs and 64 batch size, and the training process was divided into two phases. First, the discriminator was trained, followed by the encoder and generator, using the same training parameters. Adam [24] was used to optimize both phases of training, with the learning rate set to 0.001.

4.1.4 Metrics

In this experiment, four metrics, namely Accuracy, Precision, Recall, and F1 Score, are utilized to assess the efficacy of the two-classification deep learning classifier proposed in this paper.

Accuracy is defined as the ratio of the number of correctly predicted samples to the total number of samples. However, in the presence of an extremely unbalanced sample, the magnitude of accuracy may not hold much significance. Nonetheless, in this paper, accuracy still holds some relevance as, after partitioning the data, although the proportion of abnormal data is large, it accounts for approximately 80% of the total data. Its formula is:

$$\text{Accuracy} = \frac{TP + TN}{TP + TN + FP + FN} \tag{4}$$

Precision measures the proportion of true positive predictions among the total number of positive predictions made by the model. In the field of information retrieval, precision is sometimes referred to as "accuracy". Its formula is:

$$\text{Precision} = \frac{TP}{TP + FP} \tag{5}$$

Recall, also known as recall rate in the field of information retrieval, measures how many true samples are correctly identified by the model. Its formula is:

$$\text{Recall} = \frac{TP}{TP + FN} \tag{6}$$

Precision and Recall are two opposing measures, meaning that when one is very high, the other may be low. F1 Score can effectively balance both Precision and Recall, making it a reliable measure in the presence of unbalanced data. F1 Score is calculated as a weighted harmonic mean of Precision and Recall. Its formula is:

$$F1\ Score = 2 \times (\frac{Precision \times Recall}{Precision + Recall}) \tag{7}$$

4.2 Ablation Experiment

The ablation experiment is used to prove whether what we add has an effect in the experiment, so we did the experiment as shown in Table 2.

Table 2. Ablation experiment

Methods	Data sets	Accuracy	Precision	Recall	F1 Score
Add-BiGAN without add	KDDCUP99	96.77%	86.04%	99.98%	92.49%
Add-BiGAN	KDDCUP99	98.42%	93.98%	98.42%	96.11%

The ablation experiment on Add-BiGAN without add and Add-BiGAN demonstrated that the Add-BiGAN model had better effect. Add-BiGAN achieved a higher accuracy of abnormal detection for KDDCUP99 and fewer alarms. However, Add-BiGAN's recall was somewhat lower than that of Add-BiGAN without ADD. Because ADD can superimpose the extracted semantic information, it can highlight the proportion of correct classification, which is conducive to the final classification. Therefore, in the Add-BiGAN, better accuracy and higher F1 scores can be obtained. The residual structure of the Resnet [25] is based on this principle. Generally, a higher F1 score than the Add-BiGAN without add was obtained under the ablation experiment of the Add-BiGAN. The F1 score, a weighted harmonic average of Precision and Recall, is 96.11%.

4.3 Comparison Experiment

To measure the model presented in this paper, it is necessary to compare other state-of-art approaches. Therefore, the effects of all recent models are listed in Table 3.

Table 3. Performance of our approach and other state-of-art approaches

Methods	Data sets	Accuracy	Precision	Recall	F1 Score
AnoGAN[16]	KDDCUP99	---------	87.86%	82.97%	88.65%
Improved BiGAN [7] by Chen	KDDCUP99	---------	93.24%	94.73%	93.98%
Improved BiGAN [6] by Kaplan	KDDCUP99	89.5%	83.6%	99.4%	90.8%
Improved BiGAN [2] by Xu	KDDCUP99	97.85%	90.58%	99.6%	94.87%
Add-BiGAN without add	KDDCUP99	96.77%	86.04%	99.98%	92.49%
Add-BiGAN	KDDCUP99	98.42%	93.98%	98.42%	96.11%

Firstly, the results of the Add-BiGAN proposed in this paper based on KDDCUP99 data were significantly higher than the accuracy of the BiGAN proposed in the paper [7]. Chen [7] used half of the data in the KDDCUP99 dataset for training and the other half for testing. Using the Add-BiGAN presented in this paper to compare the model in the paper [6], it is possible that recall did not exceed, but the other three parameters were exceeded and the Add-BiGAN achieved a higher F1 score. Since Recall and Precision are mutually exclusive two accuracy rates, one will increase and the other will decrease appropriately. And the authors of paper [6] only selected a small portion of the data for testing. Overall, the model presented in this paper performs best. The model in paper [2], although experimented on the NSL-KDD dataset, we modified the input and performed experiments on the KDDCUP99 dataset, keeping the input consistent with our proposed Add-BiGAN. The results show that the F1 score of our model is significantly higher than that of the model in the paper [2].

The experimental results indicate that the proposed Add-BiGAN model achieved the highest F1 score of 96.11% on the KDDCUP99 dataset, suggesting that it outperforms other models at this stage.

5   Conclusion

This paper proposed an Add-BiGAN for intrusion detection. By improving BiGAN, the model can effectively solve the problems of high false positive rate and false negative rate, as well as unbalanced and unlabeled data in the intrusion detection system. It uses an add operation for semantic information superposition, which will highlight the proportion of correct classification, which is more conducive to correct classification, and the F1 score is 96.11% on the KDDCUP99 dataset. The results of ablation experiments and comparative experiments show that the F1 score of the improved model performs best in the current model. In the case that the actual scenario needs to be very strict for intrusion detection, the Add-BiGAN without add model can be used. For those who want a lower alarm rate and better identification, the Add-BiGAN can be used. In the future, we will try to apply the Add-BiGAN to other intrusion detection datasets such as CIC-IDS-2018, and use it under real working conditions to see its performance and make improvements accordingly.

Acknowledgments. This research was supported in part by the National Key R&D Program of China under Grant No. 2020YFB1707700, and the Fundamental Research Funds for the Central Universities under Grant No. 20D111201.

References

1. Yang, Z., Liu, X., Li, T., et al.: A systematic literature review of methods and datasets for anomaly-based network intrusion detection. Comput. Secur. **116**, 102675 (2022)
2. Xu, W., Jang-Jaccard, J., Liu, T., et al.: Improved bidirectional GAN-based approach for network intrusion detection using one-class classifier. Computers **11**(6), 85 (2022)
3. Xu, W., Jang-Jaccard, J., Singh, A., et al.: Improving performance of autoencoder-based network anomaly detection on nsl-kdd dataset. IEEE Access **9**, 140136–140146 (2021)

4. Sadaf, K., Sultana, J.: Intrusion detection based on autoencoder and isolation forest in fog computing. IEEE Access **8**, 167059–167068 (2020)
5. Chang, Y., Tu, Z., Xie, W., Yuan, J.: Clustering driven deep autoencoder for video anomaly detection. In: Vedaldi, A., Bischof, H., Brox, T., Frahm, J.-M. (eds.) ECCV 2020. LNCS, vol. 12360, pp. 329–345. Springer, Cham (2020). https://doi.org/10.1007/978-3-030-58555-6_20
6. Kaplan, M.O., Alptekin, S.E.: An improved BiGAN based approach for anomaly detection. Procedia Comput. Sci. **176**, 185–194 (2020)
7. Chen, H., Jiang, L.: Efficient GAN-based method for cyber-intrusion detection. arXiv preprint arXiv:1904.02426 (2019)
8. Khraisat, A., Gondal, I., Vamplew, P., et al.: Survey of intrusion detection systems: techniques, datasets and challenges. Cybersecurity **2**(1), 1–22 (2019)
9. Goodfellow, I., Pouget-Abadie, J., Mirza, M., et al.: Generative adversarial networks. Commun. ACM **63**(11), 139–144 (2020)
10. Schlegl, T., Seeböck, P., Waldstein, S.M., et al.: f-AnoGAN: fast unsupervised anomaly detection with generative adversarial networks. Med. Image Anal. **54**, 30–44 (2019)
11. An, J., Cho, S.: Variational autoencoder based anomaly detection using reconstruction probability. Special Lecture on IE **2**(1), 1–18 (2015)
12. Hsu, C W., Chang, C.C., Lin, C.J.: A practical guide to support vector classification. 1396–1400 (2003)
13. Safavian, S.R., Landgrebe, D.: A survey of decision tree classifier methodology. IEEE Trans. Syst. Man Cybern. **21**(3), 660–674 (1991)
14. Zhang, J., Zulkernine, M., Haque, A.: Random-forests-based network intrusion detection systems. IEEE Trans. Syst. Man, Cybern. Part C (Appl. Rev.), **38**(5), 649–659 (2008)
15. Aygun, R.C., Yavuz, A.G.: Network anomaly detection with stochastically improved autoencoder based models. In: 2017 IEEE 4th International confErence on Cyber Security and Cloud Computing (CSCloud). IEEE, pp. 193–198 (2017)
16. Schlegl, T., Seeböck, P., Waldstein, S. M., Schmidt-Erfurth, U., Langs, G.: Unsupervised anomaly detection with generative adversarial networks to guide marker discovery. In: Niethammer, M., Styner, M., Aylward, S., Zhu, H., Oguz, I., Yap, P.-T., Shen, D. (eds.) IPMI 2017. LNCS, vol. 10265, pp. 146–157. Springer, Cham (2017). https://doi.org/10.1007/978-3-319-59050-9_12
17. Javaid, A., Niyaz, Q., Sun, W., et al.: A deep learning approach for network intrusion detection system. In: Proceedings of the 9th EAI International Conference on Bio-inspired Information and Communications Technologies (formerly BIONETICS), pp. 21–26 (2016)
18. Akcay, S., Atapour-Abarghouei, A., Breckon, T. P.: Ganomaly: semi-supervised anomaly detection via adversarial training. In: Jawahar, C. V., Li, H., Mori, G., Schindler, K. (eds.) ACCV 2018. LNCS, vol. 11363, pp. 622–637. Springer, Cham (2019). https://doi.org/10.1007/978-3-030-20893-6_39
19. Yin, C., Zhu, Y., Fei, J., et al.: A deep learning approach for intrusion detection using recurrent neural networks. IEEE Access **5**, 21954–21961 (2017)
20. Vinayakumar, R., Soman, K.P., Poornachandran, P.: Applying convolutional neural network for network intrusion detection. In: 2017 International Conference on Advances in Computing, Communications and Informatics (ICACCI), pp. 1222–1228. IEEE (2017)
21. Roy, S. S., Mallik, A., Gulati, R., Obaidat, M. S., Krishna, P. V.: A deep learning based artificial neural network approach for intrusion detection. In: Giri, D., Mohapatra, R. N., Begehr, H., Obaidat, M. S. (eds.) ICMC 2017. CCIS, vol. 655, pp. 44–53. Springer, Singapore (2017). https://doi.org/10.1007/978-981-10-4642-1_5
22. Dumoulin, V., Belghazi, I., Poole, B., et al.: Adversarially learned inference. arXiv preprint arXiv:1606.00704 (2016)
23. Donahue, J., Krähenbühl, P., Darrell, T.: Adversarial feature learning. arXiv preprint arXiv: 1605.09782 (2016)

24. Kingma, D.P., Ba, J.: Adam: a method for stochastic optimization. arXiv preprint arXiv:1412. 6980 (2014)
25. He, K., Zhang, X., Ren, S., et al.: Deep residual learning for image recognition. In: Proceedings of the IEEE Conference on Computer Vision and Pattern Recognition, pp. 770–778 (2016)
26. Torabi, H., Mirtaheri, S.L., Greco, S.: Practical autoencoder based anomaly detection by using vector reconstruction error. Cybersecurity 6(1), 1 (2023)
27. Ren, J., Sun, Z.: GHM-DenseNet intrusion detection method based on GAN. In: 2022 IEEE 4th International Conference on Civil Aviation Safety and Information Technology (ICCASIT), pp. 1341–13489. IEEE (2022)
28. Zenati, H., Foo, C.S., Lecouat, B., et al.: Efficient GAN-based anomaly detection. arXiv preprint arXiv:1802.06222 (2018)
29. Jia, Y., Wang, M., Wang, Y.: Network intrusion detection algorithm based on deep neural network. IET Inf. Secur. 13(1), 48–53 (2019)

Washroom Occupancy Tracking and Hygiene Monitoring System Using IoT in Universities

Vinothini Kasinathan[1,2]([envelope]), Aida Mustapha[1,2], Kallychurn Dooshyant Rai[1,2], and Tham Hoong Ching[1,2]

[1] School of Computing and Technology, Asia Pacific University of Technology and Innovation, 57000 Kuala Lumpur, Malaysia
vinothini@apu.edu.my

[2] Faculty of Applied Sciences and Technology, Universiti Tun Hussein Onn Malaysia, 84600 Panchor, Johor, Malaysia

Abstract. The accelerated technological growth majorly influencing our everyday lives, Internet of Things (IoT) has been a trending topic and current interest in the contemporary world. IoT has benefited in revolutionising lifestyles, improving quality of life. Therefore, with the help of IoT, the study proposes a prototype for washroom occupancy tracking and hygiene monitoring system called the Washroomium. The prototype is evaluated with targeted users within the Asia Pacific University campus and received favourable feedback. It is hoped that this prototype would be able to provide a pleasant washroom experience for the stakeholders of university by bringing them an at-desk indication on the occupancy and hygiene status of washroom cubicles, alleviating queues and disappointment.

Keywords: Knowledge Management · Internet of Things · Washroom · Mobile Applications

1 Introduction

The beginning of the second decade of the 21st century saw the rise of the fourth industrial revolution, Industry 4.0 (IR 4.0). This innovation has been defined as a strategic initiative introduced by Germany, aimed at the transformation of industrial manufacturing through digitalization and exploitation the potentials of new technologies, such as the Internet of things (IoT) [6]. Today, the Internet has become omnipresent, and it has undoubtedly influenced almost every sector globally, impacting numerous people in unimaginable ways. However, this is only the beginning. We are entering an era of even more pervasive connectivity where a very wide variety of appliances will be connected to the web, known as the Internet of Things (IoT). This term has been defined by many authors in several different ways. The Internet of Things is simply defined as an interaction between the physical and digital worlds.

The digital world interacts with the physical world using a plethora of sensors and actuators [8]. IoT can also be defined as a paradigm in which computing, and networking capabilities are embedded in any kind of conceivable object [4]. We are now living in

L. Uden and I-H. Ting (Eds.): KMO 2023, CCIS 1825, pp. 375–386, 2023.
https://doi.org/10.1007/978-3-031-34045-1_30

a world with smartphones, smart televisions, smart fridges or other smart appliances in our daily life. Washrooms are now becoming part of this advancement. In a highly active environment such as a workplace or university, people have limited time to spare for washroom breaks. Having to queue up to use a washroom cubicle due to full occupancy is a waste of valuable time. This leads to sanitation issue that arises with shared washrooms. While waiting for an unoccupied cubicle, the user also expects a certain level of hygiene.

One crucial aspect in a public washroom that should be considered is hygiene and sanitation. According to the study carried out by the World Health Organisation (WHO), the United Nations estimated that 4.2 billion people are living on this earth without safely managed sanitation. 1.6 million lives are lost per year, suffering from diarrhoea due to lack of sanitation and hygiene [7]. Shared toilets are known to be a common transmission medium of infectious diseases due to environmental contamination [9]. Therefore, these respective researchers have made the developer understood clearly in the point of view of public health that better hygiene measures are the most effective to reduce the risk of diarrhoea and gastrointestinal diseases, as well as control the outbreak of novel infectious diseases such as the COVID-19. At present, in highly active environments which are largely populated, a general issue faced by people is having to make a trip to the washroom, only to see that the cubicles are already fully occupied and therefore must queue up or walk back to their desks. These environments often have a limited number of washrooms and washrooms are located far from frequented areas. In a highly active university that runs on a tight schedule, where students are attending back-to-back classes, lecturers rushing from one place to another, and other office staff have minimal time, the matter could result in time wastage and bringing dissatisfaction to specific students and personnel.

Connecting to the above problem, another issue to factor in is the case of hygiene. Hygiene is defined as the degree to which people keep themselves or their environment clean, mainly to prevent disease [2]. Environment in this context would be related to the washroom. Any individual would prefer a clean, hygienic washroom over a washroom with poor sanitation. Proper hygiene and sanitation are common problems faced with shared washrooms either in private institutions or public washrooms. Moreover, there an additional risk of getting infected by the COVID-19 with a lack of sanitation in public toilets [1]. As a solution of the for the above-mentioned issues, a system of updating the washroom users on the availability and cleanliness of the washroom cubicles while they remain in their respective locations is proposed. This will not only comfort and ease users with facilitated washroom usage, but also the washroom maintenance team. The system will make use of the potential of IoT by using devices that can collect and send information, receive and act on information or do both.

This study attempts to develop a washroom occupancy tracking and hygiene monitoring system for universities like Asia Pacific University (APU) through the application of IoT in solving complications encountered by washroom users. There are more than 12,000 students from more than 130 countries studying at Asia Pacific University where an average of 8,000 students are present on campus on a normal working day. Moreover, there is an approximate number of 600 staff including, lecturers, department executives, security guards and cafeteria personnel. Also, there are reoccurring Open Days that happen each week, where the university welcomes around 100–200 visitors and students.

Simultaneously, another key user will be the washroom team supervisor and his cleaning team. The reason of conducting this research at Asia Pacific University is because of its ever-growing student population and limited number of washrooms. The demand is not meeting the supply, therefore making it the perfect case study. The developer will be targeting around 7,500 on campus daily washroom user.

Asia Pacific University (APU) in Malaysia has a large and growing student population. In addition, that are numerous staff members on campus during the standard working hours. Previously, washrooms were located in only one block, Block E, which proved inefficient to the university's large student and staff population. Most of the time, regardless of peak hours, almost all washroom cubicles were occupied. Users would either wait in a queue with an average of 4–6 min of waiting time before accessing a free washroom cubicle. However, in urgent situations, users would have to rush from one floor to another, to find a free washroom to prevent any embarrassing accidents. A set of washrooms has been opened in another block, Block B, to resolve the full occupancy of washroom cubicles issue. This solution has not been entirely successful as there are peak hours, such as lunchtime, where a large percentage of the campus population uses the facilities. Moreover, increasing the number of washrooms does not solve the issue of hygiene in those areas.

On many occasions, there are unpleasant odours that linger in the washrooms, which can be traced back to those washrooms' hygiene and sanitation levels. These issues are linked to inefficient cleaning and maintaining service provided by a limited number of cleaning crew. According to the cleaning team's supervisor, washrooms are only cleaned at certain times of the day. As people around the world continues to struggle with the COVID-19 pandemic, hygiene in shared washrooms should be considered primordial. The cleaning team supervisor will have reports and notifications on when and which washrooms need cleaning and maintenance, so the required human resources are deployed to the required washroom locations. The only expenses will be for the low-cost sensors and components at a one-time cost of approximately RM20 per cubicle. Having a cleaner and more hygienic environment means better health for students and staff, eventually increasing productivity.

The system will facilitate Asia Pacific University's stakeholders, of both genders, in locating the nearest unoccupied washroom cubicles based on their respective locations within the campus Washrooms at APU are found at an average distance of 25 m from other facilities. Usually, it will take someone and an average of 7 to 10 min to take a washroom trip. As a result, valuable time is lost, whether a student is missing part of their lecture or staff pausing their work. The system will allow users to save time from displacing and waiting in washroom queues, eventually making them more productive. The data collected from the proposed IoT-based system will also serve a bigger knowledge management requirement in APU since the large amounts of data over time can be analysed to provide insights and improve decision-making processes. By integrating IoT data into knowledge management processes, APU would be able to improve their ability to learn from their students experiences, adapt to changes, and make data-driven decisions.

The remainder of this paper is organized as follows. Section 2 presents the materials and methods to design and develop the prototype of Washroomium mobile application.

Section 3 presents the evaluation methods, and finally Sect. 4 concludes with plans for future development.

2   Materials and Methods

This study proposed a prototype for washroom occupancy tracking and hygiene monitoring system called the Washroomium based on the design thinking framework [3, 5]. The central technology to this prototype is the Internet of Things (IoT), which interconnect the sensors, Washroomium application, and Internet connectivity to collect and exchange data. The following are characteristics of the proposed Washroomium mobile system:

- To provide washroom users real-time data on the occupancy status of washroom cubicles.
- To suggest washroom users with the nearest washrooms from their location.
- To motivate washroom users to keep the washrooms clean after usage.
- To assist the washroom cleaning team in optimising the cleaning method of washroom cubicles.
- To notify the washroom cleaning team whenever and wherever a washroom cubicle needs to be cleaned.
- To design and develop a Washroom Occupancy Tracking and Hygiene Monitoring mobile application.
- To have an ergonomic user interface to encourage washroom users to use the system without any difficulty and to cater for better user experience.
- To create an IoT integrated prototype model to simulate scenarios.

Washroomium will be developed as a mobile application using the Flutter Framework along with the Dart programming language on the Android Studio IDE. The microcontroller, NodeMCU ESP8266 will be programmed using the C language on the Arduino IDE. The main sensor to detect the occupancy of each washroom cubicle will be a low-cost Passive Infrared sensor. To further enhance the mobile application, a set of libraries and packages have been short-listed, to be added to the development process. Moreover, Google Firebase was identified as the most suitable database for this IoT driven project due to its Realtime database feature. As mentioned above, Flutter gives the ability to develop cross-platform applications; therefore, Washroomium will be available on both Android and the iOS mobile operating systems.

2.1   Design

The proposed Washroomium system has the following specifications: NodeMCU ESP8266 with 2 Washroom Cubicles, Passive Infrared Sensors, and Simulated Washroom Cubicles for Male and Female. All sensors are connected to a Raspberry Pi Model 3B+ and the Pi is connected to the Internet through its Wi-Fi module. Each cubicle and the sensors installed inside are individually identified using an identification number. All sensors have been programmed using the Python programming language to interact with the Raspberry Pi when collecting data and Firebase database is used to store sensors' data in real-time.

Figure 1 and Fig. 2 show the system architecture of Washroomium. When the cubicle is in use, the PIR sensor is activated and communicates with the Raspberry Pi and is becomes idle once the person leaves the cubicle. Bearing in mind that when a person uses the cubicle, the flush tank is full, and the distance of the water surface and tank lid is only few centimetres apart.

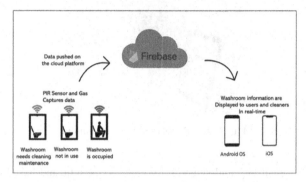

Fig. 1. System Architecture of Washroomium.

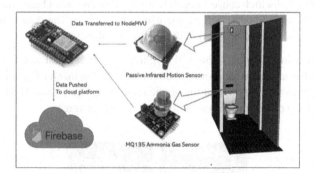

Fig. 2. Rich Diagram of Washroomium.

When leaving the cubicle, the user flushes the toilet, and the water level goes to and exceed a certain threshold set to know then flushing occurred. In an event where the water has not reached that threshold, a notification and SMS is sent to the janitor with the identification detail of that cubicle. This is because there is a high probability that the toilet was left unflushed by the user.

2.2 Prototype

The system architecture for Washroomium is translated into a working prototype model and evaluated in a real-time environment.

IoT Prototype. A prototype of the Washroomium mobile application is developed with two (2) washroom cubicles for male and female as in the real-life scenario. The Passive

Infrared Sensors (PIR) are embedded inside the roof of each cubicle just above the toilet. The PIR sensors are connected to the NodeMCU ESP8266 powered by a 5V current. Figure 3 shows the IoT implementation of Washroomium prototype.

Fig. 3. IoT Prototype of Washroomium.

The sensors sensitivity and sensing distance can be adjusted based on the size of the cubicles. The sensors has two slots made of IR sensitive materials which senses the same amount of IR when the sensor is idle. When a warm body passes by, one half of the sensor is intercepted which cause a negative differential change. These changes are what is detected, which in this case are people using the cubicle. The data is then collected by the microcontroller and updated in the real-time database.

Mobile Application. Figure 4 shows the onboarding screen that will launch when the user clicks on the icon of Washroomium on the application menu of the phone. The user will be directed to the first page of the application for the first time. The landing screen will have the logo of Washroomium and a welcoming message.

Fig. 4. User Interface of Washroomium.

To have access to the application the user has to click on "Continue as a washroom user" for anonymous login. This also has the Read Privacy Policy button. Even though Washroomium does not need the user to explicitly sign into the application, it is considered as a good approach to the able to uniquely identify them. This may be for security or analytics purposes. Anonymous sign-in method is also provided to provide an extra layer of security; therefore, it can be detected when a request comes in from an authenticated user.

Figure 5 shows that the washroom cubicles are not being used by anyone. Therefore, the Passive Infrared Sensors (PIR) in both male and female cubicles are not detecting any change in heat inside the cubicle. The information is shown in sent to Firebase Realtime database and retrieved from the Washroomium application on its washroom state page. If the normal cubicle temperature raises to body temperature and the sensors also detect moving objects, Washroomium will be triggered. These data are transmitted to the microcontroller which feeds the database.

Fig. 5. Testing Washroomium in Action.

The user can then view the occupancy in real-time regardless of his or her location. Similarly, when infrared radiation is detected by the sensor inside the female cubicle, the cubicle will light up Red and labelled as 'Occupied' to inform the user that the cubicle is in use. As such, the user can use the back button and select another nearest washroom. The colour red is used to show that a cubicle is occupied as it works as a metaphor of 'Stop'. Consequently, green colour works as an international meaning of 'Go', therefore suitable to use when the cubicles are empty. In a real-life scenario, the PIR sensor detecting range is calibrated to give reading of a certain range only, and in this case the sensor can be adjusted to one metre depending on the size of the cubicle.

Additional Features. The Washroomium state page also consist of a 'Report' button in an event when the user found a dirty cubicle and wishes to inform the cleaning team. Washroomium retains the washroom location based on the particular washroom the user is trying to lodge the report from, which in terms of user experience helps the user for not keying in the washroom location again. A dropdown with a list of several washroom issues are provided to the user. The user may select one or more washroom issues ranging from wet floors to unflushed toilets to bad smell. The list of selected issues are shown to the user after being selected.

Users can upload a picture, a feature when lodging a report. The user will be prompted with a dialog box for him or her to make a choice on whether to use the phone gallery or phone camera to take a picture. In an event when the user chooses the gallery option, the application will open the phone gallery allowing the user to select a picture he or she wants to upload. In an event when the user decides to take a picture using the phone's camera, the application will launch the camera feature whereby the user can snap a picture. A cropper feature has been added which can allow the user to crop the image taken to the desired size.

3 Evaluation

To evaluate the prototype of Washroomium, a User Acceptance Testing (UAT) was carried out in-person with students and staff at the university. UAT is the last phase of the software testing process. UAT is carried out to ensure that the system would behave as expected in its actual environment based on the given specifications. With 'user' as the prime word, this phase of testing in important to verify that the solution is working for the intended user and bringing amendments and correcting defects to suit the expectation of the user.

UAT also called beta testing and is done before rolling out the software on the market. The users are given the chance to interact with the system and checks if all features are working properly, overlooked features and any miscommunication that might have happened. The developer will design a test which would encompass all the functional scenarios in layman terms so that the non-technical testers better understand the application. 20 UAT forms were distributed to the targeted audience including the washroom supervisor. The UAT testing sheets is a questionnaire where they 'real' end-users grade the software to know if whether it is fulfilling its purpose and ensuring to provide business benefits as shown in Fig. 6.

Washroomium: A Washroom Occupancy Tracking and Hygiene Monitoring System using IoT in Asia Pacific University (APU)

User Acceptance Testing for Washroom Users
Kallychurn Dooshyant Rai
TP050544
UC3F2011SE
BSc (HONS) in Software Engineering

Section A: Respondents Details

Date:	01.07.2021	Participant's Name:	Louise Ange Uwase
Time Start:	12:00		
Time End:	12:30	Participant's occupation	Student Ambassador at APU

Section B: Condition of Technical Components (Features and Functionalities)

Component	Test Result Accept	Test Result Reject	Score (1-10)	Comment (Optional)
Washroom user can use the app without credentials and personal info	✓		10	
Sensor captures non-vison-based data	✓		10	
Washroom user can locate himself/herself	✓		8	I believe there could have been better way to implement the location of user
Washroom user is suggested nearest washroom	✓		8	
Washroom user can view occupancy status of cubicles in real time.	✓		10	
Washroom user can lodge a report to the cleaning team.	✓		10	
Washroom user is able to access application on android or iOS.	✓		10	

Section C: User Interaction and User Experience

Component	Test Result Accept	Test Result Reject	Score (1-10)	Comment (Optional)
Solves target users' problems	✓		10	
Achieves aims and objectives.	✓		10	
Promotes productivity.	✓		10	
Promotes hygiene in washroom.	✓		8	Washroom user could have a feature to see the reports too.
Ergonomic (User-friendly) interface.	✓		9	
Reduce queueing up.	✓		10	
User acceptance	✓		9	
Overall performance	✓		9	

Remarks: I suggest using better icons and images in app. These little things can improve UI. Overall, the application style and initiative are on point. Also, the hardware technology used are really interesting.

Participant:

Signature:	*Louise Ange Uwase*	Name:	Louise Ange Uwase

Developer:

Signature:		Name:	Kallychurn Dooshyant Rai

Fig. 6. User Acceptance Test (UAT) form for Washroomium.

Next, Fig. 7 shows the scenario respondents are using Washroomium. During the UAT, respondents were provided with the *.apk* file and *.ipa* file on their android phones and iPhones. They will be briefed on the flow of the system and provided a demo.

Fig. 7. Scenario during User Acceptance Test (UAT) of Washroomium.

The results from the questionnaire distributed were very positive with most of the users giving good and constructive feedback and explain their desires of having the system implemented at Asia Pacific University washroom facilities. Figure 8 shows user feedback on whether they would continue to use Washroomium.

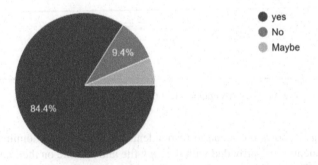

Fig. 8. Would you continue to use Washroomium?

Next, Fig. 9 shows user feedback on whether Washroomium is sufficient to cater their needs.

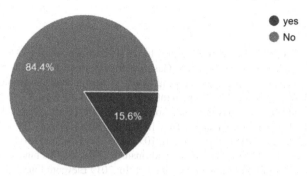

yes
No

84.4%

15.6%

Fig. 9. Is Washroomium sufficient to cater your needs?

It can be analysed from the results that the solution has a high acceptance rate among the users which can be deduced that the system has passed all the required component testing as well passed all five-user acceptance testing.

4 Conclusion

To address real life problems effectively, the use of modern technology, creativity and innovation plays a major role. Problems have to be viewed from different angles and perspectives through various ideas generation methods. This study proposed a mobile application based on Internet of Things (IoT) technology called Washroomium, which is a washroom occupancy tracking and hygiene monitoring system. Washroomium is designed to cater individual's personal experience navigating a new space to find a public washroom in a rather urgent situation. Washroomium has been duly developed as a prototyped and evaluated by 20 targeted users in Asia Pacific University of Technology and Innovation campus. The IoT-based mobile app has received positive response and is planned to enter market validation stage to be pivoted to suit the market demand of the application.

At present, the selection of user location is restricted to only two variables, which are the level and the block the user is at. In an event of implementing the system in a more complex building, the flow of selecting several variables to determine the user location will not prove to be the best approach. Moreover, displaying the three washrooms only after user location selection might cause an issue in an instance where all there, washrooms have their cubicles occupied although it is quite unlikely to happen. Furthermore, the method of optimizing washroom cleaning can be made more efficient and accurate in the future.

Acknowledgement. This project is supported by the Asia Pacific University of Technology and Innovation. Washroomium has won several innovation competitions such as the International Research and Symposium and Exposition (RISE 2021) with Silver medal, Asia International Innovation Exhibition (AIINEX 2021) with Gold Innovation Video Challenge award.

References

1. Furfaro, F., et al.: SFED recommendations for IBD endoscopy during Covid-19 pandemic: Italian and French experience. Nat. Rev. Gastroenterol. Hepatol. **17**(8), 507–516 (2020)
2. Kalra, S., et al.: Stethoscope hygiene: a call to action. Recommendations to update the CDC guidelines. Infect. Control Hosp. Epidemiol. **42**(6), 740–742 (2021)
3. Kostrzewski, M.: One design issue – many solutions. different perspectives of design thinking – case study. In: Uden, L., Hadzima, B., Ting, I.-H. (eds.) KMO 2018. CCIS, vol. 877, pp. 179–190. Springer, Cham (2018). https://doi.org/10.1007/978-3-319-95204-8_16
4. Rashid, R.A., Chin, L., Sarijari, M.A., Sudirman, R., Ide, T.: Machine learning for smart energy monitoring of home appliances using IoT. In: 2019 Eleventh International Conference on Ubiquitous and Future Networks (ICUFN), pp. 66–71. IEEE (2019)
5. Roberts, J.P., Fisher, T.R., Trowbridge, M.J., Bent, C.: A design thinking framework for healthcare management and innovation. In: Healthcare, pp. 11–14. Elsevier (2016)
6. Rojko, A.: Industry 4.0 concept: background and overview. Int. J. Interact. Mob. Technol. (iJIM) **11**(5), 77 (2017). https://doi.org/10.3991/ijim.v11i5.7072
7. Roser, M., Ochmann, S., Behrens, H., Ritchie, H., Dadonaite, B.: Eradication of diseases. Our World in Data (2014)
8. Vermesan, O., Friess, P.: Internet of Things: Converging Technologies for Smart Environments and Integrated Ecosystems. River Publishers (2013)
9. Wu, S., Wang, Y., Jin, X., Tian, J., Liu, J., Mao, Y.: Environmental contamination by SARS-CoV-2 in a designated hospital for coronavirus disease 2019. Am. J. Infect. Control **48**(8), 910–914 (2020)

Experience-Based Knowledge Management with a Conversational AI Chatbot: Taking Hand-Shaken Tea Service in Taiwan as an Example

Yu-Hsuan Wu[✉] and Fu-Ren Lin

National Tsing Hua University, Hsinchu, Taiwan
unawu1010@gmail.com, frlin@iss.nthu.edu.tw

Abstract. We human beings accumulate experience through daily practice with memory, and, we grow our knowledge through concrete experiences with an experiential learning cycle. Experience-based knowledge management (EBKM), by virtual of information technologies especially artificial intelligence (AI), could be realized nowadays to support individual daily life in experiential learning to enhance their happiness and wellbeing. The goal of the research is to explore the benefit of EBKM system with conversational AI chatbot interface to facilitate experiential learning. In the research, we designed the framework of the conversational AI chatbot with RASA's NLU, Neo4j, and LINE. Then, we adopted scenario-based survey to evaluate the perceived value from the interaction between a designated user and the prototyping chatbot. In the survey, we designed four interaction scenarios containing different dialogue episodes aiming to order drinks from hand-shaken tea shops. We recruited 214 participants and assigned them to experience these four scenarios according to their status of difficulties in choosing hand-shaken brands or drinks. From the results, we found that the conversational AI chatbot can really help people to reduce their decision-making time on choosing drinks with better purchase experience. Moreover, we can conclude that the conversational AI chatbot can realize the vendor relationship management (VRM) that customers could make good choices from a wide range of vendors. We anticipate that, in the future, EBKM can be realized with the conversational AI chatbot for VRM.

Keywords: experience-based knowledge management · conversational AI chatbot · scenario survey · hand-shaken tea service · vendor relationship management

1 Introduction

We human beings accumulate experience with memory in daily practice. Tacit knowledge in daily experience became habits for individuals. Without explicating it and storing it in a retrievable form, people tend to forget it gradually. Sometimes, people may pay the

L. Uden and I-H. Ting (Eds.): KMO 2023, CCIS 1825, pp. 387–400, 2023.
https://doi.org/10.1007/978-3-031-34045-1_31

price to repeat the bad experiences they should avoid if they can retrieve their prior experience. There comes the need for experience-based knowledge management (EBKM). EBKM covers the ranges from individual, group, organization, to inter-organization as knowledge management practices in general. However, due to different schemas among different people in daily activities for their daily routines, it is not a trivial issue in facilitating the development of EBKM systems to support individual daily life in experiential learning to enhance their happiness and wellbeing.

In Wikipedia, experience is the knowledge or mastery of an event or subject gained through involvement in or exposure to it. In theory of knowledge, there are two types of knowledge: empiricism and rationalism. Experiential learning is the process of gaining empirical knowledge through involvement in various activities. According to Kolb's experiential learning cycle [8] containing four stages: concrete experience, reflective observation, abstract conceptualization, and active experimentation, experience-based knowledge management could facilitate experiential learning process. Following the classical knowledge creation process proposed by Nonaka [15] containing four stages of tacit and explicit knowledge transformation process: socialization, externalization, combination, and internalization (SECI), experiential learning serves as a process to create knowledge from concrete experiences to active experimentation. Experiential learning can be enhanced by taking the transformative SECI process between tacit and explicit knowledge. Thus, the experience-based knowledge management could leverage the information technology to externalize individual tacit experiences and facilitate the knowledge exchange among people.

By virtue of information technology, especially artificial intelligence (AI), we could leverage personal smartphone's communication and data processing capabilities and back-end cloud computation to record, retain, exchange, and update our daily experiences to support EBKM. However, it is still rare nowadays to realize these theoretical ideas with real and up running systems. It implies that there is a vacancy in academia to know how to engage individuals to perform EBKM, and in practice to build and operate EBKM service systems. To mend the gap between thinking and doing, in this study, we want to create an experience to understand the value propositions for people to adopt EBKM service systems.

This research takes hand-shaken tea service as an example to investigate how daily ad hoc or routine experiences can be enhanced by the EBKM service system. The reason we decided to take hand-shaken tea service as a demonstration of the target EBKM system is that it is easy to encounter in Taiwan's daily life to order hand-shaken beverages from shops on the street or even order it through Uber Eats or Foodpanda. Thus, it is easy for us to reach out to various types of people while doing the evaluation of the built system. One more reason is that for an individual, there are so many kinds of drinks offered by different brand shops, it causes panic sometimes for individuals to choose one at the moment they have the needs. Therefore, to manage the experiences from different brands and drinks to ease their decision panic is crucial for people to enjoy drinking beverages from these shops. By applying the EBKM system, it could also realize vendor relationship management (VRM) when customers want to benefit from their prior experiences with different brands.

Based on the scenarios anticipated by a conversational AI chatbot to interact with users, in this paper, we would like to report the study of users' responses toward scenarios which demonstrate the interaction between a user and the chatbot system while choosing the beverage from different brands. Instead of waiting for the full fledged system up running to evaluate its performance, we adopt a scenario-based survey by demonstrating the interactive scenarios for respondents to evaluate their perception and perceived value from the service. The results show the distinct benefits for users in different situations faced while they plan to order the beverages, and guide the fully fledged system development. Besides the value created by the EBKM practice for users to enjoy hand-shaken tea service, the EBKM service system enables VRM.

2 Literature Review

2.1 Experience-Based Knowledge Management (EBKM)

Experience presents a meaning of a barrier that has been cleared and has a full understanding by people. Emotion can act as one of the important sources of information transition [17]. There are several experience-based activities in our daily lives [6]. Experience-based that applies in this study can also be referred to as customer experience-based. Satisfaction is also one of the important factors in experience-based marketing theory. There are few coverages by literature that take customers as autonomous actors for them to integrate their experiences across different service experiences.

The importance of knowledge management (KM) has been raised rapidly. There are two main categories of knowledge: tacit and explicit knowledge [10]. The first generation of KM is mainly focused on the value derived from knowledge sharing, and the second generation of KM is mainly focused on expanding the overall reach of KM [11]. KM is an effort to increase useful knowledge within the organization [12]. Good knowledge management can assist businesses to boost their efficiency [20]. In this research, we would like to transform tacit knowledge into explicit knowledge by applying knowledge management mechanisms.

This study took a prototyping conversational AI chatbot that was proposed and is under development by co-authors' team, and leverages the features of experience-based knowledge management to propose various scenarios for users to interact with the chatbot.

2.2 A Framework of Experience-Based Knowledge Management System

There are two important factors to building a good experience-based knowledge management system: content and system logistics. Content contains explicit knowledge that people can access via various cues, such as keywords or contextual clues [1]. The proposed experience-based knowledge management system is built with related technologies and theories by adopting NLP, RASA's NLU, and a graph database Neo4j.

Natural language processing (NLP) is a subfield of linguistics [14], and it is also one of the major important research fields in artificial intelligence (AI) recently [7]. There are some basic phases in NLP: (1) phonetics, (2) pragmatics, (3) morphology, (4) syntax, and (5) semantics [7]. Chatbots with NLP can help to analyze the intentions and extract some key information to identify or implicate the meaning from the users based on these phases [3].

RASA's NLU is an open-source tool that can easily build a conversational AI service system [7]. It is an open source to process Natural Language Processing (NLP) and Machine Learning (ML) techniques. Graph analysis can help businesses to understand complex relationships between linked entity data in a single network or a graph [16]. A graph database is composed of nodes and edges, and the attributes and properties to denote nodes and edges, respectively [18]. The conversational AI chatbot model in this research adopted Neo4j as the graphic database management system (DBMS) to store the actors' experiences and the interactions among actors.

2.3　Conversational AI Chatbot

A conversational chatbot is an artificially intelligent (AI) creature that can communicate with humans [9]. There are two main kinds of conversational AI chatbots: text-based and voice-based. Chatbots are increasingly seen as a valuable complement to customer service in recent years [4]. According to the recent Gartner report, 31% of interviewed organizations already had the conversational chatbot service [5]. For building chatbots, the problem was considered as translating the user's utterance to the chatbot's answer [13]. There might be many queries in one request or ambitious segmentation for some information provided on the Internet [3]. The chatbot can also become a medium in the advertising landscape, by targeting the right market segment can make business promotion easier [19]. The conversational AI chatbot is using it in customer service as a key application domain [2].

3　Scenario-Based Survey

We adopted a scenario-based survey to collect respondents' feedback on the interactive scenarios between a designated user and the chatbot. We designed a total of 28 questions organized as five sections: (1) general information, (2) hand-shaken beverage drinking habits, (3) questions about respondents' difficulty in choosing brands or drinks to assign respondents to go through different scenarios, (4) questions for users to evaluate their experience on interacting with chatbot, and (5) conclusion questions as shown in Fig. 1.

In the general information section, we aimed to collect basic data, such as gender, age group, and geographical region. In collecting hank-shaken beverage drinking habits, we asked about their preference for hand-shaken drink brands and frequency. Before seeing the scenario, participants will answer whether they had difficulties in decision-making on choosing hank-shaken drinks. Then, after going through the scenario, the participants will be asked to feed back their perception of using the conversational AI chatbot.

The participants were recruited via various social media, such as Facebook, Instagram, LinkedIn, and social networks we could access. We provided incentives to join the lucky draw at the end of the survey period to increase the probability that people will answer the questionnaire. Moreover, a referral mechanism is implemented for people to refer their acquaintances to fill out the survey to increase the probability to win the presents.

In different groups, we designed different scenarios regarding the interactions between a designated user and the chatbot to assist them to engage in the conversational AI chatbot service. According to their difficulties in choosing brands and products, we could classify users into four different user groups in the context of ordering hand-shaken tea. We run the statistical analysis to conclude the findings and generate insight for follow-up experience-based knowledge management system development.

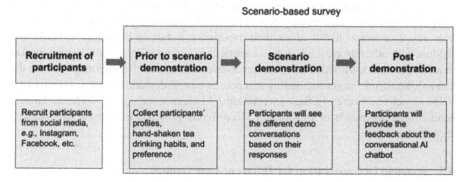

Fig. 1. The work flow of the scenario-based survey

3.1 Scenario Design

In this study, the conversational AI chatbot as the interactive interface between a user and the experience-based knowledge management system is called *"Drink Ba"* dedicated to assisting users' hand-shaken tea service experience. The chatbot is under development at the moment. The scenario design served as an MVP (Minimum Viable Product) testing to obtain potential users' responses in order to refine the system features and operations. The scenario design is described as follows. Based on the decision-making process, *Drink Ba* has different paths to meet users' need to order beverages. The interaction process starts with asking what brands a user prefers, then going through the products. After knowing the brands and products, the conversational AI chatbot will record the experiences of the users, and will remind users to record their hand-shaken tea drinking experience after users had tasted it. For chatbots to remind users to record their assessment of the experience, users' tacit knowledge in terms of how they feel and taste the drink could be externalized for future retrieval and integration. By accumulating and integrating users' prior experiences, if users can't decide which brands or drinks they want to order from, the conversational AI chatbot will guide them to make the decision by asking questions, such as "Which kind of tea do you like, black tea or green tea?" or "Do you prefer having pearls in your black tea?" to narrow down from a wide range of choices to ease their decision difficulty.

The conversational AI chatbot also can remind users if they have had negative prior experiences with specific hand-shaken tea choices, the conversational AI chatbot will alert users when they try to query the specific drinks, such as "You are used to have a negative experience when you have this drink, do you still want to drink it this time?" Hope this alert can trigger users' previous hand-shaken tea drinking experiences and prevent them from experiencing another possible negative drinking experience. In order to retain a user's prior experiences, *Drink Ba* will ask the user for feedback on their experiences every time when they consume the hand-shaken tea they just drank in order to guide the user to reflect the fresh memory of their tastes of the drink and the interactive experiences with the shop. Table 2 shows a snap of an episode of the scenario seen by Group 1 respondents.

Through the support of *Drink Ba*, we anticipate that users are able to leverage their prior experiences to make an easy choice for the moment of ordering beverages. Moreover, if a user would like to share their experience in tasting beverages in brand and product with other users, the common experiences among users would create a market trend for providers, by which more customer-oriented service offerings may enhance the hand-shaken drink bar service quality to meet customers' demands; in turn, it realizes the VRM objectives. Currently, the conversational AI chatbot includes 10 different famous hand-shaken tea brands in Taiwan and 516 different products from these hand-shaken tea brands.

3.2   Scenario Demonstration for Different User Groups

Based on the potential difficulties of choosing brand or drinks in hand-shaken tea service context, we composed four scenarios to demonstrate the interaction flows between a designated user and the chatbot. These four scenarios respond to four groups of customers as shown in Table 1. For users in Group 1 (No difficulties in choosing both brands and drinks), we designed a scenario in which the user can easily point out the brand and the product they want to drink. It also demonstrated the use case that if the user planned to reorder the drinks they didn't like previously, *Drink Ba* will pop up the notification to alert the user that they had a negative experience before. After drinking the hand-shaken tea, *Drink Ba* will ask about the user's hand-shaken tea drinking experience. In the scenario, the user would like to fix the user's feeling about the sweetness of the drinks, and *Drink Ba* helps the user to fix the latest drinking experience and assist the user in future upcoming purchases next time. Table 2 illustrates the scenario designed for Group 1 users in the survey.

In Group 2 (No difficulties in choosing brands but difficulties with drinks), we designed the conversation scenario that will guide the user to pick their preference for tea and topping ingredients. After knowing the user's preference for hand-shaken drinks, the conversational AI chatbot will recommend the user drinks from the graph relational database. However, the user might not be satisfied with the recommendation after the drink. So, when *Drink Ba* asks the user about their drinking experience, the user would respond with negative feedback. Therefore, *Drink Ba* can assist the user to fix their negative hand-shaken tea drinking experience.

In Group 3 (No difficulties in choosing drinks, have difficulties with brands), we designed the scenario that the user likes the common hand-shaken drink (*e.g.*, bubble tea). Since bubble tea can be found in most hand-shaken tea brands, it might be hard for the user to decide which brand should the user orders. However, the flavor between these brands might be a little bit different since different brands use different tea leaves, different ratios of milk, and other options, so that the user might not like the brand they picked prior to this time. In this situation, *Drink Ba* can assist the user to memorize the experience to prevent future negative purchase experiences.

In Group 4 (Having difficulties in choosing both brands and drinks), we designed the scenario a little bit similar to that for Group 2 to assist the user to find out their preference for drinks and topping ingredients. The additional step is to ask which brands the user wants to pick and purchase since they also have no idea from which brand they want to order. This step can help the user narrow down the wide range of the brands and shorten the decision-making process time. Due to the page limitation, we do not illustrate four scenarios in this manuscript.

Table 1. The four scenarios for corresponding four groups of respondents

	Without difficulties in choosing brands	With difficulties in choosing brands
Without difficulties in choosing drinks	**Group 1**	**Group 2**
With difficulties in choosing drinks	**Group 3**	**Group 4**

4 Analytical Results

4.1 Participant Profiles

The survey was distributed from January 6 to 26, 2023. A total of 214 participants (n = 214, 59.72% female and 39.35% male) completed the survey via an online participant questionnaire with various drinking habits on hand-shaken tea. Among them, 138 respondents (64%) range 18–30 years old; 36 respondents (17%) range 31–40 years old. Geographically, 85, 107, and 22 respondents were living in the North, Central, and South Taiwan, respectively. Based on two questions for respondents to answer their situations in choosing hand-shaken drinks in brands and products, respectively, we assigned them to go through corresponding scenarios. 82 (38.32%), 14 (6.54%), 52(24.30%), and 66 (30.84%) respondents were assigned to Groups 1, 2, 3, and 4, respectively.

4.2 Analytical Results

In the survey, each respondent answered seven questions containing six measurements to seek their feedback of experiencing *Drink Ba* after they read through the episodes of assigned scenarios and passed the manipulation test. These seven measurements are (1) to find the preferred brand in a short time, (2) to find the preferred drink in a short time, (3) mitigating the difficulties in choosing brands; (4) mitigating the difficulties in choosing drinks; (5) the improvement of purchase experience, (6) shortening the time to choose products, and (7) willingness to recommend to others. We analyzed the results by comparing the differences in these measurements under different scenario groups, age groups, genders, and geographical regions to discover the users' perception of conversational AI chatbot. We report the results which have significant differences in the following subsections.

Table 2. Scenario elaboration of Group 1 (No difficulties on both brands and drinks)

Scenario demonstration	Scenario elaboration
	Dink Ba! notifies the user "Una" her previous hand-shaken tea experience. Bot: Which drink would you like to have from "Da Yuan Zi"? User: Pomelo drink. Bot: However, seems like you had a bad experience last time, would you still like to order? User: Can I change to bubble tea? Bot: Sure, I will come back to you later.

* Due to the page limitation, we only display an episode of the interaction flow in Group 1.

4.2.1 The Improvement of Purchase Experience, Recommendation Rate, and to Find Preferred Brands in a Short Time in 4 Scenario Groups

We found that the average score on the helpfulness of the conversational AI chatbot is 3.58 out of 5 (n = 214, SD = 1.012), and the overall recommendation rate is 68.69%. In general, the scenarios demonstrating the interactions between a designated user and the chatbot obtain positive feedback in terms of the improvement of purchase experience and the willingness to recommend to others. Specifically, we show the scores and recommendation rates from different groups of participants in Table 3. Respondents with difficulties in choosing brands and drinks (Group 4) have the highest recommendation rate compared with respondents in other groups. It indicates that the marginal benefit of chatbot perceived by customers having difficulties in choosing brands and drinks motivates them to share this chatbot service with others. The improvement of purchase experience among four group users, people without difficulties in choosing brands and drinks show the highest score (3.76 out of 5), which indicates that the chatbot could bring up their prior experiences to prevent them from reordering drinks they did not like. By comparing the respondents among four groups regarding the frequency of purchase, the age, gender, geographical distribution, there are no significant differences. It indicates the general effect of chatbot on improving users' purchase experiences and recommendation rate, especially in scenarios 1 and 4 groups.

Table 3. Average scores on the improvement of purchase experience and recommendation rate in different scenario groups

Group#	Characteristics of choosing beverages	Improvement of purchase experience	Recommendation rate
Group 1	Without difficulties in choosing both brands and drinks	3.76	69.51%
Group 2	With difficulties in choosing brands; without difficulties in choosing drinks	3.46	50.00%
Group 3	Without difficulties in choosing brands; With difficulties in choosing drinks	3.17	59.62%
Group 4	With difficulties in choosing both brands and drinks	3.61	78.79%

In terms of the perceived benefit of finding preferred brands, the average score of four groups is 3.73 out of 5. Respondents in Group 4 perceive the highest benefit using chatbot with the score 3.94 compared with those of groups 1, 2, and 3 with scores 3.74, 3.50 and 3.36, respectively. From the pairwise t-test, we identify the significant difference between users in Group 3 and 4 (p = 0.0023*). These results show the marginal benefits of the conversational AI chatbot for users to find their preferred brand in a short time.

4.2.2 Mitigating the Difficulties in Choosing Drinks in Different Age Groups

Based on the response, we found out the comments from participants showed a trend. It seems like more participants at young ages mentioned the help from the chatbot to release their difficulties in choosing hand-shaken tea. Thus, we segment the data into three age groups to see if there are any characteristics among them. Table 4 shows the conversational AI chatbot obtains the highest score (3.87) for age group A, aged below 25 years old, to mitigate the difficulties in choosing drinks. The average score of the conversational AI chatbot that can cut down the barriers while choosing the hand-shaken tea is 3.74. We ran the pairwise t-test and obtained the result that age group A has a significant difference with age group C, aged above 36 years old, with a p-value of 0.0054. From the composition of each age group, we can identify the proportion of respondents in age group A are with difficulties in choosing brands and drinks, which can feel the marginal benefit of chatbot service.

4.2.3 Results of Mitigating the Difficulties in Choosing Drinks in Gender Groups

We also compare the benefits of using conversational AI chatbot between male and female users. The average score of the conversational AI chatbot that can mitigate the difficulties in choosing drinks for both gender groups is 3.74, and the female participants have an average score of 3.84 vs 3.55 for male. With pairwise t-test, there is a significant difference between the male and female participants with a p-value of 0.044 in mitigating the difficulties in choosing drinks as shown in Table 4.

Table 4. Average score on the helpfulness perceived by three age groups

Age group	Age range	Percentage of scenario Groups 1, 2, 3, and 4	Number of respondents	Mitigating the difficulties in choosing drinks
A	<25	26.83%, 35.71%, 57.69%, 60.61%	97	3.87
B	26–35	34.14%, 50.00%, 25.00%, 27.27%	66	3.86
C	>35	39.02%, 14.29%, 17.31%, 12.12%	51	3.35

4.2.4 Mitigating the Difficulties in Choosing Drinks in Geographical Regions

Table 5 shows the score of shortening the time to choose a product for participants from three geographical regions. From the geographical region, we found out that users who live in southern Taiwan gain more benefit from the conversational AI chatbot's assistance, in terms of shortening their time in choosing products and experiencing a better purchasing process. Moreover, they tend to be willing to recommend the conversational AI chatbot to others. The average score that the conversational AI chatbot can shorten the time of choosing hand-shaken tea is 3.71, and the score from the participants who live in the south is 4.39. From the results of the pairwise t-test shown, there is a significant difference between the participants in geo group Z with those in geo groups X and Y with p values 0.0007 and 0.000002, respectively. From the composition of the respondents in scenario groups, we can conclude that the high score from geo group Z is mainly contributed by users in scenario group 4 though the number of participants in geo group Z is the smallest size. It shows the main effect from the marginal benefit of users with the difficulties in choosing brands and drinks.

Table 5. Average score in mitigating the time in the decision for users from different regions

Geo groups	Regions	Percentage of scenario groups 1, 2, 3, and 4	Score
X	North (Taipei, New Taipei, & Keelung)	26.83%, 42.86%, 51.92%, 45.45%	3.80
Y	Central (Taoyuan, Hsinchu, Miaoli, Taichung, Changhua, & Nantou)	63.41%, 57.14%, 42.31%, 36.36%	3.53
Z	South (Yunlin, Jiayi, Tainan, Kaohsiung, & Pingtung)	9.72%, 0.00%, 5.77%, 16.67%	4.39

5 Discussions

In the endeavor of developing conversational AI chatbots to support users to better manage their daily experiences, we discovered the perceived value from potential users through a scenario-based survey. Based on the analysis of the result in Sect. 4, we elaborate on the implications in the following subsections.

5.1 Market Segmentation Strategies with the Conversational AI Chatbot

For users facing different levels of difficulties in choosing products and brands, we proposed different marketing strategies to the best use of the conversational AI chatbot.

Group 1. No difficulties on both brands and drinks: From the scenario presented to them, the conversational AI chatbot may ask users about their favorite hand-shaken tea, then just notify their previous experience or notify them of the promotion campaign from their favorite brands or products to reduce their time on the conversation with the bot, and the conversational AI chatbot can focus more on recording the experiences for their experience management benefit.

Group 2. No difficulties with drinks have difficulties with brands: The conversational AI chatbot service can shorten their time to find out which brands have their favorite drinks to narrow down their candidate brands. Maybe in the future marketing strategies can focus on how to boost the core value of the drinks and strengthen brand awareness to let this segment of customers quickly come up with the brand when they want to order the drink.

Group 3. No difficulties on brands have difficulties with drinks: The conversational AI chatbot service can guide them quickly to find the drinks they would like to have or try. For the segment marketing strategies, brands can send out the new product discount coupon to encourage users to try new products.

Group 4. Have difficulties with both brands and drinks: In this group, the market segmentation strategies for the brand could try to increase brand awareness and enhance brand loyalty first. The brand can use promotion coupons or buy one get one free to attract them to come to the same brand first and then can try to increase the frequency of this group of customers to purchase in the future. From the survey, this group has the highest recommendation rate (78%) for the conversational AI chatbot, so it can be a good group to engage to promote the conversational AI chatbot.

5.2 User Experiences of the Conversational AI Chatbot

Based on the responses from the survey, participants are willing to have this kind of conversational AI chatbot service to assist them to decide what kind of hand-shaken drinks they are going to order, and it can enhance their customer purchase experience and shorten their decision-making time (overall with a 3.58 out of 5 on the improvement of purchase experience). Especially, using the NLP model can make users feel they are talking to a real person not just a robot. Based on the response from participants, 68.69% of participants would like to recommend this service to their family and friends. According to the metrics, it shows people have good expectations of conversational chatbot services, and also the chatbot for their daily needs. Choosing hand-shaken drinks can be one of the best practices in daily life.

5.3 VRM as a Marketing Tool

The conversational AI chatbot not only reduces the decision-making time but also can query drinks across different brands in a short time. It is a great marketing tool for users to discover what other users like and would like to try in the future. Moreover, the conversational AI chatbot can help users to prevent drinking the hand-shaken tea they didn't like in the past based on prior experiences. It shows that integrating data from different brands can reduce users' time from searching the menu across brands on the Internet.

Users with no difficulties in choosing brands but having difficulties in choosing drinks, as group 3 in this study, marked an average score of 4.04 out of 5 (overall score is 3.75) that conversational AI chatbot can enhance their intention to try different hand-shaken tea in the future. It would also be great if the conversational AI chatbot can use API to connect with their Customer Relationship Management (CRM) service from the brand itself. It can definitely assist customers to make their customer experience (CX) more complete and can unify the data from online to offline. This move can facilitate customers' purchase process.

5.4 Knowledge Management

Based on the responses from participants, we can say that if there's one assistant who can help users record their experiences in purchasing hand-shaken drinks, it can enhance people's mood when they can prevent them from ordering the drinks they didn't like previously. It shows the importance of managing daily experiences especially when it is not routinely operated; for example, once in a while, we want to buy some drinks for any reason. This study supports the benefit of adopting a conversational AI chatbot to support experience-based knowledge management, as it shows an average score of 3.77 out of 5 that all participants like this feature and content of the conversational AI chatbot to help them choose hand-shaken drinks.

Users having both difficulties in choosing brands and drinks, as group 4 in this study, have the highest positive feedback (78% of recommendation rate) on the feature of the conversational AI chatbot. This group of participants seldom have a chance to try different brands and different hand-shaken tea, so they might not memorize every drink they had before. Thus, this feature can benefit them to memorize their hand-shaken drinks experience.

5.5 Conclusive Remarks and Future Research

In summary, this research serves as user research via scenario-based survey to assess the usability of potential users in different contexts in choosing their beverages. The analytic results could guide the follow-up conversational AI chatbot development. In this study, we focused on the user experiences in choosing beverages and brands as the initial stage of purchase, and the rest of the order fulfillment process could be a follow-up study when trying to integrate the chatbot service with other order fulfillment process activities, such as payment, delivery, etc.

The development of a conversational AI chatbot benefits from this user research with scenario-based survey in this study. In the future, the conversational AI chatbot not only can query for people's needs but also can be used for users to receive information from peers in the network. Thus, we could extend this service via peer-to-peer (P2P) networks with conversational AI chatbots to enable the shared experience-based knowledge management.

References

1. Chait, L.P.: Creating a successful knowledge management system. J. Bus. Strategy **20**(2), 23 (1999). https://idm.nthu.ust.edu.tw/sso/886UST_NTHU/saml2/login/?next=/saml2/idp/login/process/?url=https://www.proquest.com/scholarly-journals/creating-successful-knowledge-management-system/docview/1295105997/se-2
2. Drift: The 2018 State of chatbots report. Technical report, Drift (2018)
3. Handoyo, E., Arfan, M., Soetrisno, Y.A.A., Somantri, M., Sofwan, A., Sinuraya, E.W.: Ticketing chatbot service using serverless NLP technology. In: 2018 5th International Conference on Information Technology, Computer, and Electrical Engineering (ICITACEE), Semarang, Indonesia, pp. 325–330 (2018). https://doi.org/10.1109/ICITACEE.2018.8576921
4. Følstad, A., Taylor, C.: Investigating the user experience of customer service chatbot interaction: a framework for qualitative analysis of chatbot dialogues. Qual. User Experience **6**(1), 1–17 (2021). https://doi.org/10.1007/s41233-021-00046-5
5. Gartner: Market guide for virtual customer assistants. Technical report, Gartner (2019). https://www.gartner.com/en/documents/3947357/market-guide-for-virtual-customer-assistants
6. Grewal, D., Levy, M., Kumar, V.: Customer experience management in retailing: an organizing framework. J. Retail. **85**(1), 1–14 (2009). https://doi.org/10.1016/j.jretai.2009.01.001
7. Jiao, A.: An intelligent chatbot system based on entity extraction using RASA NLU and neural network. In: Journal of Physics: Conference Series (2020). https://iopscience.iop.org/article/10.1088/1742-6596/1487/1/012014/pdf. Accessed 1 Jan 2023
8. Kolb, D.A.: Experiential Learning: Experience as the Source of Learning and Development, vol. 1. Prentice-Hall, Englewood Cliffs (1984)
9. Lalwani, T., Bhalotia, S., Pal, A., Rathod, V., Bisen, S.: Implementation of a chatbot system using AI and NLP. Int. J. Innov. Res. Comput. Sci. Technol. (IJIRCST) **6**(3) (2018). SSRN: https://ssrn.com/abstract=3531782 or https://doi.org/10.2139/ssrn.3531782
10. Mårtensson, M.: A critical review of knowledge management as a management tool. J. Knowl. Manag. **4**(3), 204–216 (2000). https://doi.org/10.1108/13673270010350002

11. McElroy, M.W.: The New Knowledge Management. Taylor & Francis eBooks (2002). https://www.taylorfrancis.com/books/mono/10.4324/9780080512655/new-knowledge-man agement-mark-mcelroy. Accessed 16 Jan 2023
12. McInerney, C.: Knowledge management and the dynamic nature of knowledge. J. Am. Soc. Inf. Sci. Technol. (2002). https://asistdl.onlinelibrary.wiley.com/doi/abs/10.1002/asi.10109? casa_token=eBhFf5XT2DIAAAAA%3AqNIImpmzFya7CCEBKN-IirwpqoIEFfZtXI_3-D2qyqPJKeWmT8MYGbFCDL-BAJar9oMvig2DP94-J-vy. Accessed 25 Dec 2022
13. Mnasri, M.: Recent advances in conversational NLP: towards the standardization of Chatbot building. YouTube. arXiv (2019). Accessed 25 Dec 2022
14. Natural language processing in Wikipedia (2023). https://en.wikipedia.org/wiki/Natural_lang uage_processing
15. Nonaka, I.: A dynamic theory of organizational knowledge creation. Organ. Sci. 5(1), 14–37 (1994)
16. NVIDIA: Graph Analytics – What is it and Why Does it Matter? NVIDIA (n.d.). https://www.nvidia.com/en-us/glossary/data-science/graph-analytics/. Accessed 11 Dec 2022
17. Palmer, A.: Customer experience management: a critical review of an emerging idea. J. Serv. Mark. 24(3), 196–208 (2010). https://doi.org/10.1108/08876041011040604
18. Rodriguez, M.A., Neubauer, P.: Constructions from dots and lines. Bull. Am. Soc. Inf. Sci. Technol. 36(6), 35–41 (2010). https://doi.org/10.1002/bult.2010.1720360610
19. Van den Broeck, E., Zarouali, B., Poels, K.: Chatbot advertising effectiveness: when does the message get through? Comput. Hum. Behav. 98, 150–157 (2019). https://doi.org/10.1016/j.chb.2019.04.009
20. Wiig, K.M.: Knowledge management: an introduction and perspective. J. Knowl. Manag. 1(1), 6–14 (1997). https://doi.org/10.1108/13673279710800682

Healthcare

Healthcare

Implementation of Quality Management Tools and Process-Based Management in Commercializing Organizations of Orthopaedic Devices in Colombia

Mayra Samara Ordoñez-Díaz[1](✉) and Ivanhoe Rozo-Rojas[2] (iD)

[1] Fundación Universitaria de Ciencias de la Salud - FUCS, Bogota D.C., Colombia
msordonez@fucsalud.edu.co
[2] Universidad Católica de Colombia, Bogota D.C., Colombia
irozo@ucatolica.edu.co

Abstract. Quality Management Tools (QMT) are used for heading issues that affect the process performance in healthcare organizations (HCO) and improving key performance indicators related to stakeholders. QMT implementation in HCO is relevant to enhance the patient safety policy, risk mitigation, and prevent adverse event and cost increasing as in clinics and hospitals as in medical devices providers. The article aims to identify the quality management tools implemented in the logistics process in Colombian orthopaedic medical devices as initiative for strengthens the patient safety policy. A 15-questions electronic structured questionnaire was applied in 17 Colombian orthopaedic medical devices which was answered by its logistic coordinators as the process' leaders. The results show that the three QMT most implemented are 5W + 1H, PDCA cycle and Six Sigma methodology. Furthermore, the HCO which have quality management indicators in reverse logistic processes perceive impacts as result of semester or annual internal audits. To conclude, orthopaedic medical devices organizations combine quality management systems with other methodologies and tools for enhancing the satisfaction of the stakeholders. Specifically, in the logistic process, organizations involve people and technology for getting better results focusing value-added assessment. Future works may be orientated to cover the whole logistic chain and integrate the impact evaluation with clinic and hospitals' processes.

Keywords: Healthcare · Quality Management · Quality Management Tools · Logistics · Medical Devices · Orthopaedic

1 Introduction

Traditionally, some definitions related to the customer satisfaction come from manufacturing facilities, and it has been adjusted according to the criteria or perception, based on models and frameworks. Hence, ISO 9000 defines quality as the degree to which a set of inherent characteristics fulfils requirement [1]. In healthcare, quality is defined by the Worldwide Health Organization (WHO) as the degree to which health services for individuals and populations increase the likelihood of desired health outcomes [2]. It is based on evidence-based professional knowledge and is critical for achieving universal health coverage. On the other hand, Donabedian proposes a specific model for measuring quality care designed on three components (structure, process, and outcomes) which are developed in indicators [3].

Quality management tools are defined as techniques or procedures which support organizational purposes to measure the processes' performance to reduce quality issues and improve planning activities, productivity, and customer service [4]. As the WHO states the quality care definition, the quality should be focused on patient satisfaction and care processes, generating positive impacts on wellness and reduce economic losses.

In orthopedics, quality and process improvement is essential because products are incorporated in parts of the body which require stability and avoid adverse events in patients [5, 6]. Furthermore, quality management tools and techniques are widely used for enhancing the Patient Safety Policy and indicators of the processes [7] as showed in the literature review. The Fig. 1 shows the co-occurrence of keywords used in the search equation in the Scopus database:

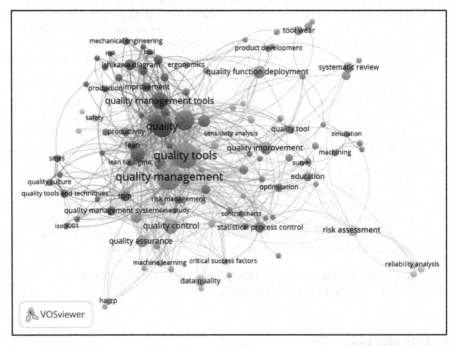

Fig. 1. Keywords co-occurrence about quality management tools in Scopus.

Using filters by year and language, a total of 1.078 documents were reported from 2015 to 2023 written in English. As we mentioned, quality management tools are used in quality assurance and risk evaluation or assessment with frameworks as ISO 9001 or Lean Six Sigma for enhancing its capabilities [14, 15]. The applications involve production and service organizations which mainly use observational and before-after studies [12] as methodological design.

The tools mentioned in the literature as 7 Quality Control Tools (7QCT) for improvement in organizations have influence in processes which can be used for collecting data, analyze data, identify root causes, measure results, track and make easier actions. In detail, 7QCT are composed by Pareto Diagram, Cause & Effect Diagram (Ishikawa Diagram), Histogram, Control Charts, Scatter Diagrams, Graphs and Check-sheets [13]. However, current studies expand the concept and involve other quality management tools as follow (Table 1):

Table 1. Quality management tools in healthcare.

Tool	Description
Flowchart	A process mapping technique that describes, through specific symbols, each step of a process. It allows us to verify how the components of a system are connected and related, besides facilitating the location of deficiencies and providing the understanding of any changes that are proposed in the existing systems
Pick chart	Possible, Implement, Challenge and Killé Chart is a visual LSS tool used to organize process improvement ideas. PICK charts are used after brainstorming sessions to help identify which ideas can be easily implemented and have a high reward
Pareto Diagram	Diagram that assumes that 20% of the defects in a given system are responsible for 80% of the existing problems. The tool allows the identification and classification of the most important problems that should be corrected first
Cause and Effect Diagram	Visual representation of multiple causes for a specific problem or effect by drawing a diagram representing the skeleton of a fish. Categorizes the potential causes of a problem into successive details to define the root cause, showing the relationship of causes and effects to each other
5S (seiri, seiton, seiso, siketsu, shitsuke)	Japanese method of organizing the workspace in a clean, efficient, and safe manner to achieve a productive work environment. The method includes 5 phases: Sort (Seiri), remove what is not necessary; Set in Order (Seiton), prepar necessary items in an organized and systematic way; Shine (Seiso), regular cleaning of equipment and workplaces; Standardize (Seikutsu), document and standardize the method; Sustain (Shitsuke), continuously maintain established procedures, audit work methods, making 5S a habit integrated into the culture
Kanban	The tool is a system of visual control of materials and tasks, using cards that are removed and placed on a board or screen, passing from step to step in the process. The main features are: the regulaition of the flow of global items through visual controls, simplification of administrative work, and ease of transmitting information in a quick and organized way

(*continued*)

Table 1. (*continued*)

Tool	Description
PDCA (Plan, Do, Check, Act)	It is a process or system management method formed by 4 phases: Plan, where the goals are determined; Do, where there is the clarification of goals and plans for those involved to understand and support the proposal; Check, where there is the checking of the data obtained through the goal; Action, where the strategy that worked well is transformed into the current way of executing the activities
Value Stream Mapping	It is a diagram that shows the detailed steps of a work process, contemplating the flow of people, materials, and information. The purpose of the VSM is to facilitate the visualization and understanding of the work process and to allow improvement by eliminating steps that do not add value to the customer, considering whether there is a safer, more efficient, or more effective option
DMAIC (Define, Measure, Analyze, Improve and Control)	The Six Sigma method is divided into five stages, where each letter constitutes one of the phases: Define, Measure, Analyze, Improve and Control. It is used to improve existing processes, besides eliminating defects, increasing customer satisfaction and, mainly, increasing the profitability of companies
FMEA (Failure Mode and Effect Analysis)	A tool that aims to eliminate potential failures, problems, and errors in systems, designs, processes, and services. The goal of FMEA is to list all potential failure modes, analyze the cause of each failure and its effects on the system. Critically analyses of failure modes and usually based on the three risk parameters of severity (S), occurrence (O) and detection (D) whose product returs the risk priority number (RPN)
FMECA (Failure Modes, Effects and Criticality Analysis)	It is an extension of FMEA and represents a valid support method for semi-quantitatively measuring system failure mode criticality
HFMEA (Healthcare Failure Mode and Effect Analysis)	FMEA adapted for healthcare. It was introduced by the Joint Comission International on Accreditation of Healthcare Organizations (JCAHO) for improving healthcare services and preventing errors
Lean Six Sigma	Lean thinking is a method for improving performance, being a strategy for changing people's mental model, the essence of the organization's culture, the way tasks are performed, plans are made and management of processes and people. It is a way to specify value, aligning, in the best sequence, the actions that create value, and performing such activities without interruption and in an increasingly efficient manner

Source: Cunha-Reis, A. et al. [12]

In this way, many organizations have implemented the quality tools, but comparison studies are not developed in orthopedic logistic processes in healthcare organizations [8, 12]. This is a necessity for identifying approaches and best practices and establishing improvement actions focused on specific opportunities in logistics, even in cost calculation [9–11].

2 Methodology

2.1 Methodological Design

A transversal-descriptive methodological design was deployed in 15-structured questions for logistic coordinators in orthopaedic medical devices. The coordinators selected to answer the questionnaire were linked to companies' representative of the sector. In order for this sample to be adequate, the researchers selected those that most frequently provide supplies for orthopedic surgery to hospitals, which had high coverage at the national level and finally the multinationals. Taken into account the limitations to access to the information and permissions to answer the survey, the methodology was based on a convenience sampling of the organizations (N = 41). Sensitive data and information were protected for confidentiality purposes. The Fig. 2 shows the methodological design in four steps:

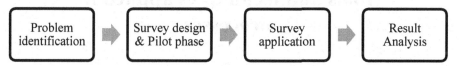

Fig. 2. Methodological design. Source: authors.

The study was intended for obtain information about the type of products, the use of quality management tools, knowledge about quality management systems, and its applications to improve their processes.

2.2 Survey Design and Pilot Phase

For the survey construction, the variables established by the researchers were taken into account, and these variables were constructed from the thematic review about the quality tools implemented in the health sector institutions. The variables that formed the analysis categories of the survey were: institution characterization, knowledge about quality tools and use or implementation of the tools in the institutions. Once these categories were established and the specific questions were raised, the pilot phase was carried out, which consisted of applying the instrument to two experts in quality and logistics reviewed the questions. Subsequently, the corresponding adjustments were made to improve the quality of the survey. The survey was applied in some cases personally and in others cases by telephone.

In the same way, to guarantee the validity of the information, interviewers were trained in order to carry out the correct application of the instrument and resolve the participants doubts.

3 Results

The survey was answered by 17 leaders of quality and logistics processes (36,5%) who were selected with the criteria mentioned in the methodological design and were authorized to answer the survey. The core business of those organizations is mainly orientated in providing osteosynthesis supplies (68% in trauma and 51% in articular prosthesis and spine). Evaluating the training in quality, 64,7% of respondents 64.7% (n = 11) indicate that have a medium level of knowledge of quality management systems which is comparable with 52,9% (n = 9) who explain that have knowledge about the ISO 9001 requirements.

Only 11.7% (n = 2) responded that have low-level knowledge about quality management systems and ISO 9001. A total of 41.1% (n = 7) participants affirm that their knowledge about quality management tools and its applications on reverse logistic process and 29.4% (n = 5) indicate that have high knowledge about it. As we mentioned before, one of the main purposes of this initiative was identify the main tools used in the processes as is shown in Fig. 3.

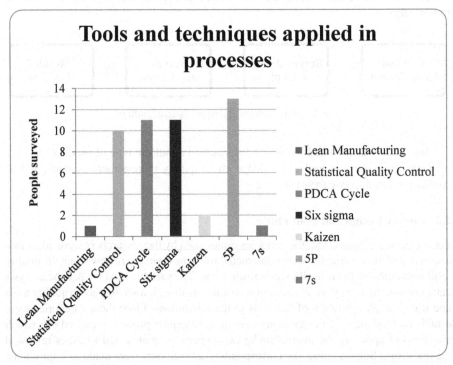

Fig. 3. Most used quality management tools in Colombian Orthopaedic Organizations reverse logistics' processes.

Another key aspect that was defined for questioning is the records of the processes to maintain information and data about the activities which is satisfactory for the 88.2% (n = 15) due to the fact that is mandatory to implement controls in all the steps of the process. Consequently, the frequency of the internal audits as verification method of quality management system's efficacy was checked, evidencing 41.1% (n = 7) practice it in 6-month period, 29.4% (n = 5) each 2 months and the others each year (Fig. 4).

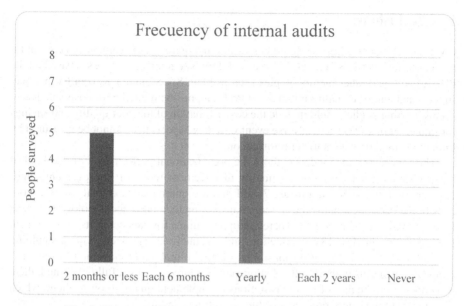

Fig. 4. Frequency of internal audits in the quality management systems

Finally, the quality management systems are involved into a measurement criterion that is important to make decisions and evaluate the performance in the processes. This element was pointed by 88,2% (n = 15) of the sample, where indicate that quality indicators in the logistic process are measured, and 76.4% (n = 13) consider that their clients (healthcare organizations providers) use quality management tools as well.

4 Discussion

According to the literature review's articles which we took concepts and approaches on QMT, previous studies reveals that those tools and techniques are not wide applied to the reverse logistics processes in orthopaedic commercialization enterprises or do not mention it which represent the most value finding of this study. The organizations have strong capabilities in knowledge and use of QMT, where they demonstrate that have orientation to the operational excellence, such as 5P, the most used tool, and combined with ISO 9001 requirements, different of the Kaizen Events as the articles reported.

The similarity of findings in previous studies is that records are physical and digital filled to keep information and data, providing support to making decision process and improving the Quality Management System. This knowledge is valuable to the people and the empowerment to develop improving cycles but is necessary to renew the learning baseline and include other QMT and its applicability into the medical and administrative processes for strengthen the capabilities and the Patient Safety Policy.

5 Conclusions

QMT are relevant for improving processes into the quality management systems and it processes. ISO 9001, KPI and QMT are useful tools to maintain processes based on the PDCA cycle and other methodologies such as Lean Six Sigma or Kaizen Events may support and enhance quality initiatives. QMT support the reduction of costs in adverse events. Further studies could include the cost estimation of the poor quality and savings for implementing QMT and adverse event were key aspects that cannot be measured by limitations in permissions to get information.

The survey provide evidence about the organizational performance of this kind of business and its appropriation on quality management tools for improvement. Findings reported that organizations use 7QMT and use internal and external audits as controls in the processes, but some of them consider include other methodologies such as Lean Thinking and Six Sigma. There are opportunities for enhancing its improvement processes adopting ISO 18404 guidelines and execute Kaizen projects as quality culture.

Although the relation of responsibility of the Colombian Orthopedic Commercializing Organizations in the results of surgical procedures is not yet fully regulated, there is a concern on the part of these institutions to implement quality tools in them, which contributes to the safety processes of the patient in hospitals.

References

1. International Standardization Organization. ISO 9001:2015 Quality Management Systems. Requirements. Geneva
2. Kuyken, W.: The World Health Organization quality of life assessment (WHOQOL): position paper from the World Health Organization. Soc. Sci. Med. 41(10), 1403–1409 (1995)
3. McCullough, K., et al.: An examination of primary health care nursing service evaluation using the Donabedian model: a systematic review. Res. Nurs. Health 46(1), 159–176 (2023)
4. Rozo-Rojas, I., et al.: Identification of key factors in the implementation of quality management practices in Sterilization Centers. In: Proceedings of the LACCEI International Multiconference for Engineering Education and Technology (2017). https://doi.org/10.18687/LACCEI2017.1.1.279
5. Pinney, S.J., Page, A.E., Jevsevar, D.S., Bozic, K.J.: Current concept review: quality and process improvement in orthopedics. Orthop. Res. Rev. 8, 1–11 (2016)
6. Shukla, S., et al.: Implementation of adverse event reporting for medical devices India. Bull. World Health Organ. 98(3), 206–211 (2020)
7. Bamford, D.R., Greatbanks, R.W.: The use of quality management tools and techniques: a study of application in everyday situations. Int. J. Qual. Reliab. Manag. 22(4), 376–392 (2005). https://doi.org/10.1108/02656710510591219
8. Martelli, N., et al.: New European regulation for medical devices: what is changing? Cardiovasc. Intervent. Radiol. 42(9), 1272–1278 (2019). https://doi.org/10.1007/s00270-019-02247-0
9. Dellifraine, J.L., Wang, Z., McCaughey, D., Langabeer, J.R., Erwin, C.O.: The use of six sigma in health care management: are we using it to its full potential? Qual. Manag. Health Care 22(3), 210–223 (2013)
10. Chassin, M.R.: Is health care ready for Six Sigma quality? Milbank Q. 76(4), 565–591 (1998)
11. Egbosimba, D.: Medical devices industry: the problem of clinical evaluation reports. Ann. Biol. Clin. (Paris). 77(5), 514–516 (2019)

12. Cunha Reis, A., et al.: Quality management tools applied to drug dispensing in hospital pharmacy: a scoping review. **19**, 582–590 (2023)
13. George, J., Singh, A., Kumar, A.: A study of basic 7 quality control tools and techniques for continuous improvement. In: 2nd International Conference on Emerging Trends in Mechanical Engineering, Bhopal (2018)
14. Rozo-Rojas, I., Díaz-Piraquive, F.N., de Jesús Muriel-Perea, Y., Ordoñez-Díaz, M.S., Ospina-Prieto, L.A.: Risk management framework as technovigilance support at sterilization unit in the San Jose hospital (Colombia). In: Uden, L., Hadzima, B., Ting, I.-H. (eds.) KMO 2018. CCIS, vol. 877, pp. 437–451. Springer, Cham (2018). https://doi.org/10.1007/978-3-319-95204-8_37
15. Rozo-Rojas, I., et al.: Identificación de las causas de variación en los procesos de esterilización de un hospital privado a través de la metodología Six SIGMA: Fases definir–medir. Conferencia Desarrollo e Innovación en Ingeniería, pp. 434–449 (2019)

How Ethnic Differences in Television Watching and Low Physical Activity in UK Adults Affect Type 2 Diabetes

Uduakobong Ayoade[1]([⊠]) and Nnenna Joy Eze[2]

[1] School of Health and Wellbeing, University of Glasgow, Clarice Pears Building (Level 3), 90 Byres Road, Glasgow G12 8TBZ, UK
ntuk.uduak@gmail.com
[2] Faculty of Health, Education and Life Sciences, Birmingham City University, Seacole Building - City South Campus, Westbourne Road, Edgbaston, Birmingham B15 3TN, UK

Abstract. Type 2 diabetes is increasing globally. However, those from South Asian and Black ethnic descent are more susceptible to the disease compared to those from European White descent. The reasons for this disparity are unknown. Lifestyle behaviours like low physical activity and sedentary behaviour are shown to be risk factors associated with type 2 diabetes. This link has been found in predominantly White ethnic groups. This study aims to examine whether the varying magnitude time spent watching television and physical activity contribute to the high risk of diabetes in minority ethnic groups compared to the majority Whites using the UK Biobank data. This is a cross-sectional study of middle-aged individuals from South Asian, Black and White ethnic backgrounds. Adjusting for age, socioeconomic status and BMI, television viewing as a sedentary behaviour and low physical activity were significant risk factors for the development of type 2 diabetes in south Asians and Whites but not Blacks which was evident with mediation by BMI. The non-significance in Blacks maybe due to other underlying factors. There is a need to develop effective interventions that can promote improved lifestyle behaviours in these populations including promoting the knowledge on the risk of sedentary behaviours and diabetes.

Keywords: Type 2 diabetes · minority ethnic groups · South Asian · Black · television viewing · physical activity · United Kingdom · epidemiology

1 Introduction

Minority ethnic groups generally have poorer health than the general population, but the reasons are many and much debated [1, 2]. In the United Kingdom, studies show that there is a huge disparity in diabetes risk among ethnic minorities [3]. Minority ethnic groups are at greater odds of having diabetes at lower obesity levels and being more active significantly reduces the risk of diabetes in these group [3]. However, modern society and technological advances have led to highly prevalent sedentary lifestyle which is increasingly considered a distinct risk factor for health problems and diseases. A

L. Uden and I-H. Ting (Eds.): KMO 2023, CCIS 1825, pp. 412–429, 2023.
https://doi.org/10.1007/978-3-031-34045-1_33

sedentary behaviour that has seen a dramatic rise over the years is screen watching [4]. Whilst the evidence for the association between television viewing and diabetes risk are known, whether this relationship differs across varying ethnicities has been largely unstudied particularly in the high-risk population of south Asians and Black ethnic groups, which is of concern given the prevalence of type 2 diabetes is substantially higher in non-white populations [5, 6].

Consequently, if sitting time is established to be independently associated with type 2 diabetes, and considering the associated complications of type 2 diabetes that minority ethnic groups have to combat, elucidating the association of television watching hours with type 2 diabetes is crucial. Clinical and public health recommendations should explicitly address sitting in addition to physical activity for minority ethnic groups; currently they do not [4, 7]. Adults from minority ethnic groups-particularly in the westernized countries-reportedly do not participate regularly in exercise activities [8, 9], it might be possible to reduce the risk of nonparticipation by restricting sitting time (e.g. television watching) and increasing nonexercised activity (e.g. standing and ambulating) throughout the day [10–12]. The latter approach might be more promising in terms of long-term adherence, because it will involve more subtle changes and fewer of the commonly cited barriers to lifestyle exercise program in this population. There have been relative studies on the implications of sitting and reduced physical activity on depression [13, 14], obesity [15] and other condition [16] across different ethnic, however, there is a dearth of studies examining both sitting time and physical activity concurrently in ethnic minority groups, to make evidence-based recommendations to contribute to implementing effective ethnic-specific interventions which would potentially constrict the ethnic disparity in type 2 diabetes.

Therefore, this research investigates and hypothesizes that the association between television viewing and type 2 diabetes varies by ethnicity in south Asian, Black and white adult participants using the UK Biobank data and to assess the extent/pattern to which this association is based on ethnicity is independent of PA and BMI. The objectives of the research are to: first, investigate the dose-response associations of television time with type 2 diabetes, independent of physical activity in the study population across different ethnic groups. The second objective was to determine the joint association of both television time and physical activity with type 2 diabetes across the ethnic groups.

2 Literature Review

A sedentary behaviour that has seen a dramatic rise over the years is screen watching. With the increasing use of screens such as televisions, computers, mobile phones, among others, more time is spent in front of screens than outside engagement and less likely to exert in physical activity [17, 18]. Among the different domains of screen watching, television viewing is reported to be the most reliable and validated indicator of sedentary behaviour. Watching television is the behaviour that occupies the most time in the leisure setting and this has led to increasing concern about the rising prevalence of television viewing and its health implications [19, 20]. The association with television viewing in studies are stronger than those for total sedentary behaviour in different outcomes, including hypertension, adiposity and diabetes [21]. Guo et al. conducted a meta-analysis of 1,071,967 participants from 48 articles showed that for each 1-h/day increase in total sedentary behaviour, the risk of type 2 diabetes increased by 5%, while the associated risk of type 2 diabetes increased by 8% for each 1-h/day increase in tv viewing (Guo et al. 2020). In another study, Paterson and colleagues performed a meta-analysis specifically focused on television watching associated with diabetes risk. The 182,568 participants from 7 studies reported increase in diabetes risk with increasing TV viewing with an estimate relative risk (RR of 1,12 (1.08–116) with each additional hour of TV viewing. This was attenuated when adjusted for physical activity [22].

Whilst the evidence for the association between television viewing and diabetes risk are known, whether this relationship differs across varying ethnicities has been largely unstudied particularly in the high-risk population of south Asians and Black ethnic groups, which is of concern given the prevalence of type 2 diabetes is substantially higher in non-white populations [5] and less physically active [8, 23]. Furthermore, studies have indicated that south Asian women spend more time at sedentary behaviours than other populations [8, 16, 23], but how prolonged television watching impacts the risk of type 2 diabetes in this population has not been explored. To our knowledge only three studies has considered the association between television watching time and diabetes risk in Black populations. The Black Women's Health Study (BWHS) reported 1.9-fold risk of diabetes amongst black women who spent more than 5 h watching television in a day relative to those who spent less than 1 h per day of television viewing [24]. In contrast, amongst the Black participants in the Multi-Ethnic Study of Atherosclerosis (MESA) and Jackson Health study, there was no statistically significant graded association between television viewing and type 2 diabetes [25, 26]. Therefore, understanding how television viewing contributes to type 2 diabetes in varying ethnic groups is an important area in need of more research. Time spent sitting in television viewing is a particularly relevant target because it is a major contributor to diabetes risk [27–29] and is potentially modifiable [29]. This will provide knowledge sharing on the risk of type 2 diabetes and help to promote healthy living amongst South Asians and Blacks.

3 Methodology

3.1 Study Design

This is a cross-sectional analysis on baseline data from the UK Biobank obtained between 2007 and 2010. The UK Biobank is a large, population-based cohort study examining the inter-relationships between environmental, lifestyle and genetic factors in adults aged between 37–73 years old. Participant written informed consent was obtained prior to data collection.

3.2 Study Population

The present research used data from UK Biobank participants who identified as White, South Asian or Black ancestry.

3.3 Exclusion Criteria

Excluded participants who reported a diagnosis of heart disease (n = 28,543) and cancers (n = 38,021) or to avoid potential reverse causation, as these groups are more likely to be sedentary, hence avoid biased estimates of sedentary behaviour [30–36]. Participants with missing information on television viewing and physical activity, those who reported ethnicity other than white, south Asian or Black were also excluded.

3.4 Primary Outcome

Participants who were entered as having 'diabetes' or 'type 2 diabetes' were selected. Those taking insulin within their first year, and were <35 years old at diagnosis were excluded to reduce the likelihood of type 1 and monogenic forms of diabetes.

3.5 Independent Measures

3.5.1 Television Viewing

TV viewing was determined from respondents' answer to the number of hours spent watching TV on a typical day, based on previous work by Hu et al. [37]. Those who responded spending >8 h on TV viewing were questioned twice, therefore high values were deemed robust [9, 38].

3.5.2 Physical Activity

Participants were classified as 'low' (not meeting criteria for the 'moderate' or 'high' categories), 'moderate' (at least 20 min of vigorous-intensity physical activity on three or more days/week; at least 30 min of moderate-intensity physical activity or walking on five or more days/week; five or more days/week spent in any combination of walking, moderate- or vigorous-intensity physical activity achieving at least 600 MET minutes/week) or 'high' (at least three days/week of vigorous-intensity physical activity achieving at least 1,500 MET minutes/week; at least seven days/week spent in any combination of walking, moderate- or vigorous-intensity physical activity achieving at least 3,000 MET minutes/week) activity levels. All data processing followed the standardised IPAQ-SF scoring guidance [39].

3.6 Assessment of Covariates

Other lifestyle behaviour factors which could act as potential confounders were identified a priori based on the established relationship of these variables to diabetes and television viewing/physical activity. These include: Body mass index (BMI), Townsend Score for socioeconomic status and smoking.

3.7 Statistical Analysis

All data analyses were performed using 14.2 (Stata Corporation, College Station, Texas, USA). The demographic and lifestyle characteristics of each ethnic group were summarized using the median and interquartile range for continuous variables, and frequencies and percentages for categorical data. The statistical significance of differences between ethnic groups was tested using the Kruskal-Wallis test for continuous variables and Pearson's chi-squared test for categorical variables. Potential interactions between television viewing and physical activity variables and ethnicity, sex, of diabetes were tested by the insertion of an interaction term in the model and calculation of the p-value using the likelihood-ratio test. Significant interactions were detected between ethnicity and television time/physical activity for diabetes ($p < 0.001$), and sex interaction for the relationship between television time/physical activity and diabetes ($p < 0.001$). Therefore, all the analyses were reported stratified by ethnicity and sex.

Cut-points for TV viewing time categories were defined a priori into 3 groups: <2 h, 2–4 h, <4 h. The choice of 2 h/day as a threshold for the lowest screen time group is consistent with recommendations that make specific references to TV viewing (Stamatakis et al. 2011). Total physical activity groups were labelled as 'low physical activity' (≤ 600 MET-min/week), 'moderate physical activity' (≥ 600 MET-min/week) and 'high physical activity' (≥ 3000 MET-minutes/week), in accordance with the Guidelines for the data processing and analysis of the International Physical Activity Questionnaire (http://www.ipaq.ki.se/).

Cuzick test for trend across ordered levels of television time and physical activity categories in progressive models with diabetes outcome as the dependent variable [40].

Multivariate binary logistic regression models were then used to examine the associations between levels of TV viewing and diabetes risk, using TV viewing time <2 h/day serving as the referent model separately for each ethnic groups by sex. Initial model adjusted for age, and socioeconomic status (model 1). Model 2 was adjusted for age, socioeconomic status, smoking and BMI (model 2). Model 3 was a further adjustment for physical activity within each ethnic group, in separate analyses for men and women. Physical activity was included in the third model, as a continuous variable because we were interested in examining whether television watching time was associated with type 2 diabetes, independent of leisure-time moderate or vigorous physical activity.

To examine whether the association between television watching time and type 2 diabetes was consistent across the range of physical activity the joint association risk of diabetes was assessed by creating nine groups based on combined tertiles of TV viewing and physical activity and using logistic regression to estimate the odds of diabetes separately among each ethnicity group by sex adjusting for the same confounders. Analyses included adjustment for age, and socioeconomic status (model 1); model 1 plus smoking and BMI (model 2). The p-values for all hypothesis tests were two-sided and $p < 0.05$ was interpreted as statistically significant.

4 Results

4.1 Characteristics of the Study Population

Table 1. shows the characteristics of the study population by sex and ethnic groups. In total 486,665 participants (264,105 women (54.27%), 222,560 men (45.73%) were included in this analysis because they belonged to the eligible ethnic groups, had for diabetes and all the independent variables. Out of this subset of participants 469,269 (96.43%) were White; 9,624 (1.98%) were South Asians and 7,772 (1.60%) were Blacks. Blacks were younger in age (52 years) compared to South Asians (55 years) and Whites (60 years). A greater proportion of Blacks (64.0% women; 65.3% men) were in the most deprived socioeconomic category compared with South Asians (35.7% women; 41.0%) and Whites (18.4% women; 19.4% men). Greater proportion of Blacks spent more than four hours watching television (up to 20.5%) compared with South Asians (up to 10.8%) and Whites (up to 12.3%). BMI values was highest in Black women (29.7 kg/m2) in the study population. Time spent in total physical activity was significantly higher ($p < 0.001$) among Whites (women: 2,533 MET-mins/wk; men: 2,648 MET-mins/wk) and lowest in than South Asians (women: 2,226 MET-mins/wk; men: 2,162 MET-mins/wk.

Overall, the crude diabetes prevalence was higher in men than in women. Age distribution was similar between men and women. Women had higher values of BMI compared to men. The crude prevalence of diabetes was highest in South Asians, followed by Blacks in comparison with Whites. Amongst the women, diabetes prevalence was 13.7% in South Asians and 10.1% in Blacks. Among men, the diabetes prevalence was 20.5% in South Asians and 12.8% in Blacks (Table 1.).

Overall, the Pearson correlation showed television time weakly correlated with total physical activity ($r = -0.07$ ($P < 0.0001$), reinforcing the argument that these are separate domains and, hence, separate risk factors.

4.2 Ethnic Difference in Television Viewing and Diabetes Risk

Table 2. shows the dose-response association of television viewing and diabetes risk by ethnic groups. Amongst South Asians and Whites, graded the risk of diabetes was significantly higher in those reporting longer duration of television viewing, when fully adjusted for age, Townsend index, smoking and alcohol status, BMI and physical activity (Ptrend < 0.05). However, there was no significant graded association between television time and diabetes amongst the Blacks (Ptrend > 0.05) for both women and men.

Data showed the risk of watching television for those who watched 2–4 h of television or more than 4 h of television was highest in South Asians (Women: OR 1.64; 95%CI (1.36–1.99) and OR 2.69; 95%CI (2.10–3.45) respectively; Men OR:1.53; 95%CI (1.32–1.78) and OR 2.31; 95%CI (1.88–2.86). Ethnic differences in joint association between television viewing and physical activity with diabetes risk.

4.3   Ethnic Differences in Joint Association Between Television Viewing and Physical Activity with Diabetes Risk

Table 3. depicts the joint association of television viewing time and physical activity categories in Whites, South Asians and Blacks, adjusted for age, SES, smoking and BMI. A linear relationship of diabetes was observed between higher time spent on television viewing with lower levels of physical activity. Among those who the who spent more than 4 h of TV viewing and performed ≥3000 MET-minutes/week of physical activity compared with the reference group, the risk of diabetes was more than 2 times higher in South Asians (Women: OR 2.06; 95%CI (1.19–3.57); men: OR 2.34;95CI (1.48–3.70)). In Whites, the risk was in Women: OR 1.89; 95%CI (1.67–2.15); Men OR 2.14; 95%CI (1.94–2.36). In Blacks the risk was women: OR 1.17; 95%CI (0.65–2.10); Men OR 1.50; 95%CI (0.84–2.67).

Table 1. Characteristics of study participants by ethnicity and sex

	Women			Men		
	white N = 255,180	South Asian N = 4,444	Black N = 4,481	White N = 214,368	South Asian N = 5,152	Black N = 3,353
	med (IQR)	med (IQR)	med (IQR)	med (IQR)	med (IQR)	med (IQR)
Age (years)	60 (52–65)	54 (48–61)	52 (47–59)	60 (53–66)	55 (47–62)	52 (46–59)
BMI (kg/m²)	26·1 (23·4–29·6)	26.7 (24·0–30·0)	29·7 (26·1–33·7)	27·3 (24·9–30·1)	26·5 (24·4–29·1)	27·9 (25·5–30·6)
Physical Activity (MET-mins/wk)	2,533 (1,455–4,547)	2,226 (1,215–4,053)	2,300 (1,299–4,053)	2,648 (1,448–5,092)	2,162 (1,158–3,908)	2,415 (1,273–4,938)
	N (%)	N (%)	N (%)	N (%)	N (%)	N (%)
Diabetes	8,710 (3·4)	599 (13·7)	451 (10·1)	13,906 (6·5)	1,042 (20·5)	414 (12·8)
Missing	471	75	37	615	108	42
TV Viewing (hr)						
<2 h	120,612 (47.3)	2,537 (57.1)	1,934 (43.2)	99,403(46.4)	2,960 (57.1)	1,517 (46.1)
2–4 h	101,914 (39.9)	1,428 (32.1)	1,630 (36.4)	85,526 (39.9)	1,691 (32.6)	1,139 (34.6)
>4 h	32,654 (12.8)	479 (10.8)	917 (20.5)	29,160 (13.6)	529 (10.2)	635 (19.3)
Smoking status						
None	150,297 (58.6)	4,144 (91.0)	3,590 (77.7)	103,816 (48.4)	3,396 (65.1)	2,029 (60.0)
Previous	83,181 (32.4)	260 (5.7)	617 (13.3)	84,320 (39.3)	1,035 (19.9)	772 (22.8)
Current	23,126(9.0)	151(3.3)	416(9.0)	26,396 (12.3)	783 (15.0)	579 (17.1)
Deprivation						
1 (least)	52,586 (20·5)	454 (9·9)	125 (2·7)	44,358 (20·6)	453 (8·6)	91 (2·7)
2	52,766 (20·5)	446 (9·8)	212 (4·6)	44,009 (20·5)	476 (9·0)	146 (4·3)
3	52,837 (20·5)	699 (15·3)	380 (8·2)	42,988 (20·0)	734 (14·0)	264 (7·8)

(*continued*)

Table 1. (*continued*)

	Women			Men		
4	51,600 (20·1)	1,337 (29·3)	953 (20·5)	41,774 (19·5)	1,445 (27·4)	675 (19·4)
5 (most)	47,197 (18·4)	1,625 (35·7)	2,964 (64·0)	4,1607 (19·4)	2,158 (41·0)	2,210 (65·3)
Alcohol Frequency						
Never	20,964 (8·15)	2,472 (54·4)	1,125 (24·4)	56,163 (26.3)	692 (23·1)	690 (20·4)
Daily	43,026 (16·7)	131 (2·9)	184 (4·0)	57,547 (26.9)	404 (13·5)	327 (9·7)
3–4/week	54,723 (21·3)	202 (4·5)	329 (7·1)	56,029 (26.2)	464 (15·5)	446 (13·2)
1–2/week	67,868 (26·4)	424 (9·3)	761 (16·5)	18,937 (8.9)	667 (22·3)	822 (24·3)
1–3/month	33,734 (13·1)	311(6·8)	648 (14·0)	14,373 (6.72)	289 (9·7)	409 (12·1)
Occasional	36,807 (14·3)	1,004 (22·1)	1,570 (34·0)	10,900 (5.1)	480 (16·0)	696 (20·5)

p-value < 0.0001 for all variables; med median; IQR interquartile range; BMI body mass index

Table 2. Association between Television viewing and risk of diabetes by Ethnicity and sex

	Women			Men		
	White	South Asian	Black	White	South Asian	Black
Model 1 Television viewing (hours)						
<2 h	1.00 (ref)	1.00 (ref)	1.00 (ref)	1.00 (ref)	1.00 (ref)	1.00 (ref)
2–4 h	1.54(1.46–1.62)	1.45(1.20–1.77)	1.04(0.82–1.31)	1.47(1.41–1.53)	1.30(1.14–1.52)	1.00(0.78–1.28)
>4 h	2.60(2.45–2.76)	2.21(1.71–2.85)	1.44(1.12–1.86)	2.29(2.18–2.40)	1.85(1.49–2.31)	1.42(1.08–1.86)
P-trend	<0.001	<0.001	0.01	<0.001	<0.001	0.02
Model 2 Television viewing (hours)						
<2 h	1.00 (ref)	1.00 (ref)	1.00 (ref)	1.00 (ref)	1.00 (ref)	1.00 (ref)
2–4 h	1.17(1.11–1.23)	1.32(1.08–1.63)	1.06(0.83–1.36)	1.20(1.15–1.25)	1.22(1.04–1.44)	0.98(0.76–1.28)
>4 h	1.54(1.44–1.64)	1.75(1.34–2.30)	1.25(0.95–1.65)	1.46(1.38–1.53)	1.59(1.26–2.01)	1.43(1.07–1.91)
P-trend	<0.001	<0.001	0.13	<0.001	0.001	0.04
Model 3 Television viewing (hours)						
<2 h	1.00 (ref)	1.00 (ref)	1.00 (ref)	1.00 (ref)	1.00 (ref)	1.00 (ref)
2–4 h	1.17(1.10–1.25)	1.28(1.01–1.63)	1.00(0.75–1.33)	1.19(1.14–1.25)	1.22(1.02–1.47)	0.93(0.69–1.25)
>4 h	1.52(1.41–1.64)	1.61(1.16–2.24)	1.19(0.87–1.64)	1.42(1.34–1.50)	1.55(1.18–2.03)	1.30(0.93–1.83)
P-trend	<0.001	0.002	0.32	<0.001	0.001	0.22

Values are odds ratios (with 95% confidence intervals) for the association of television viewing in each sex and ethnicity group. P trend refer to the dose-response levels of television viewing. Statistical models are as follow:
Model 1: Adjusted for age, and socioeconomic status
Model 2: Model 1, plus adjustment for smoking and BMI
Model 3: Model 2, plus adjustment for physical activity.

Table 3. Joint association between television viewing and physical activity with risk of diabetes in white, Black and South Asian men and women

	white			South Asian			Black		
	TV viewing < 2 h	TV viewing 2–4 h	TV Viewing > 4 h	TV viewing < 2 h	TV Viewing 2–4 h	TV Viewing > 4 h	TV Viewing < 2 h	TV Viewing 2–4 h	TV Viewing > 4 h
Women									
Model 1									
High PA	1.00 (reference)	1.53 (1.39–1.69)	2.38 (2.10–2.71)	1.00 (reference)	1.80 (1.19–2.71)	2.08 (1.08–4.00)	1.00 (reference)	1.11 (0.71–1.73)	1.56 (0.92–2.64)
Moderate PA	1.14 (1.03–1.26)	1.77 (1.61–1.94)	2.72 (2.43–3.05)	1.35 (0.94–1.94)	1.60 (1.08–2.37)	2.32 (1.39–3.87)	1.21 (0.79–1.86)	1.26 (0.82–1.94)	1.90 (1.20–3.03)
Low PA	1.78 (1.59–2.00)	2.64 (2.38–2.93)	4.61 (4.11–5.18)	1.44 (0.95–2.17)	1.89 (1.22–2.95)	3.49 (2.11–5.77)	1.57 (0.96–2.58)	1.25 (0.73–2.13)	1.81 (1.06–3.09)
P-trend < 0.001									
Model 2									
High PA	1.00 (reference)	1.18 (1.07–1.31)	1.52 (1.33–1.74)	1.00 (reference)	1.63 (1.07–2.49)	1.71 (0.86–3.38)	1.00 (reference)	1.02 (0.64–1.63)	1.19 (0.67–2.09)
Moderate PA	1.05 (0.95–1.16)	1.23 (1.12–1.36)	1.56 (1.40–1.77)	1.26 (0.87–1.81)	1.37 (0.93–2.07)	1.76 (1.03–3.01)	1.04 (0.66–1.62)	1.15 (0.73–1.80)	1.47 (0.90–2.40)
Low PA	1.25 (1.11–1.42)	1.44 (1.29–1.61)	1.89 (1.67–2.15)	1.13 (0.74–1.73)	1.37 (0.86–2.20)	2.06 (1.19–3.57)	1.33 (0.79–2.23)	1.05 (0.59–1.86)	1.17 (0.65–2.10)
P-trend < 0.001									

(continued)

Table 3. (*continued*)

Men		white			South Asian			Black		
Model 1	High PA	1.00 (reference)	1.39 (1.29–1.50)	1.94 (1.76–2.14)	1.00 (reference)	1.51 (1.10–2.06)	2.01 (1.23–3.30)	1.00 (reference)	0.84 (0.54–1.31)	1.51 (0.92–2.48)
	Moderate PA	1.22 (1.13–1.32)	1.87 (1.74–2.01)	2.63 (2.41–2.87)	1.41 (1.08–1.86)	1.94 (1.45–2.59)	2.57 (1.71–3.85)	1.15 (0.77–1.74)	1.13 (0.72–1.78)	1.24 (0.74–2.09)
	Low PA, P-trend < 0.001	1.80 (1.65–1.97)	2.61 (2.41–2.83)	4.33 (3.97–4.73)	1.72 (1.28–2.31)	1.80 (1.28–2.54)	3.13 (2.03–4.82)	0.87 (0.51–1.46)	1.22 (0.73–2.06)	1.56 (0.91–2.68)
	High PA	1.00 (reference)	1.17 (1.08–1.26)	1.33 (1.21–1.48)	1.00 (reference)	1.44 (1.05–1.99)	1.41 (0.82–2.42)	1.00 (reference)	0.82 (0.52–1.31)	1.43 (0.84–2.43)
Model 2	Moderate PA	1.19 (1.03–1.29)	1.45 (1.34–1.56)	1.66 (1.51–1.82)	1.37 (1.03–1.81)	1.73 (1.28–2.33)	2.29 (1.49–3.51)	1.16 (0.76–1.76)	1.04 (0.64–1.67)	1.16 (0.67–2.02)
	Low PA, P-trend < 0.001	1.41 (1.29–1.55)	1.67 (1.53–1.82)	2.14 (1.94–2.36)	1.59 (1.17–2.16)	1.48 (1.03–2.12)	2.34 (1.48–3.70)	0.82 (0.48–1.40)	1.07 (0.62–1.85)	1.50 (0.84–2.67)

Values are odds ratios (and 95% confidence intervals) for diabetes in different television and physical activity categories and ethnic groups, with the Whites with low TV viewing and high physical activity levels as the reference category for each sex.
Model 1: Adjusted for age, and socioeconomic status; Model 2: Model 1, plus adjustment for smoking and BMI

5 Discussion

To our knowledge, this is the first study to describe the association between television viewing and diabetes risk among multi-ethnic women and men in a UK. This research, aimed to assess the impact of higher levels of television viewing time, independent of leisure-time moderate and vigorous physical activity, associated with type 2 diabetes in Whites, South Asians and Blacks. The overall findings showed that the increased television viewing was associated with increased risk of type 2 diabetes which persisted following adjustment for potential intermediate comorbidities, which were explained by further adjustment of adiposity. However, finding also showed that the link between television viewing and Type 2 Diabetes may not always be plausible, and it may be influenced by ethnicity. According to this study's finding using participants from the UK Biobank, television viewing was not associated with T2DM risk in Blacks, whereas television viewing was strongly linked to T2DM in Whites and South Asian men and women. Secondly, the findings showed that even moderate leisure physical activity with less television watching is beneficial in reducing type 2 diabetes in South Asians and White ethnic groups.

Amongst South Asian and White ethnic groups, higher levels of television time were more strongly associated with diabetes risk in women than men irrespective of ethnicity and was independent of BMI and physical activity. Adjusting for BMI attenuated the association between TV viewing and diabetes prevalence overall, but in south Asians this attenuation was less pronounced, suggesting that the contribution of TV viewing per se, rather than associated effects on BMI, may make a larger contribution to diabetes risk in South Asians. This may reflect differences in underlying physiological factors or in ethnic differences in other behaviours clustering with TV viewing (such as eating energy dense foods), which warrant further investigation. Further investigation is also needed to determine the extent to which this association is likely to be causal. If causality can be demonstrated, these data suggest that ethnic specific interventions to reduce sedentary behaviour for people from south Asian ethnic origin should potentially be explored.

The findings show that television viewing is associated with an increased higher risk with type 2 diabetes, while increased physical activity is protective of the disease in Whites. This confirms and extends to previous studies examining the relation between television viewing and diabetes this ethnic group [41]. Recently, using a two-sample Mendelian randomization analysis method, Deng and colleagues examined the risk of diabetes in association with time watching television and physical activity. They found that spent watching television was associated with a 2.35 increased risk of type 2 diabetes (OR: 2.35 (1.9–2.9)), while inverse associations between self-reported moderate PA (OR: 0.30 (0.18–0.54) and vigorous PA (OR: 0.27 (0.14–0.54) with type 2 diabetes risk were found, respectively [41]. Findings from the UK Whitehall study found that after following a cohort of civil servants for 12 years, there was no link between television sitting and incident diabetes after adjusting for BMI (RR: 1.31(0.96 to 1.76) [42]. The MESA study looked at the association of physical activity, sedentary behaviours and incidence of type 2 diabetes in multiple ethnic groups including Whites and Blacks. In this study, the graded independent associations of physical activity were statistically significant in Whites across all increased levels of physical activity, whilst there was no significant association with television watching for those who spent up to 4 h of television watching RR:1.50 (0.91 to 2.49) [26]. The deleterious effect of television watching was only observed in Whites who spent more than 6 h of their time watching television RR:4.54 (1.42 to 14.49) [26].

To our knowledge this is the first research to explicitly examine the risk of television viewing time and type 2 diabetes in South Asians. Earlier studies with smaller sample sizer for South Asians, have assessed the relative contribution of sedentary behaviour with glycemia or type 2 diabetes. Waidyatilaka and colleagues observed that amongst dysglycaemic South Asian women, physical activity and television viewing contributed to dysglycaemia after adjustment for family history, diet, systolic blood pressure and Body Mass Index [16]. In that study, 85% of people with dysglycaemia could attribute their condition to viewing TV > 85 min a day; 78% attributed their condition to performing <1435.3 MET-minutes/week on walking and <2640.0 MET-minutes/week in moderate and vigorous physical activity [16]. The findings of links between television viewing and physical activity in the current research, in addition to other studies of impact of high sedentary time, and low physical activity in South Asians indicate the need to focus health promotion efforts on shifting sedentary time into leisure physical activity while trying to increase moderate-to Vigorous physical activity. Findings on Blacks did not show a significant dose-response effect, between time spent watching television and diabetes risk, despite a relatively high diabetes prevalence. Although this cannot be readily explained physiologically, it is consistent with a previous study by Healy and colleagues using the NHANES data, found that higher accelerometery-derived sedentary time was unrelated to insulin and insulin sensitivity - which is a condition that increases the risk of developing type 2 diabetes in the Black subpopulation [43]. Contrastingly, findings from some studies that have examined the relationship between television watching and the risk of developing type 2 diabetes in Black population in the United States, suggest a significant positive association between the two. In a study of African American women, it was found that greater television viewing was associated with a higher incidence of type 2 diabetes, independent of physical activity levels [24]. The authors suggested that reducing sedentary behaviour, particularly television watching, could be an important strategy for preventing the development of type 2 diabetes in this high-risk population. Nevertheless, it is possible that the lack of relationship between sedentary behaviour and type 2 diabetes in Black adults in this study may be influenced by unmeasured confounding lifestyle, and environmental factors that vary by geopolitical location. The US study was conducted in obese, low socioeconomic status and highly sedentary participants, whilst the participants in the UK Biobank data are reported to be more affluent, educated and healthier than the overall UK population [44, 45]. Additionally, the United Kingdom as a welfare state provides relatively high spending on healthcare for its population, whilst the US is based on health insurance which is majorly the responsibility of its citizens. However, more research on Black ethnic groups in the UK setting is needed to fully understand these potential interactions.

From a public health standpoint, it is important to understand why differences exist in sedentary behaviours among ethnic subgroups in a population. This knowledge could inform future interventions aimed at reducing sedentary time among people across ethnic origins which could in turn transform workplace cultures. However, people from south Asian ethnic background may benefit the most from efforts aimed at replacing some time spent watching television with other non-screen time activities. Culturally tailored interventions that incorporate traditional activities and values may also be effective in promoting physical activity in ethnic minority groups.

From animal studies, sedentary time is related to lipoprotein lipase regulation which is linked to local contractile activity, leading to increased plasma triacylglycerol and reduced high density lipoprotein levels [46–48]. Immobility also affects the skeletal muscle which leads to peripheral insulin resistance [9, 38, 49]. Lifestyle interventions such as the Diabetes Prevention Program (DPP) shows that increase in physical activity also reduce sedentary behaviours including television watching [50]. Additionally, in early 2017 the American Diabetes Association published updated guidelines on the lifestyle management, containing sedentary behaviour be interrupted with periods of physical activity every 30 min [51].

6   Strengths and Limitations of the Study

In addition to the large sample size, a major strength of our study was our ability to compare several ethnic groups living in the same country within the same study. The results were robust to adjustment for potentially confounding factors including socioeconomic status, smoking behaviour and age allowing for broad generalization of the findings. BMI and physical activity were adjusted, enabling an examination of their mediating role in the model. Despite the strength of the study, there were few limitations. The analyses focused on television viewing because it is the most performed form of sedentary lifestyle. However, we cannot generalize our findings to other specific sedentary behaviours (e.g., computer, driving, and work-related sitting). Nonetheless, based on recent findings in American adults, showing significant but fair associations between TV viewing time and total sedentary time derived from accelerometery, TV viewing time has been suggested to be a potentially useful indicator for total sedentary time in epidemiological analyses. In this research, the data showed that of all the different type of sedentary behaviour - TV viewing, computer time and driving - the association between TV viewing and diabetes was the strongest. This is in concordance with other studies that have reported the strong link between TV viewing and adverse health outcomes such as cancer, cardiovascular disease and mortality [52, 53].

TV viewing and physical activity were self-reported and are thus affected by recall bias and measurement error. Measurement error in potential confounders and other types of sedentary behaviour correlating with television viewing leading to residual confounding may have weakened the observed associations within the ethnic groups, however, data from objectively measured (i.e., accelerometer) data could potentially provide important complementary information on context of sedentary behaviours and their interaction with TV viewing across ethnicity. It has been argued that both domain-specific and overall (objective) measures of sedentary time are desirable [20, 31, 54, 55] sources for obtaining information for sedentary behaviour. We did not have data on eating habits during TV screen time. We also did not record sleep duration in this study. TV viewing time has been shown to be associated with short sleep duration which is in turn associated with cardio-metabolic biomarkers [56, 57]. As this is cross-sectional study, we cannot definitively infer causality. Even though we excluded participants with relevant diagnosed diseases to minimise risk reverse causation, it is never possible to do this fully in a cross-sectional study design.

7   Conclusion

While this study confirms how the association between TV viewing and diabetes affects different ethnic groups in variable magnitude, it also suggests that even a slight increase in physical activity combined with low television-viewing time can significantly reduce the risk of type 2 diabetes particularly in specific ethnic minority. However, TV viewing time is a complex construct that appears to include obesity since the risk of association with diabetes significantly increased after adjusting for BMI. Even after controlling for potential mediators including socioeconomic status and physical activity, part of the association between TV viewing and diabetes in south Asians and in whites remained unexplained in our study. This suggests that TV viewing per se may have adverse consequences to higher diabetes risk. Given the prominent role that TV has in modern society, further research is warranted to better understand why this behaviour is associated with diabetes. As there are few studies in the UK on this type of research it is clear that this field of research needs to expand beyond predominantly white populations and to explore this heterogeneity and avoid potentially inappropriate generalization of findings, whether the ethnic differences are biological, or due to unmeasured confounding factors. It is hoped that, this study makes a meaningful contribution not just in raising awareness but also translates to building a better knowledge management system for healthcare providers. This may facilitate the development of public health interventions that more effectively address the ethnic disparities.

In conclusion, sedentary behaviour is a significant risk factor for the development of type 2 diabetes, and ethnic minority groups may be at higher risk due to cultural, social, and environmental factors. Findings from this study provide evidence that television viewing (as sedentary proxy) and physical activity is associated with higher diabetes risk in south Asians and whites but not Blacks and with evidence of mediation by BMI. These findings add to growing evidence that sedentary behaviour, separated from activity, influences health even though uncertainties remain regarding underlying pathways. Therefore, there is a need to develop effective interventions that can promote physical activity and reduce sedentary behaviour in these populations.

References

1. Matthews, D.: Sociology in nursing 4: the impact of ethnicity on health inequalities. Nurs. Times **111**(44), 18–20 (2015). https://www.nursingtimes.net/. Accessed 03 Nov 2019
2. Lillie-Blanton, M., Parsons, P.E., Gayle, H., Dievler, A.: Racial differences in health: not just black and white, but shades of gray. Annu. Rev. Public Health **17**(1), 411–448 (1996). https://doi.org/10.1146/annurev.pu.17.050196.002211
3. Goff, L.M.: Ethnicity and type 2 diabetes in the UK. Diabet. Med. **36**(8), 927–938 (2019). https://doi.org/10.1111/dme.13895
4. McLaughlin, M., et al.: Worldwide surveillance of self-reported sitting time: a scoping review. Int. J. Behav. Nutr. Phys. Act. **17**(1), 111 (2020). https://doi.org/10.1186/s12966-020-01008-4

5. Ntuk, U.E., Gill, J.M., Mackay, D.F., Sattar, N., Pell, J.P.: Ethnic-specific obesity cutoffs for diabetes risk: cross-sectional study of 490,288 UK biobank participants. Diabetes Care **37**(9), 2500–2507 (2014)

6. Eastwood, S.V., Mathur, R., Sattar, N., Smeeth, L., Bhaskaran, K., Chaturvedi, N.: Ethnic differences in guideline-indicated statin initiation for people with type 2 diabetes in UK primary care, 2006–2019: a cohort study. PLoS Med. **18**(6), e1003672 (2021). https://doi.org/10.1371/journal.pmed.1003672

7. Stamatakis, E., Ekelund, U., Ding, D., Hamer, M., Bauman, A.E., Lee, I.M.: Is the time right for quantitative public health guidelines on sitting? A narrative review of sedentary behaviour research paradigms and findings. Br. J. Sports Med. **53**(6), 377–382 (2019). https://doi.org/10.1136/bjsports-2018-099131

8. Yates, T., Henson, J., Edwardson, C., Bodicoat, D.H., Davies, M.J., Khunti, K.: Differences in levels of physical activity between White and South Asian populations within a healthcare setting: impact of measurement type in a cross-sectional study. BMJ Open **5**(7), e006181 (2015). https://doi.org/10.1136/bmjopen-2014-006181

9. Wilmot, E.G., et al.: Sedentary time in adults and the association with diabetes, cardiovascular disease and death: systematic review and meta-analysis. Diabetologia **55**(11), 2895–2905 (2012). https://doi.org/10.1007/s00125-012-2677-z

10. James, C.V., Moonesinghe, R., Wilson-Frederick, S.M., Hall, J.E., Penman-Aguilar, A., Bouye, K.: Racial/ethnic health disparities among rural adults—United States, 2012–2015. MMWR Surveill. Summ. **66**(23), 1 (2017). https://doi.org/10.15585/mmwr.ss6623a1

11. Matthews, K.A., et al.: Health-related behaviors by urban-rural county classification-united states, 2013. MMWR Surveill. Summ. **66**(5) (2017). https://doi.org/10.15585/mmwr.ss6605a1

12. Egan, B.M.: Physical activity and hypertension: knowing is not enough; we must apply. Willing is not enough; we must do—von Goethe. Hypertension **69**(3), 404–406 (2017)

13. Major, L., Simonsick, E.M., Napolitano, M.A., DiPietro, L.: Domains of sedentary behavior and cognitive function: the health, aging, and body composition study, 1999/2000 to 2006/2007. J. Gerontol. A (2023). https://doi.org/10.1093/gerona/glad020

14. Werneck, A.O., et al.: Independent and combined associations of sugar-sweetened beverage consumption, TV viewing, and physical activity with severe depressive symptoms among 59,402 adults. Braz. J. Psychiatry **43**, 574–583 (2020). https://doi.org/10.1590/1516-4446-2020-1073

15. Pulsford, R.M., Stamatakis, E., Britton, A.R., Brunner, E.J., Hillsdon, M.M.: Sitting behavior and obesity: evidence from the Whitehall II study. Am. J. Prev. Med. **44**(2), 132–138 (2013)

16. Waidyatilaka, I., Lanerolle, P., Wickremasinghe, R., Atukorala, S., Somasundaram, N., de Silva, A.: Sedentary behaviour and physical activity in South Asian women: time to review current recommendations? PLoS ONE **8**(3), e58328 (2013). https://doi.org/10.1371/journal.pone.0058328

17. Cha, S.S., Seo, B.K.: Smartphone use and smartphone addiction in middle school students in Korea: prevalence, social networking service, and game use. Health Psychol. Open **5**(1), 2055102918755046 (2018). https://doi.org/10.1177/2055102918755046

18. Lee, J., Ahn, J.S., Min, S., Kim, M.H.: Psychological characteristics and addiction propensity according to content type of smartphone use. Int. J. Environ. Res. Public Health **17**(7), 2292 (2020). https://doi.org/10.3390/ijerph17072292

19. Clark, B.K., Sugiyama, T., Healy, G.N., Salmon, J., Dunstan, D.W., Owen, N.: Validity and reliability of measures of television viewing time and other non-occupational sedentary behaviour of adults: a review. Obes. Rev. **10**(1), 7–16 (2009). https://doi.org/10.1111/j.1467-789X.2008.00508.x

20. Chu, A.H., Ng, S.H., Koh, D., Müller-Riemenschneider, F.: Domain-specific adult sedentary behaviour questionnaire (ASBQ) and the GPAQ single-item question: a reliability and validity study in an Asian population. Int. J. Environ. Res. Public Health **15**(4), 739 (2018). https://doi.org/10.3390/ijerph15040739

21. Guo, C., et al.: Association of total sedentary behaviour and television viewing with risk of overweight/obesity, type 2 diabetes and hypertension: a dose–response meta-analysis. Diabetes Obes. Metab. **22**(1), 79–90 (2020). https://doi.org/10.1111/dom.13867

22. Patterson, R., et al.: Sedentary behaviour and risk of all-cause, cardiovascular and cancer mortality, and incident type 2 diabetes: a systematic review and dose response meta-analysis. Eur. J. Epidemiol. **33**(9), 811–829 (2018). https://doi.org/10.1007/s10654-018-0380-1

23. Blüher, S., et al.: Who should we target for diabetes prevention and diabetes risk reduction? Curr. Diab. Rep. **12**, 147–156 (2012). https://doi.org/10.1007/s11892-012-0255-x

24. Krishnan, S., Rosenberg, L., Palmer, J.R.: Physical activity and television watching in relation to risk of type 2 diabetes: the Black Women's Health Study. Am. J. Epidemiol. **169**(4), 428–434 (2009). https://doi.org/10.1093/aje/kwn344

25. Joseph, J.J., et al.: Modifiable lifestyle risk factors and incident diabetes in African Americans. Am. J. Prev. Med. **53**(5), e165–e174 (2017). https://doi.org/10.1016/j.amepre.2017.06.018

26. Joseph, J.J., et al.: Physical activity, sedentary behaviors and the incidence of type 2 diabetes mellitus: the Multi-Ethnic Study of Atherosclerosis (MESA). BMJ Open Diabetes Res. Care **4**(1), e000185 (2016). https://doi.org/10.1136/bmjdrc-2015-000185

27. Stamatakis, E., Gill, J.M.: Sitting behaviour and physical activity: two sides of the same cardiovascular health coin? Br. J. Sports Med. **53**(14), 852–853 (2019). https://doi.org/10.1136/bjsports-2018-099640

28. Ding, D., Rogers, K., van der Ploeg, H., Stamatakis, E., Bauman, A.E.: Traditional and emerging lifestyle risk behaviors and all-cause mortality in middle-aged and older adults: evidence from a large population-based Australian cohort. PLoS Med. **12**(12), e1001917 (2015). https://doi.org/10.1371/JOURNAL.PMED.1001917

29. Owen, N., Sugiyama, T., Eakin, E.E., Gardiner, P.A., Tremblay, M.S., Sallis, J.F.: Adults' sedentary behavior: determinants and interventions. Am. J. Prev. Med. **41**(2), 189–196 (2011). https://doi.org/10.1016/j.amepre.2011.05.013

30. Bodde, A.E., Seo, D.C., Frey, G.C., Van Puymbroeck, M., Lohrmann, D.K.: Correlates of moderate-to-vigorous physical activity participation in adults with intellectual disabilities. Health Promot. Pract. **14**(5), 663–670 (2013). https://doi.org/10.1177/1524839912462395

31. Wijndaele, K., et al.: Reliability and validity of a domain-specific last 7-d sedentary time questionnaire. Med. Sci. Sports Exerc. **46**(6), 1248 (2014). https://doi.org/10.1249/MSS.0000000000000214

32. Lynch, B.M.: Sedentary behavior and cancer: a systematic review of the literature and proposed biological mechanisms. Cancer Epidemiol. Biomarkers Prev. **19**(11), 2691–2709 (2010). https://doi.org/10.1158/1055-9965.EPI-10-0815

33. Mathew, A., et al.: Physical activity levels among urban and rural women in south India and the risk of breast cancer: a case-control study. Eur. J. Cancer Prev. **18**(5), 368–376 (2009). https://doi.org/10.1097/CEJ.0b013e32832e1c46

34. Katzmarzyk, P.T., Church, T.S., Craig, C.L., Bouchard, C.: Sitting time and mortality from all causes, cardiovascular disease, and cancer. Med. Sci. Sports Exerc. **41**(5), 998–1005 (2009). https://doi.org/10.1249/MSS.0b013e3181930355

35. Rimmer, J.H., Marques, A.C.: Physical activity for people with disabilities. Lancet **380**(9838), 193–195 (2012). https://doi.org/10.1016/S0140-6736(12)61028-9

36. Rimmer, J.H., Riley, B., Wang, E., Rauworth, A., Jurkowski, J.: Physical activity participation among persons with disabilities: barriers and facilitators. Am. J. Prev. Med. **26**(5), 419–425 (2004). https://doi.org/10.1016/j.amepre.2004.02.002

37. Hu, F.B., Li, T.Y., Colditz, G.A., Willett, W.C., Manson, J.E.: Television watching and other sedentary behaviors in relation to risk of obesity and type 2 diabetes mellitus in women. JAMA **289**(14), 1785–1791 (2003). https://doi.org/10.1001/jama.289.14.1785

38. Wilmot, E.: The hazards of sedentary behaviour. Pract. Diabetes **31**(2), 50–51 (2014). https://doi.org/10.1002/pdi.1829

39. Ipaq Research Committee: Guidelines for data processing and analysis of the International Physical Activity Questionnaire (IPAQ) – short and long forms. Ipaq (2005)

40. Cuzick, J.: A Wilcoxon-type test for trend. Stat. Med. **4**(1), 87–90 (1985). http://www.ncbi.nlm.nih.gov/pubmed/3992076. Accessed 03 July 2017

41. Deng, M.G., Cui, H.T., Lan, Y.B., Nie, J.Q., Liang, Y.H., Chai, C.: Physical activity, sedentary behavior, and the risk of type 2 diabetes: a two-sample Mendelian Randomization analysis in the European population. Front. Endocrinol. **13** (2022). https://doi.org/10.3389/fendo.2022.964132

42. Stamatakis, E., et al.: Sitting behaviour is not associated with incident diabetes over 13 years: the Whitehall II cohort study. Br. J. Sports Med. **51**(10), 818–823 (2017). https://doi.org/10.1136/bjsports-2016-096723

43. Healy, G.N., Matthews, C.E., Dunstan, D.W., Winkler, E.A., Owen, N.: Sedentary time and cardio-metabolic biomarkers in US adults: NHANES 2003–06. Eur. Heart J. **32**(5), 590–597 (2011). https://doi.org/10.1093/eurheartj/ehq451

44. Batty, G.D., Gale, C.R., Kivimäki, M., Deary, I.J., Bell, S.: Generalisability of results from UK Biobank: comparison with a pooling of 18 cohort studies. SSRN Electron. J. (2020). https://doi.org/10.2139/ssrn.3437793

45. Fry, A., et al.: Comparison of sociodemographic and health-related characteristics of UK Biobank participants with those of the general population. Am. J. Epidemiol. **186**(9), 1026–1034 (2017). https://doi.org/10.1093/AJE/KWX246

46. Allison, M.A., Jensky, N.E., Marshall, S.J., Bertoni, A.G., Cushman, M.: Sedentary behavior and adiposity-associated inflammation: the multi-ethnic study of atherosclerosis. Am. J. Prev. Med. **42**(1), 8–13 (2012). https://doi.org/10.1016/j.amepre.2011.09.023

47. Hamilton, M.T., Hamilton, D.G., Zderic, T.W.: Role of low energy expenditure and sitting in obesity, metabolic syndrome, type 2 diabetes, and cardiovascular disease. Diabetes **56**(11), 2655–2667 (2007). https://doi.org/10.2337/db07-0882.CVD

48. Larsen, R.N., et al.: Breaking up of prolonged sitting over three days sustains, but does not enhance, lowering of postprandial plasma glucose and insulin in overweight and obese adults. Clin. Sci. **129**(2), 117–127 (2015). https://doi.org/10.1042/CS20140790

49. Henson, J., et al.: Breaking up prolonged sitting with standing or walking attenuates the post-prandial metabolic response in postmenopausal women: a randomized acute study. Diabetes Care **39**(1), 130–138 (2016). https://doi.org/10.2337/dc15-1240

50. Rockette-Wagner, B., et al.: The impact of lifestyle intervention on sedentary time in individuals at high risk of diabetes. Diabetologia **58**(6), 1198–1202 (2015). https://doi.org/10.1007/s00125-015-3565-0

51. ADA: Standards of medical care in diabetes – 2017. Diabetes Care **40**(1), 386–390 (2017). https://doi.org/10.2337/dc14-S014

52. Hamer, M., Stamatakis, E.: Screen-based sedentary behavior, physical activity, and muscle strength in the English longitudinal study of ageing. PLoS ONE **8**(6), e66222 (2013). https://doi.org/10.1371/journal.pone.0066222

53. Grøntved, A., Hu, F.B.: Television viewing and risk of type 2 diabetes, cardiovascular disease, and all-cause mortality: a meta-analysis. JAMA **305**(23), 2448–2455 (2011)

54. Bennie, J.A., et al.: Total and domain-specific sitting time among employees in desk-based work settings in Australia. Aust. N. Z. J. Public Health **39**(3), 237–242 (2015). https://doi.org/10.1111/1753-6405.12293

55. Chu, A.H.Y., Van Dam, R.M., Biddle, S.J.H., Tan, C.S., Koh, D., Müller-Riemenschneider, F.: Self-reported domain-specific and accelerometer-based physical activity and sedentary behaviour in relation to psychological distress among an urban Asian population. Int. J. Behav. Nutr. Phys. Act. **15**, 1–14 (2018). https://doi.org/10.1186/s12966-018-0669-1
56. Tasali, E., Leproult, R., Spiegel, K.: Reduced sleep duration or quality: relationships with insulin resistance and type 2 diabetes. Prog. Cardiovasc. Dis. **51**(5), 381–391 (2009). https://doi.org/10.1016/j.pcad.2008.10.002
57. Cassidy, S., Chau, J.Y., Catt, M., Bauman, A., Trenell, M.I.: Cross-sectional study of diet, physical activity, television viewing and sleep duration in 233 110 adults from the UK Biobank; the behavioural phenotype of cardiovascular disease and type 2 diabetes. BMJ Open **6**(3), e010038 (2016). https://doi.org/10.1136/bmjopen-2015-010038

Potential Role of ChatGPT in Healthcare in the Prevention and Management of Non-communicable Diseases

Aravind Kumaresan[1], Lorna Uden[2], and Shazad Ashraf[3](✉)

[1] Optimists (Product of KeplerTechno Private Ltd.), University of Vaasa, Chennai 600017, India
ak@optimists.in

[2] School of Computing, Staffordshire University, College Road, Stoke-on-Trent ST4 2DE, UK
L.uden@staffs.ac.uk

[3] Institute of Cancer and Genomic Sciences, University of Birmingham, Edgbaston, Birmingham B15 2TT, UK
s.ashraf.2@bham.ac.uk

Abstract. The recent release of ChatGPT has rapidly gained popularity and become one of the world's fastest-growing applications. ChatGPT has the potential to have a significant impact on the research community and the public by revolutionising the way we perform tasks such writing articles and making decisions. ChatGPT is known for its human-like interactions and "engaging" conversation. Because of this, alarming ethical and practical challenges emerge from its uses, this is particularly relevant in the medical field and the overall impact it may have on health systems and their efficiencies. This paper gives a brief overview of the potential benefits and risks of using ChatGPT for health care services. To make sure that it is implemented without any risks to society especially the public, there should be a regulatory framework to monitor the use of this new and untested technology. In this paper we show how ChatGPT can be used to as a potential tool in the field of Non-Communicable Diseases.

Keywords: ChatGPT · Non-Communicable diseases · efficiency

1 Introduction

Although the advance of digital technology, robotics, innovation and improved diagnostics, prevention therapeutics can improve health care and treatments, they also raise ethical, legal and social challenges [1]. This is especially true of the arrival of ChatGPT (Generative Pretrained Transformer) in 2022 [2]. It is a chatbot that we can converse with as if it were a fellow human being [3]. ChatGPT was released by OpenAI (based in San Francisco) in November 2022 [4]. ChatGPT users with an interest in healthcare have already started to use it to perform simple tasks that normally require a healthcare professional [5]. For example, writing sickness certificates, patient letters or medical insurance letters. ChatGPT can act as a high-level personal assistant to speed up mundane tasks and give physicians more time to perform duties that involve direct patient

L. Uden and I-H. Ting (Eds.): KMO 2023, CCIS 1825, pp. 430–442, 2023.
https://doi.org/10.1007/978-3-031-34045-1_34

interaction [6]. It can also assist in more complex tasks such as decision making, for example stratifying patients in terms of their priority for limited health resources such as access to kidney dialysis or intensive care beds [5].

Although there are many potential benefits of using ChatGPT in healthcare, there are many serious ethical concerns that arise using this sophisticated chatbot in patient care. The use of it can lead to unintended and unwelcome issues, such as consent, quality of care, confidentiality, inequality, and reliability.

It is too early to assess the implications of using ChatGPT in healthcare and research. But as the technology advances and its uses become common, it is important to ask questions regarding the potential risk-benefits and governance around use of ChatGPT in healthcare. Because of the potential risks listed above and general ethical issues concerning ChatGPT, a standardised and accepted governance framework must be implemented. This requires a consensus from a committee with diverse expertise and representation from AI experts, data analysts, computer scientists, academics, healthcare professionals, patient representatives, data regulators and Big Tech [7].

Non-communicable diseases (NCDs) are a group of chronic diseases that are not caused by infectious agents but rather by a combination of lifestyle factors, environmental factors, and genetic predisposition. NCDs is a significant global public health concern, as they utilize a large proportion of the healthcare expenditure across borders. The four main types of NCDs are cardiovascular diseases (CVDs), cancer, chronic respiratory diseases, and diabetes. CVDs are the leading cause of death in India, accounting for nearly 28% of all deaths. Cancer is the second leading cause of death, accounting for approximately 13% of deaths. Chronic respiratory diseases and diabetes are also major health concerns in India, accounting for a significant proportion of the disease burden. Several factors contribute to the high prevalence of NCDs in India, including unhealthy dietary intake, physical inactivity, tobacco use and alcohol consumption [8]. Additionally, environmental factors such as air pollution, which is a significant problem in many major cities in India, can also contribute to the development of NCDs [8]. Efforts to address NCDs in India have included public health campaigns to promote healthy lifestyles, policies to reduce tobacco use and alcohol consumption, and efforts to improve access to healthcare services. However, there is still a significant need for further research, policy development, and implementation of effective interventions to prevent and manage NCDs in India. In this paper we explore the potential use of GPT technology in preventing and controlling NCDs in India as a case study to demonstrate how ChatGPT can be used effectively.

This paper begins with a brief literature review of ChatGPT and NCPs. This is followed by how ChatGPT can be used in healthcare and the risks and ethical issues involved. The authors believe that there is an urgent need to design a set of regulations around governance to mitigate against the potential risks that may arise. A case study of use of ChatGPT in NCDs is described. It is followed by discussions on the benefits and risks of ChatGPT for health care. The paper concludes with Future Research Priorities for ChatGPT in Healthcare.

1.1 Literature Review

ChatGPT is a type of artificial intelligence language model developed by OpenAI. It uses deep learning techniques to analyze and generate human-like language based on large datasets of text. GPT models are pre-trained on large amounts of text data, allowing them to learn the patterns and structures of language. This pre-training enables the model to generate coherent and contextually relevant text in response to a given prompt or input.

GPT language models can process large amounts of text data and generate human-like language, which makes them well-suited for a variety of healthcare applications [9]. GPT was constantly improved with more advanced versions. The first version of GPT-1was released in 2018, and was the first model in the GPT series. It had 117 million parameters and was trained on a large corpus of text data from the internet. Despite its relatively small size, GPT-1 was able to generate coherent and grammatically correct text. GPT-2 was released in 2019 and was a significant improvement over GPT-1, with 1.5 billion parameters. It was trained on a massive corpus of text data and could generate high-quality text that was difficult to distinguish from text written by humans. GPT-3 was released in 2020 and is the most advanced GPT model to date, with 175 billion parameters [10, 11]. It can generate extremely high-quality text and can perform a wide range of natural language processing tasks [12]. GPT-3 has received a lot of attention for its impressive language capabilities. GPT-4 was released in early 2023 and is OpenAI's most advanced system, producing safer and more useful responses. When GPT-4 was tested by medical experts from Microsoft without any specialized prompt crafting, it exceeded the passing score on USMLE by over 20 points and outperformed earlier general-purpose models (GPT-3.5) as well as models specifically fine-tuned on medical knowledge (Med-PaLM, a prompt-tuned version of Flan-PaLM 540B) [13].

1.2 Research Significance

The GPT technology has significant research significance in the field of healthcare and in NCDs due to its natural language processing capabilities [14]. These capabilities can be leveraged to improved patient outcomes, clinical decision-making, and healthcare efficiency. One potential use case for ChatGPT in addressing NCDs is in medical record analysis. Medical records often contain a vast amount of unstructured data that can be challenging to analyze and interpret. GPT models can be trained on large amounts of medical text data to recognize patterns and relationships between symptoms, diagnoses, and treatments. This could enable more accurate and efficient diagnosis and treatment planning. Another potential use case for GPT in healthcare is in patient communication. GPT models can generate personalized responses to patient inquiries and concerns, which could improve patient engagement and satisfaction. Overall, GPT technology has the potential to revolutionize healthcare by enabling more efficient and accurate clinical decision-making, improving patient outcomes, and enhancing the patient experience. However, as with any new technology, it is vitally important to approach the use of GPT in healthcare with caution and carefully consider the ethical implications of its implementation.

1.3   ChatGPT for Healthcare

A systematic review was conducted by Sallam (2023) using records in PubMed/MEDLINE and Google Scholar to examine the impact of ChatGPT in the context of health care education, research, or practice [15]. Sallam found that the benefits of ChatGPT were cited in 51/60 (85.0%) records that include: (1) improved scientific writing and enhancing research equity and versatility; (2) utility in health care research (efficient analysis of datasets, code generation, literature reviews, saving time to focus on experimental design, and drug discovery and development); (3) benefits in health care practice (streamlining the workflow, cost saving, documentation, personalized medicine, and improved health literacy); and (4) benefits in health care education including improved personalized learning and the focus on critical thinking and problem-based learning [7, 16–19].

ChatGPT is being touted as a tool that could transform healthcare, because it is capable of mirroring intuitive human conversation. It works by learning from human feedback and can answer follow-up questions, admit its own mistakes, challenge incorrect premises, and reject inappropriate requests. These capabilities have triggered excitement over the use of this technology. ChatGPT can be used to streamline multiple clinical workflows with possible cost savings and increased efficiency in health care delivery [20–22].

According to Patel & Lam (2023) ChatGPT can produce efficient patient discharge summaries, which can be valuable in reducing the burden of documentation in health care [23]. ChatGPT has great transformational potential in health care practice via enhancing diagnostics, prediction of disease risk and outcome, and drug discovery among other areas in translational research [17, 24]. Rao *et al.* (2023) reported that ChatGPT showed moderate accuracy in determining the imaging steps needed in breast cancer screening and in the evaluation of breast pain, which can be a promising application in decision making in radiology [25]. Many researchers have shown that ChatGPT in health has the exciting prospect of refining personalized medicine and the ability to improve health literacy by providing easily accessible and understandable health information to the public [26–28].

Sallam specifically described the healthcare benefits of ChatGPT including improved documentation, as well as personalized medicine, prediction of disease risk and outcome, streamlining clinical workflows and improved diagnostics [12, 15]. All these incrementally result in an overall improvement in cost utilisation and health literacy. Sallam further highlighted the benefits of ChatGPT in scientific research, including the ability to analyse massive data including electronic health records and other Big Datasets such as genomic information [12, 15]. It also has efficacy in experimental drug design and discovery. This ultimately releases free time for health professionals to perform more patient orientated tasks. There are considerable educational benefits when using ChatGPT to generate accurate and versatile clinical vignettes, improved personalized learning experience as well as and being an acting as a "free" adjunct in group learning.

1.4   Concerns Regarding ChatGPT Use in Health Care

Despite the benefits of ChatGPT for health care, there are major concerns that can be divided into five domains. Firstly, there is the major recurring ethical issue of the risk of bias and transparency [24, 25]. Secondly, ChatGPT can generate inaccurate content which has severe negative consequences in health. There is also concern regarding the ability of ChatGPT to provide justification for incorrect decisions [25]. There are issues of interpretability, reproducibility and the handling of uncertainty that can have harmful consequences in health care settings including health care research [29]. Finally, there is the issue of paradigm shifts in health care education, research, and practice [15]. Thus, the use of ChatGPT for health care must be undertaken and implemented in a careful manner by careful consideration of each of these domains [30].

2 Methodology

2.1 Dataset

For this study, we have used a patient dataset to train and fine tune the GPT model to customize it for our purpose. This dataset was derived from a Functional Medicine Health Questionnaire collected from over 1000 patients over a 10-year period along with their standard health diagnoses over this same period [31]. Functional medicine is an approach to healthcare that focuses on understanding and addressing the cause of a patient's health concerns, rather than simply treating the symptoms. It is a patient-centered, holistic approach that considers the genetic, environmental, and lifestyle factors that contribute to a patient's health status. Functional medicine is often used to address chronic health conditions, such as autoimmune diseases, digestive disorders, hormonal imbalances, and cardiovascular disease. Functional Medicine Practitioners (FMPs) use a wide range of tools and techniques to identify and address underlying health problems (nutritional deficiencies, hormonal imbalances, inflammation, and digestive tract dysfunction). The data comes contains information such as laboratory testing, nutritional interventions, lifestyle modifications, stress reduction techniques and targeted supplementation. FMPs work closely with patients to develop individualized treatment plans that consider the patient's unique needs, preferences, and lifestyle factors. The goal is to help optimize overall patient health using data.

2.2 Ethics

Research ethics was obtained from the local board before study commencement. Informed patient consent was obtained from all patients whose data was included within the training dataset. They were specifically informed that their data would be analyzed by clinicians and computer experts to develop AI powered algorithms to make better health prediction models.

We requested 5 research participants to take the functional medicine health questionnaire and evaluated the prediction responses from ChatGPT against expert functional medicine practitioners.

2.3 Research Design

Case study research methodology was utilised for this study. This involves collecting a vast array of data through various sources such as interviews, observation, archival research, and document analysis. The data is usually analysed using a variety of qualitative data analysis techniques, including content analysis, thematic analysis, and narrative analysis. Case study research methodology has several advantages over other research methods for this study. Firstly, it allows researchers to investigate complex and dynamic phenomena that cannot be adequately explained by quantitative methods. Secondly, it enables researchers to explore the perspectives, experiences, and underlying message of the participants. Thirdly, it allows researchers to generate rich and detailed data, which can be used to develop new theories or refine existing ones. In this study we use FM master questionnaire as the base for the in-depth interview with the patients.

2.4 Please Describe How ChatGPT is Used in Your Study

ChatGPT was fine-tuned with the previously collected FM master questionnaires and its inferred results manually reported by clinical experts. This knowledge was used to fine tune the Chat GPT to infer the results of the study participants. Fine-tuning the chat GPT (Generative Pre-trained Transformer) refers to the process of customizing a pre-trained language model to perform a specific task or set of tasks. In this context, fine-tuning involves training the chat GPT on a specific dataset or set of inputs that are relevant to a particular task, such as answering questions, engaging in conversation, or generating text. The process of fine-tuning typically involves several steps, including selecting a relevant dataset, preparing the data for training, and adjusting the hyperparameters of the model to optimize its performance on the specific task. Once the model has been fine-tuned, it can be used to generate responses or predictions based on new inputs. Fine-tuning the chat GPT is an effective way to create conversational agents or chatbots that can understand and respond to natural language inputs. By training the model on relevant data, it can learn to generate more accurate and relevant responses, leading to a more engaging and effective conversational experience for users. Overall, fine-tuning the chat GPT is a crucial step in developing advanced conversational AI systems that can understand and respond to a wide range of inputs and contexts. It enables the creation of chatbots that can converse more naturally and effectively with users, leading to improved user experiences and increased engagement.

2.5 Describe How the Research Was Conducted

All the participants gave informed consent for the data collection process and subsequent analysis. Also, all the research study ethical considerations were explained clearly to the participants. After the agreement, the participants were asked to complete the FM master questionnaire with the help of a clinical expert. The questionnaire took approximately about 1 h to complete and involved answering 260 questions to give an overview of a wide range of health aspects of individual participants.

2.6 What Was the Aim of This Research?

The aim of the research is to fine tune the ChatGPT with the FM questionnaires and responses to infer the patient's potential health conditions.

2.7 Why Was a Specific Research Sample Used?

We have used specific demographics data to fine tune the ChatGPT, so the research sample used was based on that pre-set demographics to understand and evaluate the ChatGPT responses accurately.

3   ChatGPT in Tackling NCDs Through Medical Diagnostics

Medical diagnostics refers to the process of identifying and determining the cause of a patient's health condition or symptoms. The diagnostic process typically involves a combination of medical history assessments, physical examinations, laboratory tests, imaging studies and genetic testing. Medical diagnostics can be used to diagnose a wide range of health conditions, including infectious diseases, genetic disorders, chronic illnesses, and acute injuries. The overriding objective of medical diagnostics is to accurately identify a diagnosis for a patient's condition so that appropriate treatment can be initiated. The Functional Medicine Master Health Survey (FM MHS) is a comprehensive health questionnaire and detailed blood tests used by FMPs to assess a patient's health status and identify potential underlying health problems. It is a tool that helps FMPs to understand a patient's health history, symptom pattern and lifestyle habits so that a personalized treatment plan can be set out. The FM MHS includes questions about a wide range of factors that can affect health, including nutrition, sleep, exercise, stress, emotional well-being, environmental exposures, and a detailed past medical history. It also includes questions about specific symptoms and conditions, such as digestive issues, hormonal imbalances, and cardiovascular disease. The survey is typically administered to patients before their initial consultation with an FMP. The practitioner reviews the patient's responses to identify potential underlying imbalances and develop a personalized treatment plan that addresses the underlying cause of the patient's health concerns. The FM MHS is a valuable tool for FMPs because it provides a comprehensive overview of a patient's health status and helps identify areas that may require further testing or intervention. It also helps practitioners track progress over time and adjust treatment plans to optimize patient outcomes. Thus, fine tuning the GPT with the capability to understand the user's response to the FM MHS and interpret the result will enable FMPs to analyse data in an efficient manner.

4   Ethical Issues and Problems

The use of GPT technology in healthcare, as with any new technology, raises important ethical issues and problems that need to be carefully considered. Some of the key ethical issues and problems associated with using GPT in healthcare include:

(1) *Data privacy*: GPT models require access to large amounts of text data for training to be effective. This raises concerns about the security of patient privacy and the potential for sensitive information to be inadvertently disclosed [32]. It is of vital importance to ensure that appropriate measures are in place to protect patient data and that patients are fully informed about how their data is being used. In essence, the security level of the "firewall" around patient data needs to be comparable with the level around online banking.

(2) *Bias*: GPT models can reflect the biases that are present in the data that they are trained on. This can result in discriminatory outcomes for patients based on factors such as race or gender [33]. It is important to carefully consider the selection and curation of the data used to train GPT models and to test for bias in the resulting models.

(3) *Accountability*: As GPT models become more advanced, they can generate text that is difficult to distinguish from text written by humans [18]. This raises concerns about accountability for decisions made based on GPT-generated text. It is important to establish clear guidelines for the use of GPT-generated text in decision-making and to ensure that there is a clear chain of "author" responsibility for any decisions made based within this context.

(4) *Informed consent*: Patients need to be aware that their data will be used to train GPT models and so need to fully understand the potential implications of its use within such an environment. It is therefore important to obtain informed consent around the use of GPT methodology from patients before using their data to train GPT models.

(5) *Transparency*: GPT models can be opaque, meaning that it can be difficult to understand how they arrived at a particular decision or generated a particular piece of text [18]. It is therefore important to ensure that GPT models are transparent and that the decision-making process is explainable to patients and healthcare providers. While the use of GPT technology in healthcare has the potential to improve patient outcomes and efficiency, careful consideration of the ethical implications of its use needs to be made as well as taking the necessary steps to mitigate against potential risks and problems.

4.1 Regulatory Framework

There is an urgent need to develop guidelines for ChatGPT use in scientific research, considering the issues of accountability, integrity, transparency, and honesty. The use of ChatGPT in health care should be carried out in a highly ethical and responsible manner, considering the potential risks and concerns it entails. A regulatory framework around the use of ChatGPT is necessary to allow for appropriate safeguarding in research and validation. Mira Murati, the Chief Scientific Officer, of ChatGPT is in favour of regulation to mitigate against and minimise malicious uses of the technology [34]. Currently, in the USA currently there is no binding U.S. regulatory restraints on generative AI although the Biden Administration's Blueprint for an AI Bill of Rights provides principles for responsible AI implementation, including calls for "algorithmic discrimination protections". The EU aims to regulate the commercial and government use of AI, including generative AI (known as AI ACT). According to Glorin Sebastian (2023), that regulators should implement data protection laws to protect users' privacy by regulating the collection and use of data generated through the AI system [35]. Another suggestion made by Sebastian, (2023) is to use intellectual property laws to protect against the unauthorized use of copyrighted material by chatbot programs [35].

An editorial in *Computing* journal reported that 1000 researchers, CEOs (including Elon Musk, Steve Wozniak (Apple) and Stuart Russell) are calling for a pause in the training of powerful AI systems due to the potential risks to society and humanity [31, 36]. We concur with this report for AI labs and independent experts to come together urgently to develop and implement a set of verifiable shared safety protocols for advanced AI design and development. AI developers should also work with policymakers to "dramatically accelerate" the development of AI governance systems. The governance systems around these should be appropriately validated at pace to ensure appropriate safety is in place. It is our belief that this can be achieved by the co-creation of a shared value among the various stakeholders involved [26, 37, 38].

5 Discussion

ChatGPT has received mixed reports regarding the risk-benefits of advanced AI technologies. We discuss the use of ChatGPT within healthcare systems considering the potential high benefit as well as suggesting measures in how to minimise risks to safeguard both the healthcare providers and users.

Although ChatGPT has the potential to transform healthcare, there are questions surrounding how quickly the tool may start to be integrated into healthcare workflows and what its limitations will be [39]. ChatGPT will no doubt be helpful to physicians in minimising the administrative burden [12]. There are many benefits that ChatGPT can offer heath care including assistance with patient education, appointment scheduling, documentation, and general navigation. Prior to a patient appointment with a healthcare professional, scheduling, appointment confirmations and background healthcare synopsis could be prepared and delivered to both the patient and doctor. The tool could also help clinicians to order tests, provide clinical decision-support tools, and produce discharge instructions and follow-up. It can also take on the administrative tasks such as providing responses to prior authorisations and insurance claim denials. ChatGPT can also enhance clinical decision-making by summarising patient records and extracting the pertinent information that is needed to meet the patient's care needs at any consultation.

ChatGPT has the potential to assist clinicians in in "data complex" environments. For example, within Intensive Care Units (ICU) there is dense multi-patient longitudinal datasets from continuous patient monitoring as well changes in the patient condition which may result in changes in treatment [40]. This often needs to be analysed with linked laboratory values, microbiological results, and fluid balance calculation. This may be particularly useful in helping to provide information about recognised ICU protocols. ChatGPT can be also used to analyse dense data systems and identify patterns within the textual data that it has been trained on when given a specific set of instructions. It can function by gathering, contextualising and utilising information more rapidly than humans. Secondly, ChatGPT can be used to generate clinical notes by providing succinct information, such as daily updates and discharge summaries, which can potentially save time for clinical practitioners and increase the "signal-noise" ratio. Thirdly, ChatGPT can assist physicians to determine appropriate treatment options when given clinical information, laboratory values, past medical history, and other relevant data provided that human users are cognisant of potential limitations around bias and errors. This is an evolving technology that is continuously being developed. Fourthly, future ChatGPT to be trained to automatically extract and understand all the relevant information from electronic health records and by analysing patient data, such as vital signs, laboratory results, and medical history, helping doctors to quickly access patient information, providing recommendations for interventions, and allowing more fast and comprehensive decisions. Despite the huge potential, it is important to keep in mind that ChatGPT must always be used in combination with the accepted expertise and judgement of human experts. Over time its performance needs to be validated before becoming standardised in clinical practice.

While GPT is a powerful language model with many potential applications, it does have several limitations [39]. Firstly, due to the lack of real-world knowledge, GPT relies on pre-existing training data to generate responses and does not have access to real-world knowledge or experiences outside of that data. This means that it may generate responses that are factually inaccurate or not reflective of real-world situations.

Secondly, the training data used to train GPT may be biased or contain inaccuracies, which can result in biased or inaccurate responses. For example, if the training data contains gender or racial biases, GPT may generate responses that reflect these biases [33].

Thirdly, GPT lacks emotional intelligence. It is not designed to recognize or respond to emotional cues, such as sarcasm or humor. This can result in responses that are tone-deaf or inappropriate for the situation.

Fourthly, limited domain-specific knowledge will reduce the effectiveness when compared to human experts. GPT is trained on a wide range of topics, but it may not have deep knowledge in specific domains or industries. This can limit its ability to generate accurate or relevant responses in certain contexts. Finally, GPT requires significant computational resources to operate, which can make it challenging to deploy in certain applications or in widespread settings [41].

5.1 Limitations and Recommendations for Future Work

The data set required for the training of the NCD cases was very limited and that affects the ChatGPT responses accordingly. Also, currently the study only focused on feeding the model with the FM MHS data but along with that the blood work data is equally essential to improve the data model. There is lot of scope to extend this model to improve the patient interaction in addressing their health queries on time. The model can be further trained with metadata around nutrition, supplements, fitness, and wellness programs to come up with suggestions about personalized treatment plans. Owing to the limited space for this paper, it is not possible to describe the regulatory framework around ChatGPT in detail. Our future work will improve the training of the data set and address other issues of around using ChatGPT on NCD datasets. To address the governance or regulation issue, it is necessary to develop a framework to guide the standardized use of ChatGPT in health care.

6   Conclusion

ChatGPT is the most cutting-edge AI language model ever built and has gained widespread interest. It has the potential to transform many sectors of society, especially health care. It can help streamline clinical workflow with possible cost savings in healthcare and increased efficiency within the healthcare ecosystem. ChatGPT also has the prospects of further refining personalized medicine and the ability to improve health literacy by providing easily accessible and understandable health information to the public. Despite these many benefits, there are several concerns. Ethical issues such as the risk of bias and transparency within ChatGPT is a recurring major concern. There is also the generation of inaccurate content that can have severe negative consequences in health care. Therefore, the implementation of ChatGPT in healthcare must be approached with more caution than in educational and administrative work. There must be standardised and accepted regulation concerning its use. We need urgent conversations amongst stakeholders about what the key priority areas are when using this tool. Currently, ChatGPT is still in the process of developing, so its use in healthcare must be careful monitored. ChatGPT should not be used as a replacement for human judgment. It is imperative that its performance should undergo a period of validation against humans within trusted and secure research environments. Its performance, safety and risks need to be evaluated carefully in the short to long term by experts before being deployed into mainstream practice, particularly around critical decision-making tasks. There is substantially more research to be undertaken to address the impact of ChatGPT, specifically, around governance, patient safety and the resulting effect on healthcare systems.

References

1. Perlman, P.: The Implications of ChatGPT for Legal Services and Society SSRN (2022). https://doi.org/10.2139/ssrn.4294197
2. ChatGPT: New AI chatbot has everyone talking to it [press release] (2022)
3. Chatterjee, J., Dethlefs, N.: This new conversational AI model can be your friend, philosopher, and guide … and even your worst enemy. Patterns (N Y). **4**(1), 100676 (2023)
4. OpenAI. OpenAI: Models GPT-3 (2023). https://betaopenai.com/docs/models
5. Bruce, B., Diaz, N., Carbajal, E.: The promises and pitfalls of ChatGPT: 10 digital leaders on how hospitals might use it (2023). https://www.beckershospitalreviewcom/healthcare-inf ormation-technology/the-promises-and-pitfalls-of-ChatGPT-10-digital-leaders-on-how-hos pitals-might-use-ithtml
6. Budzianowski, P., Vulić, I.: Hello, it's GPT-2—how can I help you? towards the use of pre-trained language models for task-oriented dialogue systems (2019). https://doi.org/10.48550/ arXiv.1907.05774
7. Lund, B.D., Wang, T.: Chatting about ChatGPT: how may AI and GPT impact academia and libraries? Library Hi Tech News (2023)
8. Puri, P., Singh, S.K.: Exploring the non-communicable disease (NCD) network of multi-morbid individuals in India: a network analysis. PLOS Glob. Public Health. **2**(6), e0000512 (2022)
9. Hallsworth, J.E., et al.: Scientific novelty beyond the experiment. Microb Biotechnol. (2023)
10. Dale, R.: GPT-3: what's it good for? Nat. Lang. Eng. **27**, 113–118 (2021)
11. Brown, T., et al.: Language models are few-shot learners. In: Advances in Neural Information Processing Systems, vol. 33, pp. 1877–901 (2020)
12. Anderson, N., et al.: AI did not write this manuscript, or did it? Can we trick the AI text detector into generated texts? The potential future of ChatGPT and AI in Sports & Exercise Medicine manuscript generation. BMJ Open Sport Exerc. Med. **9**(1), e001568 (2023)
13. Mbakwe, A.B., Lourentzou, I., Celi, L.A., Mechanic, O.J., Dagan, A.: ChatGPT passing USMLE shines a spotlight on the flaws of medical education. PLOS Digit. Health **2**(2), e0000205 (2023)

14. Radford, A., Narasimhan, K., Salimans, T., Sutskever, I.: Improving language understanding by generative pre-training (2018). https://www.csubcca/~amuham01/LING530/papers/radfor d2018improvingpdf
15. Sallam, M.: ChatGPT utility in healthcare education, research, and practice: systematic review on the promising perspectives and valid concerns. Healthcare (Basel) **11**(6) (2023)
16. Stokel-Walker, C.: AI bot ChatGPT writes smart essays - should professors worry? Nature (2022)
17. Mann, D.L.: Artificial intelligence discusses the role of artificial intelligence in translational medicine: a JACC: basic to translational science interview with ChatGPT. JACC Basic Transl. Sci. **8**(2), 221–223 (2023)
18. Gordijn, B., Have, H.T.: ChatGPT: evolution or revolution? Med. Health Care Philos. **26**(1), 1–2 (2023)
19. George, A.S., George, A.H.: A review of ChatGPT AI's impact on several business sectors. Partners Univ. Int. Innov. J. **23**, 4–6 (2023)
20. Jeblick, K., et al.: ChatGPT makes medicine easy to swallow: an exploratory case study on simplified radiology reports (2022). arXiv:2212.14882
21. Shen, Y., et al.: ChatGPT and other large language models are double-edged swords. Radiology 230163 (2023)
22. Mijwil, M., Aljanabi, M., Ali, A.H.: ChatGPT: exploring the role of cybersecurity in the protection of medical information. Mesopotamian J. Cybersecurity (2023). https://doi.org/ 10.58496/MJCS/2023/004
23. Patel, S.B., Lam, K.: ChatGPT: the future of discharge summaries? Lancet Digit. Health **5**(3), e107–e108 (2023)
24. Sharma, G., Thakur, A.: ChatGPT in drug discovery. ChemRxiv (2023). https://doi.org/10. 26434/chemrxiv-2023-qgs3k
25. Rao, A.S., Pang, M., Kim, J.: Assessing the utility of ChatGPT throughout the entire clinical workflow. medRxiv (2023). https://doi.org/10.1101/2023.02.21.23285886
26. Yeo, Y.H., et al.: Assessing the performance of ChatGPT in answering questions regarding cirrhosis and hepatocellular carcinoma. Clin. Mol. Hepatol. (2023)
27. Ahn, C.: Exploring ChatGPT for information of cardiopulmonary resuscitation. Resuscitation **185**, 109729 (2023)
28. D'Amico, R.S., White, T.G., Shah, H.A., Langer, D.J.: I asked a ChatGPT to write an editorial about how we can incorporate chatbots into neurosurgical research and patient care. Neurosurgery **92**(4), 663–664 (2023)
29. Duong, D., Solomon, B.D.: Analysis of large-language model versus human performance for genetics questions. medRxiv (2023)
30. Strubell, E., Ganesh, A., McCallum, A.: Energy and policy considerations for deep learning in NLP. In: Proceedings of the Annual Meeting of the Association for Computational Linguistics, vol. 57, pp. 3645–3650 (2019)
31. Osborne, S.: Elon Musk and experts say AI development should be paused immediately. Sky (2023). https://news.sky.com/story/elon-musk-and-others-sign-open-letter-calling-for-pause-on-ai-development-12845039
32. Mijwil, M., Aljanabi, M.: Towards artificial intelligence-based cybersecurity: the practices and ChatGPT generated ways to combat cybercrime. Iraqi J. Comput. Sci. Math. **4**, 65–70 (2023)
33. Lucy, L., Bamman, D.: Gender and representation bias in GPT-3 generated stories. Partners Univ. Int. Innov. J. **3**, 48–55 (2021)
34. OpenAI. OpenAI Charter (2023). https://openai.com/charter
35. Sebastian, G.: Do ChatGPT and Other AI Chatbots Pose a Cybersecurity Risk? - An Exploratory Study. SSRN (2023). https://doi.org/10.2139/ssrn.4363843

36. Kundaliya, D.: Generative AI will disrupt white collar workers in US and Europe, report warns. Computing (2023). https://www.computing.co.uk/news/4087342/generative-ai-disrupt-white-collar-workers-us-europe-report-warns

37. Brugmann, J., Prahalad, C.K.: Cocreating business's new social compact. Harv. Bus. Rev. **85**(2), 80–90, 156 (2007)

38. Uden, L., Kumaresan, A.: Sustainable smart city business model framework. In: 2021 5th International Conference on Vision, Image and Signal Processing (ICVISP), pp. 181–187 (2021). https://doi.org/10.1109/ICVISP54630.2021

39. Borji, A.: Categorical archive of ChatGPT failures (2023). arXiv:2302.03494

40. Salvagno, M., Taccone, F.S., Gerli, A.G.: Correction to: can artificial intelligence help for scientific writing? Crit Care **27**(1), 99 (2023)

41. Zhou, X., Chen, Z., Jin, X., Wang, W.Y.: An energy efficiency benchmark platform for responsible natural language processing. In: Proceedings of the Conference of the European Chapter of the Association for Computational Linguistics: System Demonstrations, vol. 16, pp. 329–336 (2021)

Author Index

L. Uden and I-H. Ting (Eds.): KMO 2023, CCIS 1825, pp. 443–444, 2023.
https://doi.org/10.1007/978-3-031-34045-1

Printed in the United States
by Baker & Taylor Publisher Services